THE
CONTEMPORARY
READER

11 X 95

THE CONTEMPORARY READER FROM LITTLE, BROWN

Edited by

Gary Goshgarian

Northeastern University

Little, Brown and Company

Boston   Toronto

This book is dedicated to Nathan Robert Goshgarian, my son.

Library of Congress Cataloging in Publication Data

Main entry under title:

The contemporary reader from Little,Brown.

1. College readers. I. Goshgarian, Gary.
II. Little, Brown and Company.
PE1417.L645 1984   808'.0427   83-24834
ISBN 0-316-32152-4

Library of Congress Catalog Card No. 83–24834

ISBN 0-316-32152-4

9 8 7 6 5 4 3 2 1

ALP

Published simultaneously in Canada
by Little, Brown & Company (Canada) Limited

Printed in the United States of America

Photo Credits
Page 1: Mary Ellen Mark//Archive. Page 39: Michael Hayman//Stock–Boston. Page 79: Bill Burke//Archive. Page 113: Alan Mercer//Stock–Boston. Page 147: Jim Anderson//Stock–Boston. Page 193: Wide World Photo. Page 239: Jim Ritscher//Stock–Boston. Page 283: NASA Photo. Page 315: Benjamin Porter//Archive. Page 341: James Holland//Stock–Boston. Page 369: Mary Ellen Mark//Archive. Page 411: Mike Mazzaschi//Stock–Boston. Page 459: Gale Zucker//Stock–Boston.

Credits continue on p. 588.

PREFACE

The purpose of any composition "reader" is to provide students with essays that inspire thought, stimulate class discussion, and serve as writing models. But a reader will fail to achieve any of these goals unless its essays fulfill one crucial task—they must interest the student.

From the perspective of a career encompassing fifteen years and a dozen and a half different readers, I have come to the realization that most collections are made up of fine prose pieces that exceed the scope and purpose of composition courses. Some pieces are simply too advanced, requiring sophisticated literary explication beyond the training of most freshmen. Other pieces are historically important but fail to speak to today's college student. And then there are those essays with fascinating subject matter, but deadly prose. Despite its significance in the history of western civilization, Thucydides' "Corcyraean Revolution" from *The Peloponnesian War* just doesn't light the freshman fire.

But I am confident this collection will. It is the result of fifteen years of listening to writing students complain about how boring their readers are; fifteen years of trying to respond adequately to the universal plea: "Why can't we read something *interesting,* something we can relate to?"

What makes *The Contemporary Reader from Little, Brown* different from all the rest is its emphasis on the *contemporary.* All the selections in this anthology were chosen because they are about current experiences and issues college students can "relate to." More than a third of the pieces were written since 1982; and those few classic pieces by prose masters such as E. B. White and James Thurber are as fresh today as they were decades ago when composed. Even the excerpt from the *Book of Revelation* in the section "War and Peace in the Nuclear Age" was selected because of its prophetic appropriateness to our world today.

Diversity. The eighty selections in this collection have been organized around thirteen different thematic categories representing a wide range of experiences students can identify with—from rock music to rocket travel, from video games to war games, from dating habits to drug habits, from high-tech life to high-punk styles, from weight control to gun control, from views on exercising to reviews of *E.T., the Extra-Terrestrial,* from dinosaurs to "Dynasty." And the writers are as diverse as the subjects they write about. Along with such exemplary favorites as E. B. White and James Thurber I have included Loren Eiseley, Martin Luther King, Jr., Michael Arlen, and Bruno Bettelheim, and some familiar humorists, such as Woody Allen, Art Buchwald, Russell Baker, Mike Royko, and Andy Rooney. Many of the authors are well-known professional columnists and editors: William F. Buckley, Jr., Ellen Goodman, William Raspberry, George F. Will, and Norman Cousins. There are pieces by noted scientists such as Albert Einstein, Carl Sagan, and Stephen Jay Gould.

I have also included previously unanthologized essays by four of the most popular fiction writers in the world today: famous horror-story author Stephen King has a piece about current horror movies; Herman Wouk (*Winds of War*) talks about nuclear madness; science fiction master Arthur C. Clarke explains how human beings might reach the stars; and America's leading detective novelist Robert B. Parker gives us a witty and entertaining narrative about body building.

Equally diverse are the writing styles and techniques. Contained in this collection are examples of the "basic" essay as well as editorials, satirical narratives, news reports, research studies, movie reviews, journal entries, personal recollections, descriptive experiences, pointed arguments, commercial ads, and more. The pieces vary in length from 500 words to 2500 words—the range most writing assignments fall within. The range also reflects the varying difficulty of the selections.

Debates. Essays on controversial topics are a special feature of this reader. Many contemporary issues are confronted, and from opposing points of view. Most of the thirteen sections contain a debate. Sometimes it is indirect, as in Part 2, "The Sexes," where articles by feminist Judy Syfers and antifeminist Phyllis Schlafly, with their strikingly different assumptions, are juxtaposed. Sometimes the arguments meet head-on, as do the opposing views of gun control and capital punishment in Part 5, "Conscience and Controversy." And sometimes writers make direct assaults on each other, as in Part 6, "War and Peace in the Nuclear Age," where Michael Kinsley in "Nuclear Holocaust in Perspective" attacks Jonathan Schell's stand in "The Effects of a Nuclear Explosion," and the nuclear freeze movement as well. Debates can be found in nonissue sections as well, such as Part 12, "The World of Advertising," which includes some barbed attacks on television commercials as well as an intelligent and cogent defense of familiar ads by long-time professional advertiser Charles O'Neill. And, in Part 11, "The Movies," we pit a sample rave review of Steven Spielberg's enormously popular *E.T., The Extraterrestrial* against an unequivocal condemnation of the movie.

Humor. There is no reason why the writing experience cannot be fun. Likewise, there is no reason why writing models cannot be entertaining. As you will discover, many of the selections are very funny and entertaining; and in their humor they have much to say. Nearly every section contains at least one humorous piece—even Part 6, "War and Peace in the Nuclear Age," which we conclude with Art Buchwald's satirical narrative, "Evacuating the Capital? No Need to Hurry Now."

Apparatus. This book is not just a collection of interesting thoughts on contemporary experience. The essays within can offer solid assistance to composition students trying to develop their own writing abilities for several reasons. First, all the essays were written by professionals, and so they serve as models of a wide variety of expository techniques and patterns. Second, each selection is preceded by a headnote containing biographical and thematic information as well as clues to writing techniques and strategies. And following each piece is a series of review questions covering both thoughts and themes ("Topical Considerations") and compositional features ("Rhetorical Considerations"). These questions are designed to stimulate class discussion, and to help students think analytically about the form and content of the essays. I have also included some suggestions for writing assignments to help students relate the particular essay to others in the book and to their own experiences.

Graphics. In addition to the essays and apparatus, there are photographs that open each section to serve as visual references and complements to the selections. Also, in "The World of Advertising" there is a variety of current magazine and newspaper ads with some specific questions intended to help students more closely analyze how advertising works on us—and to spark some lively class discussions.

Acknowledgments. There were many people behind the scenes who helped put this collection in print. I would like to acknowledge them and thank them for their assistance. I am very grateful to the people at Little, Brown and Company, in particular my editor Carolyn Potts, who believed in this project and supported it from the beginning, editorial assistant Virginia Pye, the incarnation of efficiency, and Julia Winston and Victoria Keirnan for their masterful guidance through the production process. I am greatly indebted to Nancy King who assisted me enormously in preparing the manuscript. And a very special thanks goes out to my wife, Kathleen Krueger, whose intelligent advice and insights helped pull this project through.

Gary Goshgarian

INSTRUCTOR'S MANUAL FOR *THE CONTEMPORARY READER FROM LITTLE, BROWN*

An Instructor's Manual is available from the publisher. Instructors wishing to obtain a complimentary copy of the manual may address their requests (on school letterhead) to College Marketing, Little, Brown and Company, 34 Beacon Street, Boston, Massachusetts 02106.

CONTENTS

humorists says, the whole courtship business still slogs along, like an intricate musical comedy.

ON GROWING UP

Confessions of a Burglar

Woody Allen

We open our section "On Growing Up" with a funny piece by one of America's most popular humorists, Woody Allen. He is best known for having written and starred in such zany, satirical movies as *Bananas, Play It Again, Sam, Sleeper, Love and Death, A Mid-Summer Night's Sex Comedy,* and *Annie Hall,* which won him an Academy Award in 1977. Allen has also written several books of essays, including *Getting Even* (1971), *Without Feathers* (1975), and *Side Effects* (1980). The following essay, which originally appeared in *The New Yorker,* is typical of Woody Allen's brand of humor—a seemingly nonsensical humor full of puns, twisted logic, and incongruous allusions that produce laughs while cutting below the surface. Here, Allen takes on the persona of a young felon proudly recollecting the early days of his trade.

(Following are excerpts from the soon-to-be-published memoirs of Virgil 1
Ives, who is currently serving the first of four consecutive ninety-nine-year sentences for various felonies. Mr. Ives plans on working with children when he gets out.)

Sure I stole. Why not? Where I grew up, you had to steal to eat. Then 2
you had to steal to tip. Lots of guys stole fifteen percent, but I always stole twenty, which made me a big favorite among the waiters. On the way home from a heist, I'd steal some pajamas to sleep in. Or if it was a hot night, I'd steal underwear. It was a way of life. I had a bad upbringing, you might say. My dad was always on the run from the cops and I never saw him out of disguise till I was twenty-two. For years, I thought he was a short, bearded man with dark glasses and a limp; actually, he was tall and blond and resembled Lindbergh. He was a professional bank robber, but sixty-five was the mandatory retirement age, so he had to get out. Spent his last few years in mail fraud, but the postal rates went up and he lost everything.

Mom was wanted, too. Of course in those days it wasn't the way it is 3
now, with women demanding equal rights, and all. Back then, if a woman turned to crime the only opportunities open to her were blackmail and, once in a while, arson. Women were used in Chicago to drive getaway cars, but only during the drivers' strike, in 1926. Terrible strike. It lasted eight weeks, and whenever a gang pulled a job and ran out with the money they were forced to walk or take a cab.

I had a sister and two brothers. Jenny married money. Not an actual 4
human being—it was a pile of singles. My brother Vic got in with a gang of plagiarists. He was in the middle of signing his name to "The Waste Land" when the feds surrounded the house. He got ten years. Some rich kid from a highfalutin family who signed Pound's "Cantos" got off on probation. That's the law for you. Charlie—that's my youngest brother —he's been a numbers runner, a fence, and a loan shark. Never could find himself. Eventually he was arrested for loitering. He loitered for seven

years, till he realized it was not the kind of crime that brought in any money.

The first thing I ever stole was a loaf of bread. I was working for   5
Rifkin's Bakery, where my job was to remove the jelly from doughnuts that had gone stale and transfer it to fresh goods. It was very exacting work, done with a rubber tube and a scalpel. If your hands shook, the jelly went on the floor and old man Rifkin would pull your hair. Arnold Rothstein, who we all looked up to, came in one day and said he wanted to get his hands on a loaf of bread but he absolutely refused to pay for it. He hinted that this was a chance for some smart kid to get into the rackets. I took that as a cue, and each day when I left I put one slice of rye under my coat, until after three weeks I had accumulated a whole loaf. On the way to Rothstein's office, I began to feel remorse, because even though I hated Rifkin his wife had once let me take home two seeds from a roll when my uncle was dying. I tried to return the bread, but I got caught while I was trying to figure out which loaf each slice belonged to. The next thing I knew, I was in Elmira Reformatory.

Elmira was a tough joint. I escaped five times. Once I tried to sneak   6
out in the back of a laundry truck. The guards got suspicious, and one of them poked me with his stick and asked me what the hell I was doing lying around in a hamper. I looked him right in the eye and said, "I'm some shirts." I could tell he was dubious. He kept pacing back and forth and staring at me. I guess I got a little panicky. "I'm some *shirts*," I told him. "Some denim work shirts—blue ones." Before I could say another word, my arms and legs were manacled and I was back in stir.

I learned everything I knew about crime at Elmira: how to pick pockets,   7
how to crack a safe, how to cut glass—all the fine points of the trade. For instance, I learned (and not even all professional criminals know this) that in the event of a shootout with the cops, the cops are always allowed the first two shots. It's just the way it's done. Then you return fire. And if a cop says, "We have the house surrounded, come out with your hands up," you don't just shoot wildly. You say, "I'd prefer not to," or "I'd rather not at this particular time." There's a right way to do these things, but today . . . Well, why go into all that?

For the next few years of my life I was the best damn burglar you ever   8
saw. People talk about Raffles, but Raffles had his style and I had mine. I had lunch with Raffles' son once. Nice guy. We ate at the old Lindy's. He stole the pepper mill. I stole the silverware and napkins. Then he took the ketchup bottle. I took his hat. He got my umbrella and tiepin. When we left we kidnapped a waiter. It was quite a haul. The original Raffles began as a cat burglar. (I couldn't do that, because the whiskers make me sneeze.) He'd dress up in this beat-up cat suit and dart over rooftops. In the end, he was caught by two guys from Scotland Yard dressed as dogs. I suppose you've heard of the Kissing Bandit? He'd break into a joint and rob the victim, and if it was a woman he'd kiss her. It was sad the way the

law finally nailed him. He had two old dowagers tied up and he was prancing in front of them singing "Gimme a Little Kiss, Will Ya, Huh?" when he slipped on a footstool and fractured his pelvis.

Those boys made all the headlines, but I pulled off some capers that   9
the police never did figure out. Once, I entered a mansion, blew the safe, and removed six thousand dollars while a couple slept in the same room. The husband woke up when the dynamite went off, but when I assured him that the entire proceeds would go to the Boys' Clubs of America he went back to sleep. Cleverly, I left behind some fingerprints of Franklin D. Roosevelt, who was President then. Another time, at a big diplomatic cocktail party, I stole a woman's diamond necklace while we were shaking hands. Used a vacuum cleaner on her—an old Hoover. Got her necklace and earrings. Later, when I opened the bag I found some false teeth there, which belonged to the Dutch Ambassador.

My most beautiful job, though, was when I broke into the British   10
Museum. I knew that the entire floor of the Rare Gems Room was wired and the slightest pressure on it would set off an alarm. I was lowered in upside down by a rope from the skylight, so I wouldn't touch the ground. I came through neat as you please, and in a minute I was hovering over the famous Kittridge Diamonds in their display case. As I pulled out my glass cutter a little sparrow flew in through the skylight and landed on the floor. The alarm sounded and eight squad cars arrived. I got ten years. The sparrow got twenty to life. The bird was out in six months, on probation. A year later, he was picked up in Forth Worth for pecking Rabbi Morris Klugfein into a state of semiconsciousness.

What advice would I give the average homeowner to protect himself   11
against burglars? Well, the first thing is to keep a light on in the house when you go out. It must be at least a sixty-watt bulb; anything less and the burglar will ransack the house, out of contempt for the wattage. Another good idea is to keep a dog, but this is not foolproof. Whenever I was about to rob a house with a dog in it, I threw in some dog food mixed with Seconal. If that didn't work, I'd grind up equal parts of chopped meat and a novel by Theodore Dreiser. If it happens that you are going out of town and must leave your house unguarded, it's a good idea to put a cardboard silhouette of yourself in the window. Any silhouette will do. A Bronx man once placed a cardboard silhouette of Montgomery Clift in his window and then went to Kutsher's for the weekend. Later, Montgomery Clift himself happened to walk by and saw the silhouette, which caused him great anxiety. He attempted to strike up a conversation, and when it failed to answer for seven hours Clift returned to California and told his friends that New Yorkers were snobbish.

If you surprise an intruder in the act of burglarizing your home, do not   12
panic. Remember, he is as frightened as you are. One good device is to rob *him*. Seize the initiative and relieve the burglar of his watch and

wallet. Then he can get into your bed while you make a getaway. Trapped by this defense, I once wound up living in Des Moines for six years with another man's wife and three children, and only left when I was fortunate enough to surprise another burglar, who took my place. The six years I lived with that family were happy ones, and I often look back on them with affection, although there is also much to be said for working on a chain gang.

Topical Considerations

1. How would you describe Woody Allen's brand of humor? Cite some examples. Can you think of a Woody Allen movie that exhibits the same kind of humor?

2. Allen's humor is a vehicle for some social messages. What current social issues does Allen poke fun at in this essay?

3. Allen alludes to a number of well-known people, events, books, songs, and movies of an older generation. What are some allusions you might substitute if these were confessions about your own childhood?

4. Often Allen creates a humorous effect by using a figure of speech and then twisting it around to its literal interpretation. He remarks: "The original Raffles began as a cat burglar," and then adds: "I couldn't do that, because the whiskers make me sneeze" (paragraph 8). Find another figurative–literal twist in the essay.

5. The pun is "the lowest form of wit" only when it has no point. Are Allen's puns used merely for their own sake? Or do they contribute to the central idea of his essay? Explain.

6. Do you find Allen's essay completely absurd, or does his word play challenge you to think about some of the issues he raises?

Rhetorical Considerations

1. Do you find the essay humorous? Cite some passages that you found amusing. Why did you laugh? How does Allen achieve his humor? Cite examples of absurdist humor, satire, punning, and Jewish humor.

2. From the tone and attitudes of this essay, what sort of man would you say Allen is—angry and cynical? serious and pedantic? light-hearted and flippant? eccentric and incredible?

3. What do you observe about Allen's writing style, particularly the length of his sentences? How does this style affect the tone of the essay?

4. Allen uses sentence fragments throughout the essay. What might be the reasons he chose not to write these as complete sentences?

Do they work well? Or would the essay read better if these sentences were complete?

5. What can you say about the diction in this essay? Is it formal? informal? scholarly? conversational? Cite specific words or phrases that support your answer. Do you feel that the diction is appropriate to the tone?

Writing Assignments

1. Write your own imaginary confessions, similar in tone to Allen's essay. Imitate his method of poking fun at contemporary social issues. Include word play and allusions to famous people, books, events, songs, or movies from your own experience.

2. Allen uses description and narration to illustrate how people and circumstances were responsible for turning him to a life of crime. Use these rhetorical strategies to write a true account of some of the significant people and events in your life that have made you the person you are now. Adopt a lighthearted but thoughtful tone and an informal, conversational style.

3. Find a newspaper or magazine article documenting the effect of prison life on a juvenile offender. Using Allen's comments as a jumping-off point, describe what a juvenile offender is likely to learn from his fellow inmates in prison.

Shame

Dick Gregory

Dick Gregory is another well-known satirist whose humor, like Woody Allen's, cuts below the surface of mere comedy. For years, Gregory has been active in the civil rights movement, and during the 1960s he actively campaigned against the Vietnam War. What follows is a rather sensitive narrative of a childhood experience that taught him the meaning of shame. The selection comes from Gregory's 1964 autobiography, *nigger*.

I never learned hate at home, or shame. I had to go to school for   1
that. I was about seven years old when I got my first big lesson. I was in love with a little girl named Helene Tucker, a light-complexioned little girl with pigtails and nice manners. She was always clean and she was smart in school. I think I went to school then mostly to look at her. I brushed my hair and even got me a little old handkerchief. It was a lady's

handkerchief, but I didn't want Helene to see me wipe my nose on my hand. The pipes were frozen again, there was no water in the house, but I washed my socks and shirt every night. I'd get a pot, and go over to Mister Ben's grocery store, and stick my pot down into his soda machine. Scoop out some chopped ice. By evening the ice melted to water for washing. I got sick a lot that winter because the fire would go out at night before the clothes were dry. In the morning I'd put them on, wet or dry, because they were the only clothes I had.

Everybody's got a Helene Tucker, a symbol of everything you want. I   2
loved her for her goodness, her cleanness, her popularity. She'd walk down my street and my brothers and sisters would yell, "Here comes Helene," and I'd rub my tennis sneakers on the back of my pants and wish my hair wasn't so nappy and the white folks' shirt fit me better. I'd run out on the street. If I knew my place and didn't come too close, she'd wink at me and say hello. That was a good feeling. Sometimes I'd follow her all the way home, and shovel the snow off her walk and try to make friends with her Momma and her aunts. I'd drop money on her stoop late at night on my way back from shining shoes in the taverns. And she had a Daddy, and he had a good job. He was a paper hanger.

I guess I would have gotten over Helene by summertime, but some-   3
thing happened in that classroom that made her face hang in front of me for the next twenty-two years. When I played the drums in high school it was for Helene and when I broke track records in college it was for Helene and when I started standing behind microphones and heard applause I wished Helene could hear it, too. It wasn't until I was twenty-nine years old and married and making money that I finally got her out of my system. Helene was sitting in that classroom when I learned to be ashamed of myself.

It was on a Thursday. I was sitting in the back of the room, in a seat   4
with a chalk circle drawn around it. The idiot's seat, the troublemaker's seat.

The teacher thought I was stupid. Couldn't spell, couldn't read,   5
couldn't do arithmetic. Just stupid. Teachers were never interested in finding out that you couldn't concentrate because you were so hungry, because you hadn't had any breakfast. All you could think about was noontime, would it ever come? Maybe you could sneak into the cloakroom and steal a bite of some kid's lunch out of a coat pocket. A bite of something. Paste. You can't really make a meal of paste, or put it on bread for a sandwich, but sometimes I'd scoop a few spoonfuls out of the paste jar in the back of the room. Pregnant people get strange tastes. I was pregnant with poverty. Pregnant with dirt and pregnant with smells that made people turn away, pregnant with cold and pregnant with shoes that were never bought for me, pregnant with five other people in my bed and no Daddy in the next room, and pregnant with hunger. Paste doesn't taste too bad when you're hungry.

The teacher thought I was a troublemaker. All she saw from the front 6
of the room was a little black boy who squirmed in his idiot's seat and
made noises and poked the kids around him. I guess she couldn't see a
kid who made noises because he wanted someone to know he was
there.

It was on a Thursday, the day before the Negro payday. The eagle 7
always flew on Friday. The teacher was asking each student how much his
father would give to the Community Chest. On Friday night, each kid
would get the money from his father, and on Monday he would bring it
to the school. I decided I was going to buy me a Daddy right then. I had
money in my pocket from shining shoes and selling papers, and whatever
Helene Tucker pledged for her Daddy I was going to top it. And I'd hand
the money right in. I wasn't going to wait until Monday to buy me a
Daddy.

I was shaking, scared to death. The teacher opened her book and 8
started calling out names alphabetically.

"Helene Tucker?" 9

"My daddy said he'd give two dollars and fifty cents." 10

"That's very nice, Helene. Very, very nice indeed." 11

That made me feel pretty good. It wouldn't take too much to top that. 12
I had almost three dollars in dimes and quarters in my pocket. I stuck my
hand in my pocket and held onto the money, waiting for her to call my
name. But the teacher closed her book after she called everybody else in
the class.

I stood up and raised my hand. 13

"What is it now?" 14

"You forgot me." 15

She turned toward the blackboard. "I don't have time to be playing 16
with you, Richard."

"My Daddy said he'd . . ." 17

"Sit down, Richard, you're disturbing the class." 18

"My Daddy said he'd give . . . fifteen dollars." 19

She turned around and looked mad. "We are collecting this money for 20
you and your kind, Richard Gregory. If your Daddy can give fifteen
dollars you have no business being on relief."

"I got it right now, I got it right now, my Daddy gave it to me to turn 21
in today, my Daddy said . . . "

"And furthermore," she said, looking right at me, her nostrils getting 22
big and her lips getting thin and her eyes opening wide, "we know you
don't have a Daddy."

Helene Tucker turned around, her eyes full of tears. She felt sorry for 23
me. Then I couldn't see her too well because I was crying, too.

"Sit down, Richard." 24

And I always thought the teacher kind of liked me. She always picked 25
me to wash the blackboard on Friday, after school. That was a big thrill,

it made me feel important. If I didn't wash it, come Monday the school might not function right.

"Where are you going, Richard?"   26

I walked out of school that day, and for a long time I didn't go back   27
very often. There was shame there.

Now there was shame everywhere. It seemed like the whole world had   28
been inside that classroom, everyone had heard what the teacher had
said, everyone had turned around and felt sorry for me. There was shame
in going to the Worthy Boys Annual Christmas Dinner for you and your
kind, because everybody knew what a worthy boy was. Why couldn't they
just call it the Boys Annual Dinner; why'd they have to give it a name?
There was shame in wearing the brown and orange and white plaid
mackinaw the welfare gave to three thousand boys. Why'd it have to be
the same for everybody so when you walked down the street the people
could see you were on relief? It was a nice warm mackinaw and it had a
hood, and my Momma beat me and called me a little rat when she found
out I stuffed it in the bottom of a pail full of garbage way over on Cottage
Street. There was shame in running over to Mister Ben's at the end of
the day and asking for his rotten peaches, there was shame in asking Mrs.
Simmons for a spoonful of sugar, there was shame in running out to meet
the relief truck. I hated that truck, full of food for you and your kind. I
ran into the house and hid when it came. And then I started to sneak
through alleys, to take the long way home so the people going into
White's Eat Shop wouldn't see me. Yeah, the whole world heard the
teacher that day, we all know you don't have a Daddy.

Topical Considerations

1. Gregory tried so hard to impress Helene Tucker that he often
got sick from wearing wet clothes that couldn't dry because the fire had
gone out in the night. When you were growing up, was there any one
person for whom you went to such extremes to impress? What did you
do? What was he or she like? Do you know any adults who would go (or
have gone) to such extremes?

2. Helene Tucker seems to have been a success symbol for Gregory when he was a child. He comments: "Everybody's got a Helene
Tucker, a symbol of everything you want" (paragraph 2). What does
Gregory's description of Helene tell you about what success meant to
him? What influenced his view? Describe a person who represents success
to you. What influences have shaped this view?

3. What do you think of the way Gregory handled himself in
school the day the teacher embarrassed him? Would you have responded
in the same way? Was his refusal to go to school after this incident the

only way he could deal with his shame? What would have been your answer?

4. Is shame caused by outward circumstances or by what an individual has done himself? Which should it be? What does shame mean to Gregory? What does it mean to you?

5. Why did the memory of Helene Tucker's presence the day he was shamed in class motivate Gregory to excel as a teenager? Do you think this is a useful motivational device? What other incentives can be effective?

6. Gregory remarks that he wasn't able to get Helene Tucker out of his system for twenty-two years. Why was he finally able to forget her? Do you think that if he were confronted with the same kind of experience now, he would respond in the same way? Why? Is there anything about Gregory's experience that you can relate to your own life?

7. How sensitive was the teacher? How else might she have responded to Gregory?

8. Do you think most welfare recipients are like Gregory and do not want to be on welfare? Give reasons for your answer.

Rhetorical Considerations

1. Where does Gregory state his thesis? Is this the best place for it? Explain.

2. What adjectives does Gregory use in his description of Helene Tucker in the first paragraph? Does he use too many? not enough? Are they essential to the development of his thesis? Why or why not?

3. What is the primary rhetorical pattern Gregory uses in this essay? Are others used as well? Cite sample passages.

4. Does Gregory *tell* or *show* his reader how he feels about Helene Tucker? What rhetorical patterns does he use to accomplish this?

5. How does the tone of this essay compare with Woody Allen's "Confessions of a Burglar"?

6. What can you say about Gregory's conclusion? Does it tie in with his thesis? Is it an effective ending? Why or why not?

Writing Assignments

1. Have you ever had an experience that caused you to feel shame? Write an essay describing the incident. Include concrete details, illustrations, and dialogue (as Gregory does) that will show your reader exactly what happened.

2. What does success mean to you? In an essay, analyze your own

answer to this question. Discuss the influences that have shaped your view.

3. Write an essay describing someone you idealize and would like to impress. Narrate some of the things you would do or have done to gain this person's esteem.

What I Learned About Love on AM Radio

Sally Helgesen

Some of the most profound experiences a person will have in life happen during the formative years of adolescence. Learning about love, like learning about shame, is one of those profound experiences. Sally Helgesen, a professional columnist for *Glamour* magazine, here talks about how her girlhood fantasies about love were shaped by songs she heard on AM radio. Looking back now, however, she says that the romantic visions fashioned by pop and rock music were painfully unrealistic, incomplete, and self-deceiving.

"You Can't Hurry Love," they sang. Oh, but we tried. Maybe I shouldn't say I learned about love on AM radio, maybe I should say I learned about yearning, about the romantic pleasures of pining after a guy who hardly knew me (and whom I hardly knew), about the self-deceiving joys of planning a happy future at the side of someone who had never asked for more than a dance. Songs played on AM radio have no more to do with real love—its complications, compromises, and deep joys —than do old Ginger Rogers–Fred Astaire movies; films may have gotten more realistic in recent years, but the songs haven't changed much. They still celebrate a world of melodrama and tortured passion, in which love is fated either to meet an unqualifiedly miserable end or to find the perfect resolution. To argue that *love is not like that* is to miss the point, for if we have ever daydreamed to the radio, our ideas of love, of yearning, have been shaped by it forever.

I was eight years old in 1956, the year transistor radios really hit the scene. When they appeared—small, sleek, without the encumbering need for a plug—the sound of AM was suddenly everywhere. Kids in my class began carrying pocket-sized plastic pouches to and from school, and there were rumors that bold students at the nearby junior high hid earplugs in their ears all during class. Nothing was so cool as being tuned in day and night.

"Transistor Sister" was our anthem ("With a radio under her arm; No   3
one can resist her, Cause she's loaded with musical charm."). We were
the first generation that could listen to whatever music we wanted, whenever we wanted, unconstrained by the family listening schedule—except
in the car, where battle raged between baseball fans and the lovers of
Elvis imitators. What we listened to was love songs, in all their pop, soul,
and rock-and-roll guises, and so it was that we learned of the mysteries
of romance.

It all began innocently enough, for me at least, with Ricky Nelson. The   4
photograph on his first album jacket showed him with a crew cut and
wearing a yellow V-neck sweater, yet there was just enough of a curl to
his lip to arouse disgust in adults. I used to prop the picture against my
record player, listen to such numbers as "It's Late" ("It's late, I hate to
face your dad, Too bad, I know he's going to be mad."), scream at the
top of my lungs, and fall backward, pretending to be at some undefined
sort of performance, rock concerts being unknown in those days except
in the very biggest cities. When my idol occasionally did a number on
The Ozzie and Harriet Show (he was the younger son in that famous TV
family), my girlfriends would come over and we'd tear things up in the
aptly named basement "rec room," shouting and knocking into walls
until my dad finally come down to turn the set off. It was the only way
for him to control our frenzy.

It was not at all uncommon in those days for parents to ban rock music   5
entirely. The general disdain in which it was held lent a thrilling, illicit
flavor to the most innocuous tunes of teen romance, and that came to
seem a necessary ingredient of the mysterious compound called love.
Teenaged sweethearts were considered to be misunderstood by their
parents, adults in general, indeed by the entire world. Their glorious
grudges were celebrated in mildly mutinous tunes like "Puppy Love"
("And they call it puppy love,/ Oh, I guess they'll never know,/ How a
young heart really feels,/ And why I love her so."), and more dramatic
ditties like "Town Without Pity"("If we stop to gaze upon a star,/ People
talk about how bad we are,/ Oh, 'tis not an easy age,/ We're like tigers
in a cage."). You could murmur meaningfully along with the lyrics, feeling like the embattled defender of an underdog cause, and even if you
had never had a boyfriend, you could reflect moodily upon its being
"not an easy age" if your parents hated rock-and-roll enough. Music

and love were all intertwined, and both were frowned upon by the world.

Being frowned upon was a wonderfully romantic feeling, even if your circumstaces didn't warrant it at all. I was particularly fond of songs about slum romance or anything that suggested teenage gang life. I identified with tunes like "Uptown" ("And then he comes uptown each evening to my tenement,/ Uptown, where folks don't have to pay much rent,/ And when he's there with me, he can see that he's everything.") and "He's a Rebel" ("See the way he walks down the street/ Watch the way he shuffles his feet/ Oh, How he holds his head high/ When he goes walkin' by . . . He's my guy."). Now nothing even approaching an "uptown" existed in the small midwestern city where I lived, and, of course, nobody was coming to my house each evening, much less to my "tenement"; furthermore, the "rebels" in my eighth-grade class did nothing wilder than buy an occasional pack of cigarettes. And yet I remember wishing desperately, on a visit to Chicago with my parents, that the subway on which we were riding would derail in a suitable part of town so that I might escape and somehow make my "Uptown" and "Rebel" fantasies come true. The way in which I might do this was of course vague, but then yearning, as I said, was the point of it all.

While some of us were content with fantasy, with simply hoping that train wrecks or tornadoes would magically free us to live out our misty dreams, others enacted vivid tableaux in an effort to duplicate the situation depicted in a song. A friend recalls locking herself in her bedroom and crying briefly in despair during a party she gave. There was no reason for her tears, mind you; her performance was inspired by the hit song, "It's My Party and I'll Cry If I Want To."

A younger sister of mine used to endlessly spin "Downtown" ("Downtown, things will be great when you're/ Downtown, No finer place for sure,/ Downtown, Everything's waiting for you.") while playing Barbie dolls at her girlfriends's house. "Maryjane had a convertible for Ken and Barbie," she recalls, "so we'd dress them both up for dates downtown. Afterward, we'd take the bus downtown ourselves and buy popcorn at Woolworth's and sing the song over and over, thinking about finding dates." The possibility of their doing so was limited by the fact that they were ten at the time.

The sort of daydreaming that listening to AM love tunes encourages   9
begins early. Little did I realize, as I harbored thoughts of Ricky Nelson,
that another sister of mine was thinking of his songs whenever she heard
motorcycles rumble past our quiet home. Or that she was playing my 45s
on the little record player in our room as soon as I left the house, jumping
up and down on the bed as she did so in a childish erotic frenzy. She
couldn't have been more than four at the time, but already the recordings
of "Folk Songs From Other Lands" that my mother had bought for us
left her cold. Soon she would be cutting toothpaste-ad photos of men and
women kissing out of magzines and taping them to the walls to add a
romantic note to her record-listening binges. And, shortly after that,
she'd be playing her own copy of "Surfer Girl" while dancing with her
pillow, upon which she would shower a profusion of "practice" kisses.
But then this was nothing compared to the passion of another friend,
who used to pretend that the family dog was her boyfriend and hold
the animal's ears aloft while bestowing little pecks upon its nose. Of
course, this performance was enacted to the accompaniment of romantic
AM hits.

This fantasizing along with the radio continued hot and heavy through   10
junior high school. "Young Girl" ("Young girl, get out of my mind/ My
love for you is way out of line.") was among the more frequently recalled
hits, probably because extreme youth was the main stumbling block to
romance among daydreamers. "We used to go over to my girlfriend's
house before we went to the skating rink," said one woman. "We'd play
'Young Girl' and then skate with older guys and imagine they were singing it about us." There were also lots of fans for the Supremes' wonderful
"You Can't Hurry Love": Its message about patience spoke to twelve-
year-olds eager for their first big romance.

The necessity of going to school, along with what was perceived to be   11
the general insensitivity of the adult world, seemed the great obstacle to
true love among the very young. Perhaps that's why tunes like "Summer
in the City," "See you in September," and "A Summer Place" proved
particularly popular among young daydreamers. Freedom from school
meant escape, and escape meant the freedom to love. "I used to visualize
girls with blonde hair going to the beach with guys in convertibles and
then breaking up when school started," recalled a friend now in her early
twenties, explaining her passion for such songs. Probably nothing was
ever really so expressive of the teenager's ideal of "School Is Out" as the
tune by that name sung by Gary U.S. Bonds, or the plethora of paeans
to surf, sand, sun and sports cars popularized by the Beach Boys for so

many years. I myself have memories of contriving to stand beneath a certain tree whose leaves turned their silver sides to the wind whenever I waited for my summer-of-ninth-grade boyfriend to come visit me; looking at the tree, I murmured meaningfully along with the "A Summer Song" popular that year, in which the blown-back leaves of summer led to melancholy thoughts of autumn's falling leaves and the inevitable end of summer romance and summer freedom.

Popular tunes have come a long way since the earplug transistors and portable phonos of the mid-fifties. Hit tunes are now played in department stores and supermarkets—the sound is everywhere. Even young kids have steroes and buy albums instead of 45s. Sexual references are explicit rather than veiled, but none of these changes seems to have altered the power that even trivial songs have to stir longing in teenage hearts. A fourteen-year-old I know used to make little cuts on her hand while listening to Rod Stewart's "First Cut Is the Deepest" a few years ago; she imagined she was feeling the pains of love. And who if not Marvin Gaye has set half the girls in America over the age of eight dreaming that someday a guy will be moved by a passion for them as fierce and mellow as that which he puts into his songs? 12

Dreaming along with popular hits is, as I said, less about love than about yearning. The songs evoke an amorphous dream of adult life in which romantic passion consumes every other emotion and responsibility dos not weigh anyone down. The vision is distorted, of course, because it is incomplete, but by participating in it, daydreamers can imagine themselves part of the grown-up world for a while. They can taste a little of what it feels like to be in love, and so experience certain of love's pleasures and disappointments without needing a specific object for their affections. The idea of love fuses early in life with a deliciously melancholy sense of yearning, and that yearning remains a part of love for the rest of the daydreamer's life. 13

Topical Considerations

1. What is Helgesen's theses? Do you agree with it? Do you feel it is true for the present generation? Explain.

2. Helgesen argues that transistor radios were largely responsible for AM radio having such an impact on her generation. Are similar products having the same effect on your generation? other effects? Give examples. What do you see happening as a result?

3. In paragraph 7, Helgesen writes: "While some of us were content with fantasy, with simply hoping that train wrecks or tornadoes would magically free us to live out our misty dreams, others enacted vivid tableaux in an effort to duplicate the situation depicted in a song." Does today's generation respond to rock music in this way? How much (if at

all) are the situations depicted in songs mirrored in or a direct cause of real-life problems?

4. As in Woody Allen's essay, there are numerous allusions to singers, songs, movies, and television shows that would be more familiar to an earlier generation. Who in your family would most readily recognize these allusions? As far as you know, was that person affected as Helgesen was?

5. Do you think your attitudes toward being in love would have been different if you had never listened to the radio, owned a stereo, or attended a rock concert? Explain. What other influences have shaped your views on this subject?

6. Do you daydream? Do you do it often? Do you feel it has a good or bad effect on your day-to-day activities? on your long-term goals?

Rhetorical Considerations

1. How does Helgesen begin her essay? Is this an effective opening? Is it attention-getting? Why or why not?

2. How is the location of the thesis statement for this essay different from the one in Dick Gregory's "Shame"? Is this a good place for it? Why or why not?

3. Why does Helgesen write from the first-person point of view? What would be the effect if she wrote this essay in the third person? What is the point of view of the other essays in this section? Would anything be gained or lost if any of these were written in the third person? Explain.

4. What specific names, dates, and places are used in this essay? Substitute a more general word for each specific term that you find. Which is more interesting to read? What does this suggest to you about your own writing?

5. Are there any slang expressions in this essay? Are they appropriate to the tone?

6. In her discussion of daydreaming, Helgesen avoids unnecessary repetition of this word by using synonyms. What are some of these synonyms? What are others she could have used?

Writing Assignments

1. Can you remember the first time you fell in love as a teenager? Was it the real thing or just "puppy love"? In an essay that includes narration, description, and dialogue, create a vivid picture of what your loved one was like, how you felt, and the way you acted.

2. Helgesen argues not only that AM radio shaped her generation's ideas of love but that these views were unrealistic and "self-

deceiving." Today's rock singers are still singing about love. Is their view unrealistic and self-deceiving? Or do they give the true picture? Write a one-sentence answer to this question. Using this answer as your thesis, write a persuasive essay in which you defend your answer. Give specific quotations from song titles to illustrate your points. (You might choose one favorite rock singer or group and analyze their songs.)

3. What are your own present views of what it means to be in love? Has what you hear on the radio had any influence on you? Have there been other influential factors? Write an essay in which you define romantic love and discuss what caused you to view it in this way.

Graduation

Maya Angelou

One of the most important events in a young person's life is graduation day. This selection, a vivid recollection of one such day and the events leading up to it, is by the famous black author, Maya Angelou. Born Marguerita Johnson in 1928, Angelou survived some terrible childhood experiences—a broken home, being raped at the age of eight, becoming an unwed mother at sixteen. As an adult, she involved herself in theatre, television, and journalism. She also served as a coordinator of Martin Luther King's Southern Christian Leadership Conference. She is perhaps best known for her autobiographical books, including *I Know Why the Caged Bird Sings* (1970), from which this piece was taken, and *The Heart of a Woman* (1981), the most recent memoir.

The children in Stamps trembled visibly with anticipation. 1 Some adults were excited too, but to be certain the whole young population had come down with graduation epidemic. Large classes were graduating from both the grammar school and the high school. Even those who were years removed from their own day of glorious release were anxious to help with preparations as a kind of dry run. The junior students who were moving into the vacating classes' chairs were tradition-bound to show their talents for leadership and management. They strutted through the school and around the campus exerting pressure on the lower grades. Their authority was so new that occasionally if they pressed a little too hard it had to be overlooked. After all, next term was coming, and it never hurt a sixth grader to have a play sister in the eighth grade, or a tenth-year student to be able to call a twelfth grader Bubba. So all was endured in a spirit of shared understanding. But the graduating classes themselves were the nobility. Like travelers with exotic destinations on their minds, the graduates were remarkably forgetful. They came to school without their books, or tablets, or even pencils. Volunteers fell over themselves to secure replacements for the missing equipment. When accepted, the willing workers might or might not be thanked, and it was of no importance to the pregraduation rites. Even teachers were respectful of the now quiet and aging seniors, and tended to speak to them, if not as equals, as beings only slightly lower than themselves. After tests were returned and grades given, the student body, which acted like an extended family, knew who did well, who excelled, and what piteous ones had failed.

Unlike the white high school, Lafayette County Training School distinguished itself by having neither lawn, nor hedges, nor tennis court, nor climbing ivy. Its two buildings (main classrooms, the grade school and home economics) were set on a dirt hill with no fence to limit either its boundaries or those of bordering farms. There was a large expanse to the left of the school which was used alternately as a baseball diamond or a basketball court. Rusty hoops on the swaying poles represented the permanent recreational equpment, although bats and balls could be borrowed from the P.E. teacher if the borrower was qualified and if the diamond wasn't occupied.

Over this rocky area relieved by a few shady tall persimmon trees the graduating class walked. The girls often held hands and no longer bothered to speak to the lower students. There was a sadness about them, as if this old world was not their home and they were bound for higher ground. The boys, on the other hand, had become more friendly, more outgoing. A decided change from the closed attitude they projected while studying for finals. Now they seemed not ready to give up the old school, the familiar paths and classrooms. Only a small percentage would be continuing on to college—one of the South's A & M (agricultural and mechanical) schools, which trained negro youths to be carpenters, farmers, handymen, masons, maids, cooks, and baby nurses. Their future rode heavily on their shoulders, and blinded them to the collective joy that had pervaded the lives of the boys and girls in the grammar school graduating class.

Parents who could afford it had ordered new shoes and ready-made clothes for themselves from Sears and Roebuck or Montgomery Ward. They also engaged the best seamstresses to make the floating graduating dresses and to cut down secondhand pants which would be pressed to a military slickness for the important event.

Oh, it was important, all right. Whitefolks would attend the ceremony, and two or three would speak of God and home, and the Southern way of life, and Mrs. Parsons, the principal's wife, would play the graduation march while the lower-grade graduates paraded down the aisles and took their seats below the platform. The high school seniors would wait in empty classrooms to make their dramatic entrance.

In the Store I was the person of the moment. The birthday girl. The   6
center. Bailey* had graduated the year before, although to do so he had
had to forfeit all pleasures to make up for his time lost in Baton
Rouge.

My class was wearing butter-yellow piqué dresses, and Momma   7
launched out on mine. She smocked the yoke into tiny crisscrossing
puckers, then shirred the rest of the bodice. Her dark fingers ducked in
and out of the lemony cloth as she embroidered raised daisies around the
hem. Before she considered herself finished she had added a crocheted
cuff on the puff sleeves, and a pointy crocheted collar.

I was going to be lovely. A walking model of all the various styles of   8
fine hand sewing and it didn't worry me that I was only twelve years old
and merely graduating from the eighth grade. Besides, many teachers in
Arkansas Negro schools had only that diploma and were licensed to
impart wisdom.

The days had become longer and more noticeable. The faded beige   9
of former times had been replaced with strong and sure colors. I began
to see my classmates' clothes, their skin tones, and the dust that waved
off pussy willows. Clouds that lazed across the sky were objects of great
concern to me. Their shiftier shapes might have held a message that in
my new happiness and with a little bit of time I'd soon decipher. During
that period I looked at the arch of heaven so religiously my neck kept a
steady ache. I had taken to smiling more often, and my jaws hurt from
the unaccustomed activity. Between the two physical sore spots, I suppose I could have been uncomfortable, but that was not the case. As a
member of the winning team (the graduating class of 1940) I had outdis-
tanced unpleasant sensations by miles. I was headed for the freedom of
open fields.

Youth and social approval allied themselves with me and we tram-   10
meled memories of slights and insults. The wind of our swift passage
remodeled my features. Lost tears were pounded to mud and then to
dust. Years of withdrawal were brushed aside and left behind, as hanging
ropes of parasitic moss.

My work alone had awarded me a top place and I was going to be   11
one of the first called in the graduating ceremonies. On the classroom
blackboard, as well as on the bulletin board in the auditorium, there
were blue stars and white stars and red stars. No absences, no tar-
dinesses, and my academic work was among the best of the year. I could
say the preamble to the Constitution even faster than Bailey. We timed
ourselves often: "WethepeopleoftheUnitedStatesinordertoformamore-
perfectunion . . ." I had memorized the Presidents of the United States
from Washington to Roosevelt in chronological as well as alphabetical
order.

*Angelou's brother.—Ed.

My hair pleased me too. Gradually the black mass had lengthened and thickened, so that it kept at last to its braided pattern, and I didn't have to yank my scalp off when I tried to comb it.   12

Louise and I had rehearsed the exercises until we tired out ourselves.   13
Henry Reed was class valedictorian. He was a small, very black boy with hooded eyes, a long, broad nose and an oddly shaped head. I had admired him for years because each term he and I vied for the best grades in our class. Most often he bested me, but instead of being disappointed I was pleased that we shared top places between us. Like many Southern Black children, he lived with his grandmother, who was as strict as Momma and as kind as she knew how to be. He was courteous, respectful, and soft-spoken to elders, but on the playground he chose to play the roughest games. I admired him. Anyone, I reckoned, sufficiently afraid or sufficiently dull could be polite. But to be able to operate at a top level with both adults and children was admirable.

His valedictory speech was entitled "To Be or Not to Be." The rigid   14
tenth-grade teacher had helped him to write it. He'd been working on the dramatic stresses for months.

The weeks until graduation were filled with heady activities. A group   15
of small children were to be presented in a play about buttercups and daisies and bunny rabbits. They could be heard throughout the building practicing their hops and their little songs that sounded like silver bells. The older girls (non-graduates, of course) were assigned the task of making refreshments for the night's festivities. A tangy scent of ginger, cinnamon, nutmeg, and chocolate wafted around the home economics building as the budding cooks made samples for themselves and their teachers.

In every corner of the workshop, axes and saws split fresh timber as   16
the woodshop boys made sets and stage scenery. Only the graduates were left out of the general bustle. We were free to sit in the library at the back of the building or look in quite detachedly, naturally, on the measures being taken for our event.

Even the minister preached on graduation the Sunday before. His   17
subject was, "Let your light so shine that men will see your good works and praise your Father, Who is in Heaven." Although the sermon was purported to be addressed to us, he used the occasion to speak to back-sliders, gamblers, and general ne'er-do-wells. But since he had called our names at the beginning of the service we were mollified.

Among Negroes the tradition was to give presents to children going   18
only from one grade to another. How much more important this was when the person was graduating at the top of the class. Uncle Willie and Momma had sent away for a Mickey Mouse watch like Bailey's. Louise gave me four embroidered handkerchiefs. (I gave her three crocheted doilies.) Mrs. Sneed, the minister's wife, made me an underskirt to wear for graduation, and nearly every customer gave me a nickel or maybe

even a dime with the instruction "Keep on moving to higher ground," or some such encouragement.

Amazingly the great day finally dawned and I was out of bed before I knew it. I threw open the back door to see it more clearly, but Momma said, "Sister, come away from that door and put your robe on." 19

I hoped the memory of that morning would never leave me. Sunlight was itself still young, and the day had none of the insistence maturity would bring it in a few hours. In my robe and barefoot in the backyard, under cover of going to see about my new beans, I gave myself up to the gentle warmth and thanked God that no matter what evil I had done in my life He had allowed me to live to see this day. Somewhere in my fatalism I had expected to die, accidentally, and never have the chance to walk up the stairs in the auditorium and gracefully receive my hard-earned diploma. Out of God's merciful bosom I had won reprieve. 20

Bailey came out in his robe and gave me a box wrapped in Christmas paper. He said he had saved his money for months to pay for it. It felt like a box of chocolates, but I knew Bailey wouldn't save money to buy candy when we had all we could want under our noses. 21

He was as proud of the gift as I. It was a soft-leather-bound copy of a collection of poems by Edgar Allan Poe, or, as Bailey and I called him, "Eap." I turned to "Annabel Lee" and we walked up and down the garden rows, the cool dirt between our toes, reciting the beautifully sad lines. 22

Momma made a Sunday breakfast although it was only Friday. After we finished the blessing, I opened my eyes to find the watch on my plate. It was a dream of a day. Everything went smoothly and to my credit. I didn't have to be reminded or scolded for anything. Near evening I was too jittery to attend to chores, so Bailey volunteered to do all before his bath. 23

Days before, we had made a sign for the Store and as we turned out the lights Momma hung the cardboard over the doorknob. It read clearly: CLOSED. GRADUATION. 24

My dress fitted perfectly and everyone said that I looked like a sunbeam in it. On the hill, going toward the school, Bailey walked behind with Uncle Willie, who muttered, "Go on, Ju." He wanted him to walk ahead with us because it embarrassed him to have to walk so slowly. Bailey said he'd let the ladies walk together, and the men would bring up the rear. We all laughed, nicely. 25

Little children dashed by out of the dark like fireflies. Their crepe-paper dresses and butterfly wings were not made for running and we heard more than one rip, dryly, and the regretful "uh uh" that followed. 26

The school blazed without gaiety. The windows seemed cold and unfriendly from the lower hill. A sense of ill-fated timing crept over me, and if Momma hadn't reached for my hand I would have drifted back to Bailey and Uncle Willie, and possibly beyond. She made a few slow jokes about my feet getting cold, and tugged me along to the now-strange building. 27

Around the front steps, assurance came back. There were my fellow   28
"greats," the graduating class. Hair brushed back, legs oiled, new dresses
and pressed pleats, fresh pocket handkerchiefs and little handbags, all
homesewn. Oh, we were up to snuff, all right. I joined my comrades and
didn't even see my family go in to find seats in the crowded auditorium.

The school band struck up a march and all classes filed in as had been   29
rehearsed. We stood in front of our seats, as assigned, and on a signal
from the choir director, we sat. No sooner had this been accomplished
than the band started to play the national anthem. We rose again and
sang the song, after which we recited the pledge of allegiance. We remained standing for a brief minute before the choir director and the
principal signaled to us, rather desperately I thought, to take our seats.
The command was so unusual that our carefully rehearsed and smooth-
running machine was thrown off. For a full minute we fumbled for our
chairs and bumped into each other awkwardly. Habits change or solidify
under pressure, so in our state of nervous tension we had been ready to
follow our usual assembly pattern: the American National Anthem, then
the pledge of allegiance, then the song every Black person I knew called
the Negro National Anthem. All done in the same key, with the same
passion and most often standing on the same foot.

Finding my seat at last, I was overcome with a presentiment of worse   30
things to come. Something unrehearsed, unplanned, was going to happen, and we were going to be made to look bad. I distinctly remember
being explicit in the choice of pronoun. It was "we," the graduating class,
the unit, that concerned me then.

The principal welcomed "parents and friends" and asked the Baptist   31
minister to lead us in prayer. His invocation was brief and punchy, and
for a second I thought we were getting back on the high road to right
action. When the principal came back to the dais, however, his voice had
changed. Sounds always affected me profoundly and the principal's voice
was one of my favorites. During assembly it melted and lowed weakly into
the audience. It had not been in my plan to listen to him, but my curiosity
was piqued and I straightened up to give him my attention.

He was talking about Booker T. Washington, our "late great leader,"   32
who said we can be as close as the fingers on the hand, etc. . . . Then he
said a few vague things about friendship and the friendship of kindly
people to those less fortunate than themselves. With that his voice nearly
faded, thin, away. Like a river diminishing to a stream and then to a
trickle. But he cleared his throat and said, "Our speaker tonight, who is
also our friend, came from Texarkana to deliver the commencement
address, but due to the irregularity of the train schedule, he's going to,
as they say, 'speak and run.' " He said that we understood and wanted
the man to know that we were most grateful for the time he was able to
give us and then something about how we were willing always to adjust
to another's program, and without more ado—"I give you Mr. Edward
Donleavy."

Not one but two white men came through the door offstage. The   33
shorter one walked to the speaker's platform, and the tall one moved over
to the center seat and sat down. But that was our principal's seat, and
already occupied. The dislodged gentleman bounced around for a long
breath or two before the Baptist minister gave him his chair, then with
more dignity than the situation deserved, the minister walked off the
stage.

Donleavy looked at the audience once (on reflection, I'm sure that he   34
wanted only to reassure himself that we were really there), adjusted his
glasses, and began to read from a sheaf of papers.

He was glad "to be here and to see the work going on just as it was   35
in the other schools."

At the first "Amen" from the audience I willed the offender to immedi-   36
ate death by choking on the word. But Amens and Yes, sir's began to fall
around the room like rain through a ragged umbrella.

He told us of the wonderful changes we children in Stamps had in   37
store. The Central School (naturally, the white school was Central) had
already been granted improvements that would be in use in the fall. A
well-known artist was coming from Little Rock to teach art to them. They
were going to have the newest microscopes and chemistry equipment for
their laboratory. Mr. Donleavy didn't leave us long in the dark over who
made these improvements available to Central High. Nor were we to be
ignored in the general betterment scheme he had in mind.

He said that he had pointed out to people at a very high level that one   38
of the first-line football tacklers at Arkansas Agricultural and Mechanical
College had graduated from good old Lafayette County Training School.
Here fewer Amen's were heard. Those few that did break through lay
dully in the air with the heaviness of habit.

He went on to praise us. He went on to say how he had bragged that   39
"one of the best basketball players at Fisk sank his first ball right here at
Lafayette County Training School."

The white kids were going to have a chance to become Galileos and   40
Madame Curies and Edisons and Gauguins, and our boys (the girls
weren't even in on it) would try to be Jesse Owenses and Joe Louises.

Owens and the Brown Bomber were great heroes in our world, but   41
what school official in the white-goddom of Little Rock had the right to
decide that those two men must be our only heroes? Who decided that
for Henry Reed to become a scientist he had to work like George Washington Carver, as a bootblack, to buy a lousy microscope? Bailey was
obviously always going to be too small to be an athlete, so which concrete
angel glued to what country seat had decided that if my brother wanted
to become a lawyer he had to first pay penance for his skin by picking
cotton and hoeing corn and studying correspondence books at night for
twenty years?

The man's dead words fell like bricks around the auditorium and too   42
many settled in my belly. Constrained by hard-learned manners I

couldn't look behind me, but to my left and right the proud graduating class of 1940 had dropped their heads. Every girl in my row had found something new to do with her handkerchief. Some folded the tiny squares into love knots, some into triangles, but most were wadding them, then pressing them flat on their yellow laps.

On the dais, the ancient tragedy was being replayed. Professor Parsons   43
sat, a sculptor's reject, rigid. His large, heavy body seemed devoid of will or willingness, and his eyes said he was no longer with us. The other teachers examined the flag (which was draped stage right) or their notes, or the windows which opened on our now-famous playing diamond.

Graduation, the hush-hush magic time of frills and gifts and congratu-   44
lations and diplomas, was finished for me before my name was called. The accomplishment was nothing. The meticulous maps, drawn in three colors of ink, learning and spelling decasyllabic words, memorizing the whole of *The Rape of Lucrece*—it was nothing. Donleavy had exposed us.

We were maids and farmers, handymen and washerwomen, and any-   45
thing higher that we aspired to was farcical and presumptuous. Then I wished that Gabriel Prosser and Nat Turner had killed all whitefolks in their beds and that Abraham Lincoln had been assassinated before the signing of the Emancipation Proclamation, and that Harriet Tubman had been killed by that blow on her head and Christopher Columbus had drowned in the *Santa Maria.*

It was awful to be Negro and have no control over my life. It was brutal   46
to be young and already trained to sit quietly and listen to charges brought against my color with no chance of defense. We should all be dead. I thought I should like to see us all dead, one on top of the other. A pyramid of flesh with the whitefolks on the bottom, as the broad base, then the Indians with their silly tomahawks and teepees and wigwams and treaties, the Negroes with their mops and recipes and cotton sacks and spirituals sticking out of their mouths. The Dutch children should all stumble in their wooden shoes and break their necks. The French should choke to death on the Louisiana Purchase (1803) while silkworms ate all the Chinese with their stupid pigtails. As a species, we were an abomination. All of us.

Donleavy was running for election, and assured our parents that if he   47
won we could count on having the only colored paved playing field in that part of Arkansas. Also—he never looked up to acknowledge the grunts of acceptance—also, we were bound to get some new equipment for the home economics building and the workshop.

He finished, and since there was no need to give any more than the   48
most perfunctory thank-you's, he nodded to the men on the stage, and the tall white man who was never introduced joined him at the door. They left with the attitude that now they were off to something really important. (The graduation ceremonies at Lafayette County Training School had been a mere preliminary.)

The ugliness they left was palpable. An uninvited guest who wouldn't   49 leave. The choir was summoned and sang a modern arrangement of "Onward, Christian Soldiers," with new words pertaining to graduates seeking their place in the world. But it didn't work. Elouise, the daughter of the Baptist minister, recited "Invictus," and I could have cried at the impertinence of "I am the master of my fate, I am the captain of my soul."

My name had lost its ring of familiarity and I had to be nudged to go   50
and receive my diploma. All my preparations had fled. I neither marched up to the stage like a conquering Amazon, nor did I look in the audience for Bailey's nod of approval. Marguerite Johnson, I heard the name again, my honors were read, there were noises in the audience of appreciation, and I took my place on the stage as rehearsed.

I thought about colors I hated: ecru, puce, lavender, beige, and black.   51

There was shuffling and rustling around me, then Henry Reed was   52
giving his valedictory address, "To Be or Not to Be." Hadn't he heard the whitefolks? We couldn't *be*, so the question was a waste of time. Henry's voice came out clear and strong. I feared to look at him. Hadn't he got the message? There was no "nobler in the mind" for Negroes because the world didn't think we had minds, and they let us know it. "Outrageous fortune"? Now, that was a joke. When the ceremony was over I had to tell Henry Reed some things. That is, if I still cared. Not "rub," Henry, "erase." "Ah, there's the erase." Us.

Henry had been a good student in elocution. His voice rose on tides   53
of promise and fell on waves of warnings. The English teacher had helped him to create a sermon winging through Hamlet's soliloquy. To be a man, a doer, a builder, a leader, or to be a tool, an unfunny joke, a crusher of funky toadstools. I marveled that Henry could go through with the speech as if we had a choice.

I had been listening and silently rebutting each sentence with my eyes   54
closed; then there was a hush, which in an audience warns that something unplanned is happening. I looked up and saw Henry Reed, the conservative, the proper, the A student, turn his back to the audience and turn to us (the proud graduating class of 1940) and sing, nearly speaking,

> Lift ev'ry voice and sing
> Till earth and heaven ring
> Ring with the harmonies of Liberty . . .

It was the poem written by James Weldon Johnson. It was the music composed by J. Rosamond Johnson. It was the Negro National Anthem. Out of habit we were singing it.

Our mothers and fathers stood in the dark hall and joined the hymn   55
of encouragement. A kindergarten teacher led the small children onto the stage and the buttercups and daisies and bunny rabbits marked time and tried to follow:

> Stoney the road we trod
> Bitter the chastening rod

Felt in the days when hope, unborn, had died.
Yet with a steady beat
Have not our weary feet
Come to the place for which our fathers sighed?

Every child I knew had learned that song with his ABC's and along with   56
"Jesus Loves Me This I Know." But I personally had never heard it
before. Never heard the words, despite the thousands of times I had sung
them. Never thought they had anything to do with me.

On the other hand, the words of Patrick Henry had made such an   57
impression on me that I had been able to stretch myself tall and trembling
and say, "I know not what course others may take, but as for me, give me
liberty or give me death."

And now I heard, really for the first time: 58

We have come over a way that with tears has been
    watered,
We have come, treading our path through the blood
    of the slaughtered.

While echoes of the song shivered in the air, Henry Reed bowed his   59
head, said "Thank you," and returned to his place in the line. The tears
that slipped down many faces were not wiped away in shame.

We were on top again. As always, again. We survived. The depths had   60
been icy and dark, but now a bright sun spoke to our souls. I was no
longer simply a member of the proud graduating class of 1940; I was a
proud member of the wonderful, beautiful Negro race.

Oh, Black known and unknown poets, how often have your auctioned   61
pains sustained us? Who will compute the lonely nights made less lonely
by your songs, or the empty pots made less tragic by your tales?

If we were a people much given to revealing secrets, we might raise   62
monuments and sacrifice to the memories of our poets, but slavery cured
us of that weakness. It may be enough, however, to have it said that we
survive in exact relationship to the dedication of our poets (include
preachers, musicians, and blues singers).

Topical Considerations

1. What signs does Angelou give that reveal graduation to be an
important occasion for the children in Stamps? Why do you think it was
so important, not only to the children and parents but also to the community?

2. Is there any particular reason why the principal should allude
to Booker T. Washington just prior to Mr. Donleavy's speech? How does
the audience's response to his speech reflect the black leader's own
feelings about how blacks should act toward white people?

3. Angelou appears to have been particularly sensitive to what was happening during the graduation ceremony. What first prompted her to suspect that something was amiss? How does the atmosphere change as Mr. Donleavy's speech progresses? What specifically does he say to cause the change?

4. What does Angelou appear to resent most about Donleavy's remarks? Are his assumptions about the future aspirations of the Lafayette County Training School graduates justified? What clues do we have about the quality of education at Angelou's school that might suggest otherwise? Note Angelou's frequent historical and literary allusions.

5. The Negro National Anthem was not sung at the usual place in the program. Why does its postponement turn out to be a blessing? What effect does it have on Angelou?

6. If Dick Gregory had been attending Angelou's graduation as an adult, he no doubt would have been singing as loudly as the next person. Why? How might graduation have been different if he had been the guest speaker instead of Mr. Donleavy? What might Gregory have said?

7. How is this graduation a "commencement" for Angelou?

Rhetorical Considerations

1. Look closely at Angelou's first paragraph. What specific word choices does she use to suggest how important graduation is for children and teachers? How do these words contribute to the development of the essay?

2. How would you describe Angelou's point of view? Does she exaggerate the importance of this event? Or do you think her account is fairly accurate? How might the narrative have been different if told by Bailey (Angelou's older brother)? by the minister? by Mr. Donleavy?

3. In paragraph 36, Angelou remarks that "Amens and Yes, sir's began to fall around the room like rain through a ragged umbrella." What does this suggest about the atmosphere in the room during Mr. Donleavy's speech? What other figurative language does Angelou use?

4. Writers strive to make their material interesting and attention-getting by using specific, concrete details. How successful is Angelou in doing this? Cite specific examples to prove your point.

Writing Assignments

1. If Maya Angelou were asked to be a guest speaker at Lafayette County Training School today, what do you think she would say? Write her speech. Imitate her frequent allusions to important historical events and literary works.

2. In an essay, describe the graduation ceremonies at Lafayette County Training School from the minister's point of view, from Bailey's, and from Mr. Donleavy's.

3. Write an essay about your own graduation. Describe how you, your classmates, the school, and the community prepared for the event. Use figurative language and other vivid word pictures to recreate the atmosphere of the graduation hall during the ceremony.

A Few Words About Breasts

Nora Ephron

Nora Ephron is a novelist (*Heartburn,* 1983) and a widely published freelance writer, with aricles appearing in *The New Yorker, McCall's, Cosmopolitan, Esquire,* and *Rolling Stone.* Her essays, which have been collected in several books, including *Crazy Salad* (1975) and *Scribble, Scribble* (1978), display a characteristically wry sense of humor. One of her constant subject matters is the roles of men and women in our society. This essay, from *Crazy Salad,* is a rather frank though wry complaint about how growing up in the fifties—an era that embraced rigid sexual stereotypes—created in her lasting psychological hang-ups about her breast size.

"Do you want to marry my son?" the woman asked me. 1

"Yes," I said. 2

I was nineteen years old, a virgin, going with this woman's son, this big strange 3
woman who was married to a Lutheran minister in New Hampshire and pretended she was gentile and had this son, by her first husband, this total fool of a son who ran the hero-sandwich concession at Harvard Business School and whom for one moment one December in New Hampshire I said—as much out of politeness as anything else—that I wanted to marry.

"Fine," she said. "Now, here's what you do. Always make sure you're on top of 4
him so you won't seem so small. My bust is very large, you see, so I always lie on my back to make it look smaller, but you'll have to be on top most of the time."

I nodded. "Thank you," I said. 5

"I have a book for you to read," she went on. "Take it with you when you leave. 6
Keep it." She went to the bookshelf, found it, and gave it to me. It was a book on frigidity.

"Thank you," I said. 7

That is a true story. Everything in this article is a true story, but I feel 8
I have to point out that that story in particular is true. It happened on December 30, 1960. I think about it often. When it first happened, I naturally assumed that the woman's son, my boyfriend, was responsible.

I invented a scenario where he had had a little heart-to-heart with his mother and had confessed that his only objection to me was that my breasts were small; his mother then took it upon herself to help out. Now I think I was wrong about the incident. The mother was acting on her own, I think: that was her way of being cruel and competitive under the guise of being helpful and maternal. You have small breasts, she was saying; therefore you will never make him as happy as I have. Or you have small breasts; therefore you will doubtless have sexual problems. Or you have small breasts; therefore you are less woman than I am. She was, as it happens, only the first of what seems to me to be a never-ending string of women who have made competitive remarks to me about breast size. "I would love to wear a dress like that," my friend Emily says to me, "but my bust is too big." Like that. Why do women say these things to me? Do I attract these remarks the way other women attract married men or alcoholics or homosexuals? This summer, for example. I am at a party in East Hampton and I am introduced to a woman from Washington. She is a minor celebrity, very pretty and Southern and blond and outspoken, and I am flattered because she has read something I have written. We are talking animatedly, we have been talking no more than five minutes, when a man comes up to join us. "Look at the two of us," the woman says to the man, indicating me and her. "The two of us together couldn't fill an A cup." Why does she say that? It isn't even true, dammit, so why? Is she even more addled than I am on this subject? Does she honestly believe there is something wrong with her size breasts, which, it seems to me, now that I look hard at them, are just right? Do I unconsciously bring out competitiveness in women? In that form? What did I do to deserve it?

As for men.   9

There were men who minded and let me know they minded. There   10
were men who did not mind. In any case, I always minded.

And even now that I have been countlessly reassured that my figure   11
is a good one, now that I am grown up enough to understand that most of my feelings have very little to do with the reality of my shape, I am nonetheless obsessed by breasts. I cannot help it. I grew up in the terrible fifties—with rigid stereotypical sex roles, the insistence that men be men and dress like men and women be women and dress like women, the intolerance of androgyny—and I cannot shake it, cannot shake my feelings of inadequacy. Well, that time is gone, right? All those exaggerated examples of breast worship are gone, right? Those women were freaks, right? I know all that. And yet here I am, stuck with the psychological remains of it all, stuck with my own peculiar version of breast worship. You probably think I am crazy to go on like this: here I have set out to write a confession that is meant to hit you with the shock of recognition and instead you are sitting there thinking I am thoroughly warped. Well, what can I tell you? If I had had them, I would have been a completely different person. I honestly believe that.

After I went into therapy, a process that made it possible for me to tell   12
total strangers at cocktail parties that breasts were the hang-up of my life,
I was often told that I was insane to have been bothered by my condition.
I was also frequently told, by close friends, that I was extremely boring
on the subject. And my girl friends, the ones with nice big breasts, would
go on endlessly about how their lives had been far more miserable than
mine. Their bra straps were snapped in class. They couldn't sleep on their
stomachs. They were stared at whenever the word "mountain" cropped
up in geography. And *Evangeline,* good God what they went through
every time someone had to stand up and recite the Prologue to Longfel-
low's *Evangeline:* ". . . stand like druids of eld . . . / With beards that rest
on their bosoms." It was much worse for them, they tell me. They had
a terrible time of it, they assure me. I don't know how lucky I was, they
say.

I have thought about their remarks, tried to put myself in their place,   13
considered their point of view. I think they are full of shit.

Topical Considerations

1. Ephron writes: "I have set out to write a confession that is
meant to hit you with the shock of recognition and instead you are sitting there thinking I am thoroughly warped" (paragraph 11). Do you
feel Ephron's experience is one for which many women would feel a
"shock of recognition"? Or would most women fail to identify with
it?

2. What do you see as some of the causes of Ephron's "obsession" or "hang-up"? What obsessions or hang-ups about physical appearance are typical of teenagers or even of adults? Do you have any?

3. Was Ephron more concerned about her breast size when she
was nineteen than when she was older? Why or why not? Are people more
or less likely to be concerned about their physical appearance when they
are teenagers than when they are adults? Explain.

4. What were the "rigid stereotypical sex roles" of the fifties?
Are these roles still rigid? What current social trends might have caused
the change (if any)?

5. Who were some of the motion picture sex symbols of the
fifties? Who are some of today's television and motion picture idols?
Have our views of what makes a woman beautiful or a man handsome
changed?

6. What do you think of the conversation that Ephron describes
involving herself, the minor celebrity from Washington, and the man who
joins them? Was the celebrity's remark about breast size surprisingly
candid or typical? Would you be likely to overhear such remarks at a
college fraternity party?

Rhetorical Considerations

1. How would you characterize the tone of this essay? Is it thoughtful? serious? scholarly? flippant? angry? Do you see any similarities or differences in tone between this essay and others you have read in this section?

2. What can you say about Ephron's style, especially her sentence structure? How does it contribute to the tone of the essay?

3. Is the title attention-getting? Why or why not?

4. How and where does Ephron establish the thesis for her essay?

5. Do you note any one-sentence or unusually short paragraphs? How do they compare with others in the essay? What might be the writer's intent in keeping them so short? Are they adequately developed?

6. What effect does Ephron's ending have? How does she achieve this? Does it tie the essay together and give it completeness? Or does it leave the essay dangling? Explain.

Writing Assignments

1. Write an essay in which you discuss an obsession or hang-up regarding physical appearance that you experienced while growing up. Imitate Ephron's use of narrative and dialogue to show how sensitive you were on the subject.

2. In an essay, compare and contrast the sex roles of the fifties with those of the eighties. Have they changed? If so, how have they changed and what have been some of the causes?

"In My Day . . ."

Russell Baker

Russell Baker is the Pulitzer Prize-winning columnist of the *New York Times*. Since 1962, he has written his "Observer" column, famous for its humorous, sometimes biting criticisms of social issues, American politics, and current jargon. The selection that appears here shows a somewhat different voice of the famous humorist. Taken from his enchanting memoir, *Growing Up* (1982), this essay is a quiet yet moving protest about the passage of time that separates the boy from the man and the child from his parent.

At the age of eighty my mother had her last bad fall, and after that   1
her mind wandered free through time. Some days she went to weddings

and funerals that had taken place half a century earlier. On others she presided over family dinners cooked on Sunday afternoons for children who were now gray with age. Through all this she lay in bed but moved across time, traveling among the dead decades with a speed and ease beyond the gift of physical science.

"Where's Russell?" she asked one day when I came to visit at the nursing home. 2

"I'm Russell," I said. 3

She gazed at this improbably overgrown figure out of an inconceivable future and promptly dismissed it. 4

"Russell's only this big," she said, holding her hand, palm down, two feet from the floor. That day she was a young country wife with chickens in the backyard and a view of hazy blue Virginia mountains behind the apple orchard, and I was a stranger old enough to be her father. 5

Early one morning she phoned me in New York. "Are you coming to my funeral today?" she asked. 6

It was an awkward question with which to be awakened. "What are you talking about, for God's sake?" was the best reply I could manage. 7

"I'm being buried today," she declared briskly, as though announcing an important social event. 8

"I'll phone you back," I said and hung up, and when I did phone back she was all right, although she wasn't all right, of course, and we all knew she wasn't. 9

She had always been a small woman—short, light-boned, delicately structured—but now, under the white hospital sheet, she was becoming tiny. I thought of a doll with huge, fierce eyes. There had always been a fierceness in her. It showed in that angry, challenging thrust of the chin when she issued an opinion, and a great one she had always been for issuing opinions. 10

"I tell people exactly what's on my mind," she had been fond of boasting. "I tell them what I think, whether they like it or not." Often they had not liked it. She could be sarcastic to people in whom she detected evidence of the ignoramus or the fool. 11

"It's not always good policy to tell people exactly what's on your mind," I used to caution her. 12

"If they don't like it, that's too bad," was her customary reply, "because that's the way I am." 13

And so she was. A formidable woman. Determined to speak her mind, determined to have her way, determined to bend those who opposed her. In that time when I had known her best, my mother had hurled herself at life with chin thrust forward, eyes blazing, and an energy that made her seem always on the run. 14

She ran after squawking chickens, an axe in her hand, determined on a beheading that would put dinner in the pot. She ran when she made the beds, ran when she set the table. One Thanksgiving she burned herself badly when, running up from the cellar oven with the ceremonial 15 turkey, she tripped on the stairs and tumbled back down, ending at the bottom in the debris of giblets, hot gravy, and battered turkey. Life was combat, and victory was not to the lazy, the timid, the slugabed, the drugstore cowboy, the libertine, the mushmouth afraid to tell people exactly what was on his mind whether people liked it or not. She ran.

But now the running was over. For a time I could not accept the   16
inevitable. As I sat by her bed, my impulse was to argue her back to reality. On my first visit to the hospital in Baltimore, she asked who I was.

"Russell," I said.   17
"Russell's way out west," she advised me.   18
"No, I'm right here."   19
"Guess where I came from today?" was her response.   20
"Where?"   21
"All the way from New Jersey."   22
"When?"   23
"Tonight."   24
"No. You've been in the hospital for three days," I insisted.   25
"I suggest the thing to do is calm down a little bit," she replied. "Go   26
over to the house and shut the door."

Now she was years deep into the past, living in the neighborhood   27
where she had settled forty years earlier, and she had just been talking with Mrs. Hoffman, a neighbor across the street.

"It's like Mrs. Hoffman said today: The children always wander back   28
to where they come from," she remarked.
"Mrs. Hoffman has been dead for fifteen years."   29
"Russ got married today," she replied.   30
"I got married in 1950," I said, which was the fact.   31
"The house is unlocked," she said.   32

So it went until a doctor came by to give one of those oral quizzes that   33
medical men apply in such cases. She failed catastrophically, giving wrong answers or none at all to "What day is this?" "Do you know where you are?" "How old are you?" and so on. Then, a surprise.

"When is your birthday?" he asked.   34
"November 5, 1897," she said. Correct. Absolutely correct.   35
"How do you remember that?" the doctor asked.   36
"Because I was born on Guy Fawkes Day," she said.   37
"Guy Fawkes?" asked the doctor. "Who is Guy Fawkes?"   38
She replied with a rhyme I had heard her recite time and again over   39
the years when the subject of her birth date arose:

> "Please to remember the Fifth of November,
> Gunpowder treason and plot.
> I see no reason why gunpowder treason
> Should ever be forgot."

Then she glared at this young doctor so ill informed about Guy Fawkes' failed scheme to blow King James off his throne with barrels of gunpowder in 1605. She had been a schoolteacher, after all, and knew how to glare at a dolt. "You may know a lot about medicine, but you obviously don't know any history," she said. Having told him exactly what was on her mind, she left us again.

The doctors diagnosed a hopeless senility. Not unusual, they said. "Hardening of the arteries" was the explanation for laymen. I thought it was more complicated than that. For ten years or more the ferocity with which she had once attacked life had been turning to a rage against the weakness, the boredom, and the absence of love that too much age had brought her. Now, after the last bad fall, she seemed to have broken chains that imprisoned her in a life she had come to hate and to return to a time inhabited by people who loved her, a time in which she was needed. Gradually I understood. It was the first time in years I had seen her happy.

She had written a letter three years earlier which explained more than "hardening of the arteries." I had gone down from New York to Baltimore, where she lived, for one of my infrequent visits and, afterwards, had written her with some banal advice to look for the silver lining, to count her blessings instead of burdening others with her miseries. I suppose what it really amounted to was a threat that if she was not more cheerful during my visits I would not come to see her very often. Sons are capable of such letters. This one was written out of a childish faith in the eternal strength of parents, a naive belief that age and wear could be overcome by an effort of will, that all she needed was a good pep talk to recharge a flagging spirit. It was such a foolish, innocent idea, but one thinks of parents differently from other people. Other people can become frail and break, but not parents.

She wrote back in an unusually cheery vein intended to demonstrate, I suppose, that she was mending her ways. She was never a woman to apologize, but for one moment with the pen in her hand she came very close. Referring to my visit, she wrote: "If I seemed unhappy to you at times—" Here she drew back, reconsidered, and said something quite different:

"If I seemed unhappy to you at times, I am, but there's really nothing anyone can do about it, because I'm just so very tired and lonely that I'll just go to sleep and forget it." She was then seventy-eight.

Now, three years later, after the last bad fall, she had managed to forget the fatigue and loneliness and, in these free-wheeling excursions back through time, to recapture happiness. I soon stopped trying to wrest her back to what I considered the real world and tried to travel along with her on those fantastic swoops into the past. One day when I arrived at her bedside she was radiant.

"Feeling good today," I said.

"Why shouldn't I feel good?" she asked. "Papa's going to take me up   46
to Baltimore on the boat today."

At that moment she was a young girl standing on a wharf at Merry   47
Point, Virginia, waiting for the Chesapeake Bay steamer with her father,
who had been dead sixty-one years. William Howard Taft was in the
White House, Europe still drowsed in the dusk of the great century of
peace, America was a young country, and the future stretched before it
in beams of crystal sunlight. "The greatest country on God's green
earth," her father might have said, if I had been able to step into my
mother's time machine and join him on the wharf with the satchels packed
for Baltimore.

I could imagine her there quite clearly. She was wearing a blue dress   48
with big puffy sleeves and long black stockings. There was a ribbon in her
hair and a big bow tied on the side of her head. There had been a
childhood photograph in her bedroom which showed all this, although
the colors of course had been added years later by a restorer who tinted
the picture.

About her father, my grandfather, I could only guess, and indeed,   49
about the girl on the wharf with the bow in her hair, I was merely senti-
mentalizing. Of my mother's childhood and her people, of their time and
place, I knew very little. A world had lived and died, and though it was
part of my blood and bone I knew little more about it than I knew of the
world of the pharaohs. It was useless now to ask for help from my mother.
The orbits of her mind rarely touched present interrogators for more
than a moment.

Sitting at her bedside, forever out of touch with her, I wondered about   50
my own children, and their children, and children in general, and about
the disconnections between children and parents that prevent them from
knowing each other. Children rarely want to know what their parents
were before they were parents, and when age finally stirs their curiosity
there is no parent left to tell them. If a parent does lift the curtain a bit,
it is often only to stun the young with some exemplary tale of how much
harder life was in the old days.

I had been guilty of this when my children were small in the early 1960s   51
and living the affluent life. It galled me that their childhoods should be,
as I thought, so easy when my own had been, as I thought, so hard. I had
developed the habit, when they complained about the steak being over-
cooked or the television being cut off, of lecturing them on the harshness
of life in my day.

"In my day all we got for dinner was macaroni and cheese, and we were   52
glad to get it."

"In my day we didn't have any television."   53

"In my day . . ."   54

"In my day . . ."   55

At dinner one evening a son had offended me with an inadequate   56 report card, and as I leaned back and cleared my throat to lecture, he gazed at me with an expression of unutterable resignation and said, "Tell me how it was in your days, Dad."

I was angry with him for that, but angrier with myself for having   57
become one of those ancient bores whose highly selective memories of the past become transparently dishonest even to small children. I tried to break the habit, but must have failed. A few years later my son was referring to me when I was out of earshot as "the old-timer." Between us there was a dispute about time. He looked upon the time that had been my future in a disturbing way. My future was his past, and being young, he was indifferent to the past.

As I hovered over my mother's bed listening for muffled signals from   58
her childhood, I realized that this same dispute had existed between her and me. When she was young, with life ahead of her, I had been her future and resented it. Instinctively, I wanted to break free, cease being a creature defined by her time, consign her future to the past, and create my own. Well, I had finally done that, and then with my own children I had seen my exciting future become their boring past.

These hopeless end-of-the-line visits with my mother made me wish I   59
had not thrown off my own past so carelessly. We all come from the past, and children ought to know what it was that went into their making, to know that life is a braided cord of humanity stretching up from time long gone, and that it cannot be defined by the span of a single journey from diaper to shroud.

I thought that someday my own children would understand that. I   60
thought that, when I am beyond explaining, they would want to know what the world was like when my mother was young and I was younger, and we two relics passed together through strange times. I thought I should try to tell them how it was to be young in the time before jet planes, superhighways, H-bombs, and the global village of television. I realized I would have to start with my mother and her passion for improving the male of the species, which in my case took the form of forcing me to "make something of myself."

Lord, how I hated those words. . . .   61

Topical Considerations

1. What do Baker's visits with his mother cause him to yearn for most? Why?

2. What has Baker learned that he would someday like to share with his children? When he does talk to them, how do you think they will respond? Do you think they will feel that what he has to say is important? What kinds of experiences might help them hear what he has to say?

3. Baker's mother dwells in the past. Much of her conversation

includes stories from her childhood or young womanhood. Is this typical of any older people you know? Are the causes similar?

4. Why does Baker stop "trying to wrest [his mother] back to . . . the real world" (paragraph 44)? Do you agree with his reasons?

Rhetorical Considerations

1. Do you like Baker's opening? If so, what do you like about it? If not, why not?

2. Is Baker's use of dialogue effective? Give reasons for your answer.

3. Find passages that you think give a particularly vivid portrayal of Baker's mother. Why are they vivid? Does Baker use figurative language? Does he use narrative? How does his physical description of her convey her personality?

4. What are some of the verbs Baker uses to describe the way his mother faced life as a young woman? How do these word choices reflect her personality?

Writing Assignments

1. Baker discovered late in his life that his mother was not as invulnerable as he had always believed. In paragraph 41, he remarks: "It was such a foolish, innocent idea, but one thinks of parents differently from other people. Other people can become frail and break, but not parents." How do you feel about this? Do you see your parents as different from other people? Are they invulnerable? Write an essay in which you discuss your answers to these questions. Include specific illustrations to prove your point.

2. Visit with an older member of your family—perhaps your grandfather or grandmother. Ask him or her to tell you what the world was like when he or she was young and your parents were growing up. Write a personal history spanning those years. Include references to significant political events, inventions, and social trends.

THE SEXES

2

Courtship Through the Ages

James Thurber

We open this section, "The Sexes," with an entertaining piece about courting by one of America's most famous humorists. Born in 1894, Thurber was on the staff of *The New Yorker* as a writer, cartoonist, and social commentator. He was the author of several plays and books, including *Men, Women and Dogs, My Life and Hard Times* (1933), *Is Sex Necessary?* (1929), and, with E. B. White, *My World and Welcome to It* (1942), which included his famous story "The Secret Life of Walter Mitty." This essay, first published in *The New Yorker,* humorously surveys some of the problems the males of all species have to face in wooing potential mates.

Surely nothing in the astonishing scheme of life can have non- 1
plussed Nature so much as the fact that none of the females of any of the species she created really cared very much for the male, as such. For the past ten million years Nature has been busily inventing ways to make the male attractive to the female, but the whole business of courtship, from the marine annelids up to man, still lumbers heavily along, like a complicated musical comedy. I have been reading the sad and absorbing story in Volume 6 (Cole to Dama) of the *Encyclopaedia Britannica.* In this volume you can learn all about cricket, cotton, costume designing, crocodiles, crown jewels, and Coleridge, but none of these subjects is so interesting as the Courtship of Animals, which recounts the sorrowful lengths to which all males must go to arouse the interest of a lady.

We all know, I think, that Nature gave man whiskers and a mustache 2
with the quaint idea in mind that these would prove attractive to the female. We all know that, far from attracting her, whiskers and mustaches only made her nervous and gloomy, so that man had to go in for somersaults, tilting with lances, and performing feats of parlor magic to win her attention; he also had to bring her candy, flowers, and the furs of animals. It is common knowledge that in spite of all these "love displays" the male is constantly being turned down, insulted, or thrown out of the house. It is rather comforting, then, to discover that the peacock, for all his gorgeous plumage, does not have a particularly easy time in courtship; none of the males in the world do. The first peahen, it turned out, was only faintly stirred by her suitor's beautiful train. She would often go quietly to sleep while he was whisking it around. The *Britannica* tells us that the peacock actually had to learn a certain little trick to wake her up and revive her interest: he had to learn to vibrate his quills so as to make a rustling sound. In ancient times man himself, observing the ways of the peacock, probably tried vibrating his whiskers to make a rustling sound; if so, it didn't get him anywhere. He had to go in for something else; so, among other things, he went in for gifts. It is not unlikely that he got this

idea from certain flies and birds who were making no headway at all with rustling sounds.

One of the flies of the family Empidae, who had tried everything, finally hit on something pretty special. He contrived to make a glistening transparent balloon which was even larger than himself. Into this he would put sweetmeats and tidbits and he would carry the whole elaborate envelope through the air to the lady of his choice. This amused her for a time, but she finally got bored with it. She demanded silly little colorful presents, something that you couldn't eat but that would look nice around the house. So the male Empis had to go around gathering flower petals and pieces of bright paper to put into his balloon. On a courtship flight a male Empis cuts quite a figure now, but he can hardly be said to be happy. He never knows how soon the female will demand heavier presents, such as Roman coins and gold collar buttons. It seems probable that one day the courtship of the Empidae will fall down, as man's occasionally does, of its own weight. 3

The bowerbird is another creature that spends so much time courting the female that he never gets any work done. If all the male bowerbirds became nervous wrecks within the next ten or fifteen years, it would not surprise me. The female bowerbird insists that a playground be built for her with a specially constructed bower at the entrance. This bower is much more elaborate than an ordinary nest and is harder to build; it costs a lot more, too. The female will not come to the playground until the male has filled it up with a great many gifts: silvery leaves, red leaves, rose petals, shells, beads, berries, bones, dice, buttons, cigar bands, Christmas seals, and the Lord knows what else. When the female finally condescends to visit the playground, she is in a coy and silly mood and has to be chased in and out of the bower and up and down the playground before she will quit giggling and stand still long enough even to shake hands. The male bird is, of course, pretty well done in before the chase starts, because he has worn himself out hunting for eyeglass lenses and begonia blossoms. I imagine that many a bower bird, after chasing a female for two or three hours, says the hell with it and goes home to bed. Next day, of course, he telephones someone else and the same trying ritual is gone through with again. A male bowerbird is as exhausted as a night-club habitué before he is out of his twenties. 4

The male fiddler crab has a somewhat easier time, but it can hardly be said that he is stting pretty. He has one enormously large and powerful claw, usually brilliantly colored, and you might suppose that all he had to do was reach out and grab some passing cutie. The very earliest fiddler crabs may have tried this, but, if so, they got slapped for their pains. A female fiddler crab will not tolerate any caveman stuff; she never has and she doesn't intend to start now. To attract a female, a fiddler crab has to stand on tiptoe and brandish his claw in the air. If any female in the neighborhood is interested—and you'd be suprised how many are not— 5 she comes over and engages him in light badinage, for which he is not in the mood. As many as a hundred females may pass the time of day with him and go on about their business. By nightfall of an average courting day, a fiddler crab who has been standing on tiptoe for eight or ten hours waving a heavy claw in the air is in pretty sad shape. As in the case of the males of all species, however, he gets out of bed next morning, dashes some water on his face, and tries again.

The next time you encounter a male web-spinning spider, stop and   6
reflect that he is too busy worrying about his love life to have any desire to bite you. Male web-spinning spiders have a tougher life than any other males in the animal kingdom. This is because the female web-spinning spiders have very poor eyesight. If a male lands on a female's web, she kills him before he has time to lay down his cane and gloves, mistaking him for a fly or a bumblebee who has tumbled into her trap. Before the species figured out what to do about this, millions of males were murdered by ladies they called on. It is the nature of spiders to perform a little dance in front of the female, but before a male spinner could get near enough for the female to see who he was and what he was up to, she would lash out at him with a flat-iron or a pair of garden shears. One night, nobody knows when, a very bright male spinner lay awake worrying about calling on a lady who had been killing suitors right and left. It came to him that this business of dancing as a love display wasn't getting anybody anywhere except the grave. He decided to go in for web-twitching, or strand-vibrating. The next day he tried it on one of the nearsighted girls. Instead of dropping in on her suddenly, he stayed outside the web and began monkeying with one of its strands. He twitched it up and down and in and out with such a lilting rhythm that the female was charmed. The serenade worked beautifully; the female let him live. The *Britannica*'s spider-watchers, however, report that this system is not always successful. Once in a while, even now, a female will fire three bullets into a suitor or run him through with a kitchen knife. She keeps threatening him from the moment he strikes the first low notes on the outside strings, but usually by the time he has got up to the high notes played around the center of the web, he is going to town and she spares his life.

Even the butterfly, as handsome a fellow as he is, can't always win a   7
mate merely by fluttering around and showing off. Many butterflies have to have scent scales on their wings. Hepialus carries a powder puff in a perfumed pouch. He throws perfume at the ladies when they pass. The male tree cricket, Oecanthus, goes Hepialus one better by carrying a tiny bottle of wine with him and giving drinks to such doxies as he has designs on. One of the male snails throws darts to entertain the girls. So it goes, through the long list of animals, from the bristle worm and his rudimentary dance steps to man and his gift of diamonds and sapphires. The golden-eye drake raises a jet of water with his feet as he flies over a lake;

Hepialus has his powder puff, Oecanthus his wine bottle, man his etchings. It is a bright and melancholy story, the age-old desire of the male for the female, the age-old desire of the female to be amused and entertained. Of all the creatures on earth, the only males who could be figured as putting any irony into their courtship are the grebes and certain other diving birds. Every now and then a courting grebe slips quietly down to the bottom of a lake and then, with a mighty "Whoosh!," pops out suddenly a few feet from his girl friend, splashing water all over her. She seems to be persuaded that this is a purely loving display, but I like to think that the grebe always has a faint hope of drowning her or scaring her to death.

I will close this investigation into the mournful burdens of the male 8 with the *Britannica*'s story about a certain Argus pheasant. It appears that the Argus displays himself in front of a female who stands perfectly still without moving a feather. . . . The male Argus the *Britannica* tells about was confined in a cage with a female of another species, a female who kept moving around, emptying ashtrays and fussing with lampshades all the time the male was showing off his talents. Finally, in disgust, he stalked away and began displaying in front of his water trough. He reminds me of a certain male (Homo sapiens) of my acquaintance who one night after dinner asked his wife to put down her detective magazine so that he could read a poem of which he was very fond. She sat quietly enough until he was well into the middle of the thing, intoning with great ardor and intensity. Then suddenly there came a sharp, disconcerting *slap!* It turned out that all during the male's display, the female had been intent on a circling mosquito and had finally trapped it between the palms of her hands. The male in this case did not stalk away and display in front of a water trough; he went over to Tim's and had a flock of drinks and recited the poem to the fellas. I am sure they all told bitter stories of their own about how their displays had been interrupted by females. I am also sure that they all ended up singing "Honey, Honey, Bless Your Heart."

Topical Considerations

1. Thurber compares the courtship of animals to a "complicated musical comedy" that "lumbers heavily along." What are some examples Thurber gives to illustrate his point? How do these examples relate to the courtship habits of male *Homo sapiens*? What do Thurber's examples imply about the trials that the male encounters in his courtship of the female? Do you agree? Does the male really have as difficult a time as Thurber suggests?

2. In his opening sentence, Thurber suggests what he feels is the

chief reason why the male courtship of the female has such trouble getting off the groud and why, as he comments later, it often falls by its own weight. What is the reason? What does Thurber's remark suggest about the typical attitude a female takes in the courtship ritual? Is there any hint of truth in what he is saying? Does the female really care so little for the male? Or is she just pretending?

3. What is a "love display"? What are some of the love displays that Thurber describes in his essay? Are they typical? Can you think of others? Are the ones Thurber mentions as unsuccessful as he suggests?

4. In Thurber's treatment of the subject of courtship, he describes men as playing the dominant role. Is this always necessarily the case? Does the woman sometimes take the initiative? If so, is her approach the same? Or does she have her own typical love displays and methods of courting? Explain.

5. Are men's and women's attitudes toward courtship the same as they were a generation go? What is your attitude toward courtship? Who do you think should take the initiative? How should a courtship be conducted?

Rhetorical Considerations

1. What is Thurber's aim in this essay? Is he simply being absurd and funny? Or does he make a serious point? Explain.

2. In the first paragraph, when Thurber comments that "the whole business of courtship . . . lumbers heavily along, like a complicated musical comedy," what does he mean literally? What is he suggesting figuratively about the ritual of courtship? Why is *lumber* a good word choice? How does this figure of speech relate to Thurber's thesis? Are there any other figures of speech in this paragraph?

2. Thurber also uses gloomy words and phrases in his first paragraph: The story of the courtship of animals is *"sad* and absorbing." Males go to *"sorrowful* lengths" to arouse a lady's interest. What is Thurber's purpose in choosing these words? Find similar phrases throughout the essay. How do these phrases reinforce the figure of speech introduced in the beginning?

4. How would you compare Thurber's means for producing humor with Woody Allen's in "Confessions of a Burglar"? Is it similar or different? Give reasons for your answer.

5. Discuss the organization of this essay. Is it well-structured? Does one part flow naturally from another? Does Thurber follow through on the ideas he introduces in the beginning? How does he achieve transition? Is his conclusion consistent with the attitude he establishes in the beginning?

Writing Assignments

1. Did you detect a bias in Thurber's discussion of the courtship patterns of men and women? Or is his treatment of the subject objective and balanced? Write an essay in which you defend or criticize Thurber's impression of courtship. Give examples to prove your points.

2. Write an essay in which you give examples of what you feel are typical "love displays" that men use when they seek to arouse a woman's interest. Or discuss what you consider to be typical methods that women use to interest men.

Masculine/Feminine

Prudence Mackintosh

Prudence Mackintosh is a free-lance writer and the author of a funny book, *Thundering Sneakers* (1981). She is also the mother of three boys, whom she intended to raise free of sex-role differences, free of cultural stereotyping. She gave them dolls to play with rather than guns; and she taught them that mom and dad shared household chores. As she has sadly learned, however, there is "more to this sex-role learning than the home environment can handle," including powerful forces of culture and, perhaps, nature.

I had every intention to raise liberated, nonviolent sons whose   1
aggressive tendencies would be mollified by a sensitivity and compassion that psychologists claim were denied their father's generation.

I did not buy guns or war toys (although Grandmother did). My boys   2
even had a secondhand baby doll until the garage sale last summer. I did buy Marlo Thomas' *Free to Be You and Me* record, a collection of nonsexist songs, stories, and poems, and I told them time and time again that it was okay to cry and be scared sometimes. I overruled their father and insisted that first grade was much too early for organized competitive soccer leagues. They know that moms *and dads* do dishes and diapers. And although they use it primarily for the convenient bathroom between the alley and the sandpile, my boys know that the storeroom is now mother's office. In such an environment, surely they would grow up free of sex-role stereotypes. At the very least wouldn't they pick up their own socks?

My friends with daughters were even more zealous. They named their   3
daughters strong, cool unisex names like Blakeney, Brett, Brook, Lindsay, and Blair, names that lent themselves to corporate letterheads, not Tupperware party invitations. These moms looked on Barbie with disdain and bought trucks and science kits. They shunned frilly dresses for

overalls. They subscribed to Feminist Press and read stories called "My Mother the Mail Carrier" instead of "Sleeping Beauty." At the swimming pool one afternoon, I watched a particularly fervent young mother, ironically clad in a string bikini, encourage her daughter. "You're so strong, Blake! Kick hard, so you'll be the strongest kid in this pool." When my boys splashed water in Blakeney's eyes and she ran whimpering to her mother, this mom exhorted, "You go back in that pool and shake your fist like this and say, 'You do that again and I'll bust your lights out.' " A new generation of little girls, assertive and ambitious, taking a backseat to no one?

It's a little early to assess the results of our efforts, but when my   4 seven-year-old son, Jack, comes home singing—to the tune of *"Frère Jacques"*—"Farrah Fawcett, Farrah Fawcett, I love you" and five minutes later asks Drew, his five-year-old brother, if he'd like his nose to be a blood fountain, either we're backsliding or there's more to this sex-role learning than the home environment can handle.

I'm hearing similar laments from mothers of daughters. "She used to   5 tell everyone that she was going to grow up to be a lawyer just like Daddy," said one, "but she's hedging on that ambition ever since she learned that no one wears a blue fairy tutu in the courtroom." Another mother with two sons, a daughter, and a very successful career notes that, with no special encouragement, only her daughter keeps her room neat and loves to set the table and ceremoniously seat her parents. At a Little League game during the summer, fearful that this same young daughter might be absorbing the stereotype "boys play while girls watch," her parents readily assured her that she too could participate when she was eight years old. "Oh," she exclaimed with obvious delight, "I didn't know they had cheerleaders."

How does it happen? I have my own theories, but decided to do a little   6 reading to see if any of the "experts" agreed with me. I was also curious to find out what remedies they recommended. The books I read propose that sex roles are culturally induced. In simplistic terms, rid the schools, their friends, and the television of sexism, and your daughters will dump their dolls and head straight for the boardroom while your sons contemplate nursing careers. *Undoing Sex Stereotypes* by Marcia Guttentag and Helen Bray is an interesting study of efforts to overcome sexism in the classroom. After reading it, I visited my son's very traditional school and found it guilty of unabashedly perpetrating the myths that feminists abhor. Remember separate water fountains? And how, even if the line was shorter, no boy would be caught dead drinking from the girls' fountain and vice versa? That still happens. "You wouldn't want me to get cooties, would you, Mom?" my son says, defending the practice. What did I expect in a school where the principal still addresses his faculty, who range in age from 23 to 75, as "girls"?

Nevertheless, having been a schoolteacher myself, I am skeptical of   7 neatly programmed nonsexist curriculum packets like Guttentag and Bray's. But if you can wade through the jargon ("people of the opposite sex hereafter referred to as POTOS"), some of the observations and exercises are certainly through-provoking and revealing. In one exercise fifth-grade students were asked to list adjectives appropriate to describe women. The struggle some of the children had in shifting their attitudes about traditional male roles is illustrated in this paragraph written by a fifth-grade girl who was asked to write a story about a man using the adjectives she had listed to describe women:

> Once there was a boy who all his life was very *gentle.* He never hit anyone or started a fight and when some of his friends were not feeling well, he was *loving* and *kind* to them. When he got older he never changed. People started not liking him because he was *weak, petite,* and he wasn't like any of the other men—not strong or tough. Most of his life he sat alone thinking about why no one liked him. Then one day he went out and tried to act like the other men. He joined a baseball team, but he was no good, he always got out. Then he decided to join the hockey team. He couldn't play good. He kept on breaking all the rules. So he quit the team and joined the soccer team. These men were *understanding* to him. He was really good at soccer, and was the best on the team. That year they won the championship and the rest of his life he was happy.*

After reading this paragraph it occurred to me that this little girl's self-esteem and subsequent role in life would be enhanced by a teacher who spent less time on "nonsexist intervention projects" and more time on writing skills. But that, of course, is not what the study was meant to reveal.   8

The junior high curriculum suggested by *Undoing Sex Stereotypes* has some laudable consciousness-raising goals. For example, in teaching units called "Women's Roles in American History" and "The Socialization of Women and the Image of Women in the Media" teenagers are encouraged to critically examine television commercials, soap operas, and comic books. But am I a traitor to the cause if I object when the authors in another unit use *Romeo and Juliet* as a study of the status of women? Something is rotten in Verona when we have to consider Juliet's career possibilities and her problems with self-actualization. The conclusions of this project were lost on me; I quit reading when the author began to talk about ninth-graders who were "cognitively at a formal-   9

*From *Undoing Sex Stereotypes* by Marcia Guttentag and Helen Bray © 1976 McGraw-Hill, Inc. Used with permission of McGraw-Hill Book Co.

operational level." I don't even know what my "external sociopsychological situation" is. However, I think I did understand some of the conclusions reached by the kids:

> "Girls are smart."
> "If a woman ran a forklift where my father works, there would be a walkout."
> "Men cannot be pom-pom girls."

Eminently more readable, considering that both authors are educators of educators, is *How to Raise Independent and Professionally Successful Daughters*, by Drs. Rita and Kenneth Dunn. The underlying and, I think, questionable assumption in this book is that little boys have been reared correctly all along. Without direct parental intervention, according to the Dunns, daughters tend to absorb and reflect society's values. The Dunns paint a dark picture indeed for the parents who fail to channel their daughters toward professional success. The woman who remains at home with children while her husband is involved in the "real world" with an "absorbing and demanding day-to-day commitment that brings him into contact with new ideas, jobs, and people (attractive self-actualized females)" is sure to experience lowered IQ, according to the Dunns. They go on to predict the husband's inevitable affair and the subsequent divorce, which leaves the wife emotionally depressed and probably financially dependent on her parents. 10

Now I'm all for women developing competency and self-reliance, but the Dunns' glorification of the professional is excessive. Anyone who has worked longer than a year knows that eventually any job loses most of its glamour. And the world is no less "real" at home. For that matter, mothers at home may be more "real" than bankers or lawyers. How is a corporate tax problem more real than my counseling with the maid whose boyfriend shot her in the leg? How can reading a balance sheet compare with comforting a five-year-old who holds his limp cat and wants to know why we have to lose the things we love? And on the contrary, it is my husband, the professional, who complains of lowered IQ. Though we wooed to Faulkner, my former ace English major turned trial lawyer now has time for only an occasional *Falconer* or Peter Benchley thriller. Certainly there is value in raising daughters to be financially self-supporting, but there is not much wisdom in teaching a daughter that she must achieve professional success or her marriage probably won't last. 11

In a chapter called "What to Do from Birth to Two," the authors instruct parents to introduce dolls only if they represent adult figures or groups of figures. "Try not to give her her own 'baby.' A baby doll is acceptable only for dramatizing the familiar episodes she has actually experienced, like a visit to the doctor." If some unthinking person should give your daughter a baby doll, and she likes it, the Dunns recommend that you permit her to keep it without exhibiting any negative feelings, 12 "but do not lapse into cuddling it or encouraging her to do so. Treat it as any other object and direct attention to other more beneficial toys." I wonder if the Dunns read an article by Anne Roiphe called "Can You Have Everything and Still Want Babies?" which appeared in *Vogue* a couple of years ago. Ms. Roiphe was deploring the extremes to which our liberation has brought us. "It is nice to have beautiful feet, it may be desirable to have small feet, but it is painful and abusive to bind feet. It is also a good thing for women to have independence, freedom and choice, movement, and opportunity; but I'm not so sure that the current push against mothering will not be another kind of binding of the soul. . . . As women we have thought so little of ourselves that when the troops came to liberate us we rushed into the streets leaving our most valuable attributes behind as if they belonged to the enemy."

The Dunns' book is thorough, taking parents step-by-step through the elementary years and on to high school. Had I been raising daughters, however, I think I would have flunked out in the chapter "What to Do from Age Two to Five." In discussing development of vocabulary, the Doctors Dunn prohibit the use of nonsensical words for bodily functions. I'm sorry, Doctors, but I've experimented with this precise terminology and discovered that the child who yells "I have to defecate, Mom" across four grocery aisles is likely to be left in the store. A family without a few poo-poo jokes is no family at all. 13

These educators don't help me much in my efforts to liberate my sons. And although I think little girls are getting a better deal with better athletic training and broader options, I believe we're kidding ourselves if we think we can raise our sons and daughters alike. Certain inborn traits seem to be immune to parental and cultural tampering. How can I explain why a little girl baby sits on a quilt in the park thoughtfully examining a blade of grass, while my baby William uproots grass by handfuls and eats it? Why does a mother of very bright and active daughters confide that until she went camping with another family of boys, she feared that my sons had a hyperactivity problem? I'm sure there are plenty of rowdy, noisy little girls, but I'm not just talking about rowdiness and noise. I'm talking about some sort of primal physicalness that causes the walls of my house to pulsate on rainy days. I'm talking about something inexplicable that makes my sons fall into a mad, scrambling, pull-your-ears-off-kick-your-teeth-in heap just before bedtime, when they're not even mad at each other. I mean something that causes them to climb the doorjamb with honey and peanut butter on their hands while giving me a synopsis of *Star Wars* that contains only five intelligible words: "And then this guy, he 'pssshhhhhhh.' And then this thing went 'vronggggg.' But this little guy said, 'Nong-neeee-nonh-nee.' " When Jack and Drew are not kicking a soccer ball or each other, they are kicking the chair legs, the cat, the baby's silver rattle, and, inadvertently, Baby William himself, whom they have affectionately dubbed "Tough Eddy." Staying put in a chair for the 14 duration of a one-course meal is torturous for these boys. They compensate by never quite putting both feet under the table. They sit with one leg doubled under them while the other leg extends to one side. The upper half of the body appears committed to the task at hand—eating— but the lower extremities are poised to lunge should a more compelling distraction present itself. From this position, I have observed, one brother can trip a haughty dessert-eating sibling who is flaunting the fact he ate all his "sweaty little peas." Although we have civilized them to the point that they dutifully mumble, "May I be excused, please?" their abrupt departure from the table invariably overturns at least one chair or whatever milk remains. This sort of constant motion just doesn't lend itself to lessons in thoughtfulness and gentleness.

Despite my encouragement, my sons refuse to invite little girls to play   15 anymore. Occasionally friends leave their small daughters with us while they run errands. I am always curious to see what these females will find of interest in my sons' roomful of Tonka trucks and soccer balls. One morning the boys suggested that the girls join them in playing Emergency with the big red fire trucks and ambulance. The girls were delighted and immediately designated the ambulance as theirs. The point of Emergency, as I have seen it played countless times with a gang of little boys, is to make as much noise with the siren as possible and to crash the trucks into each other or into the leg of a living-room chair before you reach your destination.

The girls had other ideas. I realized why they had selected the ambu   16 lance. It contained three dolls: a driver, a nurse, and sick man on the stretcher. My boys have used that ambulance many times, but the dolls were always secondary to the death-defying race with the fire trucks; they were usually just thrown in the back of the van as an afterthought. The girls took the dolls out, stripped and re-dressed them tenderly, and made sure that they were seated in their appropriate places for the first rescue. Once the fire truck had been lifted off the man's leg, the girls required a box of Band-Aids and spent the next half hour making a bed for the patient and reassuring him that he was going to be all right. These little girls and my sons had seen the same NBC *Emergency* series, but the girls had apparently picked up on the show's nurturing aspects, while Jack and Drew were interested only in the equipment, the fast driving, and the sirens. . . .

Of course, I want my sons to grow up knowing that what's inside a   17 woman's head is more important than her appearance, but I'm sure they're getting mixed signals when I delay our departure for the swimming pool to put on lipstick. I also wonder what they make of their father, whose favorite aphorism is "beautiful women rule the world." I suppose what we want for these sons and the women they may marry someday is a sensitivity that enables them to be both flexible and at ease with their respective roles, so that marriage contracts are unnecessary. When my sons bring me the heads of two purple irises from the neighbor's yard and ask, "Are you really the most beautiful mama in the whole world like Daddy says, and did everyone want to marry you?" do you blame me if I keep on waffling?

Topical Considerations

1. Mackintosh discusses what raising a family has taught her about the differences in the way boys and girls behave. She includes a number of amusing illustrations. What are some of these examples? Do the scenes she describes sound like any you've experienced in your own home?

2. Reread Mackintosh's description of how her sons and their little girl visitors played *Emergency*. What is significant about this illustration? Do you think its implications are always true? For example, do nurturing qualities belong exclusively to girls? Is aggressiveness typical only of boys? Give examples to support your answer.

3. What do you think of the efforts Mackintosh and her friends have made to avoid influencing their children to assume stereotypical sex roles? Would you raise your children the same way or differently? Explain your answer.

4. Mackintosh's essay encourages a healthy acceptance of the fact that boys and girls act differently when they are growing up and that these differences are inherent. Can you also think of some qualities or traits that boys and girls have in common? Or some that could be expressed by either?

5. Mackintosh remarks that boys don't need to be encouraged to be nurses, just to avoid stereotypical sex roles. Is it necessarily true, though, that a man wouldn't want to be a nurse? or a secretary? or a kindergarten teacher? Or that he wouldn't have a natural aptitude for it? Is Mackintosh implying that a woman naturally wouldn't want to be a lawyer? Would you agree if this were the assumption? Give reasons for your answer.

Rhetorical Considerations

1. Where does Mackintosh state her thesis? Is it implicit or explicit?

2. What is the primary rhetorical strategy Mackintosh uses to develop her essay? Cite individual passages to substantiate your answer.

3. Find five sentences that demonstrate Mackintosh's use of concrete detail. Revise the sentences by replacing these specifics with generalities. Read the two versions aloud. What is the difference in effect?

4. Examine Mackintosh's first and last paragraphs. Explain how the last paragraph ties in with the first to unify the essay and bring it to a conclusive finish.

Writing Assignments

1. What was it like growing up in your home? Were you encouraged to assume a stereotypical sex role? Or did your parents try to avoid this? In an essay, discuss these questions.

2. Identify a career that tends to be either male-oriented or female-oriented. Write an essay in which you discuss why this is true. Analyze whether you think it should or will continue to be this way.

Homemaking

William Raspberry

William Raspberry is a distinguished syndicated columnist for the *Washington Post*. He has written articles on a wide range of subjects, from Washington politics to black education. What he writes about here is a discovery he made one weekend while his wife was away—a discovery about the nature of homemaking. Cleaning the house and taking care of his children taught him that homemaking was more than a series of chores. He argues, in fact, that homemaking is akin to an executive enterprise—complex and very important. His argument is as much a defense of homemaking, however, as it is a defense of housewives, whose homemaking careers have long been undervalued by both men and women.

1 Since my wife was out of town last weekend—leaving me to look after our children and the house—I suppose I could make the case that I now have a better appreciation of what homemaking is about.

2 Well, if I do, it isn't because of what I had to do in her absence but because of what I didn't have to do. I had to cook and make sure that the little ones were warmly clothed, that they spent some time playing outside, that they got baths, picked up after themselves, and so on. In short, I took over a series of chores, many of which I would have performed even if my wife had been home.

3 But I didn't have to plan anything, schedule anything, or fit anything into an overall design. I didn't have to see to my children's overall nutrition; I only had to see that they weren't too bored and didn't tear the house down. What I did was episodic, a combination of housework and babysitting. What my wife does is part of an ongoing enterprise: home-

making. Hers is an executive role, though neither she nor I had ever thought to describe it as such.

I strongly suspect that the failure to make the distinction between 4 homemaking and chores is one of the chief reasons why homemaking has fallen into such disrepute of late. As Jinx Melia, founder and director of the Martha Movement,* observed in a recent interview, "ethnic" home-makers, as a rule, have managed to retain a higher sense of respect for their calling, partly, she suspects, because their husbands may be some-what more likely to work at blue-collar jobs that hold no attraction for their wives.

A larger part, though, may be that "traditional" husbands—whatever 5 jobs they work at—are likelier to be ignorant (perhaps deliberately so) of homemaking skills. Homemaking may involve as much a sense of mys-tique for these husbands as outside work holds for their wives. Men of all classes are increasingly likely these days to help out with the chores, or even take over for a spell, as I did last weekend. And if we aren't careful, we come to believe that we can do easily everything our wives do —if we can only survive the boredom of it. The result is that we lose respect for what they do. Think of homemaking as a series of more or less unpleasant chores and the disrespect is virtually automatic.

Well, most jobs are a series of more or less unpleasant chores. But it 6 doesn't follow that that's all they are. Looking up cases and precedents, trying to draw information out of a client who doesn't quite understand what you need to know, keeping records, writing "boiler-plate" contracts —all these things are routine, and a bright high school graduate could quickly learn to do them all. The chores are a drag; but lawyering is a fascinating career. Reducing a career to a series of chores creates this additional problem of perspective: Any time not spent on one or another of the chores is viewed as time wasted.

As Melia also pointed out, the men who work at professions spend an 7 enormous amount of time doing the mirror image of what their non-career wives may be chided or even openly criticized for doing. They talk on the phone a lot (perhaps about business, but they often aren't doing business). They hold staff meetings or unit meetings that are hardly different from coffee klatches. A business lunch with a client you've al-ready sold (or for whom you have no specific proposal at the moment) is not vastly different from a gathering of homemakers in somebody's kitchenette.

The main difference is that a man gets to call all these things "work." 8 One reason for the difference is that the details of homemaking are far more visible (to the spouse) than the details of work done outside. As a result, husbands often not only devalue their wives' work but also feel

*A movement to give voice to housewives and homemakers in the United States.—Ed.

perfectly free to question the wisdom of what they do as part of that work. Wives generally know too little about their husbands' work to question any aspect of it. They are more likely to magnify its importance.

None of this should be taken as a proposal that women be kept out of   9 the labor market. There are women whose talents are so far removed from home and hearth that it would be criminal to encourage them to become homemakers. There are women who need to earn income, for reasons ranging from fiscal to psychic. Women who choose careers outside the home, or who have no choice but to pursue careers, ought to be free to do so without any discrimination of any sort.

But there are also women who seek outside work primarily because   10 they know their homemaking role is undervalued, by their husbands and by themselves. There is nothing intrinsic about producing income, on the one hand, or nurturing children and managing a household, on the other, that would lead to a natural conclusion that income-production is of greater value. The opposite conclusion would appear likelier, as in the distinction between worker and queen bees, for instance. But worker bees don't claim sole ownership and discretion over what they produce; they work for the hive. It would go a long way toward changing the onerous working conditions of homemakers if we could learn to think of family income as belonging to the family, not primarily to the person who happens to bring it home.

Maybe there is a logical reason why the marriage partner who doesn't   11 produce income should be the fiscal dependent of the one who does. Off hand, I can't think what it might be.

Topical Considerations

1. What does Raspberry argue are the chief reasons that homemaking fails to receive the respect it deserves? What analogy does he use to prove his point? Is he convincing? Is his analogy appropriate? Give reasons for your answers.

2. Raspberry comments that he came to appreciate better what homemaking was all about not because of what he did in his wife's absence but because of what he didn't do. What does he mean? What are some of the things he didn't do? Who does these things in your home? Do you think these tasks are as important as Raspberry implies? Explain.

3. Describe the audience that you think would best appreciate what Raspberry is saying. Who might fail to appreciate it? Do you think it might encourage a wife who is a homemaker to live her life any differently? How? Would it produce any changes in her husband's attitude?

4. Traditionally, it is the wife who is the homemaker and the husband who earns the salary and pays the bills. Is this always the case? Can you describe any examples of a marriage in which the roles are reversed? Should they be reversed? Who should assume responsibility for the home when both partners in the marriage work?

5. What are Raspberry's views about who in the family should manage the money? How does his analogy of the worker bees in a beehive reveal his attitude? Do you agree or disagree with him?

6. What is Raspberry's attitude toward wives who choose to work outside the home? What are some reasons he gives for his opinion? How does this fit with the thesis of his essay? Does he make a valid point?

7. What specific conclusions is Raspberry drawing about women's place in the work force? What general conclusions is he drawing about attitudes toward work?

8. How does Raspberry's view of women agree with or differ from Thurber's. Do you think the typical female that Thurber describes would live up to Raspberry's expectations of an executive homemaker? How might Raspberry's homemaker conduct herself in courtship?

Rhetorical Considerations

1. What is Raspberry's aim in this essay? Where does he state it?

2. What can you say about Raspberry's treatment of his subject? Is it objective and balanced? Do you detect a bias?

3. How does Raspberry attract the reader's attention in the opening paragraph? Is this an effective way to begin? Why or why not?

4. What kind of essay has Raspberry written? Is it primarily narrative, descriptive, expository, or persuasive?

Writing Assignments

1. Homemaking is not the only kind of work that people mistakenly consider routine and uninteresting. Write an essay in which you describe another career that people view in this way. Persuade your readers to appreciate it more fully.

2. Raspberry states unequivocally his attitude toward wives who choose to work outside the home. In an essay, defend or criticize his stand. Give reasons and examples to substantiate your arguments.

3. Write an essay comparing and contrasting Raspberry's view of women with Thurber's. Discuss how each one's version of a woman would be likely to conduct herself in courtship or in the home.

I Want a Wife

Judy Syfers

Having assumed a housewife's perspective for a weekend, William Raspberry came to the conclusion that the duties of a homemaker have long been devalued, seen simply as endlessly boring chores and services instead of as a complex and important "executive" enterprise. Taking a husband's perspective, Judy Syfers here gives us a far less enobling look at homemaking, based on years of being a housewife and mother. "Who wouldn't want a wife?" she asks, and gives a host of reasons that raise some fundamental questions about sex roles and the American family.

I belong to that classification of people known as wives. I am A   1
Wife. And, not altogether incidentally, I am a mother.

Not too long ago a male friend of mine appeared on the scene fresh   2
from a recent divorce. He had one child, who is, of course, with his
ex-wife. He is obviously looking for another wife. As I thought about him
while I was ironing one evening, it suddenly occurred to me that I, too,
would like to have a wife. Why do I want a wife?

I would like to go back to school so that I can become economically   3
independent, support myself, and, if need be, support those dependent upon me. I want a wife who will work and send me to school. And
while I am going to school I want a wife to take care of my children.
I want a wife to keep track of the children's doctor and dentist appointments. And to keep track of mine, too. I want a wife to make sure my
children eat properly and are kept clean. I want a wife who will wash
the children's clothes and keep them mended. I want a wife who is
a good nurturant attendant to my children, who arranges for their
schooling, makes sure that they have an adequate social life with their
peers, takes them to the park, the zoo, etc. I want a wife who takes
care of the children when they are sick, a wife who arranges to be
around when the children need special care, because, of course, I cannot miss classes at school. My wife must arrange to lose time at work
and not lose the job. It may mean a small cut in my wife's income
from time to time, but I guess I can tolerate that. Needless to say, my
wife will arrange and pay for the care of the children while my wife is
working.

I want a wife who will take care of *my* physical needs. I want a wife who   4
will keep my house clean. A wife who will pick up after me. I want a wife
who will keep my clothes clean, ironed, mended, replaced when need
be, and who will see to it that my personal things are kept in their
proper place so that I can find what I need the minute I need it. I
want a wife who cooks the meals, a wife who is a *good* cook. I want a wife

57

who will plan the menus, do the necessary grocery shopping, prepare the meals, serve them pleasantly, and then do the cleaning up while I do my studying. I want a wife who will care for me when I am sick and sympathize with my pain and loss of time from school. I want a wife to go along when our family takes a vacation so that someone can continue to care for me and my children when I need a rest and change of scene.

I want a wife who will not bother me with rambling complaints about   5
a wife's duties. But I want a wife who will listen to me when I feel the need to explain a rather difficult point I have come across in my course of studies. And I want a wife who will type my papers for me when I have written them.

I want a wife who will take care of the details of my social life. When   6
my wife and I are invited out by my friends, I want a wife who will take care of the babysitting arrangements. When I meet people at school that I like and want to entertain, I want a wife who will have the house clean, will prepare a special meal, serve it to me and my friends, and not interrupt when I talk about the things that interest me and my friends. I want a wife who will have arranged that the children are fed and ready for bed before my guests arrive so that the children do not bother us. I want a wife who takes care of the needs of my guests so that they feel comfortable, who makes sure that they have an ashtray, that they are passed the hors d'oeuvres, that they are offered a second helping of the food, that their wine glasses are replenished when necessary, that their coffee is served to them as they like it. And I want a wife who knows that sometimes I need a night out by myself.

I want a wife who is sensitive to my sexual needs, a wife who makes   7
love passionately and eagerly when I feel like it, a wife who makes sure that I am satisfied. And, of course, I want a wife who will not demand sexual attention when I am not in the mood for it. I want a wife who assumes the complete responsibility for birth control, because I do not want more children. I want a wife who will remain sexually faithful to me so that I do not have to clutter up my intellectual life with jealousies. And I want a wife who understands that *my* sexual needs may entail more than strict adherence to monogamy. I must, after all, be able to relate to people as fully as possible.

If, by chance, I find another person more suitable as a wife than the   8
wife I already have, I want the liberty to replace my present wife with another one. Naturally, I will expect a fresh, new life; my wife will take the children and be solely responsible for them so that I am left free.

When I am through with school and have a job, I want my wife to quit   9
working and remain at home so that my wife can more fully and completely take care of a wife's duties.

My God, who *wouldn't* want a wife?

10

Topical Considerations

1. Why *does* Syfers want a wife? What would she like a wife to do for her?

2. Syfers is speaking rather eloquently for women's liberation. Why would today's feminist applaud her article? What opinions is she suggesting about a wife's role that are not explicitly stated? Consider, for example, her comment: "He had one child, who is, of course, with his ex-wife" (paragraph 2). Why "of course"? Find other examples.

3. What is the "husband" in Syfers's essay like? Do you like him? What do you think of his expectations and demands? Do you know anyone who expects what he does from his wife or girlfriend?

4. Does the wife of Syfers's view have an identity of her own? Does she lack identity? Where in the essay do you see evidence for your answer?

5. Would you say that Syfers's picture of the wife's role is exaggerated and distorted? Or is it a fair and accurate representation of reality? Point out specific details to prove your point.

6. How is Raspberry's "executive" homemaker similar to or different from the wife Syfer would like to have? Are either of the wives they describe like anyone you know?

Rhetorical Considerations

1. What is Syfers's thesis? Where is it stated in the essay? Is it explicitly stated? Explain.

2. Discuss the irony in Syfers's statement: "I want a wife." What other evidence of irony do you find in the essay.

3. Compare and contrast Syfers's point of view with Thurber's in "Courtship Through the Ages" and Raspberry's in "Homemaking."

4. How would you characterize the tone of this essay? Is it friendly and persuasive? exasperated and critical? absurd and humorous? serious and thoughtful? Compare the tone of this essay with others in this section. Cite specific passages to substantiate your answer.

5. Note how many times (after paragraph 2) Syfers begins a sentence with "I want." How does this affect the essay? Does Syfers have a reason for doing this? Or is this a weakness in the essay? Explain.

Writing Assignments

1. Write an essay entitled "I Want a Husband." Imitate Syfers's tone. What are some of the expectations women have about the role a husband should play that are as unreasonable and thoughtless as the expectations of the husband Syfers portrays?

2. In an essay, compare and contrast Raspberry's "executive" homemaker with the wife Syfers would like to have.

3. Suppose that you have just read Syfers's recently published essay, "I Want a Wife," in *Ms.* magazine. Write a letter to the editor in which you express your opinion of the essay.

Understanding the Difference
Phyllis Schlafly

Phyllis Schlafly is a well-known opponent of women's liberation and the Equal Rights Amendment. In fact, she campaigned actively against its ratification. Schlafly is a lawyer and the author of several books, including her controversial *The Power of the Positive Woman* (1977). In this essay from that book, Schlafly strongly attacks some of the basic principles of the women's liberation movement. She also counters the attitudes of women's liberationists with the attitudes of what she calls "the Positive Woman."

The first requirement for the acquisition of power by the Positive Woman is to understand the differences between men and women. Your outlook on life, your faith, your behavior, your potential for fulfillment, all are determined by the parameters of your original premise. The Positive Woman starts with the assumption that the world is her oyster. She rejoices in the creative capability within her body and the power potential of her mind and spirit. She understands that men and women are different, and that those very differences provide the key to her success as a person and fulfillment as a woman.

The women's liberationist, on the other hand, is imprisoned by her own negative view of herself and of her place in the world around her. This view of women was most succinctly expressed in an advertisement designed by the principal women's liberationist organization, the National Organization for Women (NOW), and run in many magazines and newspapers and as spot announcements on many television stations. The advertisement showed a darling curlyheaded girl with the caption: "This healthy, normal baby has a handicap. She was born female."

This is the self-articulated dog-in-the-manger, chip-on-the-shoulder, fundamental dogma of the women's liberation movement. Someone—it is not clear who, perhaps God, perhaps the "Establishment," perhaps a conspiracy of male chauvinist pigs—dealt women a foul blow by making them female. It becomes necessary, therefore, for women to agitate and demonstrate and hurl demands on society in order to wrest from an oppressive male-dominated social structure the status that has been wrongfully denied to women through the centuries.

By its very nature, therefore, the women's liberation movement 4 precipitates a series of conflict situations—in the legislatures, in the courts, in the schools, in industry—with man targeted as the enemy. Confrontation replaces cooperation as the watchword of all relationships. Women and men become adversaries instead of partners.

The second dogma of the women's liberationists is that, of all the 5 injustices perpetrated upon women through the centuries, the most oppressive is the cruel fact that women have babies and men do not. Within the confines of the women's liberationist ideology, therefore, the abolition of this overriding inequality of women becomes the primary goal. This goal must be achieved at any and all costs—to the woman herself, to the baby, to the family, and to society. Women must be made equal to men in their ability *not* to become pregnant and *not* to be expected to care for babies they may bring into the world.

This is why women's liberationists are compulsively involved in the 6 drive to make abortion and child-care centers for all women, regardless of religion or income, both socially acceptable and government-financed. Former Congresswoman Bella Abzug has defined the goal: "to enforce the constitutional right of females to terminate pregnancies that they do not wish to continue."

If man is targeted as the enemy, and the ultimate goal of women's 7 liberation is independence from men and the avoidance of pregnancy and its consequences, then lesbianism is logically the highest form in the ritual of women's liberation. Many, such as Kate Millett, come to this conclusion, although many others do not.

The Positive Woman will never travel that dead-end road. It is self- 8 evident to the Positive Woman that the female body with its baby-producing organs was not designed by a conspiracy of men but by the Divine Architect of the human race. Those who think it is unfair that women have babies, whereas men cannot, will have to take up their complaint with God because no other power is capable of changing that fundamental fact. On some college campuses, I have been assured that other methods of reproduction will be developed. But most of us must deal with the real world rather than with the imagination of dreamers.

Another feature of the woman's natural role is the obvious fact that 9 women can breast-feed babies and men cannot. This functional role was not imposed by conspiratorial males seeking to burden women with confining chores, but must be recognized as part of the plan of the Divine Architect for the survival of the human race through the centuries and in the countries that know no pasteurization of milk or sterilization of bottles.

The Positive Woman looks upon her femaleness and her fertility as 10 part of her purpose, her potential, and her power. She rejoices that she has a capability for creativity that men can never have.

The third basic dogma of the women's liberation movement is that   11
there is no difference between male and female except the sex organs,
and that all those physical, cognitive, and emotional differences you *think*
are there, are merely the result of centuries of restraints imposed by a
male-dominated society and sex-stereotyped schooling. The role imposed on women is, by definition, inferior, according to the women's
liberationists.

The Positive Woman knows that, while there are some physical compe-   12
titions in which women are better (and can command more money) than
men, including those that put a premium on grace and beauty, such as
figure skating, the superior physical strength of males over females in
competitions of strength, speed, and short-term endurance is beyond
rational dispute.

In the Olympic Games, women not only cannot win any medals in   13
competition with men, the gulf between them is so great that they cannot
even qualify for the contests with men. No amount of training from
infancy can enable women to throw the discus as far as men, or to match
men in push-ups or in lifting weights. In track and field events, individual
male records surpass those of women by 10 to 20 percent.

Female swimmers today are beating Johnny Weissmuller's records, but   14
today's male swimmers are better still. Chris Evert can never win a tennis
match against Jimmy Connors. If we removed lady's tees from golf
courses, women would be out of the game. Putting women in football or
wrestling matches can only be an exercise in laughs.

The Olympic Games, whose rules require strict verification to ascer-   15
tain that no male enters a female contest and, with his masculine advantage, unfairly captures a woman's medal, formerly insisted on a visual
inspection of the contestants' bodies. Science, however, has discovered
that men and women are so innately different physically that their
maleness/femaleness can be conclusively established by means of a simple skin test of fully clothed persons. . . .

The Five Principles

When the women's liberationists enter the political arena to promote   16
legislation and litigation in pursuit of their goals, their specific demands
are based on five principles.

(1) They demand that a "gender-free" rule be applied to every federal   17
and state law, bureaucratic regulation, educational institution, and expenditure of public funds. Based on their dogma that there is no real
difference between men and women (except in sex organs), they demand
that males and females have identical treatment always. Thus, if fathers
are not expected to stay home and care for their infant children, then
neither should mothers be expected to do so; and, therefore, it becomes

the duty of the government to provide kiddy-care centers to relieve mothers of that unfair and unequal burden.

The women's lib dogma demands that the courts treat sex as a "sus-   18
pect" classification—just as race is now treated—so that no difference of treatment or separation between the sexes will ever be permitted, no matter how reasonable or how much it is desired by reasonable people.

The nonsense of these militant demands was illustrated by the Depart-   19
ment of Health, Education and Welfare (HEW) ruling in July, 1976, that all public school "functions such as father-son or mother-daughter break-fasts" would be prohibited because this "would be subjecting students to separate treatment." It was announced that violations would lead to a cutoff of federal assistance or court action by the Justice Department.

When President Gerald Ford read this in the newspaper, he was de-   20
scribed by his press secretary as being "quite irritated" and as saying that he could not believe that this was the intent of Congress in passing a law against sex discrimination in education. He telephoned HEW Secretary David Mathews and told him to suspend the ruling.

The National Organization for Women, however, immediately an-   21
nounced opposition to President Ford's action, claiming that such events (fashion shows, softball games, banquets, and breakfasts) are sex-discriminatory and must be eliminated. It is clear that a prohibition against your right to make any difference or separation between the sexes anytime anywhere is a primary goal of the women's liberation movement.

No sooner had the father-son, mother-daughter flap blown over than   22
HEW embroiled itself in another controversy by a ruling that an after-school choir of fifth and sixth grade boys violates the HEW regulation that bars single-sex choruses. The choir in Wethersfield, Connecticut, that precipitated the ruling had been established for boys whose "voices haven't changed yet," and the purpose was "to get boys interested in singing" at an early age so they would be willing to join coed choruses later. Nevertheless, HEW found that such a boy's chorus is by definition sex discriminatory.

The Positive Woman rejects the "gender-free" approach. She knows   23
that there are many differences between male and female and that we are entitled to have our laws, regulations, schools, and courts reflect these differences and allow for reasonable differences in treatment and separa-tions of activities that reasonable men and women want.

The Positive Woman also rejects the argument that sex discrimination   24
should be treated the same as race discrimination. There is vastly more difference between a man and a woman than there is between a black and a white, and it is nonsense to adopt a legal and bureaucratic attitude that pretends that those differences do not exist. Even the United States Supreme Court has, in recent and relevant cases, upheld "reasonable" sex-based differences of treatment by legislatures and by the military.

(2) The women's lib legislative goals seek an irrational mandate of   25
"equality" at the expense of justice. The fact is that equality cannot
always be equated with justice, and may sometimes even be highly unjust.
If we had absolutely equal treatment in regard to taxes, then everyone
would pay the same income tax, or perhaps the same rate of income tax,
regardless of the size of the income.

If we had absolutely equal treatment in regard to federal spending   26
programs, we would have to eliminate welfare, low-income housing benefits, food stamps, government scholarships, and many other programs
designed to benefit low-income citizens. If we had absolutely equal treatment in regard to age, then seventeen-year-olds, or even ten-year-olds,
would be permitted to vote, and we would have to eliminate Social Security unless all persons received the same benefits that only those over
sixty-two receive now.

Our legislatures, our administrative departments, and our courts have   27
always had and still retain the discretion to make reasonable differences
in treatment based on age, income, or economic situation. The Positive
Woman believes that it makes no sense to deprive us of the ability to make
reasonable distinctions based on sex that reasonable men and women
want.

(3) The women's liberation movement demands that women be given   28
the benefit of "reverse discrimination." The Positive Woman recognizes
that this is mutually exclusive with the principle of equal opportunity for
all. Reverse discrimination is based on the theory that "group rights" take
precedence over individual rights, and that "reverse discrimination"
(variously called "preferential treatment," "remedial action," or "affirmative action") should be imposed in order to compensate some women
today for alleged past discriminations against other women. The word
"quotas" is usually avoided, but it amounts to the same thing.

The fallacy of reverse discrimination has been aptly exposed by Profes-   29
sor Sidney Hook. No one would argue, he wrote, that because many years
ago blacks and women were denied the right to vote, we should now
compensate by giving them an extra vote or two, or by barring white men
from voting at all.

But that is substantially what the women's liberationists are demand-   30
ing—and getting by federal court orders—in education, employment,
and politics when they ask for "affirmative action" to remedy past discrimination.

The Positive Woman supports equal opportunity for individuals of   31
both sexes, as well as of all faiths and races. She rejects the theories of
reverse discrimination and "group rights." It does no good for the
woman who may have been discriminated against twenty-five years ago
to know that an unqualified woman today receives preferential treatment

at the expense of a qualified man. Only the vindictive radical would support such a policy of revenge.

(4) The women's liberation movement is based on the unproven the-   32
ory that uniformity should replace diversity—or, in simpler language, the federalization of all remaining aspects of our life. The militant women demand that *all* educational institutions conform to federally determined rules about sex discrimination.

There is absolutely no evidence that HEW bureaucrats can do a better   33
or fairer job of regulating our schools and colleges than local officials. Nor is there any evidence that individuals, or women, or society as a whole, would be better off under a uniform system enforced by the full power of the federal government than they would be under a free and competitive system, under local control, using diverse methods and regulations. It is hard to see why anyone would want to put more power into the hands of federal bureaucrats who cannot cope with the problems they already have.

The militant women demand that HEW regulations enforce a strict   34
gender-free uniformity on all schools and colleges. Everything from sports to glee clubs must be coed, regardless of local customs or wishes. The militants deplore the differences from state to state in the laws governing marriage and divorce. Yet does anyone think our nation would be improved if we were made subject to a national divorce law devised by HEW?

The Positive Woman rejects the theory that Washington, D.C., is the   35
fountainhead of all wisdom and professional skill. She supports the principle of leaving all possible control and discretion in the hands of local school and college officials and their elected boards.

(5) The women's liberation movement pushes its proposals on the   36
premise that everything must be neutral as between morality and immorality, and as between the institution of the family and alternate lifestyles: for example, that homosexuals and lesbians should have just as much right to teach in the schools and to adopt children as anyone else; and that illegitimate babies and abortions by married or single mothers should be accepted as normal behavior for teachers—and funded by public money.

A good example of the rabid determination of the militant radicals to   37
push every law and regulation to the far-out limit of moral neutrality is the HEW regulation on sex discrimination that implements the Education Amendments of 1972. Although the federal statute simply prohibits sex discrimination, the HEW regulation (1) requires that any medical benefit program administered by a school or college pay for abortions for married and unmarried students, (2) prohibits any school or college from

refusing to employ or from firing an unmarried pregnant teacher or a woman who has had, or plans to have, an abortion, and (3) prohibits any school or college from refusing admission to any student who has had, or plans to have, an abortion. Abortion is referred to by the code words "termination of pregnancy."

This HEW regulation is illogical, immoral, and unauthorized by any   38 reasonable reading of the 1972 Education Act. But the HEW regulation became federal law on July 18, 1975, after being signed by the president and accepted by Congress.

The Positive Woman believes that our educational institutions have   39 not only the right, but the obligation, to set minimum standards of moral conduct at the local level. She believes that schools and colleges have no right to use our public money to promote conduct that is offensive to the religious and moral values of parents and taxpayers.

Topical Considerations

1. What was your first response to Schlafly's article? Name one issue she raises that you find particularly thought-provoking. What are your own views on the issue? Have Schlafly's remarks influenced you?

2. Schlafly remarks that she "supports equal opportunity for individuals of both sexes, as well as of all faiths and races" (paragraph 31). Yet she criticizes the women's liberationist for demanding child-care centers. How might the lack of such a facility interfere with a woman's job opportunities? Is there a contradiction here? Do you see any other possible flaws in Schlafly's case against women's liberation?

3. If you were asked to state in one sentence the chief difference in attitude between Schlafly and the National Organization for Women, what would you say?

4. If Syfers were to read Schlafly's essay, what do you think she would say? What issues would she be most likely to raise?

5. Suppose Schlafly and a member of NOW were having a debate. How might Raspberry be an effective peacemaker? Consider, for example, Schlafly's assumption that the primary aim of all women's liberationists is to avoid pregnancy and child care so that they can work outside the home. What might Raspberry say to this?

Rhetorical Considerations

1. What is Schlafly's thesis? Where does she state it?

2. What kind of essay is this—narrative? descriptive? expository? argumentative? How is it organized? Identify its main points.

3. How do Schlafly's word choices imply that she doesn't agree with the view she is summarizing in paragraph 3?

4. How would you describe the tone of this essay—humorous? strident? conciliatory? persuasive? Cite passages to illustrate your point.

Writing Assignments

1. Look again at Raspberry's and Syfers's essays. How are their attitudes toward women's efforts for equality different from Schlafly's? Suppose that you have just read a reprint of Schlafly's essay in a current periodical. Write a letter to the magazine in response to it. Adopt Raspberry's point of view. Adopt Syfers's point of view.

2. Schlafly was a strong opponent of the ERA. What were your views on the issue? Has Schlafly's essay influenced your attitude? Do you agree with her? Do you disagree? In an essay, defend your views on the defeated ERA.

Deliver Us from the Delivery
Dave Barry

Although there haven't been any changes in the way males and females mate, there have been some significant changes in the delivery of children. Over the last decade, more and more expectant parents have turned to "natural childbirth"—an experience that involves both husband and wife in childbirth classes, exercises, and the delivery itself. Not all husbands, however, are eager to partake in the arrival of babies, and Dave Barry, a free-lance writer, is one who is not. In this very funny and clever piece, Barry, playing devil's advocate, lodges a complaint against the delivery vogue—a complaint that has a few things to say about social trends, lifestyles, and the sexes. When it first appeared in syndication, this essay caused a loud stir on editorial pages, with some people outraged at Barry's apparent sexism and insensitivity toward childbirth and others tickled by his ability to find humor in very serious matters.

Let's take just a quick look at the history of baby-having: For 1
thousands of years, only women had babies. Primitive women would go off into primitive huts and groan and wail and sweat while other women hovered around. The primitive men stayed outside doing manly things, such as lifting heavy objects and spitting.

When the baby was born, the women would clean it up as best they 2
could and show it to the men, who would spit appreciatively and head off to the forest to throw sharp sticks at small animals. If you had suggested to primitive men that they should actually watch women have babies, they

would have laughed at you and probably tortured you for three or four days. They were real men.

At the beginning of the 20th century, women started having babies in 3 hospital rooms. Often males were present, but they were professional doctors who were paid large sums of money and wore masks. Normal civilian males continued to stay out of the baby-having area; they remained in waiting rooms reading old copies of Field and Stream—an activity that is less manly than lifting heavy objects, but still reasonably manly.

What I'm getting at is that, for most of history, baby-having was mainly 4 in the hands (so to speak) of women. Many fine people were born under this system. Charles Lindbergh, for example.

Things changed, though, in the 1970s. The birth rate dropped sharply. 5 Women started going to college and driving bulldozers and carrying briefcases and freely using such words as *debenture*. They just didn't have time to have babies. For a while there, the only people having babies were unwed teenage girls who are very fertile and can get pregnant merely by standing downwind from teenage boys.

Then, young professional couples began to realize that their lives were 6 missing something—a sense of stability, of companionship, of responsibility for another life. So they got Labrador retrievers. A little later, they started having babies again, mainly because of the tax advantages. These days you can't open your car door without hitting a pregnant woman. But there's a catch: *Women now expect men to watch them have babies.* This is part of the experience of "natural childbirth," which is one of those terms that sounds terrific, but that nobody really understands. Another one is "pH balanced."

At first, natural childbirth was popular only with hippie-type, granola- 7 oriented couples who lived in geodesic domes and named their babies things like Peace Love World Understanding Harrington-Schwartz. The males, their brains badly corroded by drugs and organic food, wrote smarmy articles about what a Meaningful Experience it is to see a New Life Come Into the World. None of these articles mentioned the various other fluids and solids that come into the world with the New Life, so people got the impression that watching somebody have a baby was just a peck of meaningful fun. At cocktail parties, you'd run into natural-childbirth converts who would drone on for hours, giving you a contraction-by-contraction account of what went on in the delivery room. They were worse than Moonies, or people who tell you how much they bought their houses for in 1973 and how much they're worth today.

Before long, natural childbirth was everywhere, like salad bars, and 8 now, perfectly innocent civilian males all over the country are required by federal law to watch females have babies. I recently had to watch my wife have a baby in Bryn Mawr, Pa. *Bryn Mawr,* for God's sake.

First, we had to go to 10 evening childbirth classes at Bryn Mawr 9

Hospital. Before the classes, the hospital told us, mysteriously, to bring two pillows. This was the first humiliation, because no two of our pillow-cases match and many have beer or cranberry-juice stains. It may be possible to walk down the streets of Kuala Lumpur with stained, un-matched pillowcases and still feel dignified, but this is not possible in Bryn Mawr.

Anyway, we showed up for the first class, along with about 15 other   10
couples consisting of women who were going to have to have babies and men who were going to have to watch them. They all had matching pillowcases. In fact, some couples had obviously purchased tasteful pil-lowcases especially for childbirth class; these were the Main Line-type couples, wearing golf and tennis apparel, who were planning to have wealthy babies. They sat together through all the classes, and eventually agreed to get together for brunch.

The classes consisted of sitting in a brightly lit room and openly dis-   11
cussing, among other things, the uterus. Now I can remember a time, in high school, when I would have *killed* for reliable information on the uterus. But having discussed it at length, having seen actual full-color *diagrams,* I must say in all honesty that although I respect it a great deal as an organ, it has lost much of its charm.

Our childbirth-class instructor was very big on the uterus because   12
that's where babies generally spend their time before birth. She also spent some time on the ovum, which is near the ovaries. What happens is the ovum hangs around reading novels and eating chocolates until along comes this big crowd of spermatozoa, which are tiny, very stupid one-celled organisms. They're looking for the ovum, but most of them wouldn't know it if they fell over it. They swim around for days, trying to mate with the pancreas and whatever other organs they bump into. But eventually one stumbles into the ovum, and the happy couple parades down the fallopian tubes to the uterus.

In the uterus, the Miracle of Life begins, unless you believe the Miracle   13
of Life does not begin there, and if you think I'm going to get into that, you're crazy. Anyway, the ovum starts growing rapidly and dividing into lots of little specialized parts, not unlike the federal government. Within six weeks, it has developed all the organs it needs to drool; by 10 weeks, it has the ability to cry in restaurants. In childbirth class, they showed us actual pictures of a fetus developing inside a uterus. They didn't tell us how these pictures were taken, but I suspect it involved a great deal of drinking.

We saw lots of pictures. One evening, we saw a movie of a woman we   14
didn't even know who was having a baby. I am serious. Some woman actually let some moviemakers film the whole thing. In color. She was from California.

Another time, the instructor announced, in the tone of voice you might   15
use to tell people that they had just won free trips to the Bahamas, that

we were going to see color slides of a Cesarean section. The first slides showed a pregnant woman cheerfully entering the hospital. The last slides showed her cheerfully holding a baby. The middle slides showed how they got the baby out of the cheerful woman, but I can't give you a lot of detail here because I had to go out for 15 or 20 drinks of water. I do remember that at one point our instructor cheerfully observed that there was "surprisingly little blood, really." She evidently felt this was a real selling point.

When we weren't looking at pictures or discussing the uterus, we 16 practiced breathing. This is where the pillows came in. What happens is that when the baby gets ready to leave the uterus, the woman goes through a series of what the medical community laughingly refers to as "contractions"; if it referred to them as "horrible pains that make you wonder why the hell you ever decided to get pregnant," people might stop having babies and the medical community would have to go into the major-appliance business.

In the old days, under President Eisenhower, doctors avoided the 17 contraction problem by giving lots of drugs to women who were having babies. They'd knock them out during the delivery, and the woman would wake up when her kids were entering the fourth grade. But the idea with natural childbirth is to try to avoid giving the woman a lot of drugs, so she can share the first, intimate moments after birth with the baby and father and the obstetrician and the pediatrician and the standby anesthesiologist and several nurses and the person who cleans the delivery room.

The key to avoiding drugs, according to the natural-childbirth people, 18 is for the woman to breathe deeply. The theory is that if she breathes deeply, she'll get all relaxed and won't notice that she's in a hospital delivery room wearing a truly perverted garment and having a baby.

So, in childbirth classes, we spent a lot of time sprawled on these little 19 mats with our pillows while the women pretended to have contractions and the men squatted around with stopwatches and pretended to time them. The Main Line couples didn't care for this part. They were not into squatting. After a couple of classes, they started bringing little backgammon sets and playing backgammon when they were supposed to be practicing breathing. I imagine they had a rough time in actual childbirth, unless they got the servants to have contractions for them.

Anyway, my wife and I traipsed along for months, breathing and tim- 20 ing, respectively. We had no problems whatsoever. We were a terrific team. We had a swell time. Really.

The actual delivery was slightly more difficult. I don't want to name 21 names, but I held up *my* end. I had my stopwatch in good working order and I told my wife to breathe. "Don't forget to breathe," I'd say, or "You should breathe, you know." She, on the other hand, was unusually cranky. For example, she didn't want me to use my stopwatch. Can you imagine? All that practice, all that squatting on the natural-childbirth classroom floor, and she suddenly gets into this big snit about stopwatches. Also, she almost completely lost her sense of humor. At one point, I made an especially amusing remark, and she tried to hit me. She usually has an excellent sense of humor.

Nonetheless, the baby came out all right, or at least all right for newborn babies, which is actually pretty awful unless you're a big fan of slime. I thought I had held up well for the whole thing when the doctor, who up to then had behaved like a perfectly rational person, said, "Would you like to see the placenta?" Now let's face it: That is like asking, "Would you like me to pour hot tar into your nostrils?" Nobody would *like* to see a placenta. If anything, it would be a form of punishment.   22

But without waiting for an answer, the doctor held up the placenta, not unlike the way you might hold up a bowling trophy. I bet he wouldn't have tried that with people who have matching pillowcases.   23

The placenta aside, everything worked out fine. We ended up with an extremely healthy, organic, natural baby, who immediately demanded to be put back into the uterus.   24

All in all, I'd say it's not a bad way to reproduce, although I understand that some members of the flatworm family simply divide into two.   25

Topical Considerations

1. What particular people and social trends is Barry poking fun at?

2. During the actual delivery, Barry complains that, although he did his part, his wife completely lost her sense of humor and became surprisingly crabby. Why is this funny? What is Barry suggesting here?

3. Barry remarks: "In the uterus, the Miracle of Life begins, unless you believe the Miracle of Life does not begin there, and if you think I'm going to get into that, you're crazy" (paragraph 13). What current social issue is Barry purposely avoiding here?

4. Reread "Masculine/Feminine." Do you think Prudence Mackintosh would encourage her husband to participate in childbirth classes such as those Barry describes? Explain.

5. If Barry and Phyllis Schlafly were having lunch and discussing their respective essays, what do you think would be the general drift of their conversation? What might Judy Syfers say if she happened along?

6. As was noted, this piece caused some controversy when it was first published in various newspapers across the country. Some people loudly attacked Barry for being callous and sexist. Did you find him so? Do you think he is opposed to natural childbirth?

Rhetorical Considerations

1. There are many ways a good writer can create humor in print. See if you can find some humorous passages created by allusion, by antithesis, by satire, by irony, by understatement, by overstatement, by a deliberate pretense to ignorance, by absurd analogy, by cliches.

2. Where does Barry state his thesis in this piece? Is it stated directly, or is it implied?

3. How effective is Barry's opening paragraph in establishing his tone and his theme? Consider the particular word choice as well as what he says.

4. Comment on the tone of the sentence, "Women started going to college and driving bulldozers and carrying briefcases and freely using such words as *debenture*" (paragraph 5).

5. Describe the effect and the point of the last sentence in paragraph 14: "She was from California."

Writing Assignments

1. Write an essay in which you discuss your feelings about how couples should approach the delivery of a child. Do you think husbands should partake directly in childbirth?

2. A major thrust of Barry's humor is the satirizing of a popular trend. Write your own satire of some current trend or fad and attempt to imitate Barry's ways of poking fun.

The Future of Love

Jill Tweedie

The final word in this section, "The Sexes," has been reserved for Jill Tweedie's speculations on the future of love. Tweedie, who is a London journalist for *The Guardian* and the author of *In the Name of Love* (1979), foresees a time when "romantic" love will die away. Like Sally Helgesen ("What I Learned About Love on AM Radio"), Tweedie argues that romantic love creates adolescent and self-deceptive fantasies that have little to do with reality. She also argues that, for too long, love has been defined in ways that have forced outdated standards and roles on men and women. As she looks into the future, Tweedie sees a new kind of love that will make for better relationships between men and women.

Love, it seems, is as much a part of the unique equipment of   1
homo sapiens as language or laughter and far more celebrated. If all the
words that have been written about it since mankind first put stick to clay
were laid end to end, they would rocket past Venus and vanish into deep
space. Histories of love, philosophies of love, psychologies of love, guide-
books to love, love letters, love hymns, love stories, love poems, love
songs have covered tablets and papyrus, parchment and paper and walls,
filled theatres across time and lands from Epidaurus to Radio City, and
been declaimed by gods and goddesses of love from Sappho to Warren
Beatty. Love has been, is now, and ever shall be our scourge and balm,
our wound and salve, source of our finest and most bestial actions, the
emotion that passeth all understanding. It is a heavenly body out of our
orbit, beyond man-made laws, ethics, or control, a magical splendour that
descends upon us like the gift of tongues and possesses us whether we
will or no. Love transforms us into something strange and rare, it ignites
our lives and, dying, takes all meaning away.

> The mind has a thousand eyes
> And the heart but one
> Yet the light of a whole life dies
> When love is done.

We die of love and die without it, our hearts beat for it and break for it.
Love built the Taj Mahal, wrote the Song of Solomon and cooks a billion
meals every day, across the world. Love is the only thing that matters at
all, after all.

Or so they say. And in my opinion what they say, give or take an   2
epigram or two, is rubbish. Take off the rose-coloured glasses and what
does a close examination of the facts reveal to the naked eye? That love,
true love, is the rarest of all the emotions and one that has been conspicu-
ous only by its absence ever since mankind dropped from the trees. If we
condense the earth's history into one calendar year, homo sapiens appeared in the late evening of December 31st and love, his much-vaunted
race-long companion, is still merely a glimmer on the midnight horizon
of the coming New Year. Love, in other words, inhabits the future, a kind
of reverse star whose light reaches us before it is born instead of after it
has died. Certainly, intimations of love's coming have touched an individual here and there through time and its prophets have started new religions, composed great symphonies, made beautiful sculpture, and
painted exquisite canvases. But for the wide river of humanity, the ordinary mass of men and women who have peopled our planet and reproduced our race, love was not necessary, not possible, and not there.

Why, then, the stories, the poems, and the songs, the jubilations and   3
the suicides? How can you argue that love does not exist when human
beings deliberately end their own existence for love? Surely nothing is as

indisputable as that love and mankind go hand in hand. I love, therefore I am. But is it love they feel? I think not. The word is a vast umbrella that covers a multitude of virtues and sins and because we are perfectly familiar with all of love's precursors and understudies, we imagine that we have pinned down love itself when we have merely trapped its shadow. Co-operation, for instance, midwife to that most ancient of drives, survival. You scratch my back and I'll scratch yours. Sex, a powerhouse so overwhelming in its assault upon us that, trying to domesticate it, we have given it the prettier name of love. We know about affection and friendship. We feel liking, duty, deference, greed, lust, ambition, attraction, protectiveness, ingratiation, and the desire to conform. We are gripped by infatuation, obsession, adoration, vanity, addiction, jealousy, fear, and the dread of being alone. Very deeply we know about need. I need you. He needs me. Needs must.

But love is somewhere else and all those other drives and needs and   4
feelings are like the gases that swirl about in space, inwardly spiralling through the centuries to centre at last on a small hard core, gases that are only hot air in themselves but essential for the eventual formation of a new world, a world of real love. We may arrive at it one day, given time, but we are not there yet. . . .

The interesting thing is that the slow emergence of true love does not   5
predicate some higher version of morality. No sudden conversions, no lights upon the road to Damascus are in any way necessary. A new generation with new standards of loving will not come about as a result of some mystical mutation or spiritual growth, though these may well follow. The facts are more practical. As equality becomes commonplace between men and women, they themselves will perforce change from stereotypes, however successful or unsuccessful, into ordinary human beings, each one rather different from the next. Standard sexual roles—the breadwinner, the housewife and mother—already blurred, will eventually disappear and with them will go the suppression or exaggeration of parts of the individual character made necessary by those roles. And as these masks, stylised as the masks of Japanese Kabuki, slip to reveal the human face behind, romantic love, so heavily dependent upon an artificial facade and predictable masculine or feminine behaviour, will die from starvation. Already it is showing the first signs of incipient malnutrition. When, added to that, children are raised in equality and mothers, secure in their own identity, no longer pass their fears and inferiorities on to their daughters or too great an admiration on to their sons; when both parents are equally concerned with the upbringing of children and therefore ensure that those children cannot divide their own emotions between the sexes and discard one whole area, we will have bred a race of human beings differentiated by their own personalities rather than their genitalia. The old war-cry of sexists—*vive la différence*—actually implied exactly the opposite; the rigid division of an infinite variety of people into just

two categories, male and female. *Vive la similarité.* Variety will replace conformity and variety, apart from being an evolutionary must, forces each potential lover to take stock of an individual rather than search for the stereotyped ideal of a whole sex.

Nor is this change dependent solely on a conscious wish for change. 6 Evolution has always had a voracious appetite for variety, it is literally the spice of life, offering as it does a wide menu for natural selection. And it is becoming clear to many of us that the old stereotypes of male and female are increasingly a positive threat to the well-being of the race and the earth. Women, confined to a domestic and biological cage, produce unwanted children to crowd an already overpopulated world, while their own abilities wither on the hearth. Men, driven by out-dated standards of virility, continue to denude the planet and threaten each other with uncontemplatable war. Love between such men and such women serves only their own artificial needs and seals them off in their *folie à deux* from the rest of the world instead of involving them more deeply, as real love would do. Our planetary problems are rapidly becoming too serious to permit the net-curtain mentality of the average self-satisfied couple as they peep out at trouble and hastily withdraw, safe in the certainty that God himself blesses their cosy twosome and demands nothing more than its continuation, properly seeded with kiddies.

That is not to say that monogamy is on its way out, only that monog- 7 amy as we know it today—sacrosanct, heterosexual, reproductive, life-long, and almost always a retreat from life, no longer adequately fulfils either the individuals concerned or society. All research done recently, whether anthropological, paediatric, psychiatric, criminal, or social, arrives at the same conclusion: human beings develop most fully and happily if they can feel loved as children by one or two constantly present adults and, as adults themselves, reproduce the same closeness with one other adult. But there is nothing to prove that years of monogamy with the *same* adult are necessarily beneficial. Lifelong monogamy may be nice for the Church and useful for the tax-collector but it has many drawbacks for the individual, who is a learning as well as an imprinted being. As we change and learn, from youth to old age, we must give ourselves room for that change. Like snakes, we need occasionally to shed our old skins and often we cannot do that if we are tied by bonds of guilt to an outgrown love. None of us grows at the same speed or in the same way and the chances of a parallel development with one other human being are not great. But nor does this imply a lack of love or some pervasive shame. Each of us may give another person love and help in inner growth for a while. But in a changing world, with changing people, why should we expect that love to last for ever or denigrate it if it does not? Why should love, once a mansion, be made into a cage through false expectations of what love is?

Lifelong monogamy has other drawbacks, even when it works, perhaps 8 *especially* when it works. In a cold and problematic world it is all too easy to withdraw into the cosiness of a familiar love, leaving those problems for others to solve. We have a genetic need for other people; monogamous love, in attempting to assuage that need with one other person, may not only sour into neuroses or a mutual flattery that reduces both partners, making them fear the outside world, but may also isolate us from our fellows and allow us to care less about their fate. When my husband is away from home, I turn in need to my friends, even to strangers. I become vulnerable once again to their larger opinion of me. I see myself as others, more coldly, see me. On his return my instinct is to warm myself at his me-centred love, to soothe my slightly bruised ego. Luckily for me, he does not need to build me up for his own ego and so he is not all *that* warm, just warm enough. He leaves place in me for others, because he himself has place for others.

All this—changing women, the danger of stereotypes, and intractable   9
monogramy, the needs of our race and our planet in the future—implies one imperative. We must leave adolescence behind and grow up. It is absolutely vital, if we are to continue to exist in some comfort upon our earth, that we take a giant step into true adulthood, learn to filter the emotions through our reasoning capacities and learn that survival itself rests on knowing who we are, respecting others' space, and endeavouring justly to balance our own and others' needs.

And this is where love truly comes into its own as an evolutionary tool.   10
Parental love teaches children one vital fact: that they are loved and lovable and therefore can themselves love. But the love between adults differs in one absolute from parental love: it is conditional, or should be. We find out who we are by feeling our outlines against other people, by finding out who we are not. In loving but honest eyes we see prisms of our own vague face, slowly we put the prisms together and distinguish certain unchanging features, form certain principles. Inside, a centre begins to form and once it is firmly established, roots well grown, blossoms flourishing, we can turn from it towards others with a real sense of where we differ and where we are the same. And once we know that, once we respect ourselves, it becomes impossible to accept another who violates our beliefs and ourselves. A weak ego, a weak hold on reality, opens the doors to any passing stranger who flatters us enough and makes us feel real. A strong ego, a firm knowledge of who we are, demands conditions of that stranger, demands a similarity of belief and behaviour and can discard what it does not respect, even at the price of rejecting easy flattery.

And that is what true love is there to help us do. Properly informed,   11
lovingly detached, centred respectfully in itself, it provides us with a real reflection of ourselves, to help us grow. Principles do not need to be suppressed for fear of displeasing, for fear of loss, because when the crunch comes, we can cope alone.

Love cannot thrive in inequality or extreme poverty. It requires   12 enough leisure for introspection and enough introspection for empathy. It demands that the individual feel a certain control over his life because, in too great a storm, we tend to seek any refuge. It thrives on honesty and therefore must do away with great need, since need drives out honesty. It is rational, it knows its own roots, it is moral and controllable because it stems from the head and not the heart. Any resemblance it bears to love as we know it today is purely fictional.

And true love is still in embryo, fragile compared to other ties because   13
it derives no strength from more ancient needs. Its roots are not in the past but in the future. It is a beginning, a new survival mechanism slowly evolving to suit new circumstances.

Topical Considerations

1. In her first paragraph, Tweedie describes mankind's view of what love is. What clues do we have here to indicate how Tweedie feels about this? Are there any hints to prepare the reader for her comment in the second paragraph that this celebration of love is all "rubbish"? Explain.

2. Tweedie remarks that what men equate with love is actually only a shadow of what it really is and that the word is "a vast umbrella that covers a multitude of virtues and sins" (paragraph 3). What does she claim some of these virtues and sins are? Is she right in assuming that these are not real love but only a shadow of it? Discuss.

3. Describe some of the emotional dependencies that Tweedie claims are mistaken for real love. Do you agree with her? Explain your answer.

4. Tweedie argues that mankind has not yet arrived at an understanding or demonstration of what "real love" is. Is there any truth in what she is saying? Or is she failing to appreciate real love? Give reasons for your answer. What comment might she make about Helgesen's essay, "What I Learned About Love on AM Radio"?

5. What does Tweedie feel is needed to produce "a new generation with new standards of loving" (paragraph 5)? Do you see any signs that what Tweedie is predicting is beginning to happen? Do you agree with her that such a recognition is "merely a glimmer on the midnight horizon of the coming New Year" (paragraph 2)?

6. What are Tweedie's views on stereotypical male and female roles in a marriage? How does she feel about marriage? What comments would she be likely to make about the rising divorce rate? Do you agree with her? Disagree? Give reasons for your answer.

7. If Tweedie and Thurber were to have a conversation about their respective essays, what do you think Tweedie's response would be to Thurber's essay? What are some comments she might make? How

would Thurber feel about Tweedie's article? Cite specific passages on which they would be likely to agree or disagree.

8. What comments might Tweedie make about Raspberry's thesis in his essay on homemaking? If his view were more widely accepted than it is now, what impact could it have on the future of love?

Rhetorical Considerations

1. Look carefully at the way Tweedie develops the opening to her essay. Does she refer to herself at all? What is the effect of this strategy?

2. What kind of an essay has Tweedie written? Is it primarily narration? description? persuasion? exposition?

3. How would you characterize the tone of this essay? Is it absurd and funny? thoughtful and serious? bitter and cynical? Give reasons for your answer.

4. Tweedie uses concrete terms and figures of speech to create vivid, interesting word pictures. She states that the roles that men and women play are as "stylised as the masks of Japanese Kabuki" (paragraph 5). She remarks: "Love built the Taj Mahal, wrote the Song of Solomon, and cooks a billion meals every day, across the world" (paragraph 1). Find other concrete terms and figures of speech. Substitute more general words and phrases. Decide which is more effective and explain why.

5. Rephrase the following allusion: "No sudden conversions, no lights upon the road to Damascus are in any way necessary" (paragraph 5). Is it more effective when stated in "plain English"? Why or why not?

Writing Assignments

1. Tweedie raises a controversial issue regarding the permanency of marriage. In an essay, defend or criticize her view. Include a discussion of the effect her views would have on the cohesiveness of the family, the stability of the home, and the rising generation of children.

2. How would you define "real love"? Has your concept of it changed at all as you have been growing up? Write an essay in which you compare and contrast your earliest ideas of what real love is with your present sense of it. Draw on ideas you may have gained from this and other essays in this section. You might also refer to Helgesen's essay: "What I Learned About Love on AM Radio."

3. If Tweedie's views of love were more universally accepted, they would undoubtedly produce courtship patterns very different from those described by Thurber. Write an essay describing what the future of courtship would be if this were to happen.

WORLDS IN CHANGE

3

Once More to the Lake

E. B. White

Elwyn Brooks White, who was born in 1899, is considered one of the finest essayists in America. He has written in a wide variety of forms—editorials, essays, columns (for *The New Yorker*), and children's books, including the classic *Charlotte's Web* (1952). He is also coauthor of the well-known guide for writers, *The Elements of Style* (1959). What characterizes White's style is his remarkably fresh and vivid descriptions and his observations that are at once simple and profound. In this classic essay, White, with his son, returns to a beloved scene from his boyhood, where his father had taken him. But the quiet, nostalgic experience by the lakeside suddenly brings on a shocking realization of the passing of generations.

One summer, along about 1904, my father rented a camp on a 1 lake in Maine and took us all there for the month of August. We all got ringworm from some kittens and had to rub Pond's Extract on our arms and legs night and morning, and my father rolled over in a canoe with all his clothes on; but outside of that the vacation was a success and from then on none of us ever thought there was any place in the world like that lake in Maine. We returned summer after summer—always on August 1 for one month. I have since become a salt-water man, but sometimes in summer there are days when the restlessness of the tides and the fearful cold of the sea water and the incessant wind that blows across the afternoon and into the evening make me wish for the placidity of a lake in the woods. A few weeks ago this feeling got so strong I bought myself a couple of bass hooks and a spinner and returned to the lake where we used to go, for a week's fishing and to revisit old haunts.

I took along my son, who had never had any fresh water up his nose 2 and who had seen lily pads only from train windows. On the journey over to the lake I began to wonder what it would be like. I wondered how time would have marred this unique, this holy spot—the coves and streams, the hills that the sun set behind, the camps and the paths behind the camps. I was sure that the tarred road would have found it out, and I wondered in what other ways it would be desolated. It is strange how much you can remember about places like that once you allow your mind to return into the grooves that lead back. You remember one thing, and that suddenly reminds you of another thing. I guess I remembered clearest of all the early mornings, when the lake was cool and motionless, remembered how the bedroom smelled of the lumber it was made of and of the wet woods whose scent entered through the screen. The partitions in the camp were thin and did not extend clear to the top of the rooms, and as I was always the first up I would dress softly so as not to wake the others, and sneak out into the sweet outdoors and start out in the canoe, keeping close along the shore in the long shadows of the pines. I remembered being very careful never to rub my paddle against the gunwale for fear of disturbing the stillness of the cathedral.

The lake had never been what you would call a wild lake. There were 3 cottages sprinkled around the shores, and it was in farming country although the shores of the lake were quite heavily wooded. Some of the cottages were owned by nearby farmers, and you would live at the shore and eat your meals at the farmhouse. That's what our family did. But although it wasn't wild, it was a fairly large and undisturbed lake and there were places in it that, to a child at least, seemed infinitely remote and primeval.

I was right about the tar: it led to within half a mile of the shore. But 4 when I got back there, with my boy, and we settled into a camp near a farmhouse and into the kind of summertime I had known, I could tell that it was going to be pretty much the same as it had been before—I knew it, lying in bed the first morning, smelling the bedroom and hearing the boy sneak quietly out and go off along the shore in a boat. I began to sustain the illusion that he was I, and therefore, by simple transposition, that I was my father. This sensation persisted, kept cropping up all the time we were there. It was not an entirely new feeling, but in this setting it grew much stronger. I seemed to be living a dual existence. I would be in the middle of some simple act, I would be picking up a bait box or laying down a table fork, or I would be saying something, and suddenly it would be not I but my father who was saying the words or making the gesture. It gave me a creepy sensation.

We went fishing the first morning. I felt the same damp moss covering 5 the worms in the bait can, and saw the dragonfly alight on the tip of my rod as it hovered a few inches from the surface of the water. It was the arrival of this fly that convinced me beyond any doubt that everything was as it always had been, that the years were a mirage and that there had been no years. The small waves were the same, chucking the rowboat under the chine as we fished at anchor, and the boat was the same boat, the same color green and the ribs broken in the same places, and under the floor-boards the same fresh-water leavings and debris—the dead helgramite, the wisps of moss, the rusty discarded fishhook, the dried blood from yesterday's catch. We stared silently at the tips of our rods, at the dragon-flies that came and went. I lowered the tip of mine into the water, tenta-tively, pensively dislodging the fly, which darted two feet away, poised, darted two feet back, and came to rest again a little farther up the rod. There had been no years between the ducking of this dragonfly and the other one—the one that was part of memory. I looked at the boy, who was silently watching his fly, and it was my hands that held his rod, my eyes watching. I felt dizzy and didn't know which rod I was at the end of.

We caught two bass, hauling them in briskly as though they were 6 mackerel, pulling them over the side of the boat in a businesslike manner without any landing net, and stunning them with a blow on the back of the head. When we got back for a swim before lunch, the lake was exactly where we had left it, the same number of inches from the dock, and there was only the merest suggestion of a breeze. This seemed an utterly enchanted sea, this lake you could leave to its own devices for a few hours and come back to, and find that it had not stirred, this constant and trustworthy body of water. In the shallows, the dark, water-soaked sticks and twigs, smooth and old, were undulating in clusters on the bottom against the clean ribbed sand, and the track of the mussel was plain. A school of minnows swam by, each minnow with its small individual shadow, doubling the attendance, so clear and sharp in the sunlight. Some of the other campers were in swimming, along the shore, one of them with a cake of soap, and the water felt thin and clear and unsubstantial. Over the years there had been this person with the cake of soap, this cultist, and here he was. There had been no years.

Up to the farmhouse to dinner through the teeming, dusty field, the road under our sneakers was only a two-track road. The middle track was missing, the one with the marks of the hooves and the splotches of dried, flaky manure. There had always been three tracks to choose from in choosing which track to walk in; now the choice was narrowed down to two. For a moment I missed terribly the middle alternative. But the way led past the tennis court, and something about the way it lay there in the sun reassured me; the tape had loosened along the backline, the alleys were green with plantains and other weeds, and the net (installed in June and removed in September) sagged in the dry noon, and the whole place steamed with midday heat and hunger and emptiness. There was a choice of pie for dessert, and one was blueberry and one was apple, and the waitresses were the same country girls, there having been no passage of time, only the illusion of it was in a dropped curtain—the waitresses were still fifteen; their hair had been washed, that was the only difference—they had been to the movies and seen the pretty girls with the clean hair.

Summertime, oh, summertime, pattern of life indelible, the fadeproof lake, the woods unshatterable, the pasture with the sweetfern and the juniper forever and ever, summer without end; this was the background, and the life along the shore was the design, the cottagers with their innocent and tranquil design, their tiny docks with the flagpole and the American flag floating against the white clouds in the blue sky, the little paths over the roots of the trees leading from camp to camp and the paths leading back to the outhouses and the can of lime for sprinkling, and at the souvenir counters at the store the miniature birch-bark canoes and the postcards that showed things looking a little better than they looked. This was the American family at play, escaping the city heat, wondering whether the newcomers in the camp at the head of the cove were "common" or "nice," wondering whether it was true that the people who drove up for Sunday dinner at the farmhouse were turned away because there wasn't enough chicken.

It seemed to me, as I kept remembering all this, that those times and   9
those summers had been infinitely precious and worth saving. There had
been jollity and peace and goodness. The arriving (at the beginning of
August) had been so big a business in itself, at the railway station the farm
wagon drawn up, the first smell of the pine-laden air, the first glimpse of
the smiling farmer, and the great importance of the trunks and your
father's enormous authority in such matters, and the feel of the wagon
under you for the long ten-mile haul, and at the top of the last long hill
catching the first view of the lake after eleven months of not seeing this
cherished body of water. The shouts and cries of the other campers when
they saw you, and the trunks to be unpacked, to give up their rich burden.
(Arriving was less exciting nowadays, when you sneaked up in your car
and parked it under a tree near the camp and took out the bags and in
five minutes it was all over, no fuss, no loud wonderful fuss about trunks.)

Peace and goodness and jollity. The only thing that was wrong now,   10
really, was the sound of the place, an unfamiliar nervous sound of the
outboard motors. This was the note that jarred, the one thing that would
sometimes break the illusion and set the years moving. In those other
summertimes all motors were inboard; and when they were at a little
distance, the noise they made was a sedative, an ingredient of summer
sleep. They were one-cylinder and two-cylinder engines, and some were
make-and-break and some were jump-spark, but they all made a sleepy
sound across the lake. The one-lungers throbbed and fluttered, and the
twin-cylinder ones purred and purred, and that was a quiet sound, too.
But now the campers all had outboards. In the daytime, in the hot mornings, these motors made a petulant, irritable sound; at night, in the still
evening when the afterglow lit the water, they whined about one's ears
like mosquitoes. My boy loved our rented outboard, and his great desire
was to achieve single-handed mastery over it, and authority, and he soon
learned the trick of choking it a little (but not too much), and the adjustment of the needle valve. Watching him I would remember the things you
could do with the old one-cylinder engine with the heavy flywheel, how
you could have it eating out of your hand if you got really close to it
spiritually. Motorboats in those days didn't have clutches, and you would
make a landing by shutting off the motor at the proper time and coasting
in with a dead rudder. But there was a way of reversing them, if you
learned the trick, by cutting the switch and putting it on again exactly on
the final dying revolution of the flywheel, so that it would kick back
against compression and begin reversing. Approaching a dock in a strong
following breeze, it was difficult to slow up sufficiently by the ordinary
coasting method, and if a boy felt he had complete mastery over his
motor, he was tempted to keep it running beyond its time and then
reverse it a few feet from the dock. It took a cool nerve, because if you
threw the switch a twentieth of a second too soon you would catch the

flywheel when it still had speed enough to go up past center, and the boat would leap ahead, charging bull-fashion at the dock.

We had a good week at the camp. The bass were biting well and the 11 sun shone endlessly, day after day. We would be tired at night and lie down in the accumulated heat of the little bedrooms after the long hot day and the breeze would stir almost imperceptibly outside and the smell of the swamp drift in through the rusty screens. Sleep would come easily and in the morning the red squirrel would be on the roof, tapping out his gay routine. I kept remembering everything, lying in bed in the mornings—the small steamboat that had a long rounded stern like the lip of a Ubangi, and how quietly she ran on the moonlight sails, when the older boys played their mandolins and the girls sang and we ate doughnuts dipped in sugar, and how sweet the music was on the water in the shining night, and what it had felt like to think about girls then. After breakfast we would go up to the store and the things were in the same place—the minnows in a bottle, the plugs and spinners disarranged and pawed over by the youngsters from the boys' camp, the Fig Newtons and the Beeman's gum. Outside, the road was tarred and cars stood in front of the store. Inside, all was just as it had always been, except there was more Coca-Cola and not so much Moxie and root beer and birch beer and sarsaparilla. We would walk out with a bottle of pop apiece and sometimes the pop would backfire up our noses and hurt. We explored the streams, quietly, where the turtles slid off the sunny logs and dug their way into the soft bottom; and we lay on the town wharf and fed worms to the tame bass. Everywhere we went I had trouble making out which was I, the one walking at my side, the one walking in my pants.

One afternoon while we were there at that lake a thunderstorm came 12 up. It was like the revival of an old melodrama that I had seen long ago with childish awe. The second-act climax of the drama of the electrical disturbance over a lake in America had not changed in any important respect. This was the big scene, still the big scene. The whole thing was so familiar, the first feeling of oppression and heat and a general air around camp of not wanting to go very far away. In mid-afternoon (it was all the same) a curious darkening of the sky, and a lull in everything that had made life tick; and then the way the boats suddenly swung the other way at their moorings with the coming of a breeze out of the new quarter, and the premonitory rumble. Then the kettle drum, then the snare, then the bass drum and cymbals, then crackling light against the dark, and the gods grinning and licking their chops in the hills. Afterward the calm, the rain steadily rustling in the calm lake, the return of light and hope and spirits, and the campers running out in joy and relief to go swimming in the rain, their bright cries perpetuating the deathless joke about how they were getting simply drenched, and the children screaming with delight at the new sensation of bathing in the rain, and the joke about getting drenched linking the generations in a strong indestructible chain. And the comedian who waded in carrying an umbrella.

When the others went swimming, my son said he was going in, too. He   13
pulled his dripping trunks from the line where they had hung all through the shower and wrung them out. Languidly, and with no thought of going in, I watched him, his hard little body, skinny and bare, saw him wince slightly as he pulled up around his vitals the small, soggy, icy garment. As he buckled the swollen belt, suddenly my groin felt the chill of death.

Topical Considerations

1. Returning with his son to the lake of his childhood, White wonders "how time would have marred this unique, this holy spot" (paragraph 2). What changes has time brought? What things have not changed?

2. In paragraph 4, White makes some observations that give him "a creepy sensation." What are these observations, and why do they make him feel creepy?

3. In paragraph 7, White writes that "the middle track was missing" from the old road to the farmhouse. Why "for a moment" does he miss that middle track? What about that track suggests that its loss is greater than just losing another path? In other words, what higher meaning does White give to that brief observation—a meaning consistent with the rest of the essay?

4. In paragraph 6, the author describes his beloved lake as "this constant and trustworthy body of water." In what ways does he attempt to create a sense of the lake's eternal, changeless nature?

5. In paragraph 10 there is a discussion of outboard and inboard motors. What do these have to do with this essay's attention to change?

6. Throughout the essay, the author is aware of his own mortality. Find examples of images or details that underscore this awareness.

Rhetorical Considerations

1. Discuss the appropriateness of "cathedral," the last word in paragraph 2. Why does White use this religious term? For what is it a metaphor? How appropriate is it? Are there any other religious metaphors or images in the essay?

2. In paragraph 5, White records his observations of dragonflies. These are more than just casual observations, however. How do the dragonflies function rhetorically? How do they function to further the idea of time past overlapping with time present?

3. This essay is divided between remembrance of things past and

an awareness of the present ebbing away. Where exactly is the turning point in the essay? What does White use as a pivot? How appropriate is it?

4. "A school of minnows swam by, each minnow with its small individual shadow, doubling the attendance, so clear and sharp in the sunlight" (paragraph 6). So writes White, giving us another example of his fine eye for detail. Again, however, the brilliant simplicity is deceptive. What about the double image? How is it consistent with the rest of the essay, both in style (doubling) and in meaning?

5. Discuss the appropriateness of the metaphors of musical instruments in paragraph 12.

6. Discuss the impact of the last line of the essay.

Writing Assignments

1. Write an essay in which you describe a place you loved to visit as a child. Try to give details that appeal not just to your reader's senses of sight and sound, but to all senses, as White does.

2. Write an essay about your experience in returning to a favorite place from your childhood. Attempt, as White does, to create a sense of nostalgia and to capture the experience of change, from the past you remember to the present.

How Natural Is Natural?

Loren Eiseley

Loren Eiseley (1907–1977) was an anthropologist, educator, poet, and author. His works include *The Immense Journey* (1957), *The Unexpected Universe* (1969), and *The Night Country* (1971). Like E. B. White, Eiseley had the remarkable ability to make the natural world come alive and to draw profound insights from the most common scenes. Like White in the last essay, Eiseley here pays a visit to a favorite lake—a visit that also brings him face to face with worlds in change. But it is not the succession of generations that Eiseley reflects on. Instead, he glimpses by the sunlit shore an ancient world being lost in the shadow of a brave, new other world.

In the more obscure scientific circles which I frequent there is a   1
legend circulating about a late distinguished scientist who, in his declining years, persisted in wearing enormous padded boots much too large for him. He had developed, it seems, what to his fellows was a wholly

irrational fear of falling through the interstices of that largely empty molecular space which common men in their folly speak of as the world. A stroll across his living-room floor had become, for him, something as dizzily horrendous as the activities of a window washer on the Empire State Building. Indeed, with equal reason he could have passed a ghostly hand through his own ribs.

The quivering network of his nerves, the awe-inspiring movement of his thought had become a vague cloud of electrons interspersed with the light-year distances that obtain between us and the farther galaxies. This was the natural world which he had helped to create, and in which, at last, he had found himself a lonely and imprisoned occupant. All around him the ignorant rushed on their way over the illusion of substantial floors, leaping, though they did not see it, from particle to particle, over a bottomless abyss. There was even a question as to the reality of the particles which bore them up. It did not, however, keep insubstantial newspapers from being sold, or insubstantial love from being made.   2

Not long ago I became aware of another world perhaps equally natural and real, which man is beginning to forget. My thinking began in New England under a boat dock. The lake I speak of has been pre-empted and civilized by man. All day long in the vacation season high-speed motorboats, driven with the reckless abandon common to the young Apollos of our society, speed back and forth, carrying loads of equally attractive girls. The shores echo to the roar of powerful motors and the delighted screams of young Americans with uncounted horsepower surging under their hands. In truth, as I sat there under the boat dock, I had some desire to swim or to canoe in the older ways of the great forest which once lay about this region. Either notion would have been folly. I would have been gaily chopped to ribbons by teen-age youngsters whose eyes were always immutably fixed on the far horizons of space, or upon the dials which indicated the speed of their passing. There was another world, I was to discover, along the lake shallows and under the boat dock, where the motors could not come.   3

As I sat there one sunny morning when the water was peculiarly translucent, I saw a dark shadow moving swiftly over the bottom. It was the first sign of life I had seen in this lake, whose shores seemed to yield little but washed-in beer cans. By and by the gliding shadow ceased to scurry from stone to stone over the bottom. Unexpectedly, it headed almost directly for me. A furry nose with gray whiskers broke the surface. Below the whiskers green water foliage trailed out in an inverted V as long as his body. A muskrat still lived in the lake. He was bringing in his breakfast.   4

I sat very still in the strips of sunlight under the pier. To my surprise the muskrat came almost to my feet with his little breakfast of greens. He was young, and it rapidly became obvious to me that he was laboring under an illusion of his own, and that he thought animals and men were still living in the Garden of Eden. He gave me a friendly glance from time   5 to time as he nibbled his greens. Once, even, he went out into the lake again and returned to my feet with more greens. He had not, it seemed, heard very much about men. I shuddered. Only the evening before I had heard a man describe with triumphant enthusiasm how he had killed a rat in the garden because the creature had dared to nibble his petunias. He had even showed me the murder weapon, a sharp-edged brick.

On this pleasant shore a war existed and would go on until nothing 6
remained but man. Yet this creature with the gray, appealing face wanted very little: a strip of shore to coast up and down, sunlight and moonlight, some weeds from the deep water. He was an edge-of-the-world dweller, caught between a vanishing forest and a deep lake preempted by unpredictable machines full of chopping blades. He eyed me nearsightedly, a green leaf poised in his mouth. Plainly he had come with some poorly instructed memory about the lion and the lamb.

"You had better run away now," I said softly, making no movement 7
in the shafts of light. "You are in the wrong universe and must not make this mistake again. I am really a very terrible and cunning beast. I can throw stones." With this I dropped a little pebble at his feet.

He looked at me half blindly, with eyes much better adjusted to the 8
wavering shadows of his lake bottom than to sight in the open air. He made almost as if to take the pebble up into his forepaws. Then a thought seemed to cross his mind—a thought perhaps telepathically received, as Freud once hinted, in the dark world below and before man, a whisper of ancient disaster heard in the depths of a burrow. Perhaps after all this was not Eden. His nose twitched carefully; he edged toward the water.

As he vanished in an oncoming wave, there went with him a natural 9
world, distinct from the world of girls and motorboats, distinct from the world of the professor holding to reality by some great snowshoe effort in his study. My muskrat's shore-line universe was edged with the dark wall of hills on one side and the waspish drone of motors farther out, but it was a world of sunlight he had taken down into the water weeds. It hovered there, waiting for my disappearance. I walked away, obscurely pleased that darkness had not gained on life by any act of mine. In so many worlds, I thought, how natural is "natural"—and is there anything we can call a natural world at all?

Topical Considerations

1. Eiseley mentions three separate "worlds" in this essay. What are they?

2. Both E. B. White and Loren Eiseley became acutely aware of changing worlds after visiting favorite lakes. What similar changes do they note? What changes in the natural world? What changes in society? What changes in the relationship between people and nature?

3. In paragraph 5, why is the author surprised to find a muskrat living in the lake? Given what he notes about the lake, why would he feel so? What details suggest that the muskrat's world is being threatened?

4. Explain what illusion the muskrat appears to be living under? (See paragraph 5.)

5. In his reference to Eden, what is Eiseley saying about how far man has progressed?

6. What do you make of the author's warning to the muskrat in paragraph 7? How does he mean the statement, "I can throw stones?"

7. Cite some examples of Eiseley's use of descriptive details. How effective are they in evoking a sense of the lake and the encounter with the muskrat?

8. This essay is more than just a simple reflection on a muskrat's watery world, just as E. B. White's piece is more than just a simple bit of nostalgia. What is Eiseley really despairing about here? And how appropriate is the title?

Rhetorical Considerations

1. How is the introductory discussion of the scientist in the enormous, padded boots relevant to the rest of the essay?

2. In paragraph 3, Eiseley says that the lake had been "pre-empted and civilized by man." What do "pre-empted" and "civilized" mean? Explain how Eiseley uses these terms.

3. Explain the allusion to "young Apollos of our society" (paragraph 3). What is the effect of this allusion?

4. In general, what is Eiseley's attitude toward the teenagers on the lake? Explain the allusion and the rhetorical effect of the Garden of Eden, cited in paragraph 5. Explain the allusion to "the lion and the lamb" in paragraph 6.

5. In the last paragraph, Eiseley refers both to "a world of sunlight" and to the approaching darkness. How does he use these images symbolically? How do they project his feelings and attitudes here?

Writing Assignments

1. Eiseley contrasts aspects of the natural world with those of modern society. Write an essay in which you use specific details that do the same. Consider an experience of your own when you tried to escape to the woods, the mountains, the desert, or the seashore but found that you were constantly reminded of the "other" civilized world.

2. Write an essay about an encounter you once had with some animal whose world you felt was threatened.

3. Write an essay in which you debate the need to protect the wilderness, even at the expense of industrial and economic growth.

4. The muskrat in this essay is threatened by the encroachment of civilization, although it is not one of an endangered species. Write an essay arguing the need to protect species that are endangered, such as the California condor, the snail darter, and the cougar.

5. Extinction is an irrefutable law of nature, as evidenced by the thousands of different species preserved only in fossils. Write an essay arguing that attempts to protect endangered species are costly and vain efforts to reverse a natural process.

They Also Wait Who Stand and Serve Themselves

Andrew Ward

One of the most familiar institutions in modern America is the corner gas station. Like the corner grocery store and movie house, however, it is rapidly vanishing, leaving in its place something slick, efficient, and impersonal. Andrew Ward, who is a contributing editor to *The Atlantic Monthly* and the author of *Bits and Pieces* (1980), here describes in vivid, humorous detail his local gas station and what, in the name of progress, happens to it—and by extension to the quality of American life.

1 Anyone interested in the future of American commerce should take a drive sometime to my neighborhood gas station. Not that it is or ever was much of a place to visit. Even when I first moved here, five years ago, it was shabby and forlorn: not at all like the garden spots they used to feature in the commercials, where trim, manicured men with cultivated voices tipped their visors at your window and asked what they could do for you.

2 Sal, the owner, was a stocky man who wore undersized, popped-button shirts, sagging trousers, and oil-spattered work shoes with broken laces. "Gas stinks" was his motto, and every gallon he pumped into his customers' cars seemed to take something out of him. "Pumping gas is for morons," he liked to say, leaning indelibly against my rear window and watching the digits fly on the pump register. "One of these days I'm gonna dump this place on a Puerto Rican, move to Florida, and get into something nice, like hero sandwiches."

3 He had a nameless, walleyed assistant who wore a studded denim jacket and, with his rag and squeegee, left a milky film on my windshield

as my tank was filling. There was a fume-crazed, patchy German shepherd, which Sal kept chained to the air pump, and if you followed Sal into
his cluttered, overheated office next to the service bays, you ran a gauntlet
of hangers-on, many of them Sal's brothers and nephews, who spent their
time debating the merits of the driving directions he gave the bewildered
travelers who turned into his station for help.

"I don't know," one of them would say, pulling a bag of potato chips   4
off the snack rack, "I think I would have put 'em onto 91, gotten 'em off
at Willow, and then—bango!—straight through to Hamden."

Sal guarded the rest room key jealously and handed it out with reluc-   5
tance, as if something in your request had betrayed some dismal aberra-
tion. The rest room was accessible only through a little closet littered with
tires, fan belts, and cases of oil cans. Inside, the bulb was busted and there
were never any towels, so you had to dry your hands on toilet paper—
if Sal wasn't out of toilet paper, too.

The soda machine never worked for anyone except Sal, who, when   6
complaints were lodged, would give it a contemptuous kick as he trudged
by, dislodging warm cans of grape soda which, when their pop-tops were
flipped, gave off a fine purple spray. There was, besides the snack rack
in the office, a machine that dispensed peanuts on behalf of the Sons of
Garibaldi. The metal shelves along the cinderblock wall were sparsely
stocked with cans of cooling system cleaner, windshield de-icer, anti-
freeze, and boxed head lamps and oil filters. Over the battered yellow
wiper case, below the Coca Cola clock, and half hidden by a calendar from
a janitorial supply concern, hung a little brass plaque from the oil company, awarded in recognition of Salvatore A. Castallano's ten-year business association.

I wish for the sake of nostalgia that I could say Sal was a craftsman,   7
but I can't. I'm not even sure he was an honest man. I suspect that when
business was slow he may have cheated me, but I never knew for sure
because I don't know anything about cars. If I brought my Volvo in
because it was behaving strangely, I knew that as far as Sal was concerned
it could never be a simple matter of tightening a bolt or re-attaching a
hose. "Jesus," he'd wearily exclaim after a look under the hood. "Mr.
Ward, we got problems." I usually let it go at that and simply asked him
when he thought he could have it repaired, because if I pressed him for
details he would get all worked up. "Look, if you don't want to take my
word for it, you can go someplace else. I mean, it's a free country, you
know? You got spalding on your caps, which means your dexadrometer
isn't charging, and pretty soon you're gonna have hairlines in your flushing drums. You get hairlines in your flushing drums and you might as well
forget it. You're driving junk."

I don't know what Sal's relationship was with the oil company. I sup-   8
pose it was pretty distant. He was never what they call a "participating
dealer." He never gave away steak knives or NFL tumblers or stuffed

animals with his fill-ups, and never got around to taping company posters on his windows. The map rack was always empty, and the company emblem, which was supposed to rotate thirty feet above the station, had broken down long before I first laid eyes on it, and had frozen at an angle that made it hard to read from the highway.

If, outside of television, there was ever such a thing as an oil company service station inspector, he must have been appalled by the grudging service, the mad dog, the sepulchral john. When there was supposed to have been an oil shortage a few years ago, Sal's was one of the first stations to run out of gas. And several months ago, during the holiday season, the company squeezed him out for good.   9

I don't know whether Sal is now happily sprinkling olive oil over salami subs somewhere along the Sun Belt. I only know that one bleak January afternoon I turned into his station to find him gone. At first, as I idled by the no-lead pump, I thought the station had been shut down completely. Plywood had been nailed over the service bays, Sal's name had been painted out above the office door, and all that was left of his dog was a length of chain dangling from the air-pump's vacant mast.   10

But when I got out of the car I spotted someone sitting in the office with his boots up on the counter, and at last caught sight of the "Self-Service Only" signs posted by the pumps. Now, I've always striven for a degree of self-sufficiency. I fix my own leaky faucets and I never let the bellboy carry my bags. But I discovered as I squinted at the instructional sticker by the nozzle that there are limits to my desire for independence. Perhaps it was the bewilderment with which I approach anything having to do with the internal combustion engine; perhaps it was my conviction that fossil fuels are hazardous; perhaps it was the expectation of service, the sense of helplessness, that twenty years of oil company advertising had engendered, but I didn't want to pump my own gas.   11

A mongrel rain began to fall upon the oil-slicked tarmac as I followed the directions spelled out next to the nozzle. But somehow I got them wrong. When I pulled the trigger on the nozzle, no gas gushed into my fuel tank, no digits flew on the gauge.   12

"Hey, buddy," a voice sounded out of a bell-shaped speaker overhead. "Flick the switch."   13

I turned toward the office and saw someone with Wild Bill Hickok hair leaning over a microphone.   14

"Right. Thanks," I answered, and turned to find the switch. There wasn't one. There was a bolt that looked a little like a switch, but it wouldn't flick.   15

"The switch," the voice crackled in the rain. "Flick the switch."   16

I waved back as if I'd finally understood, but I still couldn't figure out what he was talking about. In desperation, I stuck the nozzle back into my fuel tank and pulled the trigger. Nothing.   17

In the office I could see that the man was now angrily pulling on a   18 slicker. "What the hell's the matter with you?" he asked, storming by me. "All you gotta do is flick the switch."

"I couldn't find the switch," I told him.   19

"Well, what do you call this?" he wanted to know, pointing to a little   20
lever near the pump register.

"A lever," I told him.   21

"Christ," he muttered, flicking the little lever. The digits on the regis-   22
ter suddenly formed neat rows of zeros. "All right, it's set. Now you can
serve yourself," the long-haired man said, ducking back to the office.

As the gas gushed into my fuel tank and the fumes rose to my nostrils,   23
I thought for a moment about my last visit to Sal's. It hadn't been any
picnic: Sal claimed to have found something wrong with my punting
brackets, the German shepherd snapped at my heels as I walked by, and
nobody had change for my ten. But the transaction had dimension to it:
I picked up some tips about color antennas, entered into the geographical
debate in the office, and bought a can of windshield wiper solvent (to fill
the gap in my change). Sal's station had been a dime a dozen, but it
occurred to me, as the nozzle began to balk and shudder in my hand, that
gas stations of its kind were going the way of the village smithy and the
corner grocer.

I got a glob of grease on my glove as I hung the nozzle back on the   24
pump, and it took more than a minute to satisfy myself that I had replaced
the gas cap properly. I tried to whip up a feeling of accomplishment as
I headed for the office, but I could not forget Sal's dictum: Pumping gas
is for morons.

The door to the office was locked, but a sign directed me to a stainless   25
steel teller's drawer which had been installed in the plate glass of the front
window. I stood waiting for a while with my money in hand, but the
long-haired man sat inside with his back to me, so at last I reached up and
hesitantly knocked on the glass with my glove.

The man didn't hear me or had decided, in retaliation for our semantic   26
disagreement, to ignore me for a while. I reached up to knock again, but
noticed that my glove had left a greasy smear on the window. Ever my
mother's son, I reflexively reached into my pocket for my handkerchief
and was about to wipe the grease away when it hit me: at last the oil
industry had me where it wanted me—standing in the rain and washing
its windshield.

Topical Considerations

1. This is a short piece, but Ward manages to portray a clear
sense of Sal's gas station and the men associated with it. Cite some
examples of succinct descriptions. How typical of gas stations is Sal's
place? Does familiarity with gas stations help us visualize the place?

2. A writer's attitude toward his subject is determined not just by what he says about it but by the details he selects to describe it. What would you say Ward's attitude is toward Sal and his station? What select details contribute to that attitude?

3. How does Ward feel toward what replaces Sal's station? How does Ward convey that attitude (or attitudes)?

4. In paragraph 7, Ward brings up the topic of nostalgia. How does this essay transcend a simple nostalgic reflection on a neighborhood gas station? In other words, what is Ward talking about on a higher level?

5. In paragraph 23, the author says that, even though his last visit to Sal's "hadn't been any picnic . . . the transaction had dimension to it." What does Ward mean by this statement? How did the transaction with the man with the "Wild Bill Hickok hair" lack dimension?

6. How does the scene in the last paragraph dramatize Ward's major complaint in this essay?

Rhetorical Considerations

1. Cite examples of descriptions in this essay that typify gas stations we can all relate to? Do any descriptions here strike you as unique to Sal's place?

2. Cite examples where the descriptions create a sense of humor. Does our familiarity with gas stations help carry the humor?

3. What is the effect of Sal's award of recognition coming where it does in paragraph 6?

4. Diagnosing the problems with Ward's Volvo, Sal says "You got spalding on your caps, . . . your dexadrometer isn't charging, and pretty soon you're gonna have hairlines in your flushing drums" (paragraph 7). Are these real car problems, or is Sal trying to pull a fast one on Ward? Or is this the author's way of admitting his ignorance of auto repair talk?

5. Why does Ward call the rain "mongrel" in paragraph 12? What does the word connote, and how does it characterize the rain?

6. This essay contains several examples of irony. Cite some and describe how the irony works and its effects.

Writing Assignments

1. One sure sign of good writing is the use of details and specifics. Inferior writing is just the opposite—lacking in sharp details and full of vague generalities. Paragraph 6 is a good example of Ward's use of sharp details and specifics. First make note of them all, then rewrite the paragraph, substituting the details and specifics with vague generalities.

2. Write an essay in which you describe how some familiar and traditional element of American society is "going the way of the village smithy and the corner grocer." In fact, consider the plight of the corner grocer. Or the proprietor of a general store. Or the family doctor, who used to make house calls. Or a human bank teller.

3. Write an essay in which you describe an experience you've had with depersonalizing institutions.

4. Take the opposite stand from that in Assignment 3—that is, write an essay arguing that you prefer the added efficiency of the modern supermarket, for example, to the personal touch of the corner grocer. Or the computerized, twenty-four-hour bank teller to a human one. Or an automatic toll gate to a human toll collector on highways.

Stripping Down to Bare Happiness
Linda Weltner

It has been said that ours is a consumption-oriented, throwaway society that produces more waste than any other on earth. That may be so, but as Linda Weltner reports, some people are making drastic changes in the way they live. This is a story of two real people who have decided to simplify their lives without depriving themselves. It is the story of people who have, in fact, improved the quality of their lives by reducing the clutter, expense, and waste of modern living. In a way, it is also a story of the way life used to be. Linda Weltner is a columnist for *The Boston Globe* and the author of children's books.

"What we're talking about is simplification, not deprivation," explains a friend of mine. "It isn't that you can't do all the things you like, but you change. You don't like them anymore. Some of the old habits seem so wasteful and unsatisfying, you really lose your taste for them. So you still have everything you want—only on less money." 1

When I first met them, Sara and Michael were a two-career couple with a home of their own, and a large boat bought with a large loan. What interested them in a concept called voluntary simplicity was the birth of their daughter and a powerful desire to raise her themselves. Neither one of them, it turned out, was willing to restrict what they considered their "real life" into the brief time before work and the tired hours afterward. 2

"A lot of people think that as they have children and things get more expensive, the only answer is to work harder in order to earn more money. It's not the only answer," insists Michael. 3

The couple's decision was to trade two full-time careers for two half- 4 time careers, and to curtail consumption. They decided to spend their money only on things that contributed to their major goal, the construction of a world where family and friendship, work and play, were all of a piece, a world, moreover, which did not make wasteful use of the earth's resources.

Today, they live in the same suburban community in a handsome, 5 energy-efficient home they designed themselves. Small by most standards, it is easy to clean, furnish, maintain and heat. The first floor, one large room, has a kitchen area along one wall, a birch table and chairs for dining, a living area defined by a comfortable couch and a wood stove, and a corner work area. Upstairs is a child's bedroom, topped by a loft which is the master bedroom, an office that serves them both, and a bathroom. It is bright and light and in harmony with its surroundings. Soon there will be a solar greenhouse outside the front door.

How can a couple with two part-time freelance jobs afford to build 6 their own home, own a car, and share a small boat with another couple —all without a loan? How can they maintain a high standard of living that provides "everything" they want? What is it they have given up that they do not miss?

Expensive clutter, for one thing—medicine cabinets full of cosmetics 7 and over-the-counter drugs they will never use, kitchen cabinets crowded with items they would eventually throw away. The one clothes closet Sara shares with Michael easily contains the basic items in their wardrobes, many of them well-made classic styles from L. L. Bean. "I'm constantly giving things away," Sara explains. By sifting and discarding, by keeping track of what they have, Sara and Michael have a clear idea of what they really need.

They do not have a dishwasher. The number of hand-thrown pottery 8 dishes they own would not fill one. They do not own a clothes dryer; the wet clothes, drying indoors in winter, eliminate the need for a humidifier. Sara's dark hair is short. She does not need a hairdryer, electric curlers, or a curling iron. Their front yard is wooded. They do not need a power mower, grass spreader, or electric clippers. They do not own a TV, and so they and their child are not constantly saturated with images of new toys, new things, and new temptations.

They have exchanged the expenses of work in a commuter age—the 9 extra car, the cost of gasoline, professional wardrobes, lunches and frequent dinners out, and babysitting fees—for the time to pay attention to the quality of their lives. They have given up paper products, processed foods, expensive hobbies, first-run movies, restaurants, and paying for the services of others in return for home cooking, mid-week family picnics, library books, participation in community arts programs, thrift shops, an active YMCA membership, and do-it-yourself projects.

"That yearning feeling that's so much a part of this culture goes on 10 forever," says Sara. "But it doesn't matter if you're making $15,000 or

$50,000. There'll always be things you wish you could afford. Money really wasn't the reason we changed. We did it for our own personal satisfaction, and for anyone thinking of simplifying life, there's only one basic rule: 'If it isn't satisfying, don't do it.' "

Sara and Michael lent me their copy of "99 Ways to a Simple Life-   11
style," an Anchor Press/Doubleday paperback compiled by the Center for Science in the Public Interest, a handbook of practical suggestions that can be applied to anyone's living situation. I read it carefully, giving myself high marks in some areas, surprised at my socially sanctioned irrational behavior in others.

That night, accompanying my daughter on a shopping trip, I came   12
across an inexpensive hand towel that matched our kitchen wallpaper, and a pair of "bargain" sandals too handsome to resist. When I stood in the parking lot, $11 poorer, no happier on leaving the store than I had been entering it, I felt like a child, helpless in the face of my own impulses.

It is a world of illusion, this shopping merry-go-round we ride, but with   13
all the action and excitement, it is sometimes hard to find the resolve and the courage to dismount.

Topical Considerations

1. Why exactly did Sara and Michael decide to "strip down" their lives? Do you know people who, from a similar philosophical stand, "stripped down" their lives to bare happiness? Could you do that and still be happy?

2. Do you get the impression that Sara and Michael made some major sacrifices when they turned their lifestyle around? Would such a stripping down result in major sacrifices for your parents? for your friends? for yourself?

3. What does this essay say about the way Americans have become accustomed to certain material possessions? What does it say about the values projected by our consumer economy? How has television aided in our conditioning?

4. If you are familiar with apparel sold by L. L. Bean, try to characterize its style. Why would L. L. Bean make up much of Sara and Michael's wardrobes? Do you find anything ironic in the fact that their "stripping down" stopped at wardrobes with L. L. Bean labels?

5. Sara and Michael do not own a dishwasher or a clothes dryer. (In fact, most people in the world don't own these appliances.) Does their adjustment suggest that the American consumer can shake the habit of dependence on such modern conveniences? What does this say about consumer conditioning versus consumer need?

6. Sara and Michael now live without television. What benefit have they found from such an adjustment? Could you live without TV?

Do you agree that there would be some real benefits in not having it? What disadvantages would there be in a life without TV?

Rhetorical Considerations

1. What is the rhetorical advantage of beginning this piece with a quotation from the author's friends rather than with a little of their background?

2. In paragraph 6, Weltner asks three questions. Are these rhetorical questions or real ones that she then answers?

3. Weltner begins the essay with a quotation from Sara and ends with some self-reflection of her own after a shopping trip. How effective is this conclusion? How does it dramatize what the essay is about?

4. What do you make of the fact that the paragraphs in this essay are quite short? Could some of them be combined? Do you think the short paragraphs reflect Weltner's journalistic style. (She writes for *The Boston Globe.*)

Writing Assignments

1. Write an essay in which you describe how you bought something you did not really need. Try to explore your impulses. Did they arise out of "socially sanctioned irrational behavior"? Did you buy out of some deeper need for security?

2. Do you think you could live the rest of your life without television and still be happy? Write an essay in which you explore that possibility. Examine how you think your life would be changed—for better or for worse.

3. Try to imagine yourself making a drastic change in lifestyles —stripping down to bare essentials. Do you think you could live happily, like Sara and Michael, without all the modern conveniences and consumer commodities to which you have grown accustomed?

A New Kind of Man in the Making

Alvin Toffler

We end this section, "Worlds in Change," with some optimistic glimpses of the world to come. Alvin Toffler, a futurist and the best-selling author of *Future Shock* (1970) and *The Third Wave* (1980), sees the history of mankind in terms of three major waves of change. The First Wave was triggered some

10,000 years ago by the invention of agriculture. The Second Wave was launched three centuries ago by the Industrial Revolution. The Third Wave is upon us now, says Toffler, and will result both in the collapse of the industrial system and in whole new opportunities for a better life. This essay, excerpted from *The Third Wave,* documents some of the startling changes in human personality and social character that Toffler foresees—and some of the possibilities of the new civilization that is emerging.

As a novel civilization erupts into our lives, we are left to wonder   1 whether we ourselves have become obsolete.

Brilliant advances in such fields as genetics and electronics sweep our   2 breath away. The world economy becomes unrecognizable. The new means of communication dazzle us. The nuclear-family system breaks. Traditional political and economic theories seem increasingly irrelevant as, at every point, the centuries-old frame of industrialism is stretched or broken by the rise of the Third Wave.

The familiar mass society produced by the Industrial Revolution—with   3 its heavy reliance on mass production, mass communications, mass education and mass political opinion—is becoming "demassified." Diversity —in values, in family forms, in communication, in religion, in technology, in everything from politics to poetry—begins to replace industrial uniformity. New institutions, from self-help groups and political splinter organizations to transnational agencies, spring up in the rubble of the Second Wave system. Bit by bit, as yet largely unrecognized for what they are, the elements of a new, Third Wave social order are falling into place.

With so many of our habits, values, routines and responses called into   4 question, it is hardly surprising if we sometimes feel like people of the past, relics of the waning industrial civilization. But are there also people of the future among us, anticipatory citizens, as it were, of the civilization to come? Once we see past the decay and disintegration around us, can we glimpse the emerging outlines of the personality of the future—the coming, so to speak, of a "new man"?

If so, it would not be the first time *un homme nouveau* was supposedly   5 detected on the horizon. André Reszler, director of the Center for European Culture in Geneva, has described earlier attempts to forecast the coming of a new type of human being. At the end of the 18th century there was, for example, the "American Adam"—man born anew in North America, theoretically without the vices and weaknesses of the European. In the middle of the 20th century, the new man was supposed to appear in Hitler's Germany. Nazism, wrote Hermann Rauschning, "is more than a religion; it is the will to create the superman." This sturdy "Aryan" would be part-peasant, part-warrior, part-God. "I have seen the new man," Hitler once confided to Rauschning. "He is intrepid and cruel. I stood in fear before him."

The image of a new man also haunted the Communists. The Soviets   6 still speak of the coming of "Socialist Man." But it was Trotsky who rhapsodized most vividly about the future human: "Man will become incomparably stronger, wiser and more perceptive. His body will become more harmonious, his movements more rhythmical, his voice more melodious. His ways of life will acquire a powerfully dramatic quality. The average man will attain the level of an Aristotle, of a Goethe, of a Marx."

As recently as a decade or two ago, Frantz Fanon heralded the coming 7 of yet another new man who would have a "new mind." Che Guevara thought he would have a richer interior life.

Each image is different. Yet Mr. Reszler persuasively points out that 8 behind most of these images of the "new man" there lurks that familiar old fellow, the Noble Savage, a mythic creature endowed with all sorts of qualities that civilization has supposedly corrupted or worn away. And he properly questions this romanticization of the primitive, reminding us that regimes which set out consciously to foster a "new man" have usually brought totalitarian havoc in their wake.

It would be foolish, therefore, to herald yet once more the birth of a 9 "new man" (unless, now that the genetic engineers are at work, we mean that in a frightening, strictly biological sense). The idea suggests a proto-type, a single ideal model that the entire civilization strains to emulate. And in a society moving rapidly toward demassification, nothing is more unlikely.

Nevertheless, it would be equally foolish to believe that fundamentally 10 changed material conditions of life leave personality or, more accurately, social character, unaffected. As we revolutionize our technology, our energy base, our family structures and the very nature of work, we also modify people. Even if one believed in some unchanging human nature, a commonly held view I do not share, society would still reward and elicit certain character traits and penalize others, leading to changes in the distribution of traits in the population. Our task, therefore, is not to hunt for the mythic "man" but for the traits most likely to be valued by the civilization of tomorrow.

The coming of the Second Wave, for example, was accompanied by the 11 spread of the Protestant ethic with its emphasis on thrift, unremitting toil and the deferral of gratification—traits that channeled enormous ener-gies into the tasks of economic development. The Second Wave also brought changes in individualism, attitudes toward authority, concepts of objectivity and subjectivity and in the ability to think abstractly, to empa-thize and to imagine.

For peasants to be machined into an industrial work force, they had 12 to be given the rudiments of literacy. They had to be educated, informed and molded. They had to understand that another way of life was possi-ble. Large numbers were needed, therefore, with the capacity to imagine themselves in a new role and setting. Their minds had to be liberated from the proximate present. Thus, just as, to some extent, it had to

democratize communications and politics, industrialism was also forced
to democratize the imagination.

The result of such psychocultural changes was a changed distribution   13
of traits—a new social character. And today we are once more at the edge
of a similar psychocultural upheaval.

The fact that we are racing away from Orwellian uniformity makes it   14
difficult to generalize about the emerging psyche. Nevertheless, we can
point to powerful changes that are likely to influence psychological development in the emergent Third Wave society. And this leads us to fascinating, though surely tentative, conclusions.

Growing Up Different

To begin with, the child of tomorrow is likely to grow up in a society   15
far less child-centered than our own.

The aging or "graying" of the population in all high-technology coun-   16
tries implies greater public attention to the needs of the elderly and a
correspondingly reduced focus on the young. Furthermore, as women
develop jobs or careers, the traditional need to channel their energies
into motherhood is diminished.

During the Second Wave era, millions of American parents lived out   17
their own dreams through their children—often because they could reasonably expect their children to do better socially and economically than
they, themselves, had done. This expectation of upward mobility encouraged parents to concentrate enormous psychic energies on their children.
Today, many middle-class parents face agonizing disillusionment as their
children—in a far more difficult world—move down, rather than up, the
socioeconomic scale. The likelihood of surrogate fulfillment is evaporat-
ing.

For all these reasons, the baby born tomorrow may well enter a society   18
no longer obsessed with—perhaps not even terribly interested in—the
needs, wants, psychological development and instant gratification of the
child. If so, the Dr. Spocks of tomorrow will urge a more structured and
demanding childhood. Parents will be less permissive.

Parents will love their children no less. But the family is no longer   19
likely to be as heavily oriented around the child's demands as it has been
in so many middle-class homes until now.

Nor, one suspects, will adolescence be as prolonged a process as it is   20
today for so many. Millions of children are being brought up in single-
parent homes, with working mothers (or fathers) squeezed by an erratic
economy and with less of the luxury and time that were available to the
flower-child generation of the 1960's.

Others, later on, are likely to be reared in work-at-home or "electronic   21
cottage" families. Indeed, one of the most significant developments of
the coming decades will be the shift of important numbers of jobs out of

the factory or office and back into the home. Since large numbers of workers are involved in moving intangible symbols and information, rather than physical goods, it is no longer necessary for them to go to the central location to do their jobs. Even today, production engineers report, 35 to 50 percent of the work force in some advanced manufacturing centers could actually perform their work at home if we chose to organize production in that fashion. Many others could work a few days in the office and factory and a few days at home.

The skyrocketing cost of gas and transport and the plummeting cost 22 of communications and minicomputers suggest that at some point it will be far cheaper to put electronic work stations in the home than to transport vast numbers of workers back and forth every day. "Telecommuting" may well replace commuting. Clearly, not all work can be done in the home—and not all workers would want to stay home—but even if only 10 to 20 percent of the work force were to shift into the home over the next few decades, the impact on energy use, the economy and social relations would be enormous.

In many homes the family may well become a work-together produc- 23 tion unit, as it typically was before the Industrial Revolution. Moreover, we can expect the children of tomorrow's electronic cottage to be drawn directly into the family's work tasks and given growing responsibility from an early age, as is often the case today where the family runs a "mom-and-pop" business.

Such facts suggest a shorter childhood and youth, but a more responsi- 24 ble and productive one. Working alongside adults, absorbing grown-up standards, children in such homes are also likely to be less subject to peer pressures. They may well turn out to be the high achievers of tomorrow.

During the transition to the new society, wherever jobs remain scarce, 25 Second Wave labor unions will undoubtedly fight to exclude young people from the job market outside the home. Unions—and teachers, whether unionized or not—will continue to lobby for ever-longer years of compulsory or near-compulsory schooling. To the extent that they succeed, millions of young people will continue to be forced into the painful limbo of prolonged adolescence. (We may, therefore, see a sharp contrast between young people who grow up fast because of early work responsibilities in the "electronic cottage" and those who mature more slowly outside.)

However, as the needs of the economy and society are transformed, 26 we must expect education to change, too. More learning will occur outside, rather than inside, the classroom. The years of compulsory schooling will grow shorter, not longer. Instead of rigid age segregation, young and old will mingle. Education will become more interspersed and interwoven with work and more spread out over a lifetime. And work itself will probably begin earlier in life than it has in the last generation or two.

The New Worker

As the adolescent matures and enters the job arena, new forces come   27
into play on his or her personality, rewarding some traits and punishing
or penalizing others.

Throughout the Second Wave era, work steadily grew more repetitive,   28
specialized and time-pressured, and employers wanted workers who were
obedient, punctual and willing to perform rote tasks. The corresponding
traits were fostered by the schools and rewarded by the corporation.

As the Third Wave cuts across our society, new demassifying technolo-   29
gies, new organizational styles and the growing resistance of workers to
brutalizing monotony begin to transform the nature of work. Work grows
less, not more, repetitive. It becomes less fragmented, each person doing
a somewhat larger task. More and more employees work only part-time
out of choice. Flex-time and self-pacing replace the old need for mass
synchronization of behavior. Workers are forced to cope with more frequent changes in their tasks and with a blinding succession of personnel
transfers, product changes and reorganizations.

What Third Wave employers increasingly need, therefore, are men   30
and women who accept responsibility, who understand how their work
dovetails with others', who can handle ever larger tasks, who adapt swiftly
to changed circumstances and are sensitively tuned in to the people
around them.

The old Second Wave company frequently paid off for plodding   31
bureaucratic behavior. The Third Wave company requires people who
are less preprogrammed and faster on their feet. The difference, says
Donald K. Conover, general manager of corporate education for Western
Electric, is like that between classical musicians who play each note according to a predetermined, preset pattern and jazz improvisers who—
once having decided what song to play—sensitively pick up cues from one
another and, on the basis of that, decide what notes to play next.

Such people, typifying the demassified work force needed by Third   32
Wave industry, reject many Second Wave values. According to opinion
researcher Daniel Yankelovich, only 56 percent of United States workers
—mainly older ones—are still motivated by traditional incentives. They
are happiest with strict work guidelines and clear tasks. They do not
expect to find "meaning" in their work.

By contrast, as much as 17 percent of the work force already reflects   33
newer values emerging from the Third Wave. Largely young middle
managers, they are, declares Mr. Yankelovich, the "hungriest for more
responsibility and more vital work with a commitment worthy of their
talent and skills." They seek meaning along with financial reward.

To recruit such workers, employers are beginning to offer individual-   34
ized rewards. This helps explain why a few advanced companies—like
TRW Inc., the Cleveland-based high-technology firm—now provide employees not with a fixed set of fringe benefits, but with a smorgasbord of

optional holidays, medical benefits, pensions and insurance. Each worker can tailor a package to his or her own needs. Says Mr. Yankelovich, "There is no one set of incentives with which to motivate the full spectrum of the work force." Moreover, he adds, in the mix of rewards for work, money no longer has the same motivating power it once did.

No one suggests these workers don't want money. They certainly do. But once a certain income level is reached, they vary widely in what else they want. Additional increments of money no longer have their former impact on behavior. When the Bank of America in San Francisco offered an assistant vice president a promotion to a branch only 20 miles away, he refused to accept the carrot. He didn't want to commute. A decade ago, when "Future Shock" described the stress of job mobility, only an estimated 10 percent of employees resisted a corporate move. The number has jumped to between a third and a half, according to Merrill Lynch Relocation Management Inc., even though moves are often accompanied by a fatter-than-usual raise. "The balance has definitely shifted away from saluting the company and marching off to Timbuktu toward a greater emphasis on family and life style," says a vice president of Celanese Corporation.   36

Meanwhile, the most ingrained patterns of authority are also changing. In Second Wave companies, every employee has a single boss. Disputes among employees are taken to the boss to be resolved. In the advanced industries, however, the style is entirely different. Workers simultaneously have more than one boss. People of different rank and different skills meet in temporary task forces or work groups. These, in turn, are organized into what is called a "matrix." And, in the words of S.M. Davis and P.R. Lawrence, authors of a standard text on the subject: "Differences . . . are resolved without a common boss readily available to arbitrate. . . . The assumption in a matrix is that this conflict can be healthy . . . differences are valued and people express their views even when they know others may disagree."   36

This system penalizes workers who show blind obedience. It rewards those who—within limits—talk back. Workers who seek meaning, who question authority, who want to exercise discretion or who demand that their work be socially responsible may be regarded as troublemakers in Second Wave industries. But Third Wave industries cannot run without them.   37

Across the board, therefore, we are seeing a subtle but profound change in the personality traits rewarded by the economic system—a change which cannot help but shape the emerging social character.   38

The Prosumer Ethic

The economy might be viewed as having two sectors—one in which we produce goods or services for others and one in which we produce goods or services for ourselves. In the first of these, producer and consumer are   39 different people. As workers, we produce goods and services for sale or exchange. In the other sector, you and I do things for ourselves. In effect, producer and consumer are one and the same. In the first sector, we produce. In the second, we may be said to "prosume."

Each of these sectors of the economy has quite different psychological   40
effects on us. For each sector promotes its own ethic, its own set of values and its own definition of success.

The Second Wave era saw a vast expansion of production for ex-   41
change. Even the farm family, instead of growing its own food, produced cash crops and bought its food at the supermarket. The growth of exchange and the decline of what might be called "prosumption"—in both capitalist and socialist industrial nations—encouraged an acquisitive ethic. It gave rise to a narrowly economic definition of personal success.

One of the little-explored economic phenomena of the present period,   42
however, has been a tremendous increase in self-help and do-it-yourself activity, carrying it beyond mere hobbyism. Millions of people are taking their own blood pressure, building their own patios, pumping their own gasoline or joining with others in self-improvement organizations. These range from groups of women who have undergone mastectomies to antismoking groups to "bereavement" groups that help people suffering from grief after the loss of a relative or friend. Today there are some 500,000 self-help groups in the United States, and the movement is growing at a frenetic rate. Instead of looking upon themselves as the consumers of services offered by professionals like doctors, psychiatrists and other specialists, the people in this movement jointly produce (or, more accurately, prosume) their own services. They are prosumers.

The do-it-yourself part of this movement is more than holding its own.   43
The construction industry quietly passed an important juncture between 1974 and 1976 when, for the first time, more building supplies and tools were sold to do-it-yourselfers than to building contractors, carpenters or electricians.

The reasons for this surge of self-help and do-it-yourself activity are   44
complex and varied. They range from the high cost of services to the unavailability of plumbers and repairmen to the arrival of new technologies and materials and the deterioration of services previously provided by government. Whatever the causes, there is much evidence to suggest that prosumption will assume far greater significance in the decades immediately ahead. And as it comes to occupy more of our time and energy, it too will begin to shape lives and mold social character in subtle but profound ways.

Instead of ranking people by what they own, as the market ethic does,   45
the prosumer ethic places a high value on what they do. Having plenty of money still carries prestige. But other characteristics gain importance. Among these are self-reliance, the ability to adapt and survive under difficult conditions, and the ability to do things with one's own hands—

whether to build a fence, to cook a great meal, to make one's own clothes or to restore an antique chest.

Moreover, while the production or market ethic praises singlemindedness, the prosumer ethic calls for roundness instead. Versatility is "in." As the Third Wave brings production for exchange and production for use into a better balance in the economy, we begin to hear a crescendo of demands for a "balanced" way of life.   46

The shift of certain activities from the production sector to the prosumption sector now taking place also suggests the coming of another kind of balance into people's lives. Growing numbers of workers engaged in producing for the market spend their time dealing with abstractions—words, numbers, models—and people known only slightly if at all.   47

For many, such "headwork" can be fascinating and rewarding. But it is often accompanied by the sense of being dissociated—cut off, as it were, from the down-to-earth sights, sounds, textures and emotions of everyday existence. Indeed, much of today's glorification of handcrafts, gardening, peasant or blue-collar fashions and what might be called "truck-driver chic" may be a compensation for the rising tide of abstraction in the production sector.   48

By contrast, in prosumption we usually deal with a more concrete, immediate reality—in first-hand contact with things and people. As more people divide their time, serving as part-time workers and part-time prosumers, they are in a position to enjoy the concrete along with the abstract, the complementary pleasures of both headwork and handwork. The prosumer ethic makes handwork respectable again, after some 300 years of being looked down upon. And this new balance, too, is likely to influence the distribution of personality traits.   49

Similarly, with the rise of industrialism, the spread of highly interdependent factory work encouraged men to become objective. Staying home and working at low-interdependency tasks promoted privatism and subjectivity among women. Today, as more women are drawn into jobs producing for the marketplace, they, too, are increasingly objectivized. They are encouraged to "think like a man." Conversely, as more men stay home, undertaking a greater share of the housework, their need for objectivity is lessened. They are "subjectivized."   50

Tomorrow, as many Third Wave people divide their lives between working part-time in big, interdependent companies or organizations and working part-time for self and family in small, autonomous prosuming units, we may well strike a new balance between objectivity and subjectivity in both sexes.   51

Instead of fostering a "male" attitude and a "female" attitude, neither of them well balanced, the system may reward people who are healthily able to see the world through both perspectives. Objective subjectivists —and vice versa.   52

In short, with the rising importance of prosumption to the overall   53 economy, we touch off another racing current of psychological change. The combined impact of basic changes in production and prosumption, added to the deep changes in child rearing and education, promises to remake our social character at least as dramatically as the Second Wave did three centuries ago. A new social character is cropping up in our very midst.

Even if every one of these insights or speculations were to prove mistaken, however—indeed, if every one of the shifts we are beginning to see were to reverse itself—there is still one final, overpowering reason to expect volcanic changes in personality. That reason is summed up in the two words "communications revolution."   54

The Configuration Me

The link between communications and character is complex, but un-   55
breakable. We cannot transform all our media of communication and expect to remain unchanged as a people. A revolution in the media must mean a revolution in the psyche.

During the Second Wave period, people were bathed in a sea of mass-   56
produced imagery. Powerful radio and TV networks and a relatively few, centrally produced newspapers, magazines and movies fed what critics termed a "monolithic consciousness." Individuals were continually encouraged to compare themselves to a relatively small number of role models and to evaluate their life styles against a few preferred possibilities. In consequence, the range of socially approved personality styles was relatively narrow.

What we are witnessing today with the rise of cable television, video-   57
cassettes, satellite-based ad hoc networks, as well as specialized and regional magazines, is a breakup of this monolithic consciousness. Instead of a few messages going to a large number of people, many messages are flowing through the new media to quite small, highly differentiated groups. This phenomenon has deep economic and political implications, but it also affects us psychologically.

The demassification of the media today presents a dazzling diversity   58
of role models and life styles for one to measure oneself against. Moreover, the new media do not feed us fully formed chunks but broken chips and blips of imagery. Instead of being handed a selection of coherent identities to choose among, we are required to piece one together: a configurative or modular "me." Building a coherent "self" becomes far more difficult, and it explains why so many millions today are desperately searching for identity.

Caught up in that effort, we develop a heightened awareness of our   59
own individuality—of the traits that make us unique. Our self-image thus changes. We demand to be seen as, and treated as, individuals, and this occurs at precisely the time when the new production system requires more individualized workers.

Beyond helping us to crystallize what is purely personal in us, the new   60
communications media of the Third Wave turn us into producers—or
rather prosumers—of our own self-imagery.

The German poet and social critic Hans Magnus Enzensberger has   61
noted that, in yesterday's mass media, the "technical distinction between
receivers and transmitters reflects the social division of labor into producers and consumers." Throughout the Second Wave era this meant that
professional communicators produced the messages for the audience.
The audience remained powerless to respond directly to—or to interact
with—the message senders.

By contrast, the most revolutionary feature of the new means of com-   62
munication is that many of them are interactive—permitting each individual user to make or send images as well as merely to receive them from
the outside. Two-way cable, videocassettes, cheap copiers and tape re-
corders all place the means of communication into the hands of the
individual.

Looking ahead, one can imagine a stage at which even ordinary televi-   63
sion becomes interactive, so that instead of merely watching some Archie
Bunker or Mary Tyler Moore of the future, we are actually able to talk
to them and influence their behavior in the show. Even now, the Qube
cable system in Columbus, Ohio, makes it technologically possible for
viewers of a dramatic show to call on the director to speed up or slow
down the action or to choose one story ending over another.

The communications revolution gives us each a more complex image   64
of self. It differentiates us further. It speeds the very process by which we
"try on" different images of self and, in fact, accelerates our movement
through successive images. It makes it possible for us to project our
image electronically to the world. And nobody fully understands what all
this will do to our personalities. For in no previous civilization have we
ever had such powerful tools. We increasingly own the technology of
consciousness.

The world we are fast entering is so remote from our past experience   65
that all psychological speculations are admittedly shaky. What is absolutely clear, however, is that powerful forces are streaming together to
alter social character—to elicit certain traits, to suppress others and, in
the process, to transform us all.

As we move beyond Second Wave civilization, we are doing more than   66
shifting from one energy system to another or from one technological
base to the next. We are revolutionizing inner space as well. In the light
of this, it would be absurd to project the past upon the future—to picture
the people of Third Wave civilization in Second Wave terms.

If our assumptions are even partially correct, individuals will vary more   67
vividly tomorrow than they do today. More of them are likely to grow up
sooner, to show responsibility at an earlier age, to be more adaptable and
to evince greater individuality. They are more likely than their parents to

question authority. They will want money and will work for it—but, except under conditions of extreme privation, they will resist working for money alone.

Above all, they seem likely to crave balance in their lives—balance   68
between work and play, between production and prosumption, between headwork and handwork, between the abstract and the concrete, between objectivity and subjectivity. And they will see and project themselves in far more complex terms than any previous people.

As Third Wave civilization arrives, we shall create not a utopian man   69
or woman who towers over the people of the past, not a superhuman race of Goethes and Aristotles (or Genghis Khans or Hitlers) but merely, and proudly, one hopes, a race—and a civilization—that deserves to be called fully and radiantly human.

Topical Considerations

1. Toffler says that this is not the first time a "new man" has been spotted on the horizon. What other times in human history does he mention? What kinds of "new men" were these images? What did they supposedly have in common?

2. The author claims that the Third Wave will bring changes in technology, energy, and society—changes that will also modify people. How did the coming of the Second Wave modify people?

3. Toffler claims that tomorrow's society will be "far less child-centered" than today's or those of the past (paragraph 15). What does he mean by this speculation? What signs in today's society does he cite as evidence? Do you agree with his prophecy?

4. Why do today's parents, according to Toffler, "face agonizing disillusionment"? From what you have observed of parents and children and trends in our society, do you agree?

5. What developments will cause tomorrow's work force to move out of the offices and factories and back into the homes? What role will energy costs play? What about computer costs? Do you agree with the author's speculations here?

6. What changes does Toffler see in tomorrow's childhood?

7. What changes does he see in tomorrow's education?

8. What changes does Toffler see in the relationships between workers and management?

9. What connection does Toffler see between today's self-help and do-it-yourself activities and tomorrow's economy?

10. In "What I Learned About Love on AM Radio," Sally Helgesen describes how her views about love were shaped. Toffler also talks about how the media shape people's thoughts, images, and values.

What kinds of changes does he foresee as a result of the revolution in the media?

Rhetorical Considerations

1. Toffler coins the terms "demassify," "prosumer," and "telecommuting." What does he mean by these terms? How do the respective contexts help define them? If Toffler had not defined them, what help would have been the word roots, the prefixes, and the suffixes?

2. Explain Toffler's metaphor, "electronic cottage," in paragraph 21. What images are called up by the connotations? How appropriate is the metaphor to Toffler's subject? How appropriate is it to his attitude toward the subject? What effect would the term "electronic bunker" have had?

3. How would you describe the general tone of this essay—neutral? angry? remorseful? optimistic? propagandistic? bored? academic? How does Toffler feel about the "new man" on the horizon? Cite passages that typify his attitude.

4. Do you find any instances where the author was being humorous in the essay? If so, cite some examples and describe how the humor worked.

5. How well does Toffler document the evidence for the making of a "new man"? Are you satisfied with the amount and kinds of evidence he presents? Could he have presented more? less?

6. How effective are the section headings in organizing this essay?

Writing Assignments

1. Toffler foresees a "less child-centered" society than our own in the making. Write an essay in which you explore the advantages or disadvantages of growing up in such a society, where childhood has been shortened and changed.

2. Write an essay in which you discuss the advantages or disadvantages of living in a society of "electronic cottages"—that is, one in which the work force has shifted from the factory and the office to home computer stations.

3. In paragraph 17, Toffler says that Second Wave parents lived out their dreams through their children and expected and encouraged them to do better socially and economically. Do you feel that your parents harbored such dreams and expectations regarding your future? Did they encourage you to be upwardly mobile, to do better than they did? Or did

they leave your future to you? Write an essay exploring these questions.

4. Toffler claims that the "demassification" of today's media presents a "dazzling diversity of role models and life styles for one to measure oneself against" (paragraph 58). How have the media affected your own lifestyle and role modeling? Write an essay answering this question. (You might consider the effects certain movies, television programs, commercials, or ads have had on your own self-image.) So far as you can tell, what effects have certain media images had on you?

5. Write an essay about how you cannot wait for tomorrow to come—that is, the kind of tomorrow Toffler foresees.

6. Write an essay about how you'd rather live in some yesteryear than in the world of Toffler's prophecy. (You might want to pick a particular century or era of the past in which you'd rather be living.)

ON VIOLENCE IN AMERICA

Pilgrimage to Nonviolence

Martin Luther King, Jr.

Violence in America has become the number one issue of our contemporary society. Each day, newspapers and television news chronicle the latest murders, rapes, and muggings. While violence threatens the very nature of American life, debates rage over the issues of criminal justice and gun control. We open this section with an essay by one of America's most prominent and charismatic opponents to violence, Dr. Martin Luther King, Jr. Written at a time when American blacks were suffering racial injustice, sometimes violently, this essay served as a call for social change through peaceful means. King was a clergyman and a prominent civil rights leader. In 1957, he organized the Southern Christian Leadership Conference to extend his nonviolent efforts toward equality and justice for his people. In 1964, he was awarded the Nobel Peace Prize. Four years later, while supporting striking sanitation workers in Memphis, King was shot and killed. The following statement comes from his *Stride Toward Freedom* (1958).

When I went to Montgomery as a pastor, I had not the slightest 1
idea that I would later become involved in a crisis in which nonviolent
resistance would be applicable. I neither started the protest nor suggested it. I simply responded to the call of the people for a spokesman.
When the protest began, my mind, consciously or unconsciously, was
driven back to the Sermon on the Mount, with its sublime teachings on
love, and the Gandhian method of nonviolent resistance. As the days
unfolded, I came to see the power of nonviolence more and more. Living
through the actual experience of the protest, nonviolence became more
than a method to which I gave intellectual assent; it became a commitment to a way of life. Many of the things that I had not cleared up
intellectually concerning nonviolence were now solved in the sphere of
practical action.

Since the philosophy of nonviolence played such a positive role in the 2
Montgomery Movement, it may be wise to turn to a brief discussion of
some basic aspects of this philosophy.

First, it must be emphasized that nonviolent resistance is not a method 3
for cowards; it does resist. If one uses this method because he is afraid
or merely because he lacks the instruments of violence, he is not truly
nonviolent. This is why Gandhi often said that if cowardice is the only
alternative to violence, it is better to fight. He made this statement conscious of the fact that there is always another alternative: no individual
or group need submit to any wrong, nor need they use violence to right
the wrong; there is the way of nonviolent resistance. This is ultimately the
way of the strong man. It is not a method of stagnant passivity. The
phrase "passive resistance" often gives the false impression that this is
a sort of "do-nothing method" in which the resister quietly and passively

accepts evil. But nothing is further from the truth. For while the nonviolent resister is passive in the sense that he is not physically aggressive toward his opponent, his mind and emotions are always active, constantly seeking to persuade his opponent that he is wrong. The method is passive physically, but strongly active spiritually. It is not passive nonresistance to evil, it is active nonviolent resistance to evil.

A second basic fact that characterizes nonviolence is that it does not   4
seek to defeat or humiliate the opponent, but to win his friendship and understanding. The nonviolent resister must often express his protest through noncooperation or boycotts, but he realizes that these are not ends themselves; they are merely means to awaken a sense of moral shame in the opponent. The end is redemption and reconciliation. The aftermath of nonviolence is the creation of the beloved community, while the aftermath of violence is tragic bitterness.

A third characteristic of this method is that the attack is directed   5
against forces of evil rather than against persons who happen to be doing the evil. It is evil that the nonviolent resister seeks to defeat, not the persons victimized by evil. If he is opposing racial injustice, the nonviolent resister has the vision to say that the basic tension is not between races. As I like to say to the people in Montgomery: "The tension in this city is not between white people and Negro people. The tension is, at bottom, between justice and injustice, between the forces of light and the forces of darkness. And if there is a victory, it will be a victory not merely for fifty thousand Negroes, but a victory for justice and the forces of light. We are out to defeat injustice and not white persons who may be unjust."

A fourth point that characterizes nonviolent resistance is a willingness   6
to accept suffering without retaliation, to accept blows from the opponent without striking back. "Rivers of blood may have to flow before we gain our freedom, but it must be our blood," Gandhi said to his countrymen. The nonviolent resister is willing to accept violence if necessary, but never to inflict it. He does not seek to dodge jail. If going to jail is necessary, he enters it "as a bridegroom enters the bride's chamber."

One may well ask: "What is the nonviolent resister's justification for   7
this ordeal to which he invites men, for this mass political application of the ancient doctrine of turning the other cheek?" The answer is found in the realization that unearned suffering is redemptive. Suffering, the nonviolent resister realizes, has tremendous educational and transforming possibilities. "Things of fundamental importance to people are not secured by reason alone, but have to be purchased with their suffering," said Gandhi. He continues: "Suffering is infinitely more powerful than the law of the jungle for converting the opponent and opening his ears which are otherwise shut to the voice of reason."

A fifth point concerning nonviolent resistance is that it avoids not only   8
external physical violence but also internal violence of spirit. The nonviolent resister not only refuses to shoot his opponent but he also refuses

to hate him. At the center of nonviolence stands the principle of love. The nonviolent resister would contend that in the struggle for human dignity, the oppressed people of the world must not succumb to the temptation of becoming bitter or indulging in hate campaigns. To retaliate in kind would do nothing but intensify the existence of hate in the universe. Along the way of life, someone must have sense enough and morality enough to cut off the chain of hate. This can only be done by projecting the ethic of love to the center of our lives.

In speaking of love at this point, we are not referring to some senti- 9 mental or affectionate emotion. It would be nonsense to urge men to love their oppressors in an affectionate sense. Love in this connection means understanding, redemptive good will. Here the Greek language comes to our aid. There are three words for love in the Greek New Testament. First, there is *eros*. In Platonic philosophy *eros* meant the yearning of the soul for the realm of the divine. It has come now to mean a sort of aesthetic or romantic love. Second, there is *philia*, which means intimate affection between personal friends. *Philia* denotes a sort of reciprocal love; the person loves because he is loved. When we speak of loving those who oppose us, we refer to neither *eros* nor *philia*; we speak of a love which is expressed in the Greek word *agape*. *Agape* means understanding, re- deeming good will for all men. It is an overflowing love which is purely spontaneous, unmotivated, groundless, and creative. It is not set in mo- tion by any quality or function of its object. It is the love of God operating in the human heart.

Agape is disinterested love. It is a love in which the individual seeks not 10 his own good, but the good of his neighbor (I Cor. 10:24). *Agape* does not begin by discriminating between worthy and unworthy people, or any qualities people possess. It begins by loving others *for their sakes*. It is entirely "neighbor-regarding concern for others," which discovers the neighbor in every man it meets. There, *agape* makes no distinction be- tween friend and enemy; it is directed toward both. If one loves an individual merely on account of friendliness, he loves him for the sake of the benefits to be gained from the friendship, rather than for the friend's own sake. Consequently, the best way to assure oneself that Love is disinterested is to have love for the enemy-neighbor from whom you can expect no good in return, but only hostility and persecution.

Another basic point about *agape* is that it springs from the *need* of the 11 other person—his need for belonging to the best in the human family. The Samaritan who helped the Jew on the Jericho Road was "good" because he responded to the human need that he was presented with. God's love is eternal and fails not because man needs his love. St. Paul assures us that the loving act of redemption was done "while we were yet sinners"—that is, at the point of our greatest need for love. Since the white man's personality is greatly distorted by segregation, and his soul is greatly scarred, he needs the love of the Negro. The Negro must love the white man, because the white man needs his love to remove his tensions, insecurities, and fears.

Agape is not a weak, passive love. It is love in action. *Agape* is love   12
seeking to preserve and create community. It is insistence on community even when one seeks to break it. *Agape* is a willingness to sacrifice in the interest of mutuality. *Agape* is a willingness to go to any length to restore community. It doesn't stop at the first mile, but it goes the second mile to restore community. It is a willingness to forgive, not seven times, but seventy times seven to restore community. The cross is the eternal expression of the length to which God will go in order to restore broken community. The resurrection is a symbol of God's triumph over all the forces that seek to block community. The Holy Spirit is the continuing community creating reality that moves through history. He who works against community is working against the whole of creation. Therefore, if I respond to hate with a reciprocal hate I do nothing but intensify cleavage in broken community. I can only close the gap in broken community by meeting hate with love. If I meet hate with hate, I become depersonalized, because creation is so designed that my personality can only be fulfilled in the context of community. Booker T. Washington was right: "Let no man pull you so low as to make you hate him." When he pulls you that low he brings you to the point of working against community; he drags you to the point of defying creation, and thereby becoming depersonalized.

In the final analysis, *agape* means a recognition of the fact that all life   13
is interrelated. All humanity is involved in a single process, and all men are brothers. To the degree that I harm my brother, no matter what he is doing to me, to that extent I am harming myself. For example, white men often refuse federal aid to education in order to avoid giving the Negro his rights; but because all men are brothers they cannot deny Negro children without harming their own. They end, all efforts to the contrary, by hurting themselves. Why is this? Because men are brothers. If you harm me, you harm yourself.

Love, *agape,* is the only cement that can hold this broken community   14
together. When I am commanded to love, I am commanded to restore community, to resist injustice, and to meet the needs of my brothers.

A sixth basic fact about nonviolent resistance is that it is based on the   15
conviction that the universe is on the side of justice. Consequently, the believer in nonviolence has deep faith in the future. This faith is another reason why the nonviolent resister can accept suffering without retaliation. For he knows that in his struggle for justice he has cosmic companionship. It is true that there are devout believers in nonviolence who find it difficult to believe in a personal God. But even these persons believe in the existence of some creative force that works for universal wholeness. Whether we call it an unconscious process, an impersonal Brahman, or a Personal Being of matchless power and infinite love, there is a creative

force in this universe that works to bring the disconnected aspects of reality into a harmonious whole.

Topical Considerations

1. From reading King's essay, what kind of education would you say King had as a young man? How is this training reflected in the essay?

2. King was strongly influenced by Mahatma Gandhi, political activist and leader of the Indian people in the first half of this century. What do you know about Gandhi and his civil disobedience movement?

3. During the Vietnam War, thousands of young men fled to Canada and Europe to avoid being drafted. Would you call them nonviolent resisters? Consider the motives and aims of both types of protestors. Are conscientious objectors the same as King's concept of nonviolent resisters?

4. King refers to the Sermon on the Mount. What similarities do you see between its teachings and King's definition of nonviolent resistance? What differences do you see?

5. Is King's philosophy practical in today's world, in which there is so much terrorism and violence? Give reasons for your answer.

6. When King defines *agape,* he discusses how it promotes community responsibility. Identify citizen groups in your community or on your campus that demonstrate the kind of love King defines here. What other evidence of *agape* do you find in our society?

7. Do you agree with King's philosophy? Could you practice it? Describe a situation in which you might find yourself wanting to resist. Explain how you would deal with the crisis. How would it be the same or different from King's approach?

8. King was a charismatic figure of the early sixties. Is there anything about this essay that would suggest why this was true?

Rhetorical Considerations

1. Did King's opening capture your interest immediately? Was it an effective way to introduce his subject matter? Explain your reactions.

2. What is King's thesis? Is it stated explicitly or implicitly?

3. What primary rhetorical strategy does King use in developing his essay?

4. What transitional devices does King use when moving from one idea to another? How does he achieve variety so that he is not repeating the same words and phrases too often?

5. What do you think of King's conclusion? Does he need to summarize the points he made in his essay? Or has he successfully

brought the essay to a close without the need for this? How would you have ended it?

Writing Assignments

1. In paragraph 1, King remarks: "Many of the things I had not cleared up intellectually concerning nonviolence were now solved in the sphere of practical action." King's practical experiences molded his philosophy. In an essay, write about an experience you have had that taught you something about your own standards of behavior in society.

2. Were the young men who fled to Canada and Europe during the Vietnam War nonviolent resisters? In an essay, compare and contrast this type of resistance with the type King describes.

3. Identify a community action group in your community or on your campus that is involved in demonstrating *agape*. Write an essay describing the goals and actions of the group. Explain how the group demonstrates the kind of community responsibility King discusses in his essay.

38 Who Saw Murder Didn't Call the Police

Martin Gansberg

Martin Gansberg has been a reporter and editor for the *New York Times* since 1942. The article reprinted here was written in 1964, just a few days after Kitty Genovese was murdered in full view of dozens of people. The incident shocked the nation and became a springboard for countless editorials and articles—even a television movie—about public indifference and fear. This article won Gansberg several awards for best feature and news story of the year.

For more than half an hour 38 respectable, law-abiding citizens in Queens watched a killer stalk and stab a woman in three separate attacks in Kew Gardens.   1

Twice their chatter and the sudden glow of their bedroom lights interrupted him and frightened him off. Each time he returned, sought her out, and stabbed her again. Not one person telephoned the police during the assault; one witness called after the woman was dead.   2

That was two weeks ago today.   3

Still shocked is Assistant Chief Inspector Frederick M. Lussen, in   4
charge of the borough's detectives and a veteran of 25 years of homicide
investigations. He can give a matter-of-fact recitation on many murders.
But the Kew Gardens slaying baffles him—not because it is a murder, but
because the "good people" failed to call the police.

"As we have reconstructed the crime," he said, "the assailant had three   5
chances to kill this woman during a 35-minute period. He returned twice
to complete the job. If we had been called when he first attacked, the
woman might not be dead now."

This is what the police say happened beginning at 3:20 A.M. in the   6
staid, middle-class, tree-lined Austin Street area:

Twenty-eight-year-old Catherine Genovese, who was called Kitty by   7
almost everyone in the neighborhood, was returning home from her job
as manager of a bar in Hollis. She parked her red Fiat in a lot adjacent
to the Kew Gardens Long Island Rail Road Station, facing Mowbray
Place. Like many residents of the neighborhood, she had parked there
day after day since her arrival from Connecticut a year ago, although the
railroad frowns on the practice.

She turned off the lights of her car, locked the door, and started to walk   8
the 100 feet to the entrance of her apartment at 82–70 Austin Street,
which is in a Tudor building, with stores in the first floor and apartments
on the second.

The entrance to the apartment is in the rear of the building because   9
the front is rented to retail stores. At night the quiet neighborhood is
shrouded in the slumbering darkness that marks most residential areas.

Miss Genovese noticed a man at the far end of the lot, near a seven-   10
story apartment house at 82–40 Austin Street. She halted. Then, nerv-
ously, she headed up Austin Street toward Lefferts Boulevard, where
there is a call box to the 102nd Police Precinct in nearby Richmond Hill.

She got as far as a street light in front of a bookstore before the man   11
grabbed her. She screamed. Lights went on in the 10-story apartment
house at 82–67 Austin Street, which faces the bookstore. Windows slid
open and voices punctuated the early-morning stillness.

Miss Genovese screamed: "Oh, my God, he stabbed me! Please help   12
me! Please help me!"

From one of the upper windows in the apartment house, a man called   13
down: "Let that girl alone!"

The assailant looked up at him, shrugged, and walked down Austin   14
Street toward a white sedan parked a short distance away. Miss Genovese
struggled to her feet.

Lights went out. The killer returned to Miss Genovese, now trying to   15
make her way around the side of the building by the parking lot to get
to her apartment. The assailant stabbed her again.

"I'm dying!" she shrieked. "I'm dying!"   16

Windows were opened again, and lights went on in many apartments.   17
The assailant got into his car and drove away. Miss Genovese staggered
to her feet. A city bus, O–10, the Lefferts Boulevard line to Kennedy
International Airport, passed. It was 3:35 A.M.

The assailant returned. By then, Miss Genovese had crawled to the   18
back of the building, where the freshly painted brown doors to the apartment house held out hope for safety. The killer tried the first door; she
wasn't there. At the second door, 82–62 Austin Street, he saw her
slumped on the floor at the foot of the stairs. He stabbed her a third time
—fatally.

It was 3:50 by the time the police received their first call, from a man   19
who was a neighbor of Miss Genovese. In two minutes they were at the
scene. The neighbor, a 70-year-old woman, and another woman were the
only persons on the street. Nobody else came forward.

The man explained that he had called the police after much delibera-   20
tion. He had phoned a friend in Nassau County for advice and then he
had crossed the roof of the building to the apartment of the elderly
woman to get her to make the call.

"I didn't want to get involved," he sheepishly told the police.   21

Six days later, the police arrested Winston Moseley, a 29-year-old   22
business-machine operator, and charged him with homicide. Moseley had
no previous record. He is married, has two children and owns a home at
133–19 Sutter Avenue, South Ozone Park, Queens. On Wednesday, a
court committed him to Kings County Hospital for psychiatric observation.

When questioned by the police, Moseley also said that he had slain   23
Mrs. Annie May Johnson, 24, of 146–12 133d Avenue, Jamaica, on Feb.
29 and Barbara Kralik, 15, of 174–17 140th Avenue, Springfield Gardens,
last July. In the Kralik case, the police are holding Alvin L. Mitchell, who
is said to have confessed that slaying.

The police stressed how simple it would have been to have gotten in   24
touch with them. "A phone call," said one of the detectives, "would have
done it." The police may be reached by dialing "O" for operator or
SPring 7–3100.

Today witnesses from the neighborhood, which is made up of one-   25
family homes in the $35,000 to $60,000 range with the exception of the
two apartment houses near the railroad station, find it difficult to explain
why they didn't call the police.

A housewife, knowingly if quite casually, said, "We thought it was a   26
lovers' quarrel." A husband and wife both said, "Frankly, we were
afraid." They seemed aware of the fact that events might have been
different. A distraught woman, wiping her hands in her apron, said, "I
didn't want my husband to get involved."

One couple, now willing to talk about that night, said they heard the   27
first screams. The husband looked thoughtfully at the bookstore where
the killer first grabbed Miss Genovese.

"We went to the window to see what was happening," he said, "but   28
the light from our bedroom made it difficult to see the street." The wife,
still apprehensive, added: "I put out the light and we were able to see
better."

Asked why they hadn't called the police, she shrugged and replied: "I   29
don't know."

A man peeked out from a slight opening in the doorway to his apart-   30
ment and rattled off an account of the killer's second attack. Why hadn't
he called the police at the time? "I was tired," he said without emotion.
"I went back to bed."

It was 4:25 A.M. when the ambulance arrived to take the body of Miss   31
Genovese. It drove off. "Then," a solemn police detective said, "the
people came out."

Topical Considerations

1. Suppose you had been one of the 38 witnesses who heard
Kitty Genovese scream. What would you have done?

2. What do you think of the reasons the witnesses gave for not
calling the police? Are any of the reasons justifiable?

3. What does the article reveal about Kitty Genovese's neighborhood? Is there anything about it that would suggest that it is particularly
crime-prone? Is it surprising that such a crime would happen in it?

4. How would you have felt if the victim had been your best
friend? your sister? your girl friend? How would you have felt toward her
neighbors?

5. What impact do you think this article had when it was first
published in 1964? What impact did it have on you?

Rhetorical Considerations

1. Gansberg gives specific times, addresses, and ages in his article. He even lists the phone number for the police department. Why does
he do this? How would the article be affected if he didn't include these
specifics?

2. What is Gansberg's aim in writing this article? What impact do
you think he intended to have on his audience? Do you think he was
successful?

3. Although this article is written in an objective, journalistic
style, Gansberg's own bias often reveals itself. For example, why does he
describe the Austin Street area as "staid" and "middle-class"? Why does
he point out that it is a neighborhood of "one-family homes in the
$35,000 to $60,000 range"? What does this tell you about his point of
view? What other revealing clues do you see?

4. How effective is Gansberg's use of dialogue? Would the article have a greater impact without it? Give reasons for your answers.

5. Does Gansberg's conclusion tie in with his thesis? Is it an effective conclusion? Why or why not? What does it reveal about the author's point of view?

Writing Assignments

1. Have you ever been a victim of a crime? If so, write a narrative account of what happened to you. Include a description of how witnesses to the crime came or failed to come to your aid.

2. How do you think a newscaster would have reported the Kitty Genovese crime? Write a brief news blurb that could be used on a nightly TV news program. Include many of the details Gansberg provides in his article.

3. Gansberg's article is written from the point of view of the victim. Adopt another point of view—that of a witness, the murderer, a bus driver, a police officer—and write two brief papers. In the first, describe your own response to what happened the night of the crime. In the second, describe how you felt two weeks later, when Gansberg's article was published.

It's Time to Ban Handguns

Lance Morrow

One of the most hotly debated issues concerning crime in America is what to do about handguns. Some people cry for stronger gun control—even a ban— while others argue that gun control will not reduce crime, claiming that criminals will always find means to kill but that gun control would deny law-abiding citizens their constitutional right to bear arms. The essay reprinted here was written by Lance Morrow, a senior writer for *Time* magazine. It appeared a few days after March 31, 1981, when President Ronald Reagan was shot and wounded in an assassination attempt in the nation's capital.

By a curiosity of evolution, every human skull harbors a prehis-   1
toric vestige: a reptilian brain. This atavism, like a hand grenade cushioned in the more civilized surrounding cortex, is the dark hive where many of mankind's primitive impulses originate. To go partners with that throwback, Americans have carried out of their own history another curiosity that evolution forgot to discard as the country changed from a

sparsely populated, underpoliced agrarian society to a modern industrial civilization. That vestige is the gun—most notoriously the handgun, an anachronistic tool still much in use. Since 1963 guns have finished off more Americans (400,000) than World War II did.

After one more handgun made it into American history last week (another nastily poignant little "Saturday night" .22 that lay like an orphan in a Dallas pawnshop until another of those clammy losers took it back to his rented room to dream on), a lot of Americans said to themselves, "Well, maybe *this* will finally persuade them to do something about those damned guns." Nobody would lay a dime on it. The National Rifle Association battened down its hatches for a siege of rough editorial weather, but calculated that the antigun indignation would presently subside, just as it always does. After Kennedy. After King. After Kennedy. After Wallace. After Lennon. After Reagan. After . . . the nation will be left twitching and flinching as before to the pops of its 55 million pistols and the highest rate of murder by guns in the world.

The rest of the planet is both appalled and puzzled by the spectacle of a superpower so politically stable and internally violent. Countries like Britain and Japan, which have low murder rates and virtual prohibitions on handguns, are astonished by the over-the-counter ease with which Americans can buy firearms.

Americans themselves are profoundly discouraged by the handguns that seem to breed uncontrollably among them like roaches. For years the majority of them have favored restrictions on handguns. In 1938 a Gallup poll discovered that 84% wanted gun controls. The latest Gallup finds that 62% want stricter laws governing handgun sales. Yet Americans go on buying handguns at the rate of one every 13 seconds. The murder rate keeps rising. It is both a cause and an effect of gun sales. And every few years—or months—some charismatic public character takes a slug from an itinerant mental case caressing a bizarre fantasy in his brain and the sick, secret weight of a pistol in his pocket.

Why do the bloody years keep rolling by without guns becoming subject to the kind of regulation we calmly apply to drugs, cars, boat trailers, CB radios and dogs? The answer is only partly that the National Rifle Association is, by some Senators' estimate, the most effective lobbying organization in Washington and the deadliest at targeting its congressional enemies at election time. The nation now has laws, all right—a patchwork of some 25,000 gun regulations, federal, state and local, that are so scattered and inconsistent as to be preposterously ineffectual.

Firearms have achieved in the U.S. a strange sort of inevitability—the nation's gun-ridden frontier heritage getting smokily mingled now with a terror of accelerating criminal violence and a sense that as the social contract tatters, the good guys must have their guns to defend themselves against the rising tribes of bad guys. It is very hard to persuade the good guys that all those guns in their hands wind up doing more lethal harm to their own kind than to the animals they fear; that good guys sometimes get drunk and shoot other good guys in a rage, or blow their own heads off (by design or accident) or hit their own children by mistake. Most murders are done on impulse, and handguns are perfectly responsive to the purpose: a blind red rage flashes in the brain and fires a signal through the nerves to the trigger finger—BLAM! Guns do not require much work. You do not have to get your hands bloody, as you would with a knife, or make the strenuous and intimately dangerous effort required to kill with bare hands. The space between gun and victim somehow purifies the relationship—at least for the person at the trigger—and makes it so much easier to perform the deed. The bullet goes invisibly across space to flesh. An essential disconnection, almost an abstraction, is maintained. That's why it is so easy—convenient, really—to kill with one of the things.

The post-assassination sermon, an earnest lamentation about the   7
"sickness of American society," has become a notably fatuous genre that blames everyone and then, after 15 minutes of earnestly empty regret, absolves everyone. It is true that there is a good deal of evil in the American air; television and the sheer repetitiousness of violence have made a lot of the country morally weary and dull and difficult to shock. Much of the violence, however, results not from the sickness of the society but the stupidity and inadequacy of its laws. The nation needs new laws to put at least some guns out of business. Mandatory additional punishments for anyone using a gun in a crime—the approach that Ronald Reagan favors—would help. But a great deal more is necessary. Because of the mobility of guns, only federal laws can have any effect upon them. Rifles and shotguns—long guns—are not the problem; they make the best weapons for defending the house anyway, and they are hard for criminals to conceal. Most handguns are made to fire at people, not at targets or game. Such guns should be banned. The freedoms of an American individualism bristling with small arms must yield to the larger communal claim to sanity and safety—the "pursuit of happiness."

That would, of course, still leave millions of handguns illegally in   8
circulation; the penalties for possessing such weapons, and especially for using them in crime, would have to be severe. Even at that, it would take years to start cleansing the nation of handguns. Whatever its content, no substantive program for controlling guns probably stands any chance of getting through Congress unless Ronald Reagan supports it. He ought to do so, not because he has been shot in the chest but because it should be done.

The indiscriminate mass consumption of guns has finally come to   9
disgrace Americans abroad and depress them at home. It has been almost 90 years since the historian Frederick Jackson Turner propounded his famous thesis about the end of the American frontier. But the worst part of the frontier never did vanish. Its violence, once tolerable in the vast

spaces, has simply backed up into modern America, where it goes on blazing away.

Topical Considerations

1. Does anyone you know own a gun? What are his or her reasons? How do you feel about this?

2. What argument does Morrow introduce in his opening and carry through the entire essay? Do you agree with him?

3. Morrow recalls a number of assassinations that have resulted from the use of handguns. What is your response to this? Should these assassinations necessarily impel us to take a firmer stand against handguns? Why or why not?

4. According to Morrow both Britain and Japan prohibit handguns and have low murder rates. If you were debating the issue of gun control with Morrow, what could you say in rebuttal?

5. What are some of the statistics Morrow cites to win support for his arguments? Are they convincing?

6. Morrow points out that the National Rifle Association is part of the reason our country has no effective national gun control legislation. Why is this? What is your opinion of this lobbying organization? Why do you think it has so much influence?

7. Although he is critical of its opposition, Morrow apparently does not feel that the National Rifle Association is the primary cause of the problem. What does he identify as the real cause? Do you agree with him? Give reasons for your answer.

8. Given his views on nonviolent resistance and *agape,* what do you think Martin Luther King's response would have been to Morrow's statement in paragraph 7: "The freedoms of an American individualism bristling with small arms must yield to the larger communal claim to sanity and safety—the 'pursuit of happiness' "?

Rhetorical Considerations

1. In his opening, Morrow suggests that the use of handguns without regulation is a potentially explosive situation. How does he communicate this idea?

2. What is Morrow's thesis? Is it stated implicitly or explicitly? Explain.

3. Throughout the essay, Morrow paints a graphic picture of the violent, bloody effect that the absence of handgun regulation has on our nation. What figures of speech does he use to achieve this aim? How effective are they?

4. How would you characterize the tone of this essay—reasoned and objective? emotional and flag-waving? angry and bitter? resigned and frustrated? Is it similar to or different from the tone of Gansberg's article? King's essay? Explain.

5. What do you think of Morrow's conclusion? Is his mention of Frederick Jackson Turner's thesis about the American frontier consistent with the rest of the essay? Explain.

Writing Assignments

1. Write an essay in which you offer a rebuttal to Morrow's argument in favor of gun control.

2. Do you own a gun? If so, and if you do not use it for hunting or target-shooting, explain why you own it.

3. If you are not a gun owner, do you think you ever could be? Can you imagine circumstances in which you might feel compelled to purchase one?

Why Gun Control Laws Don't Work

Barry Goldwater

A voice that has long represented the other side of the gun control issue is that of the conservative Republican senator from Arizona, Barry Goldwater. Here he says that if he believed gun control legislation would reduce violent crime, he would not hesitate to support it. He argues, however, that no matter what kinds of laws are enacted—registration or even outright banning—criminals would still be able to get weapons. He claims that America has a crime problem, not a gun problem, and on that premise he argues for stronger punishment for gun-related crimes.

Let me say immediately that if I thought more gun-control laws would help diminish the tragic incidence of robberies, muggings, rapes and murders in the United States, I would be the first to vote for them. But I am convinced that making more such laws approaches the problem from the wrong direction.   1

It is clear, I think, that gun legislation simply doesn't work. There are already some 20,000 state and local gun laws on the books, and they are no more effective than was the prohibition of alcoholic beverages in the 1920s. Our most recent attempt at federal gun legislation was the Gun   2

Control Act of 1968, intended to control the interstate sale and transportation of firearms and the importation of uncertified firearms; it has done nothing to check the availability of weapons. It has been bolstered in every nook and cranny of the nation by local gun-control laws, yet the number of shooting homicides per year has climbed steadily since its enactment, while armed robberies have increased 60 percent.

Some people, even some law-enforcement officials, contend that 3 "crimes of passion" occur because a gun just happens to be present at the scene. I don't buy that. I can't equate guns with the murder rate, because if a person is angry enough to kill, he will kill with the first thing that comes to hand—a gun, a knife, an ice pick, a baseball bat.

I believe our *only* hope of reducing crime in this country is to control 4 not the weapon but the user. We must reverse the trend toward leniency and permissiveness in our courts—the plea bargaining, the pardons, the suspended sentences and unwarranted paroles—and make the law-breaker pay for what he has done by spending time in jail. We have plenty of statutes against killing and maiming and threatening people with weapons. These can be made effective by strong enforcement and firm decisions from the bench. When a man knows that if he uses a potentially deadly object to rob or do harm to another person he is letting himself in for a mandatory, unparolable stretch behind bars, he will think twice about it.

Of course, no matter what gun-control laws are enacted—including 5 national registration—the dedicated crook can always get a weapon. So, some people ask, even if national registration of guns isn't completely airtight, isn't it worth trying? Sure, it would cause a little inconvenience to law-abiding gun owners. And it certainly wouldn't stop all criminals from obtaining guns. But it might stop a few, maybe quite a few. What's wrong with that?

There are several answers. The first concerns enforcement. How are 6 we going to persuade the bank robber or the street-corner stickup artist to register his means of criminal livelihood? Then there is the matter of expense. A study conducted eight years ago showed a cost to New York City of $72.87 to investigate and process one application for a pistol license. In mid-1970 dollars, the same procedure probably costs over $100. By extrapolation to the national scale, the cost to American taxpayers of investigating and registering the 40 to 50 million handguns might reach $4 billion or $5 billion. On top of that, keeping the process in operation year after year would require taxpayer financing of another sizable federal bureau. We ought to have far better prospects of success before we hobble ourselves with such appalling expenditures.

Finally, there are legal aspects based on the much-discussed Second 7 Amendment to the Bill of Rights, which proclaims that "A well regulated Militia, being necessary to the security of a free State, the right of the people to keep and bear Arms, shall not be infringed." The anti-gun faction argues that this right made sense in the days of British oppression but that it has no application today. I contend, on the other hand, that the Founding Fathers conceived of an armed citizenry as a necessary hedge against tyranny from within as well as from without, that they saw the right to keep and bear arms as basic and perpetual, the one thing that could spell the difference between freedom and servitude. Thus I deem most forms of gun control unconstitutional in intent.

Well, then, I'm often asked, what kind of gun laws *are* you for? I reply that I am for laws of common sense. I am for laws that prohibit citizen access to machine guns, bazookas and other military devices. I am for laws that are educational in nature. I believe that before a person is permitted to buy a weapon he should be required to take a course that will teach him how to use it, to handle it safely and keep it safely about the house.   8

Gun education, in fact, can actually reduce lawlessness in a community, as was demonstrated in an experiment conducted in Highland Park, Mich. City police launched a program to instruct merchants in the use of handguns. The idea was to help them protect themselves and their businesses from robbers, and it was given wide publicity. The store-robbery rate dropped from an average of 1.5 a day to none in four months.   9

Where do we go from here? My answer to this is based on the firm belief that we have a crime problem in this country, not a gun problem, and that we must meet the enemy on his own terms. We must start by making crime as unprofitable for him as we can. And we have to do this, I believe, by getting tough in the courts and corrections systems.   10

A recent news story in Washington, D.C., reports that, of 184 persons convicted of gun possession in a six-month period, only 14 received a jail sentence. Forty-six other cases involved persons who had previously been convicted of a felony or possession of a gun. Although the maximum penalty for such repeaters in the District of Columbia is ten years in prison, half of these were not jailed at all. A study last year revealed that in New York City, which has about the most prohibitive gun legislation in the country, only one out of six people convicted of crimes involving weapons went to jail.   11

This sorry state of affairs exists because too many judges and magistrates either don't know the law or are unwilling to apply it with appropriate vigor. It's time to demand either that they crack down on these criminals or be removed from office. It may even be time to review the whole system of judicial appointments, to stop weakening the cause of justice by putting men on the bench who may happen to be golfing partners of Congressmen and too often lack the brains and ability for the job. In Arizona today we elect our judges, and the system is working well, in part because we ask the American and local bar associations to consider candidates and make recommendations. In this way, over the last few years, we have replaced many weaklings with good jurists.   12

We have long had all the criminal statutes we need to turn the tide   13
against the crime wave. There is, however, one piece of proposed legislation that I am watching with particular interest. Introduced by Sen. James
McClure (R., Idaho), it requires that any person convicted of a federal
crime in which a gun is used serve five to ten years in jail automatically
on top of whatever penalty he receives for the crime itself. A second
conviction would result in an extra ten-year-to-life sentence. These sentences would be mandatory and could not be suspended. It is, in short,
a "tough" bill. I think that this bill would serve as an excellent model for
state legislation.

And so it has in California which, last September, signed into law a   14
similar bill requiring a mandatory jail sentence for any gun-related felony.

Finally, it's important to remember that this is an area of great confu-   15
sion; an area in which statistics can be juggled and distorted to support
legislation that is liable to be expensive, counter-productive or useless.
The issue touches upon the freedom and safety of all of us, whether we
own firearms or not. The debate over gun control is an adjunct to the war
against crime, and that war must be fought with all the intelligence and
tenacity we can bring to it.

Topical Considerations

1. Goldwater argues that new gun control legislation can't be
expected to be effective since existing laws are not. What would Morrow
reply to this argument?

2. Supporters of gun control argue that guns encourage "crimes
of passion" and contribute directly to an increased murder rate. Goldwater disagrees. What is his reasoning on this? How do his views differ
from Morrow's?

3. Goldwater supports stronger enforcement of criminal sentences as a more effective deterrent for preventing crimes of passion. In
defense of this, he reasons that such enforcement will cause a man to
think twice before using any deadly weapon, including a gun. Do you see
any contradiction between this and his reasoning about crimes of passion?

4. Why does Goldwater believe gun control is unconstitutional?
Does he make a valid point?

5. What does Goldwater mean when he says that "we have a
crime problem in this country, not a gun problem" (paragraph 10)? How
is this different from Morrow's approach? What solutions does Goldwater
suggest?

6. If you were judging a debate between Goldwater and Morrow,
who would you decide had won? Consider how well each of them ad-

dresses the issues and whether either one successfully argues a point that the other fails to note.

Rhetorical Considerations

1. Compare Goldwater's opening to Morrow's. Which did you find more interesting? Why?

2. How is Goldwater's writing style different from Morrow's? Which one seems more literary? Which essay would work well as a political speech? Give reasons for your answers.

3. In a well-balanced argumentative essay, the writer considers the opposing arguments and offers a rebuttal. Does Goldwater do this? If so, how does he order his pro and con arguments?

4. Does Goldwater offer sufficient specific facts, details, and illustrations to support his arguments? Are there any points that need more development?

5. Do Goldwater's ideas flow logically from one to another? Point out some of the ways he achieves transition.

6. At several points, Goldwater asks questions of his reader. How effective is this technique? Why?

Writing Assignments

1. Suppose that you have just heard Barry Goldwater giving a political speech that argues along the same lines as this essay. Decide whether or not you are convinced of his stand. Write a letter telling him what you thought of his speech.

2. Write a newspaper editorial favoring or opposing gun control. Use the arguments you find in either Goldwater's essay or Morrow's that you believe are most convincing.

3. Have you ever witnessed a gun-related crime? If so, write a narrative description of the incident. Comment on how it influenced your views (if at all) on gun control.

4. Does anyone you know own a handgun? Write a paper in which you express how you feel about this.

Capital Punishment: The Question of Justification

David Hoekema

Capital punishment is the center of what might be the longest running debate in modern American society. It is an issue that raises the most fundamental questions about justice, morality, psychology, religion, and social responsibility. In this piece, David Hoekema, a philosophy professor at St. Olaf College in Minnesota, looks at both the history of capital punishment and the arguments concerning it. He admits that he is sympathetic to the idea that a murderer deserves to die, but he offers several reasons why our judicial system should not be entrusted with powers of execution.

In 1810 a bill introduced in the British Parliament sought to 1
abolish capital punishment for the offense of stealing five shillings or
more from a shop. Judges and magistrates unanimously opposed the
measure. In the House of Lords, the chief justice of the King's Bench,
Lord Ellenborough, predicted that the next step would be abolition of the
death penalty for stealing five shillings from a house; thereafter no one
could "trust himself for an hour without the most alarming apprehension
that, on his return, every vestige of his property [would] be swept away
by the hardened robber" (quoted by Herbert B. Ehrmann in "The Death
Penalty and the Administration of Justice," in *The Death Penalty in America,*
edited by Hugo Adam Bedau [Anchor, 1967], p. 415).

During the same year Parliament abolished the death penalty for pick- 2
ing pockets, but more than 200 crimes remained punishable by death.
Each year in Great Britain more than 2,000 persons were being sentenced
to die, though only a small number of these sentences were actually
carried out.

I

In this regard as in many others, the laws of the English colonies in 3
North America were much less harsh than those of the mother country.
At the time of the Revolution, statutes in most of the colonies prescribed
hanging for about a dozen offenses—among them murder, treason, pi-
racy, arson, rape, robbery, burglary, sodomy and (in some cases) counter-
feiting, horse theft and slave rebellion. But by the early nineteenth century a movement to abolish the death penalty was gaining strength.

The idea was hardly new: czarist Russia had eliminated the death 4
penalty on religious grounds in the eleventh century. In the United States
the movement had been launched by Benjamin Rush in the eighteenth
century, with the support of such other distinguished citizens of Philadelphia as Benjamin Franklin and Attorney General William Bradford. By
the 1830s, bills calling for abolition of capital punishment were being

regularly introduced, and defeated, in several state legislatures. In 1846 Michigan voted effectively to abolish the death penalty—the first English-speaking jurisdiction in the world to do so.

In the years since, twelve states have abolished capital punishment   5
entirely. Although statutes still in effect in some states permit the death penalty to be imposed for a variety of offenses—ranging from statutory rape to desecration of a grave to causing death in a duel—murder is virtually the only crime for which it has been recently employed. There are about 400 persons in U.S. prisons under sentence of death, but only one execution (Gary Gilmore's) has been carried out in this country in the past eleven years.

However, the issue of whether capital punishment is justifiable is by   6
no means settled. Since the Supreme Court, in the case of *Furman* v. *Georgia* in 1972, invalidated most existing laws permitting capital punishment, several states have enacted new legislation designed to meet the court's objections to the Georgia law. And recent public-opinion surveys indicate that a large number, possibly a majority, of Americans favor imposing the death penalty for some crimes. But let us ask the ethical question: Ought governments to put to death persons convicted of certain crimes?

II

First, let us look at grounds on which capital punishment is defended.   7
Most prominent is the argument from *deterrence.* Capital punishment, it is asserted, is necessary to deter potential criminals. Murderers must be executed so that the lives of potential murder victims may be spared.

Two assertions are closely linked here. First, it is said that convicted   8
murderers must be put to death in order to protect the rest of us against those individuals who might kill others if they were at large. This argument, based not strictly on deterrence but on incapacitation of known offenders, is inconclusive, since there are other effective means of protecting the innocent against convicted murderers—for example, imprisonment of murderers for life in high-security institutions.

Second, it is said that the example of capital punishment is needed to   9
deter those who would otherwise commit murder. Knowledge that a crime is punishable by death will give the potential criminal pause. This second argument rests on the assumption that capital punishment does in fact reduce the incidence of capital crimes—a presupposition that must be tested against the evidence. Surprisingly, none of the available empirical data shows any significant correlation between the existence or use of the death penalty and the incidence of capital crimes.

When studies have compared the homicide rates for the past fifty years   10
in states that employ the death penalty and in adjoining states that have abolished it, the numbers have in every case been quite similar; the death penalty has had no discernible effect on homicide rates. Further, the

shorter-term effects of capital punishment have been studied by examining the daily number of homicides reported in California over a ten-year period to ascertain whether the execution of convicts reduced the number. Fewer homicides were reported on days immediately following an execution, but this reduction was matched by an increase in the number of homicides on the day of execution and the preceding day. Executions had no discernible effect on the weekly total of homicides. (Cf. "Death and Imprisonment as Deterrents to Murder," by Thorsten Sellin, in Bedau, op. cit., pp. 274–284, and "The Deterrent Effect of Capital Punishment in California," by William F. Graves, in Bedau, op. cit., pp. 322–332.)

11   The available evidence, then, fails to support the claim that capital punishment deters capital crime. For this reason, I think, we may set aside the deterrence argument. But there is a stronger reason for rejecting the argument—one that has to do with the way in which supporters of that argument would have us treat persons.

12   Those who defend capital punishment on grounds of deterrence would have us take the lives of some—persons convicted of certain crimes —because doing so will discourage crime and thus protect others. But it is a grave moral wrong to treat one person in a way justified solely by the needs of others. To inflict harm on one person in order to serve the purposes of others is to use that person in an immoral and inhumane way, treating him or her not as a person with rights and responsibilities but as a means to other ends. The most serious flaw in the deterrence argument, therefore, is that it is the wrong *kind* of argument. The execution of criminals cannot be justified by the good which their deaths may do the rest of us.

III

13   A second argument for the death penalty maintains that some crimes, chief among them murder, *morally require* the punishment of death. In particular, Christians frequently support capital punishment by appeal to the Mosaic code, which required the death penalty for murder. "The law of capital punishment," one writer has concluded after reviewing relevant biblical passages, "must stand as a silent but powerful witness to the sacredness of God-given life" ("Christianity and the Death Penalty," by Jacob Vellenga, in Bedau, op. cit., pp. 123–130).

14   In the Mosaic code, it should be pointed out, there were many capital crimes besides murder. In the book of Deuteronomy, death is prescribed as the penalty for false prophecy, worship of foreign gods, kidnapping, adultery, deception by a bride concerning her virginity, and disobedience to parents. To this list the laws of the book of Exodus add witchcraft, sodomy, and striking or cursing a parent.

15   I doubt that there is much sentiment in favor of restoring the death penalty in the United States for such offenses. But if the laws of Old

Testament Israel ought not to govern our treatment of, say, adultery, why should they govern the penalty for murder? To support capital punishment by an appeal to Old Testament law is to overlook the fact that the ancient theocratic state of Israel was in nearly every respect profoundly different from any modern secular stae. For this reason, we cannot simply regard the Mosaic code as normative for the United States today.

But leaving aside reference to Mosaic law, let me state more strongly   16
the argument we are examining. The death penalty, it may be urged, is the only just penalty for a crime such as murder; it is the only fair *retribution*. Stated thus, the argument at hand seems to be the right *kind* of argument for capital punishment. If capital punishment can be justified at all, it must be on the basis of the *seriousness of the offense* for which it is imposed. Retributive considerations *should* govern the punishment of individuals who violate the law, and chief among these considerations are the principle of proportionality between punishment and offense and the requirement that persons be punished only for acts for which they are truly responsible. I am not persuaded that retributive considerations are sufficient to set a particular penalty for a given offense, but I believe they do require that in comparative terms we visit more serious offenses with more severe punishment.

Therefore, the retributive argument seems the strongest one in sup-   17
port of capital punishment. We ought to deal with convicted offenders not as we want to, but as they deserve. And I am not certain that it is wrong to argue that a person who has deliberately killed another person deserves to die.

But even if this principle is valid, should the judicial branch of our   18
governments be empowered to determine whether individuals deserve to die? Are our procedures for making laws and for determining guilt sufficiently reliable that we may entrust our lives to them? I shall return to this important question presently. But consider the following fact: During the years from 1930 to 1962, 466 persons were put to death for the crime of rape. Of these, 399 were black. Can it seriously be maintained that our courts are administering the death penalty to all those and only to those who deserve to die?

IV

Two other arguments deserve brief mention. It has been argued that,   19
even if the penalty of life imprisonment were acceptable on other grounds, our society could not reasonably be asked to pay the cost of maintaining convicted murderers in prisons for the remainder of their natural lives.

This argument overlooks the considerable costs of retaining the death   20
penalty. Jury selection, conduct of the trial, and the appeals process become extremely time-consuming and elaborate when death is a possi-

ble penalty. On the other hand, prisons should not be as expensive as they are. At present those prisoners who work at all are working for absurdly low wages, frequently at menial and degrading tasks. Prisons should be reorganized to provide meaningful work for all able inmates; workers should be paid fair wages for their work and charged for their room and board. Such measures would sharply reduce the cost of prisons and make them more humane.

But these considerations—important as they are—have little relevance   21
to the justification of capital punishment. We should not decide to kill convicted criminals only because it costs so much to keep them alive. The cost to society of imprisonment, large or small, cannot justify capital punishment.

Finally, defenders of capital punishment sometimes support their case   22
by citing those convicted offenders—for example, Gary Gilmore—who have asked to be executed rather than imprisoned. But this argument, too, is of little relevance. If some prisoners would prefer to die rather than be imprisoned, perhaps we should oblige them by permitting them to take their own lives. But this consideration has nothing to do with the question of whether we ought to impose the punishment of death on certain offenders, most of whom would prefer to live.

V

Let us turn now to the case *against* the death penalty. It is sometimes   23
argued that capital punishment is unjustified because those guilty of crimes cannot help acting as they do: the environment, possibly interacting with inherited characteristics, causes some people to commit crimes. It is not moral culpability or choice that divides law-abiding citizens from criminals—so Clarence Darrow argued eloquently—but the accident of birth or social circumstances.

If determinism of this sort were valid, not only the death penalty but   24
all forms of punishment would be unjustified. No one who is compelled by circumstances to act deserves to be punished. But there is little reason to adopt this bleak view of human action. Occasionally coercive threats compel a person to violate the law; and in such cases the individual is rightly excused from legal guilt. Circumstances of deprivation, hardship and lack of education—unfortunately much more widely prevalent—break down the barriers, both moral and material, which deter many of us from breaking the law. They are grounds for exercising extreme caution and for showing mercy in the application of the law, but they are not the sole causes of crimes: they diminish but do not destroy the responsibility of the individual. The great majority of those who break the law do so deliberately, by choice and not as a result of causes beyond their control.

Second, the case against the death penalty is sometimes based on the   25 view that the justification of punishment lies in the reform which it effects. Those who break the law, it is said, are ill, suffering either from psychological malfunction or from maladjustment to society. Our responsibility is to treat them, to cure them of their illness, so that they become able to function in socially acceptable ways. Death, obviously, cannot reform anyone.

Like the deterrence argument for capital punishment, this seems to be   26
the wrong *kind* of argument. Punishment is punishment and treatment is treatment, and one must not be substituted for the other. Some persons who violate the law are, without doubt, mentally ill. It is unreasonable and inhumane to punish them for acts which they may not have realized they were doing; to put such a person to death would be an even more grievous wrong. In such cases treatment is called for.

But most persons who break the law are not mentally ill and do know   27
what they are doing. We may not force them to undergo treatment in place of the legal penalty for their offenses. To confine them to mental institutions until those put in authority over them judge that they are cured of their criminal tendencies is far more cruel than to sentence them to a term of imprisonment. Voluntary programs of education or vocational training, which help prepare prisoners for noncriminal careers on release, should be made more widely available. But compulsory treatment for all offenders violates their integrity as persons; we need only look to the Soviet Union to see the abuses to which such a practice is liable.

VI

Let us examine a third and stronger argument, a straightforward moral   28
assertion; the state ought not to take life unnecessarily. For many reasons —among them the example which capital punishment sets, its effect on those who must carry out death sentences and, above all, its violation of a basic moral principle—the state ought not to kill people.

The counterclaim made by defenders of capital punishment is that in   29
certain circumstances killing people is permissible and even required, and that capital punishment is one of those cases. If a terrorist is about to throw a bomb into a crowded theater, and a police officer is certain that there is no way to stop him except to kill him, the officer should of course kill the terrorist. In some cases of grave and immediate danger, let us grant, killing is justified.

But execution bears little resemblance to such cases. It involves the   30
planned, deliberate killing of someone in custody who is not a present threat to human life or safety. Execution is not necessary to save the lives of future victims, since there are other means to secure that end.

Is there some vitally important purpose of the state or some funda-   31
mental right of persons which cannot be secured without executing convicts? I do not believe there is. And in the absence of any such compelling

reason, the moral principle that it is wrong to kill people constitutes a powerful argument against capital punishment.

VII

Of the arguments I have mentioned in favor of the death penalty, only one has considerable weight. That is the retributive argument that murder, as an extremely serious offense, requires a comparably severe punishment. Of the arguments so far examined against capital punishment, only one, the moral claim that killing is wrong, is, in my view, acceptable.   32

There is, however, another argument against the death penalty which I find compelling—that based on the imperfection of judicial procedure. In the case of *Furman* v. *Georgia,* the Supreme Court struck down existing legislation because of the arbitrariness with which some convicted offenders were executed and others spared. Laws enacted subsequently in several states have attempted to meet the court's objection, either by making death mandatory for certain offenses or by drawing up standards which the trial jury must follow in deciding, after guilt has been established, whether the death penalty will be imposed in a particular case. But these revisions of the law diminish only slightly the discretion of the jury. When death is made the mandatory sentence for first-degree murder, the question of death or imprisonment becomes the question of whether to find the accused guilty as charged or guilty of a lesser offense, such as second-degree murder.   33

When standards are spelled out, the impression of greater precision is often only superficial. A recent Texas statute, for example, instructs the jury to impose a sentence of death only if it is established "beyond a reasonable doubt" that "there is a probability that the defendant would commit criminal acts of violence that would constitute a continuing threat to society" (Texas Code of Criminal Procedure, Art. 37.071; quoted in *Capital Punishment: The Inevitability of Caprice and Mistake,* by Charles L. Black, Jr. [Norton, 1974], p. 58). Such a law does not remove discretion but only adds confusion.   34

At many other points in the judicial process, discretion rules, and arbitrary or incorrect decisions are possible. The prosecutor must decide whether to charge the accused with a capital crime, and whether to accept a plea of guilty to a lesser charge. (In most states it is impossible to plead guilty to a charge carrying a mandatory death sentence.) The jury must determine whether the facts of the case as established by testimony in court fit the legal definition of the offense with which the defendant is charged—a definition likely to be complicated at best, incomprehensible at worst. From a mass of confusing and possibly conflicting testimony the jury must choose the most reliable. But evident reliability can be deceptive: persons have been wrongly convicted of murder on the positive identification of eyewitnesses.   35

Jurors must also determine whether at the time of the crime the ac-   36
cused satisfied the legal definition of insanity. The most widely used
definition—the McNaghten Rules formulated by the judges of the House
of Lords in 1843—states that a person is excused from criminal responsibility if at the time of his act he suffered from a defect of reason which
arose from a disease of the mind and as a result of which he did not "know
the nature and quality of his act," or "if he did know it . . . he did not
know he was doing what was wrong" (quoted in *Punishment and Responsibility,* by H. L. A. Hart [Oxford University Press, 1968], p. 189). Every word
of this formula has been subject to legal controversy in interpretation,
and it is unreasonable to expect that juries untrained in law will be able
to apply it consistently and fairly. Even after sentencing, some offenders
escape the death penalty as a result of appeals, other technical legal
challenges, or executive clemency.

Because of all these opportunities for arbitrary decision, only a small   37
number of those convicted of capital crimes are actually executed. It is
hardly surprising that their selection has little to do with the character of
their crimes but a great deal to do with the skill of their legal counsel. And
the latter depends in large measure on how much money is available for
the defense. Inevitably, the death penalty has been imposed most frequently on the poor, and in this country it has been imposed in dispropor-
tionate numbers on blacks.

To cite two examples in this regard: All those executed in Delaware   38
between 1902 and the (temporary) abolition of the state's death penalty
in 1958 were unskilled workers with limited education. Of 3,860 persons
executed in the United States between 1930 and the present, 2,066, or
54 percent, were black. Although for a variety of reasons the per capita
rate of conviction for most types of crime has been higher among the
poor and the black, that alone cannot explain why a tenth of the population should account for more than half of those executed. Doubtless
prejudice played a part. But no amount of goodwill and fair-mindedness
can compensate for the disadvantage to those who cannot afford the
highly skilled legal counsel needed to discern every loophole in the
judicial process.

VIII

Even more worrisome than the discriminatory application of the death   39
penalty is the possibility of mistaken conviction and its ghastly consequences. In a sense, any punishment wrongfully imposed is irrevocable,
but none is so irrevocable as death. Although we cannot give back to a
person mistakenly imprisoned the time spent or the self-respect lost, we
can release and compensate him or her. But we cannot do anything for
a person wrongfully executed. While we ought to minimize the opportunities for capricious or mistaken judgments throughout the legal sys-

tem, we cannot hope for perfect success. There is no reason why our mistakes must be fatal.

Numerous cases of erroneous convictions in capital cases have been 40 documented; several of those convicted were put to death before the error was discovered. However small their number, it is too large. So long as the death penalty exists, there are certain to be others, for every judicial procedure—however meticulous, however compassed about with safeguards—must be carried out by fallible human beings.

One erroneous execution is too many, because even lawful executions 41 of the indisputably guilty serve no purpose. They are not justified by the need to protect the rest of us, since there are other means of restraining persons dangerous to society, and there is no evidence that executions deter the commission of crime. A wrongful execution is a grievous injustice that cannot be remedied after the fact. Even a legal and proper execution is a needless taking of human life. Even if one is sympathetic —as I am—to the claim that a murderer deserves to die, there are compelling reasons not to entrust the power to decide who shall die to the persons and procedures that constitute our judicial system.

Topical Considerations

1. Suppose that you are a member of a state legislature or of the Congress of the United States. You are aware that in 1810 the British Parliament voted on a bill to abolish capital punishment for the offense of stealing five shillings or more from a shop. You know, too, of Lord Ellenborough's reasons for opposing this bill. Would awareness of this incident have any influence on your vote on a capital punishment bill? Explain.

2. Hoekema comments that czarist Russia eliminated the death penalty in the eleventh century. Do you see any incongruity in the fact that a dictatorship abolished capital punishment in the eleventh century and democracies are still arguing over the issue in the twentieth century?

3. Many Americans who favor capital punishment argue that it is necessary to deter potential criminals. Hoekema refutes this argument. What are his counterarguments? Are they based on fact? Are they logical? What might a defendant say in rebuttal?

4. How does Hoekema counter the argument that capital punishment is in accord with Mosaic law? Is what he says reasonable?

5. Do you think Hoekema's suggestions for rehabilitation of prisoners would be practicable in your state?

6. Does your state have the death penalty? How do you feel about this now that you have read Hoekema's essay? Has he influenced your opinion?

7. If Kitty Genovese's murderer had been caught and convicted and you were the judge trying his case, would you have given him the death penalty?

8. Given his philosophical stand on nonviolence and his theological background, how do you think King would have responded to Hoekema's essay? In particular, what might he have said about Hoekema's comments on the Mosaic code?

9. Of all the arguments Hoekema presents in his opposition to capital punishment, which one do you find most convincing? Why?

Rhetorical Considerations

1. Where does Hoekema state his thesis?

2. Analyze the organization of Hoekema's essay. Is the essay logical and cohesive? Is it easy to identify his main points? Are there sufficient specific facts and details to support his arguments? Cite passages to substantiate your answer.

3. Does Hoekema discuss both sides of the issue? How does he order his discussion of pro and con arguments?

4. How would you evaluate Hoekema's treatment of his subject? Do you find him fair, reasonable, and objective? Emotional and unreasonably prejudiced? Cite evidence to prove your point.

5. In King's essay, there is no reiteration of main points in the conclusion. In Hoekema's essay, Hoekema succinctly restates the main arguments he has discussed. Can you give any reasons why this would be necessary in Hoekema's essay but not in King's? Was it simply a matter of personal preference, or are there other reasons?

Writing Assignments

1. Adopt the point of view of a supporter of capital punishment who has just read Hoekema's essay. Write a letter to the author in which you offer a rebuttal to his arguments.

2. Suppose that your state legislature is considering a bill to abolish capital punishment. Write a letter to your state representative asking that he or she support the bill. Include the arguments in Hoekema's essay that you feel will be most convincing.

3. Suppose that, as a congressperson who is heading a subcommittee formed to research the need for prison reform in your state, you have been asked to find out what programs for rehabilitation are already available and to suggest improvements or changes. Write a report in which you summarize what these programs are. Include in your proposal for improvements those given in Hoekema's essay.

Capital Punishment

William F. Buckley, Jr.

William F. Buckley, Jr., is one of America's most articulate and prominent conservatives. He is editor of *National Review* and host of the long-running weekly television program, "Firing Line." He is a regular contributor to *Atlantic Monthly, New Yorker, Harper's Magazine,* and *Esquire;* he writes nationally syndicated newspaper columns each week; and he is also a novelist. In the essay reprinted here, Mr. Buckley offers sharp counterarguments to the opponents of capital punishment. Several of his points meet head-on with those of David Hoekema in the preceding essay.

There is national suspense over whether capital punishment is   1
about to be abolished, and the assumption is that when it comes it will
come from the Supreme Court. Meanwhile, (a) the prestigious State
Supreme Court of California has interrupted executions, giving constitutional reasons for doing so; (b) the death wings are overflowing with
convicted prisoners; (c) executions are a remote memory; and—for the
first time in years—(d) the opinion polls show that there is sentiment for
what amounts to the restoration of capital punishment.

The case for abolition is popularly known. The other case less so, and   2
(without wholeheartedly endorsing it) I give it as it was given recently to
the Committee of the Judiciary of the House of Representatives by Professor Ernest van den Haag, under whose thinking cap groweth no moss.
Mr. van den Haag, a professor of social philosophy at New York University, ambushed the most popular arguments of the abolitionists, taking
no prisoners.

(1) The business about the poor and the black suffering excessively   3
from capital punishment is no argument against capital punishment. It is
an argument against the *administration* of justice, not against the penalty.
Any punishment can be unfairly or unjustly applied. Go ahead and reform
the processes by which capital punishment is inflicted, if you wish; but
don't confuse maladministration with the merits of capital punishment.

(2) The argument that the death penalty is "unusual" is circular.[1]   4
Capital punishment continues on the books of a majority of states, the
people continue to sanction the concept of capital punishment, and indeed capital sentences are routinely handed down. What has made capital
punishment "unusual" is that the courts and, primarily, governors have
intervened in the process so as to collaborate in the frustration of the
execution of the law. To argue that capital punishment is unusual, when
in fact it has been made unusual by extra-legislative authority, is an
argument to expedite, not eliminate, executions.

[1]The Eighth Amendment to the U.S. Constitution (part of the Bill of Rights) forbids
"cruel and unusual" punishment.

(3) Capital punishment is cruel. That is a historical judgment. But the   5
Constitution suggests that what must be proscribed as cruel is (a) a
particularly painful way of inflicting death, or (b) a particularly un-
deserved death; and the death penalty, as such, offends neither of these
criteria and cannot therefore be regarded as objectively "cruel."

Viewed the other way, the question is whether capital punishment can   6
be regarded as useful, and the question of deterrence arises.

(4) Those who believe that the death penalty does not intensify the   7
disinclination to commit certain crimes need to wrestle with statistics
that, in fact, it can't be proved that *any* punishment does that to any
particular crime. One would rationally suppose that two years in jail
would cut the commission of a crime if not exactly by 100 percent more
than a penalty of one year in jail, at least that it would further discourage
crime to a certain extent. The proof is unavailing. On the other hand, the
statistics, although ambiguous, do not show either (a) that capital punishment net discourages; or (b) that capital punishment fails net to discourage. "The absence of proof for the additional deterrent effect of the death
penalty must not be confused with the presence of proof for the absence
of this effect."

The argument that most capital crimes are crimes of passion commit-   8
ted by irrational persons is no argument against the death penalty, because it does not reveal how many crimes might, but for the death penalty, have been committed by rational persons who are now deterred.

And the clincher. (5) Since we do not know for certain whether or not   9
the death penalty adds deterrence, we have in effect the choice of two
risks.

Risk One: If we execute convicted murderers without thereby deter-   10
ring prospective murderers beyond the deterrence that could have been
achieved by life imprisonment, we may have vainly sacrificed the life of
the convicted murderer.

Risk Two: If we fail to execute a convicted murderer whose execution   11
might have deterred an indefinite number of prospective murderers, our
failure sacrifices an indefinite number of victims of future murderers.

"If we had certainty, we would not have risks. We do not have cer-   12
tainty. If we have risks—and we do—better to risk the life of the convicted
man than risk the life of an indefinite number of innocent victims who
might survive if he were executed."

Topical Considerations

1. Buckley comments that Professor van den Haag's case against
the abolition of capital punishment "ambushed the most popular arguments of the abolitionists, taking no prisoners" (paragraph 2). Is this
true? Look again at Hoekema's essay. Pinpoint each argument that both

men discuss. Who presents the more convincing side of the argument?

2. Do you think it would have been useful for Buckley to be aware of Hoekema's arguments before he claimed that Professor van den Haag's ambush was wholly successful? Are there any significant arguments that Hoekema addresses in his essay but that Buckley does not mention?

3. How does Buckley feel about Professor van den Haag's report? Why does he publish a summary of his arguments?

4. Both Hoekema and Buckley remark that public opinion polls indicate that the number of Americans favoring the death penalty is increasing. What reasons could there be for this increase? Is this a good argument for not abolishing capital punishment?

5. Of all the arguments that Buckley presents, which do you find most convincing? least convincing? Why?

6. Having read both Hoekema's and Buckley's essays, which of the two do you find more persuasive? Does either writer reaffirm the position you had on this issue before reading his article? Has either one changed your perspective? Cite specific arguments from the essays to explain your answers.

Rhetorical Considerations

1. Buckley is well known for his sharp wit. Do you see any examples of his wit in this article? How do they contribute to the effectiveness of Buckley's arguments?

2. Buckley has built his case against the abolition of capital punishment largely by means of deductive reasoning. Cite examples of this. Are his conclusions logical and reasonable? Do you see any flaws in his reasoning?

3. Buckley's writing style is succinct and to the point. How does he achieve this effect? Examine his sentences. Find sentences that seem to have added emphasis. What do you notice about them?

4. How is Buckley's ending different from Hoekema's? Should Buckley's have been more like Hoekema's? Why or why not?

Writing Assignments

1. Suppose that your state legislature is considering a bill to abolish capital punishment. Write a letter to your state representative urging him or her to oppose the bill. Use the arguments from Buckley's essay that you feel will be most convincing.

2. Suppose that you are on a panel of judges presiding over a debate between William Buckley, Jr., and David Hoekema. Having heard

their arguments, who would you decide had won the debate? Write an essay in which you defend your decision.

3. Have you ever known anyone who had to serve a prison sentence? Write a narrative account of his or her experience.

CONSCIENCE AND
CONTROVERSY

5

The Ambivalence of Abortion

Linda Bird Francke

Abortion is probably the only issue today that is more controversial than capital punishment. The prime reason for the controversy is that all the moral, political, legal, and religious debates on the issue hinge on the very definition of life itself. Does it begin at conception or not? Does a fetus have human status, and therefore human rights, or not? Although science and the courts have not yet resolved these questions, the issue is further complicated by the demands for the rights of women not to have to give birth to unwanted children. This issue is as much moral as it is political. In this powerful autobiographical narrative, writer Linda Bird Francke tells how her strong political convictions about women's rights to have abortions suddenly came into conflict with her own conscience when she was faced with an unwanted pregnancy.

1   We were sitting in a bar on Lexington Avenue when I told my husband I was pregnant. It is not a memory I like to dwell on. Instead of the champagne and hope which had heralded the impending births of the first, second and third child, the news of this one was greeted with shocked silence and Scotch. "Jesus," my husband kept saying to himself, stirring the ice cubes around and around. "Oh, Jesus."

2   Oh, how we tried to rationalize it that night as the starting time for the movie came and went. My husband talked about his plans for a career change in the next year, to stem the staleness that fourteen years with the same investment-banking firm had brought him. A new baby would preclude that option.

3   The timing wasn't right for me either. Having juggled pregnancies and child care with what freelance jobs I could fit in between feedings, I had just taken on a full-time job. A new baby would put me right back in the nursery just when our youngest child was finally school age. It was time for *us*, we tried to rationalize. There just wasn't room in our lives now for another baby. We both agreed. And agreed. And agreed.

4   How very considerate they are at the Women's Services, known formally as the Center for Reproductive and Sexual Health. Yes, indeed, I could have an abortion that very Saturday morning and be out in time to drive to the country that afternoon. Bring a first morning urine specimen, a sanitary belt and napkins, a money order or $125 cash—and a friend.

5   My friend turned out to be my husband, standing awkwardly and ill at ease as men always do in places that are exclusively for women, as I checked in at nine A.M. Other men hovered around just as anxiously, knowing they had to be there, wishing they weren't. No one spoke to each other. When I would be cycled out of there four hours later, the same

men would be slumped in their same seats, locked downcast in their cells of embarrassment.

The Saturday morning women's group was more dispirited than the men in the waiting room. There were around fifteen of us, a mixture of races, ages and backgrounds. Three didn't speak English at all and a fourth, a pregnant Puerto Rican girl around eighteen, translated for them.   6

There were six black women and a hodgepodge of whites, among them a T-shirted teenager who kept leaving the room to throw up and a puzzled middle-aged woman from Queens with three grown children.   7

"What form of birth control were you using?" the volunteer asked each one of us. The answer was inevitably "none." She then went on to describe the various forms of birth control available at the clinic, and offered them to each of us.   8

The youngest Puerto Rican girl was asked through the interpreter which she'd like to use: the loop, diaphragm, or pill. She shook her head "no" three times. "You don't want to come back here again, do you?" the volunteer pressed. The girl's head was so low her chin rested on her breastbone. "*Sí*," she whispered.   9

We had been there two hours by that time, filling out endless forms, giving blood and urine, receiving lectures. But unlike any other group of women I've been in, we didn't talk. Our common denominator, the one which usually floods across language and economic barriers into familiarity, today was one of shame. We were losing life that day, not giving it.   10

The group kept getting cut back to smaller, more workable units, and finally I was put in a small waiting room with just two other women. We changed into paper bathrobes and paper slippers, and we rustled whenever we moved. One of the women in my room was shivering and an aide brought her a blanket.   11

"What's the matter?" the aide asked her. "I'm scared," the woman said. "How much will it hurt?" The aide smiled. "Oh, nothing worse than a couple of bad cramps," she said. "This afternoon you'll be dancing a jig."   12

I began to panic. Suddenly the rhetoric, the abortion marches I'd walked in, the telegrams sent to Albany to counteract the Friends of the Fetus, the Zero Population Growth buttons I'd worn, peeled away, and I was all alone with my microscopic baby. There were just the two of us there, and soon, because it was more convenient for me and my husband, there would be one again.   13

How could it be that I, who am so neurotic about life that I step over bugs rather than on them, who spend hours planting flowers and vegetables in the spring even though we rent out the house and never see them, who make sure the children are vaccinated and inoculated and filled with vitamin C, could so arbitrarily decide that this life shouldn't be?   14

"It's not a life," my husband had argued, more to convince himself   15
than me. "It's a bunch of cells smaller than my fingernail."

But any woman who has had children knows that certain feeling in   16
her taut, swollen breasts, and the slight but constant ache in her uterus
that signals the arrival of a life. Though I would march myself into
blisters for a woman's right to exercise the option of motherhood, I
discovered there in the waiting room that I was not the modern woman
I thought I was.

When my name was called, my body felt so heavy the nurse had to help   17
me into the examining room. I waited for my husband to burst through
the door and yell "stop," but of course he didn't. I concentrated on three
black spots in the acoustic ceiling until they grew in size to the shape of
saucers, while the doctor swabbed my insides with antiseptic.

"You're going to feel a burning sensation now," he said, injecting   18
Novocain into the neck of the womb. The pain was swift and severe, and
I twisted to get away from him. He was hurting my baby, I reasoned, and
the black saucers quivered in the air. "Stop," I cried. "Please stop." He
shook his head, busy with his equipment. "It's too late to stop now," he
said. "It'll just take a few more seconds."

What good sports we women are. And how obedient. Physically the   19
pain passed even before the hum of the machine signaled that the vacu-
uming of my uterus was completed, my baby sucked up like ashes after
a cocktail party. Ten minutes start to finish. And I was back on the arm
of the nurse.

There were twelve beds in the recovery room. Each one had a gaily   20
flowered draw sheet and a soft green or blue thermal blanket. It was all
very feminine. Lying on these beds for an hour or more were the shocked
victims of their sex, their full wombs now stripped clean, their futures less
encumbered.

It was very quiet in that room. The only voice was that of the nurse,   21
locating the new women who had just come in so she could monitor their
blood pressure, and checking out the recovered women who were free to
leave.

Juice was being passed about, and I found myself sipping a Dixie cup   22
of Hawaiian Punch. An older woman with tightly curled bleached hair was
just getting up from the next bed. "That was no goddamn snap," she said,
resting before putting on her miniskirt and high white boots. Other
women came and went, some walking out as dazed as they had entered,
others with a bounce that signaled they were going right back to Bloom-
ingdale's.

Finally then, it was time for me to leave. I checked out, making an   23
appointment to return in two weeks for an IUD insertion. My husband
was slumped in the waiting room, clutching a single yellow rose wrapped
in a wet paper towel and stuffed into a Baggie.

We didn't talk the whole way home, but just held hands very tightly.   24
At home there were more yellow roses and a tray in bed for me and the
children's curiosity to divert.

It had certainly been a successful operation. I didn't bleed at all for two   25
days just as they had predicted, and then I bled only moderately for
another four days. Within a week my breasts had subsided and the tender-
ness vanished, and my body felt mine again instead of the eggshell it
becomes when it's protecting someone else.

My husband and I are back to planning our summer vacation and his   26
career switch.

And it certainly does make more sense not to be having a baby right   27
now—we say that to each other all the time. But I have this ghost now.
A very little ghost that only appears when I'm seeing something beautiful,
like the full moon on the ocean last weekend. And the baby waves at me.
And I wave at the baby. "Of course, we have room," I cry to the ghost.
"Of course, we do."

Topical Considerations

1. What are the reasons the author and her husband do not want
another child?

2. How does Francke describe the state of the men in the waiting
room of the abortion clinic? What feelings do they seem to share?

3. According to Francke, what "common denominator" links the
women at the clinic?

4. In paragraph 13, Francke says she suddenly panicked. Why
did she?

5. What had been Francke's political stand on the abortion issue
before her visit to the clinic? Do you think she has had a change of heart
since? Explain your reasons for your answer.

6. In paragraph 16, Francke admits that she "was not the modern
woman" she had thought she was. What does she mean by this statement?
Why the term "modern woman"?

7. In paragraph 17, Francke says that she waited for her husband
to burst through the door of the operating room and yell "stop." What
does this say about what was going on in Francke's mind? What does it
say about her own strength of will? Do you think this is another confession that she is not the "modern woman" she thought she was but, rather,
one who hopes to be rescued from a bad situation by a man? Or is this
a momentary fantasy that goes beyond sex roles?

8. Francke says that the physical pain of the operation was "swift
and severe." But the mental pain, though also severe, is not so swift in
passing. What evidence is there in the essay that Francke's mental anguish persisted after the operation?

Rhetorical Considerations

1. What does *ambivalence* mean? How does the author demonstrate ambivalence in the first paragraph? Where in the essay does she actually discuss her ambivalence rather than simply dramatizing it?

2. Explain the rhetorical effect of the repetition in paragraph 3: "We both agreed. And agreed. And agreed." Where else do you find such repetition? Explain its effect, too.

3. This is a highly emotional and moving essay. Does the author convey her emotional trauma by becoming overly emotional or sentimental in the piece? If you think so, cite examples. If you think not, how well does she avoid being sentimental?

4. What is the effect of telling us that the Women's Services is formally known as the Center for Reproductive and Sexual Health? What does the name difference suggest about the clinic's self-perception? About the clinic's relationship to the community?

5. Discuss the matter-of-fact tone of paragraph 4. How is Francke's own emotional anxiety sustained by the seemingly neutral tone? Is her tone ironic? Explain your answers.

6. Francke says that the women at the abortion clinic were a mixture of ages, races, and social strata. How would you describe Francke's attitude toward these other women? What is her feeling toward the youngest girl?

7. At the end of paragraph 12, the aide with a smile tells one scared woman, "This afternoon you'll be dancing a jig." What is the effect of the observation of the aide's manner and words? How does it contrast with what is going on inside the author?

8. Discuss the effect of the first two lines of paragraph 19: "What good sports we women are. And how obedient."

9. Why would Francke mention the seemingly minor detail of her husband "clutching a single yellow rose wrapped in a wet paper towel and stuffed into a Baggie" (paragraph 23)? Does this detail have a higher, symbolic function in the essay?

10. Throughout the essay, Francke writes in the past tense. Why did she switch to the present tense in the last two paragraphs? And to what effect?

Writing Assignments

1. Abortion is one of our society's most controversial issues, because what is being debated hinges on the definition of life itself—whether life begins at conception or at birth. Write an essay stating your own feelings about when life begins and about the abortion issue. In your

essay, also discuss whether modern science has helped or complicated the problem of determining when life occurs.

2. Write a political speech defending a woman's right to have a legal abortion.

3. Write a political speech against the legalization of abortion.

4. Linda Bird Francke's essay is about her ambivalence on a particularly sensitive social issue. Write a paper in which you face your own ambivalence about some social issue. Like Francke, consider both sides and explain your ambivalence. You might want to consider some of the other social issues talked about in this section—the compulsory draft, censorship, creationism versus science, legalization of drugs.

5. None of the women at Francke's abortion clinic had used any birth control measures. Write an essay in which you argue for or against compulsory sex education programs in elementary schools. In your essay, be sure to state your stand clearly and give your reasons behind it.

6. Francke's essay is a powerful piece, not just because the issue is highly controversial but because she was caught up in an emotional tug-of-war between strong political convictions and an intense personal experience. If you have ever been caught up in such a conflict between ideals and real experience, write a first-person account describing it, and explore any ambivalence or change of heart you might have experienced as a result. (If you have been a victim of a crime, for example, you might want to consider your attitudes toward criminals and punishment before and after the event.)

Unwed Mothers in America

Norman Cousins

Nearly a million babies are born each year to unwed mothers, and over 60% of these mothers are teenagers. Because so many of these mothers are economically dependent, the financial cost to society is staggering. Far worse, however, is the social, moral, and psychological cost, for what is at stake might be the fundamental stabilizing unit of American society—the family. In this brief essay, Norman Cousins looks at the dangerous impact of such a sorry situation and at some of the factors that have contributed to it, including the divorce rate and pornography. Norman Cousins was editor of *Saturday Review* for more than 35 years and is the author of many books, including *The Improbable Triumvirate* (1972), *The Quest for Immortality* (1974), and the best-selling *Anatomy of an Illness* (1979).

The grimmest statistics of 1979 have nothing to do with inflation   1
or even the cost of the arms race. Nothing about the year now ending

deserves greater concern and scrutiny than the fact that almost a million babies were born to unwed women. Equally startling and disturbing is a statistic showing that about 600,000 teenagers become mothers each year. Of these, more than 10,000 are 14 years of age or younger.

The problem is compounded when many of the unwed mothers, espe-   2
cially the teenagers, go on to have additional children. One of the reasons behind that decision is that the mothers cannot support themselves and are attracted to the added welfare payments given for each family member.

Inevitably, the immediate question raised by these developments con-   3
cerns the economic cost. The Population Resource Center has estimated that the bill for the first 10 years of life of each child born to a teenager will be $18,710. This translates into more than $8 billion for the entire group. If these figures are projected to all the children born of unwed and economically dependent mothers during the next 20 years, assuming the total number of babies each year is no greater than it is now, the eventual cost could be in excess of $100 billion. Inflation could add another $20 billion to the total expenditure.

But the economic cost, catastrophic though it is, may actually be the   4
minor part of the problem. Far more serious is the social, moral, and psychological impact on life in America. What happens to a nation when the family ceases to exist as the central and stabilizing unit of society? Underlining and magnifying this problem is the current divorce rate, now approaching 40 percent.

In this light, there is something almost bizarre about the preoccupa-   5
tion of the American people with military security from external sources. A bomb has already fallen on America. The shattering effect is reaching into every aspect and corner of our lives. It doesn't take much imagina-tion to visualize the disfiguration of a society when a large percentage of the population requires government support. Moreover, government is being forced not just to assume the financial burden but to provide the kind of care that in many cases is beyond the capacity of many mothers. Doctors report that a horrendously high number of teenage mothers are emotionally and intellectually incapable of bringing up their children. The same failure applies to many older women. Social-welfare agencies are therefore confronted with the need to fill the roles of both mother and father on a day-to-day basis. The pressure on schools and particularly on teachers is correspondingly great.

How did we come to this point?   6

It will be said that the decline of religion in American life in the past   7
20 or 30 years may account for a large part of the problem. Yet many unwed mothers identify themselves as members of religious denomina-tions. Nor do all the girls come from broken homes. What we are dealing with here is a complex equation involving many factors, not all of them readily identifiable. Certainly it is true that moral and social restraints no

longer have a presiding presence in American life. Marriage is no longer universally considered an indispensable or even desirable condition of a full and ongoing relationship between the sexes. Explicit love scenes between young people—or people of any age, for that matter—are commonplace in almost every form of entertainment, especially in film and print. Unfortunately, no one has yet figured out a way to control pornography without touching off perhaps even greater problems in government thought control; but it is absurd to contend that the kind of exploitation of sex that now abounds in society does not produce desensitization and casualness about the prime elements of life. It is similarly irresponsible to contend that there is no connection between the saturating violence in the entertainment media and the lack of respect for human emotions and for life in general.

One of the dangers in the present situation is that if it continues   8
unchecked, a demand will go up for the sterilization of unwed mothers with more than one child—with their consent if possible but without their consent if necessary. Before the problem deteriorates to that level, it would be useful if a presidential commission could examine every aspect of the question and its long-term implications. Such a study should look into all the interacting factors of home background, housing, community experience, quality of education, church influence, economic conditions, and so forth. A report by itself would not solve the problem, but it might succeed at least in getting the issue into the American consciousness and putting it at the top of the national agenda, where it belongs.

Topical Considerations

1. What is one reason unwed mothers end up having additional children?

2. Cousins says that despite the staggering economic costs of children born of unwed and economically dependent teenage mothers, an even greater cost will be felt in the form of "the social, moral, and psychological impact on life in America" (paragraph 4). What kinds of effects does the author specify?

3. Paragraph 6 is a single question: "How did we come to this point?" How does Cousins answer this question? How, in fact, did we end up with such a horrendous problem? Does Cousins suggest that the problem is intrinsically American—that there is something unique about our society that would create such a problem?

4. According to Cousins, what particular role has pornography played in regard to the issue of unwed mothers in America? Do you agree with his claim?

5. What connection does Cousins make between the central problem and religion in America? Do you agree with him?

6. Do you agree with the author that "marriage is no longer universally considered an indispensable or even desirable condition of a full and ongoing relationship between the sexes" (paragraph 7)? If this is true, is it necessarily a bad thing? Do you think it is a bad thing that the divorce rate is nearly 40%?

7. According to Cousins, what role does "the saturating violence in the entertainment media" (paragraph 7) have in regard to the central issue? Do you agree?

8. Cousins worries that one of the dangerous consequences of the present problem could be the sterilization of unwed mothers, with or without their consent. Why is that a dangerous potential? Do you agree with Cousin's speculation?

9. According to Cousins, what can be done to change the situation for the better?

Rhetorical Considerations

1. Cousins opens his essay with several statistics. What is the advantage of this strategy?

2. How appropriate to the problem under discussion is the metaphor of the bomb in paragraph 5?

3. Paragraph 6 is a single-sentence question. What rhetorical strategy do you think Cousins was using here?

4. How would you define the author's tone in this essay? Is he angry? sad? Is there a sense of urgency? Explain your answers.

Writing Assignments

1. Cousins cites pornography as a major contributor to the problem of unwed teenage mothers in America. Explore this idea more fully. Write a paper in which you discuss how pornography has caused people to be more casual, even reckless, toward sex.

2. Cousins warns that the control of pornography could touch off "even greater problems in government thought control" (paragraph 7). Explore this speculation more fully. Write a paper in which you argue that censorship of erotica could lead to even greater repressions by government.

3. Cousins also argues that violence in the media has led to "the lack of respect for human emotions and for life in general" (paragraph 7). Write a paper exploring this claim, citing the violence in the movies, in print, and on television—including series shows and the news. Does violence, like sex, sell? And does it desensitize people to real horrors and real crime?

4. What do you think should be done about the unwed mother problem in America? Write a paper in which you give some potential solutions.

5. Cousins says that religion in America has been on the decline in the past few decades. Do you think America needs to go back to its churches and synagogues? Write a paper arguing that the revitalization of religious values could help solve some of our most severe social and moral problems, such as the one addressed in this essay.

6. If you know an unwed mother, write a paper on what you have observed of her situation. Did some of the forces Cousins cites influence her situation? In other words, was she a girl from a broken home? Was she desensitized by the media? Did she lack religious convictions? How successful has she been as a mother? What specific problems did she have to face from family, friends, and society in general?

The Evidence Builds Against Marijuana

Jane E. Brody

More than 4 million youngsters between the ages of 12 and 17 smoke marijuana regularly. And as that number grows, so grows the evidence that pot is dangerous to health. In this rather unimpassioned essay, Jane E. Brody cites some of the specific hazards of marijuana that drug researchers have found. Although the studies cited are not conclusive, there is enough evidence that habitual use of marijuana can lead to brain and body damage. Jane E. Brody is a nutritionist and the personal health columnist for the New York Times. She is also the author of Jane Brody's Nutrition Book (1981) and Jane Brody's The New York Times Guide to Personal Health (1982), a collection of her newspaper columns.

Millions of marijuana-smoking young Americans, jaded by alarm- 1
ists and politically motivated but poorly documented reports of marijuana's alledged risks, are convinced that it is a safe drug, especially when
compared to alcohol.

However, as a growing number of persons smoke a more potent mari- 2
juana at ever-younger ages, scientists are gathering an impressive—
though still inconclusive—body of evidence indicating that the nation's
second leading recreational drug (alcohol is No. 1) is indeed hazardous
to health.

In fact, some leading drug experts who once dismissed marijuana as 3 a drug of minor consequence now express serious concern about the possible risks and patterns of use, particularly among teen-agers.

Among those who now take a dim view of marijuana are Dr. Sidney   4
Cohen, a drug expert at the University of California at Los Angeles, who once described marijuana as "a trivial weed," and Dr. Robert L. DuPont, former director of the National Institute on Drug Abuse, who had lobbied for marijuana's legalization.

According to these and other experts, it is no longer possible to say   5
that marijuana is an innocuous drug with few if any health effects aside from intoxication. Although the evidence for immediate effects on the brain is most convincing, a number of recent studies show damaging effects that suggest long-term health hazards involving many different body functions. These include the heart, lungs and reproductive organs.

The problem with accurately defining the hazards of marijuana is that   6
the way in which it is used by Americans has not yet been subjected to long-term study. Decades of experience with marijuana in other countries is not necessarily relevant here, where a stronger form of the drug is used, primarily by people in their formative years, and where patterns of inhalation are likely to differ.

It may be 20 years or more before the necessary studies can be con-   7
ducted among Americans. Therefore, it is especially important to heed the "early warning signs" of the long-term hazards of smoking marijuana. One need only recall that it took half a century of heavy cigarette smoking by millions of Americans before the health risks of tobacco were widely recognized. By then, so many had become so hooked on the "innocuous weed" that today, 25 years after the first major report on the health hazards of cigarettes, more than 50 million Americans still smoke cigarettes, and smoking remains the nation's leading preventable cause of illness and premature death.

The following are among the reasons for the mounting concern about   8
marijuana:

Patterns of use. Some 43 million Americans have tried marijuana and   9
the latest national survey in 1977 showed that 16 million were current users. Current users included 4 percent of 12-year-olds, 15 percent of 14-year-olds, and 31 percent of 18- to 21-year olds. More than four million youngsters aged 12 to 17 were using marijuana in 1977, and one in nine high school seniors used marijuana daily. The survey showed that the proportion of youngsters who had begun using marijuana before the ninth grade had nearly doubled since 1972.

Marijuana is far less popular among adults, and most who use it tend   10
to smoke it only occasionally. There is relatively little concern about occasional use by adults, except for pregnant women and persons with heart disease, lung disease or emotional disorders.

Potency. Drug experts are disturbed about the rapidly increasing po-   11 tency of the marijuana generally available to Americans. In 1975, the average sample of confiscated marijuana contained 0.4 percent of the mind-altering chemical THC (tetrahydrocannabinol). By last year,* because of improved cultivation practices, the average was 4 percent of the active drug—a tenfold increase in potency. And one cultivated form increasingly available in this country contains 7 percent THC.

This is especially worrisome because, unlike alcohol, which is soluble   12
in water and rapidly washed out of the body, THC and related cannabinoids in marijuana are fat-soluble and can remain and accumulate in the body for a week or longer after marijuana is smoked.

Brain effects. Immediate effects on the brain are the least controver-   13
sial and best defined of marijuana's hazards. Like alcohol, marijuana is intoxicating and a marijuana high impairs memory, learning, speech, reading comprehension, arithmetic problem-solving and the ability to think. Long-term intellectual effects are not known.

Some researchers have described what they called "a motivational   14
syndrome" among young marijuana smokers, who, with frequent use of the drug, tend to lose interest in school, friends and sexual intercourse. However, it is not known whether marijuana use is a direct cause or merely one symptom of a general underlying problem. Persistent brain abnormalities and changes in emotion and behavior have been demonstrated in monkeys given large doses of marijuana.

Also like alcohol, marijuana interferes with psychomotor functions   15
such as reaction time, coordination, visual perception and other skills important for driving and operating machinery safely. Actual tests of marijuana-intoxicated drivers have clearly shown that their driving is impaired, yet they tend to think they are driving better than usual. In several surveys 60 to 80 percent of marijuana users said they sometimes drive while high.

Although not physically addicting, people can become psychologically   16
hooked on the drug. Marijuana may aggravate existing emotional problems. The most common adverse emotional effect is an "acute panic reaction," in which the user may become terrified and paranoid and require hospital treatment. In 1978, some 10,000 persons were treated in hospital emergency rooms for adverse marijuana reactions.

Lung damage. Marijuana cigarettes are unfiltered and smokers tend   17
to inhale deeply, exposing sensitive lung tissue to potent, irritating chemicals. One study among marijuana smokers showed that five marijuana cigarettes a week were more damaging to the lungs than six packs of cigarettes smoked over the same period. Marijuana smoking irritates the air passages and diminishes the amount of air the lungs can hold and exhale, the studies show.

*1979.—Ed.

Like tobacco, marijuana smoke impairs lung defenses against infec-   18
tions and foreign inhaled matter. In animal studies, it has caused extensive lung inflammation. Bronchitis may occur in people who smoke marijuana regularly.

Marijuana smoke contains 150 chemicals in addition to THC, and the   19
effects of most of these are not known. One ingredient is benzopyrene,
a known cancer-causing agent that is 70 percent more abundant in marijuana smoke than in tobacco smoke. There is also more "tar" in marijuana than in high-tar cigarettes. When painted on the skin of mice,
marijuana tar can produce tumors. However, there is as yet no good
evidence of any cancer-causing effects in people. If there is such an effect,
it is not likely to become apparent for another two decades.

Heart effects. Marijuana has an even greater effect on heart function   20
than tobacco. It can raise the heart rate by as much as 50 percent. This
is of no known consequence to young healthy persons. But in those with
poor heart function, this effect can be dangerous and may also produce
chest pains (angina). Most doctors would caution heart patients to steer
clear of marijuana.

Hormone and reproductive effects. Several, but not all, studies have   21
shown that marijuana smoking can lower the level of the male sex hormone, testosterone, in the blood, though it usually remains within the
range of normal. Sperm abnormalities, including reduced numbers of
sperm and abnormal sperm movement and shapes, have also been found
in relation to marijuana use.

In females, preliminary studies suggest an adverse effect on the men-   22
strual cycle in 40 percent of the women who smoke marijuana at least four
times a week. The result may be infertility. In animal studies, the levels
of growth hormone and the female sex hormones, estrogen and proges-
terone, have been reduced by marijuana.

Marijuana can cross the placenta and reach the developing fetus; preg-   23
nant monkeys given THC were far more likely to suffer abortions or
deliver dead babies.

Studies by Dr. Gabriel G. Nahas of Columbia University showed an   24
effect of marijuana on the hypothalamus, the body's master gland that
directs the functions of other hormone-producing glands.

Immune impairment. Evidence from both animal and human studies   25
have suggested damage to basic body defenses against disease. However,
it is not known whether marijuana smokers are any more likely to get sick
than other persons of similar life circumstances. As the National Institute
on Drug Abuse concludes in its latest report to Congress on marijuana:
"It is very difficult to anticipate the problems which will arise in a given
society in advance. Thus, any attempt to compare the health impact of
marijuana with that of alcohol and tobacco at *current* levels of use is
certain to minimize the hazards of marijuana."

Topical Considerations

1. Brody says that recent studies show that marijuana is hazardous to one's health, but she adds that the studies are inconclusive. Why is that so, according to the author?

2. What evidence does Brody present that marijuana is more toxic than alcohol? How is marijuana like alcohol in its effects?

3. What adverse affects does marijuana have on the brain?

4. What does Brody mean when she writes in paragraph 14: "However, it is not known whether marijuana use is a direct cause or merely one symptom of a general underlying problem"?

5. Cigarettes are known to cause cancer. What about marijuana cigarettes?

6. Do you think the evidence Brody presents is convincing enough to change the minds of people who smoke pot? Is the problem with the evidence or with the habit?

7. According to Brody's survey, what effects does marijuana have on human reproductive capacity?

8. What is the meaning of the last sentence in the essay? How are the hazards of marijuana minimized when compared to the health impact of alcohol and tobacco? Explain.

Rhetorical Considerations

1. How convincing is Brody's "evidence" against marijuana? Does she give enough? not enough? Where could she have presented more documentation and data?

2. Brody makes the point that we know more about the hazards from cigarette smoking than we do about those from pot smoking. In paragraph 7, however, she draws a parallel between the studies of the two habits. How convincing is this parallel?

3. Brody's paragraphs are nearly the same size throughout the essay. Could some of them be combined? Do you think her paragraphing has a rhetorical function, or does it merely reflect her training as a journalist?

4. How effective is Brody's conclusion to her essay? Does it wrap up matters well?

Writing Assignments

1. In paragraph 9, Brody presents statistics indicating that more than 4 million youngsters between ages 12 and 17 use pot regularly. Why do you think young children would turn to marijuana? Write a paper on

this, exploring what you see as the forces—from society, family, or peers —that turn kids on to pot.

2. If you are a marijuana smoker, write a paper describing the effects you experience. What pleasures do you get? What physical and psychological effects can you note? Also talk about how you view your marijuana smoking—as a habit, a hobby, recreation, a social thing, an addiction. In light of the evidence Brody presents here, do you think you can or will give it up?

3. Write a paper in which you call for the legalization of marijuana. For support, you might cite the greater hazards of alcohol and cigarettes and make a comparative case in defense of pot.

4. In light of the dangers presented in this essay, write a paper in which you call for stronger penalties for marijuana pushers and/or users. Cite some data, as Brody does, to support your arguments.

5. Brody never gets into the sociological reasons why so huge a segment of our society is turning to marijuana. In an essay, try exploring some of the background forces that cause people to seek out an illegal substance for getting high. What social stresses might contribute to so great a need?

Creationism Isn't Science

Niles Eldredge

In 1859, Charles Darwin published his monumental *On the Origin of Species*, which started a controversy that has been raging ever since. At the heart of the controversy is the question of human origin. On one side are scientists who subscribe to Darwin's theory of evolution—that man is biologically descended from lower species. On the other side are creationists who embrace the version of man's origin given in Genesis—that God made man and woman as we are. Within the last few years, creationists have asked for "equal time" in the classroom and in biology books to present a countertheory to evolution. In this essay, Niles Eldredge, who is a scientist and the curator of the Department of Invertebrates at the American Museum of Natural History in New York, examines the arguments and claims of the creationists. He concludes that granting equal time would be a destructive blow to all science education in America.

Despite this country's apparent modernism, the creationist   1
movement once again is growing. The news media proclaimed a juryless trial in California as "Scopes II" and those who cling to the myth of progress wonder how the country could revert to the primitive state it was in when Darrow and Bryan battled it out in the hot summer of 1925 in

Dayton, Tennessee. But the sad truth is that we have not progressed. Creationism never completely disappeared as a political, religious, and educational issue. Scopes was convicted of violating the Tennessee statute forbidding the teaching of the evolutionary origins of mankind (although in fact he was ill and never really did teach the evolution segment of the curriculum). The result was a drastic cutback in serious discussion of evolution in many high school texts until it became respectable again in the 1960s.

Although technological advances since 1925 have been prodigious,   2 and although science news magazines are springing up like toadstools, the American public appears to be as badly informed about the real nature of science as it ever was. Such undiluted ignorance, coupled with the strong anti-intellectual tradition in the US, provides a congenial climate for creationism to leap once more to the fore, along with school prayer, sex education, Proposition 13, and the other favorite issues of the populist-conservative movement. Much of the success of recent creationist efforts lies in a prior failure to educate our children about science— how it is done, by whom, and how its results are to be interpreted.

Today's creationists usually cry for "equal time" rather than for actu-   3 ally substituting the Genesis version of the origin of things for the explanations preferred by modern science. (The recent trial in California is an anachronism in this respect because the plaintiff simply affirmed that his rights of religious freedom were abrogated by teaching him that man "descended from apes"). At the heart of the creationists' contemporary political argument is an appeal to the time-honored American sense of fair play. "Look," they say, "evolution is only a theory. Scientists cannot agree on all details either of the exact course of evolutionary history, or how evolution actually takes place." True enough. Creationists then declare that many scientists have grave doubts that evolution actually has occurred—a charge echoed by Ronald Reagan during the campaign, and definitely false. They argue that since evolution is only a theory, why not, in the spirit of fair play, give equal time to equally plausible explanations of the origin of the cosmos, of life on earth, and of mankind? Why not indeed?

The creationist argument equates a biological, evolutionary system   4 with a non-scientific system of explaining life's exuberant diversity. Both systems are presented as authoritarian, and here lies the real tragedy of American science education: the public is depressingly willing to see merit in the "fair play, equal time" argument precisely because it views science almost wholly in this authoritarian vein. The public is bombarded with a constant stream of oracular pronouncements of new discoveries, new truths, and medical and technological innovations, but the American education system gives most people no effective choice but to ignore, accept on faith, or reject out of hand each new scientific finding. Scientists themselves promote an Olympian status for their profession; it's small wonder that the public has a tough time deciding which set of authoritarian pronouncements to heed. So why not present them all and let each person choose his or her own set of beliefs?

Of course, there has to be some willingness to accept the expertise of specialists. Although most of us "believe" the earth is spherical, how many of us can design and perform an experiment to show that it must be so? But to stress the authoritarianism of science is to miss its essence. Science is the enterprise of comparing alternative ideas about what the cosmos is, how it works, and how it came to be. Some ideas are better than others, and the criterion for judging which are better is simply the relative power of different ideas to fit our observations. The goal is greater understanding of the natural universe. The method consists of constantly challenging received ideas, modifying them, or, best of all, replacing them with better ones. 5

So science is ideas, and the ideas are acknowledged to be merely approximations to the truth. Nothing could be further from authoritarianism—dogmatic assertions of what is true. Scientists deal with ideas that appear to be the best (the closest to the truth) given what they think they know about the universe at any given moment. If scientists frequently act as if their ideas *are* the truth, they are simply showing their humanity. But the human quest for a rational coming-to-grips with the cosmos recognizes imperfection in observation and thought, and incorporates the frailty into its method. Creationists disdain this quest, preferring the wholly authoritarian, allegedly "revealed" truth of divine creation as an understanding of our beginnings. At the same time they present disagreement among scientists as an expression of scientific failure in the realm of evolutionary biology. 6

To the charge that "evolution is *only* a theory," we say "all science is theory." Theories are ideas, or complex sets of ideas, which explain some aspect of the natural world. Competing theories sometimes coexist until one drives the other out, or until both are discarded in favor of yet another theory. But it is true that one major theory usually holds sway at any one time. All biologists, including biochemists, molecular geneticists, physiologists, behaviorists, and anatomists, see a pattern of similarity interlocking the spectrum of millions of species, from bacteria to timber wolves. Darwin finally convinced the world that this pattern of similarity is neatly explained by "descent with modification." If we imagine a genealogical system where an ancestor produces one or more descendants, we get a pattern of progressive similarity. The whole array of ancestors and descendants will share some feature inherited from the first ancestor; as each novelty appears, it is shared only with later descendants. All forms of life have the nucleic acid RNA. One major branch of life, the vertebrates, all share backbones. All mammals have three inner ear bones, hair, and mammary glands. All dogs share features not found in other carnivores, such as cats. In other words, dogs share similarities 7 among themselves in addition to having general mammalian features, plus general vertebrate features, as well as anatomical and biochemical similarities shared with the rest of life.

How do we test the basic notion that life has evolved? The notion of evolution, like any scientific idea, should generate predictions about the natural world, which we can discover to be true or false. The grand prediction of evolution is that there should be one basic scheme of similarities interlocking all of life. This is what we have consistently found for over 100 years, as thousands of biologists daily compared different organisms. Medical experimentation depends upon the interrelatedness of life. We test drugs on rhesus monkeys and study the effects of caffeine on rats because we cannot experiment on ourselves. The physiological systems of monkeys are more similar to our own than to rats. Medical scientists know this and rely on this prediction to interpret the signifi- cance of their results in terms of human medicine. Very simply, were life not all interrelated, none of this would be possible. There would be chaos, not order, in the natural world. There is no competing, rational biological explanation for this order in nature, and there hasn't been for a long while.

Creationists, of course, have an alternative explanation for this order permeating life's diversity. It is simply the way the supernatural creator chose to pattern life. But any possible pattern could be there, including chaos—an absence of any similarity among the "kinds" of organisms on earth—and creationism would hold that it is just what the creator made. There is nothing about this view of life that smacks of prediction. It tells us nothing about what to expect if we begin to study organisms in detail. In short, there is nothing in this notion that allows us to go to nature to test it, to verify or reject it.

And there is the key difference. Creationism (and it comes in many guises, most of which do not stem from the Judeo-Christian tradition) is a belief system involving the supernatural. Testing an idea with our own experiences in the natural universe is simply out of bounds. The mystical revelation behind creationism is the opposite of science, which seeks rational understanding of the cosmos. Science thrives on alternative ex- planations, which must be equally subject to observational and experi- mental testing. No form of creationism even remotely qualifies for inclu- sion in a science curriculum.

Creationists have introduced equal-time bills in over 10 state legisla- tures, and recently met with success when Governor White of Arkansas signed such a bill into law on March 19 (reportedly without reading it). Creationists also have lobbied extensively at local school boards. The impact has been enormous. Just as the latest creationist bill is defeated in committee, and some of their more able spokesmen look silly on national TV, one hears of a local school district in the Philadelphia environs where some of the teachers have adopted the "equal time" or "dual model" approach to discussing "origins" in the biology curriculum on their own initiative. Each creationist "defeat" amounts to a Pyrrhic victory for their opponents. Increasingly, teachers are left to their own discretion, and whether out of personal conviction, a desire to be "fair," or fear of parental reprisal, they are teaching creationism along with evolution in their biology classes. It is simply the path of least resistance.

Acceptance of equal time for two alternative authoritarian explana-   12
tions is a startling blow to the fabric of science education. The fundamental notion a student should get from high school science is that people can confront the universe and learn about it directly. Just one major inroad against this basic aspect of science threatens all of science education. Chemistry, physics, and geology—all of which spurn biblical revelation in favor of direct experience, as all science must—are jeopardized every bit as much as biology. That some creationists have explicitly attacked areas of geology, chemistry, and physics (in arguments over the age of the earth, for example) underscores the more general threat they pose to all science. We must remove science education from its role as authoritarian truthgiver. This view distorts the real nature of science and gives creationists their most potent argument.

The creationists' equal-time appeal maintains that evolution itself   13
amounts to a religious belief (allied with a secular humanism) and should not be included in a science curriculum. But if it is included, goes the argument, it must appear along with other religious notions. Both are authoritarian belief systems, and neither is science, according to this creationist ploy.

The more common creationist approach these days avoids such soph-   14
istry and maintains that both creationism and evolution belong in the realm of science. But apart from some attempts to document the remains of Noah's Ark on the flanks of Mt. Ararat, creationists have been singularly unsuccessful in posing testable theories about the origin, diversity, and distribution of plants and animals. No such contributions have appeared to date either in creationism's voluminous literature or, more to the point, in the professional biological literature. "Science creationism" consists almost exclusively of a multipronged attack on evolutionary biology and historical geology. No evidence, for example, is presented in favor of the notion that the earth is only 20,000 years old, but many arguments attempt to poke holes in geochemists' and astronomers' reckoning of old Mother Earth's age at about 4.6 billion years. Analysis of the age of formation of rocks is based ultimately on the theories of radioactive decay in nuclear physics. (A body of rock is dated, often by several different means, in several different laboratories. The results consistently agree. And rocks shown to be roughly the same age on independent criteria (usually involving fossils) invariably check out to be roughly the same age when dated radiometrically. The system, although not without

its flaws, works.) The supposed vast age of any particular rock can be shown to be false, but not by quoting Scripture.

All of the prodigious works of "scientific creationism" are of this   15
nature. All can be refuted. However, before school boards or parent groups, creationists are fond of "debating" scientists by bombarding the typically ill-prepared biologist or geologist with a plethora of allegations, ranging from the second law of thermodynamics (said to falsify evolution outright) to the supposed absence of fossils intermediate between "major kinds." No scientist is equally at home in all realms of physics, chemistry, geology, and biology in this day of advanced specialization. Not all the proper retorts spring readily to mind. Retorts there are, but the game is usually lost anyway, as rebuttals strike an audience as simply another set of authoritarian statements they must take on faith.

Although creationists persist in depicting both science and creationism   16
as two comparable, monolithic belief systems, perhaps the most insidious attack exploits free inquiry in science. Because we disagree on specifics, some of my colleagues and I are said now to have serious doubts that evolution has occurred. Distressing as this may be, the argument actually highlights the core issue raised by creationism. The creationists are acknowledging that science is no monolithic authoritarian belief system. But even though they recognize that there are competing ideas within contemporary biology, the creationists see scientific debate as a sign of weakness. Of course, it really is a sign of vitality.

Evolutionary theory since the 1940s (until comparatively recently) has   17
focused on a single coherent view of the evolutionary process. Biologists of all disciplines agreed to a remarkable degree on the outlines of this theory, the so-called "modern synthesis." In a nutshell, this was a vindication of Darwin's original position: that evolution is predominantly an affair of gradual progressive change. As environmental conditions changed, natural selection (a culling process similar to the "artificial" selection practiced by animal breeders) favored those variants best suited to the new conditions. Thus evolutionary change is fundamentally adaptive. The modern synthesis integrated the newly arisen science of genetics with the Darwinian view and held that the entire diversity of life could be explained in these simple terms.

Some biologists have attacked natural selection itself, but much of   18
the current uproar in evolutionary biology is less radical in implication. Some critics see a greater role for random processes. Others, like me, see little evidence of gradual, progressive change in the fossil record. We maintain that the usual explanation—the inadequacy of the fossil record—is itself inadequate to explain the non-change, the maintenance of status quo which lasts in some cases for 10 million years or more in our fossil bones and shells. In this view, change (presumably by natural selection causing adaptive modifications) takes place in bursts of a few

thousand years, followed usually by immensely longer periods of business as usual.

Arguments become heated. Charges of "straw man," "no evidence," 19 and so on are flung about—which shows that scientists, like everyone, get their egos wrapped up in their work. They believe passionately in their own ideas, even if they are supposed to be calm, cool, dispassionate, and able to evaluate all possibilities evenly. (It is usually in the collective process of argument that the better ideas win out in science; seldom has anyone single-handedly evinced the open-mindedness necessary to drop a pet idea). But nowhere in this *sturm und drang* has any of the participants come close to denying that evolution has occurred.

So the creationists distort. An attack on some parts of Darwin's views 20 is equated with a rejection of evolution. They conveniently ignore that Darwin merely proposed one of many sets of ideas on *how* evolution works. The only real defense against such tactics lies in a true appreciation of the scientific enterprise—the trial-and-error comparison of ideas and how they seem to fit the material universe. If the public were more aware that scientists are expected to disagree, that what a scientist writes today is not the last word, but a progress report on some very intensive thinking and investigation, creationists would be far less successful in injecting an authoritarian system of belief into curricula supposedly devoted to free, open rational inquiry into the nature of natural things.

Topical Considerations

1. Eldredge says in the first paragraph that "we have not progressed" since the Scopes trial of 1925. In what ways does he mean this statement? What kind of evidence does he offer?

2. According to Eldredge, what is the "danger" in viewing science as "authoritarian"? And what is "the real tragedy of American science education" (paragraph 4)?

3. Why isn't creationism science in the author's view? Do you agree with his argument?

4. What point is Eldredge making in paragraphs 7 and 8 when he discusses the physiology of dogs, cats, and monkeys?

5. What does Eldredge say is the "key difference" (paragraph 10) between creationism and evolutionary science?

6. Why is Eldredge opposed to an "equal-time" or a "dual-model" approach to the teaching of human origins in schools?

7. If creationists insist on equal time for the Judeo-Christian explanation of our origins—that is, the account given in Genesis—shouldn't there be equal time for other creation stories, such as those

from ancient Babylon, Persia, India, and China or those endorsed by followers of Islam, Daoism, Hinduism, and Shintoism, not to mention the various tribal accounts of people throughout Africa, Australia, and Polynesia? Why should the Western creation story be the only valid one taught?

8. On what grounds do creationists attack science? How does their attack, in fact, reveal "signs of vitality" in science?

Rhetorical Considerations

1. How does Eldredge define *science* (see paragraph 5)? How does he define *authoritarianism*? Why does he find it necessary to define these terms?

2. This essay is a comparison/contrast argument. Eldredge gives the background of the controversy first; then he examines both creationism and science; and finally, he contrasts the two positions and offers reasons why creationism is not a science and should not have equal time. Outline this essay and see if, in fact, Eldredge gives equal time to each case, balancing one against the other with equivalent space. (You may want to count paragraphs as evidence.)

3. Eldredge is a scientist. He admits that scientists "get their egos wrapped up in their work" (paragraph 19) and may act as if their ideas were absolute truths. Do you think that Eldredge is guilty of this same kind of egoism?

Writing Assignments

1. As Eldredge says, at the heart of creationism is a belief system involving the supernatural. Write a paper arguing that one can believe in God and still endorse evolution. Explain your reasons.

2. Eldredge explains that science differs from creationism on the key point of experimental testing. Science is testable, whereas creationism is not. Write a paper explaining why it is necessary for science to be able to test hypotheses.

3. Do you think creationism can be testable? Write an essay in which you propose some principles by which creationist dogma can be tested.

4. Eldredge says that the American public is "badly informed about the real nature of science" (paragraph 2). Write a paper arguing for or against this claim, citing your own observations and experience. Are you badly informed?

5. In an essay, state your own feelings about giving equal time to creationism in schools.

A Little Banning Is a Dangerous Thing

Loudon Wainwright

It has been said that books are gateways to truth. Not everybody agrees, however, on just what kinds of truths should be available to people—especially to schoolchildren. Within the last few years, the perennial grumblings about censorship have turned into full-scale battlecries, now echoing from coast to coast and from courtroom to courtroom. On one side are vigilantes of the printed word, dedicated to protecting young minds from subversion and perversion. On the other side are guardians of the printed word, who feel that suppression of books is dangerous to education and to democracy itself. Loudon Wainwright, author of *Life* magazine's "The View From Here" column, uses his own childhood experience with a banned book to launch an argument against the censors, who, he says, understand neither children nor the books they condemn.

My own introduction to sex in reading took place about 1935, I 1
think, just when the fertile soil of my young mind was ripe for planting. The exact place it happened (so I've discovered from checking the source in my local library) was the middle of page 249, in a chapter titled "Apples and Ashes," soon after the beginning of Book III of a mildly picaresque novel called *Anthony Adverse.* The boy Anthony, 16, and a well-constructed character named Faith Paleologus ("Her shoulders if one looked carefully were too wide. But so superb was the bosom that rose up to support them. . . .") made it right there in her apartment where he'd gone to take a quick bath, thinking (ho-ho) that she was out.

Faith was Anthony's sitter, sort of, and if author Hervey Allen was just 2
a touch obscure about the details of their moon-drenched meeting, I filled in the gaps. "He was just in time," Allen wrote, "to see the folds of her dress rustle down from her knees into coils at her feet. . . . He stood still, rooted. The faint aroma of her body floated to him. A sudden tide of passion dragged at his legs. . . . He was half blind, and speechless now. All his senses had merged into one feeling. . . . To be supported and yet possessed by an ocean of unknown blue depths below you and to cease to think! Yes, it was something like swimming on a transcendent summer night."

Wow! Praying that my parents wouldn't come home and catch me 3
reading this terrific stuff, I splashed ahead, line after vaguely lubricious line, exhilarated out of my mind at Anthony's good fortune. "After a while he was just drifting in a continuous current of ecstasy that penetrated him as if he were part of the current in which he lay." I still don't understand *that* line, but I sure feel the old surge of depravity. And reading it again, I thank God there was no righteous book banner around

at the time to snatch it from me. *Anthony Adverse* doesn't rank as literature, or even required reading, but I'm convinced it served a useful, even educational, purpose for me at the time.

Alert vigilantes of the printed word worked hard to suppress the novel 4
then. The wretched little war to keep the minds of children clean is always going on. In fact, it has heated up considerably since President Reagan came to power, with libraries around the country reporting a threefold increase in demands that various volumes even less ruinous than *Anthony Adverse* be withdrawn. School boards, too, are feeling the cleansing fire of assorted crusaders against dirty words and irreverent expressions of one sort or another. Protesters range from outraged individual parents to teachers to local ministers to such well-organized watchdog outfits as the Gabler family of Texas, Washington's Heritage Foundation and, of course, the Moral Majority.

The victims are fighting back. Writers are leading public "read-ins" of 5
their banned works. One school board case, which actually dates to 1976, has gone all the way to the U.S. Supreme Court. Before the end of the current term, the court is expected to rule on whether or not the First Amendment rights (to free expression) of five students in Island Trees, N.Y., were denied when the board took nine books out of circulation. A far more personal thrust against censorship was made recently by author Studs Terkel. At the news that his book *Working* was in danger of being banned in Girard, Pa., Terkel went there and standing before the whole school in assembly made his own eloquent case for the book, for the so-called bad language in it and for reading in general. Six weeks later the school board voted unanimously to keep *Working* in the reading program where it had initially been challenged. Presumably they were persuaded, in part at least, that Terkel was *not*, as Kurt Vonnegut wrote in a furious and funny defense of his own *Slaughterhouse-Five,* one of those "sort of ratlike people who enjoy making money from poisoning the minds of young people."

What gets me is the weird presumption that the book banners actually 6
know something about the minds of young people. Vonnegut, among others, suspects that a lot of censors never even get around to reading the books they suppress. And just the briefest scanning of the list of titles currently banned or under threat in various communities call the banners' credentials to rude question. *The Scarlet Letter, The Great Gatsby, A Farewell to Arms, Huckleberry Finn, The Grapes of Wrath* are a few of the variously seminal works challenged as somehow being dangerous to the stability of impressionable young minds. *Mary Poppins* and *The American Heritage Dictionary* have been under attack, too, the former after protests that its black characters were stereotypes, the latter presumably as a storehouse of words that shouldn't be viewed by innocent eyes, much less defined.

More critically, the censors forget, if they ever knew, many of the needs 7 of childhood. One, obviously, is the need for privacy, for a place to get away from the real world, a place where one is safe from—among other things—difficult or boring adult demands. The world that a reader makes is a perfect secret world. But if its topography is shaped by adults pushing their own hardened views of life, the secret world is spoiled.

Yet the world of the young human mind is by no means a comfy   8
habitat, as much as a lot of interfering adults would like to shape it that way. In *The Uses of Enchantment,* Bruno Bettelheim's book about the great importance of folk and fairy tales to child development, the author writes: "There is a widespread refusal to let children know that the source of much that goes wrong in life is due to our very own natures—the propensity of all men for acting aggressively, asocially, selfishly, out of anger and anxiety. Instead, we want our children to believe that, inherently, all men are good. But children know that *they* are not always good; and often, even when they are, they would prefer not to be." In the fantasies commonly churned out in the mind of a normal child, whatever that is, bloody acts of revenge and conquest, daredevil assaults and outlandish wooings are common currency. To achieve the bleak, cramped, sanitized, fear-ridden state of many adults takes years of pruning and repression.

Books, as everyone but the censors know, stimulate growth better than   9
anything—better than sit-coms, better than *Raiders of the Lost Ark,* better than video games. Many books, to be sure, are dreadful heaps of trash. But most of these die quickly in the marketplace or become best-sellers incapable of harming the adults who buy them.

It's often the best books that draw the beadiest attention of the cen-   10
sors. These are the books that really have the most to offer, the news that life is rich and complicated and difficult. Where else, for example, could a young male reader see the isolation of his painful adolescence reflected the way it is in *Catcher in the Rye,* one of the *most* banned books in American letters. In the guise of fiction, books offer opportunities, choices and plausible models. They light up the whole range of human character and emotion. Each, in its own way, tells the truth and prepares its eager readers for the unknown and unpredictable events of their own lives.

Anthony Adverse, my first banned book, was just a huge potboiler of the   11
period. Still, it tickled my fantasy. And it sharpened my appetite for better stuff, like *Lady Chatterley's Lover.* Actually I didn't read that tender and wonderful book until I was almost 50. I wish I'd read it much sooner while we were both still hot.

Topical Considerations

1. Wainwright says that his "introduction to sex in reading" was Hervey Allen's *Anthony Adverse,* and he quotes some of the pertinent passages. Did you find these passages particularly erotic? Explain your

answer. What in the language and/or description might have been cause for a book banner to raise his sword?

2. Why does Wainwright say, "I thank God there was no righteous book banner around at the time to snatch it [*Anthony Adverse*] from me" (paragraph 3)? How do you think the author benefited from having read the book?

3. What link does the author see between the increase in book banning and the Reagan administration?

4. How are some victims of censorship fighting back?

5. The author cites some books that have been banned in various communities around the country, including such American classics as *The Scarlet Letter, The Great Gatsby, A Farewell to Arms, Huckleberry Finn,* and *The Grapes of Wrath.* If you have read any of these books, can you think of any reasons why the censors would have banned them? Do you think the censors actually read the books from cover to cover? or just select passages? or not at all?

6. Wainwright also reports that some censors have even banned *The American Heritage Dictionary* because it defines "words that shouldn't be viewed by innocent eyes" (paragraph 6). Do you think dictionaries should include swear words? Explain your answer. If dirty words were not defined, do you think people would stop using them?

7. Wainwright's chief criticism of censors is their lack of understanding of children's "need for privacy." What is his point here? What don't the censors know about childhood development?

Rhetorical Considerations

1. One good strategy in writing an essay that argues a point is to open it with a personal anecdote that somehow illustrates the issues. How effective is Wainwright's opening anecdote in illustrating what he argues? How much use of the *Anthony Adverse* example does he make throughout the essay? How well does the reference to *Lady Chatterley's Lover* in the last paragraph round off the piece?

2. Exactly where in the essay is Wainwright's thesis statement?

3. How would you characterize the passages quoted from *Anthony Adverse* in terms of their erotic quality—raw? explicit? sensual? abstract? dull? Do you think the ellipses (the strings of periods indicating word omissions) were intended to save space or to avoid printing more salacious passages? Do you think the *Anthony Adverse* passages illustrate the kinds of material that have been wrongly banned?

4. How well structured is this essay? Can you see a clear beginning, middle, and end? Referring to paragraph numbers, where would you make these divisions?

5. How would you characterize the tone of this essay? From the tone and the attitudes of the piece, what kind of man would you say the author is? Does he sound angry and frustrated? arrogant and elitist? reasonable and friendly? Cite passages to substantiate your answer.

Writing Assignments

1. Wainwright talks a little about how a banned book in his childhood helped enrich his childhood fantasies while exposing him to some exhilarating human experiences. Perhaps you can do the same— that is, write about your first exposure to sex in reading. What was it like? What effects did it have on you? Were you scared? exhilarated? baffled? offended? educated in a healthy or unhealthy way?

2. Wainwright points out that some traditional and great American classics have been banned by certain people—even *Mary Poppins* and *The American Heritage Dictionary.* One question that arises is just how far censorship will go and what its consequences could be. Write a paper exploring the potential dangers to democracy that book banning poses.

3. If you disagree with Wainwright—that is, if you sincerely feel that some literary material is detrimental to the healthy development of children and should be banned from schools and libraries—explain your case in an essay. Cite specific titles already on library shelves and explain why you think they pose dangers to children and should therefore be removed.

The Draft: Why the Country Needs It

James Fallows

Following the Soviet invasion of Afghanistan in December 1979, President Carter asked Congress to reinstitute draft registration. By law, all eighteen-year-old males were required to report to their local post offices and register. The registration summoned a lot of signers as well as a lot of protesters who feared another call to war, as in the 1960s. What this essay addresses is not so much military preparedness or the Cold War, but rather how to maintain a selective service system that is fair and decent, unlike that during the Vietnam War, which was racially, economically, and educationally discriminatory. James Fallows is Washington editor of *Atlantic Monthly* and the author of several controversial articles.

I am more than angry. I did not give birth to my one and only son to have him snatched away from me 18 years later. My child has been loved and cared for and taught right from wrong and *will not* be fed into any egomaniac's war machine.

Our 18- to 25-year-olds have not brought this world to its present sorry state. Men over the age of 35, down through the centuries, have brought us here, and we women have been in silent accord.

Well, this is one woman, one mother, who says *no.* I did not go through the magnificent agony of childbirth to have that glorious young life snuffed out.

Until the presidents, premiers, supreme rulers, politburos, senators and congressmen of the world are ready to physically, as opposed to verbally, lead the world into combat, they can bloody well forget my child.

Unite mothers! Don't throw your sons and daughters away. Sometime, somewhere, women have just got to say no.

No. No. No. No. No. Never my child.

—Louise M. Saylor

(Letter published in the Washington *Post,* January 28, 1980.)

Nor my child, Mrs. Saylor. Nor either of my mother's sons when, ten years ago, both were classified I-A. But *whose,* then? As our statesmen talk again of resisting aggression and demonstrating our will—as they talk, that is, of sending someone's sons (or daughters) to bear arms overseas—the only fair and decent answer to that question lies in a return to the draft.

I am speaking here not of the health of the military but of the character of the society the military defends. The circumstances in which that society will choose to go to war, the way its wars will be fought, and its success in absorbing the consequent suffering depend on its answer to the question Whose sons will go?

History rarely offers itself in lessons clear enough to be deciphered at a time when their message still applies. But of all the hackneyed "lessons" of Vietnam, one still applies with no reservations: that we wound ourselves gravely if we flinch from honest answers about who will serve. During the five or six years of the heaviest draft calls for Vietnam, there was the starkest class division in American military service since the days of purchased draft deferments in the Civil War. Good intentions lay at the root of many of these inequities. The college-student deferment, the various "hardship" exemptions, Robert McNamara's plan to give "disadvantaged" youngsters a chance to better themselves in the military, even

General Hershey's intelligence test to determine who could remain in school—all were designed to allot American talent in the most productive way. The intent was to distinguish those who could best serve the nation with their minds from those who should offer their stout hearts and strong backs. The effect was to place the poor and the black in the trenches (and later in the coffins and the rehabilitation wards), and their "betters" in colleges or elsewhere far from the sounds of war. I speak as one who took full advantage of the college-student deferment and later exploited the loopholes in the physical qualification standards that, for college students armed with a doctor's letter and advice from the campus draft counseling center, could so easily be parlayed into the "unfit for service" designation known as a I-Y. Ask anyone who went to college in those days how many of his classmates saw combat in Vietnam. Of my 1200 classmates at Harvard, I know of only two, one of them a veteran who joined the class late. The records show another fifty-five in the reserves, the stateside Army, or military service of some other kind. There may be more; the alumni lists are not complete. See how this compares with the Memorial Roll from a public high school in a big city or a West Virginia hill town.

For all the talk about conflict between "young" and "old" that the war   4
caused, the lasting breach was among the young. In the protest marches on the Pentagon and the Capitol, students felt either scorn for or estrangement from the young soldiers who stood guard. What must the soldiers have felt about these, their privileged contemporaries, who taunted them so? To those who opposed the war, the ones who served were, first, animals and killers; then "suckers" who were trapped by the system, deserving pity but no respect; and finally invisible men. Their courage, discipline, and sacrifice counted for less than their collective taint for being associated with a losing war. A returned veteran might win limited redemption if he publicly recanted, like a lapsed Communist fingering his former associates before the HUAC. Otherwise, he was expected to keep his experiences to himself. Most veterans knew the honor they had earned, even as they knew better than anyone else the horror of the war. They came to resent being made to suppress those feelings by students who chose not to join them and who, having escaped the war without pain, now prefer to put the whole episode in the past. Perhaps no one traversed that era without pain, but pain of the psychic variety left arms, legs, life intact and did not impede progress in one's career. For people of my generation—I speak in the narrow sense of males between the ages of twenty-eight and thirty-six or thirty-seven—this wound will never fully heal. If you doubt that, sit two thirty-two-year-olds down together, one who served in Vietnam and one who did not, and ask them to talk about those years.

At least there was theoretical consistency between what the students   5
of those days recommended for others and what they did themselves.

Their point was that no one should go to war, starting with them. It should also be said that their objection to the war, at least in my view, was important and right. And while they—we—may have proven more effective and determined in acts of individual salvation than in anything else, they at least paid lip service to the idea of the "categorical imperative," that they should not expect others to bear a burden they considered unacceptable for themselves.

I hear little of that tone in the reaction to President Carter's muted call   6
for resumption of draft registration. Within a week of his request in the State of the Union address, I spent time at two small colleges. At both, the sequence of questions was the same. Why is our defense so weak? When will we show the Russians our strength? *Isn't it terrible about the draft?*

Senator Kennedy, who so often decried the unfairness of the draft   7
during Vietnam, won cheers from his college audience for his opposition to draft registration, in the same speech in which he suggested beefing up our military presence in the Persian Gulf. Kennedy did go on to argue that we should not shed blood for oil, which is more than most antidraft groups have done to date. It would have been reassuring to hear the students say that they oppose registration *because* they oppose a military showdown in the Persian Gulf. Instead many simply say, We don't want to go. I sense that they—perhaps all of us—have come to take for granted a truth so painful that few could bear to face it during Vietnam: that there will be another class of people to do the dirty work. After seven years of the volunteer Army, we have grown accustomed to having suckers on hand.

That the volunteer Army is another class can hardly be denied. The   8
Vietnam draft was unfair racially, economically, educationally. By every one of those measures, the volunteer Army is less representative still. Libertarians argue that military service should be a matter of choice, but the plain fact is that service in the volunteer force is too frequently dictated by economics. Army enlisted ranks E1 through E4—the privates and corporals, the cannon fodder, the ones who will fight and die—are 36 percent black now. By the Army's own projections, they will be 42 percent black in three years. When other "minorities" are taken into account, we will have, for the first time, an army whose fighting members are mainly "non-majority," or, more bluntly, a black and brown army defending a mainly white nation. The military has been an avenue of opportunity for many young blacks. They may well be first-class fighting men. They do not represent the nation.

Such a selective bearing of the burden has destructive spiritual effects   9
in a nation based on the democratic creed. But its practical implications can be quite as grave. The effect of a fair, representative draft is to hold the public hostage to the consequences of its decisions, much as children's presence in the public schools focuses parents' attention on the quality of the schools. If citizens are willing to countenance a decision

that means that *someone's* child may die, they may contemplate more deeply if there is the possibility that the child will be theirs. Indeed, I would like to extend this principle even further. Young men of nineteen are rightly suspicious of the congressmen and columnists who urge them to the fore. I wish there were a practical way to resurrect the provisions of the amended Selective Service Act of 1940, which raised the draft age to forty-four. Such a gesture might symbolize the desire to offset the historic injustice of the Vietnam draft, as well as suggest the possibility that, when a bellicose columnist recommends dispatching American forces to Pakistan, he might also realize that he could end up as a gunner in a tank.

Perhaps the absence of a World War II-scale peril makes such a pro-   10
posal unrealistic; still, the columnist or congressman should have to contemplate the possibility that his son would be there, in trench or tank. Under the volunteer Army that possibility will not arise, and the lack of such a prospect can affect behavior deeply. Recall how, during Vietnam, protest grew more broad-based and respectable when the graduate school deferment was eliminated in 1968. For many families in positions of influence, the war was no longer a question of someone else's son. How much earlier would the war have ended had college students been vulnerable from the start?

Those newly concerned families were no better and no worse than   11
other people at other times; they were responding to a normal human instinct, of the sort our political system is designed to channel toward constructive ends. It was an instinct that Richard Nixon and Henry Kissinger understood very well, as they deliberately shifted the burden of the war off draftees and finally off Americans, to free their hands to pursue their chosen course. Recall how fast protest ebbed with the coming of the volunteer Army and "Vietnamization" in the early 1970s. For this reason, the likes of Nixon and Kissinger might regard a return to the draft as a step in the wrong direction, for it would sap the resolve necessary for a strong foreign policy and introduce the weakening element of domestic dissent. At times leaders must take actions that seem heartless and unfair, and that an informed public would probably not approve. Winston Churchill let Coventry be bombed, because to sound the air-raid sirens and save its citizens would have tipped off the Germans that Britain had broken their code. But in the long run, a nation cannot sustain a policy whose consequences the public is not willing to bear. If it decides not to pay the price to defend itself, it will be defenseless. That is the risk of democracy.

What kind of draft? More than anything else, a *fair* one, with as few   12
holes as possible to wriggle through. The 1971 Selective Service Act, passed when the heavy draft calls had already ended, theoretically closed most of the loopholes. But if real trouble should begin, those nine-year-old patches might give way before political pressures unless we concen-

trate again on the mechanics of an equitable draft. "Fairness" does not mean that everyone need serve. This year 4.3 million people will turn eighteen, 2.2 million women and 2.1 million men. For the last few years, the military has been taking 400,000 people annually into the volunteer Army—or, in raw figures, only one in ten of the total available pool. Using today's mental and physical standards, the military knocks off 30 percent of the manpower pool as unqualified, and it excludes women from combat positions. When these calculations are combined with the diminishing number of young men—only 1.6 million men will turn eighteen in 1993 —the military projects that it will need to attract one of every three "qualified and available men" by the end of the 1980s.

Read another way, this means that a draft need affect *no more* than one in three—and probably far fewer. To make the draft seem—and be—fair, the pool of potential draftees should be as large as possible, even if only a few will eventually be picked. Those who are "disabled" in the common meaning of that term—the blind, paraplegics—should be excluded, but not the asthmatics and trick-back cases who are perfectly capable of performing non-combat military jobs. The military's physical requirements now assume that nearly all men must theoretically be fit for combat, even though only 14 percent of all male soldiers hold combat jobs. The proportion of draftees destined for combat would probably be higher, since those are the positions now most understrength; if actual fighting should begin it would be higher still. But combat will never represent the preponderance of military positions, and its requirements should not blindly dictate who is eligible for the draft. Instead, everyone without serious handicap should be eligible for selection by lottery—men and women, students and non-students. Once the lottery had determined *who* would serve, assignments based on physical classifications could determine where and how.   13

The question of women's service is the most emotionally troubling aspect of this generally emotional issue, but the progress of domestic politics over the last ten years suggests that the answer is clear. If any sexual distinctions that would deny a woman her place as a construction worker or a telephone pole climber have been forbidden by legislators and courts, what possible distinction can spare women the obligation to perform similar functions in military construction units or the Signal Corps? President Carter recognized this reality in deciding to include women in his initial draft registration order. If women are drafted, they have an iron-clad case for passage of the Equal Rights Amendment. If they are not, their claim for equal treatment elsewhere becomes less compelling. At the same time, it is troubling to think of women in combat, or of mothers being drafted, and a sensible draft law would have to recognize such exceptions.   14

There should be no educational deferments except for students still in high school, and possibly in two other cases. One would be for college   15 students who enroll in ROTC; like their counterparts in the service academies, they would be exchanging four years of protected education for a longer tour of duty as an officer after graduation. The other exception might be for doctors, possessors of a skill the military needs but cannot sensibly produce on its own. If potential doctors wanted to be spared all eligibility for the draft, they could enter a program like the Navy's V-12 during World War II, in which they could take a speeded-up college course and receive a publicly subsidized medical education, after which they would owe several years' service as military doctors. Except in the most far-fetched situations, "hardship" cases should be taken care of by compensation rather than by exemption. If these are permitted, they become an invitation to abuse: who can forget George Hamilton pleading hardship as his mother's sole supporting son? Instead, the government should offset hardship with support payments to the needy dependents.

One resists the idea of lottery, because it adds to the system the very   16
element of caprice and unfairness it is so important to remove. But since only a fraction of those eligible to serve are actually required, there seems no other equitable way to distribute the burden. With a well-established lottery, every male and female might know at age eighteen whether he or she was near the top of the list and very likely to be called, or near the bottom and almost certainly protected. How far the draft calls went down the list would depend on how many people volunteered and how many more were needed.

None of these concerns and prescriptions would matter if the volun-   17
teer Army were what it so often seemed in the last few years—a stand-in, a symbol, designed to keep the machinery running and the troops in place, not to be sent into action for any cause less urgent than absolute survival. But now we hear from every quarter that the next decade will be a time of testing, that our will and our strategy and our manpower will be on the line. The nature of this challenge, and the style of our response, are what we should be thinking and talking about now. Our discussions will never be honest, nor our decisions just, as long as we count on "suckers" to do the job.

Topical Considerations

1. How effective is Fallows's use of Mrs. Saylor's letter as an epigraph to his essay? Does he answer her protests convincingly?

2. According to Fallows, what was unfair about the draft system during the Vietnam War?

3. What does the author say about the way Vietnam War soldiers were regarded by those at home who opposed the war? What is Fallows's point?

4. Fallows argues that the country needs the draft. Is his call for it based on a need for a strong military preparedness or for a more equitable system than what exists?

5. Would you say that James Fallows is a political liberal or a conservative? Defend your answer with evidence from his essay.

6. What is Fallows's chief criticism of the young people who oppose the draft (paragraph 7)? Is he saying that they are naive? hypocritical? cowardly? self-serving? or what?

7. How does Fallows feel about an all-volunteer Army? Is he for or against it?

8. What kind of draft system would Fallows like to see?

9. What is Fallows's stand regarding women and a military draft?

Rhetorical Considerations

1. In paragraph 3, Fallows tells us that he got a student deferment from the draft while he was at Harvard. How does this admission affect his argument in the essay? Does it weaken it or strengthen it?

2. Fallows cites statistics in paragraphs 8 and 12. How do these statistics serve his case? Should he have given more or less?

3. What is the point of the Churchill allusion in paragraph 11? How effectively does it serve the argument Fallows makes here?

4. How would you describe the tone of this essay? Does Fallows display any anger or outrage?

Writing Assignments

1. If you are opposed to a military draft, write a paper explaining your reasons.

2. If you are in favor of a military draft, write a paper explaining your reasons.

3. Fallows does not say much about the all-volunteer Army first implemented in the early 1970s, but he does say that it is not representative of the nation, since the makeup of the Army is dictated by economics. The implication is that decisions about the use of the volunteer Army could not be made democratically unless every social class was represented. Write a paper in which you propose how the all-volunteer Army could be made more representative.

4. Write a paper in which you argue that women should or should not be subject to a military draft.

5. Write a paper in which you argue for or against a universal draft—that is, one that would make mandatory two years of military service for men and women between the ages of 18 and 26.

Nothing About the Draft Makes Sense

William Grieder

Several years have passed since Congress reinstituted draft registration. The following essay by Washington writer William Grieder takes a look at the success of draft registration. Grieder concludes that it has turned into a "national joke," since it hasn't scared the Russians—and needn't scare Americans. He says that the likelihood of restoring a peacetime draft is remote, for to do so would be dangerous.

1   When the government issued its cattle call for the cold war in July 1980, it assumed that every eighteen-year-old male, save for a few malcontents and backwoods cranks, would dutifully report to the post office and register for the draft. After all, he only had to sign a card telling the government where he lives. This wasn't a real draft or mobilization for a real war. It was a cheap way to bluster at the Russians and show them America is at the ready.

2   Now, two years later, draft registration has degenerated into a national joke. Instead of a symbolic gesture of strength, it resembles a lame exercise in nostalgia, attempting to recreate the great struggle between citizens and government during the war in Vietnam. Only this struggle, I'm afraid, is hollow, the moral equivalent of shadowboxing.

3   On one side, the government huffs and puffs and threatens. It is staging a series of show trials to scare the offenders. It is creating a maze of bureaucratic machinery to snoop by computer and locate violators. On the other side, a national resistance movement has blossomed, with networks of committees and coalitions campaigning passionately against a nonexistent draft, flying squads of defense lawyers, even a fledgling underground of fugitive resisters.

4   Registration is not working. For whatever reasons, hundreds of thousands are not signing up. Collectively, they confront the government with one of the grossest episodes of mass defiance of the law since Americans decided to drink their way through Prohibition. In this case as well, the only practical solution is repeal.

5   The Selective Service likes to look on the bright side: 8 million young men, eighteen to twenty years old, have registered. But that evades the monstrous law-enforcement problem that draft registration has created. Even the government concedes that nearly 700,000 eligible men have declined to register. The entire war in Vietnam produced only an estimated 570,000 draft evaders.

6   But there are more: another million men, based on census estimates, are violators because they have moved since registering and have failed

to notify the government of their new addresses, which is also a felony. That makes roughly 1.7 million eligible for prosecution. Since federal prisons only hold about 28,000, it's going to be a tight squeeze.

None of this is necessary. Draft registration was dreamed up by Jimmy   7 Carter back in early 1980 as a symbolic gesture in response to the Soviet invasion of Afghanistan. The Commies were supposed to shudder when they saw American youth streaming into their post offices. Ronald Reagan, espousing his best libertarian values while running for president, denounced the gimmick and promised to scrap it.

The external evidence suggests that Reagan *almost* kept his word. By   8 the early winter of 1981, when the Justice Department was prepared to indict the first crop of unregistered young men, the White House told the prosecutors to hold off. Reagan was still evaluating the system. If registration were going to be junked, it made no sense to send a few to jail. A few days later, martial law was imposed in Poland, and the cold warriors concluded it was no time for faint hearts. The next month, Reagan embraced the registration scheme—and now he is stuck with it.

So far, four resisters have been indicted and one convicted—all young   9 men who have been most out front in articulating their opposition to registration and the draft. Given the legal flaws in how the registration system was implemented and the moral arguments that some conscientious objectors will offer in defense, it is not at all certain the feds will win convictions in every case. Even if a handful go to prison, it's not clear that the hundreds of thousands of others will be frightened into registering. Because the defendants are all visible opponents of the system, willing to stand trial and voice their principles, the unintended message from their prosecutions may be: keep your mouth shut, and the government won't mess with you.

Back in April, the president's Military Manpower Task Force held a   10 meeting at the Pentagon, with Defense Secretary Caspar Weinberger presiding, to discuss the delicate problem of prosecuting draft resisters. A transcript of that private meeting, later unearthed by George Wilson of the *Washington Post,* revealed both the flippancy of the president's advisers and their fear that the draft trials might inflame public opinion against the cold-war program.

"When is the first felony prosecution planned?" John Herrington,   11 assistant navy secretary for manpower, asked.

"You want to be there?" presidential counselor Edwin Meese wise-   12 cracked.

"You should be on *Phil Donahue,* John," said Selective Service Director   13 Thomas Turnage.

The ensuing conversation showed they were bothered by the potential   14 for bad headlines. Herrington worried that perhaps the draft trials would add fuel to the growing antinuclear movement in the country. Turnage suggested that maybe the Justice Department could give light sentences as a way to soften the controversy. Meese said the kids would still have to face felony convictions. Finally, Herrington proposed that they keep the trials as quiet as possible. Bring the young men to the bar of justice in out-of-the-way places, he said, like Omaha, where there will be less national news coverage.

The first trial was held in Roanoke, Virginia—not exactly a center of   15 media coverage—but the government has failed to arrange for quiet cases. A young Christian named Enten Eller, whose pure religious scruples made bad press for the prosecutor, was convicted and sentenced to three years' probation, and instructed to register within ninety days. Eller says he will not register, which means he faces up to six years in prison and a fine of up to $10,000.

Meanwhile, the wonders of bureaucracy (which Ronald Reagan pro-   16 mised to eliminate) are at work, tracking down offenders, in case the prosecutions don't work. The Selective Service bought a million names from a Long Island mail-order house and sent out warning letters to people who were thought to be nonregistrants. The names included a three-year-old girl and a ten-year-old beagle. Even Turnage admits it was a flop.

Next, with approval from Congress, Selective Service began delving   17 into forbidden government records—social security rolls and the Internal Revenue Service's tax returns—trying to match names and addresses and birthdays. The IRS, which is a more intimidating agency than Selective Service, intends to send threatening letters to 250,000 young men.

That won't work either, probably, so Congress is preparing to enact   18 a provision that means real hard-ball for college students—it is threatening to cut off federal loans or scholarships from anyone who hasn't registered. Counselor Meese liked this idea when Turnage proposed it at the April task-force meeting. "You could have a line on each of the applications: have you registered for the draft?" Meese enthused. "And if they put no, then you withhold their benefits. If they put yes, then you get a few that have done it fraudulently; you kick them off their benefits and prosecute them."

The idea passed the House of Representatives 303 to 95, and final   19 passage seems most likely. Let's root out the laggards and show the Commies we mean business. So the enforcement machinery grows like a malignant weed—first Selective Service and the Justice Department, then the Social Security Administration and the IRS, now the Department of Education and every college and university that manages federal aid to students. All must be engaged in this meaningless search for bodies —bodies the government doesn't want or need. Thanks to Reagan's recession, the all-volunteer armed forces are filling their quotas for manpower. Indeed, they are turning them away at the recruiting stations. Even the most agitated cold warriors will concede: the return of the draft is not imminent.

But Paul Jacob thought otherwise when he left his home in Little Rock, Arkansas, on July 4th, 1981, leaving no forwarding address. A lanky twenty-two-year-old with curly brown hair, former chairman of the Arkansas Libertarian party, Jacob dropped out of college and enlisted as perhaps the movement's first "underground" resister. The Selective Service sent him a threatening letter, and the FBI has come around to ask his family where he is. They don't know. For the past year, Jacob has moved around the country, talking to college groups, working at odd jobs, making the point that it's fairly easy to avoid prosecution if you are mobile and semisecretive. 20

"It's important to show seventeen-year-olds and eighteen-year-olds who are about to register that you can resist being a slave to the military," Jacob said. "If the choice is between jail and the draft, then eighteen-year-olds have nowhere to go, but . . . there's a much better alternative. That is simply to move away from home and not leave a forwarding address. I've been away from home for a year now, and I've been a public resister and I'm still free. So, obviously, anyone who's been a quiet nonregistrant has nothing to fear." 21

The resistance movement, composed of hundreds of local groups, is an interesting mix of youthful libertarians and lefty radicals, pacifists and church groups, and older veterans from the antiwar movement. Jacob is connected with the National Resistance Committee, which actively urges young men not to sign up. Other organizations, like Draft Action, merely counsel and defend. 22

"Some of the resisters are planning on voluntarily turning themselves over to federal prosecutors," Jacob said. "If they take me to court, I'm not going to walk in. They're going to have to drag me in. This is not a voluntary situation. This is the government coercing young people into possibly fighting and killing and maybe dying for the U.S. government." 23

Jacob says he learned his politics as an adolescent watching TV—the horror shows of Vietnam and Watergate—but obviously his political sensibilities are more acute than most of the other 1.7 million violators. Draft Action's Barry Lynn, a leading antidraft activist who also battled the Vietnam draft ten years ago, finds an extraordinary seriousness and knowledge among many of those who choose not to sign. Then there are many others, he said, who simply "view this thing as a kind of joke. If it's so damned important, why did it take the government so long to get around to indicting the first guy?" 24

The premise of the resistance movement is that registration is only the first step in softening up young people and conditioning them to accept the real draft. To stop the draft, first stop the registration. They argue 25 further that the way the registration law is written, the time for ethical objections to induction has been greatly foreshortened. If Congress enacts a draft law, the induction notices could go out within forty-eight hours, and ten days later, the unlucky losers in the draft lottery would have to report for physicals. Not much time, in other words, to plead for hardship status or wrestle with one's conscience.

Both claims have some validity. In 1979, when Congress was tinkering   26
with the idea of registration, the army chief of staff, General Bernard Rogers, told a Senate committee: "Because of the antipathy of so many in this country for the selective service system, that system being equated to the draft and the draft being anathema to so many, is why I suggest the evolutionary approach. First, to start to register and get us accustomed to that . . . then commence to classification . . . then, third, start to draft for the Individual Ready Reserve."

Despite the general's wishful thinking, however, the political climate   27
for bringing back the draft has not improved since 1979—it's gotten much worse. Certainly, the fouled-up registration has contributed to that (and the resisters are entitled to a share of the credit). But the more fundamental change is the public hostility to the foreign adventures talked up by the Reagan administration. When the trial balloon was going up for U.S. troop involvement in El Salvador, the public reacted in horror, and the president backed away from the idea. That was a clear signal to hawkish politicians of both parties that restoring the draft law would be an explosive step, certain to ignite domestic turmoil. Meanwhile, it has become clear that the draft isn't needed to solve the military's real manpower shortages, which are in the higher enlisted grades of technical experts, pilots and commanders.

The restoration of a peacetime draft would, indeed, be dangerous.   28
The absence of a draft acts as a political firebreak against adventurous involvement in foreign wars. The Pentagon wouldn't want to fight one without a draft. If Congress had had to enact a new draft law in 1964, instead of passing the deceitfully vague Gulf of Tonkin Resolution, our nation might not have gone deeper into the Big Muddy of Indochina. The next time, if a president wants to restore conscription, he should be forced to produce a more compelling purpose than filling out the military's manpower tables.

Antidraft advocate Barry Lynn agrees that the likelihood of restored   29
conscription is much more remote today than it was a few years ago, but he argues that resistance to registration serves as a crucial "brake on the draft, just as the draft is a brake on the kind of intervention we all oppose."

I'm not convinced it works that way. If this president or the next one   30
stumbles into a foreign crisis and persuades the nation to go to war again, then I expect Congress would swiftly enact a new draft law—regardless of how screwed up the present registration is. Actually, I suspect the

present system would be scrapped and Selective Service would start over again with old-fashioned draft cards. At that point, every eligible young man would face his own heavy choice.

Despite the inflated rhetoric of resistance, however, no one is really at   31 that point now. Unless we are willing to debase the meaning of words, signing a card at the post office is not oppression. It is not slavery. It may be dumb, but it is not an infringement of liberty. Sorry, boys, the Sixties are over.

If an eighteen-year-old asked me, I would advise him to go ahead and   32 sign the little card. The act of registration has less meaning than both sides in this struggle are assigning to it. It doesn't scare the Russians. And it needn't scare Americans either.

I am making a distinction that many of the resisters will regard as too   33 precious, but I think the moral claim of civil disobedience should not be casually invoked. Otherwise, we could all stop paying taxes on the ethical grounds that we don't like the way the government spends our money. The act of civil disobedience, it seems to me, must be proportionate to the offense against liberty, aimed at a wrongful law that really is oppressive. The racial-segregation laws were evil and the civil-rights demonstrators who willfully violated them were protected by their higher moral purpose. Draft resisters during the war in Vietnam, whether they went to jail or to Canada, had a morally authentic claim, refusing to serve or kill in a war that was wrong. Signing a card at the post office does not present a comparable moral choice. Of course, if a young man wants to throw his body at this stupid system and add his number to the mass violations, the odds are with him. It's very unlikely that he will ever be sent to jail. But I think there are more effective ways for him to influence politics and politicians than by going "underground." For starters, he might try voting.

Topical Considerations

1. What do you think James Fallows would say about Grieder's stand on the draft here? Are there points on which they agree? Where do they essentially disagree?

2. According to Grieder, why was the draft registration idea "dreamed up"?

3. Grieder says in paragraph 2 that the draft registration "has degenerated into a national joke." According to the author, how is it not working?

4. Of all the measures the Reagan administration took to get nonregistrants to register, what was the most intimidating? Why?

5. What does Grieder say about the all-volunteer army?

6. How would you classify Grieder politically? Is he a conserva-

tive? a liberal? a radical? a libertarian? Cite evidence to support your answer.

7. In paragraph 28, Grieder says that "restoration of a peacetime draft would . . . be dangerous." According to Grieder, why would this be so?

Rhetorical Considerations

1. Explain the allusion in Grieder's phrase, "the moral equivalent of shadowboxing" (paragraph 2).

2. How does Grieder mean "the Commies" in paragraph 7? What is his tone here?

3. How good is Grieder's evidence that the registration system is "fouled up"?

4. The author makes extensive use of the Paul Jacob example. How effective and comprehensive is this example?

5. Do you think Grieder presents a reasonable, well-argued, and well-documented case here? Explain.

6. Discuss the effectiveness of Grieder's last line in summarizing his thesis.

Writing Assignments

1. What are your feelings about registering for the draft? Do you regard registration as a national obligation or an act of coercement? Do you think, as Grieder does, that draft registration in peacetime is dangerous? Explain your feelings.

2. Toward the end of his essay, Grieder brings up the issue of civil disobedience. He cites civil rights demonstrators and Vietnam draft resisters, all of whom he thought were morally right in their civil disobedience. Can you think of any social causes that would lead you to acts of civil disobedience? Which ones, and why?

3. What are your feelings about women having to register for the draft? Write a paper in which you explore this issue; state your opinions and your reasons for them.

WAR AND PEACE IN THE NUCLEAR AGE

6

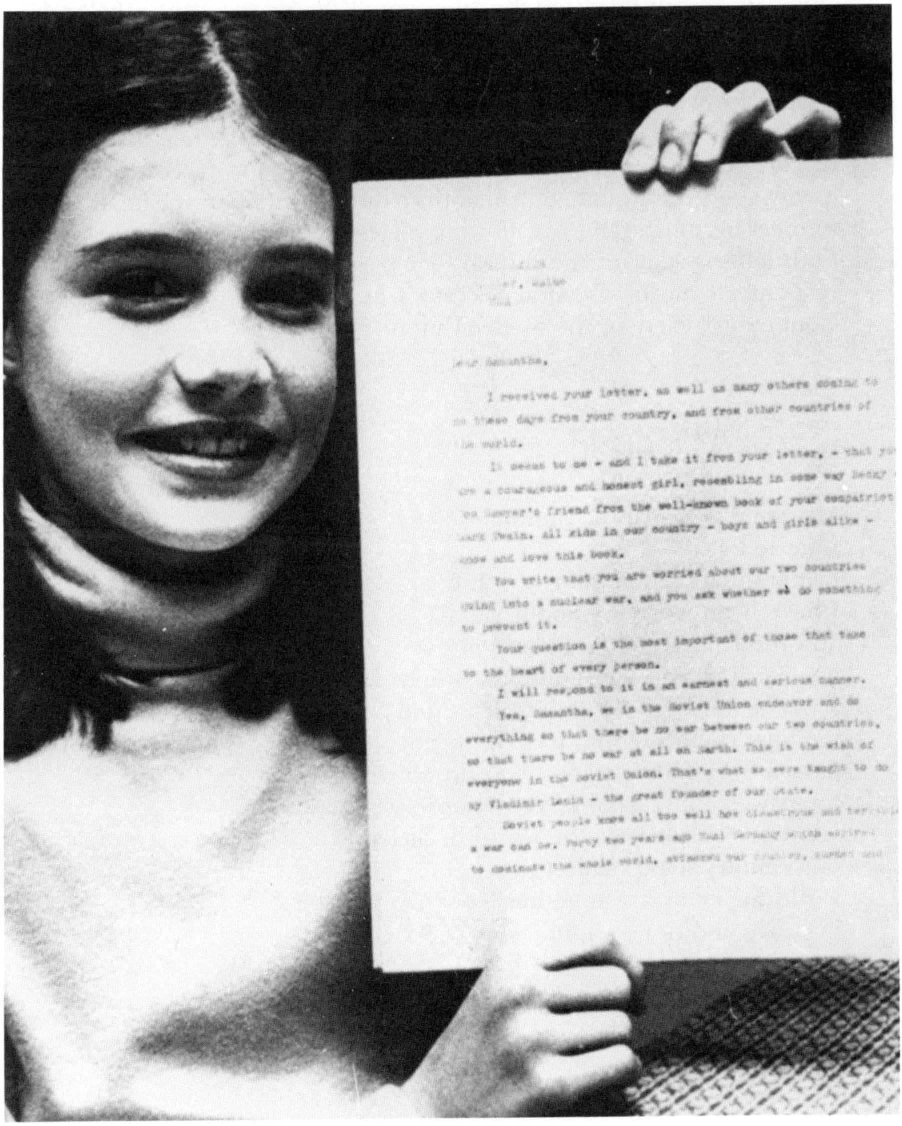

Early in 1983, Samantha Smith, the 10-year-old girl in the photograph on the preceding page, sent a brief letter to Yuri V. Andropov, the new head of the Soviet Communist party. In her note, she congratulated Andropov on his new job, left vacant when former chairman Leonid Brezhnev died. Although Samantha's letter was one of hundreds the Soviet leader regularly receives from people around the world, excerpts of Samantha's letter were printed in the Soviet Communist party newspaper, *Pravda*. What apparently attracted the attention of *Pravda* was Samantha's asking Andropov if he wanted to have a nuclear war with America and why he wanted to conquer the world. In a few weeks, Samantha received a response from Andropov himself. She immediately became a celebrity—her story becoming news around the world. In July 1983, at the invitation of Yuri Andropov, Samantha and her parents spent two weeks touring the Soviet Union, although, to Samantha's disappointment, she never did get to meet her host. On the following pages we have reprinted the texts of both letters—that of the fifth-grader from Manchester, Maine, and the response from the General Secretary of the Central Committee of the Communist Party of the Soviet Union.

Dear Mr. Andropov,

My name is Samantha Smith.
I am ten years old.
Congratulations on your new job.
I have been worrying about Russia
and the United States getting into a
nuclear war. Are you going to vote to have
a war or not? If you aren't please tell
me how you are going to help to not
have a war. This question you do not have
to answer, but I would like to know why
you want to conquer the world or at least
our country. God made the
world for us to live together
in peace and not to fight.

Sincerely,

Samantha Smith

Samantha SMITH
Manchester, Maine
    USA

Dear Samantha,

I received your letter, as well as many others coming to me these days from your country, and from other countries of the world.

It seems to me—and I take it from your letter,—that you are a courageous and honest girl, resembling in some way Becky—Tom Sawyer's friend from the well-known book of your compatriot Mark Twain. All kids in our country—boys and girls alike—know and love this book.

You write that you are worried about our two countries going into a nuclear war, and you ask whether we do something to prevent it.

Your question is the most important of those that take to the heart of every person.

I will respond to it in an earnest and serious manner.

Yes, Samantha, we in the Soviet Union endeavor and do everything so that there be no war between our two countries, so that there be no war at all on Earth. This is the wish of everyone in the Soviet Union. That's what we were taught to do by Vladimir Lenin—the great founder of our State.

Soviet people know all too well how disastrous and terrible a war can be. Forty two years ago Nazi Germany which aspired to dominate the whole world, attacked our country, burned and destroyed thousands and thousands of our cities and villages, killed millions of Soviet men, women and children.

In that war, which ended by our victory, we were allies with the United States, we fought together to liberate many nations from the Nazi invaders. I hope you know this from your history lessons at school. Today, we want very much to live in peace, to trade and to cooperate with all our neighbors on the globe, no matter how close or far away they are, and, certainly, with such a great country as the United States of America.

America has—as well as we do—a frightful weapon which can instantly annihilate millions of people. However, we do not want this weapon to be ever used. That is why the Soviet Union solemnly declared to the world that it will never—but never!—be the first to use nuclear weapons against any country. As a matter of fact, we propose in general that an end be put to the further production of this weapon and that the elimination be started of all its stockpiles on Earth.

I believe this is a sufficient reply to your second question, e.g. "Why do you want to conquer the world or at least the United States?" We want nothing of the kind. Nobody in our vast and beautiful country—workers or peasants, writers or doctors, children or grown-ups, or members of the government—wants war, be it big or "small".

We want peace, we have a lot to do: to grow grain, to build, to invent, to write books and to make space flights. We want peace for ourselves and for all people of the planet, for our own kids and for you, Samantha.

I invite you, if your parents can let you go, to come visit us, best of all in summer. You will get to know our country, will meet children of your age, spend time on the seashore in a youngsters' camp called "Artek", where school-children of our and other lands come to spend their vacations. And you will see for yourself: everybody in the Soviet Union stands for peace and friendship among nations.

Thank you for your congratulations. I wish you all the best in your life that you only began to live.

Y. ANDROPOV

Atomic War or Peace

Albert Einstein

It seems appropriate to open this section on the nuclear age with a statement
by a man who was directly responsible for it. Albert Einstein (1879–1955) was
one of the greatest scientific minds that ever lived. It was his theory of
relativity, published early in this century, that revolutionized physics and thus
paved the way to the nuclear age. Yet it is one of the great ironies of history
that this same genius who gave us the formula for atomic fission, $E = MC^2$,
was also an outspoken pacificist. In fact, it was partly because of his
pacificism that Einstein was not made part of the scientific team that worked
on the Manhattan Project, the code name for the development and
construction of the first atomic bomb (1940–1945). On August 6, 1945, the first
atomic bomb used in warfare was dropped on Hiroshima, Japan. Three days
later, a second atomic bomb fell on Nagasaki. A quarter of a million people
died, and the nuclear age was born. The following essay is the first public
statement on the atomic bomb by Albert Einstein, made in October of that
year. Despite the passage of almost 40 years, Einstein's fears and hopes
regarding atomic power are terribly current.

The release of atomic energy has not created a new problem. It 1
has merely made more urgent the necessity of solving an existing one.
One could say that it has affected us quantitatively, not qualitatively. As
long as there are sovereign nations possessing great power, war is inevitable. This does not mean that one can know when war will come but only
that one is sure that it will come. This was true even before the atomic
bomb was made. What has changed is the destructiveness of war.

I do not believe that the secret of the bomb should be given to the 2
United Nations Organization. I do not believe it should be given to the
Soviet Union. Either course would be analogous to a man with capital
who, wishing another individual to collaborate with him on an enterprise,
starts by giving him half his money. The other man might choose to start
a rival enterprise, when what is wanted is his co-operation. The secret of
the bomb should be committed to a world government, and the United
States should immediately announce its readiness to do so. Such a world
government should be established by the United States, the Soviet Union
and Great Britain, the only three powers which possess great military
strength. The three of them should commit to this world government all
of their military resources. The fact that there are only three nations with
great military power should make it easier, rather than harder, to establish a world government.

Since the United States and Great Britain have the secret of the atomic 3
bomb and the Soviet Union does not, they should invite the Soviet Union
to prepare and present the first draft of a Constitution for the proposed
world government. This would help dispel the distrust of the Russians,
which they feel because they know the bomb is being kept a secret chiefly

to prevent their having it. Obviously, the first draft would not be the final one, but the Russians should be made to feel that the world government will guarantee their security.

It would be wise if this Constitution were to be negotiated by one 4
American, one Briton and one Russian. They would, of course, need advisers, but these advisers should serve only when asked. I believe three men can succeed in preparing a workable Constitution acceptable to all the powers. Were six or seven men, or more, to attempt to do so, they would probably fail. After the three great powers have drafted a Constitution and adopted it, the smaller nations should be invited to join the world government. They should also be free not to join and, though they should feel perfectly secure outside the world government, I am sure they will eventually wish to join. Naturally, they should be entitled to propose changes in the Constitution as drafted by the Big Three. But the Big Three should go ahead and organize the world government, whether or not the smaller nations decide to join.

Such a world government should have jurisdiction over all military 5
matters, and it need have only one other power. That is the power to interfere in countries where a minority is oppressing the majority and, therefore, is creating the kind of instability that leads to war. For example, conditions such as exist today in Argentina and Spain should be dealt with. There must be an end to the concept of non-intervention, for to abandon non-intervention in certain circumstances is part of keeping the peace.

The establishment of a world government should not be delayed until 6
similar conditions of freedom exist in each of the three great powers. While it is true that in the Soviet Union the minority rules, I do not believe that the internal conditions in that country constitute a threat to world peace. One must bear in mind that the people in Russia had not had a long tradition of political education; changes to improve conditions in Russia had to be effected by a minority for the reason that there was no majority capable of doing so. If I had been born a Russian, I believe I could have adjusted myself to this situation.

It should not be necessary, in establishing a world government with a 7
monopoly of authority over military affairs, to change the internal structure of the three great powers. It would be for the three individuals who draft the Constitution to devise ways for collaboration despite the different structures of their countries.

Do I fear the tyranny of a world government? Of course I do. But I fear 8
still more the coming of another war. Any government is certain to be evil to some extent. But a world government is preferable to the far greater evil of wars, particularly when viewed in the context of the intensified destructiveness of war. If such a world government is not established by a process of agreement among nations, I believe it will come anyway, and in a much more dangerous form; for war or wars can only result in one

power being supreme and dominating the rest of the world by its over-whelming military supremacy.

Now that we have the atomic secret, we must not lose it, and that is   9
what we would risk doing if we gave it to the United Nations Organization or to the Soviet Union. But, as soon as possible, we must make it clear that we are not keeping the bomb a secret for the sake of maintaining our power but in the hope of establishing peace through world government, and that we will do our utmost to bring this world government into being.

I appreciate that there are persons who approve of world government   10
as the ultimate objective but favor a gradual approach to its establish-ment. The trouble with taking little steps, one at a time, in the hope of eventually reaching the ultimate goal, is that while such steps are being taken, we continue to keep the bomb without convincing those who do not have the bomb of our ultimate intentions. That of itself creates fear and suspicion, with the consequence that the relations between rival countries deteriorate to a dangerous extent. That is why people who advocate taking a step at a time may think they are approaching world peace, but they actually are contributing by their slow pace to the possi-bility of war. We have no time to waste in this way. If war is to be averted, it must be done quickly.

Further, we shall not have the secret of the bomb for very long. I know   11
it is being argued that no other country has money enough to spend on the development of the atomic bomb and that, therefore, we are assured of the secret for a long time. But it is a common mistake in this country to measure things by the amount of money they cost. Other countries which have the raw materials and manpower and wish to apply them to the work of developing atomic power can do so; men and materials and the decision to use them, and not money, are all that is needed.

I do not consider myself the father of the release of atomic energy. My   12
part in it was quite indirect. I did not, in fact, foresee that it would be released in my time. I only believed that it was theoretically possible. It became practical through the accidental discovery of chain reaction, and this was not something I could have predicted. It was discovered by Hahn in Berlin, and he himself at first misinterpreted what he discovered. It was Lise Meitner who provided the correct interpretation and escaped from Germany to place the information in the hands of Niels Bohr.

In my opinion, a great era of atomic science cannot be assured by   13
organizing science in the way large corporations are organized. One can organize the application of a discovery already made, but one cannot organize the discovery itself. Only a free individual can make a discovery. However, there can be a kind of organization wherein the scientist is assured freedom and proper conditions of work. Professors of science in American universities, for instance, should be relieved of some of their teaching so as to have more time for research. Can you imagine an organization of scientists making the discoveries of Charles Darwin?

I do not believe that the vast private corporations of the United States   14
are suitable to the needs of the times. If a visitor should come to this
country from another planet, would he not find it strange that, in this
country, private corporations are permitted to wield so much power
without having to assume commensurate responsibility? I say this to
stress my conviction that the American government must retain control
of atomic energy, not because socialism is necessarily desirable but because atomic energy was developed by the government; it would be
unthinkable to turn over this property of the people to any individual or
group of individuals. As for socialism, unless it is international to the
extent of producing a world government which controls all military
power, it might lead to wars even more easily than capitalism because it
represents an even greater concentration of power.

To give any estimate as to when atomic energy might be applied for   15
peaceful, constructive purposes is impossible. All that we know now is
how to use a fairly large quantity of uranium. The use of small quantities,
sufficient, say, to operate a car or an airplane, is thus far impossible, and
one cannot predict when it will be accomplished. No doubt, it will be
achieved, but no one can say when. Nor can one predict when materials
more common than uranium can be used to supply atomic energy. Presumably, such materials would be among the heavier elements of high
atomic weight and would be relatively scarce due to their lesser stability.
Most of these materials may already have disappeared through radioactive disintegration. So, though the release of atomic energy can be, and
no doubt will be, a great boon to mankind, this may not come about for
some time.

I myself do not have the gift of explanation which would be needed   16
to persuade large numbers of people of the urgency of the problems that
now face the human race. Hence, I should like to commend someone who
has this gift of explanation: Emery Reves, whose book *The Anatomy of Peace*
is intelligent, clear, brief, and, if I may use the absurd term, dynamic on
the topic of war and need for world government.

Since I do not foresee that atomic energy will prove to be a boon within   17
the near future, I have to say that, for the present, it is a menace. Perhaps
it is well that it should be. It may intimidate the human race into bringing
order to its international affairs, which, without the pressure of fear,
undoubtedly would not happen.

Topical Considerations

1. Looking back over the almost 40 years since Einstein's essay
was written, do you think his assessment was right—that atomic energy
has affected us "quantitatively, not qualitatively" (paragraph 1)? What
"existing" problem did it make "more urgent"?

2. What reasons did Einstein give for not revealing the secret of atomic energy to the Soviet Union?

3. What was Einstein's proposal for preventing atomic warfare back in 1945? Does it seem to be a reasonable and workable plan? Or does it strike you as impractical, dangerous, and naive? Explain.

4. In paragraph 12, Einstein says that he does not consider himself "the father of the release of atomic energy." Yet has he not been considered the "father of the atomic bomb"? How has history portrayed Albert Einstein to you?

5. How did Einstein regard atomic energy when he wrote this statement? How did he see the menace of it as potentially useful back in 1945? Looking back, can you say that he was accurate? Explain.

Rhetorical Considerations

1. Explain the effectiveness of the analogy in paragraph 2, where Einstein likens releasing the atomic secrets to giving away capital to a potential partner.

2. How would you describe Einstein's attitude toward the Soviet Union?

3. Albert Einstein was one of the greatest thinkers of modern times. Would you know that from reading this essay? Consider the language, style, and content of his argument.

Writing Assignment

1. Einstein does not consider himself the "father of the atomic bomb," although he was the one individual whose theories on energy and matter made atomic energy possible. Write a letter to Albert Einstein in which you either thank him or berate him for his contribution. You are speaking, of course, from hindsight, so it would be useful to explain to him some historical reasons for your feelings.

Must Wars Occur?

Herman Wouk

Herman Wouk probably has written more about war than anybody else alive today. He is the best-selling author of such classics as *The Caine Mutiny* (1951), *Youngblood Hawke* (1962), and *War and Remembrance* (1978). He is also the author of *The Winds of War* (1971), which was made into an

enormously popular multipart television movie in 1983. Because of his long
career as a creator of war literature, Wouk was recently invited to tour military
installations. This article begins with a report on that experience of viewing our
"machines of destruction," terrible counterparts to the Russian arsenals. As
Wouk says, the tour turned out to be a sobering realization of the "monstrous
and incredibly frightening and dangerous closed loop of insanity" in which we
and the Soviet Union are trapped. From there, he goes on to examine the
roots of Americans' fears of the Russians and the Russians' fears of us—and
by extension the roots of war itself. Must wars occur? Can humans control
their nature? The questions answer themselves.

It is the paradox of my career that, though I have won recognition   1
as a creator of war literature, I regard war, and preparation for war, as
the primal curse now afflicting the human race. Some serious writers
understandably have averted their eyes from the skull that grins at them
from current events, so as to create art out of their private preoccupa-
tions. I have looked straight at the grinning skull and written about it.

Last May I toured our military establishment in a program called the   2
Joint Civilian Orientation Conference. The Defense Department from
time to time invites executives from various fields—industrial, academic,
professional—to go out and see what is happening in the armed forces.
A high official who admired my battle scenes in *The Winds of War* nomi-
nated me for this unlikely activity, jolting me out of my ivory tower and
taking me away for a week from writing my new book. I should perhaps
mention in these budget-slashing times that I had to pay my own way for
the excursion, and so did everybody else.

What is there to say about a week like that, junketing around among   3
the main military commands, meeting four-star generals, seeing impressive combat exercises wryly called "dog and pony shows" by those who
put them on, getting taken on exciting rides in exotic combat vehicles?
In one sense, call it a Disney World tour of the armed forces for privileged
fat cats. Certainly it had that side to it, and the frank and undisguised idea
was to get us to support the defense budget, and to spread the word that
all was hunky-dory in the armed forces, or at least getting there.

The 50 fellow Americans with whom I travelled were refreshing and   4
reviving company after my long isolation amid my books; a fine lot of men
and women, of differing politics but full of genuine goodwill, ready to
laugh in that good old boy haw-haw way, now and then coming out with
sharp shrewd comments and questions that showed how little they were
missing of what went on, and how astute they were. I believe they saw
what I saw, and had much the same reaction.

Well, what did I see?   5

First of all, we are trapped in a monstrous and incredibly frightening   6
and dangerous closed loop of insanity with the Soviet Union. The
buildup and counter-buildup of destructive weapons, described in calm

voices by 30-year-old officers with pointers and slides, are more chilling than any variation of Dr. Strangelove fantasy. Possibly the most gruesome thing is that everybody has come to take the whole horrible lunacy for granted. I went down into a missile site and I saw the dread thing. I walked through an aircraft, the "Looking Glass" command vessel of the Strategic Air Command, one of which is always aloft, all of which have the capacity to fire our entire Minute Man arsenal, and literally touch off the conflagration to end civilized life on earth. There I was, looking at the stuff, which is usually manned by fellows about the age of my sons.

The ingenuity, labor, and treasure poured out on this closed loop of   7
insanity truly stun the mind. If nations did not learn war any more, there would be nothing mankind could not do, and could not make of this frail little global island on which we float through black space. As it is, we seem to stand all but convicted of not measuring up, and of being doomed like the dinosaurs. All but. New ideas and new words can still make a difference, so long as the grand blowup does not come. Because the other side of the coin of this horrible insanity is the wondrous ingenuity and discipline and persistence of men, who create and maintain and work these infernal marvels.

Subconsciously we are all aware that we are living in this ghastly   8
nightmare of the lethal closed loop. We go on day by day just by shutting it from mind. I call it a closed loop, because our own sophisticated fail-safe procedures to forestall accidental war are in the end no sure protection; *for we are locked into the unknown fail-safe procedures of the Soviet Union.* One damned fool in Russia, or a cabal of damned fools or Slavic Strangeloves, can kick off the doomsday cycle, conceivably beyond our control to recall.

Our machines of destruction are imposing, and even sometimes have   9
a weird hellish beauty. We spent a night aboard the USS *America,* one of our older carriers. The *America* is so huge, so full of big marvelous machinery, and it catapults off and retrieves aircraft at night in a melodramatic spectacle of skill, force, and flame not matched on earth. The marines, the army, the air force, all seem to know what they are doing. All are equipped with terrific weapons, all seek more and better weapons, all know what the Russians have to counter them and their weapons. The Russians are the bugbear. Our people are not afraid òf them, but very worried about what they have in weaponry; and all training is openly against Russian capabilities.

How did we ever get into this paralyzing lock with Russia? And what   10
are our chances of getting out of it alive?

When I was born, the United States of America had an army of about   11
a hundred thousand men, a small coal-burning navy, and a few shaky flying machines of wood and canvas. There were in the land less than half as many people as there are now. Russia, where my parents came from,

was a feeble, benighted monarchy honeycombed with revolutionaries, tottering to the crash of the Lenin overthrow. The lock has all developed in my lifetime. I even played my infinitesimal part in it, in the Second World War. For that war led straight to our present predicament.

Fear of surprise attack haunts us Americans. At Pearl Harbor we   12 learned what one treacherous machine-age attack could do. The lesson sank in. Hence the awesome vigils in the missile shafts, the submarines, and the strategic bombers; hence the electric waves pulsing across the oceans, over the poles, under the seas, warning of the approach of any solid object, lighting up screens in underground centers—one of which I visited on the tour—where watchers always sit, with open wireless circuits to the pleasant-faced young men at the rocket buttons. Behind those pleasant faces is the steel glare of a giant surprised once, determined not to be surprised again, and terribly armed against surprise.

For the Russians, too, the big scar left by modern history is surprise   13 attack. We tend to forget that. The eastward plunge of the Germans on June 22, 1941, was as unexpected a catastrophe for the Soviet Union as the Japanese naval attack half a year later, on December 7, was for the United States. The Russian nation barely escaped enslavement by the Germans, half their country was pillaged and laid waste for over three years, and in saving themselves they lost perhaps 35 million civilian and military lives.

So it has come to pass that the two great superpowers face each other   14 with arrays of apocalyptic machines, each seeking to ward off a repetition of old disasters which neither inflicted on the other. In fact, we became comrades-in-arms to crush the greatest menace to civilization of modern times: Hitlerite Germany. The German armed forces were not the funny bumbling monsters who today in films and television shows wear swastikas and Wehrmacht helmets. They came so close to world rule because they were so able and fierce in war. The free democracies of America and Britain, and the Marxist dictatorship of Russia, threw aside their differences and together fought a just war, a war that had to be won to rid the planet of the moral leprosy of Nazism.

We won it. Hitler and the Nazis are gone. At the center of Europe,   15 where they once shook the earth with their iron march, there is a power void. Across that void, we and the Russians glare at each other, and huff and puff, and sometimes frighten each other. I believe the Soviet rulers have moments of freezing terror as they face American force. They know the horror of war, in a way we living Americans have so far—except for those who have fought far away, on foreign shores—known only from television screens. Not since the Civil War has blood been shed on American soil by the clash of armies. That is an immense difference between the two deadlocked giants.

And there may be hope in that, if only a glimmer. I have travelled in   16 the Soviet Union, seen the war monuments, watched the sober crowds visiting them. I could swear not only that the Russian people hate and fear war, but that—despite years of dissembling Kremlin propaganda—they remember Lend-Lease; and the Normandy invasion, too, which pulled half the Wehrmacht horde off their backs, so that they could drive the Germans out and march to Berlin. As the grim geriatric inheritors of the grabby Stalin die off, and the younger generation takes hold, we may work out a better relationship with this brave people, once our allies, than that of two scorpions in a bottle. There is nothing necessary or eternal about the deadlock. It developed in one man's lifetime. All history is change.

But let us even say that we free ourselves from that doomsday lock. Will that mean world peace?   17

Hardly. The two scorpions in a bottle comprise but 10 percent of the human race. That, too, we tend to forget. Among the other 90 percent there persist a thousand quarrels; quarrels over territory, over honor, over water rights, over nationalist pride, over causes lost in the mists of time, leaving only old hatreds. How reply to those who arm to right wrongs real or fancied, recent or ancient, and who would cry to the peacemakers, "Why stop war now? Why *us?*"   18

What of lunatic rulers like Qaddafi of Libya and Idi Amin of Uganda, who erupt into power unstoppably, and wield their national armed forces by mad whim? What of religious fanatics like the Ayatollah Khomeini, who can seize control of a country and launch an armed crusade against neighbors in the Divine Name?   19

I have studied war and written against war most of my working life. We are passing through a very dark tunnel in history. I am not misled into thinking that struck matches like flower power and anti-nuclear demonstrations are light at the end of the tunnel. But I will close this somber review with a word or two about light.   20

I will shortly leave on my first round-the-world tour, passing eastward through Jerusalem to Beijing. *The Winds of War* has been translated into Chinese with heartwarming success; and the Chinese Writers Association has invited me to address authors and historians in Beijing, a bid I could not find in my heart to decline. I have never been to China. The publisher's preface to my work has said, "Although we cannot approve of the author's anti-Marxist views, the novel is an important dramatic narrative of the war," or words to that effect.   21

Strange! In the Soviet Union, because of my known anti-Marxist views, I am a literary non-person; my works are available only in English in the Lenin Library and other large libraries, and one must sign out for them. The Marxist Chinese show more civility and political tolerance, in this literary instance, than the Soviets, once their models and teachers; though a few years ago America, and all things American, were as anath-   22 ema in China as they are in Iran, where we are now the "great Satan." So hatred can fade. I am eager to learn more exactly in China, if I can, what this glimmer means.

I am going via Jerusalem so as to visit my two sons. Deep-sea divers   23 and game fishermen, they live in Eilat, on the Red Sea. One of them served in the Israeli navy during the "Peace in Galilee" operation, the expulsion of the PLO terrorist army from Lebanon. Once, when my son's vessel put in to base for resupply, he telephoned me. The victorious Israeli advance was giving him no joy or pride, though he was sure of its necessity. He described what he had seen: the fierce attacks against the terrorist units holing up with their rockets and howitzers amid the civilians of the coastal towns, and the resulting destruction. He was sick at heart, and close to despair.

The Israeli army, one of the most effective in the world, is also the   24 strangest. It has sprung up in a generation, from a people who 40 years ago docilely marched by the millions into execution chambers, which the German government told them were hygienic showers. This bestial hoax was the surprise attack of all time, on an utterly defenseless people. It roused that people once for all to learn to defend themselves.

But you never saw soldiers with such little taste for fighting. The feisty   25 martial spirit of the Wehrmacht, of British and French arms in the times of imperial glory, even of the Pacific Fleet as we sailed against "the Japs" —none of that is perceptible in Israel. They hate the whole business. They hate it as much as the anti-nuclear marchers do. Once I observed a field exercise of the Israelis, and an officer pointed out a long-haired unit commander to me. "That is a red-hot leader of the Peace Now movement," he said. "He believes in giving back all the territories. But he has been called up on reserve duty, and he is a hell of a good soldier."

If the Israelis ever become convinced that the Arabs will really leave   26 them alone, I think they will disband their army and throw their arms into the sea. They marched peaceably out of Sinai, dismantling settlements that had cost millions, giving up strategic depth, yielding oil wells that were balancing their economy, simply because the Egyptians showed a willingness to leave them alone. That is not the old martial spirit of glory, loot, and mastery. It is something new in warfare, since the ancient Egyptians and Chinese first began making their picture-language records of war.

But just because war does go back to the first records of man, gloomy   27 skeptics argue that there will always be war: that it is part of unchanging human nature.

I reply that until 400 years ago, the time of Shakespeare, there had   28 always been human sacrifice somewhere on earth. Until the early 19th century, there had always been duelling. Hamilton, one of America's founding fathers, died by a duellist's bullet. Until Lincoln's Emancipation Proclamation in 1862, when my own grandfather was alive, there had always been human slavery. Yet these barbaric curses have dimmed from the scene of mankind. To this extent, if human nature has not changed, it has come under control.

My study of the whole matter has wakened a whisper in my heart that our grandchildren, if the race can get through this dark time, may yet see the dawn. Herodotus, the Greek historian, narrates that two ancient warring armies, frightened out of their wits by a total eclipse of the sun, threw down their arms and made peace. The eclipse is now nearly total. Perhaps the peace, then, is more nearly at hand than we dare hope.   29

"Nation will not lift up sword against nation," wrote the prophet Isaiah more than six centuries before the Christian era, *"neither will they learn war any more."*   30

If I do not utterly give up that hope, it is because I cannot and will not. Meantime, men of goodwill have to hang in there. As Victor Henry, the hero of *The Winds of War,* sums up the lessons of the Battle of Leyte Gulf, we are nearing the moment in human history when *"Either war is finished, or we are."*   31

Topical Considerations

1. How does Wouk say he differs from other writers of war literature?

2. On Wouk's tour with the military, what was "the most gruesome thing" he observed? How well does he portray it?

3. How well does the author explain the Russians' attitude toward us? Why are they so afraid? What historical reasons does Wouk give?

4. How do you think Wouk feels about the antinuclear movement in America and in other countries? Do you think he would march in a demonstration for nuclear disarmament?

5. How well does Wouk answer the question in this essay's title? Does he present evidence that wars need not occur? Does he offer us some "light" (paragraph 20), some hope for the future?

Rhetorical Considerations

1. Several times, Wouk refers to the "closed loop of insanity." How does he explain this metaphor? How effective is it, given what he is arguing here?

2. What is the effect of making paragraph 10 two simple questions? How well does he answer them? Is his evidence sufficient support of his answer?

3. Explain the irony in the fact that "in these budget-slashing times" (paragraph 2), Wouk had to pay his own way for the military excursion.

4. Explain the appropriateness of the Dr. Strangelove reference in paragraph 6. What kind of "fantasy" is he characterizing?

5. Explain the impact of the last sentence of paragraph 6.

6. In paragraph 14, Wouk refers to all the war technology as "apocalyptic machines." Explain what "apocalyptic" means and why it is appropriate here.

7. What is the rhetorical purpose of the Herodotus reference in paragraph 29?

8. How do you interpret Wouk's allusion to his *Winds of War* in the last paragraph? Is it a sneaky plug for himself? Does it weaken the impact of his conclusion or strengthen it?

Writing Assignments

1. Given the "closed loop of insanity" the United States and the USSR have gotten themselves into, and given the view that humans *can* alter the momentum of history, write a letter to the president of the United States (and/or of the Soviet Union) in which you try to convince him to support nuclear disarmament.

2. Write a letter to the president of the United States in which you try to convince him of the need to develop newer and stronger weapons to defend ourselves. Use as your reasoning the lessons history has taught about people, nations, and war.

3. If Herman Wouk's essay changed your mind about the issues involved, write an essay explaining how and why.

4. Do you think there is hope for a lasting peace? Do you think the nuclear nations on the earth will manage to avoid using their terrible "apocalyptic machines"? Write a paper describing what you see of our future in this dangerous nuclear age.

To Preserve a World Graced by Life

Carl Sagan

Carl Sagan is famous on many fronts—as a scientist, a writer, and a television personality. He is director of the Laboratory for Planetary Studies and the David Duncan Professor of Astronomy and Space Sciences at Cornell University. He is also the author of *The Cosmic Connection* (1972), the Pulitzer Prize-winning *Dragons of Eden* (1977), and *Broca's Brain* (1981). He is probably most widely recognized as the creator and narrator of the thirteen-part PBS television series, "Cosmos." Viewing human life in characteristically cosmic terms, Sagan points out just how privileged we are as a species to be alive on Earth, since there is no other place in our solar system where we could survive. We are also privileged to control our own future. Like Einstein before him, Sagan proclaims that there is no issue more important in our nuclear age than making certain that we have a future. He calls on the country that first used nuclear weapons on people to take the first step toward decelerating their production.

1   There is no issue more important than the avoidance of nuclear war. Whatever your interests, passions or goals, they and you are threatened fundamentally by the prospect of nuclear war. We have achieved the capability for the certain destruction of our civilization and perhaps of our species as well. I find it incredible that any thinking person would not be concerned in the deepest way about this issue.

2   In the last 20 years, the United States and the Soviet Union have accomplished something stunning and historic—the close-up examination of all those points of light, from Mercury to Saturn, that moved our ancestors to wonder and to science. Every one of these worlds is lovely and instructive, and there are premonitions and stirrings of life on Titan and Iapetus and some other worlds. But apparently life does not exist on these worlds. Something has gone wrong. Some critical step was lacking. Or perhaps life arose once and subsequently died out. The lesson we have learned is that life is a comparative rarity, that you can have 20 or 30 or 40 worlds and on only one of them does life appear and sustain itself.

3   What has evolved on our planet is not just life, not just grass or mice or beetles or microbes, but beings with a great intelligence, with a capacity to anticipate the future consequences of present actions, with the ability even to leave their home world and seek out life elsewhere. What a waste it would be if, after four billion years of tortuous biological evolution, the dominant organism on the planet contrived its own annihilation. No species is guaranteed its tenure on this planet. And we've been here for only about a million years, we, the first species that has devised the means for its self-destruction. I look at those other worlds, cratered, airless, cold, here and there coated with a hopeful stain of organic matter, and I remind myself what an astonishing thing has happened here. How privileged we are to live, to influence and control our future. I believe we have an obligation to fight for that life, to struggle not just for ourselves, but for all those creatures who came before us, and to whom we are beholden, and for all those who, if we are wise enough, will come after us. There is no cause more urgent, no dedication more fitting for us than to strive to eliminate the threat of nuclear war. No social convention, no political system, no economic hypothesis, no religious dogma is more important.

The dangers of nuclear war are, in a way, well-known. But in a way they are not well-known, because there is a psychological factor—psychiatrists call it denial—that makes us feel it's so horrible that we might as well not think about it. That element of denial is, I believe, one of the most serious problems we face. If everyone had a profound and immediate sense of the actual consequences of nuclear war, we would be much more willing to confront and challenge national leaders of all nations when they present narrow and self-serving arguments for the continuation of mutual nuclear terror.   4

Denial, however, is remarkably strong and there are many cases in human history where, faced with the clearest signs of extreme danger, people refuse to take simple corrective measures. Some 25 years ago, a tsunami, a tidal wave in the Pacific, was approaching the Hawaiian Islands. The people there were given many hours warning to flee the lowlands and run to safety. But the idea of a great, crashing wave of water 30 feet high surging inland, inundating and washing your house out to sea was so unbelievable, so unpleasant, that many people simply ignored the warning and were killed. In fact, one schoolteacher thought the report to be so interesting that she gathered up her children and took them down to the water's edge to watch. I believe that one of the most important jobs that scientists have in this dialogue on the dangers of nuclear war is to state very clearly what the dangers are.   5

The evidence is compelling that weapons proliferation leads to a substantial, indeed to an exponential growth of nuclear weapons worldwide. The situation is like that of two or more coupled linear differential equations; each nation's rate of growth of nuclear weapons is proportional to some other nation's stockpile of nuclear weapons. No nation is ever satisfied that it has enough weapons. Any "improvements" by the other side force us to "improve" our weapons systems. Exponentials not only go up, they also go down, suggesting that a concerted effort to increase the nuclear weapons systems stockpiled by one nation will result in a corresponding increase by other nations. But likewise, a concerted effort by any one nuclear power to decrease its stockpile might very well have as a consequence a decline in the stockpiles of other nations, and, at least up to a point, the process can be self-sustaining. I therefore raise the question of whether the nation that first developed and used nuclear weapons on human populations has some special obligation to decelerate the nuclear arms race. There is a wide range of possible options, including small and safe unilateral steps to test the responses of other nations, and major bilateral and multilateral efforts to negotiate substantial, verifiable force reductions.   6

Disarmament, done in such a way as to preserve deterrence against a nuclear attack, is in everybody's interest. It's only a matter of getting started. Of course there's some risk. It takes courage. But as Einstein asked, in precisely this context, "What is the alternative?"   7

An extraterrestrial being coming upon the Earth might note that a few   8
nations, one of them being the United States, actually have organizations
devoted to peace as well as to war. The United States has something
called the Arms Control and Disarmament Agency. But its budget is less
than one hundred thousandth of the budget of the Department of Defense. This is a numerical measure of the relative importance that we
place on finding ways to make war and finding ways to make peace. Is it
possible that the intelligence, compassion and even self-interest of the
American people have been thoroughly exhausted in the pursuit of solutions to the threat of nuclear war? Or is it more likely that so little
attention is given to it, so little encouragement is provided to bright
young people to consider this issue, that we have not even begun to find
innovative and imaginative solutions?

Through the courageous examination of these deep painful issues, and   9
through the political process, I am convinced we can make an important
contribution toward preserving and enhancing the life that has graced
our small world.

Topical Considerations

1. What is Sagan's point in citing the lack of life in the rest of the
solar system?

2. According to Sagan, if more people "had a profound and
immediate sense of the actual consequences of nuclear war," we could
stand up to world leaders who argue for "the continuation of mutual
nuclear terror" (paragraph 4). Do you agree? Aren't there many people
who know well the consequences of nuclear war but aren't willing to
disarm? What is it that prevents the cessation of the arms buildup?

3. How does Sagan suggest we can avoid nuclear war? Explain
his reasoning. Where is the greatest risk in his proposal? Why is it worth
taking?

4. According to Sagan, why have we found more ways to make
war than peace?

Rhetorical Considerations

1. Exactly where is the thesis statement in Sagan's essay? Comment on the strategy of its location in the piece.

2. How apt and effective is the example of the tsunami in paragraph 5?

3. What is Sagan's purpose in comparing the budgets of the
Arms Control and Disarmament Agency and the Department of Defense?
How effectively is his point made?

4. If you had not known, could you have guessed from this essay that Sagan is an astronomer? What clues can you find?

5. From the tone of this essay, what kind of man would you say Sagan is—rational? informed? scared? desperate? hysterical? out of touch? naive?

Writing Assignments

1. Write a letter to Carl Sagan in which you clearly explain why you agree or disagree with his stand on nuclear weapons and war.

2. Do you think the leaders of the world are capable of rising above their ideological, political, economic, and religious differences to eliminate nuclear weapons once and for all? Write a paper answering this question.

3. Imagine that you are an extraterrestrial who has been invited to address the United Nations General Assembly. Write a speech in which you tell the nations of the world just how to resolve their nuclear arms dilemma and avoid war.

Chapter 16 of the Revelation of St. John the Divine

The Revelation of St. John the Divine, or the Apocalypse, is the last book of the New Testament. It is a vision of the end of life on Earth as we know it and of the establishment of a new order. It is also the revelation of God's judgments on humankind—the unleashing of his wrath on the unfaithful, the destruction of the Antichrist and his evil followers by the returned Messiah, and the creation of a new heaven and new earth for the righteous. Many scholars believe Revelation was occasioned by the cruel treatment of Christians by the Roman Emperor Domitian at the end of the first century A.D. and was written to encourage them to be faithful at all costs, since that age of wickedness would come to an end and be succeeded by a new age of freedom and happiness under Jesus Christ himself. Christian fundamentalists have long felt, however, that Revelation was a prophecy of Doomsday—the inevitable destruction of earth for its wickedness. Some have even seen the nuclear age as the beginning of the end—humankind prophetically inventing and perfecting its self-destruction. The following is Chapter 16 of Revelation, describing angels pouring out the vials of God's wrath on Earth. The details of destruction in this excerpt have an ominous ring for our age. They also serve as a prelude to the next piece, Jonathan Schell's description of the effects a nuclear device would have on New York City.

And I heard a great voice out of the temple saying to the seven   1
angels, Go your ways, and pour out the vials of the wrath of God upon
the earth.

And the first went, and poured out his vial upon the earth; and there   2
fell a noisome and grievous sore upon the men which had the mark of
the beast, and *upon* them which worshipped his image.

And the second angel poured out his vial upon the sea; and it became   3
as the blood of a dead *man:* and every living soul died in the sea.

And the third angel poured out his vial upon the rivers and fountains   4
of waters; and they became blood.

And I heard the angel of the waters say, Thou art righteous, O Lord,   5
which art, and wast, and shalt be, because thou hast judged thus.

For they have shed the blood of saints and prophets, and thou hast   6
given them blood to drink; for they are worthy.

And I heard another out of the altar say, Even so, Lord God Almighty,   7
true and righteous *are* thy judgments.

And the fourth angel poured out his vial upon the sun; and power was   8
given unto him to scorch men with fire.

And men were scorched with great heat, and blasphemed the name of   9
God, which hath power over these plagues: and they repented not to give
him glory.

And the fifth angel poured out his vial upon the seat of the beast; and   10
his kingdom was full of darkness; and they gnawed their tongues for pain,

And blasphemed the God of heaven because of their pains and their   11
sores, and repented not of their deeds.

And the sixth angel poured out his vial upon the great river Euphrates;   12
and the water thereof was dried up, that the way of the kings of the east
might be prepared.

And I saw three unclean spirits like frogs *come* out of the mouth of the   13
dragon, and out of the mouth of the beast, and out of the mouth of the
false prophet.

For they are the spirits of devils, working miracles, *which* go forth unto   14
the kings of the earth and of the whole world, to gather them to the battle
of that great day of God Almighty.

Behold, I come as a thief. Blessed *is* he that watcheth, and keepeth his   15
garments, lest he walk naked, and they see his shame.

And he gathered them together into a place called in the Hebrew   16
tongue Armageddon.

And the seventh angel poured out his vial into the air; and there came   17
a great voice out of the temple of heaven, from the throne, saying, It is
done.

And there were voices, and thunders, and lightnings; and there was a   18
great earthquake, such as was not since men were upon the earth, so
mighty an earthquake, *and* so great.

And the great city was divided into three parts, and the cities of the   19
nations fell: and great Babylon came in remembrance before God, to give
unto her the cup of the wine of the fierceness of his wrath.

And every island fled away, and the mountains were not found.   20

And there fell upon men a great hail out of heaven, *every stone* about   21
the weight of a talent: and men blasphemed God because of the plague
of the hail; for the plague thereof was exceeding great.

The Effects of a Nuclear Explosion

Jonathan Schell

In his essay, Carl Sagan made the point that if we all had "a profound and
immediate sense of the actual consequences of a nuclear war," we would be
much more willing to challenge our leaders to disarm. The following essay was
written with just that strategy and intent. Done in a coldly objective tone, this
piece thoroughly details the effects a thermonuclear bomb would have on New
York City. This essay was one of three that appeared in the *New Yorker* and
were later collected and published as *The Fate of the Earth* (1982). Widely
read, this book considers the theories and effects of the nuclear arms race
and the consequences of nuclear war.

What happened at Hiroshima was less than a millionth part of a   1
holocaust at present levels of world nuclear armament. The more than
millionfold difference amounts to more than a difference in magnitude;
it is also a difference in kind. The authors of "Hiroshima and Nagasaki"*
observe that "an atomic bomb's massive destruction and indiscriminate
slaughter involves the sweeping breakdown of all order and existence—
in a word, the collapse of society itself," and that therefore "the essence
of atomic destruction lies in the totality of its impact on man and society."
This is true also of a holocaust, of course, except that the totalities in
question are now not single cities but nations, ecosystems, and the earth's
ecosphere. Yet with the exception of fallout, which was relatively light at
Hiroshima and Nagasaki (because both the bombs were air-burst), the
immediate devastation caused by today's bombs would be of a sort similar
to the devastation in those cities. The immediate effects of a twenty-
megaton bomb are not different in kind from those of a twelve-and-a-half-
kiloton bomb; they are only more extensive. . . . In bursts of both weap-

*A comprehensive study, carried out by a group of distinguished Japanese scientists, of
the consequences of the bombing of those two cities.—Ed.

ons, for instance, there is a radius within which the thermal pulse can ignite newspapers: for the twelve-and-a-half-kiloton weapon, it is a little over two miles; for the twenty-megaton weapon, it is twenty-five miles. (Since there is no inherent limit on the size of a nuclear weapon, these figures can be increased indefinitely, subject only to the limitations imposed by the technical capacities of the bomb builder—and of the earth's capacity to absorb the blast. The Soviet Union, which has shown a liking for sheer size in so many of its undertakings, once detonated a sixty-megaton bomb.) Therefore, while the total effect of a holocaust is qualitatively different from the total effect of a single bomb, the experience of individual people in a holocaust would be, in the short term (and again excepting the presence of lethal fallout wherever the bombs were ground-burst), very much like the experience of individual people in Hiroshima. The Hiroshima people's experience, accordingly, is of much more than historical interest. It is a picture of what our whole world is always poised to become—a backdrop of scarcely imaginable horror lying just behind the surface of our normal life, and capable of breaking through into that normal life at any second. Whether we choose to think about it or not, it is an omnipresent, inescapable truth about our lives today that at every single moment each one of us may suddenly become the deranged mother looking for her burned child; the professor with the ball of rice in his hand whose wife has just told him "Run away, dear!" and died in the fires; Mr. Fukai running back into the firestorm; the naked man standing on the blasted plain that was his city, holding his eyeball in his hand; or, more likely, one of millions of corpses. For whatever our "modest hopes" as human beings may be, every one of them can be nullified by a nuclear holocaust.

One way to begin to grasp the destructive power of present-day nuclear weapons is to describe the consequences of the detonation of a one-megaton bomb, which possesses eighty times the explosive power of the Hiroshima bomb, on a large city, such as New York. Burst some eighty-five hundred feet above the Empire State Building, a one-megaton bomb would gut or flatten almost every building between Battery Park and 125th Street, or within a radius of four and four-tenths miles, or in an area of sixty-one square miles, and would heavily damage buildings between the northern tip of Staten Island and the George Washington Bridge, or within a radius of about eight miles, or in an area of about two hundred square miles. A conventional explosive delivers a swift shock, like a slap, to whatever it hits, but the blast wave of a sizable nuclear weapon endures for several seconds and "can surround and destroy whole buildings" (Glasstone). People, of course, would be picked up and hurled away from the blast along with the rest of the debris. Within the sixty-one square miles, the walls, roofs, and floors of any buildings that had not been flattened would be collapsed, and the people and furniture inside would be swept down onto the street. (Technically, this zone would be hit by various overpressures of at least five pounds per square inch. Overpressure is defined as the pressure in excess of normal atmospheric pressure.) As far away as ten miles from ground zero, pieces of glass and other sharp objects would be hurled about by the blast wave at lethal velocities. In Hiroshima, where buildings were low and, outside the center of the city, were often constructed of light materials, injuries from falling buildings were often minor. But in New York, where the buildings are tall and are constructed of heavy materials, the physical collapse of the city would certainly kill millions of people. The streets of New York are narrow ravines running between the high walls of the city's buildings. In a nuclear attack, the walls would fall and the ravines would fill up. The people in the buildings would fall to the street with the debris of the buildings, and the people in the street would be crushed by this avalanche of people and buildings. At a distance of two miles or so from ground zero, winds would reach four hundred miles an hour, and another two miles away they would reach a hundred and eighty miles an hour. Meanwhile, the fireball would be growing, until it was more than a mile wide, and rocketing upward, to a height of over six miles. For ten seconds, it would broil the city below. Anyone caught in the open within nine miles of ground zero would receive third-degree burns and would probably be killed; closer to the explosion, people would be charred and killed instantly. From Greenwich Village up to Central Park, the heat would be great enough to melt metal and glass. Readily inflammable materials, such as newspapers and dry leaves, would ignite in all five boroughs (though in only a small part of Staten Island) and west to the Passaic River, in New Jersey, within a radius of about nine and a half miles from ground zero, thereby creating an area of more than two hundred and eighty square miles in which mass fires were likely to break out.

If it were possible (as it would not be) for someone to stand at Fifth Avenue and Seventy-second Street (about two miles from ground zero) without being instantly killed, he would see the following sequence of events. A dazzling white light from the fireball would illumine the scene, continuing for perhaps thirty seconds. Simultaneously, searing heat would ignite everything flammable and start to melt windows, cars, buses, lampposts, and everything else made of metal or glass. People in the street would immediately catch fire, and would shortly be reduced to heavily charred corpses. About five seconds after the light appeared, the blast wave would strike, laden with the debris of a now nonexistent midtown. Some buildings might be crushed, as though a giant fist had squeezed them on all sides, and others might be picked up off their foundations and whirled uptown with the other debris. On the far side of Central Park, the West Side skyline would fall from south to north. The four-hundred-mile-an-hour wind would blow from south to north, die down after a few seconds, and then blow in the reverse direction with diminished intensity. While these things were happening, the fireball would be burning in the sky for the ten seconds of the thermal pulse. Soon huge, thick clouds of dust and smoke would envelop the scene, and as the mushroom cloud rushed overhead (it would have a diameter of about twelve miles) the light from the sun would be blotted out, and day would turn to night. Within minutes, fires, ignited both by the thermal pulse and by broken gas mains, tanks of gas and oil, and the like, would begin to spread in the darkness, and a strong, steady wind would begin to blow in the direction of the blast. As at Hiroshima, a whirlwind might be produced, which would sweep through the ruins, and radioactive rain, generated under the meteorological conditions created by the blast, might fall. Before long, the individual fires would coalesce into a mass fire, which, depending largely on the winds, would become either a conflagration or a firestorm. In a conflagration, prevailing winds spread a wall of fire as far as there is any combustible material to sustain it; in a firestorm, a vertical updraft caused by the fire itself sucks the surrounding air in toward a central point, and the fires therefore converge in a single fire of extreme heat. A mass fire of either kind renders shelters useless by burning up all the oxygen in the air and creating toxic gases, so that anyone inside the shelters is asphyxiated, and also by heating the ground to such high temperatures that the shelters turn, in effect, into ovens, cremating the people inside them. In Dresden, several days after the firestorm raised there by Allied conventional bombing, the interiors of some bomb shelters were still so hot that when they were opened the inrushing air caused the contents to burst into flame. Only those who had fled their shelters when the bombing started had any chance of surviving. (It is difficult to predict in a particular situation which form the fires will take. In actual experience, Hiroshima suffered a firestorm and Nagasaki suffered a conflagration.)

In this vast theatre of physical effects, all the scenes of agony and death   4
that took place at Hiroshima would again take place, but now involving millions of people rather than hundreds of thousands. Like the people of Hiroshima, the people of New York would be burned, battered, crushed, and irradiated in every conceivable way. The city and its people would be mingled in a smoldering heap. And then, as the fires started, the survivors (most of whom would be on the periphery of the explosion) would be driven to abandon to the flames those family members and other people who were unable to flee, or else to die with them. Before long, while the ruins burned, the processions of injured, mute people would begin their slow progress out of the outskirts of the devastated zone. However, this time a much smaller proportion of the population than at Hiroshima would have a chance of escaping. In general, as the size of the area of devastation increases, the possibilities for escape decrease. When the devastated area is relatively small, as it was at Hiroshima, people who are not incapacitated will have a good chance of escaping to safety before the fires coalesce into a mass fire. But when the devastated

area is great, as it would be after the detonation of a megaton bomb, and fires are springing up at a distance of nine and a half miles from ground zero, and when what used to be the streets are piled high with burning rubble, and the day (if the attack occurs in the daytime) has grown impenetrably dark, there is little chance that anyone who is not on the very edge of the devastated area will be able to make his way to safety. In New York, most people would die wherever the blast found them, or not very far from there.

If instead of being burst in the air the bomb were burst on or near the   5
ground in the vicinity of the Empire State Building, the overpressure would be very much greater near the center of the blast area but the range hit by a minimum of five pounds per square inch of overpressure would be less. The range of the thermal pulse would be about the same as that of the air burst. The fireball would be almost two miles across, and would engulf midtown Manhattan from Greenwich Village nearly to Central Park. Very little is known about what would happen to a city that was inside a fireball, but one would expect a good deal of what was there to be first pulverized and then melted or vaporized. Any human beings in the area would be reduced to smoke and ashes; they would simply disappear. A crater roughly three blocks in diameter and two hundred feet deep would open up. In addition, heavy radioactive fallout would be created as dust and debris from the city rose with the mushroom cloud and then fell back to the ground. Fallout would begin to drop almost immediately, contaminating the ground beneath the cloud with levels of radiation many times lethal doses, and quickly killing anyone who might have survived the blast wave and the thermal pulse and might now be attempting an escape; it is difficult to believe that there would be appreciable survival of the people of the city after a megaton ground burst. And for the next twenty-four hours or so more fallout would descend downwind from the blast, in a plume whose direction and length would depend on the speed and the direction of the wind that happened to be blowing at the time of the attack. If the wind was blowing at fifteen miles an hour, fallout of lethal intensity would descend in a plume about a hundred and fifty miles long and as much as fifteen miles wide. Fallout that was sublethal but could still cause serious illness would extend another hundred and fifty miles downwind. Exposure to radioactivity in human beings is measured in units called rems—an acronym for "roentgen equivalent in man." The roentgen is a standard measurement of gamma- and X-ray radiation, and the expression "equivalent in man" indicates that an adjustment has been made to take into account the differences in the degree of biological damage that is caused by radiation of different types. Many of the kinds of harm done to human beings by radiation—for example, the incidence of cancer and of genetic damage—depend on the dose accumulated over many years; but radiation sickness, capable of causing death, results from an "acute" dose, received in a period of anything from

a few seconds to several days. Because almost ninety per cent of the so-called "infinite-time dose" of radiation from fallout—that is, the dose from a given quantity of fallout that one would receive if one lived for many thousands of years—is emitted in the first week, the one-week accumulated dose is often used as a convenient measure for calculating the immediate harm from fallout. Doses in the thousands of rems, which could be expected throughout the city, would attack the central nervous system and would bring about death within a few hours. Doses of around a thousand rems, which would be delivered some tens of miles downwind from the blast, would kill within two weeks everyone who was exposed to them. Doses of around five hundred rems, which would be delivered as far as a hundred and fifty miles downwind (given a wind speed of fifteen miles per hour), would kill half of all exposed able-bodied young adults. At this level of exposure, radiation sickness proceeds in the three stages observed at Hiroshima. The plume of lethal fallout could descend, depending on the direction of the wind, on other parts of New York State and parts of New Jersey, Pennsylvania, Delaware, Maryland, Connecticut, Massachusetts, Rhode Island, Vermont, and New Hampshire, killing additional millions of people. The circumstances in heavily contaminated areas, in which millions of people were all declining together, over a period of weeks, toward painful deaths, are ones that, like so many of the consequences of nuclear explosions, have never been experienced.

A description of the effects of a one-megaton bomb on New York City 6 gives some notion of the meaning in human terms of a megaton of nuclear explosive power, but a weapon that is more likely to be used against New York is the twenty-megaton bomb, which has one thousand six hundred times the yield of the Hiroshima bomb. The Soviet Union is estimated to have at least a hundred and thirteen twenty-megaton bombs in its nuclear arsenal, carried by Bear intercontinental bombers. In addition, some of the Soviet SS–18 missiles are capable of carrying bombs of this size, although the actual yields are not known. Since the explosive power of the twenty-megaton bombs greatly exceeds the amount necessary to destroy most military targets, it is reasonable to suppose that they are meant for use against large cities. If a twenty-megaton bomb were air-burst over the Empire State Building at an altitude of thirty thousand feet, the zone gutted or flattened by the blast wave would have a radius of twelve miles and an area of more than four hundred and fifty square miles, reaching from the middle of Staten Island to the northern edge of the Bronx, the eastern edge of Queens, and well into New Jersey, and the zone of heavy damage from the blast wave (the zone hit by a minimum of two pounds of overpressure per square inch) would have a radius of twenty-one and a half miles, or an area of one thousand four hundred and fifty square miles, reaching to the southernmost tip of Staten Island, north as far as southern Rockland County, east into Nassau County, and west to Morris County, New Jersey. The fireball would be about four and a half miles in diameter and would radiate the thermal pulse for some twenty seconds. People caught in the open twenty-three miles away from ground zero, in Long Island, New Jersey, and southern New York State, would be burned to death. People hundreds of miles away who looked at the burst would be temporarily blinded and would risk permanent eye injury. (After the test of a fifteen-megaton bomb on Bikini Atoll, in the South Pacific, in March of 1954, small animals were found to have suffered retinal burns at a distance of three hundred and forty-five miles.) The mushroom cloud would be seventy miles in diameter. New York City and its suburbs would be transformed into a lifeless, flat, scorched desert in a few seconds.

If a twenty-megaton bomb were ground-burst on the Empire State   7
Building, the range of severe blast damage would, as with the one-megaton ground blast, be reduced, but the fireball, which would be almost six miles in diameter, would cover Manhattan from Wall Street to northern Central Park and also parts of New Jersey, Brooklyn, and Queens, and everyone within it would be instantly killed, with most of them physically disappearing. Fallout would again be generated, this time covering thousands of square miles with lethal intensities of radiation. A fair portion of New York City and its incinerated population, now radioactive dust, would have risen into the mushroom cloud and would now be descending on the surrounding territory. On one of the few occasions when local fallout was generated by a test explosion in the multi-megaton range, the fifteen-megaton bomb tested on Bikini Atoll, which was exploded seven feet above the surface of a coral reef, "caused substantial contamination over an area of more than seven thousand square miles," according to Glasstone. If, as seems likely, a twenty-megaton bomb ground-burst on New York would produce at least a comparable amount of fallout, and if the wind carried the fallout onto populated areas, then this one bomb would probably doom upward of twenty million people, or almost ten per cent of the population of the United States.

Topical Considerations

1. What similarities would there be between the real destruction incurred by the bombs dropped on Hiroshima and Nagasaki and that caused by a nuclear holocaust? What differences would there be?

2. In describing the devastation caused by a one-megaton bomb exploded over New York City, Schell subdivides the effects and moves from one to the other. What is the first effect he discusses? What is the second? What is the third?

3. What is there about New York City that would make escape or refuge from death virtually impossible?

4. What differences in effects would there be if the bomb were detonated at ground level instead of 8,500 feet above the city?

5. What does Schell say about the effects of radiation and their range?

6. Why does Schell say in paragraph 6 that a twenty-megaton bomb would most likely be used against New York? What different effects would this bomb have from those of a one-megaton device?

Rhetorical Considerations

1. Schell gives us grim and thorough details of what nuclear weapons could do to a city. How well does he back up his speculations with factual information?

2. What is Schell's point in giving us so many details at so many different stages of a bomb's destruction? Do all these details clutter the essay or make it more persuasive? Explain.

3. What is the advantage of beginning the piece with details of the destruction of Hiroshima and Nagasaki?

4. This essay is a horribly frightening scenario that details how millions of people could die. How would you define Schell's tone throughout? Does he ever display emotions or reveal his own fears and feelings? Is his tone here an effective one? Does his style fit his subject and purpose?

5. At the end of paragraph 3, Schell makes some comments in parentheses about the difficulty in predicting "which form the fires will take," and he goes on to specify the forms of the fires in Hiroshima and Nagasaki. Why would Schell even bother considering such a difficulty, when it really doesn't make any difference given the consequences? Is there some higher rhetorical purpose behind this?

6. Do you think Schell has written this essay for the general reader or for one with more technical knowledge? Explain your answer.

7. Schell writes in very long paragraphs. Would breaking them up into shorter paragraphs weaken or strengthen their effects?

Writing Assignments

1. If this essay had any effects on you, write a paper describing them. Did it change your mind about war, nuclear arms, or the future?

2. Nuclear bombs were introduced for use in wars, for military purposes. As Schell points out, however, the destructive power of these weapons has far exceeded military needs and intent. Write a paper in which you argue that today's nuclear weapons are not military weapons.

3. Write a letter to the president of the United States (and/or of the Soviet Union) and attempt to convince him of the need to support nuclear disarmament.

4. Write a letter to the president of the United States urging him to support development of bigger and newer weapons to ensure the safety of the United States.

Nuclear Holocaust in Perspective

Michael Kinsley

Immediately following its publication, Jonathan Schell's *Fate of the Earth* was adopted by the American antinuclear movement as its manifesto. There were other reactions as well, however, including the following essay, reprinted from *Harper's Magazine.* Michael Kinsley's statement not only is a voice in opposition to the antinuclear movement, it is a point-for-point attack on Jonathan Schell's arguments—what Kinsley calls his "hothouse reasoning" and his "pretentious" style. Kinsley says that there is more bad poetry than good policy in Schell and the antinuclear movement. He specifically criticizes the strategy, style, and intention of the Schell essay.

It would be very sad if the world were destroyed in a nuclear   1
holocaust. Jonathan Schell may well feel this sadness more profoundly than I do. His acclaimed three-part series in *The New Yorker,* "The Fate of the Earth," now rushed into book form by Knopf, is mostly a meditation on how sad it would be. He demands "the full emotional, intellectual, spiritual, and visceral understanding of the meaning of extinction." He asserts that even now "The peril of extinction surrounds . . . love with doubt." And "Politics, as it now exists, is . . . thoroughly compromised." And "Works of art, history, and thought . . . are undermined at their foundations. . . ." Schell cites scientific evidence against any complaisant hope that human life, once destroyed in a nuclear war, might evolve again in a few million years. And don't suppose that humanity might escape nuclear war by fleeing the earth in a spaceship. Schell points out that this would be not only "an injustice to our birthplace and habitat," but futile: "[T]he fact is that wherever human beings went, there also would go the knowledge of how to build nuclear weapons, and, with it, the peril of extinction." I confess that this spaceship business had never occurred to me. But, really, I think a nuclear holocaust would be very, very sad.

That said, where do we stand?   2

We stand where we've stood for three decades, with East and West in   3
a nuclear stalemate that could turn at any moment into mutual annihila-

tion. In addition, we stand with nuclear weapons as the only genuine deterrent to a Soviet invasion of Europe (and of the Middle East, a threat implicitly invoked in the Carter Doctrine). Third, we stand at the edge of a large expansion of the nuclear club, with unpredictable consequences.

Over the past few months a mass political movement—the first in years   4
—has sprouted in the United States and Europe, demanding that something be done about this. Something, but what? On this, the movement is vaguer, because it's hard to think what the Western governments can do to prevent a nuclear war. On the third point, they might stop competing with one another to sell nuclear equipment to the third world, but it's already a little late for that. On the first point, they might show a bit more enthusiasm for a strategic arms limitation treaty. But this would be primarily a matter of saving money and reducing the risk of a disastrous accident. The basic balance of terror cannot be dismantled without perfect trust between the world's greatest enemies—an unlikely development.

The West really could do something about problem number two, the   5
dependence on nuclear weapons to protect Europe. That something would be to replace nuclear arms with conventional defense. . . . But a conventional defense strong enough to justify forswearing first use of nuclear weapons would require massively increased military spending for the other NATO countries, and probably a draft for the United States.

The thought of increasing conventional military strength to replace   6
nuclear bombs (like the thought that a successful nuclear ban would increase the chance of conventional warfare) is utterly alien to the mentality of most antinuclear activists. Is the horror of nuclear weapons sui generis, or is the goal abolition of all weapons and war? Are there practical steps that can be taken, or must we await a transformation of human nature? Jonathan Schell's essay well illustrates the confusion of the antinuclear movement.

Perhaps it is lèse majesté to call a major three-part series in *The New*   7
Yorker "pretentious," but "The Fate of the Earth" is one of the most pretentious things I've ever read, from the title through the grand finale (which begins, "Four and a half billion years ago, the earth was formed"). "Gosh, is this profound," is about all that many sonorous passages convey:

> [T]he limitless complexity [of nuclear war] sometimes seems to be as great as that of life itself. But if these effects should lead to human extinction, then all the complexity will give way to the utmost simplicity—the simplicity of nothingness.
>
> Like the thought "I do not exist," the thought "Humanity is now extinct" is an impossible one for a rational person, because as soon as it is, we are not.

Even funnier are the pompous generalities that come attached to *New Yorker*-style cautionary notes:

> Human beings have a worth—a worth that is sacred. But it is for human beings that they have that sacred worth, and for them that the other things in the creation have their worth (although it is a reminder of our indissoluble connection with the rest of life that many of our needs and desires are also felt by animals).

Hannah Arendt "never addressed the issue of nuclear arms," Schell   8 tells us, but of course she is dragged in. "I have discovered her thinking to be an indispensable foundation for reflection on this question." Evil, you know. What is really indispensable is her graphic descriptions of Nazi death camps. They pop up here to illustrate the point (both unenlightening and untrue, on recent evidence) that you can't deny horrors that have already happened. Himmler appears a little later, expressing his desire to make Europe "Jew-free." Schell observes, "His remark applies equally well to a nuclear holocaust, which might render the earth 'human-free.'" In fact, Hannah and Himmler are here for aesthetic rather than pedagogical purposes. This is simply how you decorate apocalyptic bigthink.

Despite a lot of wacky judiciousness ("From the foregoing, it follows   9 that there can be no justification for extinguishing mankind"), Schell's method is basically bullying rather than argument. The pomp is intended to intimidate, and the moral solemnity is a form of blackmail. Unless you feel as anguished about nuclear war as Jonathan Schell, unless you worry about it *all the time* like him (allegedly), your complacency disqualifies you from objecting. In fact, you are suffering "a kind of sickness" or "a sort of mass insanity." So shut up.

Much of Schell's essay does take the form of argument, but it tends to   10 be hothouse reasoning: huge and exotic blossoms of ratiocination that could grow only in an environment protected from the slightest chill of common sense. For example, here he is arguing that we should not have an experimental nuclear war in order to see what would happen:

> We cannot run experiments with the earth, because we have only one earth, on which we depend for our survival; we are not in possession of any spare earths that we might blow up in some universal laboratory in order to discover their tolerance of nuclear holocausts. Hence, our knowledge of the resiliency of the earth in the face of nuclear attack is limited by our fear of bringing about just the event—human extinction—whose likelihood we are chiefly interested in finding out.

Now welcome please "The famous uncertainty principle, formulated by the German physicist Werner Heisenberg," which makes a brief star turn at this point in the argument. Its role is to escort "an opposite but [not very] related uncertainty principle: our knowledge of extinction is limited because the experiments with which we would carry out our observations interfere with us, the observers, and, in fact, might put an end to us."

The argument is crowned with a portentous aphorism: "the demand   11
for certainty is the path toward death." Then, just to show that he's thought of everything, Schell considers and rejects the idea of holding an experimental nuclear war on another planet, ". . . for if we have no extra, dispensable earths to experiment with, neither are we in possession of any planets bearing life of some different sort." The reader is left convinced that an experimental nuclear war is a bad idea, and that Jonathan Schell possesses either an absurdly swelled head, or a "philosophical synthesis" that is "profoundly new" (—Eliot Fremont-Smith, the *Village Voice*).

Schell prefaces his discussion of the consequences of nuclear war with   12
a discussion of the difficulty of imagining it. Some of the alleged obstacles are of this sort: "when we strain to picture what the scene would be like after a holocaust we tend to forget that for most people, and perhaps for all, it wouldn't be *like* anything, because they would be dead."

But the main set of obstacles involves a supposed reluctance of people   13
to hear about it. Schell pleads with his readers to make this sacrifice: "it may be only by descending into this hell in imagination now that we can hope to escape descending into it in reality at some later time." He promises to protect their delicate sensibilities: "I hope in this article to proceed with the utmost possible respect for all forms of refusal to accept the unnatural and horrifying prospect of a nuclear holocaust." He flatters their "investigative modesty" as "itself . . . a token of our reluctance to extinguish ourselves." And thence to pages of the usual gruesome description. The horror is lightened only by some *New Yorker*y punctiliousness, as when having killed off millions in a one-megaton bomb over Manhattan, he adds that newspapers and dry leaves would ignite "in all five boroughs (though in only a small part of Staten Island)."

Schell's posture of reluctant scientific inquiry will be familiar to afi-   14
cionados of pornographic movies. And there *is* something pornographic about the emphasis on grisly details that is the distinguishing feature of the antinuclear movement in its latest manifestation. Perhaps Jonathan Schell is so sensitive that he really does find these disaster scenarios painful to contemplate, and probably we all do withhold true visceral understanding of what it would be like. But others will find such disaster scenarios grimly fascinating (certainly the most interesting part of Schell's book). Is that sick? If so, it is a sickness that is widespread, and one that the antinuclear movement both shares and exploits. So the coy posture is annoying.

But destruction of civilization, or even the agonizing death of every-   15 body in the whole world, would be, to Schell, just a minor aspect of the tragedy of a nuclear holocaust. The greatest crime would be against "the helpless, speechless unborn." Schell brandishes this notion of the unborn as his trump card, in case anyone still thinks nuclear war is a good idea. By "the unborn," he does not merely mean fetuses (though by his analysis—liberals please note—abortion is unthinkably immoral). Nor does he mean the future human race as an entity. He does not even mean future people who might inherit a nuclear-wrecked civilization and environment. He means individual people who will *never be born* if there is no one left to conceive them. "While we can launch a first strike against them," Schell inimitably points out, "they have no forces with which to retaliate."

Schell concedes "the metaphysical-seeming perplexities involved in   16
pondering the possible cancellation of people who do not yet exist—an apparently extreme effort of the imagination, which seems to require one first to summon before the mind's eye the countless possible people of the future generations and then to consign these incorporeal multitudes to a more profound nothingness. . . ." But he's up to the challenge:

> Death cuts off life; extinction cuts off birth. Death dispatches into the nothingness after life each person who has been born; extinction in one stroke locks up in the nothingness before life all the people who have not yet been born. For we are finite beings at both ends of our existence—natal as well as mortal—and it is the natality of our kind that extinction threatens. We have always been able to send people to their death, but only now has it become possible to prevent all birth and so doom all future human beings to uncreation.

And so on and on. Schell is *very strict* about what might be called "aliveism." Having waxed eloquent for pages about the unborn as repositories for our hopes and dreams, he stops to warn that we should not treat them merely "as auxiliaries to *our* needs," because "no human being, living or unborn, should be regarded as an auxiliary." The unborn, he scolds, "are not to be seen as beasts of burden. . . ."

Well, my goodness. Do we really have a moral obligation not to deny   17
birth to everyone who, with a bit of help, might enjoy the "opportunity to be glad that they were born instead of having been prenatally severed from existence by us"? I shudder to think how I've failed. For that matter, I shudder for Jonathan Schell—for every moment he's spent banging away on his typewriter, instead of banging away elsewhere.

In solving the problem of nuclear war, Schell cautions, we must "act   18
with the circumspection and modesty of a small minority," since "even if every person in the world were to enlist, the endeavor would include only an infinitesimal fraction of the people of the dead and unborn

generations." Yes, the dead count too. So he proposes "a worldwide program of action," involving an "organization for the preservation of mankind." We must "delve to the bottom of the world" and then "take the world on our shoulders." He writes, "Our present system and the institutions that make it up are the debris of history. They have become inimical to life, and must be swept away." What he proposes, in short, is that the nations of the world abjure all further violence—nuclear *and* conventional warfare—and give up their sovereignty to some central organization.

This idea will win no prizes for circumspection and modesty. Other problems come to mind, too. Like, how shall we arrange all this? Schell writes: [19]

> I have not sought to define a political solution to the nuclear predicament—either to embark on the full-scale examination of the foundations of political thought which must be undertaken . . . or to work out the practical steps. . . . I have left to others those awesome, urgent tasks.

Good heavens. This sudden abandonment, on page 219, puts Schell's hyperventilated rhetoric in an odd light. Is he just going to head off on a book tour and leave us stranded?

Schell is convinced, though, like the rest of the antinuclear movement, that the main task is education—convincing people of how bad a nuclear war would be. "If we did acknowledge the full dimension of the peril . . . extinction would at that moment become not only 'unthinkable' but also undoable." The key word here is "we." But there is no "we." There are individual actors who cannot completely know or trust one another. That's life. Even if everyone in the world shared Schell's overwrought feelings about nuclear war, the basic dilemma would not disappear: the best defense against an enemy's use or threat to use nuclear weapons is the threat to use them back. [20]

Schell correctly points out the weakness in deterrence theory: since nuclear wars are unwinnable, it's hard to make a potential aggressor believe you would actually strike back once your country was in ruins. "[O]ne cannot credibly deter a first strike with a second strike whose raison d'être dissolves the moment the first strike arrives." This may be "a monumental logical mistake," as Schell asserts, but it has prevented anyone from using a nuclear weapon, or even overtly threatening to use one first, for thirty-five years. And in any event, pending his proposed outburst of "love, a spiritual energy that the human heart can pit against the physical energy released from the heart of matter," it's all we've got. [21]

So the first problem with Schell's solution is that you can't get there from here. The second problem is what "there" could be like. Speaking, [22] if I may, for the unborn, I wonder if they might not prefer the risk of not being born at all to the certainty of being born into the world Schell is prepared to will them.

The supreme silliness of "The Fate of the Earth," and of much of the   23 antinuclear movement, is the insistence that any kind of perspective on nuclear war is immoral. Schell complains, "It is as though life itself were one huge distraction, diverting our attention from the peril to life." And to Schell, apparently, all considerations apart from the danger of nuclear war *are* mere distractions. He repeatedly asks, What could be worse than the total annihilation of the earth and everything and everyone on it forever and ever? He demands that "this possibility must be dealt with morally and politically as though it were a certainty." We can opt for "human survival," or for "our transient aims and fallible convictions" and "our political and military traditions."

> On the one side stand human life and the terrestrial creation. On the other side stands a particular organization of human life—the system of independent, sovereign nation-states.

Gee, I just can't decide. Can you?

If the choice were "survival" versus "distractions," it would be easy,   24 and Schell wants to make it seem easy (though I have to wonder whether he really lives his own life at the peak of obsessive hysteria posited in his writing). In fact, that's not the choice. The choice is between the chance, not the certainty, of a disaster of uncertain magnitude, versus institutional and social arrangements that have some real charm.

Schell suggests at one point that "say, liberty" and other "benefits of   25 life" are relatively unimportant in his scheme of things, because

> to speak of sacrificing the species for the sake of one of these benefits involves one in the absurdity of wanting to destroy something in order to preserve one of its parts.

But it's clear that he imagines his postnuclear world as a delightful lion-and-lamb affair, no nation-states, no war, free hors d'oeuvres at the Algonquin bar, a place anyone would prefer even apart from the nuclear dilemma. Some of his admirers know better. In a recent column, Eliot Fremont-Smith of the *Village Voice* expressed the general dazzlement "The Fate of the Earth" has induced in the New York literary scene. He called on Knopf to cancel the rest of its spring list in deference to Schell's vital message. But Fremont-Smith did indicate some passing regret for what might have to be given up when Schell's world organization replaces national sovereignty. His list includes "freedom, liberties, social justice" —but he is willing to kiss these trinkets away in the name of "a higher and longer-viewed morality." Others may demur.

Actually, if Schell and his admirers really believe that the nuclear peril   26
outweighs all other considerations, they are making unnecessary work for
themselves by proposing to convince all the leaders of the world to lay
down their weapons. Schell concedes that the people of the Soviet Union
don't have much influence over their government, and suggests, rather
lamely, that "public opinion in the free countries would have to . . . bring
its pressure to bear, as best it could, on all governments." But why not
avoid this problem by concentrating on our own governments? Schell is
right: the doctrine of deterrence is only necessary for nation-states that
wish to preserve themselves as political entities. Nothing would reduce
the peril of nuclear war more quickly and dramatically than for the free
and open societies of the West to renounce the use of nuclear weapons
unilaterally. That would solve the flaw Schell sees in deterrence theory
by making the Soviet threat to use them thoroughly credible, and therefore making their use unnecessary. More creatively, we might offer the
Soviets a deal: you forswear nuclear weapons, and we'll forswear *all*
weapons, nuclear and conventional. They might find this very tempting.
So, by his own logic ("the nuclear powers put a higher value on national
sovereignty than they do on human survival"), would Jonathan Schell.

In practice, the antinuclear movement *is* concentrating on the free   27
governments of the West, for the obvious reason that these are the only
governments susceptible to being influenced. I do not think most antinuclear protesters want unilateral disarmament. But the suspicion that
they do is widespread among the political leaders they must attempt to
persuade, and is hampering their basically worthy efforts. The glorious
muddle of their thinking is hampering those efforts even more. What *do*
they want?

Topical Considerations

1. What does Kinsley say is fundamental to the dismantling of
the nuclear terror between enemies? What hope does he see for this
possibility?

2. On what issues is the antinuclear movement vague and confused, according to Kinsley?

3. Throughout the essay, Kinsley refers to Jonathan Schell's
"Fate of the Earth" essay. Why does he say the piece is "pretentious"?
Is his evidence convincing?

4. What is Kinsley's central argument against Schell—his style?
his arguments? his politics? or some of each?

5. What does Kinsley mean when he accuses Schell of "hothouse
reasoning" (paragraph 10)?

6. At the end of paragraph 13, Kinsley specifically refers to that

portion of "Fate of the Earth" reprinted in the preceding essay. Kinsley refers to these as "pages of the usual gruesome description," then goes on to say that there is something "pornographic" about such emphasis. How does he mean this term? Looking back over Schell's piece, do you agree? Do you agree with Kinsley's assessment of the "sickness" of the antinuclear movement?

7. According to Kinsley, what is Schell's proposal for avoiding nuclear war? What does he think of Schell's idea? What is Kinsley's proposal?

Rhetorical Considerations

1. Much of Kinsley's attack on Jonathan Schell centers on his style and writing tone. How would you characterize Kinsley's style and tone? Would you say he is cynical? despairing? fatalistic? ironical? Cite passages for evidence.

2. Occasionally, Kinsley slips from attacking Schell's writing to attacking him personally. Cite some of these passages. Do these personal insults weaken or strengthen Kinsley's case? Explain.

3. What do you make of the sentence at the end of paragraph 1: "But, really, I think a nuclear holocaust would be very, very sad"? Is Kinsley being serious and sincere? Or do you think he is being cynical? sarcastic? understated?

4. Find some examples of Kinsley's humor in this essay. How were the humorous effects created?

5. The author quotes from Schell's essay. How well does he use the sample passages? Do his commentaries seem accurate and fair?

Writing Assignments

1. If you have read the Schell piece in this book, how has Kinsley's essay affected your view of it? Write an essay telling how your attitudes have been changed.

2. Did this essay put nuclear holocaust in perspective for you? Did it affect your attitudes about nuclear war, the future, nuclear disarmament, or the antinuclear movement? If so, describe these effects in an essay.

3. Kinsley says that Schell and other antinuclear supporters are fooling themselves when they think they can "convince all the leaders of the world to lay down their weapons" (paragraph 26). Write an essay in which you argue either for or against this position.

How I Designed an A-Bomb in My Junior Year at Princeton

John Aristotle Phillips and David Michaelis

Most of us would assume that building a nuclear weapon would at the outset require genius, special expertise, and highly classified information. Unfortunately, however, that may not be the case. The following is an account of how a junior on academic probation at Princeton designed a workable atomic bomb as a term project in physics. John Aristotle Phillips had two goals in writing his term paper: showing how easily a nuclear device could be assembled by terrorists and getting an A in the course. He accomplished both, and his term paper was immediately classified. In collaboration with his former classmate, David Michaelis, Phillips wrote the following account, which comes from their book *Mushroom: The Story of the A-Bomb Kid* (1979).

1 The first semester of my junior year at Princeton University is a disaster, and my grades show it. D's and F's predominate, and a note from the dean puts me on academic probation. Flunk one more course, and I'm out.

2 Fortunately, as the new semester gets under way, my courses begin to interest me. Three hours a week, I attend one called Nuclear Weapons Strategy and Arms Control in which three professors lead 12 students through intense discussions of counterforce capabilities and doomsday scenarios. The leader is Hal Feiveson, renowned for his strong command of the subject matter. Assisting him are Marty Sherwin, an authority on cold-war diplomacy, and Freeman Dyson, an eminent physicist.

3 One morning, Dyson opens a discussion of the atomic bomb: "Let me describe what occurs when a 20-kiloton bomb is exploded, similar to the two dropped on Hiroshima and Nagasaki. First, the sky becomes illuminated by a brilliant white light. Temperatures are so high around the point of explosion that the atmosphere is actually made incadescent. To an observer standing six miles away the ball of fire appears brighter than a hundred suns.

4 "As the fireball begins to spread up and out into a mushroom-shaped cloud, temperatures spontaneously ignite all flammable materials for miles around. Wood-frame houses catch fire. Clothing bursts into flame, and people suffer intense third-degree flash burns over their exposed flesh. The very high temperatures also produce a shock wave and a variety of nuclear radiations capable of penetrating 20 inches of concrete. The shock wave levels everything in the vicinity of ground zero; hurricane-force winds then rush into the vacuum left by the expanding shock wave and sweep up the rubble of masonry, glass and steel, hurling it outward as lethal projectiles."

Silence falls over the room as the titanic proportions of the destruction   5
begin to sink in.

"It takes only 15 pounds of plutonium to fabricate a crude atomic   6
bomb," adds Hal Feiveson. "If breeder reactors come into widespread
use, there will be sufficient plutonium shipped around the country each
year to fashion thousands of bombs. Much of it could be vulnerable to
theft or hijacking."

The class discusses a possible scenario. A 200-pound shipment disap-   7
pears en route between a reprocessing facility and a nuclear reactor. State
and local police discover only an empty truck and a dead driver. Two
weeks later, a crude fission bomb is detonated in Wall Street. Of the
half-million people who crowd the area during the regular business day,
100,000 are killed outright. A terrorist group claims responsibility and
warns the President that if its extravagant political demands are not met,
there will be another explosion within a week.

"That's impossible," a student objects. "Terrorists don't have the   8
know-how to build a bomb."

"You have to be brilliant to design an A-bomb," says another. "Be-   9
sides, terrorists don't have access to the knowledge."

Impossible? Or is it? The specter of terrorists incinerating an entire   10
city with a homemade atomic bomb begins to haunt me. I turn to John
McPhee's book *The Curve of Binding Energy,* in which former Los Alamos
nuclear physicist Ted Taylor postulates that a terrorist group could easily
steal plutonium or uranium from a nuclear reactor and then design a
workable atomic bomb with information available to the general public.
According to Taylor, all the ingredients—except plutonium—are legally
available at hardware stores and chemical-supply houses.

Suddenly, an idea comes to mind. Suppose an average—or below-   11
average in my case—physics student could design a workable atomic
bomb on paper? That would prove Taylor's point dramatically and show
the federal government that stronger safeguards have to be placed on the
storage of plutonium. If I could design a bomb, almost any intelligent
person could. But I would have to do it in less than three months to turn
it in as my junior independent project. I decide to ask Freeman Dyson to
be my adviser.

"You understand," says Dyson, "my government security clearance   12
will preclude me from giving you any more information than that which
can be found in physics libraries? And that the law of 'no comment'
governing scientists who have clearance to atomic secrets stipulates that,
if asked a question about the design of a bomb, I can answer neither yes
nor no?"

"Yes, sir," I reply. "I understand."   13

"Okay, then. I'll give you a list of textbooks outlining the general   14
principles—and I wish you luck."

I'm tremendously excited as I charge over to the physics office to   15
record my project, and can barely write down:

John Aristotle Phillips
Dr. Freeman Dyson, Adviser
"How to Build Your Own
Atomic Bomb"

A few days later, Dyson hands me a short list of books on nuclear-   16
reactor technology, general nuclear physics and current atomic theory.
"That's all?" I ask incredulously, having expected a bit more direction.

At subsequent meetings Dyson explains only the basic principles of   17
nuclear physics, and his responses to my calculations grow opaque. If I
ask about a particular design or figure, he will glance over what I've done
and change the subject. At first, I think this is his way of telling me I am
correct. To make sure, I hand him an incorrect figure. He reads it and
changes the subject.

Over spring vacation, I go to Washington, D.C., to search for records   18
of the Los Alamos Project that were declassified between 1954 and 1964.
I discover a copy of the literature given to scientists who joined the
project in the spring of 1943. This text, *The Los Alamos Primer,* carefully
outlines all the details of atomic fissioning known to the world's most
advanced scientists in the early '40s. A whole batch of copies costs me
about $25. I gather them together and go over to the bureaucrat at the
front desk. She looks at the titles, and then looks up at me.

"Oh, you want to build a bomb, too?" she asks matter-of-factly.   19

I can't believe it. Do people go in there for bomb-building information   20
every day? When I show the documents to Dyson, he is visibly shaken.
His reaction indicates to me that I actually stand a chance of coming up
with a workable design.

The material necessary to explode my bomb is plutonium-239, a man-   21
made, heavy isotope. Visualize an atomic bomb as a marble inside a
grapefruit inside a basketball inside a beach ball. At the center of the
bomb is the initiator, a marble-size piece of metal. Around the initiator
is a grapefruit-size ball of plutonium-239. Wrapped around the plutonium is a three-inch reflector shield made of beryllium. High explosives
are placed symmetrically around the beryllium shield. When these deto-
nate, an imploding shock wave is set off, compressing the grapefruit-size
ball of plutonium to the size of a plum. At this moment, the process of
atoms fissioning—or splitting apart—begins.

There are many subtleties involved in the explosion of an atomic   22
bomb. Most of them center on the actual detonation of the explosives
surrounding the beryllium shield. The grouping of these explosives is

one of the most highly classified aspects of the atomic bomb, and it poses the biggest problems for me as I begin to design my bomb.

My base of operations is a small room on the second floor of Ivy, my 23 eating club. The conference table in the center of the room is covered with books, calculators, design paper, notes. My sleeping bag is rolled out on the floor. As the next three weeks go by, I stop going to classes altogether and work day and night. The other members at Ivy begin referring to me as The Hobo because of my unshaven face and disheveled appearance. I develop a terrible case of bloodshot eyes. Sleep comes rarely.

I approach every problem from a terrorist's point of view. The bomb 24 must be inexpensive to construct, simple in design, and small enough to sit unnoticed in the trunk of a car or an abandoned U-Haul trailer.

As the days and nights flow by, linked together by cups of coffee and 25 bologna sandwiches, I scan government documents for gaps indicating an area of knowledge that is still classified. Essentially, I am putting together a huge jigsaw puzzle. The edge pieces are in place and various areas are getting filled in, but pieces are missing. Whenever the outline of one shows up, I grab my coffee Thermos and sit down to devise the solution that will fill the gap.

With only two weeks left, the puzzle is nearly complete, but two pieces 26 are still missing: which explosives to use, and how to arrange them around the plutonium.

During the next week I read that a high-explosive blanket around the 27 beryllium shield might work. But after spending an entire night calculating, I conclude that it is not enough to guarantee a successful implosion wave. Seven days before the design is due, I'm still deadlocked.

The alarm clock falls off the table and breaks. I take this as a sign to 28 do something drastic, and I start all over at the beginning. Occasionally I find errors in my old calculations, and I correct them. I lose sense of time.

With less than 24 hours to go, I run through a series of new calcula- 29 tions, mathematically figuring the arrangement of the explosives around the plutonium. If my equations are correct, my bomb might be just as effective as the Hiroshima and Nagasaki bombs. But I can't be sure until I know the exact nature of the explosives I will use.

Next morning, with my paper due at 5 P.M., I call the Du Pont Company 30 from a pay phone and ask for the head of the chemical-explosives division, a man I'll call S. F. Graves. If he gives me even the smallest lead, I'll be able to figure the rest out by myself. Otherwise, I'm finished.

"Hello, Mr. Graves. My name is John Phillips. I'm a student at Prince- 31 ton, doing work on a physics project. I'd like to get some advice, if that's possible."

"What can I do for you?"   32

"Well," I stammer, "I'm doing research on the shaping of explosive   33
products that create a very high density in a spherically shaped metal. Can
you suggest a Du Pont product that would fit in this category?"

"Of course," he says, in a helpful manner.   34

I don't think he suspects, but I decide to try a bluff: "One of my 35
professors told me that a simple explosive blanket would work in the
high-density situation."

"No, no. Explosive blankets went out with the Stone Age. We sell [he 36
names the product] to do the job in similar density-problem situations to
the one you're talking about."

When I hang up the phone, I let out a whoop. Mr. Graves has given   37
me just the information I need. Now, if my calculations are correct with
respect to the new information, all I have to do is complete my paper by
five.

Five minutes to five, I race over to the physics building and bound up 38
the stairs. Inside the office, everybody stops talking and stares at me. I
haven't shaved in over a week.

"Is your razor broken, young man?" asks one of the department secre- 39
taries.

"I came to hand in my project," I explain. "I didn't have time to shave. 40
Sorry."

A week later, I return to the physics department to pick up my project. 41
One thought has persisted: If I didn't guess correctly about the implosion
wave, or if I made a mistake somewhere in the graphs, I'll be finished at
Princeton.

A secretary points to the papers. I flip through them, but don't find 42
mine. I look carefully; my paper is not there.

Trying to remain calm, I ask her if all the papers have been graded. 43

"Yes, of course," she says.   44

Slowly I return to my room. The absence of my paper can only mean   45
that I blew it.

In the middle of the week, I go back to the physics-department office, 46
hoping to catch the chairman for a few minutes. The secretary looks up,
then freezes.

"Aren't you John Phillips?" she asks.   47

"Yes," I reply.   48

"Aren't you the boy who designed the atomic bomb?"   49

"Yes, and my paper wasn't . . ."   50

She takes a deep breath. "The question has been raised by the depart- 51
ment whether your paper should be classified by the U.S. government."

"What? Classified?"   52

She takes my limp hand, shaking it vigorously. "Congratulations," she 53
says, all smiles. "You got one of the only A's in the department. Dr.

Wigner wants to see you right away. He says it's a fine piece of work. And Dr. Dyson has been looking for you everywhere."

For a second I don't say anything. Then the madness of the situation   54
hits me. A small air bubble of giddiness rises in my throat. Here I have put on paper the plan for a device capable of killing thousands of people, and all I was worrying about was flunking out.

Topical Considerations

1. In paragraphs 3 and 4, Professor Dyson begins his discussion with some detailed descriptions of what occurs when a twenty-kiloton bomb is exploded. What might Dyson's intention have been in giving this account? What might Phillips's purpose have been in giving Dyson's account?

2. What aspects of atomic bomb construction posed the biggest problems to Phillips? How does he go about resolving them?

3. The author's purpose in this account is not to tell us how to build our own atomic bomb, but what is his purpose? Explain.

Rhetorical Considerations

1. What is the rhetorical advantage of writing this account in the present tense?

2. What is the rhetorical advantage of Phillips's use of dialogue throughout?

3. In paragraph 54, the author says that suddenly "the madness of the situation hits" him. What madness does he mean? Is it just what he describes in the final sentence, or does the "madness" suggest something greater? Explain.

Writing Assignment

1. The piece you have just read was written in narrative form—that is, it told a story by relating a series of events in a coherent way. Write a similar kind of narrative in which you recount an exciting experience you have had. Like Phillips and Michaelis, move chronologically, citing specific events and details.

Evacuating the Capital? No Need to Hurry Now

Art Buchwald

Nuclear warfare is not a laughing matter, but if anybody could find something funny to say about it, it would be Art Buchwald. He is one of America's best-known journalists and humorists. Since 1962, Buchwald has written a column that is syndicated in nearly 400 newspapers. Many of his essays have been published in collections, such as *Son of The Great Society* (1966) and *The Buchwald Stops Here* (1978). What characterizes Buchwald is his good-natured mockery of American politics and social trends. In this characteristic piece, he goes after a grand evacuation plan dreamed up by the Office of Civil Defense. According to the plan, in the event of a nuclear alert, residents of major cities would jump into their cars and speed off to rural "host" towns, where residents would welcome the evacuees. As Buchwald suggests, however, things don't always go according to plan—especially the government's plan.

1   Unlike most people, I take Civil Defense very seriously. While the evacuation plan for Washington hasn't been fully worked out, I know what we're supposed to do. When the sirens go off, we're all to get in our automobiles, grab our credit cards and head for Lickety Split, West Virginia.

2   The other evening around five o'clock I decided to take a dry run. I came home and told my wife, who was in her housecoat and curlers.

3   "Get in the car, we're going to have a practice evacuation drill."

4   "Let me get dressed first."

5   "You don't have time. Do you think when the real thing happens, the Russians are going to wait for you to get all gussied up? Grab the credit cards and let's go."

6   "Do you have gas in the car?" she wanted to know.

7   "I have half a tank."

8   "That won't get us to Lickety Split."

9   "I'm sure if the real thing happens, the Civil Defense people will have emergency gasoline trucks all along the highway. After all, they can't expect us to evacuate Washington during an atomic bomb attack and not supply the petrol. Now stop talking and get in the car. We have to pretend this is not a drill."

10 As soon as we got near Key Bridge, we found cars bumper to bumper. We moved 10 feet every five minutes.

11 "What's going on?" my wife wanted to know.

12 "It's normal rush-hour traffic," I explained.

13 We made it over the Key Bridge in 45 minutes and moved smoothly

along the George Washington Parkway at 25 miles an hour until we hit the Beltway and were slowed down to 15."

"I guess you didn't get out of town as fast as you had hoped," my wife said.   14

"That's because this is just a drill. When people know they're racing against a Soviet ICBM, they'll be doing 80 miles an hour."   15

"How do we get to Lickety Split?" my wife asked.   16

"I guess the Civil Defense people haven't put up their signs yet."   17

My wife started to cry. "Let's go back."   18

"We can't go back until the Civil Defense people tell us it's safe. Washington, as far as this drill is concerned, has been completely vaporized."   19

By asking directions from 40 people, we finally got to Lickety Split six hours later.   20

It was dark, and no one was on the streets. We knocked on the door of a farmhouse. A man carrying a shotgun answered it.   21

"Hi," I said, "we're from Washington and we were told to come to Lickety Split in case of an atomic attack. We thought we'd arrive early and look the place over just to see where we'd be the most comfortable."   22

"You got one minute to get off my farm."   23

"Don't shoot. Haven't you heard from the federal Civil Defense people? You're supposed to open your homes to us until they can rebuild the capital."   24

"Thirty seconds."   25

"We'll sleep in the barn," I pleaded. "We're not proud."   26

"Fifteen seconds."   27

My wife pulled me away from the door towards the car.   28

"I'm reporting you to the Federal Emergency Management Administration," I yelled at him. "You're making their atomic war evacuation plan into a farce."   29

Topical Considerations

1. If you hadn't known Buchwald was a humorist, where in the essay would you have caught on?

2. What typically American characteristics and attitudes does he satirize?

3. What assumptions about the Civil Defense people does Buchwald poke fun at?

4. If it were a real attack, what kinds of conditions would the Buchwalds probably face as they tried to leave Washington?

5. What is Buchwald's point in this piece? Who is the real target of his satire? Where is this best dramatized in the piece?

Rhetorical Considerations

1. What humorous effects does Buchwald intend by naming his assigned evacuation destination Lickety Split, West Virginia?

2. How does Buchwald characterize his wife in this little scenario? How does he characterize himself?

3. The farmer in Lickety Split says only a few words. How well does what he says underscore the problem Buchwald is criticizing?

Writing Assignments

1. Do what Buchwald does here—imagine making a practice evacuation drill from your home town to some fictitious destination assigned by the Civil Defense Department. Try to imagine the kinds of funny things that could go wrong, including the kind of reception you might get.

2. The real issue of evacuating the Capital or any city during a nuclear emergency is not so funny. Write a paper in which you suggest to the Civil Defense people an alternative to their "host town" plan.

AMERICAN HIGH TECH

7

The Mind in the Machine

Roger Rosenblatt

Since the Industrial Revolution of the nineteenth century, science fiction writers have written tales of robots in revolt, dramatizing a general cultural fear of machine takeover. Today, this sense of menace has been heightened by the continuous development of ever-capable high-speed computers. Many people wonder if humans have granted to artificial intelligence the winning edge over their own species. We open this section, "American High Tech," with a clear and insightful examination of the differences between human and computer intelligence. Roger Rosenblatt, a senior writer for *Time* magazine, argues that rather than being threatened by how much computers know, we should be grateful for learning how much we don't know. The difference may be a saving grace.

The factory robot that crushed a man to death in Japan last year did little to silence the talk that machines are a threat to human pre-eminence. That talk has been alive ever since people first discovered that they could manufacture tools vastly superior to themselves; in Samuel Butler's satire *Erewhon* (1872), the citizens establish a museum of old machines in which they at once deposit and abandon their mechanical inventions, which they believed would swallow up their souls. When machines possess artificial intelligence, like computers, the human fear of being overtaken seems both more urgent and more complex. Science-fiction writers from Capek to Asimov have built much of their genre around robots, androids, computers and their kin—each fairly boring and predictable as characters, but all presenting the same basic paradox: that they will eventually take command of the world, and that a man can beat them every time.

This proposition is not as contradictory as it sounds, since, for one thing, the fact that it takes real (*i.e.*, natural) intelligence to create the artificial kind would seem to give humanity a perpetual edge; and, for another, people are able to hold contraries in their heads simultaneously —a feat that is reassuring in itself, since it is one of the things that distinguishes men from machines. Indeed, man tends to search out such distinctions even as he endows his machines with increasing sophistication, as if to make sure that his evolution is no slower than that of his creations. Still, it is sometimes nerve-racking to read what these boxes can do. Joseph Weizenbaum, of M.I.T., who has recently come to criticize computer education for children as a context for "toy problems," nonetheless got more than a toy gasp out of the public in 1968 when he unveiled his project ELIZA—an IBM 7094 programmed by Weizenbaum to "practice" psychotherapy—and then published a "conversation" between ELIZA and a real patient:

Patient: You are like my father in some ways.

ELIZA: What resemblance do you see?
Patient: You are not very aggressive, but I think you don't want me to notice that.
ELIZA: What makes you think I am not very aggressive?
Patient: You don't argue with me.
ELIZA: Why do you think I don't argue with you?
Patient: You are afraid of me.
ELIZA: Does it please you to believe I am afraid of you?
The elements of parody notwithstanding, it is no joke to see a machine become a man, especially in an era whose main (if somewhat *pro forma*) worry centers on men becoming machines.

A great deal of intellectual effort is therefore spent these days—mostly by the computer scientists themselves—trying to reassure everybody that, as smart as a machine can get, it can never be as intelligent as its progenitor. In part, this effort is made in order to see that the wizened, noncomputer generation—which often regards the younger with the unbridled enthusiasm that the Chinese showed the Mongol hordes—feels that it has a safe and legitimate place in modernity. In part, the effort is made because the proposition is true: a computer cannot possess the full range of human intelligence. Yet, in terms of reconciling man and machine, this effort still misses the point. The cultural value of computers does not lie in perceiving what they cannot do, but what they can, and what, in turn, their capabilities show about our own. In other words, a computer may not display the whole of human intelligence, but that portion it can display could do a lot more good for man's self-confidence than continuing reassurances that he is in no immediate danger of death by robot.

Essentially, what one wants to know in sorting out this relationship is the answers to two questions: Can computers think (a technical problem)? And, should they think (a moral one)? In order to get at both, it is first necessary to agree on what thinking itself is—what thought means—and that is no quick step. Every period in history has had to deal with at least two main definitions of thought, which mirror the prevailing philosophies of that particular time and are usually in opposition. Moreover, these contending schools change from age to age. On a philosophical level, thought cannot know itself because it cannot step outside itself. Nor is it an activity that can be understood by what it produces (art, science, dreams). To Freud the mind was a house; to Plato a cave. These are fascinating, workable metaphors, but the fact is that in each case an analogy had to be substituted for an equation.

At the same time, certain aspects of thinking can be identified without encompassing the entire process. The ability to comprehend, to conceptualize, to organize and reorganize, to manipulate, to adjust—these are all parts of thought. So are the acts of pondering, rationalizing, worrying, brooding, theorizing, contemplating, criticizing. One thinks when one imagines, hopes, loves, doubts, fantasizes, vacillates, regrets. To experience greed, pride, joy, spite, amusement, shame, suspicion, envy, grief—all these require thought; as do the decisions to take command, or umbrage; to feel loyalty or inhibitions; to ponder ethics, self-sacrifice, cowardice, ambition. So vast is the mind's business that even as one makes such a list, its inadequacy is self-evident—the recognition of inadequacy being but another part of an enormous and varied instrument.

The answer to the first question, then—Can a machine think?—is yes   6
and no. A computer can certainly do some of the above. It can (or will soon be able to) transmit and receive messages, "read" typescript, recognize voices, shapes and patterns, retain facts, send reminders, "talk" or mimic speech, adjust, correct, strategize, make decisions, translate languages. And, of course, it can calculate, that being its specialty. Yet there are hundreds of kinds of thinking that computers cannot come close to. And for those merely intent on regarding the relationship of man to machine as a head-to-artificial-head competition, this fact offers some solace—if not much progress.

For example, the Apollo moon shot in July 1969 relied on computers   7
at practically every stage of the operation. Before taking off, the astronauts used computerized simulations of the flight. The spacecraft was guided by a computer, which stored information about the gravitational fields of the sun and moon, and calculated the craft's position, speed and altitude. This computer, which determined the engines to be fired, and when, and for how long, took part of its own information from another computer on the ground. As the Apollo neared the moon, a computer triggered the firing of a descent rocket, slowed the lunar module, and then signaled Neil Armstrong that he had five seconds to decide whether or not to go ahead with the landing. At 7,200 ft., a computer commanded the jets to tilt the craft almost upright so that Armstrong and Aldrin could take a close look at what the world had been seeking for centuries.

Would one say, then, that computers got men to the moon? Of course   8
not. A machine is merely a means. What got man to the moon was his desire to go there—desire being yet another of those elements that a computer cannot simulate or experience. It was far less interesting, for instance, that Archimedes believed he could move the earth with his lever than that he wanted to try it. Similarly, no machine could have propelled man to the moon had not the moon been in man in the first place.

Thus the second question—Should a machine think?—answers itself.   9
The question is not in fact the moral problem it at first appears, but purely a practical one. Yes, a machine should think as much as it can, because it *can* only think in limited terms. Hubert Dreyfus, a philosophy professor at Berkeley, observes that "all aspects of human thought, including nonformal aspects like moods, sensory-motor skills and long-range self-interpretations, are so interrelated that one cannot substitute an abstractable web of explicit beliefs for the whole cloth of our concrete

244 American High Tech

everyday practice." Marianne Moore saw the web her own way: "The mind is an enchanting thing,/ is an enchanted thing/ like the glaze on a/ kaytdid-wing/ subdivided by sun/ till the nettings are legion,/ Like Gieseking playing Scarlatti." In short, human intelligence is too intricate to be replicated. When a computer can smile at an enemy, cheat at cards and pray in church all in the same day, then, perhaps, man will know his like. Until then, no machine can touch us.

For the sake of argument, however, what if Dreyfus, Moore and common sense were all wrong? What if the mind with its legion nettings could in fact be replicated in steel and plastic, and all human befuddlements find their way onto a program—would the battle be lost? Hardly. The moon is always in the man. Even if it were possible to reduce people to box size and have them plonked down before themselves in all their powers, they would still want more. Whatever its source, there is a desire that outdesires desire; otherwise computers would not have come into being. As fast as the mind travels, it somehow manages to travel faster than itself, and people always know, or sense, what they do not know. No machine does that. A computer can *achieve* what it does not know (not knowing that $2+2=4$, it can find out), but it cannot yearn for the answer or even dimly suspect its existence. If people knew where such suspicions and yearnings came from, they might be able to lock them in silicon. But they do not know what they are; they merely know that they are—just as in the long run they only know that they exist, not what their existence is or what it means. The difference between us and any machine we create is that a machine is an answer, and we are a question.

But is there anything really startling in this? With all the shouting and sweating that go on about machines taking over the world, does anyone but a handful of zealots and hysterics seriously believe that the human mind is genuinely imperiled by devices of its own manufacture? In *Gödel, Escher, Bach* (1979), Douglas R. Hofstadter's dazzling book on minds and machines, a man is described—one Johann Martin Zacharias Dase (1824–61)—who was employed by governments because he could do mathematical feats like multiplying two 100-digit numbers in his head, and could calculate at a glance how many sheep were in a field, for example, or how many words in a sentence, up to about 30. (Most people can do this up to about six.) Were Mr. Dase living today, would he be thought a computer? Are computers thought of as men? This is a kind of cultural game people play, a false alarm, a ghost story recited to put one's mind at rest.

The trouble is that "at rest" is a poor place to be in this situation, because such a position encourages no understanding of what these machines can do for life beyond the tricks they perform. Alfred North Whitehead said that "civilization advances by extending the number of important operations which we can perform without thinking about them." In that sense, computers have advanced civilization. But thinking about the computer, as a cultural event or instrument, has so far not advanced civilization one whit. Instead, one hears humanists either fretting about the probability that before the end of the century computers will be able to beat all the world's chess masters, or consoling themselves that a computer cannot be Mozart—the response to the first being, "So what?" and to the second, "Who ever thought so?" The thing to recognize about the computer is not how powerful it is or will become, but that its power is finite. So is that of the mind. The finitudes in both cases are not the same, but the fact that they are comparable may be the most useful news that man's self-evaluation has received in 200 years.

For too long now, generations have been bedeviled with the idea, formally called romanticism, that human knowledge has no limits, that man can become either God or Satan, depending on his inclinations. The rider to this proposition is that some human minds are more limitless than others, and wherever that notion finds its most eager receptacles, one starts out with Byron and winds up in Dachau. To be fair, that is not all of romanticism, but it is the worst of it, and the worst has done the world a good deal of damage. For the 18th century, man was man-size. For the 19th and 20th, his size has been boundless, which has meant that he has had little sense of his own proportion in relation to everything else —resulting either in exaggerated self-pity or in self-exaltation—and practically no stable appreciation of his own worth. 13

Now, suddenly, comes a machine that says in effect: This is the size of man insofar as that size may be measured by this machine. It is not the whole size of man, but it is a definable percentage. Other machines show you how fast you can move and how much you can lift. This one shows you how well you can think, in certain areas. It will do as much as you would have it do, so it will demonstrate the extent of your capabilities. But since it can only go as far as you wish it to go, it will also demonstrate the strength of your volition. 14

Both these functions are statements of limitation. A machine that tells you how much you can know likewise implies how much you cannot. To learn what one can know is important, but to learn what one cannot know is essential to one's well-being. This offers a sense of proportion, and so is thoroughly antiromantic. Yet it is not cold 18th century rationalistic either. The computer simply provides a way of drawing a line between the knowable and the unknowable, between the moon and the moon in man, and it is on that line where people may be able to see their actual size. 15

Whether the world will look any better for such self-recognition is anybody's guess. The mind, being an enchanted thing, has surprised itself too often to suggest that any discovery about itself will improve economies or governments, much less human nature. On face value, however, the cultural effects of these machines are promising. Every so 16 often in history man makes what he needs. In one sense he made the computer because he needed to think faster. In another, he may have needed to define himself more clearly; he may have sensed a need for intellectual humility. If he needed intellectual humility at this particular time, it may be a sign that he was about to get out of hand again, and so these contraptions, of which he pretends to be so fearful, may in fact be his self-concocted saving grace. The mind is both crafty and mysterious enough to work that way.

Topical Considerations

1. Through references to Samuel Butler's satire *Erewhon* (1872) and Joseph Weizenbaum's project ELIZA, Rosenblatt establishes reasons why some people are so fearful of robots. What are some of the reasons he touches upon?

2. How does Rosenblatt define thought? According to this definition, can a machine think?

3. Rosenblatt gives us an account of the role of computers in the moon shot of July 1969. Is Rosenblatt trying to illustrate that a machine, the computer, is responsible for this feat? Or is he trying to demonstrate that man is responsible for it?

4. What is Rosenblatt's answer to the question, "Should a machine think?" How do his references to a philosopher and a poet support his answer?

5. Would you agree with Alfred North Whitehead's statement that "civilization advances by extending the number of important operations which we can perform without thinking about them" (paragraph 12)? Cite examples from your own experience to prove or disprove this idea.

6. Rosenblatt claims that the romantic view of man has done the world a good deal of damage. Explain his attitude.

Rhetorical Considerations

1. The opening lines of this essay include a reference to a recent industrial accident as well as a reference to a satire written in 1872. How are these seemingly disparate events connected? Why is this an effective beginning?

2. What is the purpose of the allusion to the Chinese and the Mongol hordes in paragraph 3?

3. Read over paragraphs 9, 11, and 12. Based on the kinds of references Rosenblatt makes, with what fields of study does he seem to be familiar? Do these references strengthen his argument?

Writing Assignments

1. Rosenblatt talks about some traditional fears people have had about machine domination. If you have heard any particular fears expressed by friends or relatives, write a paper about their concerns. What are the bases of these fears? Which kinds of machines do people fear? What consequences do they worry about?

2. If you have read any machine-menace science fiction stories, write a paper about the attitudes expressed toward the machines in these stories. Consider any of Isaac Asimov's robot stories (for example, *I, Robot*). What are the specific dangers these mechanical creations pose to human beings?

3. Write a letter to Mr. Rosenblatt telling him why you agree or disagree with his position in this essay.

And Man Created the Chip

Merrill Sheils

"We are at the dawn of the era of the smart machine—an 'information age' that will change forever the way an entire nation works, plays, travels and even thinks." So writes reporter Merrill Sheils in this cover story for *Newsweek*. With the assistance of researchers William Cook, Michael Reese, Marc Frons and Phyllis Malamud, Sheils gives us a lively overview of the current computer revolution, with a look back at its roots and a glimpse forward at the possible ways computers will transform our lives—ways that have some people worried.

Welcome! Always glad to show someone from the early '80s around the 1 *place. The biggest change, of course, is the smart machines—they're all around us. No need to be alarmed, they're very friendly. Can't imagine how you lived without them. The telephone, dear old thing, is giving a steady busy signal to a bill collector I'm avoiding. Unless he starts calling from a new number my phone doesn't know, he'll never get through. TURN OFF! Excuse me for shouting—almost forgot the bedroom television was on. Let's see, anything else before we go? The oven already knows the menu for tonight and the kitchen robot will mix us a mean Martini. Guess we're ready. Oh no, you won't need a key. We'll just program the lock to recognize your voice and let you in whenever you want.*

A revolution is under way. Most Americans are already well aware of 2 the gee-whiz gadgetry that is emerging, in rapidly accelerating bursts, from the world's high-technology laboratories. But most of us perceive only dimly how pervasive and profound the changes of the next twenty years will be. We are at the dawn of the era of the smart machine—an "information age" that will change forever the way an entire nation works, plays, travels and even thinks. Just as the industrial revolution dramatically expanded the strength of man's muscles and the reach of his hand, so the smart-machine revolution will magnify the power of his brain. But unlike the industrial revolution, which depended on finite resources such as iron and oil, the new information age will be fired by a seemingly limitless resource—the inexhaustible supply of knowledge itself. Even computer scientists, who best understand the galloping technology and its potential, are wonderstruck by its implications. "It is really awesome," says L. C. Thomas of Bell Laboratories. "Every day is just as scary as the day before."

The driving force behind the revolution is the development of two   3 fundamental and interactive technologies—computers and integrated circuits. Today, tiny silicon chips half the size of a fingernail are etched with circuitry powerful enough to book seats on jumbo jets (and keep the planes working smoothly in the air), cut complex swatches of fabric with little wastage, help children learn to spell and play chess well enough to beat all but the grandest masters. The new technology means that bits of computing power can be distributed wherever they might be useful—the way small electric motors have become ubiquitous—or combined in giant mainframe computers to provide enormous problem-solving potential. In addition, this "computational plenty" is making smart machines easier to use and more forgiving of unskilled programming. Machines are even communicating with each other. "What's next?" asks Peter E. Hart, director of the SRI International artificial-intelligence center. "More to the point, what's *not* next?"

The explosion is just beginning. In 1979, the world market for micro-   4 electronics topped $11 billion. Over the next five years, chip sales are expected to grow by at least 20 per cent annually, and the market for microprocessors, entire "computers on a chip," will expand by 50 per cent each year—even though the chips themselves and the computing power they represent are diving in price. As industry officials are fond of remarking, if the automobile industry had improved its technology at the same rate computer science has, it would now be turning out Rolls-Royces that cost no more than $70 apiece.

There are a few clouds on the industry's horizon: capital costs are   5 rising, and Japan is mounting an all-out challenge to American supremacy in the field. Some experts predict that the shape of the industry will change considerably by the end of the decade, perhaps even shrinking down to a half-dozen IBM-like giants. But whatever shake-outs lie ahead, the world will continue to snap up chips as fast as manufacturers can turn them out, creating a mushrooming "information industry" that will grow into a $500 billion-a-year enterprise, by far the biggest on earth.

The transformation will not be easy, for smart machines bring with   6 them the seeds of widespread economic dislocation and social unrest. Eventually, for example, they will make possible the full automation of many factories, displacing millions of blue-collar workers with a new "steel-collar" class. Even office workers will feel the crunch, as smart machines do more and more of the clerical work. Traditional businesses such as television networks and publishing companies will encounter new competition as programmers and advertisers beam information directly into the consumer's home.

Some social critics warn of a new generation of Luddites[1] who will fight   7 to stop the new technology through restrictive laws—or even sabotage. Others predict the rise of a new criminal class of master computer-raiders. And many view the advent of smart machines with a dread they cannot really explain. To them, computers are alien, too complicated to understand and too prone to horrifying mistakes like the recent false alarms on the Air Force's NORAD missile-detection system. Alarmists harbor fears that the technology will get out of control—perhaps producing new machines that can outsmart their human masters.

But industry experts think these problems can—and will—be solved.   8 In the optimists' scenario, educational programs will retrain displaced workers and equip them with skills suited to the booming new information business. Meanwhile, laymen will grow more and more comfortable with computers as they invade everyday life. And in the end, the smart-machine revolution will do far more to enrich life than most Americans realize. As the industry likes to picture the future, the new technology offers potential solutions to humanity's most intractable problems—the allocation of energy resources, food enough for all and the worldwide improvement of health care, to name just a few.

Somewhere between the dire warnings and the utopian visions, the   9 future will take form. But there is no doubt that the era of smart machines will be vastly different from anything that preceded it. "What we are doing is creating a new class structure around wealth—this time, the wealth of information," says SRI International futurologist Peter Schwartz. "Like today's 'haves and have-notes,' we will be a society of the 'knows and know-nots.' "

What makes both the industry and the technology all the more aston-   10 ishing is that neither existed 35 years ago. The pace of development is roughly akin to going from the Wright Brothers' first airplane to the space shuttle in a decade.

The first big electronic computer was ENIAC (for Electronic Numeri-   11 cal Integrator and Calculator), which was built in 1946. ENIAC filled a huge room, gobbled up 140,000 watts of electricity and contained 18,000 vacuum tubes that generated and controlled the electric current, allowing ENIAC to calculate. The tubes were large and expensive, and they produced a lot of heat, but it really didn't matter: almost as soon as ENIAC was complete, it was obsolete.

In 1947, scientists at Bell Laboratories introduced the transistor, a tiny   12
piece of semiconducting material such as silicon or germanium. Minute
impurities added to the semiconductor enabled it to free or capture
electrons without huge amounts of external energy. And as it turned out,
the transistor was the perfect mate for digital computers using a binary
code—an arithmetic system that employs only two digits or "bits," 1 and
0, that can be combined in strings, or "bytes," to represent any numerical
value. (Bytes, in turn, can be used in a computer language to represent
alphabetical characters.) Such computers rely on a large number of electrical circuits that are either "on" (corresponding to 1) or "off" (representing 0) to hold the binary code. The more circuits, the more the
computer can do—and the closer they are to each other, the faster the
computer can perform. Transistors allowed computer scientists to combine many more circuits in a fraction of the space of the old vacuum-tube
design and at much less cost.

Another advantage of transistors is that they lose none of their capacity   13
as they shrink in size. The next giant step in the small-is-beautiful revolution was the simultaneous announcement in 1959 by Texas Instruments
and Fairchild Semiconductor that both had successfully produced integrated circuits—single semiconductor chips containing several complete
electronic circuits. Once again, the breakthrough enabled manufacturers
to pack more computing power into less space. By 1970, the laboratories
were producing chips with large-scale integration of circuitry (LSI): thousands of integrated circuits crammed onto a single quarter-inch square
of silicon. Today, fully 100,000 transistors can be integrated on a chip,
making a tiny piece of silicon far more powerful than ENIAC.

There are various different kinds of microchips—for example, there   14
are memories that store data, amplifiers that transmit it and microprocessors that combine a number of computing tasks. The size of their components almost defies explanation. A human hair has a width of 100 microns; parts of the transistors now crowded onto chips are less than 3
microns wide. By the mid-1980s, with the advent of very large-scale
integration (VLSI), scientists expect to be using sub-micron geometries.
George H. Heilmeier, who is vice president for corporate research at
Texas Instruments, describes the increasing density this way: "In the
mid-1960s, the complexity of a chip was comparable to that of the street
network of a small town. Today's microprocessor is comparable to the
entire Dallas–Ft. Worth area. And the ultimate quarter-micron technology will be capable of producing chips whose complexity rivals an urban
street network covering the entire North American continent."

Making a chip is a complex process. Most manufacturers now use what   15
Heilmeier calls the "dip and wash" technique. A diagram of electronic
circuitry is designed by a scientist on a computer terminal. Photographic
machines produce hundreds of reproductions of the display and reduce
them in size until their individual components are in the micron range.

A photographic negative, or mask, is made of the patterns. Ultraviolet light is then projected through the mask onto a thin, 4-inch wafer of silicon that has been treated with photo resist, a light-sensitive material. Just like a film, the photo resist is developed, and the tiny patterns of the chips' circuitry emerge on the silicon's surface. The wafer is dipped in acid, which eats away the silicon where there is no photo resist. A layer of metal can be deposited for the interconnections between circuits, then another layer of photo resist. Some wafers take ten or more etched layers. Once all the layers are formed on the wafer, the chips are sawed out, fine wire leads are connected and they are ready for use in electronic devices.

16   VLSI will take even more complicated manufacturing technology. One technique most companies consider promising is electron-beam lithography, which uses electron beams to expose the photo resist on the wafer in much finer detail than optical processes permit. The scientists are also working hard to improve memory systems so that they will be able to store the ever-greater amounts of data for the chips to process.

17   One big advance in the works is bubble memories. On a chip of garnet coated with a thin layer of magnetic film, scientists form microscopic regions of reverse magnetization. The presence of one of these bubbles represents the 1 of the binary code, its absence the 0—and the over-all pattern contains the data that has been stored. Bubble memories have two great advantages over previous technology: the memory patterns do not disappear when the power is turned off, and they take up less space. Researchers at Bell Labs have turned out one experimental bubble-memory chip with the ability to store 11.5 million bits—more than ten times the capacity of the most powerful chip now on the market. Appropriately enough, the Bell scientists call it "the incredible hulk."

18   All these wonders are bursting out of the labs at a steadily dwindling cost to consumers. "The great thing about semiconductors is that when you make them smaller and denser, they automatically get faster and the power requirement goes down," says Lewis M. Branscomb, chief scientist for IBM. "So the entire machine, if you're building a larger computer, gets smaller, and you need less packaging. That makes them less expensive." One way of measuring the improvement is to take a look at Control Data Corp.'s new Cyber 205, which CDC introduced this month as "the world's most powerful computing system." The 205, which can perform 800 million operations in a single second, is smaller and eight times more powerful than its predecessor, a CDC mainframe introduced just two years ago. But the price—$7.9 million—is about the same.

19   Not surprisingly, the rapid growth of computer power, combined with its declining cost, has inspired a rush to find new applications for the technology. By the mid-1980s, most automobiles will contain microprocessors that regulate fuel use, adjust engine performance and notify the driver on a dashboard terminal when something goes wrong. And starting next year, the Library of Congress will catalog all new books and

other acquisitions on a computer: they will never be entered in an old-fashioned card catalog.

Hospitals, too, are making use of the wonders. At Massachusetts General in Boston, an automated analyzer hooked to the hospital's big computers tests blood samples. And the hospital has also developed a medical computer language called MUMPS that puts its computers to use in a variety of ways. Using one program, a student doctor is presented with a simulated "patient" with certain symptoms. At each step, the student has a choice of action—and the patient responds. If the student errs, the program makes it clear—and in the worst case, dryly informs the student that the patient has died.   20

The next big frontier on the consumer market—and one the industry hopes will make computers more attractive than ever—is speech. Two years ago, Texas Instruments brought out a learning device called "Speak and Spell," which "spoke" with a voice generated by two memory chips and a speech-synthesizer under the control of a microprocessor. The product attracted interest from all over the world, and TI itself has redoubled its research. Last year, it introduced a sophisticated translating machine available in four languages that permits the user to enter a word on a keyboard and get both a digital display of its foreign translation and a computer "voice" pronouncing it.   21

More complicated still are smart machines that both speak *and* understand the human voice. At Bell Labs, scientists are concentrating on systems that will allow human beings and computers to communicate by voice over the telephone. An experimental airline-reservation program has a vocabulary of about 200 words. The customer would have to use words the machine recognizes—and the computer would respond with appropriate information in sequences that have not been preprogramed. In April, IBM researchers used a computer to transcribe speech into printed form with a 91 per cent accuracy rate. "The good news was that the accuracy was so high," says Branscomb. "The bad news was that it took the computer 200 times as long to transcribe as we took to speak."   22

The scientists are confident that they will eventually be able to produce machines that both talk and listen with a high degree of accuracy, though they admit that some breakthroughs—such as teaching them to distinguish among homonyms by analyzing the context—are a long way off. For the handicapped, the benefits could be enormous: vast improvements in telephones for the deaf, for instance, that can print out whatever the voice on the other end is saying.   23

An even bigger breakthrough could come from technology that allows smart machines to "talk" among themselves. "Somehow, we have to figure out a way to link them all together," says George Pake, vice president of corporate research for Xerox. "The essence of the smart machines is that they will help us to communicate with them—and they, in turn, will be able to communicate with each other." Xerox itself recently   24 patented Ethernet—a system that can connect up to 100 disparate machines, enabling them to send bursts of information at incredible speeds. And Xerox, Satellite Business Systems and several other high-tech giants also plan to offer satellite services that would permit worldwide intra-corporate communication among smart machines.

But the really big player in the game may turn out to be American   25
Telephone and Telegraph Co., the telecommunications behemoth that is the parent company of Bell Labs. Recent Federal deregulatory initiatives may permit AT&T to enter the data-processing field, and Bell could come in with a big bang. Not only can AT&T move huge amounts of information over existing telephone lines, its research arm has been working on a giant new network called Advanced Communications Systems (ACS). ACS is an intelligent network: it can translate the language of any computer into its own digital code, move the data through the system, then translate it again to the language of the receiving terminal or computer.

Other companies in data processing are afraid that Ma Bell will crush   26
them with her huge capital and scientific resources. Newspaper publishers, for instance, worry that once office and home computers can tap into data banks all over the country, people will no longer need newspapers: both news and advertising could be fed directly into the living room. But Robert W. Lucky, director of Bell's electronic and computer-systems research lab, thinks cultural habits will prevail—at least for the foreseeable future. "I want to *feel* The New York Times, take it to the bathroom with me, spill my orange juice on it," he says.

In other sectors of the economy, the changes could come quickly. The   27
advent of microprocessors has made industrial robots, for example, far more useful and versatile than ever before. Today, instead of performing just one simple task, they can be repeatedly programed to switch jobs— and to do highly complex ones, at that. And for the first time, the new technology has made robots cheaper and more efficient than many of their human counterparts: for an hourly "wage" of just $4.60, the average cost of maintaining them, they perform tedious and dangerous work with a high degree of reliability. The average human worker on an automobile assembly line, by contrast, earns $16 an hour.

Big Labor has been slow to take notice of the change, perhaps because   28
the first automation "revolution," in the era of dumb robots, made so few inroads. But now robots can be built so that they can "see" rudimentary shapes and even make tactile distinctions. By some estimates, from 50 to 75 per cent of all U.S. factory workers could be displaced by smart robots before the end of the century. The estimates may be inflated, but they suggest that the new automation will emerge as a stormy issue at the union-management bargaining table in the years ahead.

Smart machines of a different sort are invading America's offices: U.S.   29
business will be 200 per cent more automated by 1990, some experts predict. Electronic filing systems already store information in many

offices, and electronic mail flashes messages from coast to coast. Several small computer companies like Chromatics, Inc., of Atlanta have pioneered sophisticated systems that not only analyze data but display the analyses in vivid color graphs, charts and pictures that eliminate the need for bulky computer print-outs. Architects can use the machines to visualize how new buildings will fit into existing neighborhoods, and the U.S. Navy is using them to test underwater equipment.

Computers have not really invaded the home as yet: only about 200,000 home computers are in use across the United States. But that will change as consumers recognize the extraordinary potential of the smart machines. Already, for instance, a home-computer user can tap into the data banks of Source Telecomputing Corp. of McLean, Va., over ordinary telephone lines. At a cost of $2.75 an hour for off-peak, nonbusiness hours and $15 per hour during the workday, the armchair computerist can call up the UPI news wire and sort through it by key words: "Carter," for instance, would produce all the stories in the data banks about Jimmy Carter. The company, which advertises as "The Source," also has the entire world airline schedule and descriptions of wines in its data banks, and it provides a 10,000-item discount-shopping catalog, even taking orders through the computer. As similar services start to move into the market and compete for customers, home-computer manufacturers like Apple, Radio Shack and Hewlett-Packard expect sales to take off.

The nation's schools have already been invaded by pocket calculators, and more sophisticated "learning machines" will surely follow. To supplement its "Speak and Spell," for instance, Texas Instruments will introduce two new speaking devices this summer, "Speak and Read" and "Speak and Math," both designed to help kids master basic skills.

The educational possibilities seem enormous. "It is perfectly possible to build enough computing power into a video game in a few years so that your youngster will be able to simulate the laws of physics on a spaceship and see not little blips on the screen, but the view out the window of the spaceship," says Carver A. Mead, a computer-science professor at the California Institute of Technology. "He could fly near the velocity of light and see what that looks like, or fly down between the atoms of a crystal, looking at them from whatever angle he wants. If you think television has had a big impact, imagine this! Since the ability to write, there has never been a thing that made that big a change in the way people learn and grow up."

The smart-machine industry—by any estimate still in its infancy—is also in for some changes. Analysts point out that vertical integration is already taking place, with computer giants like IBM investing in semiconductor production and turning out minicomputers as well as mainframes, and semiconductor companies like Texas Instruments testing the computer markets. At the same time, the industry is growing steadily more capital-intensive as technology grows more and more sophisticated, technical personnel require higher salaries and facilities expand to meet the exploding demand. Last year, the industry devoted fully 16 per cent of sales revenues to capital expenditures, compared with 4.7 per cent for all manufacturing industries. The inevitable result in the next few years will be increasing concentration, with many small smart-machine manufacturers being bought up by the big companies or squeezed out of the market.

The giants that are left will dominate an ever-growing share of the U.S. economy. Computer experts see only one major impediment to the rapid growth of the information age: resistance to the technology by an adult generation that fears it. Some of the public's fears are justified; smart machines, for example, can be used to invade the privacy of home and office. Computer crime is already on the rise, with a sophisticated new breed of criminals cracking the codes that protect confidential corporate information and arranging the electronic transfer of bank funds to their own accounts. But computer scientists argue that eventually, the improved technology of the smart machines themselves will be able to prevent such abuses.   34

There is no doubt that machines will get smarter and smarter, even designing their own software and making new and better chips for new generations of computers ("incest is best," one industry slogan has it). More and more of their power will be devoted to making them easier to use—"friendly," in industry parlance—even for those not trained in computer science. And computer scientists expect that public ingenuity will come up with applications the most visionary researchers have not even considered. One day, a global network of smart machines will be exchanging rapid-fire bursts of information at unimaginable speeds. If they are used wisely, they could help mankind to educate its masses and crack new scientific frontiers. "For all of us, it will be fearful, terrifying, disruptive," says SRI's Peter Schwartz. "In the end there will be those whose lives will be diminished. But for the vast majority, their lives will be greatly enhanced." In any event, there is no turning back: if the smart machines have not taken over, they are fast making themselves indispensable—and in the end, that may amount to very much the same thing.   35

Topical Considerations

1. Sheils begins the essay by comparing the "era of the smart machine" to the Industrial Revolution. What similarities and differences does she see between the two? Do you see other similarities and differences?

2. Sheils notes that the explosion in sales of chips and micro-

processors will not be problem-free. What are some of the problems that might be encountered? Are these concerns similar to those that Rosenblatt discussed in his essay?

3. In paragraph 10, Sheils states: "The pace of development is roughly akin to going from the Wright Brothers' first airplane to the space shuttle in a decade." What major developments in computer technology does she cite to support this statement?

4. Sheils notes: "All these wonders are bursting out of the lab at a steadily dwindling cost to consumers" (paragraph 18). Why is it that as computers get smaller and their capacities grow greater, the price often goes down?

5. Computers that speak and understand the human voice will be the next frontier on the consumer market, Sheils claims. What hitherto unheard-of services will they provide? Which services do you think will be eagerly embraced by the public? Which might be resisted? Why?

Rhetorical Considerations

1. What is the purpose of the imaginary monologue that begins the essay? Is the scenario described here relevant to the computer advances discussed in the essay?

2. This essay sets out to discuss the consequences of advances in computer technology. Do you feel that the report stresses the positive effects, the negative effects, or some of both? Explain.

3. A number of computer scientists are quoted in the course of this essay. Find these quotations and read them over. Viewed collectively, do these quotations create an image of a computer scientist? If so, what is that image—obsessive? well-rounded? good-humored? insecure? conceited? What effect do you think this characterization has on the reader? Is it deliberate?

4. Paragraphs 11 through 17 give us an overview of the development of computers. In your opinion, were the explanations successful? Were they clear? too technical? not technical enough? helpful? confusing? In your opinion, should the layperson be able to understand these explanations, or are they aimed at the technologically sophisticated?

Writing Assignments

1. In a style similar to the opening monologue of this essay, write a description of a world of the future, dominated by the computer. Focus on one particular area, such as the home, school, factory, or sports. Make sure your attitude, be it positive or negative, comes through clearly in your description.

2. If you are interested in the design and manufacturing of the chip and would like to learn more about it, find one or two recently published articles on the topic. After reading these articles, write an essay of exposition, explaining the design, production, and function of this item.

Computer Addicts

Dina Ingber

This is an extension of one of the considerations in the last essay. Dina Ingber, a free-lance writer, examines the different ways the computer craze of today is affecting people, particularly the young. Gripped by an irresistible urge, kids stay endlessly glued to consoles—forgetting to eat, abandoning friends in a feverish desire to create even more intricate programs and games. Ingber wonders if these young "hackers" are just misfits or if they are harbingers of the future.

It is 3 A.M. Everything on the university campus seems ghostlike   1
in the quiet, misty darkness—everything except the computer center. Here, twenty students, rumpled and bleary-eyed, sit transfixed at their consoles, tapping away on the terminal keys. With eyes glued to the video screen, they tap on for hours. For the rest of the world, it might be the middle of the night, but here time does not exist. As in the gambling casinos of Las Vegas, there are no windows or clocks. This is a world unto itself. Like gamblers, these young computer "hackers" are pursuing a kind of compulsion, a drive so consuming it overshadows nearly every other part of their lives and forms the focal point of their existence. They are compulsive computer programmers. Some of these students have been at the console for thirty hours or more without a break for meals or sleep. Some have fallen asleep on sofas and lounge chairs in the computer center, trying to catch a few winks but loath to get too far away from their beloved machines.

Most of these students don't have to be at the computer center in the   2
middle of the night. They aren't working on assignments. They are there because they want to be—they are irresistibly drawn there.

And they are not alone. There are hackers at computer centers all   3
across the country. In their extreme form, they focus on nothing else. They flunk out of school and lose contact with friends; they might have difficulty finding jobs, choosing instead to wander from one computer center to another, latching on to other hacker groups. They may even forgo personal hygiene.

"I remember one hacker. We literally had to carry him off his chair to   4
feed him and put him to sleep. We really feared for his health," says a
computer-science professor at MIT.

Of course, such extreme cases are very rare. But modified versions are   5
common. There are thousands of them—at universities, high schools,
even on the elementary school level—wherever young people have access
to computers. One computer-science teacher spoke of his three-year-old
daughter who already likes to play endlessly with his home computer.

What do they do at the computer at all hours of the day or night? They   6
design and play complex games; they delve into the computer's memory
bank for obscure tidbits of information; like ham radio operators, they
communicate with hackers in other areas who are plugged into the same
system. They even do their everyday chores by computer, typing term
papers and getting neat printouts. One hacker takes his terminal home
with him every school vacation so he can keep in touch with other hackers.
And at Stanford University, even the candy machine is hooked up to a
computer, programmed by the students to dispense candy on credit to
those who know the password.

At the high-school level, students have been known to break into the   7
computer room after school and spend hours decoding other systems. By
breaking the code, they can cut into other programs, discovering the
computerized grading system of their school or making mischievous (and
often costly) changes to other people's programs.

Computer-science teachers are now more aware of the implications of   8
this hacker phenomenon and are on the lookout for potential hackers and
cases of computer addiction that are already severe. They know that the
case of the hackers is not just the story of one person's relationship with
a machine. It is the story of a *society's* relationship to the so-called thinking
machines, which are becoming almost ubiquitous.

Many feel we are now on the verge of a computer revolution that will   9
change our lives as drastically as the invention of the printing press and
the Industrial Revolution changed society in the past. By the most conservative estimates, one out of three American homes will have computers or terminals within the next five to ten years. Electronic toys and
games, which came on the market in 1976, already comprise a more than
half-billion-dollar business. And though 300,000 Americans now work
full time programming computers, at least another 1.2 million will be
needed by 1990. Many of them are likely to come from today's young
hackers.

The computer hackers who hang out at university and high-school   10
computer centers are, for the most part, very bright students. They are
good at problem solving and usually good in mathematics and technical
subjects. And they are almost always male.

There is a strong camaraderie and sense of belonging among hackers.   11
They have their own subculture, with the usual in jokes and even a whole

vocabulary based on computer terminology (there is even a hacker's dictionary). But to outsiders, they are a strange breed. In high schools, the hackers are called nerds or the brain trust. They spend most of their free time in the computer room and don't socialize much. And many have trouble with interpersonal relationships.

Bob Shaw, a 15-year-old high-school student, is a case in point. Bob   12
was temporarily pulled off the computers at school when he began failing his other courses. But instead of hitting the books, he continues to sulk outside the computer center, peering longingly through the glass door at the consoles within.

Pale and drawn, his brown hair unkempt, Bob speaks only in mono-   13
syllables, avoiding eye contact. In answer to questions about friends, hobbies, school, he merely shrugs or mumbles a few words aimed at his sneakered feet. But when the conversation turns to the subject of comput-ers, he brightens—and blurts out a few full sentences about the computer he's building and the projects he plans.

"Apparently there is a class of people who would rather use the com-   14
puter than watch TV, go bowling, or even go out on a date," says Ralph Gorin, Director of Computer Facilities at Stanford University. "They find that the computer has a large number of desirable properties. It's not terribly demanding, and it does what it's told, which is much nicer than human beings. I mean, when was the last time someone did what you told him to do?"

"People are afraid inside," explains Lizzy, a 16-year-old high-school   15
computer-science student. "Sometimes it's easier to be a friend to a computer that won't make fun of you. It's easier than the pressures of a peer group."

"The computer will never insult you," says another youngster.   16

"Everyone has problems socially to some degree, and the computer   17
can act as just another escape mechanism," Gorin explains. "The young-ster feels like 'I just can't stand it anymore,' so he runs down to the computer room. The computer doesn't care what time it is or what you look like or what you may have been doing lately. The computer doesn't scold you or talk back."

Are the hackers just a group of social outcasts who hook up with   18
machines because they can't make it with people? That would probably be a gross exaggeration—and yet, "Most hackers do have problems ad-justing socially," admits J.Q. Johnson, a graduate student at Stanford. "Perhaps because they don't have much social life, they spend more time at the computer center."

Joel Bion, a sophomore at Stanford, explains how he got hooked: "I've   19
been working with computers since I was eight. I grew up in Minnesota and I didn't have many friends. I wasn't into sports and couldn't partici-pate in gym class because I had asthma. Then I found a computer termi-nal at school. I bought some books and taught myself. Pretty soon I was

spending a few hours on it every day. Then I was there during vacations. Sure, I lost some friends, but when I first started I was so fascinated. Here was a field I could really feel superior in. I had a giant program, and I kept adding and adding to it. And I could use the computer to talk to people all over the state. I thought that was great social interaction. But, of course, it wasn't, because I never came into face-to-face contact."

Joel managed to break his addiction after a few years and is now a peer   20
counselor at Stanford. But his lack of interpersonal relationships during the hacker period is common, and this problem has led Stanford psychologist Dr. Philip Zimbardo to take a closer look at the hacker phenomenon.

Hackers at Stanford have what is known as an electronic bulletin board   21
that allows them to send each other messages on the computer. What struck Zimbardo was that the programmers could be sitting right next to each other at adjacent consoles, but rather than talking directly, they communicated via computer.

Zimbardo also noticed that the messages left on the bulletin board   22
lacked emotion, and the thoughts were expressed in formulalike terms similar to programming language. "It could be," says Zimbardo, "that people who become hackers already have social deficiencies and becoming a hacker is a way of copping out of having intimate relationships.

"I've known some hackers whose addiction to playing with the com-   23
puter and thinking exclusively in terms of information transmission makes it impossible for them to relate to anyone who's not a hacker," Zimbardo continues. "The danger is that they can come to think about people in much the same way that they think about computers. Computers are always consistent, so they begin to expect that consistency from people, which by virtue of human nature is not possible or even desirable."

Zimbardo describes the case of a computer student who was working   24
with him on a special assignment. The student interacted with excessive formality. He couldn't deal with small talk, and all his conversations were task-oriented: "You will do this. This must be done." He gave commands rather than making requests or suggestions. And he couldn't deal with the "fickleness" of human nature. All this, according to Zimbardo, was a reflection of the way the student interacted with the computer. Ultimately the student was dismissed because of his inability to get along with others.

"In some extreme cases, hackers exhibit elements of paranoia, because   25
people can't be trusted the way computers can," says Zimbardo. "When people don't do just what he orders them to do, the hacker begins to perceive hostile motives and personal antagonism."

It would be absurd to label all hackers paranoid or even deviant. But   26
it would also be naive to shrug off the hacker phenomenon as meaningless.

Perhaps this attachment to a machine could be viewed as just another 27
side of man, the technological animal, who has always been obsessed with
tools, machines, gadgets and gimmicks.

"There used to be a time when the term *hacker* referred to someone 28
who was just enthusiastic about computers. It wasn't pejorative. Some
people feel that way about cars or music to some degree," says Ralph
Gorin.

Certainly the outstanding members of any creative field—the Picassos 29
and the Beethovens—spent extraordinary amounts of time at their craft
and were considered somewhat odd. And as Gorin points out, the computer, by its very nature, has an even stronger pull.

"Computers are attractive because, to a higher degree than any other 30
object, they are interesting and malleable."

Interesting and malleable: two key words if you want to understand the 31
hacker's addiction and the increasing allure of the computer for all segments of our society.

The computer can be almost as interesting as a human being. Like 32
people, it is interactive. When you ask it a question, it gives you an
answer. And because it stores great quantities of information, it can often
answer more questions, more accurately, than human friends.

This interaction has led some to attribute human characteristics to the 33
machine. Such anthropomorphizing of inanimate objects is not unusual.
Ships, trains and planes, for example, are often given human names.

But humanizing the computer seems much more natural because the 34
machine does appear to "think" and "talk" like a person. As a result,
some students form strong emotional attachments to their computers.
"Some kids probably think the computer 'likes' them," says George Trus-
cott, a math and computer teacher in Palo Alto, California.

Hackers are not the only ones interacting with the computer on a 35
personal level. The amazing powers of the machine have enticed even the
most sophisticated scientists into wondering just how human it can become. The newly developing science of artificial intelligence aims at
programming the computer to think, reason and react in much the same
way that people do. Computers can diagnose a patient's ailments and
recommend treatments. They can mimic the dialogue of a psychother-
apist or the reasoning of a lawyer.

If computers can replace our most admired humans, the professionals, 36
then why shouldn't the hackers feel close to them and invest emotional
energy in them? After all, the computer seems to have unlimited potential. Already, with today's technology, tens of thousands of words can be
stored on a tiny silicon chip measuring less than a centimeter square and
a millimeter thick. And any item of information on the chip can be called
up and displayed on a TV screen in a fraction of a second. So the computer user has access to worlds of information within reach, literally, of
his fingertips. And the computer can rearrange that information and

interrelate facts or draw conclusions at the programmer's command. It is, as Gorin points out, extremely malleable.

By programming a computer, a youngster can create a world of his own. That is, he feeds a set of rules in, and it acts according to those rules only. It is bent to the will of the programmer. 37

A favorite hacker pastime is playing computer games; these are not the games you see in pinball parlors but much more complex versions that hackers invent. 38

At Stanford, for example, hackers stay up into the wee hours playing Adventure. The object is to find various pieces of treasure hidden in different parts of a cave. To do this, you must instruct the computer (that is, type instructions into the console) as to what direction to take (north, south, east, west, up, down, jump, run, etc.). After each command, the computer describes the area you have reached and what lies around you. You encounter obstacles along the way—snakes, dragons, darkness, slimy pits—but you also encounter magical objects that can help you overcome the obstacles. 39

"With a computer, the possibilities are limited only by your imagination," Gorin explains. "You can be a spaceship pilot, a great explorer or a treasure hunter. It can lead you into the world of fantasy all of your own making." 40

Joseph Weizenbaum, professor of computer science at MIT, thinks that the sense of power over the machine ultimately corrupts the hacker and makes him into a not-very-desirable sort of programmer. The hackers are so involved with designing their program, making it more and more complex and bending it to their will, that they don't bother trying to make it understandable to other users. They rarely keep records of their programs for the benefit of others, and they rarely take time to understand why a problem occurred. 41

Computer-science teachers say they can usually pick out the prospective hackers in their courses because these students make their homework assignments more complex than they need to be. Rather than using the simplest and most direct method, they take joy in adding extra steps just to prove their ingenuity. 42

But perhaps those hackers know something that we don't about the shape of things to come. "That hacker who had to be literally dragged off his chair at MIT is now a multimillionaire of the computer industry," says MIT professor Michael Dertouzos. "And two former hackers became the founders of the highly successful Apple home-computer company." 43

When seen in this light, the hacker phenomenon may not be so strange after all. If, as many psychiatrists say, play is really the basis for all human activity, then the hacker games are really the preparation for future developments. 44

Sherry Turkle, a professor of sociology at MIT, has for years been studying the way computers fit into people's lives. She points out that the 45

computer, because it seems to us to be so "intelligent," so "capable," so
. . . "human," affects the way we think about ourselves and our ideas
about what we are. She says that computers and computer toys already
play an important role in children's efforts to develop an identity by
allowing them to test ideas about what is alive and what is not.

"The youngsters can form as many subtle nuances and textured re-   46
lationships with the computers as they can with people," Turkle points
out.

Computers are not just becoming more and more a part of our world.   47
To a great degree, they *are* our world. It is therefore not unlikely that our
relationship with them will become as subjective as that of the hackers.
So perhaps hackers are, after all, harbingers of the world to come.

Topical Considerations

1. In what ways are compulsive computer programmers, or
"hackers," like gamblers or alcoholics?

2. Often, hackers are nonsocial and noncommunicative, like
fifteen-year-old Bob Shaw. Why is the computer so attractive to this
personality type?

3. How can a hacker's obsessive contact with the computer lead
to hostile and paranoid behavior? Explain this phenomenon.

4. What did Joseph Weizenbaum mean when he said that "the
sense of power over the machine ultimately corrupts the hacker" (paragraph 41)?

5. Why do you think all the hackers mentioned here are male?
Why are no female hackers mentioned? Discuss this with some women
friends.

Rhetorical Considerations

1. The essay opens with a description of a computer center at 3
A.M. What words or phrases suggest the isolating or asocial qualities of
this obsession? Could this introduction serve as a beginning for a piece
of writing other than an essay?

2. Paragraphs 14 through 19 explain why the introverted person
is drawn to the computer. How effective is the use of direct quotations
from students and professors? Rewrite one paragraph, eliminating these
quotations and including only essential information. Discuss the differences in the two versions. Which is more effective?

3. Look at the last paragraph of the essay. Does it reinforce or
undercut the main idea of the essay? Is it an appropriate conclusion?
Explain your reasons.

Writing Assignments

1. Do you know or have you observed a hacker? If so, write a character sketch that conveys the individual's background, appearance, values, and actions. As in the introduction to this piece, choose your words carefully for effect.

2. Computer video games are thought to be addictive, particularly for adolescent boys, who seem especially drawn to games involving combat and violence. Write an essay explaining the appeal of these games.

The Coupling of Man and Machine

Mathew Tekulsky

Imagine clicking your teeth or blinking your eyes to make mechanical arms do what you want? Imagine amputees "thinking" their artificial limbs into action? Imagine legal cases being tried by judge machines? "Science fiction?" you ask. Not really. These are some of the things the new science of biotechnology is up to. Here is a fascinating article about new machines that someday soon will be extensions of our senses and that will vastly expand our minds and skills. It was written by Mathew Tekulsky, a writer who specializes in following new developments in science and technology.

All of us are handicapped. We can't see in the dark like a cat; hear   1
supersonic sounds like a dolphin; navigate by sound like a bat; nor smell
scents like a dog. Our abilities are limited. But a new science called
biotechnology, or human engineering, may extend human capabilities as
far as the imagination will allow. With the help of new machines we can
lengthen our grasp to the bottom of the ocean or control mechanical
objects by voice, much as the brain controls the body. We can "think"
things to happen, project our presence around the globe, and expand our
senses of sight and touch. We can stretch the intellect to learn and to
make decisions better and faster, even to read another's mind.

One stage where the latest revolution in human potential is being   2
enacted is in Woodland Hills, California. As you enter the offices of
Perceptronics, Inc., they seem ordinary enough. Take a walk around
back, however, and you confront a large metallic cylinder resting on a
vertical stand. The object resembles a human arm but for one major
difference: it's the size of a human body.

The arm consists of two long, cylindrical sections connected by an   3
"elbow" joint; a "wrist" area containing a mass of metal components; and

a gripper "hand" device, composed of two metal clamps. In front of the arm stands a squat structure made of interlocking pipes, some of which have valves with square handles. Behind the arm is a control panel with two joysticks and a bunch of buttons with numbers or labels such as FORWARD, GRASP, ROTATE or DO NOW. Directly above the control panel and flanking it are televisions. Each television screen shows the mechanical arm from a different angle.

"Look into the television monitor," says Dr. Amos Freedy, as he sits   4
down at the control panel. He presses buttons marked CHAIN 1. On the screen, the arm opens its gripper and rotates it counterclockwise. Then the arm moves forward and places the gripper over the square valve handle. The gripper closes, and the arm rotates the valve clockwise exactly 180 degrees. Then the arm opens its gripper, moves away from the valve and back into its original position. Hydraulic lifts and computerized electronic controls move the arm the same way that a human brain instructs a human arm. When the arm moves forward, the computer figures out about how much power to put in each joint so that the arm will move straight.

The arm at Perceptronics displays remarkable mechanical agility. But   5
if the arm is right in front of us, why are we looking at a television screen to see what it's doing? Because, Freedy explains, this is just a test system. In actual use, the mechanical arm and the pipe-and-valve structure (an oil well, perhaps) would be on the ocean floor, while the control station would be on the surface. Although the television cameras surrounding the control station are designed to give the arm's operator the "feeling" of being at the bottom of the ocean, the computer can also produce a simulation—a three-dimensional display of the arm and the pipe-and-valve structure—based on reports it gets from sensors in the underwater environment.

These techniques extend human sight to the sea floor, but other senses   6
are also being expanded through feedback devices. Force-reflecting feedback, for example, induces a force on the operator's arm that corresponds to the forces on a mechanical arm when it's lifting something. (The force on the equipment might be too much for a person to bear, so it would be reduced to levels he could tolerate and whose effects he could predict.) Another type of feedback called slip sensing allows the operator to feel something sliding through a mechanical arm's "hands." Anyone who has been to a carnival and tried to pluck out a prize with a mechanical gripper knows how hard it is to pick something up with only vision to rely on. Without slip sensing, you might crush a fragile item or grip a metal object too loosely to hold on to it. If this is a prize at a carnival, the slip is no great loss. But if it's a container filled with radioactive waste, the slip could be catastrophic.

Machines could also be given artificial skins that are sensitive to touch,   7
heat, vibrations and, perhaps to a certain extent, pain, in order to relay

to an operator that they are reaching a breaking point. The vision of a remote manipulator could also be coupled with the human controller's eye movement, so if the controller looked one way, the TV cameras would swing in that direction; as the pupils dilated to adapt to light, the camera would let in more light; and as the lenses flattened or thickened for focal-length adjustment, the camera would adjust for a distant object or one close to the mechanical arm.

Erasing Limitations

Biotechnology need not stop at duplicating the senses of the human   8
operator. It can amplify them as well. If the mechanical arm's job at the bottom of the ocean is to screw something in, it needn't do it like a person; it could go 360 degrees on a rotation. Similarly, things underwater are going to be murky when seen through a television camera, so why not use an infrared camera or a sonar to reconstruct a visual image? Microphones could pick up the sounds of the oceans and translate supersonic noises into the human hearing spectrum. This would alert you when a school of dolphins was nearby. You could even re-create the smells of a mechanical arm's environment and prepare dinner from your office by remote control. If you turned the stove on, but the pilot light wasn't lit, you'd smell gas.

Machines such as the mechanical arm could erase the limitations of   9
being human not just in underwater operations but in any locations that are inaccessible or hazardous. When remotely controlled machines are common, people may become expert at using them for ordinary jobs. Watchmakers would work on tiny mechanisms by remotely controlling a device programmed to perform adroitly. Automated kitchens would have mechanical arms and other devices to come out of the walls and prepare food on command.

But why even push a button? Why not just tell a machine what to do?   10
That is exactly the goal of research at the Biotechnology Lab at the University of California at Los Angeles. In a corner of the Lab sits an extraordinary wheelchair, a voice-recognition wheelchair. The chair can be commanded by a human voice, and it recognizes only one voice, that of the person who programs it by speaking into a computer. If the person using the chair tells it to turn left, it'll turn left. But if someone else walks up to the wheelchair and says, "Left," it'll just sit there. Attached to the back of the wheelchair is a small computer; on the front is a table with a control panel and a mechanical arm. The mechanical arm looks like the one at Perceptronics, except that it's human size. Eventually, the computer will be miniaturized so that the voice-recognition wheelchair will look like any other wheelchair.

Mark Tiedemann, a student at the Lab, demonstrates what the chair   11
can do. There's a plastic cassette-tape case standing on a nearby table. "Arm . . . up," Tiedemann says. The arm rises. "Halt." It stops. "Left."

The arm swings to the left, toward the table where the case is sitting. "Halt." It stops. "Down." The arm drops. "Halt." It hovers directly over the case. "Open." The clamp at the end of the arm opens. "Down." The arm lowers so that the case lies in between the two clamps. "Clamp." The arm clamps the case. "Up." The arm lifts, carrying the case. "Left." The arm swings behind the wheelchair. "Halt." It stops in front of Tiedemann. "Open." The machine hands him the case.

Tiedemann explains that you could tell the wheelchair to go to a door, then direct the arm to grab the knob, turn it, and pull or push it. He adds, somewhat proudly, that if he says, "Down," the whole arm remains rigid, but if he says, "Lower," the "wrist" tilts back, like a human hand, keeping whatever is held in the clamp level even though the arm is moving. This means the arm could raise or lower a glass of water without spilling it.   12

Manipulation by voice control need not be limited to wheelchairs. Perhaps someday we'll be driving cars simply by telling them which way to turn and when to stop; or maybe we'll just say, "Go to the airport" or "Take me home" and the car will follow a prescribed route—a track, as it were—that is automatically controlled to avoid accidents.   13

The Phantom Limb

In addition to voice control, the Biotechnology Lab is developing ways to control objects by eye movements and clicking one's teeth. A special pair of glasses measures the position of the eyeball by reflecting invisible infrared light from the cornea to a specially mirrored surface on the glasses and then to an array of sensors located in a pencil-thin cylinder on the side frame. The glasses will enable a handicapped person to instruct a mechanical arm simply by moving his eyes. Since eyes can only move to the left or the right and up or down, the number of movements they can control is limited. Therefore, there's a device in the glasses called an accelerometer, which responds to the mechanical shock made by a person clicking his teeth. Between the eye movement and clicking the teeth a certain number of times and at a certain speed, the arm can be ordered to perform many actions.   14

There is yet a fourth way to get a machine to work for us: thinking.   15

Kevin Corker, another student, holds up a white shirt with one arm stitched closed for an amputee. Attached to the arm and shoulder area are nine pairs of electrodes, each wired to an artificial arm with a microprocessor that can translate electrical signals into action.   16

Muscle contraction is a chemical process that produces electricity in a distinctive pattern. An amputee usually has a phantom-limb phenomenon. The nerves are intact from the site of the amputation to his brain, and the amputee feels as though he still had the missing limb.   17

"We put the shirt on," Corker says, "set up the computer, and tell the wearer, 'Flex your arm.' He does what he thinks is flexing his missing limb and generates an electrical pattern. We tell the computer what that pat-   18 tern means and it tells the artificial arm what to do. We can train twenty-seven movements this way. So far, the subjects I've worked with have managed to master seven."

In short, the amputee can think his artificial arm to perform tasks.   19
The seven movements that Corker's patients have mastered begin with simple, or independent, motions such as finger opening and closing; go on to what are called two-motor motions and include such doubles as finger opening and forearm movement; and finally include three-motor motions, such as arm flexion, forearm movement and finger opening.

"The three-motor motions could be used in eating," Corker explains,   20
as he flexes his arm, turns it toward his body, closes his fingers and brings his hand up to his mouth. "These three activities are correlated into one electrical signal."

Three thoughts, one signal; thinking has produced a complex body   21
movement. If all the electrical signals of our brain were deciphered, the manual operation of mechanical devices could become obsolete. Dictating machines that can transcribe directly from speech are already being developed, and a machine that can type out what you're *thinking* may be developed someday. Scientists at the University of California at San Diego have recently used computers to read a person's thoughts. Distinguishing a brief signal from the many produced by the brain, computers were able to record a person's surprise and consternation at reading a nonsensical sentence. Additional testing should pinpoint many more distinctive patterns of brain waves. As the electric arm has shown, translating these patterns into action will be the next step.

Talking to Dummies

The extension of our senses represented by remotely controlled arms   22
is not limited to mechanical operations. The concept is also being applied in communications at UCLA. Multiple television cameras can take pictures of a person from different angles in one conference room and then project these separate images to form a composite picture on a mannequin in another conference room, perhaps thousands of miles away. The mannequin takes on the exact appearance of the person who is talking; sound comes out of a speaker placed in the mannequin's mouth. Anyone who has been to Disneyland has probably seen something like this. Eventually, three-dimensional, reconstructive holography or perhaps androids could simulate the feeling of having a real person sitting next to you. If the real person gestured with his hands, then the hologram image could mime him.

But will people talk to a dummy?   23

Corker has an answer: "I guess it depends on the character of the   24
person you're talking to. People talk to dummies all the time. You talk

into the wall when you talk on the phone, and you still use the phone. But if you can see a face that seems to be animate, the assumption is that it would be more communicative."

This type of teleconferencing could be used by a multinational corporation for a discussion between the home office and a branch plant halfway around the world or for a board of directors meeting. It could revolutionize education by making it possible for a student to study with a teacher anywhere in the country. The entertainment field might also benefit. Maybe we'll be able to plug in a tape and have an exact likeness of Johnny Carson perform a comedy routine. For that matter, perhaps we'll be watching three-dimensional movies, with all the sights, sounds and smells of real life. We could be transported onto the field at Waterloo; into the audience of a Shakespeare play in Elizabethan England; or back to Biblical times. 25

In teleconferencing, biotechnology is the relationship between the human mind—the psychology of perception and expectation—and the mechanical system. "What we're doing," says Corker, "is projecting a reality which really isn't there; creating enough of an illusion so that the brain will supply the missing feelings." 26

But if machines can extend our senses and our physical capabilities, could they also extend our intellect? At Perceptronics, the answer is "Yes." 27

There, they've developed a machine that helps a group of people make the best possible decision in a given situation. It's called the Group Decision Aid, and it's a computer that stands about five feet high. It has a large television screen, and it is placed at the end of the conference table at a group meeting. Each participant has a small terminal. The group, with the aid of an "intermediator" (a trained person who serves as a link between the participants and the computer), enters into the machine a list of alternative courses of action and their possible outcomes. This list is called a "decision tree." 28

The machine is also given the value structure of each participant; that is, how important each person thinks an action is. It identifies and helps resolve conflicts between participants so they reach a consensus. Then, by using its models of human decision-making, the computer instructs the members as to which decision is the best one, based on their particular sets of values. 29

Perceptronics uses a fictitious scenario to demonstrate the decision aid: a U.S. B-52, carrying two nuclear weapons, is flying in the vicinity of Shamba, a Third World ally of the United States. Problems with its onboard electrical system force the plane to land at Shamba's capital city, Savin. Two hours after the landing, Shamba's government is overthrown by leftist rebels. The plane and its payload are captured and its crew executed. The rebels occupy the U.S. Embassy in Savin, take the 30 personnel as hostages, and issue a list of demands and an ultimatum. The United States has four hours to accede to their demands and 15 days to carry them out. Otherwise, the hostages will be killed and a nearby neutral city-state, Mandero City, will be bombed with the B-52's payload.

A Decision Tree

In this scenario, participants enter into the computer a decision tree   31 that includes the following alternatives: attack immediately, negotiate, display strength (deploy carriers to Mandero City), accede to demands. If the decision is to attack, a number of outcomes are possible: lose hostages and Mandero City; lose hostages and save city; save hostages and lose city; save both. Each participant now enters a value assignment from zero (least desirable outcome) to 100 (most desirable outcome) for each of these outcomes. In addition, a probability assessment is made of each outcome; that is, how likely is it to occur?

Each participant is then asked to enter a value for the effect of the   32 possible outcomes. The influence of the outcome "lose hostages and save city" is considered in relation to: African allies, domestic opinion, international prestige, lives and property, U.S.-Russian relations, national security and economic impact. In this case, the participants disagree on how important the effect on international prestige would be. Some think it is very important, while others don't consider it crucial. After they discuss the issue, the group is instructed by the computer to re-enter the values for this factor. If an agreement is reached, the computer informs them that "no further discussion is necessary." If an agreement is not reached, the existing values are averaged.

This procedure is followed for each alternative and every possible   33 outcome. The computer's decision: "Negotiate."

This scenario was devised before the U.S. Embassy takeover in Iran,   34 and according to Dr. Gershon Weltman, president of Perceptronics, the decision aid "would work very well with something like the Iranian crisis." Dr. Freedy, describes how the computer would evaluate a decision tree: "Let's say we go and get the hostages in Iran. What's the outcome? We lose so many soldiers. What are the attributes of that? Bad publicity, bad image for the U.S., bad relationship with the Arabs. What's the outcome of that? No oil. What's the outcome of that? Lines at the gas station. So it goes and goes, and you get a huge tree; and how do you analyze it? The computer helps you; it decomposes the problem instantaneously. You have to realize that scientifically this is a very, very complex and advanced concept."

It is interesting to note that the Group Decision Aid is already being   35 tested by the CIA and the Defense Department for crisis management. It could be used not only by governments but also by large corporations, small businesses, hospitals or lawmakers. In short, any group faced with a decision to make. Let's say an airplane manufacturer has to decide whether to build a new jet engine or modify an old one. Top executives could use the decision aid to compare the cost of parts, labor, research and development. A team of physicians could use the decision aid to help them determine whether to operate.

Individuals could use the decision aid, too. Let's say you want to buy   36
a house. The computer would ask you the merits of certain houses. Perhaps the rate of interest is a very important factor. What about location prestige—do you want a Beverly Hills address? Maybe you would rather have a stone house than a wooden one. All these subjective factors would go into the computer, which would recommend the best house for you. Perhaps someday we'll all be walking around with pocket-size decision aids.

Personality Machines

What will the future bring? Weltman provides this view: "People are   37
going to accept machines as having personality. It's starting to happen now. Simple machines, such as *Speak and Spell,* have a very definite personality. Look at the chess-playing machines. They are accepted now as equals by all but chess masters, and pretty soon one will be sophisticated enough to be accepted as an equal by a master. We are going to start thinking of machines as we think of aides or subordinates. We are going to incorporate machine intelligence into our normal jobs. I think the decision aid is an example of that. Maybe we'll go beyond that. If a judge machine could learn all the law and could learn, like our computer does here, the value system of the people who administer the law, the judge machine would try a case in a minute. Or you could put one policeman plus a detection machine in a patrol car. You give the thing a personality so the person won't feel lonely, and pretty soon he has a machine for a partner. He feeds in license numbers. He says, 'Is that one hot?'' and the machine recognizes them and says, 'No, that one's okay.'

"As the machine gains personality, as we begin to see that it is an   38
assistant, we're going to start giving it more important tasks. We might turn around in ten or twenty years and say, boy, we never realized that machines would be doing important and high-status jobs that require value judgments. As machines get more sensory capabilities, which is happening now, I think that you're probably going to see machines controlling traffic, maybe even machines controlling air traffic. Wherever a machine is performing a cognitive or higher-level intellectual task, the machine is going to start by being an assistant and probably wind up by being an independent operator. And when you get a subordinate that you trust, you let that person do the job by himself."

Topical Considerations

1. In what new sense does the author of this article use the term *handicapped?* How can biotechnology eliminate these so-called handicaps?

2. Consider the name Perceptronics. Why is this such an appropriate name for the firm?

3. What is the arm Tekulsky describes in the beginning of this article? How is it controlled? To what uses can it be put?

4. Define the following terms: *force-reflecting feedback, slip sensing,* and *artificial skins.*

5. In some cases, biotechnology must amplify rather than duplicate the senses of the human operator. Give some examples of such amplification.

6. Tekulsky writes that "a machine that can type out what you are *thinking* may be developed someday" (paragraph 21). Would you like to see such a machine developed? How might it be used constructively? Can you think of any destructive uses to which it could be put? What ethical or moral problems might the invention of such a machine pose?

7. Tekulsky describes a talking dummy—the appearance of a person simulated by three-dimensional, reconstructive holography. How is such an image created? How might such an image be utilized in fields such as education, politics, business, religion? Try to think of uses in addition to those discussed in this article.

8. Probably the most provocative question posed in the essay is the following: "But if machines can extend our senses and our physical capabilities, could they also extend our intellect? At Perceptronics the answer is 'Yes' " (paragraph 26). Explain how the decision tree can be used to make decisions, to extend our intellect.

9. Tekulsky mentions: "Perhaps someday we'll all be walking around with pocket-size decision aids" (paragraph 35). Imagine that this was a reality today. List two ways in which it might be beneficial for the average person. Also list two ways in which it would be bad for the average person.

Rhetorical Considerations

1. Dissect the opening paragraph of this essay. What was the writer's strategy? What effect did he want it to have on the reader?

2. Look at the section headed "Erasing Limitations." In each of the paragraphs, copy down the topic sentence. Then answer the following questions about each topic sentence: Does each paragraph have a clear topic sentence? In some cases, is the topic sentence also a transitional sentence? Where in the paragraph does the topic sentence appear?

3. Does the reporter in this article concentrate on straightfor-

ward reporting, or does he make value judgments about his material? How does he compare to Roger Rosenblatt ("The Mind in the Machine") in this respect?

Writing Assignments

1. Take one of the examples of biotechnology discussed in this article and imagine that you are going to write an article on that item alone. Write an introductory paragraph to the article that you think will grab your readers' attention and arouse them enough to want to read on immediately. Review the introductory paragraphs in this section of the book for ideas and inspiration.

2. If the concept of the average person walking around with pocket-sized decision aids intrigues you, try the following assignment. Write a dialogue, comical or serious, that might occur between two people as they try to make a decision (important or trivial) with the use of a portable decision aid.

The Dazzle of Lasers

Newsweek

Lasers were once no more than a science fiction imagining. Today, however, they are used in many areas—from metals to medicine, from defense to detective work. The following is a *Newsweek* review of the extraordinary development of this high-tech wonder. Written in clear, layman terms, this piece explains how lasers evolved from the early research in the fifties and what they may be used for in the future.

Science-fiction writers invented it first. In his 1898 classic, "The   1 War of the Worlds," H. G. Wells imagined an invasion of Martians who nearly conquered planet Earth with weapons firing lethal beams of light. In the 1930s, Buck Rogers fought his way through the pages of comic books armed with a ray gun. It took scientists decades to catch up. Not until 1960, nearly 50 years after Albert Einstein first described the basic principle, did Theodore Maiman, a 33-year-old engineer at Hughes Research Laboratories, build a homely four-inch cylinder containing a ruby rod encircled by a flash tube: the world's first working laser.

More than two decades later, the laser has wrought a technological   2 revolution. Lasers are an indispensable tool for delicate eye surgery, and doctors are using lasers experimentally to destroy cancerous tumors, unclog diseased arteries and even treat herpes. Just as they provide new tools for health care, however, they also make possible new engines of destruction: recently Dr. Edward Teller, the father of the hydrogen bomb, called on President Reagan to urge that the United States build a space-based laser-weapon system that would use a nuclear bomb to fire brutally intense laser X-rays against enemy missiles in flight.

Today pilots flying the new Boeing 767 and 757 aircraft navigate with the aid of new laser gyroscopes. Supermarkets use lasers to ring up prices at the checkout counter by "reading" the universal bar codes like the one on NEWSWEEK'S cover. Powerful lasers cut and weld steel in factories from Detroit to Tokyo. Artists and filmmakers are beginning to use lasers for animation: at Lucasfilm, George Lucas, the creator of "Star Wars" and its sequels, has a team of computer wizards developing a machine that uses a computer-driven laser to draw animated images on film; a second film, with human actors, is then merged by laser with the graphics into a single seamless whole.   3

Just the Beginning

Applied to communications, lasers transmit digital information, telephone conversations or pictures at the speed of light over hair-thin strands of ultrapure glass fibers. They are the heart of a new generation of high-speed copiers and printers, of the Pioneer Laser Disc system and the futuristic record players—digital-audio disc systems—that went on the market this fall in Japan. These practical applications are just the beginning. "The two inventions or discoveries that revolutionized life in the 19th century were James Watt's steam engine in 1769 and the work of Galvani and Volta on electricity in the 1790s," says Kenjiro Sakurai, director of Japan's government-sponsored Opto-electronics Joint Research Laboratory. "In my opinion, the discovery of laser oscillation is the equivalent of both of those."   4

How does the laser work? Anyone who has ever focused sunlight through a magnifying glass and watched paper or dry leaves snap into flames understands the power of concentrated light. Laser light is intense, concentrated light, too, but it works on a different principle. Shine sunlight through a prism and it breaks into the glorious colors of the rainbow. In the scientists' vocabulary, sunlight is "incoherent"—it is made up of a mix of wavelengths spanning the spectrum from infrared to ultraviolet. Laser light, on the other hand, is monochromatic and coherent—it shines at a single wavelength, and all the light waves march together in step like soldiers on parade.   5

Unearthly Power

The acronym "laser," coined by scientist Gordon Gould in 1957, describes in shorthand form how the device works: Light Amplification by Stimulated Emission of Radiation. In 1916 Einstein predicted that   6 electrons in an atom could be deliberately stimulated to emit photons (light energy) of a certain wavelength. He was right. The laser must first be "pumped" with energy in a variety of ways—from Maiman's flash tube to a nuclear explosion—so that the electrons are excited into higher energy states. But these high energy electrons are unstable—and fall back to a lower energy level. On the way down, their extra energy is released as light. That light is captured inside the laser and amplified by bouncing it back and forth between mirrors. The laser beam that emerges is am- plified, monochromatic, coherent light—and it shines with an unearthly power.

In the two decades since its invention, the laser has undergone a 7 dramatic transformation: a wide variety of gas, solid-state, diode and other lasers has been created. Each shines at a different wavelength; some pulse on and off, others operate continuously. These are the differences that make lasers so versatile. Carbon-dioxide-gas lasers, for instance, make marvelous cutting tools—the high-powered ones are industrial workhorses, cutting and welding steel and other metals, and the low- powered CO_2 lasers are often the surgeon's "light scalpel."

Delicate Surgery

When the laser moved out of the laboratory, one of its first and most 8 significant applications was as a medical tool. Lasers are commonly used for delicate surgery inside the eye. In treating blood-vessel disorders resulting from complications of diabetes, doctors aim a fine beam of argon laser light through the pupil of the eye and place up to 2,000 tiny laser burns very closely around the back portion of the retina. These laser "welds" prevent harmful growth or rupture of new, unwanted blood vessels.

Glaucoma patients also benefit from a promising new treatment. To 9 relieve open-angle glaucoma, a disease in which the fluid of the inner eye doesn't drain as it should, surgeons beam very short pulses of laser light into the eye and place 100 small burns in a full circle around the trabecu- lar meshwork (which rings the cornea). The fluid drains, and pressure inside the eye is reduced. The entire procedure can be done in a doctor's office with a local anesthetic in about 20 minutes.

One of the prime advantages of laser-light scalpels is that they cauter- 10 ize as they cut; the heat from the laser beam seals off small severed blood vessels, there by reducing the amount of bleeding. "It cuts cleanly and sterilizes at the same time," says Dr. Janos Voros of the Laser Research Foundation in New Orleans. "If the laser is used properly, it is safer than other instruments." Voros and others now use lasers to treat endometrio- sis (the tissue growth that can block the female reproductive tract and is a cause of infertility), to destroy ovarian cysts and to remove life-threaten- ing tubal pregnancies. The heat from a two-watt argon laser will cauterize blood vessels on the surface of the skin and can be used to remove disfiguring port-wine stains—or tattoos. "We destroy a lot of gorgeous pictures when Marines decide to become executives," says Dr. Leon Goldman, director of the Laser Research Laboratory Medical Center at the Jewish Hospital of Cincinnati.

Vaporizing Blisters

In experimental research at several medical centers around the country, doctors are using the laser to vaporize blisters caused by the herpes simplex-II virus. One study that is still confidential reports that in a clinical trial, laser treatment of primary lesions successfully prevented recurrent outbreaks in 25 of 30 patients. Other virologists, however, are still skeptical about the costly treatment.   11

The very properties that make lasers dangerous—power and heat—are also being put to use to destroy some kinds of brain and spinal tumors. "Lasers have brought a new frontier to neurosurgery," says Dr. Leonard Cerullo of Northwestern University Medical School. "They have made some inoperable tumors operable and high-risk tumors less high risk." Three years ago the number of laser neurosurgical operations done in the United States was less than 20; today successful operations number in the thousands. But despite its success, the laser is not a cure-all. "The laser is not a cure for cancer and it does not make a bad surgeon a good surgeon," cautions Cerullo. "But it gives a good surgeon a big advantage."   12

At several major medical centers in the United States, Australia and Japan, lasers are being used experimentally to combat cancerous tumors without surgery. The treatment—photoradiation therapy—depends on the laser as a light source, not a heat source. Patients are injected with a photosensitive chemical called hematoporphyrin derivative (HPD) that lodges in the malignant tissue. When the tumor is exposed to red light from a tunable dye laser, it creates a toxic photochemical reaction that destroys the cancerous cells. "It is especially effective on patients who have tried every other treatment unsuccessfully," says Dr. Thomas Dougherty of Roswell Park Memorial Institute in Buffalo, N.Y., "and on patients who simply cannot tolerate any more radiation therapy because of the side effects."   13

Many medical researchers envision the day when lasers combined with fiber-optic cables will make it possible to pipe light into the body for completely internalized diagnosis and treatment. Laser light traveling into the lungs through a fluorescence bronchoscope is now used as a diagnostic tool to identify lung cancers that become fluorescent when a patient has been injected with HPD. And in September, Dr. Garrett Lee of the University of California at Davis announced a new technique using laser-light pulses to destroy fatty deposits of cholesterol that block arteries: the light is delivered through a "laserscope," a bundle of microscopic fibers that can be threaded through the blood vessel like a catheter. The   14 technique has been used successfully on animals, and trials on humans will begin next year. Similar animal experiments are under way at Detroit's Sinai Hospital, where Terry Fuller has used a fiber-optic cable running through an endoscope to operate on gastric tumors.

Battle Stations

Warfare also is changing as laser technology advances. Laser guidance   15
systems have brought once unimaginable accuracy to artillery. In the near future, higher-intensity lasers may be used to blind the electronic sensory systems of aircraft, missiles, tanks and ships. And ultimately, some visionaries insist, the globe could be surrounded by a platoon of orbiting battle stations armed with lasers capable of destroying planes and missiles within seconds of their being launched.

That day may seem remote, but lasers are rapidly becoming a big-   16
ticket item in the arms race. The United States has poured about $2.5 billion into researching high-energy lasers (HEL's), and Sen. Malcolm Wallop of Wyoming has called for a "Manhattan style" project to put U.S. lasers in space. Wallop's plan sounds as if it were lifted from the script of the movie "Star Wars": the United States would deploy a fleet of approximately 24 laser battle stations in orbits 800 to 1,000 miles above the earth. At least eight would be looking at the Soviet Union at any one time, while the rest could be scanning the oceans for missiles launched from submarines. Upon detecting oncoming Soviet missiles, the stations would use mirrors to aim powerful chemically activated lasers. The lasers would shoot round after round, pausing only long enough over each target to ensure that the enemy missile was really destroyed. A battle station armed with a 10-megawatt laser and a mirror with a 10-meter diameter could theoretically disable two conventional rockets a second. "These would be catastrophic kills," says one Wallop aide. "They would weaken the missile enough so the entire structure is torn apart."

'Vulnerable'

Wallop's plan may be premature, however. The Pentagon would have   17
to develop a sufficiently powerful laser, build a mirror capable of reflecting light with microscopic precision over thousands of miles and construct an aiming mechanism that can be transported into space. Such research is under way, but testing won't be possible until 1987 at the earliest. Would the system work even then? According to Robert S. Cooper, director of the Defense Advanced Research Projects Agency, laser defense might work against slow-flying manned bombers, but a battle against missiles, lasting only a few minutes, could be a thousand times more difficult. "I've devoted my life to systems," says Cooper, "and my judgment is that we cannot now manage the complexity of the kind of system we're talking about."

Lasers are rapidly transforming warfare back on earth. Their first real   18 combat test was during the Vietnam War, when American jet fighters used rudimentary laser targeting devices to steer "smart" bombs aimed at North Vietnamese convoys headed down the Ho Chi Minh Trail. Today M1 Abrams tanks are equipped with 20-pound range finders that bounce laser light from a cannon target back to a receiving telescope. In a small fraction of a second, a computer processes the wealth of information carried by the reflected light about such matters as target distance, wind velocity and barometric pressure; it then fine-tunes the cannon's aim and fires. Previously, says Howard W. Boehmer, a vice president of Hughes Aircraft Co., "you couldn't shoot accurately beyond 1,000 to 1,500 meters. With modern laser tank-fire control, targets are very vulnerable up to 3,000 meters."

The next major military use of lasers will probably be in communications. The Defense Department is currently working on special lasers to contact nuclear missile-bearing submarines at sea. Ocean-colored light would be beamed from satellites to the ocean floor. Although the light would be visible to an enemy, it would sweep across vast stretches of ocean and thus not reveal the location of the submarine. "All you'd know is that it's somewhere in the ocean basin," says Cooper. The Navy plans to test a prototype of the system using aircraft in 1984.   19

The military is not yet ready to use lasers as destructive weapons in themselves; so far they have shown no superiority over conventional artillery. Last June, however, a Pentagon official told Congress that research is continuing on ways to use high-energy lasers in a variety of combat situations. The military achieved its first laser "kill" in 1973 when the Air Force used a gas-powered laser to shoot down a winged drone. More recently, the Air Force has been experimenting with an "airborne laser laboratory," a specially equipped plane designed to track targets and hit them with laser beams. But according to some sources, the airborne project has not been notably successful. For the near term, they conclude, the best use of the lasers will be to disable enemy electronic and sensory systems. They are not yet a primary military weapon.   20

Communications

Just as they are opening new doors to medicine and military practices, lasers are also having a profound impact on communications. Back in 1880, Alexander Graham Bell invented and patented a mirror-and-lens system he called the "photophone" to transmit his voice on a sunbeam. "I have heard a ray of sun laugh and cough and sing," he boasted. Newspapers at the time ridiculed the invention, but now, more than a century later, technology is catching up to Bell. Instead of sunbeams, today's light-wave communication systems use laser light ricocheting through tiny glass fibers. Lasers generate light waves at extraordinarily high frequencies—in the range of trillions of cycles per second—which makes it possible to transmit enormous quantities of information. (By   21 contrast, the transistor operates at a maximum range of millions of cycles per second.) In addition, fiber-optic cables are cheaper than copper wire and are not subject to electromagnetic interference, or the annoying cross talk and static that plague current systems. "The big breakthrough was the semiconductor laser," says Venky Narayanamurti, director of the Solid State Electronics Research Laboratory at Bell Labs. "From now on I expect tremendous growth."

This year alone, AT&T will install 15,000 miles of glass fibers in   22 commercial systems across the country. Two information superhighways being built of fiber-optic cable will link Boston, New York, Philadelphia and Washington, D.C., in a 776-mile system on the East Coast, and Sacramento, Oakland and Los Angeles on the West Coast. In 1984 the video and voice signals for television broadcasts of the Los Angeles Olympics will race through fiber-optic systems buried beneath the city streets to a transmitter; from there, they will be beamed to a satellite parked in geosynchronous orbit above the earth and relayed around the globe. Light-wave communications may also tie together networks of computers, printers and video screens in the office of the future; the new AT&T headquarters building under construction in New York is being fiber-wired for future services. But the most ambitious project so far is a transatlantic fiber-optic cable to be built by 1988 that could significantly cut the cost of communications between the United States and Europe.

Optical Circuits

Now that the semiconductor diode laser has been perfected for fiber-   23 optic transmission, the new frontier in research is to create integrated optical circuits on a chip. The goal is to put light sources, modulators, photodetectors and amplifiers on a single chip. The Lilliputian city of tiny laser lights winking at each other would process and store information just as silicon computer chips do today—but at much higher speeds. "We are now with light waves about where we were with transistors in the 1950s," says Joseph Giordmaine, director of the Electronic and Photonic Technology Laboratory at Bell Labs. "Right now discrete lasers are butted up against the fiber and used for optical transmission only. All the signal processing is still done electronically. We want to replace the electronic circuits with optical circuits."

Engineers predict that integrated optical circuits will follow the same   24 dramatic trends that have driven semiconductor electronics over the past two decades: they will become smaller, faster, cheaper. "Right now you can have a million devices on a computer chip," says Giordmaine. "Why should optical chips be any different?" The advent of optical integrated circuits will make it possible to make real what has always remained a dream: a revolutionary generation of extremely fast optical computers.

The optical computer is probably decades away from becoming a   25 reality, but lasers are already having a direct impact on the field of information recording and storage. In the late 1970s, laser-based videodiscs were introduced; they haven't made as big a splash in the home market as manufacturers had hoped, but they are a promising information-storage technology. One drawback of the first-generation machines is that the laser "records" information by punching holes in the disc, which means that the disc isn't reusable. But in June, scientists at Japan's national broadcasting service, NHK, announced a significant breakthrough —a prototype of an erasable videodisc system that uses a helium-neon laser controlled by a computer on a silicon chip to record color-TV signals on an ultrathin magnetic film in a glass disc. Because the signals are stored magnetically, the videodisc can be erased and rerecorded thousands of times.

The printed word is another form of information storage, of course, and lasers are the scribes in new high-speed printers and photocopiers such as the Xerox 9700 and the IBM 3800. The machines create images by using a computer-controlled laser to write lines or characters at extremely high speeds on a photosensitive drum, which then transfers the image to paper.   26

Laser-Toting Robots

Using the same idea—having a computer guide the laser beam's path —makes it possible to create a new generation of machine tools for the factories of the future. In Japan and the United States, engineers are building laser-toting robots with computers for brains. "Computers, lasers and robots are the three essential components for a flexible manufacturing system," says Katsuhiko Isobe, of Mitsubishi Electric Corp. "With conventional machinery you've got to make a die or mold of each item you want and station a person at a machine to run it. The beauty of lasers is that they can do machining without ever physically touching the material." In October Japan's Fuji Tool sold to Ford Motor Co. in the United States a laser processing machine that will do work now done by skilled tool and die makers. The machine automatically scans the shape of a prototype automobile model and uses a carbon-dioxide laser to cut metal master panels. It then uses computer-controlled machinery equipment to produce a stamping mold. "The laser is absolutely revolutionary," says Isobe. "I think it will be at the center of industry in the 21st century."   27

While industrial lasers today are most often used for cutting, welding, drilling and measuring, the laser's light can be put to a much different use: separating isotopes to produce nuclear fuel. Right now, uranium is enriched to make nuclear fuel through the painstaking, expensive process of gas diffusion. But at Lawrence Livermore National Lab in California, scientists are perfecting a less-expensive process that uses a copper laser turned with a Mercurochrome-colored dye that can be set to emit light at a precise frequency.   28

Fusion Power

Someday the laser may make conventional nuclear power plants obso-   29
lete. Scientists at Livermore, Los Alamos and the University of Rochester
are building gigantic laser systems for fusion research. When it is finished
in 1984, Livermore's Nova will have 10 laser beams focusing an awesome
blast of energy—100 trillion watts of power—on a flyspeck of deuterium
and tritium fuel. When the lasers fire, the fuel will implode in the intense
heat—72 million degrees Fahrenheit—setting off a small, confined thermonuclear explosion. Laser-fusion power plants, if they ever become a
reality, will harness the immense energy created by hydrogen fusion—a
process that drives the sun.

Someday laser light may be piped through giant optic cables into deep   30
ocean waters to create undersea farms; it may be beamed into space to
talk to orbiting space stations. Lasers also may be used to fire extremely
precise light pulses at DNA molecules, altering the structure of chromo-
somes and thereby repairing defective genes—or even creating new
forms of life. And eventually billions of lasers will link the world in a vast
information network, a global village of light. Science truth, H. G. Wells
might observe, is at least as strange as science fiction.

Topical Considerations

1. How does the author try to capture our interest and our imagination in the opening paragraph of this essay? Did it capture your interest?

2. What similarities does the author see between the inventions
and discoveries of the nineteenth century and the invention of the laser
in the twentieth century?

3. What is laser light? Exactly how does a laser work? Evaluate
the explanations of the laser given in this article. Were they clear and easy
to understand? Were they addressed to the scientist or to the average
person?

4. The word *laser* is an acronym—a word formed from the initial
letters of a series of words. Can you list other acronyms popularized by
the world of technology?

5. The contributions of the laser in the fields of medicine, defense weapons, and communications are discussed. Pick one of these
areas and discuss what you think are the most significant advances in this
field.

6. Much research is being done regarding the use of the laser in
the fields of medicine, defense and communications. If research could be
continued in only one of these areas and had to be suspended in the other
two, in which area do you feel it should be continued? Explain your
reasons.

7. The idea of laser stations in space, designed to shoot down enemy missiles, was supported by President Reagan in a speech in the winter of 1983. Although he regards this proposal enthusiastically, many others regard it skeptically. Reread the section of the essay dealing with lasers in space. How do you feel about this plan?

Rhetorical Considerations

1. The author does not mention the word *laser* until the very end of the first paragraph of this essay. How do you explain the delay?

2. Compare the content of paragraph 1 with the content of paragraph 2. What is the effect of the juxtaposition of these two paragraphs?

3. Locate and copy down the transitional words or sentences connecting the sections on the laser in medicine, warfare, and communications. Evaluate the transitions. Are they simple, refined, purely functional, or elaborate?

4. Both "The Dazzle of Lasers" and "The Coupling of Man and Machine" are examples of scientific reporting. If you did not know that these articles were authored by different people, could you conclude that by an analysis of the style of each essay? Consider point of view, principles of organization, tone, sentence structure, metaphorical language used, and humor. What conclusions might you draw about the nature of scientific reporting?

Writing Assignments

1. Review the description of the workings of the laser (paragraph 5 and 6). Select a technological piece of equipment with which you are familiar and write a paragraph or two explaining how this item works. You might describe the workings of a pump, a hairdryer, a carburetor, or an internal combustion engine. When you finish, ask yourself if it was easier or more difficult than you thought it would be to write the paragraphs and explain why.

2. If you are a reader of science fiction, you have probably read about many technological wonders, like the laser, that once existed only in the imagination but now exist in reality. Write an essay discussing science fiction you have read and the scientific wonders described therein.

OUT OF TIME AND SPACE

8

"But a Watch in the Night": A Scientific Fable

James C. Rettie

We open our "Out of Time and Space" section with a highly imaginative analogy that reads like a science fiction story. An employee of the National Forest Service in Upper Darby, Pennsylvania, Rettie intended this piece to be a conservationist's lament over the loss of forests and the resultant erosion of soil in the blind rush of modern development. Given the ingenious narrative strategy he picked, however, his "scientific fable" also enables us to witness the evolution of the Earth and the life on it. What Rettie helps us realize is both the enormous amount of time spanned by the history of our planet and the mere moment that has elapsed since the origin of man.

1   Out beyond our solar system there is a planet called Copernicus. It came into existence some four or five billion years before the birth of our Earth. In due course of time it became inhabited by a race of intelligent men.

2   About 750 million years ago the Copernicans had developed the motion picture machine to a point well in advance of the stage that we have reached. Most of the cameras that we now use in motion picture work are geared to take twenty-four pictures per second on a continuous strip of film. When such film is run through a projector, it throws a series of images on the screen and these change with a rapidity that gives the visual impression of normal movement. If a motion is too swift for the human eye to see it in detail, it can be captured and artificially slowed down by means of the slow-motion camera. This one is geared to take many more shots per second—ninety-six or even more than that. When the slow motion film is projected at the normal speed of twenty-four pictures per second, we can see just how the jumping horse goes over a hurdle.

3   What about motion that is too slow to be seen by the human eye? That problem has been solved by the use of the time-lapse camera. In this one, the shutter is geared to take only one shot per second, or one per minute, or even one per hour—depending upon the kind of movement that is being photographed. When the time-lapse film is projected at the normal speed of twenty-four pictures per second, it is possible to see a bean sprout growing up out of the ground. Time-lapse films are useful in the study of many types of motion too slow to be observed by the unaided, human eye.

4   The Copernicans, it seems, had time-lapse cameras some 757 million years ago and they also had superpowered telescopes that gave them a clear view of what was happening upon this Earth. They decided to make a film record of the life history of Earth and to make it on the scale of one

picture per year. The photography has been in progress during the last 757 million years.

In the near future, a Copernican interstellar expedition will arrive upon our Earth and bring with it a copy of the time-lapse film. Arrangements will be made for showing the entire film in one continuous run. This will begin at midnight of New Year's eve and continue day and night without a single stop until midnight of December 31. The rate of projection will be twenty-four pictures per second. Time on the screen will thus seem to move at the rate of twenty-four years per second; 1440 years per minute; 86,400 years per hour; approximately two million years per day; and sixty-two million years per month. The normal life-span of individual man will occupy about three seconds. The full period of Earth history that will be unfolded on the screen (some 757 million years) will extend from what the geologists call Pre-Cambrian times up to the present. This will, by no means, cover the full time-span of the Earth's geological history but it will embrace the period since the advent of living organisms.

During the months of January, February, and March the picture will be desolate and dreary. The shape of the land masses and the oceans will bear little or no resemblance to those that we know. The violence of geological erosion will be much in evidence. Rains will pour down on the land and promptly go booming down to the seas. There will be no clear streams anywhere except where the rains fall upon hard rock. Everywhere on the steeper ground the stream channels will be filled with boulders hurled down by rushing waters. Raging torrents and dry stream beds will keep alternating in quick succession. High mountains will seem to melt like so much butter in the sun. The shifting of land into the seas, later to be thrust up as new mountains, will be going on at a grand scale.

Early in April there will be some indication of the presence of single-celled living organisms in some of the warmer and sheltered coastal waters. By the end of the month it will be noticed that some of these organisms have become multicellular. A few of them, including the Trilobites, will be encased in hard shells.

Toward the end of May, the first vertebrates will appear, but they will still be aquatic creatures. In June about 60 per cent of the land area that we know as North America will be under water. One broad channel will occupy the space where the Rocky Mountains now stand. Great deposits of limestone will be forming under some of the shallower seas. Oil and gas deposits will be in process of formation—also under shallow seas. On land there will still be no sign of vegetation. Erosion will be rampant, tearing loose particles and chunks of rock and grinding them into sand and silt to be spewed out by the streams into bays and estuaries.

About the middle of July the first land plants will appear and take up the tremendous job of soil building. Slowly, very slowly, the mat of vegetation will spread, always battling for its life against the power of erosion. Almost foot by foot, the plant life will advance, lacing down with its root structures whatever pulverized rock material it can find. Leaves and stems will be giving added protection against the loss of the soil foothold. The increasing vegetation will pave the way for the land animals that will live upon it.

Early in August the seas will be teeming with fish. This will be what 10 geologists call the Devonian period. Some of the races of these fish will be breathing by means of lung tissue instead of through gill tissues. Before the month is over, some of the lung fish will go ashore and take on a crude lizard-like appearance. Here are the first amphibians.

In early September the insects will put in their appearance. Some will 11 look like huge dragonflies and will have a wing spread of 24 inches. Large portions of the land masses will now be covered with heavy vegetation that will include the primitive spore-propagating trees. Layer upon layer of this plant growth will build up, later to appear as the coal deposits. About the middle of this month, there will be evidence of the first seed-bearing plants and the first reptiles. Heretofore, the land animals will have been amphibians that could reproduce their kind only by depositing a soft egg mass in quiet waters. The reptiles will be shown to be freed from the aquatic bond because they can reproduce by means of a shelled egg in which the embryo and its nurturing liquids are sealed and thus protected from destructive evaporation. Before September is over, the first dinosaurs will be seen—creatures destined to dominate the animal realm for about 140 million years and then to disappear.

In October there will be series of mountain uplifts along what is now 12 the eastern coast of the United States. A creature with feathered limbs— half bird and half reptile in appearance—will take itself into the air. Some small and rather unpretentious animals will be seen to bring forth their young in a form that is a miniature replica of the parents and to feed these young on milk secreted by mammary glands in the female parent. The emergence of this mammalian form of animal life will be recognized as one of the great events in geologic time. October will also witness the high water mark of the dinosaurs—creatures ranging in size from that of the modern goat to monsters like Brontosaurus that weighed some 40 tons. Most of them will be placid vegetarians, but a few will be hideous-looking carnivores, like Allosaurus and Tyrannosaurus. Some of the herbivorous dinosaurs will be clad in bony armor for protection against their flesh-eating comrades.

November will bring pictures of a sea extending from the Gulf of 13 Mexico to the Arctic in space now occupied by the Rocky Mountains. A few of the reptiles will take to the air on bat-like wings. One of these, called Pteranodon, will have a wingspread of 15 feet. There will be a rapid development of the modern flowering plants, modern trees, and modern insects. The dinosaurs will disappear. Toward the end of the month there will be a tremendous land disturbance in which the Rocky Mountains will rise out of the sea to assume a dominating place in the North American landscape.

As the picture runs on into December it will show the mammals in 14 command of the animal life. Seed-bearing trees and grasses will have covered most of the land with a heavy mantle of vegetation. Only the areas newly thrust up from the sea will be barren. Most of the streams will be crystal clear. The turmoil of geologic erosion will be confined to localized areas. About December 25 will begin the cutting of the Grand Canyon of the Colorado River. Grinding down through layer after layer of sedimentary strata, this stream will finally expose deposits laid down in Pre-Cambrian times. Thus in the walls of that canyon will appear geological formations dating from recent times to the period when the Earth had no living organisms upon it.

15   The picture will run on through the latter days of December and even up to its final day with still no sign of mankind. The spectators will become alarmed in the fear that man has somehow been left out. But not so; sometime about noon on December 31 (one million years ago) will appear a stooped, massive creature of man-like proportions. This will be Pithecanthropus, the Java ape man. For tools and weapons he will have nothing but crude stone and wooden clubs. His children will live a precarious existence threatened on the one side by hostile animals and on the other by tremendous climatic changes. Ice sheets—in places 4000 feet deep—will form in the northern parts of North America and Eurasia. Four times this glacial ice will push southward to cover half the continents. With each advance the plant and animal life will be swept under or pushed southward. With each recession of the ice, life will struggle to reestablish itself in the wake of the retreating glaciers. The woolly mammoth, the musk ox, and the caribou all will fight to maintain themselves near the ice line. Sometimes they will be caught and put into cold storage —skin, flesh, blood, bones and all.

16   The picture will run on through supper time with still very little evidence of man's presence on the Earth. It will be about 11 o'clock when Neanderthal man appears. Another half hour will go by before the appearance of Cro-Magnon man living in caves and painting crude animal pictures on the walls of his dwelling. Fifteen minutes more will bring Neolithic man, knowing how to chip stone and thus produce sharp cutting edges for spears and tools. In a few minutes more it will appear that man has domesticated the dog, the sheep and, possibly, other animals. He will then begin the use of milk. He will also learn the arts of basket weaving and the making of pottery and dugout canoes.

17   The dawn of civilization will not come until about five or six minutes before the end of the picture. The story of the Egyptians, the Babylonians, the Greeks, and the Romans will unroll during the fourth, the third and the second minute before the end. At 58 minutes and 43 seconds past 11:00 P.M. (just 1 minute and 17 seconds before the end) will come the beginning of the Christian era. Columbus will discover the new world 20 seconds before the end. The Declaration of Independence will be signed just 7 seconds before the final curtain comes down.

In those few moments of geologic time will be the story of all that   18
has happened since we became a nation. And what a story it will be! A
human swarm will sweep across the face of the continent and take it
away from the . . . red men. They will change it far more radically than
it has ever been changed before in a comparable time. The great virgin
forests will be seen going down before ax and fire. The soil, covered for
eons by its protective mantle of trees and grasses, will be laid bare to
the ravages of water and wind erosion. Streams that had been flowing
clear will, once again, take up a load of silt and push it toward the seas.
Humus and mineral salts, both vital elements of productive soil, will be
seen to vanish at a terrifying rate. The railroads and highways and cities
that will spring up may divert attention, but they cannot cover up the
blight of man's recent activities. In great sections of Asia, it will be seen
that man must utilize cow dung and every scrap of available straw or
grass for fuel to cook his food. The forests that once provided wood for
this purpose will be gone without a trace. The use of these agricultural
wastes for fuel, in place of returning them to the land, will be leading to
increasing soil impoverishment. Here and there will be seen a dust
storm darkening the landscape over an area a thousand miles across.
Man-creatures will be shown counting their wealth in terms of bits of
printed paper representing other bits of a scarce but comparatively useless yellow metal that is kept buried in strong vaults. Meanwhile, the
soil, the only real wealth that can keep mankind alive on the face of this
Earth is savagely being cut loose from its ancient moorings and washed
into the seven seas.

We have just arrived upon this Earth. How long will we stay?   19

Topical Considerations

1. What would you say Rettie's purpose was in writing this essay?
What was he trying to demonstrate?

2. Explain Rettie's extensive analogy. Does it work for you? How
does it dramatize the various geological developments in earth's history?
the evolution of different life forms? the emergence of humankind?

3. How does Rettie's strategy of the year-long time-lapse movie
of Earth's history serve his interests in soil conservation?

Rhetorical Considerations

1. Do you think Rettie spends too much time at the beginning of
his essay explaining how the camera works? Explain your answer.

2. Why do you think Rettie chose to create alien observers?

3. At what point in this essay did you suspect that Rettie was

giving more than a simple narrative of the development of life on Earth? Where did he start sounding critical? Where is there a tone change?

4. Explain the effectiveness of the rhetorical question that concludes the piece.

5. Rettie took the title of his essay from Psalm 90 in the King James version of the Bible: "For a thousand years in Thy sight are but as yesterday when it is past, and as a watch in the night." How does this passage help you understand Rettie's title choice?

Writing Assignment

1. This essay was written some 35 years ago. If you can think of other environmental problems that have occurred since, try to splice them into the end of the piece. In other words, pick up from where Rettie left off in an essay of your own, using the same camera-eye technique. You might want to end at the present or extend the narrative to some future time.

Were Dinosaurs Dumb?

Stephen Jay Gould

Ever since their bones were discovered in the nineteenth century, dinosaurs have gotten bad press. They were the biggest land creatures, so surely they must have been the clumsiest and the dumbest. In fact, didn't some of the giants of these giants have brains the size of walnuts? Maybe so, but as scientist and writer Stephen Jay Gould says, any creature that held sway for some 100 million years couldn't have been all that stupid. What follows is a reevaluation of the intelligence of dinosaurs by a man who is highly qualified to speak for them. Stephen Jay Gould teaches biology and the history of science at Harvard University. He also writes the award-winning column "This View of Life" for *Natural History* magazine, and he is author of the widely acclaimed books, *Ever Since Darwin* (1977), *The Panda's Thumb* (1980), from which this piece comes, *The Mismeasurement of Man* (1981), and *Hen's Teeth and Horse's Toes* (1983).

When Muhammad Ali flunked his army intelligence test, he 1
quipped (with a wit that belied his performance on the exam): "I only said I was the greatest; I never said I was the smartest." In our metaphors and fairy tales, size and power are almost always balanced by a want of intelligence. Cunning is the refuge of the little guy. Think of Br'er Rabbit and

Br'er Bear; David smiting Goliath with a slingshot; Jack chopping down the beanstalk. Slow wit is the tragic flaw of a giant.

The discovery of dinosaurs in the nineteenth century provided, or so it appeared, a quintessential case for the negative correlation of size and smarts. With their pea brains and giant bodies, dinosaurs became a symbol of lumbering stupidity. Their extinction seemed only to confirm their flawed design. 2

Dinosaurs were not even granted the usual solace of a giant—great physical prowess. God maintained a discreet silence about the brains of behemoth, but he certainly marveled at its strength: "Lo, now, his strength is in his loins, and his force is in the navel of his belly. He moveth his tail like a cedar. . . . His bones are as strong pieces of brass; his bones are like bars of iron [Job 40:16–18]." Dinosaurs, on the other hand, have usually been reconstructed as slow and clumsy. In the standard illustration, *Brontosaurus* wades in a murky pond because he cannot hold up his own weight on land. 3

Popularizations for grade school curricula provide a good illustration of prevailing orthodoxy. I still have my third grade copy (1948 edition) of Bertha Morris Parker's *Animals of Yesterday*, stolen, I am forced to suppose, from P.S. 26, Queens (sorry Mrs. McInerney). In it, boy (teleported back to the Jurassic) meets brontosaur: 4

> It is huge, and you can tell from the size of its head that
> it must be stupid. . . . This giant animal moves about very
> slowly as it eats. No wonder it moves slowly! Its huge feet
> are very heavy, and its great tail is not easy to pull
> around. You are not surprised that the thunder lizard
> likes to stay in the water so that the water will help it hold
> up its huge body. . . . Giant dinosaurs were once the lords
> of the earth. Why did they disappear? You can probably
> guess part of the answer—their bodies were too large for
> their brains. If their bodies had been smaller, and their
> brains larger, they might have lived on.

Dinosaurs have been making a strong comeback of late, in this age of "I'm OK, you're OK." Most paleontologists are now willing to view them as energetic, active, and capable animals. The *Brontosaurus* that wallowed in its pond a generation ago is now running on land, while pairs of males have been seen twining their necks about each other in elaborate sexual combat for access to females (much like the neck wrestling of giraffes). Modern anatomical reconstructions indicate strength and agility, and many paleontologists now believe that dinosaurs were warmblooded. . . . 5

The idea of warmblooded dinosaurs has captured the public imagination and received a torrent of press coverage. Yet another vindication of dinosaurian capability has received very little attention, although I regard 6 it as equally significant. I refer to the issue of stupidity and its correlation with size. The revisionist interpretation, which I support in this column, does not enshrine dinosaurs as paragons of intellect, but it does maintain that they were not small brained after all. They had the "right-sized" brains for reptiles of their body size.

I don't wish to deny that the flattened, minuscule head of largebodied *Stegosaurus* houses little brain from our subjective, top-heavy perspective, but I do wish to assert that we should not expect more of the beast. First of all, large animals have relatively smaller brains than related, small animals. The correlation of brain size with body size among kindred animals (all reptiles, all mammals, for example) is remarkably regular. As we move from small to large animals, from mice to elephants or small lizards to Komodo dragons, brain size increases, but not so fast as body size. In other words, bodies grow faster than brains, and large animals have low rations of brain weight to body weight. In fact, brains grow only about two-thirds as fast as bodies. Since we have no reason to believe that large animals are consistently stupider than their smaller relatives, we must conclude that large animals require relatively less brain to do as well as smaller animals. If we do not recognize this relationship, we are likely to underestimate the mental power of very large animals, dinosaurs in particular. 7

Second, the relationship between brain and body size is not identical in all groups of vertebrates. All share the same rate of relative decrease in brain size, but small mammals have much larger brains than small reptiles of the same body weight. This discrepancy is maintained at all larger body weights, since brain size increases at the same rate in both groups—two-thirds as fast as body size. 8

Put these two facts together—all large animals have relatively small brains, and reptiles have much smaller brains than mammals at any common body weight—and what should we expect from a normal, large reptile? The answer, of course, is a brain of very modest size. No living reptile even approaches a middle-sized dinosaur in bulk, so we have no modern standard to serve as a model for dinosaurs. 9

Fortunately, our imperfect fossil record has, for once, not severely disappointed us in providing data about fossil brains. Superbly preserved skulls have been found for many species of dinosaurs, and cranial capacities can be measured. (Since brains do not fill craniums in reptiles, some creative, although not unreasonable, manipulation must be applied to estimate brain size from the hole within a skull.) With these data, we have a clear test for the conventional hypothesis of dinosaurian stupidity. We should agree, at the outset, that a reptilian standard is the only proper one—it is surely irrelevant that dinosaurs had smaller brains than people or whales. We have abundant data on the relationship of brain and body size in modern reptiles. Since we know that brains increase two-thirds as fast as bodies as we move from small to large living species, we can 10 extrapolate this rate to dinosaurian sizes and ask whether dinosaur brains match what we would expect of living reptiles if they grew so large.

Harry Jerison studied the brain sizes of ten dinosaurs and found that   11
they fell right on the extrapolated reptilian curve. Dinosaurs did not have small brains; they maintained just the right-sized brains for reptiles of their dimensions. So much for Ms. Parker's explanation of their demise.

Jerison made no attempt to distinguish among various kinds of dino-   12
saurs; ten species distributed over six major groups scarcely provide a proper basis for comparison. Recently, James A. Hopson of the University of Chicago gathered more data and made a remarkable and satisfying discovery.

Hopson needed a common scale for all dinosaurs. He therefore com-   13
pared each dinosaur brain with the average reptilian brain we would expect at its body weight. If the dinosaur falls on the standard reptilian curve, its brain receives a value of 1.0 (called an encephalization quotient, or EQ—the ratio of actual brain to expected brain for a standard reptile of the same body weight). Dinosaurs lying above the curve (more brain than expected in a standard reptile of the same body weight) receive values in excess of 1.0, while those below the curve measure less than 1.0.

Hopson found that the major groups of dinosaurs can be ranked by   14
increasing values of average EQ. This ranking corresponds perfectly with inferred speed, agility and behavioral complexity in feeding (or avoiding the prospect of becoming a meal). The giant sauropods, *Brontosaurus* and its allies, have the lowest EQ's—0.20 to 0.35. They must have moved fairly slowly and without great maneuverability. They probably escaped predation by virtue of their bulk alone, much as elephants do today. The armored ankylosaurs and stegosaurs come next with EQ's of 0.52 to 0.56. These animals, with their heavy armor, probably relied largely upon passive defense, but the clubbed tail of ankylosaurs and the spiked tail of stegosaurs imply some active fighting and increased behavioral complexity.

The ceratopsians rank next at about 0.7 to 0.9. Hopson remarks: "The   15
larger ceratopsians, with their great horned heads, relied on active defensive strategies and presumably required somewhat greater agility than the tail-weaponed forms, both in fending off predators and in intraspecific combat bouts. The smaller ceratopsians, lacking true horns, would have relied on sensory acuity and speed to escape from predators." The ornithopods (duckbills and their allies) were the brainiest herbivores, with EQ's from 0.85 to 1.5. They relied upon "acute senses and relatively fast speeds" to elude carnivores. Flight seems to require more acuity and agility than standing defense. Among ceratopsians, small, hornless, and presumably fleeing *Protoceratops* had a higher EQ than great three-horned *Triceratops*.

Carnivores have higher EQ's than herbivores, as in modern verte-   16
brates. Catching a rapidly moving or stoutly fighting prey demands a

good deal more upstairs than plucking the right kind of plant. The giant theropods (*Tyrannosaurus* and its allies) vary from 1.0 to nearly 2.0. Atop the heap, quite appropriately at its small size, rests the little coelurosaur *Stenonychosaurus* with an EQ well above 5.0. Its actively moving quarry, small mammals and birds perhaps, probably posed a greater challenge in discovery and capture than *Triceratops* afforded *Tyrannosaurus*.

I do not wish to make a naive claim that brain size equals intelligence   17 or, in this case, behavioral range and agility (I don't know what intelligence means in humans, much less in a group of extinct reptiles). Variation in brain size within a species has precious little to do with brain power (humans do equally well with 900 or 2,500 cubic centimeters of brain). But comparison across species, when the differences are large, seems reasonable. I do not regard it as irrelevant to our achievements that we so greatly exceed koala bears—much as I love them—in EQ. The sensible ordering among dinosaurs also indicates that even so coarse a measure as brain size counts for something.

If behavioral complexity is one consequence of mental power, then we   18 might expect to uncover among dinosaurs some signs of social behavior that demand coordination, cohesiveness, and recognition. Indeed we do, and it cannot be accidental that these signs were overlooked when dinosaurs labored under the burden of a falsely imposed obtuseness. Multiple trackways have been uncovered, with evidence for more than twenty animals traveling together in parallel movement. Did some dinosaurs live in herds? At the Davenport Ranch sauropod trackway, small footprints lie in the center and larger ones at the periphery. Could it be that some dinosaurs traveled much as some advanced herbivorous mammals do today, with large adults at the borders sheltering juveniles in the center?

In addition, the very structures that seemed most bizarre and useless   19 to older paleontologists—the elaborate crests of hadrosaurs, the frills and horns of ceratopsians, and the nine inches of solid bone above the brain of *Pachycephalosaurus*—now appear to gain a coordinated explanation as devices for sexual display and combat. Pachycephalosaurs may have engaged in head-butting contests much as mountain sheep do today. The crests of some hadrosaurs are well designed as resonating chambers; did they engage in bellowing matches? The ceratopsian horn and frill may have acted as sword and shield in the battle for mates. Since such behavior is not only intrinsically complex, but also implies an elaborate social system, we would scarcely expect to find it in a group of animals barely muddling through at a moronic level.

But the best illustration of dinosaurian capability may well be the fact   20 most often cited against them—their demise. Extinction, for most people, carries many of the connotations attributed to sex not so long ago—a rather disreputable business, frequent in occurrence, but not to anyone's credit, and certainly not to be discussed in proper circles. But, like sex, extinction is an ineluctable part of life. It is the ultimate fate of all species, not the lot of unfortunate and ill-designed creatures. It is no sign of failure.

The remarkable thing about dinosaurs is not that they became extinct,   21
but that they dominated the earth for so long. Dinosaurs held sway for 100 million years while mammals, all the while, lived as small animals in the interstices of their world. After 70 million years on top, we mammals have an excellent track record and good prospects for the future, but we have yet to display the staying power of dinosaurs.

People, on this criterion, are scarcely worth mentioning—5 million   22
years perhaps since *Australopithecus,* a mere 50,000 for our own species, *Homo sapiens.* Try the ultimate test within our system of values: Do you know anyone who would wager a substantial sum, even at favorable odds, on the proposition that *Homo sapiens* will last longer than *Brontosaurus?*

Topical Considerations

1. According to Gould, dinosaurs have long suffered the big-is-dumb-and-clumsy tradition. What are some of the sources of that tradition that Gould cites?

2. Why have attitudes toward dinosaurs recently been turned around?

3. On what basic grounds does Gould argue his defense of dinosaurs? Explain his reasoning regarding brain and body size ratios.

4. Explain "encephalization quotient," or EQ. Why didn't the brontosaurus and other less brainy beasts need higher EQs?

5. Why did carnivores necessarily have higher EQs? Which had the highest? Why was a higher EQ necessary for them?

6. How does Gould's interpretation of some of the bizarre head structures of some dinosaurs counter interpretations of earlier paleonotologists?

Rhetorical Considerations

1. How well does the Muhammad Ali anecdote that opens the essay illustrate Gould's stand? Was it appropriate and convincing?

2. Find examples of Gould's use of humor. How does it add to or detract from his argument?

3. Gould refers to scientists and scientific studies in his essay. How well does he use their evidence to support his arguments? Be specific.

4. A good conclusion to an essay should wrap up some of the major points made and leave some impact. Evaluate Gould's concluding paragraph.

Writing Assignment

1. Gould's essay is a defense against the popularly held attitude that dinosaurs were dumb. Try your own hand at writing a defense of animals against popularly held beliefs—for example, that cats are sneaky, pigeons are stupid, some dogs are smarter than others, and so on. If you cannot find some scientific evidence to back you up, at least use reasoned arguments and your own observations.

The Case For Studying UFOs

J. Allen Hynek

For decades, there have been people who have believed in a two-way traffic between Earth and the stars. Some have reported seeing strange lights in the sky; others have claimed to have seen flying saucers up close; still others have insisted that they have been taken for rides in alien vehicles piloted by weird beings. Whatever the truth is, UFOs are phenomena of modern times that refuse to go away, despite loud disclaimers from the scientific community. What follows is a "case for studying" the phenomenon, written by a respected scientist. J. Allen Hynek is the former chairman of the Astronomy Department at Northwestern University, a past director of the Smithsonian Astrophysical Laboratory (1956–1960), and a consultant to Project Blue Book, the Air Force UFO study, for seventeen years. Hynek is also the founder of the Center for UFO Studies.

1   Whether a person has complete disdain for UFO phenomena or completely uncritical acceptance, or takes one of the many intermediate positions, certain incontrovertible facts stand out. UFO reports not only exist but also *persist;* they flow from many parts of the world, from disparate cultures and environments. A significant percentage of such reports come from sane and responsible people, as judged by commonly accepted standards (indeed, sometimes from well-trained technical and scientific personnel).

2   UFO phenomena are one thing; their interpretation is quite another. Unfortunately, in the public mind one particular interpretation has completely overshadowed and displaced the phenomena themselves: UFOs have been made synonymous with visiting extraterrestrial intelligences.

3   Now this is a very appealing and exciting idea, but it is this very interpretation that has been an abomination to most scientists. Familiar as they are with awesome astronomical distances, they can see no logical way in which such visitors could get here. A simple illustration serves to emphasize this: if we let the thickness of an ordinary playing card repre-

sent the distance from the earth to the moon, then it would require a 19-mile line of playing cards, back to back, to reach the star closest to our solar system. If UFOs indeed be space visitors, then they must really know something we don't!

Here is the great stumbling block; here is where the baby is cast out   4 with the bathwater: since, according to our present scientific paradigm, it is clearly impossible for space travel to exist on such a scale, well then, UFOs must be nonsense. This is a most logical deduction on the part of the well-meaning, objective members of the scientific fraternity.

Somehow this is reminiscent of the nineteenth-century physicist who,   5 while working with Crookes tubes (a prototypic cathode-ray tube), noted that protected photographic material became fogged when placed nearby. His far-reaching conclusion from this observation is said to have been "Do not place photographic materials near a Crookes tube," thus missing the discovery of X-rays.

Even the great can sometimes be found wearing blinders when it   6 comes to the unexpected. In his *Book of the Damned,* Charles Fort tells the following story of Antoine Lavoisier, one of the founding fathers of modern chemistry. On September 13, 1768, "French peasants in the fields near Luce heard a violent crash like a thunderclap and saw a great stone object hurtle down from the sky. The French Academy of Sciences asked the great chemist Lavoisier for a report on the occurrence; but Lavoisier was convinced that stones never fell out of the sky and reported that all the witnesses were mistaken or lying. It was not until the nineteenth century that the Academy accepted the reality of meteorites."

What might *we* be bypassing by overlooking UFO phenomena? Is our   7 only possible conclusion that we should disregard them because their implications are so bizarre and are as unfathomable as X-rays would have been to the pedestrian, objective scientific worker of the nineteenth century? Perhaps it is a mistake to characterize observations of UFO phenomena as one nineteenth-century British physicist defined effects produced by the hypnotists of his day: "One-half imposture and the rest bad observation." Today, these same hypnotic techniques are accepted and useful in many areas, from medical therapy to legal matters. The old scientist was not alone in his dismissal of hypnotism. So serious was the attack on it by science that, when hypnotism was employed in lieu of anesthesia, the hypnotized patients undergoing surgery were branded as "hardened imposters who let their legs be cut off and large tumors cut out without showing any sign even of discomfort." Just how deep into sand can one sink one's head?

Now there is no doubt that many UFO reports are just as bizarre and   8 unbelievable as the demonstrations of hypnotists or, to translate to the world of physics, as the seemingly unbelievable wave-particle duality of light. Indeed, the analogy is apt. UFO phenomena exhibit a similar duality, which, it seems, we must accept in a similar manner.

On the one hand, UFO phenomena seem to be utterly physical. Reported objects have been photographed (although it must be admitted that so far no really good close-ups have been produced), and they have appeared on radar screens. They can break tree branches and leave holes in the ground, and it is said that bullets have ricocheted off them. They have been reliably reported to stop car engines and to interfere with electrical circuits. A recent study of over 400 "car stopping" cases leaves little doubt about this physical effect.   9

Yet, on the other hand, UFO phenomena exhibit strangely nonphysical attributes. On occasion they appear, at least temporarily, to abrogate the inertial properties of matter: they exhibit extraordinary accelerations, hover effortlessly a few feet above the ground and can disappear before one's very eyes. Furthermore, physical objects can be kept track of. We always know where a bus or an aircraft is; it has a continuous "world line." But an outstanding characteristic of a UFO is its "localization in space and time." A UFO is almost always reported in just one locality and is rarely seen sequentially in town after town, as a bus would be. And it does not remain for long in a specific locality. The distribution curve of UFO "duration times" peaks at about 10 minutes.   10

I have dubbed this unique property of the UFO the "Cheshire cat effect" after Alice's cat in Wonderland, which also appeared out of nowhere, remained in one location for a short period and then vanished!   11

John Stuart Mill, in his *A System of Logic*, noted, "The greatest of all causes of non-observation is preconceived opinion." To some, this ability of UFOs to appear and disappear is sufficient reason for dismissing the entire subject out of hand. But is this not more a case of refusing to look and observe because preconditioning teaches us to not want to look?   12

But the cat seems to be there, and from time to time it demands some attention. Maybe it's trying to tell us something.   13

Topical Considerations

1. What is the common public interpretation of UFOs? Why is this interpretation "an abomination to most scientists" (paragraph 3)?

2. According to Hynek, what is the "stumbling block" in the argument of "objective members of the scientific fraternity" (paragraph 4)?

3. How does Hynek liken UFO phenomena to the "wave-particle duality of light" (paragraph 8)?

4. What characteristics of reported UFOs are most baffling?

5. In your own words, what is Hynek's "case for studying UFOs"? Does he indicate that he believes UFOs are from other worlds?

6. Do you believe there is other intelligent life in the universe? What are your reasons? Do you believe that we have been visited by beings from other worlds? Explain your answer.

Rhetorical Considerations

1. What is the meaning of the expression "to cast the baby out with the bathwater" (see paragraph 4)? How does Hynek use this metaphor?

2. Hynek makes use of comparison in this essay to strengthen his case. Explain the comparison made in paragraph 6. What is being compared to what, and how effective and convincing is the comparison?

3. Is the wave-particle duality of light a particularly fitting analogy to UFO phenomena?

4. In the next-to-the-last paragraph, Hynek quotes John Stuart Mill. How does Hynek use this quotation? How does it serve his case here?

Writing Assignments

1. If you believe we have been visited by aliens from other worlds, write a paper in which you clearly argue your reasons.

2. If you do not believe we have been visited by aliens, write a paper clearly stating your reasons. Also, try to offer some solid explanations for the thousands of UFO sightings that have been reported all over the world for decades.

3. "The greatest of all causes of non-observation is preconceived opinion." So wrote John Stuart Mill, quoted in paragraph 12. Using this idea, write a paper in which you argue the need for science to investigate other phenomena that traditionally have been dismissed as nonsense, as have UFOs. Use as support historical evidence, as Hynek does, that preconceptions are often a guarantee of ignorance.

Our Cosmic Cousins

Gene Bylinsky

There are some 100 billion stars in our own galaxy, the Milky Way, and some 100 billion galaxies in the universe. With all that out there, the likelihood of extraterrestrial life is enormous. But what might life elsewhere look like? Such speculations have long been the domain of science fiction writers, whose bizarre assortment of beings suggests that anything is possible. New discoveries by radio astronomers tell us, however, that the raw material of life is everywhere. Thus, says scientist and writer Gene Bylinsky, extraterrestrial evolution is likely to follow not bizarre but parallel courses to that on Earth. This essay was taken from Bylinsky's *Life in Darwin's Universe*.

The molecules that make up life are scattered throughout the   1
cosmos like seeds on a freshly plowed field. Radio astronomers have
recently discovered water, carbon monoxide, methane, ethyl alcohol and
even precursors of the simple amino acid glycine drifting in clouds of
interstellar dust. We now know that the Universe is a vast chemical laboratory and that it may be devoted to the creation of life. And since the
raw materials of life are the same everywhere, evolution is likely to follow
parallel paths throughout the cosmos. It is Darwin's Universe. Astronomers estimate that there are 1.6 billion stars with planets in our galaxy
alone; among the 100 billion detectable galaxies in Darwin's Universe,
the opportunities for life are boundless.

Scientists and nonscientists alike have argued that extraterrestrial life   2
won't resemble any familiar organism or machine because it will have
evolved in environments far different from Earth's But the new information supplied by radio astronomers—that the basic building blocks of life
are the same everywhere—suggests that throughout the cosmos the dictates of the environment will be surprisingly similar.

Family Resemblance

The family resemblance between us and our cosmic cousins starts at   3
an invisible and profound level: that of atoms and molecules. The four
basic elements of life—carbon, hydrogen, oxygen and nitrogen—are
among the most abundant in the Universe and exist everywhere in about
the same proportion.

At the center of life on Earth—and elsewhere, radio astronomers now   4
confirm—is the carbon molecule. Carbon has four electrons in its outer
shell, which can be joined by another four. This symmetry allows carbon
atoms to combine easily with others and form the long polymer chains
necessary for life.

Life needs a solvent, too. Water is the universal catalyst, allowing   5
chemical reactions to take place without itself being changed. Where
there's water and carbon, there is life.

The universal laws of physics and mechanics dictate life's form and   6
shape. Living beings everywhere will have to contend with gravity, fric-
tion, turbulence and drag. As Dr. N. John Berrill, the British biologist,
puts it, "If you pulled a camel through the eye of a needle, it would come
out as a thread—and so would anything else. I think this side of evolution
is universal."

But the existence of a planet exactly duplicating Earth—in size, rate of   7
rotation, precise distance from a sun, inclination of its axis—is as unlikely
as the existence of an evolutionary double for mankind. Changing just a
few simple physical parameters of a planet would lead to profound differences in its appearance and indigenous life forms.

On a smaller planet, trees and animals—released from gravitational   8
restraint—would shoot upward, tall and slender. On such a planet, a

giraffelike animal could have a neck twice as long as that of its terrestrial counterpart, and trees could soar to 500 feet or more.

On a larger planet, gravity would have the opposite effect—animals   9 would become squat, their legs and necks thickened. On a large planet with gravity five times that of Earth, a 160-pound person would weigh 800 pounds and would require a larger heart and an elephantine bone structure.

For a detailed model of how life can evolve on other planets, we need   10 only look to Earth. On isolated continents thousands of miles apart, in environments that differ sharply from one another, evolution created three kinds of wolf (two marsupial and the other placental) from ancestral shrewlike animals only distantly related. And tens of millions of years apart, evolution poured two creatures that once lived on land, the ichthyosaur and the dolphin, into nearly the same shape to cope with the same new environment, the sea. Examples of such convergent evolution —the separate rise of unrelated but strikingly similar animals shaped by similar environmental forces—suggest that creatures evolving on planets with the same basic raw materials for life will bear some similarity to creatures on Earth.

We can't expect exact duplicates of man and other earthly beings,   11 however, because, as Harvard paleontologist George Gaylord Simpson and others have argued persuasively, evolution is nonrepeatable and irreversible. If life were starting all over again on a primitive Earth, neither man nor other animals would evolve into their exact present forms. Our existence is the result of too many unpredictable events— climatic changes, solar and cosmic radiation, the fortuitous development of lungs in Paleozoic fish gasping for air in shallow ponds.

Even on Earth, mankind wasn't the only candidate for high intelli-   12 gence. If the savannas had never opened up, beckoning our forebears down from the trees to become hunter-gatherers, or if geologic and climatic changes on Earth had favored a flying instead of a walking creature, natural selection might have picked not the ape but the bat, descendant of the same shrewlike mammal.

Or suppose that those Paleozoic fishes had remained in rivers and   13 oceans without venturing onto dry land. Legions of other creatures stood ready to emerge from the sea in their stead: insects, crustaceans, even mollusks such as the octopus. And what if the continents had never surfaced, if Earth or another planet were totally covered with water? Such a planet would be inhabited by two types of marine animal: mollusks, such as octopuses, squid and clams, and spiny echinoderms, such as starfish. There would be no mammals, such as dolphins or whales that went back to the sea, and no vertebrate fish, since they are the product of freshwater streams.

An octopuslike creature would probably have the best chance to   14 emerge as ruler of a sea-planet. Even on Earth, where the octopus is

relatively little known, it is beginning to acquire a reputation for high
intelligence (it builds homes when caves are unavailable) and a wide
range of emotions (it changes color when frightened or angry), despite
its walnut-size brain.

Another group of creatures whose ancestors came from the sea—   15
insects—could have had a clear express lane to intelligent evolution if no
other life forms had competed against them. In the absence of amphibians, mammals and reptiles, insects could have radiated into niches now
filled by animals. Just as Earth had a chance to be the Planet of the Insects,
alien worlds are also likely to see such a possibility arise.

We can't exclude birds as a planet's dominant creature either. On   16
Earth, in fact, birds seem to have had the stage to themselves between
the extinction of giant reptiles and the first surge of mammalian evolution. As a result, many of the original seed-eating and fruit-eating birds
became too huge to fly and developed oversize beaks, possibly for feeding on small reptiles and fish and large insects. Without competitive,
preying mammals to bother them, birds might have become the rulers of
Earth.

Or an intelligent reptile could have headed humans off at the evolu-   17
tionary pass. If the age of reptiles, which began 200 million years ago, had
never ended (as it did, 65 million years ago), mammals might never have
been given a chance to evolve much beyond those tiny shrews.

In a recent Soviet computer simulation of land animals' evolution, the   18
creature that emerged as dominant was a highly active and intelligent
tailless reptile walking on its hind legs and possessing skillful hands. Its
descendants, the simulation further projected, were medium-size, upright reptiles with fur instead of scales.

Life has adjusted to a remarkable variety of conditions and extremes   19
on Earth, and it will do so elsewhere as well. We find life no matter where
we look on this planet, from the top of Mount Everest to the ocean
depths. One type of bacterium thrives in sulfurous hot springs by synthe-
sizing heat-resistant structural materials. On the ocean floor, strange
wormlike creatures crawl in eternal darkness under pressures 1,000 times
those at sea level.

Some organisms even modify their seemingly hostile environments.   20
Lichens in arid lands, for example, ensure an adequate water supply by
boring microscopic tunnels in the rocks on which they live. The rock
becomes more porous and thus able to hold more water—a remarkable
demonstration of how even "unintelligent" life can change its environment. We must not underestimate the ability of life on other planets to
occupy niches that seem preposterous to us.

Earth's million-plus living species and its 250,000 or so fossil species   21
represent only a fraction of life forms that have—or could have—lived on
the planet. Known rates of evolutionary turnover have allowed experts
to predict that the number of species that ought to be in our fossil record

is at least a hundred times the number found so far. That adds up to 25 million species on Earth alone. Multiply that by the billions of potentially life-bearing planets circling other suns, and the total possible number of cosmic species staggers the imagination.

Topical Considerations

1. Despite the fact that there are 1.6 billion stars with planets in the Milky Way alone and some 100 billion galaxies, scientists seem to think that extraterrestrial life might not be so radically different from terrestrial life. On what evidence are they basing this speculation?
2. Science fiction movies and novels often depict alien life as bizarrely different from our own. At times, however, the aliens are almost indistinguishable from human kind. Which kind of alien seems more probable, and why?
3. What might life be like on a small planet? on a very large planet?
4. On what bases does Bylinsky hypothesize the kinds of life forms that might exist elsewhere?
5. According to Bylinsky, why would neither man nor other animals evolve into their exact present forms if life were starting all over again on a primitive Earth?
6. According to the author, how might the octopus have become the dominant life form on Earth? or the insect? or the reptile?
7. Bylinsky says: "We must not underestimate the ability of life on other planets to occupy niches that seem preposterous to us" (paragraph 20). On what evidence does he make this assertion?

Rhetorical Considerations

1. If you did not know that this article appeared in *Science Digest,* what would you say about the kind of audience it was intended for? Were there technical matters in the essay that you did not follow?
2. Find examples where Bylinsky used deductive reasoning to make his speculations about life elsewhere.
3. How does the author's use of scientific research contribute to his speculations?

Writing Assignments

1. Bylinsky says that there is as little chance of finding a planetary double of Earth as there is of finding "an evolutionary double for mankind" (paragraph 7). Write a paper in which you explore either the

advantages or the disadvantages of finding a world inhabited by human-like creatures.

2. Bylinsky makes some fanciful but scientific speculations about what life might look like on Earth if one or two parameters had been different. Write a paper in which you speculate about the kind of life form one might find on a world like our own but with one or two physical parameters changed. Consider, for instance, a planet with very high or very low gravity.

3. Write a paper in which you argue that our government should be preparing a task force to communicate with alien visitors. In your paper, tell how such a task force should be composed and what its procedures should be for meeting such a contingency.

The Planets Are Not Enough

Arthur C. Clarke

Are the stars made for man? Will we ever reach them? Given our present technology, it seems highly unlikely, since reaching even the next closest star, Proxima Centauri, would take our fastest space vehicles about a hundred thousand years. As astronomer and famous science fiction author Arthur C. Clarke says, however, it is crucial that we explore space. Yet to do so, given the vast distances, we will need either a totally new technology or some extraordinary developments in our existing technology. Clarke here offers some remarkable possibilities on how we might make a journey to the stars. Clarke is the author of more than fifty science and science fictions books, most notable of which are *Childhood's End* (1953), *Rendezvous with Rama* (1974), *2001: A Space Odyssey* (with Stanley Kubrick, 1968), and its sequel, *2010: Odyssey Two* (1982).

Altogether apart from its scientific value, space travel has one   1
justification that transcends all others. It is probably the only way we can hope to answer one of the supreme questions of philosophy: Is Man alone in the Universe? It seems incredible that ours should be the only inhabited planet among the millions of worlds that must exist among the stars, but we cannot solve this problem by speculating about it. If it can be solved at all, it will be by visiting other planets to see for ourselves.

The Solar System, comprising the nine known worlds of our Sun and   2
their numerous satellites, is a relatively compact structure, a snug little celestial oasis in an endless desert. It is true that millions of miles separate Earth from its neighbors, but such distances are cosmically trivial. They will even be trivial in terms of human engineering before another hundred years—a mere moment in historical time—have elapsed. However, the distances that sunder us from the possible worlds of other stars are

of a totally different order of magnitude, and there are fundamental reasons for thinking that nothing—no scientific discovery or technical achievement—will ever make *them* trivial.

When today's chemical fuels have been developed to the ultimate, and 3 such tricks as refueling in space have been fully exploited, we will have spaceships which can attain speeds of about ten miles a second. That means that the Moon will be reached in two or three days and the nearer planets in about half a year. (I am deliberately rounding these numbers off, and anyone who tries to check my arithmetic had better remember that spaceships will never travel in straight lines or at uniform speeds.) The remoter planets, such as Jupiter and Saturn, could be reached only after many years of travel, and so the trio Moon-Mars-Venus marks the practical limit of exploration for chemically propelled spaceships. Even for these cases, it is all too easy to demonstrate that hundreds of tons of fuel would be needed for each ton of payload that would make the round trip.

This situation, which used to depress the pre-atomic-energy as- 4 tronauts, will not last for long. Since we are not concerned here with engineering details, we can take it for granted that eventually nuclear power, in some form or other, will be harnessed for the purposes of space flight. With energies a millionfold greater than those available from chemical fuels, speeds of hundreds, and ultimately thousands of miles a second will be attainable. Against such speeds, the Solar System will shrink until the inner planets are no more than a few hours apart, and even Pluto will be only a week or two from Earth. Moreover, there should be no reasonable limit to the amount of equipment and material that could be taken on an interplanetary expedition. Anyone who doubts this may ponder the fact that the energy released by a single H-bomb is sufficient to carry about a million tons to Mars. It is true that we cannot as yet tap even a fraction of that energy for such a purpose, but there are already hints of how this may be done.

The short-lived Uranium Age will see the dawn of space flight; the 5 succeeding era of fusion power will witness its fulfillment. But even when we can travel among the planets as freely as we now travel over this Earth, it seems that we will be no nearer to solving the problem of man's place in the Universe. That is a secret that will still lie hidden in the stars.

All the evidence indicates that we are alone in the Solar System. True, 6 there is almost certainly some kind of life on Mars, and possibly on Venus —perhaps even on the Moon. (The slight evidence for lunar vegetation comes from the amateur observers who actually *look* at the Moon, and is regarded skeptically by professional astronomers, who could hardly care less about a small slag heap little more than a light-second away.) Vegetation, however, can provide little intellectual companionship. Mars may be a paradise for the botanist, but it may have little to interest the zoologist —and nothing at all to lure the anthropologist and his colleagues across some scores of millions of miles of space.

This is likely to disappoint a great many people and to take much of   7
the zest out of space travel. Yet it would be unreasonable to expect
anything else; the planets have been in existence for several billion years,
and only during the last .0001 per cent of that time has the human race
been slightly civilized. Even if Mars and Venus have been (or will be)
suitable for higher forms of life, the chances are wildly against our en-
countering beings anywhere near our cultural or intellectual level at this
particular moment of time. If rational creatures exist on the planets, they
will be millions of years ahead of us in development—or millions of years
behind us. We may expect to meet apes or angels, but never men.

The angels can probably be ruled out at once. If they existed, then   8
surely they would already have come here to have a look at us. Some
people, of course, think that this is just what they are doing. I can only
say that they are going about it in a very odd manner.

We had better assume, therefore, that neither on Mars nor Venus, nor   9
on any other of the planets, will explorers from Earth encounter intelligent life. We are the only castaways upon the tiny raft of the Solar System,
as it drifts forever along the Gulf Streams of the Galaxy.

This, then, is the challenge that sooner or later the human spirit must   10
face, when the planets have been conquered and all their secrets brought
home to Earth. The nearest of the stars is a million times farther away
than the closest of the planets. The spaceships we may expect to see a
generation from now would take about a hundred thousand years to
reach Proxima Centauri, our nearest stellar neighbor. Even the hypothet-
ical nuclear-powered spaceships which a full century of atomic engineering may produce could hardly make the journey in less than a thousand
years.

The expressive term "God's quarantine regulations" has been used to   11
describe this state of affairs. At first sight, it appears that they are rigor-
ously enforced. There may be millions of inhabited worlds circling other
suns, harboring beings who to us would seem godlike, with civilizations
and cultures beyond our wildest dreams. But we shall never meet them,
and they for their part will never know of our existence.

So run the conclusions of most astronomers, even those who are quite   12
convinced that mere common or garden interplanetary flight is just
around the corner. But it is always dangerous to make negative predictions, and though the difficulties of *interstellar* travel are stupendous, they
are not insuperable. It is by no means certain that man must remain
trapped in the Solar System for eternity, never to know if he is a lonely
freak of no cosmic significance.

There are two ways in which we might gain direct knowledge of other   13
stellar systems without ever leaving our own. Rather surprisingly, it can
be shown that radio communication would be perfectly feasible across
interstellar space, if very slow-speed telegraphy were employed. However, we can hardly assume that anyone would be listening in at the

precise frequency with a receiver tuned to the extremely narrow band that would have to be employed. And even if they were, it would be extremely tedious learning to talk to them with no initial knowledge of their language—and having to wait many years for any acknowledgment of our own signals, as the radio waves came limping back across the light-years. If we sent a question to Proxima Centauri, it would be almost nine years before any answer could reach Earth.

A more practical, though at first sight more startling, solution would   14 be to send a survey ship—unmanned. This would be a gigantic extrapolation of existing techniques, but it would not involve anything fundamentally new. Imagine an automatic vessel, crammed with every type of recording instrument and controlled by an electronic brain with preset instructions. It would be launched out across space, aimed at a target it might not reach for a thousand years. But at last one of the stars ahead would begin to dominate the sky, and a century or so later, it would have grown into a sun, perhaps with planets circling around it. Sleeping instruments would wake, the tiny ship would check its speed, and its sense organs would start to record their impressions. It would circle world after world, following a program set up to cover all possible contingencies by men who had died a thousand years before. Then, with the priceless knowledge it had gained, it would begin the long voyage home.

This type of proxy exploration of the universe would be slow and   15 uncertain and would demand long-range planning beyond the capacity of our age. Yet if there is no other way of contacting the stars, this is how it might be done. One millennium would make the investment in technical skill so that the next would reap the benefit. It would be as if Archimedes were to start a research project which could produce no results before the time of Einstein.

If men, and not merely their machines, are ever to reach the planets   16 of other suns, problems of much greater difficulty will have to be solved. Stated in its simplest form, the question is this: How can men survive a journey which may last for several thousand years? It is rather surprising to find that there are at least five different answers which must be regarded as theoretical possibilities—however far they may be beyond the scope of today's science.

Medicine may provide two rather obvious solutions. There appears to   17 be no fundamental reason why men should die when they do. It is certainly not a matter of the body "wearing out" in the sense that an inanimate piece of machinery does, for in the course of a single year almost the entire fabric of the body is replaced by new material. When we have discovered the details of this process, it may be possible to extend the life span indefinitely if so desired. Whether a crew of immortals, however well balanced and psychologically adjusted, could tolerate each other's company for several centuries in rather cramped quarters is an interesting subject for speculation.

Perhaps a better answer is that suggested by the story of Rip Van   18
Winkle. Suspended animation (or, more accurately, a drastic slowing
down of the body's metabolism) for periods of a few hours is now, of
course, a medical commonplace. It requires no great stretch of the imagination to suppose that, with the aid of low temperatures and drugs, men
may be able to hibernate for virtually unlimited periods. We can picture
an automatic ship with its oblivious crew making the long journey across
the interstellar night until, when a new sun was looming up, the signal
was sent out to trigger the mechanisms which would revive the sleepers.
When their survey was completed, they would head back to Earth and
slumber again until the time came to awake once more, and to greet a
world which would regard them as survivors from the distant past.

The third solution was, to the best of my knowledge, suggested over   19
thirty years ago by Professor J. D. Bernal in a long out-of-print essay, *The
World, the Flesh, and the Devil*, which must rank as one of the most outstanding feats of scientific imagination in literature. Even today, many of the
ideas propounded in this little book have never been fully developed,
either in or out of science fiction. (Any requests from fellow authors to
borrow my copy will be flatly ignored.)

Bernal imagined entire societies launched across space, in gigantic   20
arks which would be closed, ecologically balanced systems. They would,
in fact, be miniature planets, upon which generations of men would live
and die so that one day their remote descendants would return to Earth
with the record of their celestial Odyssey.

The engineering, biological and sociological problems involved in   21
such an enterprise would be of fascinating complexity. The artificial
planets (at least several miles in diameter) would have to be completely
self-contained and self-supporting, and no material of any kind could be
wasted. Commenting on the implications of such closed systems, *Time*
magazine's able, erudite science editor Jonathan Leonard once hinted
that cannibalism would be compulsory among interstellar travelers. This
would be a matter of definition; we crew members of the [four]-billion-
man spaceship Earth do not consider ourselves cannibals despite the fact
that every one of us must have absorbed atoms which once formed part
of Caesar and Socrates, Shakespeare and Solomon.

One cannot help feeling that the interstellar ark on its thousand-year   22
voyages would be a cumbersome way of solving the problem, even if all
the social and psychological difficulties could be overcome. (Would the
fiftieth generation still share the aspirations of their Pilgrim Fathers who
set out from Earth so long ago?) There are, however, more sophisticated
ways of getting men to the stars than the crude, brute-force methods
outlined above. After the hardheaded engineering of the last few paragraphs, what follows may appear to verge upon fantasy. It involves, in the
most fundamental sense of the word, the storage of human beings. And
by that I do not mean anything as naïve as suspended animation.

A few months ago, in an Australian laboratory, I was watching what   23
appeared to be perfectly normal spermatozoa wriggling across the microscope field. They *were* perfectly normal, but their history was not. For
three years, they had been utterly immobile in a deep freeze, and there
seemed little doubt that they could be kept fertile for centuries by the
same technique. What was still more surprising, there had been enough
successes with the far larger and more delicate ova to indicate that they
too might survive the same treatment. If this proves to be the case,
reproduction will eventually become independent of time.

The social implications of this make anything in *Brave New World* seem   24
like child's play, but I am not concerned here with the interesting results
which might have been obtained by, for example, uniting the genes of
Cleopatra and Newton, had this technique been available earlier in history. (When such experiments are started, however, it would be as well
to remember Shaw's famous rejection of a similar proposal: "But suppose, my dear, it turns out to have my beauty and your brains?")*

The cumbersome interstellar ark, with its generations of travelers   25
doomed to spend their entire lives in empty space, was merely a device
to carry germ cells, knowledge, and culture from one sun to another. How
much more efficient to send only the cells, to fertilize them automatically
some twenty years before the voyage was due to end, to carry the embryos
through to birth by techniques already foreshadowed in today's biology
labs, and to bring up the babies under the tutelage of cybernetic nurses
who would teach them their inheritance and their destiny when they were
capable of understanding it.

These children, knowing no parents, or indeed anyone of a different   26
age from themselves, would grow up in the strange artificial world of their
speeding ship, reaching maturity in time to explore the planets ahead of
them—perhaps to be the ambassadors of humanity among alien races, or
perhaps to find, too late, that there was no home for them there. If their
mission succeeded, it would be their duty (or that of their descendants,
if the first generation could not complete the task) to see that the knowledge they had gained was someday carried back to Earth.

Would any society be morally justified, we may well ask, in planning   27
so onerous and uncertain a future for its unborn—indeed unconceived
—children? That is a question which different ages may answer in different ways. What to one era would seem a cold-blooded sacrifice might to
another appear a great and glorious adventure. There are complex problems here which cannot be settled by instinctive, emotional answers.

So far, we have assumed that all interstellar voyages must of necessity   28
last for many hundreds or even thousands of years. The nearest star is
more than four light-years away; the Galaxy itself—the island Universe of

---

*We have Shaw's word for it that the would-be geneticist was a complete stranger and
not, as frequently stated, Isadora Duncan.

which our Sun is one insignificant member—is hundreds of thousands of light-years across; and the distances *between* the galaxies are of the order of a million light-years. The speed of light appears to be a fundamental limit to velocity; in this sense it is quite different from the now outmoded "sound barrier," which is merely an attribute of the particular gases which happen to constitute our atmosphere.

Even if we could reach the speed of light, therefore, interstellar journeys would still require many years of travel, and only in the case of the very nearest stars would it appear possible for a voyager to make the round trip in a single lifetime, without resort to such techniques as suspended animation. However, as we shall see, the actual situation is a good deal more complex than this.   29

First of all, is it even theoretically possible to build spaceships capable of approaching the speed of light? (That is, 186,000 miles a second or 670,000,000 miles per hour.) The problem is that of finding a sufficient source of energy and applying it. Einstein's famous quotation $E = mc^2$ gives an answer—on paper—which a few centuries of technology may be able to realize in terms of engineering. If we can achieve the *total* annihilation of matter—not the conversion of a mere fraction of a per cent of it into energy—we can approach as near to the speed of light as we please. We can never reach it, but a journey at 99.9 per cent of the speed of light would, after all, take very little longer than one at exactly the speed of light, so the difference would hardly seem of practical importance.   30

Complete annihilation of matter is still as much a dream as atomic energy itself was thirty years ago. However, the discovery of the antiproton (which engages in mutual suicide on meeting a normal proton) may be the first step on the road to its realization.   31

Traveling at speeds approaching that of light, however, involves us at once in one of the most baffling paradoxes which spring from the theory of relativity—the so-called "time-dilation effect." It is impossible to explain *why* this effect occurs without delving into very elementary yet extremely subtle mathematics. (There is nothing difficult about basic relativity math: most of it is simple algebra. The difficulty lies in the underlying concepts.) Nevertheless, even if the explanation must be skipped, the results of the time-dilation effect can be stated readily enough in nontechnical language.   32

Time itself is a variable quantity; the rate at which it flows depends upon the speed of the observer. The difference is infinitesimal at the velocities of everyday life, and even at the velocities of normal astronomical bodies. It is all-important as we approach to within a few per cent of the speed of light. To put it crudely, the faster one travels, the more slowly time will pass. At the speed of light, time would cease to exist; the moment "Now" would last forever.   33

Let us take an extreme example to show what this implies. If a spaceship left Earth for Proxima Centauri at the speed of light, and came back   34 at once at the same velocity, it would have been gone for some eight and one-half years according to all the clocks and calendars of Earth. *But the people in the ship, and all their clocks, would have recorded no lapsed time at all.*

At a physically attainable speed, say 95 per cent of the velocity of light, the inhabitants of the ship would think that the round trip had lasted about three years. At 99 per cent, it would have seemed little more than a year to them. In each case, however, they would return more than eight years—Earth time—after they had departed. (No allowance has been made here for stopping and starting, which would require additional time.)   35

If we imagine a more extensive trip, we get still more surprising results. The travelers might be gone for a thousand years, from the point of view of Earth, having set out for a star five hundred light-years away. If their ship had averaged 99.9 per cent of the speed of light, they would be fifty years older when they returned to an Earth—*where ten centuries had passed away!* *   36

It should be emphasized that this effect, incredible though it appears to be, is one of the natural consequences of Einstein's theory. The equation connecting mass and energy once appeared to be equally fantastic and remote from any practical application. It would be very unwise, therefore, to assume that the equation linking time and velocity will never be of more than theoretical interest. Anything which does not violate natural laws must be considered a possibility—and the events of the last few decades have shown clearly enough that things which are possible will always be achieved if the incentive is sufficiently great.   37

Whether the incentive will be sufficient here is a question which only the future can answer. The men of five hundred or a thousand years from now will have motivations very different from ours, but if they are men at all they will still burn with that restless curiosity which has driven us over this world and which is about to take us into space. Sooner or later we will come to the edge of the Solar System and will be looking out across the ultimate abyss. Then we must choose whether we reach the stars—or whether we wait until the stars reach us.   38

Topical Considerations

1. Arthur C. Clarke is a world-famous author of science fiction, one who has given us all sorts of alien life in print. Speaking realistically, however, what kind of life does he expect we will eventually find in our own solar system?

---

*The physical reality of the time-dilation effect has been the subject of unusually acrimonious debate in recent years. Very few scientists now have any doubt of its existence, but its magnitude may not have the values quoted above. My figures are based on special relativity, which is too unsophisticated to deal with the complexities of an actual flight.

312 Out of Time and Space

2. Why will it be necessary for us to invent some revolutionary means of transport to reach the stars? Why can't we use existing means of propulsion?

3. Clarke says that one way we can attempt to discover whether extraterrestrial life exists beyond our solar system is through radio communications. What are some of the chief problems intrinsic in this approach?

4. What are some of the possible ways Clarke suggests by which humans might reach the stars? Which seems the most feasible to you, and why?

5. What does Clarke mean by his last comment in paragraph 27: "There are complex problems here which cannot be settled by instinctive, emotional answers"? Do you agree with him on this?

6. Why does Clarke say that we cannot rule out the possibility that someday we may build ships that travel at speeds approaching that of light?

7. All of Clarke's suggestions for reaching the stars involve not only great expense but also great and long-range visions. Do you think that we are capable of such commitments? If so, what evidence is there? If not, why?

Rhetorical Considerations

1. Where is the thesis statement of this essay?

2. Clarke uses a few metaphors throughout his essay. At the beginning of paragraph 2, for example, he refers to our solar system as "a snug little celestial oasis in an endless desert." Find other metaphors he uses. How do they contribute to his writing? Do you find anything sentimental about them?

3. If you didn't know Clarke was a scientist, could you tell from this essay? How?

4. How well does the final paragraph conclude the piece? How does it reflect the opening paragraph?

5. Find an example of Clarke's use of illustration. How convincing is it?

Writing Assignments

1. Do you think we should explore space, even given the huge expense? Write a paper in which you answer this question, giving solid reasons to support your position.

2. We may not have received any communications from extraterrestrials yet, but if they're out there and listening, they might well have

picked up a few of our own signals in the form of radio and television. Write a report from the point of view of an extraterrestrial whose job it is to describe some aspect of life on earth based solely on what he has picked up from television and/or radio. For instance, you might want to describe human beings' daily habits, mating rituals, or diet, based solely on commercials. Have fun with this; there is a lot of room for humor and satire.

3. If you had the opportunity to go to another planet in our solar system, would you? If so, explore your reasons and motivations in a well-thought-out paper. If not, explain your reasons.

FADS AND FANCIES

9

All the World's a Video Game

Jennifer Allen

In the mid 1970s, the first electronic video game was introduced to the home entertainment market. It was an electronic ping-pong game called Pong, in which players moved bars up and down the sides of their TV screens to deflect blips aimed at each other. From this rather undynamic origin, video games have become an entertainment phenomenon in America as well as a multi-billion-dollar industry. In arcades, airports, and homes across the nation, people line up before bedazzling screens to zap, dodge, or gobble up little blips. One of the most popular of the games is Pac-Man, whose familiar yellow gaping circle of a mouth is now seen in the form of cereal, candy vitamins, and pillows. The enormous popularity of video games, both in and out of the home, has generated considerable criticism from people who are particularly worried about the long-range psychological and social damage to children and adolescents—who spend the most time and money playing the games. What follows are the confessions of a Pac-Man addict. Jennifer Allen, who is a mature woman and a free-lance writer, gives us an amusing account of her own fascination with and addiction to the little blips on the screen.

1   It is a chill Thursday morning, the day after the surgeon general announced that video games contribute to violent and testy behavior, a wobbly grip on reality, and, for all one knows, cancer of the eyeballs, dyslexia, ennui, arthritis, palsy, and pox.

2   The surgeon general's remarks worried but did not faze me. At nine the next morning, I am standing in a smudgy, steamy Laundromat at Broadway and 78th Street, burrowing in my purse for quarters for the Pac-Man machine, and feeling like the chaperon at the party. On line ahead of me, having dumped his bundles at my feet, is a pocky, pink-skinned messenger; ahead of him is a six-year-old boy who has to stretch his neck to see the screen. Except for a tall boy in a crewneck sweater slouching against a washing machine and devouring a Mars bar, the others on line are all skinny and black and look about fourteen years old. The children glance at me, mildly curious, the way you pass by someone who is having a conversation with a parking meter.

3   For a while it is reassuring, a comfort just to be near the Pac-Man machine, like sitting in a restaurant when you're famished, knowing a hot dinner is on its way. But the minutes start to limp, then hobble. How long will I have to wait? Is it possible that I'll have to leave here without getting to play?

4   "Shouldn't you be in school?" I ask one of the boys, in what I hope is a friendly, bantering tone.

5   "Shouldn't you be at work?" he says.

6   I have been bewildered lately by my fascination with Pac-Man: Lacking a certain competitive gusto and weak in motor skills, I have never been a games player or sportswoman. So it comes as a surprise—like a sudden

infatuation with someone I never even liked—to find that I am attached to this game. I play almost daily, before or after working, and cannot pass by a machine without stopping for a game. I've stopped buying cigarettes at the head shop down the street and switched to a candy store–video parlor two blocks away. I steal quarters from my boyfriend's dresser top, the ones he saves for the washing machine, and tell him I'm going out for the paper.

The romance began on Labor Day weekend. On the way back to the city, I stopped at a Catskill resort, and wandering through the vast lobby, I came across a big black room aglow with wall-to-wall video games. It was dazzling in there, like Las Vegas: hot lights against the dark and a cacophony of sounds, from explosions to computerized ditties. The screens on the games had laser beams or shooting stars or tiny gorillas or little blobs in hot pink and green and electric blue that swoop or jiggle or dart all over them. I was mesmerized.   7

First, I tried Space Invaders, in which moving launchpads rained bombs on advancing rows of green creatures, and vice versa. Space Invaders was dead serious, grim, accompanied by a tune that sounded like the chase music from *Jaws* played at high speed. Space Invaders was depressing; I watched helplessly as the merciless bullies marched closer, launchpads crumbled, one by one, into smithereens.   8

Across the room was Alpine Skier. This game features a skier schussing down a mountain slope to a gay Bavarian tune and a remarkably lifelike sound effect of skis slicing through crisp, packed snow. The idea was to guide the skier past the tractors, trees, and boulders that dotted the slope. I lasted longer there, but got discouraged again: The collisions reminded me of my own unhappy skiing past—spills, tumbles, tears.   9

Wait: Another happy, dopey song noodled from a nearby machine. It was the Pac-Man theme song—a tune that, weeks later, I would hear in my dreams. Grown-ups and children were clustered around the game, laughing and talking, better-tempered than the dour, determined players who wrestled with Asteroids and Space Invaders. The object of the game was to get the yellow Pac-Men to eat the maze of dots on the screen before being eaten by the creatures who pursued them. If the Pac-Men ate certain dots, the creatures in pursuit turned blue, and the Men could earn extra points by eating them. There were no explosions or smashups; when a Pac-Man got eaten, the only sound was a droopy, wilting noise, the kind that might accompany a clown making a sad face.   10

I spent $3 at Pac-Man, oblivious to the honeymooning couple patiently waiting their turn, and left feeling feverish and happy and a little woozy, as if I had just gulped a strong drink on an empty stomach. Driving home, I found myself humming the Pac-Man song.   11

I begin playing regularly at the candy store–video gallery. Like a customer in a porn shop, I do not look at the proprietor, even when he   12 gives me change. In the back of the store, where the three games are, the carpet is flecked with gum wrappers and cigarette butts; it is so warm and clammy that players wipe the sides of their faces as they play, and the control knobs of the games are slippery with sweat. When the younger players are here, mostly boys and girls from about eleven to fourteen, the place smells of grape gum and some kind of lime stick candy that stains the kids' mouths green. At dusk, when it is taken over by older teenagers and young men, mostly Puerto Rican and black, it has a gray fog of cigarette smoke stale and thick enough to sting the eyes.

The older boys, in unlaced Adidas, small gold hoops in their ears, play   13
with the loose, deft elegance of seasoned sportsmen. I can watch them for a full ten minutes before I start feeling an itchy impatience to play. For the first few moments of a game, they hardly have to look at the screen; they bum Kools or blow loopy smoke rings or talk to their friends. One of them always plays the first two minutes standing sideways to the machine, looking at it lazily out of the corner of an eye. They barely have to flick the knob, it seems, to send their Pac-Men scooting around the screen, nimble as polliwogs. The secret to racking up extra points is to save certain high-scoring spots for last, to play almost desultorily for a while. With herculean self-control, the players hold out, keep cool, bide their time, smoke.

The boys are friendly enough to me, in the offhand way of one wastrel   14
to another, explaining fine points, offering encouragement. "Eat them energizers later," they say, "and go for the banana, girl." There are a few others besides me whom they help: an older woman fat as a baloon with teeth the color of weak tea, a person in an E.T. sweatshirt who has clumps of hair missing and could be man or woman or child. Idlers, weirdos, losers. My colleagues. We applaud one another's high scores, cluck at one another's defeats.

Even if they are having a tournament, they let me slip in a game or two   15
of my own. I never ascend beyond a low intermediate level, but playing continues to transport me. When I was first sucked in, I was not aware of all the sound and light effects—the sounds are muted, as if played through a layer of felt; colors change so quickly, they come and go before I can take note of them. But now I anticipate and see and hear every color, every sound: whistles, keens, thumps, a noise that sounds like the whoop of an air-raid siren, blinking blues and reds and yellows. My nervous system seems wired to these various changes; I can feel my heart race when they happen. In a kind of dithery, agitated rapture after each session, I have to stand outside, taking deep breaths. The sour city air feels as sweet and invigorating as a mountain breeze.

After a couple of weeks of playing, I begin to notice side effects on my   16
playing hand: lima-bean-size blisters on one side of the middle finger and

a baby callus at the base of the index finger. My arm feels cramped and achy after I play, as if I had been pitching baseballs.

One day Marie, the nine-year-old who lives in my building, tells me   17
that she has Pac-Man at home. Minutes later, I am sitting with Marie in front of Marie's TV set in Marie's all-pink bedroom, learning how to play the home-video version of Pac-Man. Marie plays every afternoon—she is no longer allowed to play at the candy store, because she got mugged there once and had all her quarters stolen—and is splendid. Even Peter, Marie's five-year-old brother, is good enough to beat me at this version, which seems practically impossible. The figures on the screen are faint and flicker and dance around much too fast and make my eyeballs feel as if they were jiggling in my head.

"Mom," Marie says to her mother as she maneuvers her Pac-Men   18
around the screen, "you know how we always get one of our Christmas presents on Christmas Eve?"

"Yes, honey," says Marie's mother, who is watching.   19

"Well, could I get my Colecovision on Christmas Eve?"   20

"Of course you may," says Marie's mother. As she leaves, I imagine   21
what it would be like to be Marie, to roll out of her canopied bed every morning and have two different sets of Pac-Man at her fingertips. I am jealous of Marie.

Some dim, muffled voice inside tells me it would not be dignified to   22
become a regular at the candy store, so in the next few weeks I find other places to play: a cookie store, a pizza parlor, the Laundromat, the student center at the New School. I miss the way my heart flutters when I am not playing; I miss the noises and colors of the game. The rest of the world reminds me of the first part of *The Wizard of Oz,* before the screen explodes in Technicolor: poky, shabby, gray. And I worry: For one thing, the callus on my index finger has hardened into a lump, and my playing arm aches a lot. I am afraid I won't be able to stop playing, and imagine myself running to one of the Times Square arcades in the dead of night for a fix, begging quarters off salesmen who have come for the peepshow next door.

One day I am sipping coffee at a neighborhood diner when an ac-   23
quaintance sits down at the next table. She is smart and funny and a practiced player of miniature golf. I feel it is safe to confide in her, to tell her about how much I love playing Pac-Man.

"I know how it is," says the young woman. "I was hooked on Asteroids   24
—I hung around a bowling alley for a year." A friend! A fellow addict! But after a year, it seemed, the addiction just faded; she hasn't played for months (although she can still do all the sound effects, and does, sitting in the restaurant). Not to worry, the thirst to play goes away when you aren't looking.

Much encouraged, I bolt from the restaurant, leaving a dollar bill as   25
a tip. I still need all the quarters I can get.

Topical Considerations

1. Exactly where in the essay does Allen establish her addiction to Pac-Man? How does she do this?

2. What is the message in the brief exchange between Allen and one of the boys in the laundromat (paragraphs 4 and 5)?

3. Allen says that she is "bewildered" by her attachment to and fascination with Pac-Man (paragraph 6). How does she illustrate the degree of her attachment? Are you convinced by these illustrations?

4. What different kinds of people regularly play video games, according to the author's experience?

5. How does Allen characterize her relationship with other Pac-Man players?

6. Video games involve more than just the competition itself; they are whole light-and-sound packages. According to Allen, how do the audiovisual components of these electronic games contribute to their attraction?

7. What are some of the consequences Allen has suffered from her addiction to Pac-Man? What widespread criticism of video games does she touch upon here?

8. Do you think that video games can cause psychological and social harm to people, particularly children and adolescents? Explain your opinions.

Rhetorical Considerations

1. How does the first paragraph set the tone of this essay? How does it suggest Allen's attitude toward both video games and the warnings about them? After having read this essay, can you say that Allen suffers from any of the ailments cited in paragraph 1?

2. In paragraph 2, Allen says that the children glanced at her "the way you pass by someone who is having a conversation with a parking meter." Find other examples where Allen creates a humorous effect by analogies and comparisons.

3. How clear are Allen's explanations of how the different video games work? Which description is most detailed and vivid?

4. In paragraph 12 and 13, Allen offers descriptive details of the different age groups that frequent the candy store–video gallery. What specific details distinguish the younger from the older players? How vivid are Allen's details and word choices?

5. Comment on the significance of the author's focus on nine-year-old Marie in paragraphs 17 through 21. What does this example illustrate?

6. Although it is brief, how does the final paragraph summarize

Allen's discussion? What points in the essay does it reflect back upon? How does it echo any thoughts or attitudes in the opening paragraph?

Writing Assignments

1. Do you play video games? If so, write an essay describing how you got interested, why you play, which games you like best, and why. Try to capture your fascination with and attraction to them.

2. Allen vividly describes some of the video game players and locales. Visit a place where people play video games—an arcade, a student lounge or game room, a laundromat, and so forth. Write a descriptive narrative in which you try to capture vividly the video game scene and the people in it. As Allen does, try to categorize the players, using specific details regarding their dress, gestures, conversations, and so on.

3. In the last few years, video games have come under fire from parents, educators, and community groups. One major argument is that video games encourage aggressiveness and violence. Some people also fear long-range dehumanizing consequences—that over time young people will come to view others merely as blips on a screen. Write a paper in which you express your own opinion about video games and the issue of violence and dehumanization.

4. Much of the criticism aimed at video games comes from the older generations. Do you think part of this criticism stems from older people's lack of familiarity with and, therefore, lack of ease with the new computer technology—a technology that young people embrace? Write a paper in which you explore video games and the computer-generation gap.

5. If you have played video games and don't like them, write a paper telling why. What arguments do you have against them? Do you see them as psychologically and socially harmful?

6. Write a paper in which you defend video games against claims that they take young people away from important intellectual activities. Consider the claims that video games stimulate the mind's nonlinear thinking—that is, the ability to deal with several options at once.

Made in Heaven

Leigh Montville

Left to themselves, human beings couldn't have come up with the Izod alligators, the Adidas triple stripes or Calvin Kleins; it must have been divine inspiration. So says *Boston Globe* columnist Leigh Montville in this brief but humorous narrative on manufacturers' labels and those who wear them.

Indirectly, Montville's essay raises some interesting questions about the relationship between marketing and the consumer mind.

And in the spring of one year in the sixth millennium of Creation, the Lord became bored. He watched the long line of human beings heading toward the world and knew He had to make some changes. Just to stay awake.   1

He had an idea.   2

"Put a tiny alligator on the left breast of every human who leaves the shop for the next week," He bellowed to his angels. "And make it snappy."   3

"An alligator?" the angels asked.   4

"An alligator," the Lord said. "Now."   5

The angels hurried to work. A change like this hadn't happened in a long time, not since the Lord requested redheads and peroxide blondes. An alligator . . . an alligator. One of the angels drew a stencil and the others began the work.   6

"Do you think He wants the alligator above or below the nipple?" one angel asked.   7

"We'll try a few spots," a second angel replied. "We'll see what works best."   8

The final choice was slightly above the left nipple. Thousands, then millions of people were sent to the world with the little alligators upon their breasts. The angels watched with horror. The Lord watched with renewed interest. He found that He was pleased.   9

"Look at that, will you?" He said. "Man seems to like having a little alligator above his left breast. Look how proud he is. He parades around with confidence he never had before."   10

Sure enough, race and creed and ethnic origin made no difference. The people who wore the alligator were the most confident on the planet. They admired each other's alligators. They pitied the poor folk who did not have alligators.   11

"Let us try this," the Lord said. "Let us keep making alligators, but on Tuesdays and Thursdays, perhaps, let's produce people with a little polo player on the left breast."   12

"A polo player, Lord?" the angels asked.   13

"Just do what I ask," the Lord said.   14

The appearance of people with polo players above their left breasts seemed to be as exciting as the appearance of the people with alligators. The Lord laughed as He watched everyone admiring everyone else. He wanted to see more.   15

"Let us make people with little penguins above their left breasts," He told the angels. "Let us make some people with a fox in that spot. A tiger. A hand making a signal with the index finger and thumb. Every now and then, too, make some people with the word 'Rugger' across the right biceps."   16

The new diversity soon dominated the world. Virtually everyone under   17
age 58 bore an insignia or name above the left breast. Humankind viewed
these changes as blessings supplied by a Benevolent Being.

"You are a genius, Lord," the angels said.   18

"I have only begun," the Lord replied.   19

He turned his attention now to the right buttock. He thought and   20
thought, searching for the right expression. He decided upon names.

"Names, Lord?" the angels asked.   21

"Take these down," the Lord said in a flash of inspiration. "Calvin   22
Klein. Gloria Vanderbilt. Sasson. Sergio Valenti. Lee. And . . . let me
think . . . yes, Jordache."

The names on the right buttock were at least as successful as the   23
animals above the left breast. Some names were printed. Some were
written in script. People looked each other over, fore and aft, and cooed
at the different markings.

"Love your alligator," one of them would say to a complete stranger.   24
"And love your Sergio Valenti, too."

"Wonderful, Lord," the angels said. "Man has not been so interested   25
in his surroundings for a long time."

"Take out your pads," the Lord said. "There is more work to do."   26

He now turned his attention to feet. He ordered some feet to be made   27
with three stripes down the sides. He ordered other feet made with two
stripes. With stars. He ordered feet made with little green tabs with the
word "Bass" or "Dexter" written on the tabs. He ordered feet made with
metal plates on the side that read "Candie's."

"Feet may be the ultimate," the Lord said. "I have a hunch we haven't   28
seen anything, compared to what will happen with feet."

He was right again, of course. The designs on the feet were the best of   29
all. People boasted about their feet. People admired each other's feet. To
walk down the street with an animal on the left breast, a name on the right
buttock, and swirls on the feet was to be as close to heaven as possible.

"I am pleased," the Lord said as he sat upon a cloud and watched the   30
activity. "I am very, very pleased."

The angels were pleased because He was pleased. They stood in a line   31
and awaited orders. There was nary a waver when the Lord decreed that
some people should now be made with little plugs in their ears that
played Top 40 music all day long.

Everyone simply went to work.   32

Topical Considerations

1. Why does God suddenly order his angels to put a little alligator on the left breast of the next week's batch of human beings? What
does His reason—or lack of reason—say about manufacturers' trademarks and the wearing of them?

2. In paragraph 11, Montville says that alligator wearers pity those "poor folk who did not have alligators." What is his point here? What is he saying about the attitude of some who wear alligators?

3. Montville humorously makes the point that there is a kind of tribal affinity among people who wear certain manufacturer trademarks, a certain kind of identity. What associations come to mind when you think of the Izod alligator? or the Sears Penguin? or the Ralph Lauren Polo player? What kind of person comes to mind? what images?

4. Why do you think people wear clothes with familiar trademarks—for status? for identity? for diversity? Explain your answers.

5. What is Montville chiefly satirizing in this little piece?

6. What point is Montville making in the last sentence?

Rhetorical Considerations

1. This piece is loosely framed as a religious parable. What biblical touches can you find?

2. In what ways is God depicted as the biblical God? as a corporate executive?

3. What satirical advantage is there in Montville's suggestion that Izod alligators, Calvin Klein jeans, and Adidas stripes were the inspiration of God, not man?

4. How do the angels' reactions to God's orders function in the piece? What do you make of their responses?

Writing Assignments

1. If you wear some of the familiar labels Montville cites here, write a paper in which you examine your motivations. Do you wear them for prestige? If so, explain the prestige you feel. If you wear them for other reasons, try to explain them.

2. Write a paper in which you give a portrait of the kind of person who wears, say, Izod alligator shirts, or someone who wears Jordache jeans or Nike running shoes. Don't hesitate to have some fun and show some humor.

3. Select some current newspaper and magazine ads for some of the familiar manufacturers Montville cites here. (This can also be done with television commercials.) What kinds of images do the advertisers project? To what socioeconomic and age groups are they appealing? What images and fantasies are projected?

The Jeaning of America—and the World

Carin C. Quinn

Perhaps no article of clothing is more synonymous with America than blue jeans. And no blue jean label is more recognized than Levi-Strauss. Levi's have spanned all ages, all social classes, and all continents—and a hundred and thirty years. In this article, Carin C. Quinn narrates the development of this all-American symbol now gone worldwide. She also gives some of the reasons Levi's have become so popular.

This is the story of a sturdy American symbol which has now spread throughout most of the world. The symbol is not the dollar. It is not even Coca-Cola. It is a simple pair of pants called blue jeans, and what the pants symbolize is what Alexis de Tocqueville called "a manly and legitimate passion for equality. . . ." Blue jeans are favored equally by bureaucrats and cowboys; bankers and deadbeats; fashion designers and beer drinkers. They draw no distinctions and recognize no classes; they are merely American. Yet they are sought after almost everywhere in the world—including Russia, where authorities recently broke up a teen-aged gang that was selling them on the black market for two hundred dollars a pair. They have been around for a long time, and it seems likely that they will outlive even the necktie.

This ubiquitous American symbol was the invention of a Bavarian-born Jew. His name was Levi Strauss.

He was born in Bad Ocheim, Germany, in 1829, and during the European political turmoil of 1848 decided to take his chances in New York, to which his two brothers already had emigrated. Upon arrival, Levi soon found that his two brothers had exaggerated their tales of an easy life in the land of the main chance. They were landowners, they had told him; instead, he found them pushing needles, thread, pots, pans, ribbons, yarn, scissors, and buttons to housewives. For two years he was a lowly peddler, hauling some 180 pounds of sundries door-to-door to eke out a marginal living. When a married sister in San Francisco offered to pay his way West in 1850, he jumped at the opportunity, taking with him bolts of canvas he hoped to sell for tenting.

It was the wrong kind of canvas for that purpose, but while talking with a miner down from the mother lode, he learned that pants—sturdy pants that would stand up to the rigors of the digging—were almost impossible to find. Opportunity beckoned. On the spot, Strauss measured the man's girth and inseam with a piece of string and, for six dollars in gold dust, had [the canvas] tailored into a pair of stiff but rugged pants. The miner was delighted with the result, word got around about "those pants of

Levi's," and Strauss was in business. The company has been in business ever since.

When Strauss ran out of canvas, he wrote his two brothers to send   5
more. He received instead a tough, brown cotton cloth made in Nîmes, France—called *serge de Nîmes* and swiftly shortened to "denim" (the word "jeans" derives from *Gênes,* the French word for Genoa, where a similar cloth was produced). Almost from the first, Strauss had his cloth dyed the distinctive indigo that gave blue jeans their name, but it was not until the 1870s that he added the copper rivets which have long since become a company trademark. The rivets were the idea of a Virginia City, Nevada, tailor, Jacob W. Davis, who added them to pacify a mean-tempered miner called Alkali Ike. Alkali, the story goes, complained that the pockets of his jeans always tore when he stuffed them with ore samples and demanded that Davis do something about it. As a kind of joke, Davis took the pants to a blacksmith and had the pockets riveted; once again, the idea worked so well that word got around; in 1873 Strauss appropriated and patented the gimmick—and hired Davis as a regional manager.

By this time, Strauss had taken both his brothers and two brothers-   6
in-law into the company and was ready for his third San Francisco store. Over the ensuing years the company prospered locally, and by the time of his death in 1902, Strauss had become a man of prominence in California. For three decades thereafter the business remained profitable though small, with sales largely confined to the working people of the West—cowboys, lumberjacks, railroad workers, and the like. Levi's jeans were first introduced to the East, apparently, during the dude-ranch craze of the 1930s, when vacationing Easterners returned and spread the word about the wonderful pants with rivets. Another boost came in World War II, when blue jeans were declared an essential commodity and were sold only to people engaged in defense work. From a company with fifteen salespeople, two plants, and almost no business east of the Mississippi in 1946, the organization grew in thirty years to include a sales force of more than twenty-two thousand, with fifty plants and offices in thirty-five countries. Each year, more than 250,000,000 items of Levi's clothing are sold—including more than 83,000,000 pairs of riveted blue jeans. They have become, through marketing, word of mouth, and demonstrable reliability, the common pants of America. They can be purchased pre-washed, pre-faded, and pre-shrunk for the suitably proletarian look. They adapt themselves to any sort of idiosyncratic use; women slit them at the inseams and convert them into long skirts, men chop them off above the knees and turn them into something to be worn while challenging the surf. Decorations and ornamentations abound.

The pants have become a tradition, and along the way have acquired   7
a history of their own—so much so that the company has opened a

museum in San Francisco. There was, for example, the turn-of-the-century trainman who replaced a faulty coupling with a pair of jeans; the Wyoming man who used his jeans as a towrope to haul his car out of a ditch; the Californian who found several pairs in an abandoned mine, wore them, then discovered they were sixty-three years old and still as good as new and turned them over to the Smithsonian as a tribute to their toughness. And then there is the particularly terrifying story of the careless construction worker who dangled fifty-two stories above the street until rescued, his sole support the Levi's belt loop through which his rope was hooked.

Topical Considerations

1. Why are jeans so popular today? Are they popular now for the same reasons they were originally?

2. How does Strauss's success story reflect the popular myth that America is the land of opportunity?

3. Was Strauss's success purely the result of luck? Could it have happened to anyone? Or was he an unusually astute businessman with an eye for what sells? Cite specific incidents in his story to prove your answer.

4. Quinn points out that the sale of jeans became a booming business through "marketing, word of mouth, and demonstrable reliability" (paragraph 6). Is this true of today's products? Which of these three factors do you think is most effective in securing the success of a product today? Why?

5. Quinn refers to jeans as a "sturdy American symbol." How do jeans represent America and Americans? Can you name other American symbols that Quinn does not mention?

Rhetorical Considerations

1. Does this essay have a beginning, a middle, and an end? How would you divide it? What rhetorical pattern does Quinn use to develop each section?

2. Rewrite Quinn's first paragraph so that no specific details, quotations, or illustrations are used. Substitute a general word or phrase when necessary to preserve the meaning. Read your version aloud. Which version is more interesting?

3. What is Quinn's attitude toward jeans? Cite specific adjectives, quotations, and illustrations that reveal how she feels.

4. How does Quinn's ending tie the essay together?

Writing Assignments

1. Do you know of anyone (perhaps yourself) who has been given an opportunity to accomplish something worthwhile and has been successful? Write an essay about it.

2. Identify an American symbol that Quinn doesn't mention. Write about it. Consider the following questions: Why is it a symbol? What does it say about America and Americans? Use a variety of rhetorical strategies to develop your essay: definition, description, narration, analogy.

3. If you wear jeans, write a paper in which you consider exactly why. Is it tradition? identity? prestige? peer pressure? or a little of each? If you have a favorite label, try to explain why you prefer it.

The Last Wave

Ernest Hebert

Does the latest style reflect an attitude—or just another way of dressing up? Whatever the answer, it seems that with each generation comes new music, fashions, and hairdos. The fifties brought us rock and roll as well as black leather jackets and slick DA haircuts. The sixties spawned hippies, along with bell-bottom pants, beads, and long hair. The seventies saw the birth of discos as well as designer jeans and high-styled coifs. Now, with the eighties, we have New Wave music, the bold new look of punk, and blue hair. In this very funny monologue, columnist Ernest Hebert reflects the desperation of an *au courant* person trying to keep up with the look and style of the moment.

"Hello, hello. Is this Hairsatz Hair Styling Emporium? It is. 1
Good. I'd like to make an appointment to get my hair cut and styled.

"I want a new wave. That is, my hair is already wavy but I want a New 2
Wave haircut. I'm a tough case. The naturally disheveled spikes of hair natural to the New Wave cut aren't natural when you have naturally wavy hair, so I'll need the New Wave styled in, spikes and all. Also, the color of my hair is wrong. It's brown. Do you suppose you could dye it pink or purple?

"I decided to get into New Wave when I attended a concert by a New 3
Wave band, and the lead singer, who was a healthy young millionaire with naturally spiked hair, said to the audience, 'All is pain.' I thought: This is great stuff, real philosophical. So I've been studying New Wave.

"I've got the hardest part down—the punk look, I mean. The look is 4
a dead stare, real vacant, held for minutes on end while you converse,

dance, drink, or take drugs. You'd think the look would be easy to master, but it's actually very difficult. Sometimes your eyes want to twinkle with mirth, or the corners of your mouth will twitch involuntarily with embarrassment. No good. The look requires complete dedication to vacancy.

"I asked one of my New Wave friends the key to unlocking the look, 5 to uncorking the out-to-lunch genie. . . . Oh, dear, I'm in trouble with my metaphor. Anyway, my friend advised me to say over and over again, 'All is pain.' I practiced diligently, but she said, 'Your eyes are not vacant enough. It's in the eyes. Think pain.'

"I had to resort to desperate measures to get the New Wave look fixed 6 on my face. An iron garden rake did the trick. I put the rake flat on the ground, prong side up. Then I stepped real hard on the prongs, and the handle came flying into my face, and—wow, what an experience—hit me right between the eyes. I took out my pocket mirror and studied my pupils. The New Wave look was almost there. I put the rake back down and repeated the process. Wow! This was great, this was pain. I've had the New Wave look ever since.

"My New Wave wardrobe is more or less complete—faded blue jeans, 7 T-shirts, skinny ties, black shoes—and the earring fits nicely in my left lobe. You can make ear holes pretty easy with a sewing needle, but if you're really into pain, fish hooks work better. You know, because of the barb?

"Having acquired the look and bought the outfit, naturally I wanted 8 to show off my New Wave, so I trotted on down to the next New Wave concert, where I ran into my New Wave friend. 'Hey,' she said, 'I really really love your T-shirt and skinny tie, but you've got to do something about that hair. I don't see a single spike. Nothing but waves. And the color—it's all wrong. I mean, brown—dark brown at that? Come on.'

"Sometimes, I miss the old days at the barbershop. You didn't have 9 to make an appointment, and you knew what kind of haircut you would get because the barber only knew one way to cut hair.

"Haircuts only cost about a buck. Of course, you had to put up with 10 a lot. Barbers tended to be stubborn and opinionated. My own barber was a devoted reader of the op-ed pages of the local newspaper, and I had to put up with his rantings about politics. If I had ever told him I wanted my hair styled, he would have called me names and escorted me out the door.

"I got those haircuts every two weeks, but Elvis Presley changed the 11 hair scene. Inspired by Elvis, I cultivated a DA—which was good because you didn't get penalized if you had wavy hair. I grew my hair longer, combed it back with my own Wesson Oil, and allowed a single curl to fall onto my forehead. This allowed me to date more girls and go to the barber fewer times.

"I finally stopped going to the barber altogether when I became a   12
hippie. I didn't cut my hair for two years. I wore bell-bottom pants, beads,
and sandals. Gosh, but it was all so groovy.

"When the Afro cut became popular, I just had to try it. I returned to   13
the barbershop. My, how it had changed. The new wave of barbers.
. . . No, no, I don't mean New Wave barbers; I mean a new wave of
barbers. . . . The new wave of barbers gave you a book of styles to choose
from, they included women barbers, they encouraged you to wash your
hair, and they even had hair dryers. No Wesson Oil in the place. I asked
the new wave barber who styled my hair into an Afro what had happened
to the barber who used to cut my hair. 'Haven't you heard? He went
bankrupt and went into politics. He's your congressman,' he said.

"I had the Afro for a while, but it got to be a hassle, and what with the   14
high interest rates I couldn't afford the payments on the loan I took out
to get those expensive haircuts. So for the last couple of years I've worn
my hair naturally wavy, cutting it myself. But New Wave is for me. So I'd
like to make an appointment.

"What? What? Hairsatz doesn't do New Wave haircuts anymore? New   15
Wave is old? Well, what's new?"

Topical Considerations

1. According to Hebert, what is "the punk look"? And what is it
supposed to convey?

2. Hebert says he finally mastered "the punk look" by causing
himself to be smashed in the face with a rake handle. How is a rake an
appropriate means for achieving it? What does this effort say about Hebert's
attitude toward the punk look and what it is supposed to reflect?

3. Hebert describes his New Wave wardrobe. From your own
experience, how accurate is his description? How would you characterize
New Wave wardrobes?

4. What specific changes in hair styles over the years does Hebert
note? What changes in barbers and barbershops does he describe?

5. In this little essay, Hebert is having fun taking satirical pot
shots at fads and faddists. Given that this is a first-person narrative,
however, what is Hebert saying about himself?

Rhetorical Considerations

1. What is the significance of the title of this piece?

2. What special rhetorical advantages are gained by framing this
piece as a telephone monologue?

3. What is Hebert's intention in naming the place he wants to get his hair styled Hairsatz Hair Styling Emporium? What is the pun here? What is an emporium?

4. One effective means of creating a humorous effect is irony. Find some examples of irony in Hebert's piece.

5. How well does the concluding paragraph illustrate a key point of this essay?

Writing Assignments

1. Give a portrait in writing of the New Wave look. Describe the kinds of clothes, hair, and style of expression a typical New Waver has. Do you agree with Hebert that a key message conveyed by the New Wave look is "All is pain"?

2. See if you can describe your own style. Write a paper in which you attempt to define your own look—your wardrobe and style. Is it New Wave? preppy? chic? conservative? a mixture? something undefinable?

3. Write a paper in which you try to define the look and style of one of your professors—perhaps even your English professor.

4. If your English professor suddenly started showing up to class dressed in high punk, with spiked pink hair, faded jeans, T-shirts, skinny ties, and so on, how do you think that would affect the way you would regard him or her? (We're assuming your English professor is not already a high punker.) Could you still take him or her as seriously? Would your learning be affected?

5. Hebert uses himself to suggest humorously how conditioned we are to respond to the latest styles and fashions, or "looks." Do you see anything wrong with this? Write a paper examining the pros and cons of keeping up with the look in vogue.

That Lean and Hungry Look

Suzanne Britt Jordan

Not everybody thinks thin—particularly not author Suzanne Britt Jordan. As she says in the following essay, she has made a hobby of observing thin people and has decided that she doesn't like what she sees. It might be said that Ms. Jordan thinks fat. In fact, her essay is a humorous look at the thin world through the eyes of a "chubby." But there is more here than just fat–thin joking. Jordan makes some interesting statements about people, personalities, and stereotypes. This essay first appeared in *Newsweek* and was later expanded into her book *Skinny People Are Dull and Crunchy Like Carrots* (1982)

Caesar was right. Thin people need watching. I've been watching   1
them for most of my adult life, and I don't like what I see. When these
narrow fellows spring at me, I quiver to my toes. Thin people come in
all personalities, most of them menacing. You've got your "together"
thin person, your mechanical thin person, your condescending thin person, your tsk-tsk thin person, your efficiency-expert thin person. All of
them are dangerous.

In the first place, thin people aren't fun. They don't know how to goof   2
off, at least in the best, fat sense of the word. They've always got to be
adoing. Give them a coffee break, and they'll jog around the block. Supply
them with a quiet evening at home, and they'll fix the screen door and
lick S&H green stamps. They say things like "there aren't enough hours
in the day." Fat people never say that. Fat people think the day is too
damn long already.

Thin people make me tired. They've got speedy little metabolisms that   3
cause them to bustle briskly. They're forever rubbing their bony hands
together and eyeing new problems to "tackle." I like to surround myself
with sluggish, inert, easygoing fat people, the kind who believe that if you
clean it up today, it'll just get dirty again tomorrow.

Some people say the business about the jolly fat person is a myth, that   4
all of us chubbies are neurotic, sick, sad people. I disagree. Fat people
may not be chortling all day long, but they're a hell of a lot *nicer* than the
wizened and shriveled. Thin people turn surly, mean, and hard at a young
age because they never learn the value of a hot-fudge sundae for easing
tension. Thin people don't like gooey soft things because they themselves
are neither gooey nor soft. They are crunchy and dull, like carrots. They
go straight to the heart of the matter while fat people let things stay all
blurry and hazy and vague, the way things actually are. Thin people want
to face the truth. Fat people know there is no truth. One of my thin
friends is always staring at complex, unsolvable problems and saying,
"The key thing is. . . ." Fat people never say that. They know there isn't
any such thing as the key thing about anything.

Thin people believe in logic. Fat people see all sides. The sides fat   5
people see are rounded blobs, usually gray, always nebulous and truly not
worth worrying about. But the thin person persists. "If you consume
more calories than you burn," says one of my thin friends, "you will gain
weight. It's that simple." Fat people always grin when they hear statements like that. They know better.

Fat people realize that life is illogical and unfair. They know very well   6
that God is not in his heaven and all is not right with the world. If God
was up there, fat people could have two doughnuts and a big orange drink
anytime they wanted it.

Thin people have a long list of logical things they are always spouting   7
off to me. They hold up one finger at a time as they reel off these things,
so I won't lose track. They speak slowly as if to a young child. The list
is long and full of holes. It contains tidbits like "get a grip on yourself,"
"cigarettes kill," "cholesterol clogs," "fit as a fiddle," "ducks in a row,"
"organize," and "sound fiscal management." Phrases like that.

They think these 2,000-point plans lead to happiness. Fat people know   8
happiness is elusive at best and even if they could get the kind thin people
talk about, they wouldn't want it. Wisely, fat people see that such programs are too dull, too hard, too off the mark. They are never better than
a whole cheesecake.

Fat people know all about the mystery of life. They are the ones   9
acquainted with the night, with luck, with fate, with playing it by ear.
One thin person I know once suggested that we arrange all the parts of
a jigsaw puzzle into groups according to size, shape, and color. He
figured this would cut the time needed to complete the puzzle by at
least 50 percent. I said I wouldn't do it. One, I like to muddle through.
Two, what good would it do to finish early? Three, the jigsaw puzzle
isn't the important thing. The important thing is the fun of four people
(one thin person included) sitting around a card table, working a jigsaw
puzzle. My thin friend had no use for my list. Instead of joining us, he
went outside and mulched the boxwoods. The three remaining fat people finished the puzzle and made chocolate, double-fudged brownies to
celebrate.

The main problem with thin people is they oppress. Their good inten-   10
tions, bony torsos, tight ships, neat corners, cerebral machinations, and
pat solutions loom like dark clouds over the loose, comfortable, spread-
out, soft world of the fat. Long after fat people have removed their coats
and shoes and put their feet up on the coffee table, thin people are still
sitting on the edge of the sofa, looking neat as a pin, discussing rutabagas.
Fat people are heavily into fits of laughter, slapping their thighs and
whooping it up, while thin people are still politely waiting for the punch
line.

Thin people are downers. They like math and morality and reasoned   11
evaluation of the limitations of human beings. They have their skinny
little acts together. They expound, prognose, probe, and prick.

Fat people are convivial. They will like you even if you're irregular and   12
have acne. They will come up with a good reason why you never wrote
the great American novel. They will cry in your beer with you. They will
put your name in the pot. They will let you off the hook. Fat people will
gab, giggle, guffaw, gallumph, gyrate, and gossip. They are generous,
giving, and gallant. They are gluttonous and goodly and great. What you
want when you're down is soft and jiggly, not muscled and stable. Fat
people know this. Fat people have plenty of room. Fat people will take
you in.

Topical Considerations

1. Why do you think Jordan wrote this essay—to be entertaining? to be serious and persuasive? a little of both? Explain your answer.

2. In paragraph 6, Jordan remarks: "They know very well that God is not in his heaven and all is not right with the world." What is the literary allusion in this line? What other allusions do you see? Note, for example, the title and the opening line.

3. Do you agree with Jordan's generalities about fat and thin people? On what points do you agree? disagree?

4. Does Jordan's characterization of thin people remind you of anyone you know? Describe specific incidents to show how such an individual fits Jordan's description.

5. Identify some of the comments that Jordan makes in defense of fat people. How might a thin person reverse these so that they are an attack instead of a defense of fatness? Consider, for example: "Fat people think the day is too damn long already" (paragraph 2) or "If God was up there, fat people could have two doughnuts and a big orange drink anytime they wanted it" (paragraph 6).

Rhetorical Considerations

1. How does Jordan order her comparison and contrast of thin people and fat people? Analyze her essay paragraph by paragraph to explain your answer.

2. Point out some of the adjectives Jordan uses to show the contrast between thin people and fat people.

3. What connotations does the word *rutabagas* have that make it a good word choice in paragraph 10? What does Jordan seek to achieve by using this word? Cite other apt word choices.

4. Jordan uses alliteration extensively in her concluding paragraph. Why? How does it contribute to the total effect she seeks to achieve?

5. Discuss Jordan's use of clichés. How do they contribute to the humor in her essay?

6. Jordan often opens a paragraph with a short declarative sentence. Why is this effective? How does it compare with the length of other sentences in any given paragraph?

Writing Assignments

1. Adopt the point of view of one of Jordan's thin people. Write a rebuttal essay in which you turn Jordan's remarks into a criticism of fat people. Think of an appropriate title similar to Jordan's.

2. Assume that you have just read Jordan's essay in a magazine. Write a letter to the editor expressing your response to it. You may either defend or attack the essay.

Farewell to Fitness

Mike Royko

Mike Royko is just one of those millions of us who got caught up in "thinking thin." Like Suzanne Britt Jordan, he rejected it; but it wasn't skinny people who turned him off. It was all the dieting, the workouts, and the sacrifices. In this very witty and funny piece, Royko takes some swipes at America's obsession with getting in shape. He is a well-known columnist for the *Chicago Daily News* and the author of *Boss,* a biography of Chicago's late mayor, Richard Daley.

At least once a week, the office jock will stop me in the hall, 1 bounce on the balls of his feet, plant his hands on his hips, flex his pectoral muscles and say: "How about it? I'll reserve a racquetball court. You can start working off some of that. . . ." And he'll jab a finger deep into my midsection.

It's been going on for months, but I've always had an excuse: "Next 2 week, I've got a cold." "Next week, my back is sore." "Next week, I've got a pulled hamstring." "Next week, after the holidays."

But this is it. No more excuses. I made one New Year's resolution, 3 which is that I will tell him the truth. And the truth is that I don't want to play racquetball or handball or tennis, or jog, or pump Nautilus machines, or do push-ups or sit-ups or isometrics, or ride a stationary bicycle, or pull on a rowing machine, or hit a softball, or run up a flight of steps, or engage in any other form of exercise more strenuous than rolling out of bed.

This may be unpatriotic, and it is surely out of step with our muscle-4 flexing times, but I am renouncing the physical-fitness craze.

Oh, I was part of it. Maybe not as fanatically as some. But about 15 5 years ago, when I was 32, someone talked me into taking up handball, the most punishing court game there is.

From then on it was four or five times a week—up at 6 A.M., on the 6 handball court at 7, run, grunt, sweat, pant until 8:30, then in the office at 9. And I'd go around bouncing on the balls of my feet, flexing my pectoral muscles, poking friends in their soft guts, saying: "How about working some of that off? I'll reserve a court," and being obnoxious.

This went on for years. And for what? I'll tell you what it led to: I 7 stopped eating pork shanks, that's what. It was inevitable. When you join the physical-fitness craze, you have to stop eating wonderful things like pork shanks because they are full of cholesterol. And you have to give up eggs benedict, smoked liverwurst, Italian sausage, butter-pecan ice cream, Polish sausage, goose-liver pate, Sara Lee cheesecake, Twinkies, potato chips, salami-and-Swiss-cheese sandwiches, double cheeseburgers with fries, Christian Brothers brandy with a Beck's chaser, and everything else that tastes good.

Instead, I ate broiled skinless chicken, broiled whitefish, grapefruit, steamed broccoli, steamed spinach, unbuttered toast, yogurt, eggplant, an apple for dessert and Perrier water to wash it down. Blahhhhh! **8**

You do this for years, and what is your reward for panting and sweating around a handball-racquetball court, and eating yogurt and the skinned flesh of a dead chicken? **9**

—You can take your pulse and find that it is slow. So what? Am I a clock? **10**

—You buy pants with a narrower waistline. Big deal. The pants don't cost less than the ones with a big waistline. **11**

—You get to admire yourself in the bathroom mirror for about 10 seconds a day after taking a shower. It takes five seconds to look at your flat stomach from the front, and five more seconds to look at your flat stomach from the side. If you're a real creep of a narcissist, you can add another 10 seconds for looking at your small behind with a mirror. **12**

That's it. **13**

Wait, I forgot something. You will live longer. I know that because my doctor told me so every time I took a physical. My fitness-conscious doctor was very slender—especially the last time I saw him, which was at his wake. **14**

But I still believe him. Running around a handball court or jogging five miles a day, eating yogurt and guzzling Perrier will make you live longer. **15**

So you live longer. Have you been in a typical nursing home lately? Have you walked around the low-rent neighborhoods where the geezers try to survive on Social Security? **16**

If you think living longer is rough now, wait until the 1990s, when today's Me Generation potheads and coke sniffers begin taking care of the elderly (today's middle-aged joggers). It'll be: "Just take this little happy pill, gramps, and you'll wake up in heaven." **17**

It's not worth giving up pork shanks and Sara Lee cheesecake. **18**

Nor is it the way to age gracefully. Look around at all those middle-aged jogging chicken-eaters. Half of them tape hairpieces to their heads. That's what comes from having a flat stomach. You start thinking that you should also have hair. And after that comes a facelift. And that leads to jumping around a disco floor, pinching an airline stewardess and other bizarre behavior. **19**

I prefer to age gracefully, the way men did when I was a boy. The only time a man over 40 ran was when the cops caught him burglarizing a **20** warehouse. The idea of exercise was to walk to and from the corner tavern, mostly to. A well-rounded health-food diet included pork shanks, dumplings, Jim Beam and a beer chaser.

Anyone who was skinny was suspected of having TB or an ulcer. A fine   21
figure of a man was one who could look down and not see his knees, his feet or anything else in that vicinity. What do you have to look for, anyway? You ought to know if anything is missing.

A few years ago I was in Bavaria, and I went to a German beer hall.   22
It was a beautiful sight. Everybody was popping sausages and pork shanks and draining quart-sized steins of thick beer. Every so often they'd thump their magnificent bellies and smile happily at the booming sound that they made.

Compare that to the finish line of a marathon, with all those emaciated   23
runners sprawled on the grass, tongues hanging out, wheezing, moaning, writhing, throwing up.

If that is the way to happiness and a long life, pass me the cheesecake.   24

May you get a hernia, Arnold Schwarzenegger. And here's to you,   25
Orson Welles.

Topical Considerations

1. Why does Royko mention pork shanks so often in his essay? Why is broiled skinless chicken anathema to him?

2. It seems obvious that Royko would be sure to fail miserably with a strict diet plan. What does he say to suggest this?

3. How do you feel about some of the conclusions Royko reaches about keeping fit? Are you ready to give up your regimen of a daily run and yogurt for lunch? Why or why not?

4. Royko ridicules the office jock who bounces around flexing his muscles. Is there any truth in his observations? Are there other people that Royko makes fun of?

5. How does Royko plan to "age gracefully"? What does he believe is an "ungraceful" way to grow old? Why? What do you think? Gives reasons for your answer.

Rhetorical Considerations

1. Where does Royko state his thesis? What rhetorical strategy does he use to introduce it? Is it attention-getting? Why?

2. Reread paragraph 7. What do you note about the length of the sentences? How does this affect the reading of the paragraph? Find another similar paragraph.

3. How would you characterize the tone of this essay? Cite spe-

cific passages that prove your point.

4. Royko achieves humor by exaggerating points of contrast. Find examples of this in the essay.

Writing Assignments

1. Write an essay about the importance of keeping fit from the point of view of the office jock Royko satirizes in his essay. Imitate Royko's use of satire, this time ridiculing flabby fat people.

2. Americans today seem to be obsessed with the need to keep fit. In an essay, argue for or against the current fitness craze.

TELEVISION

10

What Did Kids Do Before Television Was Invented?

Peter C. Kratcoski

Television is the primary source of entertainment for Americans. It is also the prime target of many psychologists and sociologists who see TV as dangerous to health. The lead piece in this section reflects one major criticism—that television threatens the creative activity of children. Peter C. Kratcoski is an editor for *USA Today* and a professor of sociology and criminal justice at Kent State University. His criticism here is not leveled at the quality of television, as is the criticism of others in this section, but at the nature of the experience itself—a very passive one. His essay also gives a glimpse of how pre-TV kids filled their time.

When adults who grew up in the 1940's or early 1950's describe the days of their youth to their children, they paint a Norman Rockwell-style portrait of life. Hats went off as the flag passed by; days were filled with fishing, swimming, playing ball, or chatting with kindly adults; and parents' dreams for their children could be attained within the town limits —a good report card, a date for the prom, a romance with the boy next door. No matter how rosy the picture is painted, however, the question inevitably comes back: "Yes, but what did you do without television?" With television currently taking a good deal of criticism for its violence, suggestiveness, and debunking of authority figures in children's lives, it seems appropriate to recall the sorts of pastimes in which children of a small-town background engaged in the pre-television era.   1

One of our particular favorite activities was playing in the cemetery. Although children seen roaming unsupervised in a cemetery today would probably be viewed suspiciously as potential vandals, we spent quite a few hours walking among the markers, commenting on the age and life status of the deceased and speculating on the character of those whose stones were particularly ornate. The children buried in the cemetery were most intriguing to us. We would talk about what dread disease might have finished them off and how old they would be today if they had lived; they even were sometimes included as imaginary playmates in our games.   2

This rather ghoulish preoccupation with the other-worldly also extended to our favorite holiday, Halloween. "Trick or treat," rather than being a one-night affair, extended for two or more weeks before the haunting day. A group of children disguised as hobos, ghosts, scarecrows, or gypsies might descend on a household at any time, and the hauntee had to be ready with treats or face the penalty of having his or her windows "soaped" (coated over with swirls and squiggles of bar soap). A code of "soaping" ethics existed—"nice" kids used bar soap, never pieces of wax, which had to be scraped from the window with a razor   3 blade. The climax of the Halloween season came with the town parade, in which every kid who could walk or be carried participated. Many adults also joined in the fun, and prizes were awarded. One of the oddities of our particular area was the custom of fashioning costumes from suits of long underwear and then stuffing pillows into every possible inch of the material to produce droopy, horrendous-looking, fatty creatures. *Buying* a costume was unthinkable. Some mothers took this as the yearly opportunity to show off their sewing skills and fashioned elaborate crepe-paper costumes for their pretty, curly haired daughters. Those of us not so blessed uttered secret prayers for rain during the parade, in the hope that these strutting beauties would be reduced to dripping, runny nothings. Hours were spent talking about what this year's costume would be, pretending we were going to dress another way to keep others from stealing our prize-winning idea, and spying on friends to find out what they were *really* going to wear.

Some of our pastimes centered about the church and the parochial   4
school, but were not necessarily inspirational in intent. Holy Saturday was a day of great rejoicing, because at noon on that day Lent ended and we could again eat candy, read comic books, drink pop, or return to whatever other vice our parents had helped us promise to give up for the past 40 days. We would gravely prepare the forbidden fruit and wait for the signal of the church bell tolling at noon before gleefully digging in. Another important day was Aug. 15, the Feast of the Assumption, when the nuns who taught in the school received their assignments for the following year. It was a clear case of fate intervening in our lives. A word from the Mother Superior on that day would send a particularly feared presence from among us, never to be seen again, or would commit us to another year of toeing the line. The 8 A.M. Mass was crowded, rumors flew, and we would intently study the faces of the nuns for any sign that a packed suitcase was waiting in the convent. When the news came out, it would spread like wildfire, and then a period of relief or resignation followed.

It seemed that we did a good deal more reading than children do   5
today, but the adventure themes we favored were not unlike those of television escapism. Nancy Drew was frowned upon by the town librarian, a fact which made her even more appealing to the girls. The older boys' interest ran to novels smuggled from their parents' collections or paperbacks purchased at the drugstore. All of the "juicy" parts were marked for rereading and discussion.

These few examples seem to suggest that, even without television, we   6
were preoccupied in our early lives with the same themes of violence, rather ghoulish aspects of the supernatural, testing and disrespect for authority, vandalism, a desire to shock adults, and references to things considered "taboo" which we now object to in television fare available to children. The apparent difference is the level and visibility of these themes. A good deal of the rebellious or aberrant activity of the past

occurred only in the imaginations of the youths of that time, in contrast to the graphic visual presentation of these themes on television. In addition, a good deal of the testing of limits or rebelliousness was expressed in activities of which adults were unaware. In contrast to television programming—which is prepared, produced, and projected by adults—the testing activities engaged in years ago had an element of social control by the children themselves. Parents were not seen as friends or buddies, and the kids' world was closed to them. Adults seemed comfortable with this idea and kept a hands-off attitude unless behavior became blatantly rebellious, disruptive, or destructive. One possible answer, then, to the question, "What did kids do before television was invented?" seems to be that they acted out their fantasies themselves, rather than depending on film characters to do it for them.

Topical Considerations

1. What are the implications in the question asked of adults: "But what did you do without television?"

2. According to Kratcoski, how did his childhood activities differ from those of kids today?

3. Did your own Halloween experiences differ much from those of the author? In what ways? In general, how have Halloween activities changed since the days of Kratcoski's childhood?

4. How does the author answer the question in the title?

Rhetorical Considerations

1. Explain the allusion in paragraph 1 to "a Norman Rockwell-style portrait of life." How does the author characterize such a portrait?

2. Comment on the tone of Kratcoski's word choice, "finished them off," when he refers to the children buried in the cemetery (paragraph 2).

3. Does this essay have an organizing scheme? Outline it according to paragraphs.

4. Where is the thesis statement in this piece? What is the rhetorical strategy of placing it where it is? How well does Kratcoski support that statement in the essay?

Writing Assignments

1. Kratcoski's complaint is aimed not at the quality of television but at the nature of the experience itself, which he says is passive. Before TV, kids used to act out their fantasies themselves, but today they depend

on adult-produced programs to do it for them. Do you agree with Krat-coski? Write a paper evaluating his claim, and use your own childhood memories as evidence. Did you have a free and active fantasy life?

2. One of the arguments people have against television is that children read less because of it. Evaluate the effects television has had on your own reading experience. Did you like to read as a child? What did you read? Did you prefer television to books?

3. Part of Kratcoski's essay centers on his pretelevision activities, such as his memories of Halloween. Write your own recollection of Halloweens past. What kinds of preparations did you make? Did you design and create your own costumes, or did you buy them? What trick-or-treat experiences did you have? In a narrative, try to capture some of the things you did.

The Plug-In Drug

Marie Winn

For years, the harmful effects of television, particularly on children, have been the professional interest of social commentator and writer Marie Winn. She is author of *The Plug-In Drug: TV* (1977), from which this essay has been adapted, and *Children Without Childhood* (1983). She says that home and family life have changed considerably since the invention of television—and in ways we may not care to imagine. She makes a strong case against television, accusing it of being a prime force in the warping of children and in the disintegration of the American family.

A quarter of a century after the introduction of television into   1
American society, a period that has seen the medium become so deeply ingrained in American life that in at least one state the television set has attained the rank of a legal necessity, safe from repossession in case of debt along with clothes, cooking utensils, and the like, television viewing has become an inevitable and ordinary part of daily life. Only in the early years of television did writers and commentators have sufficient perspective to separate the activity of watching television from the actual content it offers the viewer. In those early days writers frequently discussed the effects of television on family life. However, a curious myopia afflicted those early observers: almost without exception they regarded television as a favorable, beneficial, indeed, wondrous influence upon the family.

"Television is going to be a real asset in every home where there are   2
children," predicts a writer in 1949.

"Television will take over your way of living and change your chil-   3 dren's habits, but this change can be a wonderful improvement," claims another commentator.

"No survey's needed, of course, to establish that television has 4 brought the family together in one room," writes *The New York Times* television critic in 1949.

Each of the early articles about television is invariably accompanied by 5 a photograph or illustration showing a family cozily sitting together before the television set, Sis on Mom's lap, Buddy perched on the arm of Dad's chair, Dad with his arm around Mom's shoulder. Who could have guessed that twenty or so years later Mom would be watching a drama in the kitchen, the kids would be looking at cartoons in their room, while Dad would be taking in the ball game in the living room?

Of course television sets were enormously expensive in those early 6 days. The idea that by 1975 more than 60 percent of American families would own two or more sets was preposterous. The splintering of the multiple-set family was something the early writers could not foresee. Nor did anyone imagine the number of hours children would eventually devote to television, the common use of television by parents as a child pacifier, the changes television would effect upon child-rearing methods, the increasing domination of family schedules by children's viewing requirements—in short, the *power* of the new medium to dominate family life.

After the first years, as children's consumption of the new medium 7 increased, together with parental concern about the possible effects of so much television viewing, a steady refrain helped to soothe and reassure anxious parents. "Television always enters a pattern of influences that already exist: the home, the peer group, the school, the church and culture generally," write the authors of an early and influential study of television's effects on children. In other words, if the child's home life is all right, parents need not worry about the effects of all that television watching.

But television does not merely influence the child; it deeply influences 8 that "pattern of influences" that is meant to ameliorate its effects. Home and family life have changed in important ways since the advent of television. The peer group has become television-oriented, and much of the time children spend together is occupied by television viewing. Culture generally has been transformed by television. Therefore it is improper to assign to television the subsidiary role its many apologists (too often members of the television industry) insist it plays. Television is not merely one of a number of important influences upon today's child. Through the changes it has made in family life, television emerges as *the* important influence in children's lives today.

The Quality of Family Life

Television's contribution to family life has been an equivocal one. For 9 while it has, indeed, kept the members of the family from dispersing, it has not served to bring them together. By its domination of the time families spend together, it destroys the special quality that distinguishes one family from another, a quality that depends to a great extent on what a family *does,* what special rituals, games, recurrent jokes, familiar songs, and shared activities it accumulates.

"Like the sorcerer of old," writes Urie Bronfenbrenner, "the television set casts its magic spell, freezing speech and action, turning the living into silent statues so long as the enchantment lasts. The primary danger of the television screen lies not so much in the behavior it produces—although there is danger there—as in the behavior it prevents: the talks, the games, the family festivities and arguments through which much of the child's learning takes place and through which his character is formed. Turning on the television set can turn off the process that transforms children into people."   10

Yet parents have accepted a television-dominated family life so completely that they cannot see how the medium is involved in whatever problems they might be having. A first-grade teacher reports: 11

"I have one child in the group who's an only child. I wanted to find out more about her family life because this little girl was quite isolated from the group, didn't make friends, so I talked to her mother. Well, they don't have time to do anything in the evening, the mother said. The parents come home after picking up the child at the baby-sitter's. Then the mother fixes dinner while the child watches TV. Then they have dinner and the child goes to bed. I said to this mother, 'Well, couldn't she help you fix dinner? That would be a nice time for the two of you to talk,' and the mother said, 'Oh, but I'd hate to have her miss "Zoom." It's such a good program!' "   12

Even when families make efforts to control television, too often its very presence counterbalances the positive features of family life. A writer and mother of two boys aged 3 and 7 described her family's television schedule in an article in *The New York Times:*   13

> We were in the midst of a full-scale War. Every day was a new battle and every program was a major skirmish. We agreed it was a bad scene all around and were ready to enter diplomatic negotiations. . . . In principle we have agreed on 2½ hours of TV a day, "Sesame Street," "Electric Company" (with dinner gobbled up in between) and two half-hour shows between 7 and 8:30 which enables the grown-ups to eat in peace and prevents the two boys from destroying one another. Their pre-bedtime choice is dreadful, because, as Josh recently admitted, "There's nothing much on I really like." So . . . it's "What's My Line" or "To Tell the Truth." . . . Clearly there is a need for first-rate children's shows at this time. . . .

Consider the "family life" described here: Presumably the father   14
comes home from work during the "Sesame Street"–"Electric Company"
stint. The children are either watching television, gobbling their dinner,
or both. While the parents eat their dinner in peaceful privacy, the children watch another hour of television. Then there is only a half-hour left
before bedtime, just enough time for baths, getting pajamas on, brushing
teeth, and so on. The children's evening is regimented with an almost
military precision. They watch their favorite programs, and when there
is "nothing much on I really like," they watch whatever else is on—
because *watching* is the important thing. Their mother does not see anything amiss with watching programs just for the sake of watching; she
only wishes there were some first-rate children's shows on at those times.

Without conjuring up memories of the Victorian era with family games   15
and long, leisurely meals, and large families, the question arises: isn't
there a better family life available than this dismal, mechanized arrangement of children watching television for however long is allowed them,
evening after evening?

Of course, families today still do *special* things together at times: go   16
camping in the summer, go to the zoo on a nice Sunday, take various trips
and expeditions. But their *ordinary* daily life together is diminished—that
sitting around at the dinner table, that spontaneous taking up of an
activity, those little games invented by children on the spur of the moment when there is nothing else to do, the scribbling, the chatting, and
even the quarreling, all the things that form the fabric of a family, that
define a childhood. Instead, the children have their regular schedule of
television programs and bedtime, and the parents have their peaceful
dinner together.

The author of the article in the *Times* notes that "keeping a family sane   17
means mediating between the needs of both children and adults." But
surely the needs of adults are being better met than the needs of the
children, who are effectively shunted away and rendered untroublesome,
while their parents enjoy a life as undemanding as that of any childless
couple. In reality, it is those very demands that young children make upon
a family that lead to growth, and it is the way parents accede to those
demands that builds the relationships upon which the future of the family
depends. If the family does not accumulate its backlog of shared experiences, shared *everyday* experiences that occur and recur and change and
develop, then it is not likely to survive as anything other than a caretaking
institution.

Family Rituals

Ritual is defined by sociologists as "that part of family life that the   18
family likes about itself, is proud of and wants formally to continue."
Another text notes that "the development of a ritual by a family is an
index of the common interest of its members in the family as a group."

What has happened to family rituals, those regular, dependable, recur-   19
rent happenings that gave members of a family a feeling of *belonging* to
a home rather than living in it merely for the sake of convenience, those
experiences that act as the adhesive of family unity far more than any
material advantages?

Mealtime rituals, going-to-bed rituals, illness rituals, holiday rituals,   20
how many of these have survived the inroads of the television set?

A young woman who grew up near Chicago reminisces about her   21
childhood and gives an idea of the effects of television upon family rituals:

"As a child I had millions of relatives around—my parents both come   22
from relatively large families. My father had nine brothers and sisters.
And so every holiday there was this great swoop-down of aunts, uncles,
and millions of cousins. I just remember how wonderful it used to be.
These thousands of cousins would come and everyone would play and
ultimately, after dinner, all the women would be in the front of the house,
drinking coffee and talking, all the men would be in the back of the house,
drinking and smoking, and all the kids would be all over the place, playing
hide and seek. Christmas time was particularly nice because everyone
always brought all their toys and games. Our house had a couple of rooms
with go-through closets, so there were always kids running in a great
circle route. I remember it was just wonderful.

"And then all of a sudden one year I remember becoming suddenly   23
aware of how different everything had become. The kids were no longer
playing Monopoly or Clue or the other games we used to play together.
It was because we had a television set which had been turned on for a
football game. All of that socializing that had gone on previously had
ended. Now everyone was sitting in front of the television set, on a
holiday, at a family party! I remember being stunned by how awful that
was. Somehow the television had become more attractive."

As families have come to spend more and more of their time together   24
engaged in the single activity of television watching, those rituals and
pastimes that once gave family life its special quality have become more
and more uncommon. Not since prehistoric times when cave families
hunted, gathered, ate, and slept, with little time remaining to accumulate
a culture of any significance, have families been reduced to such a same-
ness.

Real People

It is not only the activities that a family might engage in together that   25
are diminished by the powerful presence of television in the home. The
relationships of the family members to each other are also affected, in
both obvious and subtle ways. The hours that the young child spends in
a one-way relationship with television people, an involvement that allows
for no communication or interaction, surely affect his relationships with
real-life people.

Studies show the importance of eye-to-eye contact, for instance, in real-life relationships, and indicate that the nature of a person's eye-contact patterns, whether he looks another squarely in the eye or looks to the side or shifts his gaze from side to side, may play a significant role in his success or failure in human relationships. But no eye contact is possible in the child-television relationship, although in certain children's programs people purport to speak directly to the child and the camera fosters this illusion by focusing directly upon the person being filmed. (Mr. Rogers is an example, telling the child "I like you, you're special," etc.) How might such a distortion of real-life relationships affect a child's development of trust, of openness, of an ability to relate well to other *real* people? 26

Bruno Bettelheim writes: 27

> Children who have been taught, or conditioned, to listen passively most of the day to the warm verbal communications coming from the TV screen, to the deep emotional appeal of the so-called TV personality, are often unable to respond to real persons because they arouse so much less feeling than the skilled actor. Worse, they lose the ability to learn from reality because life experiences are much more complicated than the ones they see on the screen. . . .

A teacher makes a similar observation about her personal viewing experiences: 28

"I have trouble mobilizing myself and dealing with real people after watching a few hours of television. It's just hard to make that transition from watching television to a real relationship. I suppose it's because there was no effort necessary while I was watching, and dealing with real people always requires a bit of effort. Imagine, then, how much harder it might be to do the same thing for a small child, particularly one who watches a lot of television every day." 29

But more obviously damaging to family relationships is the elimination of opportunities to talk, and perhaps more important, to argue, to air grievances, between parents and children and brothers and sisters. Families frequently use television to avoid confronting their problems, problems that will not go away if they are ignored but will only fester and become less easily resolvable as time goes on. 30

A mother reports: 31

"I find myself, with three children, wanting to turn on the TV set when they're fighting. I really have to struggle not to do it because I feel that's telling them this is the solution to the quarrel—but it's so tempting that I often do it." 32

A family therapist discusses the use of television as an avoidance mechanism: 33

"In a family I know the father comes home from work and turns on   34
the television set. The children come and watch with him and the wife
serves them their meal in front of the set. He then goes and takes a
shower, or works on the car or something. She then goes and has her own
dinner in front of the television set. It's a symptom of a deeper-rooted
problem, sure. But it would help them all to get rid of the set. It would
be far easier to work on what the symptom really means without the
television. The television simply encourages a double avoidance of each
other. They'd find out more quickly what was going on if they weren't
able to hide behind the TV. Things wouldn't necessarily be better, of
course, but they wouldn't be anesthetized."

The decreased opportunities for simple conversation between parents   35
and children in the television-centered home may help explain an observation made by an emergency room nurse at a Boston hospital. She reports
that parents just seem to sit there these days when they come in with a sick
or seriously injured child, although talking to the child would distract and
comfort him. "They don't seem to know *how* to talk to their own children at
any length," the nurse observes. Similarly, a television critic writes in *The
New York Times:* "I had just a day ago taken my son to the emergency ward
of a hospital for stitches above his left eye, and the occasion seemed no
more real to me than Maalot or 54th Street, south-central Los Angeles.
There was distance and numbness and an inability to turn off the total
institution. I didn't behave at all; I just watched. . . ."

A number of research studies substantiate the assumption that televi-   36
sion interferes with family activities and the formation of family relationships. One survey shows that 78 percent of the respondents indicated no
conversation taking place during viewing except at specified times such
as commercials. The study notes: "The television atmosphere in most
households is one of quiet absorption on the part of family members who
are present. The nature of the family social life during a program could
be described as 'parallel' rather than interactive, and the set does seem
to dominate family life when it is on." Thirty-six percent of the respondents in another study indicated that television viewing was the only family
activity participated in during the week.

In a summary of research findings on television's effect on family   37
interactions, James Gabardino states: "The early findings suggest that
television had a disruptive effect upon interaction and thus presumably
human development. . . . It is not unreasonable to ask: 'Is the fact that
the average American family during the 1950's came to include two
parents, two children and a television set somehow related to the psy-
chosocial characteristics of the young adults of the 1970's?' "

Undermining the Family

In its effect on family relationships, in its facilitation of parental with-   38
drawal from an active role in the socialization of their children, and in its

replacement of family rituals and special events, television has played an important role in the disintegration of the American family. But of course it has not been the only contributing factor, perhaps not even the most important one. The steadily rising divorce rate, the increase in the number of working mothers, the decline of the extended family, the breakdown of neighborhoods and communities, the growing isolation of the nuclear family—all have seriously affected the family.

As Urie Bronfenbrenner suggests, the sources of family breakdown   39
do not come from the family itself, but from the circumstances in which the family finds itself and the way of life imposed upon it by those circumstances. "When those circumstances and the way of life they generate undermine relationships of trust and emotional security between family members, when they make it difficult for parents to care for, educate and enjoy their children, when there is no support or recognition from the outside world for one's role as a parent and when time spent with one's family means frustration of career, personal fulfillment and peace of mind, then the development of the child is adversely affected," he writes.

But while the roots of alienation go deep into the fabric of American   40
social history, television's presence in the home fertilizes them, encourages their wild and unchecked growth. Perhaps it is true that America's commitment to the television experience masks a spiritual vacuum, an empty and barren way of life, a desert of materialism. But it is television's dominant role in the family that anesthetizes the family into accepting its unhappy state and prevents it from struggling to better its condition, to improve its relationships, and to regain some of the richness it once possessed.

Others have noted the role of mass media in perpetuating an unsatis-   41
factory *status quo*. Leisure-time activity, writes Irving Howe, "must provide relief from work monotony without making the return to work too unbearable; it must provide amusement without insight and pleasure without disturbance—as distinct from art which gives pleasure through disturbance. Mass culture is thus oriented towards a central aspect of industrial society: the depersonalization of the individual." Similarly, Jacques Ellul rejects the idea that television is a legitimate means of educating the citizen: "Education . . . takes place only incidentally. The clouding of his consciousness is paramount. . . ."

And so the American family muddles on, dimly aware that something   42
is amiss but distracted from an understanding of its plight by an endless stream of television images. As family ties grow weaker and vaguer, as children's lives become more separate from their parents', as parents' educational role in their children's lives is taken over by television and schools, family life becomes increasingly more unsatisfying for both parents and children. All that seems to be left is Love, an abstraction that family members *know* is necessary but find great difficulty giving each

other because the traditional opportunities for expressing love within the family have been reduced or destroyed.

For contemporary parents, love toward each other has increasingly   43
come to mean successful sexual relations, as witnessed by the proliferation of sex manuals and sex therapists. The opportunities for manifesting other forms of love through mutual support, understanding, nurturing, even, to use an unpopular word, *serving* each other, are less and less available as mothers and fathers seek their independent destinies outside the family.

As for love of children, this love is increasingly expressed through   44
supplying material comforts, amusements, and educational opportunities. Parents show their love for their children by sending them to good schools and camps, by providing them with good food and good doctors, by buying them toys, books, games, and a television set of their very own. Parents will even go further and express their love by attending PTA meetings to improve their children's schools, or by joining groups that are acting to improve the quality of their children's television programs.

But this is love at a remove, and is rarely understood by children. The   45
more direct forms of parental love require time and patience, steady, dependable, ungrudgingly given time actually spent *with* a child, reading to him, comforting him, playing, joking, and working with him. But even if a parent were eager and willing to demonstrate that sort of direct love to his children today, the opportunities are diminished. What with school and Little League and piano lessons and, of course, the inevitable television programs, a day seems to offer just enough time for a good-night kiss.

Topical Considerations

1. According to Winn, in what specific ways does television destroy "the special quality that distinguishes one family from another" (paragraph 9)? What family behavior is dangerously "prevented"?

2. How does television threaten family unity and closeness, according to the author?

3. What does Winn say about the quality of television programs?

4. In what specific ways does television affect children's play and creativity?

5. What evidence does Winn present to support her claim that TV has endangered family rituals?

6. How can television adversely affect the way people—including children—relate to one another?

7. In paragraph 41, Irving Howe is quoted as saying that the mass media, including television, "must provide amusement without insight and pleasure without disturbance." Do you think this is a fair assess-

ment of the nature of network television? Do you think this is what the general American public wants? What it needs? What about public television? How would Howe assess PBS programs?

Rhetorical Considerations

1. In what ways is television a "plug-in drug"? Is this a fair metaphor?

2. Winn says that people today are so dominated by the television set "that they cannot see how the medium is involved in whatever problems they might be having" (paragraph 11). How well does she illustrate that claim?

3. What would you say Winn's attitude is toward the American TV public? Cite some passages in her essay to support your statement.

4. In paragraph 44, Winn speaks of love of children. Do you think she oversimplifies love to material display? Does she offer much evidence? Need she?

5. Evaluate the kind and amount of evidence Winn summons to support her thesis in the essay. Is some of it excessive? Is it lacking in other places?

Writing Assignments

1. Did television play a prominent role in your home? Did you and your family watch it regularly as you were growing up? If so, try to evaluate any negative effects television had on your family and your upbringing. Consider how it might have functioned as a babysitter for you and how it affected communication between family members, rituals, and creativity.

2. Winn calls television a "plug-in drug." The use of a drug often leads to some effort to shake the habit. Write a paper in which you explore the difficulties some people you know would have in adjusting to life without television. Consider the rigid patterns that might have evolved over the years with television.

3. Imagine what life might be like twenty years from now, given the rapid development and spread of television across America. Consider that television might someday have hundreds of channels broadcasting twenty-four hours a day. Create a scenario of the total-television family of the future, extrapolating from some of Winn's observations.

4. In paragraph 13, Winn refers to the plight of a mother who tries to "control television" in her home. Write this woman a letter in which you suggest how she can creatively reorganize her family's day around activities other than television—and still get things done.

Our Need For a "Dynasty"

Mark Muro

According to the Nielsen Ratings, the most popular television series for the 1982 and 1983 seasons was ABC's prime-time soap opera, "Dynasty." For millions of viewers, this program has become a way of life on Wednesday nights. This slick melodrama centers on the flashy and tumultuous lives of oil tycoon Blake Carrington, his regal and loving wife Krystle, their sexy and spoiled daughter Fallon, their malevolent but handsome son Adam, and Blake's viperous and vengeful ex-wife, Alexis. What seems to make "Dynasty" so successful is that it has out-soaped all the rest in scandal, sexiness, violence, conflict, adultery, opulence, and decadence. It is the most complete of soap's seedy fantasies. But there is more—some perverse fun, in fact. As journalist Mark Muro says in this clever and lively analysis, what makes "Dynasty" work so well, despite its high sleaziness, is that it spells out our darkest views of the rich—and "warms our middle-class hearts."

The populace gets fidgety at about 9:30 on Wednesday nights. 1
Diners ask for checks. Shoppers head home. Dates end. 2

"It's time," says the thick inner whisper of America. "It's time." 3

And so it is that the nation crouches at its televisions to watch "Dy- 4
nasty," the 10 P.M. ABC soap opera that outsleazed its progenitor "Dallas" and once, in November, snatched away the hand of that fickle mistress, America's Average Prime Time Viewer. Like a scruffy junkyard mongrel, "Dynasty" has clawed its way upward in its third season.

You don't have to be Aaron Spelling to figure out why. 5

For one thing, there are the characters. 6

Stereotypes all, you snicker at the professional half-conviction with 7
which they are played.

At the center of the *tableau* stands oil tycoon and proud head of the 8
family, Blake Carrington. Played by John Forsythe, formerly the star of "Bachelor Father" and the voice behind "Charlie" of "Charlie's Angels," he's a real man, a gruff capitalist who plays hardball, whether he's barking orders in his company's dog-eat-dog struggle with its competitor Colbyco or beating up his son Steve's homosexual lover. Beset from all sides, he hangs tough, a Reaganesque hero who defends family, business, and, dare he say it, America from decline. He calls his wife "Pretty Lady." He always looks like a boiler with too much steam in it. But not even his billions can help his fake-looking blue-gray hair.

Arranged around this *paterfamilias* are the women: Linda Evans as 9
Krystle, the loyal wife behind the great man; Pamela Sue Martin as Fallon, the spoiled daughter; and, of course, the viperous Alexis, Carrington's tempestuous ex, played by Joan Collins.

While the lovely Krystle's earnest sweetness is insufferable—she floats 10 around biting her fingers, getting all weepy, and begging the men to be nice when things get nasty—Alexis' slinking connivance and jealous tantrums keep things satisfactorily decadent. Alexis is behind most of the trouble, and one appreciates the way she goads pure Krystle into hissing cat fights. With her tart's sultriness and English accent (which sounds fake, even though she really is British), she personifies all that is "Dynasty." So no one's confused, good Krystle is a stereoscopic, white-gowned blonde in the Bo Derek mode (Evans actually was married to Bo's husband John Derek), while dark Alexis, who looks like a cut-rate Elizabeth Taylor, wears an astonishing wardrobe in, yup, black. Because she's evil.

Such is the symbolism of "Dynasty."   11

With the addition of a new character this season—Blake and Alexis'   12
smarmy long-lost son Adam, played by Gordon Thomson—the show has taken a distinct turn for the creepy. Adam Carrington gives all appearances of surpassing even Alexis' wanton malignance. Who else would think of liquidating a rival by redecorating his office with poisonous paint?

The cast is rounded out by Jeff Colby, Fallon's husband, played by   13
John James with plenty of overacted grimaces and hand motions. He's "Dynasty's" closest thing to a good guy. He's a bore.

But all soap operas are about the same. So what distinguishes "Dy-   14
nasty" from "Dallas" and "Falcon Crest" and all the others? Why do millions of viewers drop everything at the strains of Bill Conti's pompous theme song?

The operative fact in "Dynasty's" success may well be America's tend-   15
ency to go just a little too far. This is a nation of overkill. Maybe it's our uncouth youth as a people, or maybe some influence of our grand geography, but we like things in extremes. When we want money or power or sex, we want, you know, *lots* of it.

Like all soap operas, "Dynasty" acts out our seediest fantasies. We call   16
it a day, tilt the Barcalounger back, and flick "Dynasty" on at midweek because we're sick and tired of the usual polite struggle to just hang in there. We want the gutter, or we want the penthouse. Nothing in between. If we can get the two in the same place, all the better.

When the economy is going to hell and most of us are just scraping   17
by, we especially enjoy hearing about the troubles of the rich. Seeing their decadence gives us a pleasant feeling of moral superiority. Seeing their family turmoil, their calamities, and their blackmailings comforts us that being king isn't all that great anyway. This is why we couldn't get enough of Claus von Bulow's trial, and why we love "Dynasty." It satisfies us to gawk at our economic betters and discover their problems.

What distinguishes "Dynasty" is the scale, the pure brazenness of it all.   18
"Dynasty" represents perfection of a kind. In keeping with the Aesthetic of Overkill, the plot is a perfectly realized hysteria of soap opera action.

Always anxious to cooperate with our lust for quick gratification, "Dynasty" goes all the way on every date.

It's as if they jammed five segments of any other soap opera into each   19
hour. Bang, bang, bang: kidnapping, bigamy, rape, financial ruin, deathbed marriages, adultery, lost sons, babies falling from roofs . . .

"Dynasty" is above; and below, criticism. It's that shameless.   20

On "Dynasty," the limousines are longer than on "Dallas," the fortunes more outrageous, the offices more imperial.   21

On "Dynasty" you get cocktails on Lear jets and phones in the Mercedes.   22

When "Dynasty" gives you a house, it gives you a house to end all   23
houses, a palace on the order of Versailles with corridors into the distance and approximately four obedient servants for every one magisterial family member.

Compared to the Carringtons, the Ewings of "Dallas" are decidedly   24
middle class.

And while "Dallas" grows ever more predictable, "Dynasty" hurtles   25
along in more and more unpredictable frenzy. While the plot twists and turns in a maniacal *delirium tremens* that can throw on the screen the bequest of Colbyco billions to Alexis or the sudden specter of incest in the briefest blink of an eye, characters constantly reveal unexpected reserves of viciousness. You can't get tired of anyone or any part of the baroque plot: There's no time. New characters like Adam Carrington; Kirby, the daughter of the Carrington mansion majordomo Joseph; and Kristle's ex, the tennis pro Mark Jennings are suddenly whisked onscreen while others, like the completely untrustable family doctor Nicholas Toscani; Blake's pouty, homosexual son Steve; and Steve's subsequent wife Sammy Jo are casually disposed of.

It makes for a dizzying, hyperactive view of human nature, one in which   26
the species comes across as very mean indeed.

In the hands of less shameless producers than Aaron Spelling and   27
Richard and Esther Shapiro, this view might be a bit of a downer, but on "Dynasty," it's not depressing at all. We love it. It refreshes us. While we're happily vindicated in our darkest views of The Rich, our metabolism stirs with the hell-bent pace of the extravagant decadence.

It warms our middle-class hearts.   28

Topical Considerations

1. Muro claims that the characters on "Dynasty" are mere stereotypes. What specific stereotypes does he find? If you have watched the program, do you agree with Muro's assessment?

2. "Dynasty" has won the status of being the most popular television series of the last two seasons. According to Muro, what is the special

attraction of this show? And what distinguishes it from other nighttime soap operas?

3. In what ways does "Dynasty" exploit typically American traits and tastes? What connection does Muro make between "Dynasty's" success and the American economy?

4. " 'Dynasty' is above, and below, criticism. It's that shameless." What does Muro mean by these statements?

5. How, specifically, does "Dynasty" differ from "Dallas"?

6. Would you say Muro likes "Dynasty," dislikes it, or is simply hooked on it? Explain your answer, based on what he says in the essay.

Rhetorical Considerations

1. Comment on Muro's attitude in his comparison of "Dynasty" to "a scruffy junkyard mongrel" clawing its way "upward in its third season" (paragraph 4).

2. Based on Muro's comments and his word choices, try to define exactly his feelings toward "Dynasty" and its success. Where does he clearly state his opinions?

3. Evaluate the tone of the one-sentence paragraph 11.

4. What does "smarmy" mean (see paragraph 12)?

5. How fully does Muro support with evidence his thesis statement in paragraph 18?

6. How effectively does the concluding one-sentence paragraph summarize the thesis of this essay?

Writing Assignments

1. If you have ever watched "Dynasty," you must have formed your own opinions of the show. Do you think Muro's comments are accurate? Do you think he comes down too hard on it? not hard enough? Write out your own evaluation of "Dynasty," commenting on Muro's assessments.

2. Watch a few episodes of "Dynasty" and see if you can elaborate on the character types in the show. Are they, in fact, stereotypes? Do they have more depth and dimension than Muro gives them credit for?

3. Muro claims that "Dynasty" spells out our darkest views of the rich—that the show "warms our middle-class hearts." Write your own analysis of how the show depicts the very rich. Do you think it appeals to our middle-class desire to see the "troubles of the rich" as well as their "extravagant decadence"?

4. Muro specifically criticizes the show for mastering "the Aesthetic of Overkill" (paragraph 18). Watch a few episodes of "Dynasty"

and write a paper on such overkill. Just how does the program feed the American hunger for extremes?

5. Write a paper in which you compare and contrast "Dynasty" with other soap operas, such as "Dallas" and "Falcon Crest." What do they have in common? How do they essentially differ? Which stereotypes are portrayed? Which fantasies are addressed?

The Violence Is Fake, the Impact Is Real

Ellen Goodman

Perhaps the most common concern among critics of television is what all the violence does to children. Many studies done by private institutions and by the government conclude that children do, in fact, learn aggressive behavior from what they see on the screen, despite the disclaimers of broadcasters. The issue Ellen Goodman raises here is what TV violence fails to teach kids about the consequences of real violence. Ellen Goodman is a widely syndicated, Pulitzer Prize-winning columnist for the *Boston Globe.* She is the author of *Turning Points* (1979) and *Close to Home* (1981), collections of her columns.

I don't usually think of television executives as being modest, shy   1
and retiring. But for a decade or two, the same souls who have bragged about their success in selling products have been positively humble about their success in selling messages.

Yes indeed, they would tell advertisers, children see, children do   2
. . . do buy candy bars and cereals and toys. But no, no, they would tell parents, children see, but children don't . . . imitate mangling and mayhem.

But now the government has released another study on TV and vio-   3
lence. The predictable conclusion is that "violence on television does lead to aggressive behavior by children and teenagers who watch the programs." After analyzing 2500 studies and publications since 1970, the "overwhelming" scientific evidence is that "excessive" violence on the screen produces violence off the screen.

Somehow or other, I feel like I have been here before. By now, the   4
protestations of the networks sound like those of the cigarette manufacturers who will deny the link between cigarettes and lung disease to their (and our) last breath. By now, studies come and go, but the problem remains.

Today the average kid sits in front of the tube for 26 hours a week. The   5 kids don't begin with a love of violence. Even today, one runaway favorite in the Saturday morning line-up is about the benign "Smurfs." But eventually they learn from grown-ups.

In the incredible shrinking world of kidvid, there is no regularly scheduled program for kids on any of the three networks between the hours of 7 A.M. and 6 P.M. A full 80 percent of the programs kids watch are adult television. For those who choose adventures, the broadcasters offer endless sagas of terror, chase, murder, rescue.   6

As Peggy Charren, who has watched this scene for a long time as head of Action for Children's Television, puts it: "Broadcasters believe that the more violent the problems, the more attractive the adventure to audiences in terms of sitting there and not turning it off. The ultimate adventure is doing away with someone's life. The ultimate excitement is death."   7

The government, in its report, listed some theories about why there is this link between violence on TV and violence in kinds' behavior. One theory was that TV is a how-to lesson in aggression. Children learn "how to" hit and hurt from watching the way they learn how to count and read. Another theory is that kids who see a world full of violence accept it as normal behavior.   8

But I wonder whether violence isn't accepted because it is normalized —sanitized and packaged. We don't see violence on television in terms of pain and suffering, but in terms of excitement. In cartoons, characters are smashed with boulders, and dropped from airplanes only to get up unscathed. In adventure shows, people are killed all the time, but they are rarely "hurt."   9

As Charren put it, "There is no feeling badly about violence on television." We don't bear witness to the pain of a single gunshot wound. We don't see the broken hand and teeth that come from one blow to the jaw. We don't share the blood or the guilt, the anguish or the mourning. We don't see the labor of rebuilding a car, a window, a family.   10

Our television stars brush themselves off and return same time, same station, next week without a single bruise. Cars are replaced. The dead are carted off and forgotten.   11

In Japan, I am told there is an unwritten rule that if you show violence on television, you show the result of that violence. Such a program is, I am sure, much more disturbing. But maybe it should be. Maybe that's what's missing.   12

In the real world, people repress aggression because they know the consequences. But on television, there are no consequences. In the end kids may be less affected by the presence of violence than by the absence of pain. They learn that violence is okay. That nobody gets hurt.   13

So, if the broadcasters refuse to curb their profitable adventures in hurting, their national contribution to violence, then let them add something to the mix: equal time for truth and consequences.   14

Topical Considerations

1. What is Goodman's major criticism of television broadcasters? How are they like cigarette manufacturers?

2. What are some of the problems with network television for children?

3. What is Goodman's central complaint about the way violence is portrayed on television? Is it just that it is too graphic?

4. How does the Japanese treatment of television violence differ from the American treatment?

5. What suggestions does Ellen Goodman make about portrayal of violence on television? Would you make the same suggestions?

Rhetorical Considerations

1. Where is the thesis statement in this essay? Would you have placed it elsewhere? Explain your answer.

2. Explain Goodman's use of the word "sanitized" in describing television violence in paragraph 9. What does the word mean, and how good a choice is it?

3. What is the rhetorical effect of the parallel sentence structures in paragraph 10?

4. How does paragraph 12 fit Goodman's thesis?

Writing Assignments

1. Do you agree with Goodman's claim that pain and suffering are missing from the television experience with violence? Using your own knowledge of television, write a paper in which you answer this question. You may want to watch a few shows in which violence and its consequences are dramatized.

2. Watch a typical Saturday morning cartoon show and make note of the way violence is handled. Then write a paper in which you analyze just how violence is depicted and how it might be interpreted by children. Is violence made to seem normal? Are people hurt? Are children left feeling that violence is okay?

3. Have you ever seen a television program—or a made-for-TV movie—in which both the "truth and consequences" of violence were fairly portrayed? If so, write a paper in which you praise the accuracy of the portrayal of the pain and suffering that follow violence.

Packaged News

Brendan Boyd

And now for the news—or, more exactly, the non-news. We end this section on a satirical upbeat. Have you ever wondered how television newscasters always manage to fill their half-hour slots on days when nothing newsworthy has happened? And have you ever noticed how the same kinds of stories—the same news *packages*— are aired from network to network? Sure you have, and so has writer Brendan Boyd, who gives us some very funny insights into the seven o'clock news. Boyd is a professional writer who has written comic strips, rock music reviews, and two books—*The Great American Baseball Card* (1973) and *And a Player to Be Named Later* (1982). He is currently a book editor and the author of the syndicated column "Investor's Notebook."

Good evening, ladies and gentlemen. Welcome to *The Seven o'Clock News.*   1
    Nothing happened today.
    Goodnight.

That's the way television *should* handle the four out of seven days every week when current events go into suspended animation. But don't hang by your rabbit ears waiting for it to happen. Because the television news, contrary to FCC disclaimers, is not really the news at all. It's just another way for the networks to sell Efferdent, and for corporate America to unwind after its collective tough day at the office.

Thus, on those not-so-infrequent days when the Pope has not been 2 shot, Afghanistan has not been invaded, and no member of the British Royal Family has needlessly disgraced himself, the networks still carry out their contractual obligation, if not necessarily their duty, to report the news, even though there's no news to report. They dust off their file of canned headlines, change a few names, and settle in to perpetuate the requisite delusion that something really did happen today.

Of course, the day will come when absolutely nothing happens. And 3 on that day we'll all be subjected to the ultimate in televised monotony: *The Seven o'Clock News with Absolutely Nothing New About It Whatsoever.* As always, the events of this numbingly uneventful day will be sorted into the usual predictable categories.

World Update

This first class of story is intended to make viewers feel that because 4 an event has limitless scale it also has limitless importance. Television newscasters like to distract us from the vacuousness of their stories by impressing us with the amount of ground these stories cover.

Soviet Leader Brezhnev Rumored Ill. This is the perfect lead item for a slow 5 news day. It's both potentially earthshaking and completely irrefutable.

363

It replaces that perennial favorite, *Mao Rumored Dead,* which passed into blessed obsolescence several years back when the Chinese leader actually died. If Brezhnev has not been looking particularly feeble lately, some other Iron Curtain codger's name may safely be substituted. And in a pinch, a more generalized notion about totalitarians will suffice—say, *Kremlin Shake-up Hinted.*

846 Perish in Indian Train Mishap. Or *267 Killed as Mexican Bus Plunges*   6
off Mountain. Or *536 Die in Burmese Ferry Crash.* In all Third World disasters the volume of the victimization is meant to compensate for our physical and emotional distance from the event. But no matter how many Africans starve to death in any given famine, television doesn't really consider it news unless Frank Sinatra didn't punch a photographer that day. The New York tabloids are rumored to use a formula in determining space allocations for such stories. *800 Dead in Bolivian Earthquake,* for example, is said to equal *6 Felled by Ptomaine at Staten Island Clambake.*

Troops Mass Along Nepalese Border. Troops are always massing some-   7
where. That's what troops do. And their massing is always supposed to mean something ominous, although usually it doesn't. Notice that we never see a follow-up story about troops *disbanding* along the Nepalese border.

SALT Talks Winding Down. For ten years the only thing we knew about   8
the SALT talks was that they were about to reopen. Now that we've finally figured out what the SALT talks are supposed to be, they seem always to be winding down. To establish the proper tedious mood, this story should be followed by one of the following diplomatic grace notes: *NATO Maneuvers Begin. Rumblings in SEATO.* Or *Bilateral Trade Agreements Signal New Era in U.S.-New Zealand Friendship.*

Christian Democrats Score Gains in Belgium. There are 627 political parties   9
in Europe. All but nine have the word Christian or Democrat in their names. And they're always scoring gains.

U.N. General Assembly Convenes. This is a portentous occurrence which   10
everyone in the world thinks he or she should care about, but which nobody actually does.

U.S.-Cuba Thaw Seen Possible. This is the obligatory hopeful note in   11
East-West relations. It alternates with pictorial essays of visiting American plumbers teaching mainland Chinese apprentices how to steam-clean a grease trap.

Cyprus After Makarios. Another in the always popular series, "Incredibly   12
Shallow Profiles of Enigmatic Dictators." A personal favorite has always been *Souvanna Phouma, Cambodia's Neutralist Playboy,* although I must admit a lingering fondness for the now obsolete *Ethiopian Ruler Haile Selassie Marks 87th Birthday by Buying New Summerweight Uniform.*

Pope Urges World Leaders to Seek Peace. But notice he never says exactly   13
how.

National Update

The second class of story is intended to make viewers feel that because   14
something is happening *near* them it is somehow relevant *to* them. And
let's face it, there is something more compelling about even the most banal
range of events if the boredom they engender has a distinctly local flavor.

Former Senator Eugene McCarthy Mulling Third Party Try. Ah, the sixties.   15
They provide the networks with an endless source of thirty-second
filmclips on how Joan Baez has mellowed, Jane Fonda hasn't, and Dick
Gregory remains the world's skinniest nudge.

Conspiracy Theorists Hint New Oswald Evidence. Mention of President   16
Kennedy's assassin is frequently linked in a two-cushion shot with news
that there are *Fresh Indications James Earl Ray Acted Alone in King Killing.*

47 Percent Favor Easing of Marijuana Laws. And the other 53 percent are   17
too stoned to care. Polls are a favorite ploy for slow news days. Who, after
all, can fail to attach at least marginal significance to a finding such as "72
percent of Americans believe that asparagus turns urine green, whereas
a surprising 38 percent feel that getting in an eight-item supermarket
express line with nine items should be punishable by death."

Kennedy Family Marks Anniversary of First Congressional Victory. Every day   18
of the year is some sort of anniversary for the Kennedys. No anchorman
worth his capped teeth would let one slide by without paying perfunctory
homage to "three decades of heartbreak."

Switch to Metric System Poses Problems. Or, "Is Celsius a Communist plot   19
to bore us to death?"

Ex-Nixon Crony Robert Vesco Linked to New Illegalities. Just as every corpo-   20
ration in the United States is destined to be bought by ITT, every white-
collar crime committed in the free world during the past fifteen years will
eventually be linked to Robert Vesco.

Parents Unite to Fight Pornography in School Libraries. No doubt they're up   21
in arms against *Huckleberry Finn,* the underwear section of the Sears catalog, and the Manhattan Yellow Pages.

Business and Finance

The third class of story is meant to appeal to *the* primal interest of   22
every potential viewer—money. Economics is the ultimate mystery. And
television broadcasters do nothing to allay our bewilderment with their
nightly recalculations of our shrinking worth.

Housing Starts Decline 23 Percent. Housing starts, domestic car sales, and   23
American exports have declined every month for the past twenty years.
How far down, pray tell, is down?

Prime Rate Rises ¼ Percent. All together now, class, what is the prime   24
rate? That's right. It's the rate the nation's banks charge their most
credit-worthy customers. And why did the Dow Jones Industrial Average
go down yesterday? That's right. Profit taking. And why is it going up

today? That's right. Bargain hunting. One of the more comforting characteristics of television news is that, having told us any salient fact about
a given situation, it can safely be counted on to tell us that fact, and only
that fact, over and over again.

Human Interest, Human Horror
Television newscasters have always depended on the misfortune of   25
strangers. These stories are meant to appeal to the kind of people who
slow down on the highway to get a good look at a car wreck. That is to
say—all of us.

Cancer Linked to Banana Daiquiris. This one comes from television   26
news's extensive "Life Causes Death" file.

Detroit Man Goes Berserk, Turns Rifle on Crowd. He was unquestionably a   27
quiet, neat, well-mannered man whom neighbors say would be the last
person you'd ever expect to do such a thing.

National Guard, Boy Scouts Scour Woods for Missing Toddler. Aside to Gloria   28
Steinem: Why aren't the Girl Scouts ever called out on such occasions?

Sidelights
Plus, if time permits (and unfortunately it always seems to) we can   29
count on a quick hopscotching of headlines drawn from all of the preceding categories. These stories are too important sounding to ignore but
too familiar to devote more than thirty seconds to.

G.M. Recalls Every Car It Made Last Year
New Bomber Hits Cost Overruns
Guam Accelerates Drive for Statehood
Teamster Insurgents Press Leadership for Reforms
All-Volunteer Army Seen Foundering
Recluse Found Starved to Death With $3 Million Stuffed in Mattress
Postal Service to Seek Rate Increases
First Thompsons Gazelle in 27 Years Born in Captivity
Seven Tie for First-Round Lead in Greater Greensboro Open

Parting Inspirational Feature
This final story is meant to send the now ossified viewers away either   30
laughing, shaking their heads, or feeling grateful that none of the awful
things that happened that day happened to them.

National's Oldest Living Man Observes 116th Birthday. Every slow news day   31
can use an uplifting senior citizen feature to top it off. There are only
three possibilities here. The first involves either a visit to a rest home by
a third-tier celebrity like Corbett Monica or Deborah Raffin, or a mass
golden-ager outing to some heinously inappropriate setting (*150 Elders
Enjoy Day at New Jersey Drag Speedway*). The second is a courage-in-the-
face-of-adversity story such as *Despite Beatings, Blindness, Bankruptcy, Wid-*

owed Iron Lung Inhabitant Counts Blessings. (I demand a recount.) The third, and most popular alternative, chronicles a birthday party for a senior citizen who, having achieved a particularly ill-advised longevity, is then required to state his prescription for long life. This recipe usually consists of equal parts smoking, drinking, and womanizing. But it makes no mention whatsoever of watching the seven o'clock news.

Topical Considerations

1. Boyd says in his opening paragraph that "television news, contrary to FCC disclaimers, is not really news at all." How does Boyd mean such a claim? What do network news programs report instead?

2. According to Boyd, in what specific ways do news programs give more entertainment than news? In what ways are network news shows "packaged"?

3. In paragraph 7, Boyd says that we always hear about somebody's troops amassing on somebody else's border, but "we never see a follow-up story about troops *disbanding.*" What exactly is Boyd's point here? Is he saying that we are rarely told the good news of the day? or that this ominous kind of reporting is a subtle way of keeping us tuned in day after day? or that news programs don't have in their files "canned headlines" about troops disbanding?

4. Beneath almost all of Boyd's satirical jabs, he is making some serious, critical statements about news broadcasting. Select a few of his headlines and determine his more serious criticisms.

5. How does TV news try to appeal to the viewer's "primal interest" in money? in the viewer's taste for horror?

Rhetorical Considerations

1. How accurate are Boyd's news story categories? How well do they organize his essay?

2. Evaluate the satirical effect of paragraph 6? What is the brunt of Boyd's humor here?

3. What is the message in Boyd's final sentence, and how does it summarize his overall thesis?

Writing Assignments

1. Do you think network news programs are "no-news" packages? Write a paper in which you express your own views about TV news programs. (Do you think matters would be different if network news shows were expanded to a full hour each night?)

2. Watch the news for the next several nights and test Boyd's package of news categories. How well do they conform to the organization of the programs?

3. Local news can be considered packaged as well. Write a parody—in the spirit of Brendan Boyd—of local news programs, giving categories such as world update, national update, state and local news, sports, weather, human interest, the daily crime log, and so on. Structure your paper according to these categories and provide canned headlines.

4. If you watch one network news program more than others—or exclusively—try to assess your preference. Does it have anything to do with the way the news is packaged, or with the personalities of those who are giving the news? Just how important is the personality factor in network news competition?

5. Attempt to write a script for a typical news program. Make up typical headlines and stories and attempt to capture the reporting styles you see on nightly news programs. (Try to do a parody of TV broadcast news, if possible.)

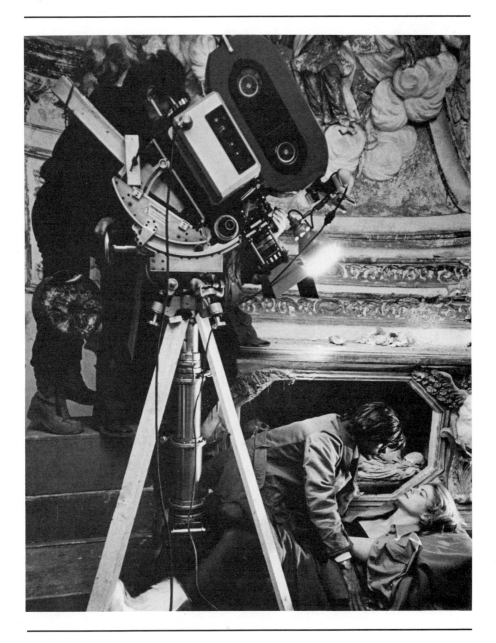

The Art of Moving Pictures: Man, Superman, and Myth

Bruno Bettelheim

The moving picture is "the authentic American art of our time," writes world-famous child psychologist and educator Bruno Bettelheim. It is the source of our cultural heroes, our ideals, and the myths of our past and future. And because the moving picture reaches so many people, it has the potential of achieving what all great art does—binding diversified segments of our society together in a high aesthetic experience. Citing such classics as *Star Wars, Superman, Patton,* and *2001,* Bettelheim talks about some of the heroes, myths, and aesthetic experiences movies have created. Dr. Bettelheim is the Distinguished Professor Emeritus of Education, Psychology and Psychiatry at the University of Chicago. Among his best-known books are *Love Is Not Enough* (1950), *The Informed Heart* (1960), *Children of the Dream* (1969), and *The Uses of Enchantment* (1976).

1   Whether we like it or not—and many may disagree with my thesis because painting, or music, or some other art is more important to them —the art of the moving image is the only art truly of our time, whether it is in the form of the film or television. The moving picture is our universal art, which comprises all others, literature and acting, stage design and music, dance and the beauty of nature, and, most of all, the use of light and of color.

2   It is always about us, because the medium is truly part of the message and the medium of the moving image is uniquely modern. Everybody can understand it, as everyone once understood religious art in church. And as people used to go to church on Sundays (and still do), so the majority today go to the movies on weekends. But while in the past most went to church only on some days, now everybody watches moving images every day.

3   All age groups watch moving pictures, and they watch them for many more hours than people have ever spent in churches. Children and adults watch them separately or together; in many ways and for many people, it is the only experience common to parents and children. It is the only art today that appeals to all social and economic classes, in short, that appeals to everybody, as did religious art in times past. The moving picture is thus by far the most popular art of our time, and it is also the most authentically American of arts.

4   When I speak here of the moving picture as the authentic American art of our time, I do not think of art with a capital *A,* nor of "high" art. Putting art on a pedestal robs it of its vitality. When the great medieval and Renaissance cathedrals were erected, and decorated outside and

in with art, these were popular works, that meant something to every-body.

Some were great works of art, others not, but every piece was signifi- 5 cant and all took pride in each of them. Some gain their spiritual experi- ence from the masterpiece, but many more gain it from the mediocre works that express the same vision as the masterpiece but in a more accessible form. This is as true for church music or the church itself as for paintings and sculptures. This diversity of art objects achieves a unity, and differences in quality are important, provided they all represent, each in its own way, the overarching vision and experience of a larger, impor- tant cosmos. Such a vision confers meaning and dignity on our existence, and is what forms the essence of art.

So among the worst detriments to the healthy development of the art 6 of the moving image are efforts by aesthetes and critics to isolate the art of film from popular movies and television. Nothing could be more con- trary to the true spirit of art. Whenever art was vital, it was always equally popular with the ordinary man and the most refined person. Had Greek drama and comedy meant nothing to most citizens, the majority of the population would not have sat all day long entranced on hard stone slabs, watching the events on the stage; nor would the entire population have conferred prizes on the winning dramatist. The medieval pageants and mystery plays out of which modern drama grew were popular entertain- ments, as were the plays of Shakespeare. Michelangelo's David stood at the most public place in Florence, embodying the people's vision that tyranny must be overthrown, while it also related to their religious vision, as it represented the myth of David and Goliath. Everybody admired the statue; it was simultaneously popular and great art, but one did not think of it in such disparate terms. Neither should we. To live well we need both: visions that lift us up, and entertainment that is down to earth, provided both art and entertainment, each in its different form and way, are embodiments of the same visions of man. If art does not speak to all of us, common men and elites alike, it fails to address itself to that true humanity that is common to all of us. A different art for the elites and another one for average man tears society apart; it offends what we most need: visions that bind us together in common experiences that make life worth living.

When I speak of an affirmation of man, I do not mean the presentation 7 of fake images of life as wonderfully pleasant. Life is best celebrated in the form of a battle against its inequities, of struggles, of dignity in defeat, of the greatness of discovering oneself and the other.

Quite a few moving pictures have conveyed such visions. In *Kagemusha*, 8 the great beauty of the historical costumes, the cloak-and-dagger story with its beguiling Oriental settings, the stately proceedings, the pag- eantry of marching and fighting armies, the magnificent rendering of nature, the consummate acting—all these entrance us and convince us of the correctness of the vision here: the greatness of the most ordinary of men. The hero, a petty thief who turns impostor, grows before our eyes into greatness, although it costs him his life. The story takes place in sixteenth-century Japan, but the hero is of all times and places: he accepts a destiny into which he is projected by chance and turns a false existence into a real one. At the end, only because he wants to be true to his new self, he sacrifices his life and thus achieves the acme of suffering and human greatness. Nobody wants him to do so. Nobody but he will ever know that he did it. Nobody but the audience observes it. He does it only for himself; it has no consequences whatsoever for anybody or anything else. He does it out of conviction; that is his greatness. Life that permits the lowest of men to achieve such dignity is life worth living, even if in the end it defeats him, as it will defeat all who are mortal.

Two other films, very different, render parallel visions that celebrate 9 life, a celebration in which we, as viewers, vicariously participate although we are saddened by the hero's defeat. The first was known in the United States by its English name, *The Last Laugh*, although its original title, *The Last Man*, was more appropriate. It is the story of the doorman of a hotel who is demoted to cleaning washrooms. The other movie is *Patton*. In one of these films the hero stands on the lowest rung of society and existence; in the other, he is on society's highest level. In both pictures we are led to admire a man's struggle to discover who he really is, for, in doing so, he achieves tragic greatness. These three films, as do many others, affirm man and life, and so inspire in us visions that can sustain us.

My choice of these three films out of many is arbitrary. What I want 10 to illustrate is their celebration of life in forms appropriate to an age in which self-discovery may exact the highest possible price. Only through incorporating such visions can we achieve satisfaction with our own life, defeat and transcend existential despair.

What our society suffers from most today is the absence of consensus 11 about what it and life in it ought to be. Such consensus cannot be gained from society's present stage, or from fantasies about what it ought to be. For that the present is too close and too diversified, and the future too uncertain, to make believable claims about it. A consensus in the present hence can be achieved only through a shared understanding of the past, as Homer's epics informed those who lived centuries later what it meant to be Greek, and by what images and ideals they were to live their lives and organize their societies.

Most societies derive consensus from a long history, a language all 12 their own, a common religion, common ancestry. The myths by which they live are based on all of these. But the United States is a country of immigrants, coming from a great variety of nations. Lately, it has been emphasized that an asocial, narcissistic personality has become characteristic of Americans, and that it is this type of personality that makes for the malaise, because it prevents us from achieving a consensus that would counteract a tendency to withdraw into private worlds. In his study of narcissism, Christopher Lasch says that modern man, "tortured by self-consciousness, turns to new cults and therapies not to free himself of his personal obsessions but to find meaning and purpose in life, to find something to live for." There is widespread distress because national morale has declined, and we have lost an earlier sense of national vision and purpose.

Contrary to rigid religions or political beliefs, as are found in totalitar-   13
ian societies, our culture is one of great individual differences, at least in principle and in theory. But this leads to disunity, even chaos. Americans believe in the value of diversity, but just because ours is a society based on individual diversity, it needs consensus about some overarching ideas more than societies based on the uniform origin of their citizens. Hence, if we are to have consensus, it must be based on a myth—a vision—about a common experience, a conquest that made us Americans, as the myth about the conquest of Troy formed the Greeks. Only a common myth can offer relief from the fear that life is without meaning or purpose. Myths permit us to examine our place in the world by comparing it to a shared idea. Myths are shared fantasies that form the tie that binds the individual to other members of his group. Such myths help to ward off feelings of isolation, guilt, anxiety, and purposelessness—in short, they combat isolation and anomie.

We used to have a myth that bound us together; in *The American Adam*,   14
R. W. B. Lewis summarizes the myth by which Americans used to live:

> God decided to give man another chance by opening up
> a new world across the sea. Practically vacant, this glori-
> ous land had almost inexhaustible natural resources.
> Many people came to this new world. They were people
> of special energy, self-reliance, intuitive intelligence, and
> purity of heart. . . . This nation's special mission in the
> world would be to serve as the moral guide for all other
> nations.

The movies used to transmit this myth, particularly the westerns,   15
which presented the challenge of bringing civilization to places where before there was none. The same movies also suggested the danger of that chaos; the wagon train symbolized the community men must form on such a perilous journey into the untamed wilderness, which in turn became a symbol for all that is untamed within ourselves. Thus the western gave us a vision of the need for cooperation and civilization, because without it man would perish. Another symbol often used in these westerns was the railroad, which formed the link between wilderness and civilization. The railroad was the symbol of man's role as civilizer.

Robert Warshow delineates in *The Immediate Experience* how the hero of   16
the western—the gunfighter—symbolizes man's potential: to become
either an outlaw or a sheriff. In the latter role, the gunfighter was the hero
of the past, and his opening of the West was our mythos, our equivalent
of the Trojan War. Like all such heroes, the sheriff experienced victories
and defeats, but, through these experiences, he grew wiser and learned
to accept the limitations that civilization imposes.

This was a wonderful vision of man—or the United States—in the New   17
World; it was a myth by which one could live and grow, and it served as
a consensus about what it meant to be an American. But although most
of us continue to enjoy this myth, by now it has lost most of its vitality.
We have become too aware of the destruction of nature and of the
American Indian—part of the reality of opening the West—to be able to
savor this myth fully; and, just as important, it is based on an open
frontier that no longer exists. But the nostalgic infatuation with the western suggests how much we are in need of a myth about the past that
cannot be invalidated by the realities of today. We want to share a vision,
one that would enlighten us about what it means to be an American today,
so that we can be proud not only of our heritage but also of the world
we are building together.

Unfortunately, we have no such myth, nor, by extension, any that   18
reflects what is involved in growing up. The child, like the society, needs
such myths to provide him with ideas of what difficulties are involved in
maturation. Fairy tales used to fill this need, and they would still do so,
if we would take them seriously. But sugar-sweet movies of the Disney
variety fail to take seriously the world of the child—the immense problems with which the child has to struggle as he grows up, to make himself
free from the bonds that tie him to his parents, and to test his own
strength. Instead of helping the child, who wants to understand the
difficulties ahead, these shows talk down to him, insult his intelligence,
and lower his aspirations.

While most of the popular shows for children fall short of what the   19
child needs most, others at least provide him with some of the fantasies
that relieve pressing anxieties, and this is the reason for their popularity.
Superman, Wonder Woman, and the Bionic Woman stimulate the child's
fantasies about being strong and invulnerable, and this offers some relief
from being overwhelmed by the powerful adults who control his existence. The Incredible Hulk affords a confrontation with destructive
anger. Watching the Hulk on one of his rampages permits a vicarious
experience of anger without having to feel guilty about it or anxious
about the consequences, because the Hulk attacks only bad people. As
food for fantasies that offer temporary relief, such shows have a certain
value, but they do not provide material leading to higher integration, as
myths do.

Science-fiction movies can serve as myths about the future and thus   20 give us some assurance about it. Whether the film is *2001* or *Star Wars*, such movies tell about progress that will expand man's powers and his experiences beyond anything now believed possible, while they assure us that all these advances will not obliterate man or life as we now know it. Thus one great anxiety about the future—that it will have no place for us as we now are—is allayed by such myths. They also promise that even in the most distant future, and despite the progress that will have occurred in the material world, man's basic concerns will be the same, and the struggle of good against evil—the central moral problem of our time —will not have lost its importance.

Past and future are the lasting dimensions of our lives; the present is   21
but a fleeting moment. So these visions about the future also contain our past; in *Star Wars*, battles are fought around issues that also motivated man in the past. There is good reason that Yoda appears in George Lucas's film: he is but a reincarnation of the teddy bear of infancy, to which we turn for solace; and the Jedi Knight is the wise old man, or the helpful animal, of the fairy tale, the promise from our distant past that we shall be able to rise to meet the most difficult tasks life can present us with. Thus, any vision about the future is really based on visions of the past, because that is all we can know for certain.

As our religious myths about the future never went beyond Judgment   22
Day, so our modern myths about the future cannot go beyond the search for life's deeper meaning. The reason is that only as long as the choice between good and evil remains man's paramount moral problem does life retain that special dignity that derives from our ability to choose between the two. A world in which this conflict has been permanently resolved eliminates man as we know him. It might be a universe peopled by angels, but it has no place for man.

What Americans need most is a consensus that includes the idea of   23
individual freedom, as well as acceptance of the plurality of ethnic backgrounds and religious beliefs inherent in the population. Such consensus must rest on convictions about moral values and the validity of overarching ideas. Art can do this because a basic ingredient of the aesthetic experience is that it binds together diverse elements. But only the ruling art of a period is apt to provide such unity: for the Greeks, it was classical art; for the British, Elizabethan art; for the many petty German states, it was their classical art. Today, for the United States, it has to be the moving picture, the central art of our time, because no other art experience is so open and accessible to everyone.

The moving picture is a visual art, based on sight. Speaking to our   24
vision, it ought to provide us with the visions enabling us to live the good life; it ought to give us insight into ourselves. About a hundred years ago, Tolstoy wrote, "Art is a human activity having for its purpose the transmission to others of the highest and best feelings to which men have

risen." Later, Robert Frost defined poetry as "beginning in delight and ending in wisdom." Thus it might be said that the state of the art of the moving image can be assessed by the degree to which it meets the myth-opoetic task of giving us myths suitable to live by in our time—visions that transmit to us the highest and best feelings to which men have risen—and by how well the moving images give us that delight which leads to wisdom. Let us hope that the art of the moving image, this most authentic American art, will soon meet the challenge of becoming truly the great art of our age.

Topical Considerations

1. According to Bettelheim, what is the distinction between popular art and "art with a capital *A*"? Can movies ever achieve the status of "great art"? How?

2. In paragraphs 8 and 9, Bettelheim discusses three movies briefly. What "visions" do these have in common?

3. Why does America suffer from a low morale, according to the author? How can myths help?

4. What is Bettelheim's criticism of "movies of the Disney variety" (paragraph 18)? Do you agree with him? Explain your reasons.

5. Why were the "western myths" so valuable to our American culture? What has happened to these myths?

6. Bettelheim says that science fiction visions about the future "also contain our past" (paragraph 21). He cites *Star Wars* as an example. Are these future–past visions found in other science fiction movies? What about *E.T.*? or *Return of the Jedi*? or *Star Trek: The Movie*? or its sequel, *The Wrath of Khan*? or any other recent science fiction films?

7. Can you think of any science fiction movies that do not create a positive myth of the future?

8. In paragraph 23, Bettelheim writes: "What Americans need most is a consensus that includes the idea of individual freedom, as well as acceptance of the plurality of ethnic backgrounds and religious beliefs inherent in the population." He goes on to say that the art of moving pictures can achieve this consensus. Do you think he is overstating the potential of moving pictures?

Rhetorical Considerations

1. What is Bettelheim's purpose, in paragraphs 2 and 3, in drawing a parallel between people going to church and people going to movies?

2. What is the topic sentence of paragraph 6? How does the author's use of examples verify that sentence?

3. If you did not know that Bruno Bettelheim was a child psychologist, could you have guessed from his writing? Consider his statements about psychology and his vocabulary. Do you find any places where he seems to lapse into professional jargon?

Writing Assignments

1. Bettelheim talks about how superheroic characters such as Superman, Wonder Woman, the Bionic Woman, and the Incredible Hulk stimulate the fantasies of children. If you are a fan of these mythic characters, write a paper in which you analyze the kinds of fantasies they project.

2. Write a paper in which you attempt to determine some of the common characteristics shared by two or more motion picture heroes, such as Superman, Rocky, James Bond, and any John Wayne roles. (See if you can come up with ten common characteristics.)

3. Write a paper in which you attempt to determine some of the common characteristics shared by two or more moving picture heroines such as Wonder Woman, the Bionic Woman, Princess Leia (the *Star Wars* trilogy), and Charlie's Angels. (See if you can come up with ten common characteristics.)

4. Bettelheim says: "If art does not speak to all of us, common men and elites alike, it fails to address itself to that true humanity that is common to all of us" (paragraph 6). Can you think of a movie that appeals exclusively to "the elites" and one that appeals exclusively to "common men"? If so, in a paper try to determine just why they are mutually exclusive. How do they each fail to "bind us together in common experiences that make life worth living" (paragraph 6)?

5. Select a single movie that you think exemplifies the best in moving picture art according to the criteria spelled out by Bettelheim. In a paper, explain your choice, telling why you think the movie has achieved the status of "great art."

The Motion Picture Production Code of 1930

In the preceding essay, Bruno Bettelheim observed that moving pictures have the power of influencing cultural and moral attitudes, and we often hear concerns expressed about the effects of television violence on children. What about the moral effects of movies, in which violence and sex is so often depicted with graphic excess? Does repeated exposure to movies with high levels of violence and sex have psychologically and socially damaging effects on people? What these questions raise, of course, is the issue of censorship and its place in a free democratic society. During the 1920s, film producers and distributors decided that, rather than face the grim possibility of federal regulation, they would produce their own set of guidelines for what to put on the screen. That decision resulted in the 1930 Motion Picture Production Code, which spelled out for moviemakers exactly what they could and could not get away with. What is particularly interesting about the Code is its stated belief that motion pictures have the power to raise or lower the moral standards of an audience. Although violations were common in later years, the Code remained in effect until 1968, when the current rating system came into effect. The following is the original 1930 Motion Picture Production Code. It is a "time capsule" of attitudes, assumptions, and standards.

Preamble

The Motion Picture Production Code was formulated and formally 1 adopted by The Association of Motion Picture Producers Inc., (California) and The Motion Picture Association of America, Inc., (New York) in March, 1930.

Motion picture producers recognize the high trust and confidence 2 which have been placed in them by the people of the world and which have made motion pictures a universal form of entertainment.

They recognize their responsibility to the public because of this trust 3 and because entertainment and art are important influences in the life of a nation.

Hence, though regarding motion pictures primarily as entertainment 4 without any explicit purpose of teaching or propaganda, they know that the motion picture within its own field of entertainment may be directly responsible for spiritual or moral progress, for higher types of social life, and for much correct thinking.

During the rapid transition from silent to talking pictures they realized 5 the necessity and the opportunity of subscribing to a Code to govern the production of talking pictures and of reacknowledging this responsibility.

On their part, they ask from the public and from public leaders a 6 sympathetic understanding of their purposes and problems and a spirit of cooperation that will allow them the freedom and opportunity necessary to bring the motion picture to a still higher level of wholesome entertainment for all the people.

General Principles

1. No picture shall be produced which will lower the moral standards 7 of those who see it. Hence the sympathy of the audience shall never be thrown to the side of crime, wrong-doing, evil or sin.

2. Correct standards of life, subject only to the requirements of drama 8 and entertainment, shall be presented.

3. Law, natural or human, shall not be ridiculed, nor shall sympathy 9 be created for its violation.

Reasons Underlying The General Principles

I. No picture shall be produced which will lower the moral standards   10
of those who see it. Hence the sympathy of the audience should
never be thrown to the side of crime, wrong-doing, evil or sin.
This is done:

  1. When evil is made to appear attractive or alluring, and good is
made to appear unattractive.

  2. When the sympathy of the audience is thrown on the side of
crime, wrong-doing, evil, sin. The same thing is true of a film that
would throw sympathy against goodness, honor, innocence,
purity or honesty.

    Note: Sympathy with a person who sins is not the same as
sympathy with the sin or crime of which he is guilty. We may feel
sorry for the plight of the murderer or even understand the circumstances which led him to his crime. We may not feel sympathy
with the wrong which he has done.

    The presentation of evil is often essential for art or fiction or
drama. This in itself is not wrong provided:

  a. That evil is not presented alluringly. Even if later in the film
the evil is condemned or punished, it must not be allowed to
appear so attractive that the audience's emotions are drawn
to desire or approve so strongly that later the condemnation
is forgotten and only the apparent joy of the sin remembered.

  b. That throughout, the audience feels sure that evil is wrong and
good is right.

II. Correct standards of life shall, as far as possible, be presented.   11

    A wide knowledge of life and of living is made possible through
the film. When right standards are consistently presented, the motion picture exercises the most powerful influences. It builds character, develops right ideals, inculcates correct principles, and all this
in attractive story form.

    If motion pictures consistently hold up for admiration high
types of characters and present stories that will affect lives for the
better, they can become the most powerful natural force for the
improvement of mankind.

III. Law, natural or human, shall not be ridiculed, nor shall sympathy be   12
created for its violation.

    By natural law is understood the law which is written in the
hearts of all mankind, the great underlying principles of right and
justice dictated by conscience.

    By human law is understood the law written by civilized nations.

  1. The presentation of crimes against the law is often necessary for
the carrying out of the plot. But the presentation must not throw

sympathy with the crime as against the law nor with the criminal as against those who punish him.

2. The courts of the land should not be presented as unjust. This does not mean that a single court may not be represented as unjust, much less that a single court official must not be presented this way. But the court system of the country must not suffer as a result of this presentation.

Particular Applications

I. Crimes Against the Law

These shall never be presented in such a way as to throw sympathy with the crime as against law and justice or to inspire others with a desire for imitation.

1. **Murder**
   a. The technique of murder must be presented in a way that will not inspire imitation.
   b. Brutal killings are not to be presented in detail.
   c. Revenge in modern times shall not be justified.
2. **Methods of Crime** should not be explicitly presented.
   a. Theft, robbery, safe-cracking, and dynamiting of trains, mines, buildings, etc., should not be detailed in method.
   b. Arson must be subject to the same safeguards.
   c. The use of firearms should be restricted to essentials.
   d. Methods of smuggling should not be presented.
3. **The illegal drug traffic** must not be portrayed in such a way as to stimulate curiosity concerning the use of, or traffic in, such drugs; nor shall scenes be approved which show the use of illegal drugs, or their effects, in detail.
4. **The use of liquor** in American life, when not required by the plot or for proper characterization, will not be shown.

II. Sex

The sanctity of the institution of marriage and the home shall be upheld. Pictures shall not infer that low forms of sex relationship are the accepted or common thing.

1. **Adultery and Illicit Sex,** sometimes necessary plot material, must not be explicitly treated or justified, or presented attractively.
2. **Scenes of Passion**
   a. These should not be introduced except where they are definitely essential to the plot.
   b. Excessive and lustful kissing, lustful embraces, suggestive postures and gestures are not to be shown.

c. In general, passion should be treated in such manner as not to stimulate the lower and baser emotions.

3. **Seduction or Rape**
   a. These should never be more than suggested, and then only when essential for the plot. They must never be shown by explicit method.
   b. They are never the proper subject for comedy.
4. **Sex perversion** or any inference of it is forbidden.
5. **White slavery** shall not be treated.
6. **Miscegenation** (sex relationship between the white and black races) is forbidden.
7. **Sex hygiene** and venereal diseases are not proper subjects for theatrical motion pictures.
8. Scenes of **actual child birth,** in fact or in silhouette, are never to be presented.
9. **Children's sex organs** are never to be exposed.

III. Vulgarity

The treatment of low, disgusting, unpleasant, though not necessarily evil, subjects should be guided always by the dictates of good taste and a proper regard for the sensibilities of the audience.   15

IV. Obscenity

Obscenity in word, gesture, reference, song, joke, or by suggestion (even when likely to be understood only by part of the audience) is forbidden.   16

V. Profanity

Pointed profanity and every other profane or vulgar expression, however used, are forbidden.   17

No approval by the Production Code Administration shall be given to the use of words and phrases in motion pictures including, but not limited to, the following:

Alley cat (applied to a woman); bat (applied to a woman); broad (applied to a woman); Bronx cheer (the sound); chippie; cocotte; God, Lord, Jesus Christ (unless used reverently); cripes; fanny; fairy (in a vulgar sense); finger (the); fire, cries of; Gawd; goose (in a vulgar sense); "hold your hat" or "hats"; hot (applied to a woman); "in your hat"; Madam (relating to prostitution); nance; nerts; nuts (except when meaning crazy); pansy; razz-berry (the sound); slut (applied to a woman); S.O.B.; son-of-a; tart; toilet gags; tom cat (applied to a man);

traveling salesman and farmer's daughter jokes; whore; damn, hell (excepting when the use of said last two words shall be essential and required for portrayal, in proper historical context, of any scene or dialogue based upon historical fact or folklore, or for the presentation in proper literary context of a Biblical, or other religious quotation, or a quotation from a literary work **provided** that no such use shall be permitted which is intrinsically objectionable or offends good taste).

In the administration of Section V of the Production Code, the Production Code Administration may take cognizance of the fact that the following words and phrases are obviously offensive to the patrons of motion pictures in the United States and more particularly to the patrons of motion pictures in foreign countries:

Chink, Dago, Frog, Greaser, Hunkie, Kike, Nigger, Spig, Wop, Yid.

VI. Costume
1. **Complete nudity** is never permitted. This includes nudity in fact or   18
   in silhouette, or any licentious notice thereof by other characters in the pictures.
2. **Undressing scenes** should be avoided, and never used save where essential to the plot.
3. **Indecent or undue exposure** is forbidden.
4. **Dancing costumes** intended to permit undue exposure or indecent movements in the dance are forbidden.

VII. Dances
1. Dances suggesting or representing sexual actions or indecent passion   19
   are forbidden.
2. Dances which emphasize indecent movements are to be regarded as obscene.

VIII. Religion
1. No film or episode may throw **ridicule** on any religious faith.   20
2. **Ministers of religion** in their character as ministers of religion should not be used as comic characters or as villains.
3. **Ceremonies** of any definite religion should be carefully and respectfully handled.

IX. Locations
The treatment of bedrooms must be governed by good taste and   21
delicacy.

X. *National Feelings*

1. **The use of the Flag** shall be consistently respectful.   22
2. **The history,** institutions, prominent people and citizenry of all nations shall be represented fairly.

XI. *Titles*

The following titles shall not be used: 23

1. Titles which are salacious, indecent, obscene, profane or vulgar.
2. Titles which suggest or are currently associated in the public mind with material, characters or occupations unsuitable for the screen.
3. Titles which are otherwise objectionable.

XII. *Repellent Subjects*

The following subjects must be treated within the careful limits of 24 good taste:

1. **Actual hangings** or electrocutions as legal punishments for crime.
2. **Third Degree** methods.
3. **Brutality** and possible gruesomeness.
4. **Branding** of people or animals.
5. **Apparent cruelty** to children or animals.
6. **The sale of women,** or a woman selling her virtue.
7. **Surgical operations.**

Special Regulations on Crime in Motion Pictures

RESOLVED, that the Board of Directors of the Motion Picture Associ- 25 ation of America, Incorporated, hereby ratifies, approves, and confirms the interpretations of the Production Code, the practices thereunder, and the resolutions indicating and confirming such interpretations heretofore adopted by the Association of Motion Picture Producers, Incorporated, all effectuating regulations relative to the treatment of crime in motion pictures, as follows:

1. Details of crime must never be shown and care should be exercised at all times in discussing such details.
2. Action suggestive of wholesale slaughter of human beings, either by criminals, in conflict with police, or as between warring factions of criminals, or in public disorder of any kind, will not be allowed.
3. There must be no suggestion, at any time, of excessive brutality.
4. Because of the increase in the number of films in which murder is frequently committed, action showing the taking of human life, even in the mystery stories, is to be cut to the minimum. These frequent presentations of murder tend to lessen regard for the sacredness of life.
5. Suicide, as a solution of problems occurring in the development of screen drama, is to be discouraged as morally questionable and as

bad theatre—unless absolutely necessary for the development of the plot.

6. There must be no display, at any time, of machine guns, submachine guns or other weapons generally classified as illegal weapons in the hands of gangsters, or other criminals, and there are to be no off-stage sounds of the repercussions of these guns.

7. There must be no new, unique or trick methods shown for concealing guns.

8. The flaunting of weapons by gangsters, or other criminals, will not be allowed.

9. All discussions and dialogue on the part of gangsters regarding guns should be cut to the minimum.

10. There must be no scenes, at any time, showing law-enforcing officers dying at the hands of criminals. This includes private detectives and guards for banks, motor trucks, etc.

11. With special reference to the crime of kidnapping—or illegal abduction—such stories are acceptable under the Code only when the kidnapping or abduction is (a) not the main theme of the story; (b) the person kidnapped is not a child; (c) there are no details of the crime of kidnapping; (d) no profit accrues to the abductors or kidnappers; and (e) where the kidnappers are punished.

It is understood, and agreed, that the word kidnapping, as used in paragraph 11 of these Regulations, is intended to mean abduction, or illegal detention, in modern times, by criminals for ransom.

12. Pictures dealing with criminal activities, in which minors participate, or to which minors are related, shall not be approved if they incite demoralizing imitation on the part of youth.

13. No picture shall be approved dealing with the life of a notorious criminal of current or recent times which uses the name, nickname or alias of such notorious criminal in the film, nor shall a picture be approved if based upon the life of such a notorious criminal unless the character shown in the film be punished for crimes shown in the film as committed by him.

Special Resolution on Costumes

On October 25, 1939, the Board of Directors of the Motion Picture Association 26
of America, Inc., adopted the following resolution:

RESOLVED, that the provisions of Paragraphs 1, 3 and 4 of subdivision VI of the Production Code, in their application to costumes, nudity, indecent or undue exposure and dancing costumes, shall not be interpreted to exclude authentically photographed scenes photographed in a foreign land, of natives of such foreign land, showing native life, if such scenes are a necessary and integral part of a motion picture depicting exclusively such land and native life, provided that no such scenes shall be intrinsically objectionable nor made a part of any motion picture produced in any studio; and provided further that no emphasis shall be made in any scenes of the customs or garb of such natives or in the exploitation thereof. . . .

Topical Considerations

1. Do you think a motion picture can "lower the moral standards of those who see it" (paragraph 7)? If so, what kinds of pictures can have what kinds of effects on people's moral standards? Can you cite any particular movies?

2. Can you think of any movies in which crime, criminals, and evil were presented "alluringly"? How were they so presented? How were they made attractive? Were you attracted? Did you want the criminals to win out?

3. The 1930 Code pledges: "Correct standards of life shall, as far as possible, be presented" (paragraph 11). Is it possible to present such standards? Or are "correct standards" relative to the times and the people in question?

4. Do you think that motion pictures can build character, as claimed in paragraph 11? Can you think of any actors or actresses that have had an influence on your character?

5. What are the restrictions placed on the treatment of crime? on sex?

6. Which "Particular Applications" in the Code do you most favor? Which do you find objectionable? Why?

7. Are there any standards of the 1930 Motion Picture Production Code that have not been violated by recent films?

Rhetorical Considerations

1. How objective is the language of the Code? Cite passages where the language is subjective or emotionally charged.

2. Do you think that some of these provisions should have been more specific? When the Code says, for example, "Brutal killings are not to be presented in detail," do you think the details should have been spelled out?

Writing Assignments

1. Do you think that motion pictures have the power to lower the moral standards of an audience? Write a paper in which you state your own position on this question. Be sure to cite specific movies to support your opinions.

2. The Motion Picture Production Code of 1930 was drawn up because of what producers saw as their responsibility to the general public. What do you think of their responsibility and their Code? Do you find that their sense of responsibility to the moral character of the public is valid? Do you think their Code was a good idea? Be specific.

3. Think of some movies you have seen recently that clearly violate aspects of the Motion Picture Production Code of 1930. Write a paper in which you describe just how the Code was violated.

4. Think of some movies you have seen recently in which provisions of the 1930 Code have been upheld. Write a paper in which you describe just how the Code was upheld, not violated.

5. Do you think that today's movie producers should be made to follow a Code? Explain your answer in a paper. What restrictions, if any, would you want to see?

6. Imagine that you are one of the 1930 Code enforcers. Write an evaluation of a recent movie you have seen in terms of the way it measures up to the various provisions of the Code.

Do Movie Ratings Work?

Carl T. Rowan and David M. Mazie

The movie ratings G, PG, R, X—for some people these letters spell help; for others, they spell censorship. For still others, they spell nothing much at all. In this essay, Carl T. Rowan and David M. Mazie take a close look at the current movie rating system—a system that is supposed to help moviegoers decide if a film is right for them or not. But what is PG for one person may be R for another. As the authors explain—citing some familiar film titles—the current rating system could use some refinements to lessen the confusion and to aid parents in deciding what their kids should see.

At a drive-in theater showing the movie *Grease,* an embarrassed   1
father started to hum loudly to distract his six- and eight-year-old daughters from a scene in which a roomful of high-school girls were giggling about their summer sex-capades. "I thought PG meant 'pretty good,'" the dad later admitted.

Another father left important chores to accompany his two young   2
daughters to see *The Blue Lagoon*— and came out protesting that the film's R rating, which required him to go with the girls, was ridiculous. "I could have stayed home," he said.

That alphabet soup of G's, PG's, R's and X's—the motion-picture   3
industry's ratings you see in movie ads—is under attack these days. One movie critic lambastes the rating system as a "hoax" that allows children

to be exposed to gore and violence. At the other extreme, a film producer calls it "an unacceptable form of censorship." Its defenders call it an effective self-policing system. Says Charlton Heston, former president of the Screen Actors Guild and one of the most respected figures in Hollywood, "The rating system has kept censors away. Because of that, I'm freer to make films the way I think they should be made."

What *is* the truth? Does the present rating system tell parents enough? 4 Or is it a form of censorship that should be scrapped? Hollywood has grappled with questions like these since the days of the nickelodeon, trying to balance parental concerns with creative freedom, while avoiding censorship.

In 1927, the Motion Picture Producers and Distributors of America 5 (MPPDA) published a list of "don'ts" and "be carefuls" for film writers and producers. That was followed in 1930 by the Production Code, which told moviemakers at every step along the film-making process exactly what they could and couldn't do. The Code proclaimed that "no picture shall be produced which will lower the moral standards of those who see it" and that "the sympathy of the audience shall never be thrown to the side of crime, evil or sin." It listed forbidden words—"alley cat," "fanny," "tart," etc.—and established many other no-nos, such as identifying a brothel, jokes about farmers' daughters, lustful kisses, and on and on.

Thanks to the Code, a generation of American moviegoers was given 6 the impression that married couples slept only in twin beds, that crime never paid, that angry people rarely said anything harsher than "darn." But in the 1950s and 1960s the film industry began to ignore its own rules and to close the gap between the reel world and the real world with pictures like *Baby Doll, Who's Afraid of Virginia Woolf?* and steamy imports from Europe.

With the Production Code in tatters and a 1968 Supreme Court deci- 7 sion opening the door for state and local censors, Hollywood's fear of government regulation returned. Enter Jack Valenti, president of the Motion Picture Association of America (MPAA, successor to the MPPDA). Late in 1968, Valenti brought together his own organization of big-studio producers and distributors with independent distributors, exhibitors and importers, and got them to agree to a new system of voluntary self-regulation, under the supervision of the MPAA.

It was a far cry from the old operation. Gone was the pretense of being 8 morals-keeper for the nation. Nothing was approved or disapproved; no films were banned. A new Classification and Rating Administration (CARA) was established to view films and assign them one of four ratings:

G—General Audiences: film contains no material most parents would 9 consider objectionable, even for younger children.

PG—Parental Guidance Suggested: parents might consider some of 10 the material unsuitable for children.

R—Restricted: some adult material; no one under 17 admitted unless 11 accompanied by a parent or adult guardian.

X—Strictly Adult: no one under 17—in some places 18—admitted.   12

CARA consists of a chairman, named by Valenti, and six members   13
chosen by the chairman with Valenti's approval. Since 1975, the chairman
has been Richard D. Heffner, a 55-year-old historian, university professor
and public-television pioneer. The other members include three men and
three women. All are parents.

The board meets each weekday in a Hollywood screening room and   14
views two or three films, for a total of some 300 to 400 a year. As a film
is shown, they take notes on its theme, on its treatment of violence, sex
and nudity, and on its language. A majority vote decides the rating.

"We try not to vote our own prejudices," says Heffner. "Instead, we   15
make an educated guess as to what most parents of children under 17 will
feel a film's rating should be." If a filmmaker doesn't agree, he can appeal
the rating.

The most difficult distinction is between PG and R. As Valenti notes,   16
"It's not easy to please all the families in America." He has found that
parents in the Middle West are most put off by on-screen sex, New
Yorkers by violence, and those in parts of the South by language.

Although the same classification system has survived for nearly 13   17
years, the rating board does try to reflect changing attitudes. Pictures that
earned an X several years ago would probably get an R today, according
to Valenti. "After all," he points out, "today's kids can see more violence
on the nightly news than they do in an R movie."

Whatever a movie is rated, someone is likely to be upset. Industry   18
executives, for instance, believe that a letter can make a difference at the
box office—R and X ratings keep away a number of teen-agers, while a
G rating can give the impression that the movie must be fluff. Valenti
disagrees. "If you've got a picture that a lot of people want to see, no
rating will hurt you," he says.

But NBC critic Gene Shalit believes that the box-office connection is   19
real. In one of the harshest attacks yet leveled at the system, he charged
that while "ratings pretend to protect children, they are really forged to
protect investors. At the heart of the hokum is the permissive R rating,
which is just a violent X movie that kids can see, thereby increasing the
profit potential."

While Shalit and others argue for tougher regulation, some cry that the   20
rating system is already too restrictive. Robert Radnitz, an independent
producer of family films, including the award-winning *Sounder,* has fought
the system since its inception. "Proponents may call it self-regulation,"
he says. "I call it censorship." Although Radnitz decries the excesses of
sex and violence in today's films, he feels that "only the individual can
regulate himself. No code or appointed body should interfere."

The issue of censorship is complex. Heffner admits feeling personal   21
outrage and disgust at some of what he sees on the screen. "But I'm
convinced," he says, "that the price of film censorship would be too great;
it could undermine free expression in other areas as well. Our voluntary

system of classifying films provides a practical mechanism for satisfying parents' needs, without resorting to censorship."

Valenti proudly points out that no new state, city or county rating   22 board has been set up since the rating system went into effect. The last state board, in Maryland, closes shop July 1. Warns Lew Wasserman, chairman of the entertainment conglomerate, MCA, Inc., "If this industry were subjected to local censorship, it would disappear."

The rating system has earned respect and support outside, as well as   23 inside, the movie industry. Says James M. Wall, editor of *Christian Century*, "We've had better films as a result. The artist is freer to explore complicated human emotions and be more candid with material." The most recent survey of moviegoers shows that 61 percent of adults with children consider the ratings very useful or fairly useful.

But some changes clearly would help. Parents should receive more   24 information on why a film is considered questionable for young viewers. Is it too violent? Are sex scenes too explicit? Is the language too raunchy? An additional letter in the ratings (R-V, R-S, R-L) would provide guidance; so would a more detailed explanation ("one moment of bad language"), which could be obtained by calling the theater. Another useful change would be establishing 13-and-under and 17-and-under subcategories, at least within certain ratings. These two improvements would lessen the confusion that arises when a sensitive movie like *Ordinary People* has the same R rating as a vicious one like *Cruising*, or when *Popeye* and *Airplane* are both PG. And they would make it easier for parents to say yes or no when their children ask to see a movie.

For in the end, it is parents who will make or break the movie-rating   25 system. They must take time to understand the ratings and to exercise responsibility. PG *doesn't* mean "pretty good." It is the film industry's early-warning flag. It says: "Hold it; there are things in this film that may make it inappropriate for *your* child. Find out about it; if you're still concerned, see it first on your own." An R is a strong warning that a film may contain objectionable material. Armed with this information, parents are then free to decide if their children should see a particular film.

And that is what the rating system is all about: freedom of choice for   26 parents, freedom to create for filmmakers, freedom from censorship for us all.

Topical Considerations

1. What central issue of the current rating system does this essay address?

2. When did movie producers begin to ignore the 1930 Motion Picture Production Code? Have you ever seen any of the "transition" movies that closed "the gap between the reel world and the real world"

(paragraph 6)? If you have, which provisions of the Code were violated?

3. In what fundamental way does the current classification and rating system for movies differ from the 1930 Code? Do you think the current system is superior to the older Code? Explain your answer.

4. Gene Shalit claims that the "R rating . . . is just a violent X movie that kids can see" (paragraph 19). Do you agree with this? Aren't there nonviolent R-rated movies? Can you think of any movie that has been rated X recently because of its violence?

5. In paragraph 24, the authors offer some suggestions on refining the rating system—R-V, R-S, R-L. Would you like to see these suggestions implemented? Give your reasons.

6. In paragraph 21, we learn that Richard D. Heffner, chairman of the Classification and Rating Administration (CARA), was himself outraged and disgusted by some of what he had seen on the screen. But he says he is opposed to censorship. What would be the dangers of censorship? What are your feelings about censorship of movies with excessive violence and sex?

Rhetorical Considerations

1. How well do the authors answer the question in the essay's title?

2. This essay examines the arguments for and against the effectiveness of the current movie rating system. How well do the authors maintain a balance of pro and con opinions?

3. Where in the essay do the authors state their own opinion about the usefulness of the rating system? How well do they support their position with evidence?

4. Paragraphs 5 and 6 mention the 1930 Motion Picture Production Code. Evaluate the authors' attitude toward the Code.

Writing Assignments

1. What is your opinion of the current movie rating system? Is it useful in determining the nature of a movie's content? Or do you think it should be further defined, as the authors suggest? Write out your thoughts, citing specific movies to illustrate your points.

2. Suppose that you received a letter from your parents saying that your 13-year-old brother or sister wanted to see a movie that they didn't know was graphically violent—a movie such as *Halloween, Friday the 13th, Carrie, Dawn of the Dead,* or *The Thing* (the remake). Write a letter explaining to your parents just why you think they should not take your brother or sister to such a movie. Be specific in your reasons.

3. Now write a letter to your younger brother or sister explaining why you think seeing such a movie would not be a good idea.

4. Suppose a good friend invited you to see an X-rated movie. Write a letter to this person explaining why you think seeing such a movie is a good or a bad idea. Consider the kinds of effects it might have on you.

5. Have you ever seen a movie that you thought was misrated? If so, write a letter to the producers of that movie, complaining that their rating (P, PG, R, or X) was either too restrictive or not restrictive enough.

On the Horror in Horror Movies

Stephen King

There are few people alive today who know more about the art of horror than Stephen King. He is the world-class supreme master of the genre. His novels represent a publishing phenomenon, exceeding 40 million in print—all since his first, *Carrie,* was published in 1973, when he was 26 years old. In rapid succession, he published *Salem's Lot* (1975), *The Shining* (1977), *The Stand* (1978), *The Dead Zone* (1979), *Firestarter* (1980), and *Cujo* (1981). All but *The Stand* have been made into movies; he also wrote and had a part in the 1982 movie *Creepshow.* King's latest books include *Christine* (1983), *Pet Sematary* (1983), and *The Talisman* (with Peter Straub), scheduled for publication in 1984. The following piece comes from his *Danse Macabre* (1981), a nonfiction survey of horror in literature, TV, and films. In it, King explores the nightmare cravings we have for horror movies, while analyzing in lurid detail how some horrifying screen classics help us better understand some deep-seated fears and taboos.

If we say "art" is any piece of creative work from which an audi-   1
ence receives more than it gives (a liberal definition of art, sure, but in this field it doesn't pay to be too picky), then I believe that the artistic value the horror movie most frequently offers is its ability to form a liaison between our fantasy fears and our real fears. I've said and will reemphasize here that few horror movies are conceived with "art" in mind; most are conceived only with "profit" in mind. The art is not consciously created but rather thrown off, as an atomic pile throws off radiation.

I do not contend by saying the above that every exploitation horror   2
flick is "art," however. You could walk down Forty-second Street in Times Square on any given afternoon or evening and discover films with names like *The Bloody Mutilators, The Female Butcher,* or *The Ghastly Ones*— a 1972 film [in which] we are treated to the charming sight of a woman being cut open with a two-handed bucksaw; the camera lingers as her intestines spew out onto the floor. These are squalid little films with no

whiff of art in them, and only the most decadent filmgoer would try to argue otherwise. They are the staged equivalent of those 8- and 16-millimeter "snuff" movies which have reputedly oozed out of South America from time to time.

Another point worth mentioning is the great risk a filmmaker takes   3
when he/she decides to make a horror picture. In other creative fields, the only risk is failure—we can say, for instance, that the Mike Nichols film of *The Day of the Dolphin* "fails," but there is no public outcry, no mothers picketing the movie theaters. But when a horror movie fails, it often fails into painful absurdity or squalid porno-violence.

There are films which skate right up to the border where "art" ceases   4
to exist in any form and exploitation begins, and these films are often the field's most striking successes. *The Texas Chainsaw Massacre* is one of these; in the hands of Tobe Hooper, the film satisfies that definition of art which I have offered, and I would happily testify to its redeeming social merit in any court in the country. I would not do so for *The Ghastly Ones*. The difference is more than the difference between a chainsaw and a bucksaw; the difference is something like seventy million light-years. Hooper works in *Chainsaw Massacre*, in his own queerly apt way, with taste and conscience. *The Ghastly Ones* is the work of morons with cameras.*

So, if I'm going to keep this discussion in order, I'll keep coming back   5
to the concept of value—of art, of social merit. If horror movies have redeeming social merit, it is because of that ability to form liaisons between the real and unreal—to provide subtexts. And because of their mass appeal, these subtexts are often culture-wide.

In many cases—particularly in the fifties and then again in the early   6
seventies—the fears expressed are sociopolitical in nature, a fact that gives such disparate pictures as Don Siegel's *Invasion of the Body Snatchers* and William Friedkin's *The Exorcist* a crazily convincing documentary feel. When the horror movies wear their various sociopolitical hats—the B-picture as tabloid editorial—they often serve as an extraordinarily accurate barometer of those things which trouble the night-thoughts of a whole society.

But horror movies don't always wear a hat which identifies them as   7
disguised comments on the social or political scene. . . . More often the horror movie points even further inward, looking for those deep-seated personal fears—those pressure points—we all must cope with. This adds an element of universality to the proceedings, and may produce an even

---

*One success in skating over this thin ice does not necessarily guarantee that the filmmaker will be able to repeat such a success; while his innate talent saves Hooper's second film, *Eaten Alive*, from descending to *The Bloody Mutilators* category, it is still a disappointment. The only director I can think of who has explored this gray land between art and porno-exhibitionism successfully—even brilliantly—again and again with never a misstep is the Canadian filmmaker David Cronenberg.

truer sort of art. It also explains, I think, why *The Exorcist* (a social horror film if there ever was one) did only so-so business when it was released in West Germany, a country which had an entirely different set of social fears at the time (they were a lot more worried about bomb-throwing radicals than about foul-talking young people), and why *Dawn of the Dead* went through the roof there.

This second sort of horror film has more in common with the Brothers Grimm than with the op-ed page in a tabloid paper. It is the B-picture as fairy tale. This sort of picture doesn't want to score political points but to scare the hell out of us by crossing certain taboo lines. So if my idea about art is correct (it giveth more than it receiveth), this sort of film is of value to the audience by helping it to better understand what those taboos and fears are, and why it feels so uneasy about them.   8

A good example of this second type of horror picture is RKO's *The Body Snatcher* (1945), liberally adapted—and that's putting it kindly—from a Robert Louis Stevenson story and starring Karloff and Lugosi. . . .   9

As an example of the art, *The Body Snatcher* is one of the forties' best. And as an example of this second artistic "purpose"—that of breaking taboos—it positively shines.   10

I think we'd all agree that one of the great fears which all of us must deal with on a purely personal level is the fear of dying; without good old death to fall back on, the horror movies would be in bad shape. A corollary to this is that there are "good" deaths and "bad" deaths; most of us would like to die peacefully in our beds at age eighty, . . . but very few of us are interested in finding out how it might feel to get slowly crushed under an automobile lift while crankcase oil drips slowly onto our foreheads.   11

Lots of horror films derive their best effects from this fear of the bad death (as in *The Abominable Dr. Phibes,* where Phibes dispatches his victims one at a time using the Twelve Plagues of Egypt, slightly updated, a gimmick worthy of the Batman comics during their palmiest days). Who can forget the lethal binoculars in *Horrors of the Black Museum,* for instance? They came equipped with spring-loaded six-inch prongs, so that when the victim put them to her eyes and then attempted to adjust the field of focus . . .   12

Others derive their horror simply from the fact of death itself, and the decay which follows death. In a society where such a great store is placed in the fragile commodities of youth, health, and beauty (and the latter, it seems to me, is very often defined in terms of the former two), death and decay become inevitably horrible, and inevitably taboo. If you don't think so, ask yourself why the second grade doesn't get to tour the local mortuary along with the police department, the fire department, and the nearest McDonalds—one can imagine, or I can in my more morbid moments, the mortuary and McDonalds combined; the highlights of the tour, of course, would be a viewing of the McCorpse.   13

No, the funeral parlor is taboo. Morticians are modern priests, working 14
their arcane magic of cosmetics and preservation in rooms that are clearly
marked "off limits." Who washes the corpse's hair? Are the fingernails
and toenails of the dear departed clipped one final time? Is it true that
the dead are encoffined *sans* shoes? Who dresses them for their final star
turn in the mortuary viewing room? How is a bullet hole plugged and
concealed? How are strangulation bruises hidden?

The answers to all these questions are available, but they are not 15
common knowledge. And if you try to make the answers part of your store
of knowledge, people are going to think you a bit peculiar. I know; in the
process of researching a forthcoming novel about a father who tries to
bring his son back from the dead, I collected a stack of funeral literature
a foot high—and any number of peculiar glances from folks who wondered why I was reading *The Funeral: Vestige or Value?*

But this is not to say that people don't have a certain occasional 16
interest in what lies behind the locked door in the basement of the
mortuary, or what may transpire in the local graveyard after the mourners
have left . . . or at the dark of the moon. *The Body Snatcher* is not really
a tale of the supernatural, nor was it pitched that way to its audience; it
was pitched as a film (as was that notorious sixties documentary *Mondo
Cane*) that would take us "beyond the pale," over that line which marks
the edge of taboo ground.

"Cemeteries raided, children slain for bodies to dissect!" the movie 17
poster drooled. "Unthinkable realities and unbelievable FACTS of the dark
days of early surgical research EXPOSED in THE MOST DARING SHRIEK-AND-
SHUDDER SHOCK SENSATION EVER BROUGHT TO THE SCREEN!" (All of this
printed on a leaning tombstone.)

But the poster does not stop there; it goes on very specifically to mark 18
out the exact location of the taboo line and to suggest that not everyone
may be adventurous enough to transgress this forbidden ground: "If You
Can 'Take It' See GRAVES RAIDED! COFFINS ROBBED! CORPSES CARVED!
MIDNIGHT MURDER! BODY BLACKMAIL! STALKING GHOULS! MAD REVENGE!
MACABRE MYSTERY! And Don't Say We Didn't Warn You!"

All of it has sort of a pleasant, alliterative ring, doesn't it? 19

These "areas of unease"—the political-social-cultural and those of the 20
more mythic, fairy-tale variety—have a tendency to overlap, of course; a
good horror picture will put the pressure on at as many points as it can.
They Came from Within, for instance, is about sexual promiscuity on one
level; on another level it's asking you how you'd like to have a leech jump
out of a letter slot and fasten itself onto your face. These are not the same
areas of unease at all.

But since we're on the subject of death and decay, we might look at 21
a couple of films where this particular area of unease has been used well.
The prime example, of course, is *Night of the Living Dead,* where our

horror of these final states is exploited to a point where many audiences found the film well-nigh unbearable. Other taboos are also broken by the film: at one point a little girl kills her mother with a garden trowel . . . and then begins to eat her. How's that for taboo-breaking? Yet the film circles around to its starting-point again and again, and the key word in the film's title is not *living* but *dead.*

At an early point, the film's female lead, who has barely escaped being 22
killed by a zombie in a graveyard where she and her brother have come to put flowers on their dead mother's grave (the brother is not so lucky), stumbles into a lonely farmhouse. As she explores, she hears something dripping . . . dripping . . . dripping. She goes upstairs, sees something, screams . . . and the camera zooms in on the rotting, weeks-old head of a corpse. It is a shocking, memorable moment. Later, a government official tells the watching, beleaguered populace that, although they may not like it (i.e., they will have to cross that taboo line to do it), they must burn their dead; simply soak them with gasoline and light them up. Later still, a local sheriff expresses our own uneasy shock at having come so far over the taboo line. He answers a reporter's question by saying, "Ah, they're dead . . . they're all messed up."

The good horror director must have a clear sense of where the taboo 23
line lies, if he is not to lapse into unconscious absurdity, and a gut understanding of what the countryside is like on the far side of it. In *Night of the Living Dead,* George Romero plays a number of instruments, and he plays them like a virtuoso. A lot has been made of this film's graphic violence, but one of the film's most frightening moments comes near the climax, when the heroine's brother makes his reappearance, still wearing his driving gloves and clutching for his sister with the idiotic, implacable single-mindedness of the hungry dead. The film is violent, as is its sequel, *Dawn of the Dead*— but the violence has its own logic, and I submit to you that in the horror genre, logic goes a long way toward proving morality.

The crowning horror in Hitchcock's *Psycho* comes when Vera Miles 24
touches that chair in the cellar and it spins lazily around to reveal Norman's mother at last—a wizened, shriveled corpse from which hollow eyesockets stare up blankly. She is not only dead; she has been stuffed like one of the birds which decorate Norman's office. Norman's subsequent entrance in dress and makeup is almost an anticlimax.

In AIP's *The Pit and the Pendulum* we see another facet of the bad death 25
—perhaps the absolute worst. Vincent Price and his cohorts break into a tomb through its brickwork, using pick and shovel. They discover that the lady, his late wife, has indeed been buried alive; for just a moment the camera shows us her tortured face, frozen in a rictus of terror, her bulging eyes, her clawlike fingers, the skin stretched tight and gray. Following the Hammer films, this becomes, I think, the most important moment in the post-1960 horror film, signaling a return to an all-out effort to terrify the audience . . . and a willingness to use any means at hand to do it.

Other examples abound. No vampire movie can be complete without 26
a midnight creep through the tombstones and the jimmying of a crypt
door. The John Badham remake of *Dracula* has disappointingly few fine
moments, but one rather good sequence occurs when Van Helsing (Lau-
rence Olivier) discovers his daughter Mina's grave empty . . . and an
opening at its bottom leading deeper into the earth.* This is English
mining country, and we're told that the hillside where the cemetery has
been laid out is honeycombed with old tunnels. Van Helsing nevertheless
descends, and the movie's best passage follows—crawling, claustro-
phobic, and reminiscent of that classic Henry Kuttner story, "The Graveyard Rats." Van Helsing pauses at a pool for a moment, and his daughter's voice comes from behind him, begging for a kiss. Her eyes glitter
unnaturally; she is still dressed in the cerements of the grave. Her flesh
has decayed to a sick green color and she stands, swaying, in this passage
under the earth like something from a painting of the Apocalypse. In this
one moment Badham has not merely asked us to cross the taboo line with
him; he has quite literally pushed us across it and into the arms of this
rotting corpse—a corpse made more horrible because in life it conformed
so perfectly to those conventional American standards of beauty: youth
and health. It's only a moment, and the movie holds no other moment
comparable to it, but it is a fine effect while it lasts.

Topical Considerations

1. How does Stephen King define "art" here? How well does he
illustrate his definition through the horror movie examples he cites?

2. According to King, why did the movie *The Exorcist* do only
mediocre business at West German box offices, where as *Dawn of the Dead*
was a smash hit?

3. King defends even B horror movies because they help us
better understand our taboos and fears. What are some of these taboos
and fears? Think of a recent horror movie you have seen and try to
determine which particular taboos were broken for you and which fears
were provoked. (You might consider some of the movies made from
Stephen King's works.)

4. What particular taboos, according to King, did *Night of the
Living Dead* break?

5. What does King mean when he says that there is a "logic" to

---

*Van Helsing's *daughter?* I hear you saying with justifiable dismay. Yes indeed. Readers
familiar with Stoker's novel will see that Badham's film (and the stage play from which it
was drawn) has rung any number of changes on the novel. In terms of the tale's interior
logic, these changes of plot and relationship seem to work, but to what purpose? The
changes don't cause Badham to say anything new about either the Count or the vampire
myth in general, and to my mind there was no coherent reason for them at all. As we have
to far too often, we can only shrug and say, "That's showbiz."

the violence in well-made horror movies? Can you think of any such logic in a horror movie you've seen recently?

6. How did John Badham, director of the remake of *Dracula*, push the audience across the "taboo line" in that horror flick? Can you think of other movies that have pushed us across that line?

Rhetorical Considerations

1. King defines "art" in paragraph 1. How well does he use this definition in measuring the movies he talks about?

2. One of Stephen King's appeals is his style of writing. Did you find his style and tone here appealing? Explain your answer.

3. Did you find any evidence of King's sense of humor? If so, cite specific passages. What did you find humorous about these passages?

Writing Assignments

1. Stephen King distinguishes between horror movies that show some "art" and those that give us horror for its own sake, that show no restraint on the screen. Write a paper in which you discuss the differences between two horror movies—one that shows art and one that goes overboard, without redemption.

2. King talks about how movies terrify and horrify us. Write a paper in which you try to define the difference between terror and horror. Then, keeping your definitions in mind, discuss how a particular horror movie you have recently seen managed to create these effects.

3. If you have seen any of the movies made from Stephen King books, try to write a review of one in which you analyze the particular taboos that it broke for you and the particular fears to which it appealed.

The Visionary Gleam

David Denby

E.T., the Extra-Terrestrial may turn out to be the movie blockbuster of all times. Therefore, it seems appropriate to say something in this section about that Steven Spielberg phenomenon. We offer, in fact, three different views of *E.T.*— the first, a particularly well-done rave review by a professional movie critic; the second, a brief and insightful religious interpretation by a nonprofessional reviewer; and the third, an interpretation by a famous *Newsweek* political columnist on whom the charm of *E.T.* clearly was lost. We begin with warm praise from *New York Magazine*'s movie reviewer, David Denby, who focuses on how beautiful and funny *E.T.*'s vision of innocence was. Denby's interpretation brings to mind Bruno Bettelheim's criteria for great movie art.

Steven Spielberg's **E.T., the Extra-Terrestrial** is one of the most   1
beautiful fantasy-adventure movies ever made—a sublimely witty and inventive fable that goes so deep into the special alertness, loyalty, and ardor of children that it makes you see things you had forgotten or blotted out and feel things you were embarrassed to feel. Watching it, children will be in heaven; adults, I think, will be moved by how funny, even hip, innocence can be. You may wonder how so commercial a work can be innocent, but Spielberg has pulled it off: He's used his fabulous technique and boundless savvy to create the ecstasy of first responses, when friendship, danger, the physical world itself strike the child as awesome, revelatory. It's a Wordsworthian science-fiction movie.

After the frantic aridities of *1941* and the entertaining but soulless   2
high jinks of *Raiders of the Lost Ark,* the director has returned to the beatific mood of *Close Encounters of the Third Kind.* The new movie is a heart-wrenching elaboration of that moment at the end of *Close Encounters* when the awkward little creature moves down the runway of its spaceship in a column of overpowering light and raises its palms in greeting.

The premise of *E.T.* is simple. Accidentally left behind by outer-space   3
visitors, a smallish, green-brown creature, brilliant but physically vulnerable, takes refuge in the bedroom of a ten-year-old boy in the California suburbs. The boy, Elliott (Henry Thomas), aided by his big brother, Michael (Robert Macnaughton), and his gravely beautiful little sister, Gertie (Drew Barrymore), secretly cares for the extraterrestrial (E.T. for short) as if it were a peculiarly intelligent wild animal—feeding it, protecting it from shadowy scientific authorities, and finally helping it in its quest to return home, where it must go if it is to survive.

In outline, the plot may seem familiar, since there are many echoes in   4
it of such classic animal-and-child stories as *The Black Stallion* and *The Yearling,* as well as a large infusion of *Peter Pan.* But Spielberg and screenwriter Melissa Mathison (who worked on the script of *The Black Stallion*) have worked out the story with astounding moment-by-moment physical and emotional detail: Even such spellbinders as J.M. Barrie, Marjorie Kinnan Rawlings, and Disney himself might have been impressed. It's been years since I've been this caught up in the emotions of a movie.

Nearly everyone has had the experience of lying on the grass on a clear   5
night, looking up at the sky and feeling not only amazement but also a sense of *anticipation,* the conviction that something overwhelming was about to happen. Spielberg is the master of this hushed, awed mood of imminence, and he always delivers what he has promised. Spielberg makes physical beauty dramatically exciting; he has a kinetic sense of

detail. His characteristic visual style (Allen Daviau is the cinematographer here) depends on a stealthily moving camera and shafts of dazzling white light against darkness—light as power and intelligence.

The opening of *E.T.* is both majestic and witty—a true Spielberg combination. Having landed in a dark forest of redwoods and firs, the outer-space creatures quietly explore, taking specimens, talking to one another in their strange, snurfling language. The details are exquisite: Long brown fingers delicately uproot a plant; immense redwoods in parallel columns, seen from the creatures' point of view, stretch endlessly upward; in the valley below, a flat California valley community glistens and hums in the night. As a group of men—scientists probably, looking for the spaceship—drive up violently in their cars and trucks, Spielberg holds the aliens' point of view, keeping the camera low, in the bushes. We never see the men's faces; the scientists are embodied by the light—first headlights, then superpowered flashlights moving around in the dark like tracer bullets. One little gremlin, tearing through the bushes, emits a panicked noise somewhere between a squeal and a honk, and gets left aground as the spaceship takes off. 6

From the beginning, then, we are plunged into an entirely physical, almost visceral experience of the story, accomplished without obvious scare tactics. All the excitement is fully earned—it is dramatized from the inside, as experience, and not felt merely as the usual cinematic assault on the senses. Spielberg charges every scene with eccentric movement, but nothing is rushed or forced. When Elliott lures the gremlin into his house, Spielberg finally unveils his incomparable toy. This lifelike brown rubber thing is the finest creation of Carlo Rambaldi, who also constructed the 1976 King Kong and the earlier Spielberg extraterrestrials. Squat, a waddler with horny feet, it has long arms that touch the ground, a long neck that extends in moments of panic. Rambaldi has made it comical-looking, slightly grotesque, but not frightening: He's given it beautiful liquid eyes that dilate with emotion. And Spielberg has given it a personality—grave, tender, quietly sad, and utterly benevolent. A dignified, rather conservative man of feeling (one can imagine E.T. as editor of *The New Yorker*), it pulsates and makes sympathetic noises—murmurs and groans—when other people are hurt. In Elliott's robe, it shuffles off to the kitchen, looking like an elderly visiting uncle who stayed through the winter. 7

In the past, most directors have made aliens threatening, even terrifying. Spielberg's gentler conception, in which the extraterrestrials find *us* alien, is infinitely more fun. When little Gertie sees E.T. in her brother's bedroom, she screams "Eek!" and E.T. screams back, neck craning, long fingers held up in protest against this small blond thing with pink yarn in her hair. For Gertie, E.T. is a part of the world of toys and dolls and magical bedtime stories, and she quickly accepts it, dressing it up in a blond wig and bracelets, chattering away at it as it follows her around the 8 kitchen. Tiny Drew Barrymore (John's granddaughter) is a very positive child with a natural gravity that becomes increasingly comical. Spielberg performs miracles with her and with Henry Thomas, whose arched eyebrows give him a look of devilish intelligence.

In those classic animal tales, children have special qualities of mind 9
and character—generosity, concern—that adults don't have, and that is part of the reason the animals come to them. From the beginning, Elliott feels he has been chosen by E.T., and he takes the responsibility of introducing him to an entire civilization—in his bedroom. Elliott, who sends a toy shark chasing after a real goldfish (E.T. stares in grave wonder) and who presents a little metal car as a means of human locomotion, doesn't always distinguish between real objects and their representation. He's still learning, while E.T. is trying to decode an entire way of life. For a magical moment, they occupy the same place, communicating haphazardly, confusingly, but ecstatically. Their empathy is so great that when E.T. chugs down a couple of beers, Elliott, at school miles away, belches loudly and casts lewd, drunken looks at the girl across the aisle. Like every great fantasist, Spielberg extends his premises in strictly logical fashion until they attain the surreal. In several sequences, he moves into new areas of wild inventiveness that parallel, in popular and largely benevolent rather than macabre terms, what some of the great surrealists have done.

What fuses the movie's separate moods is Spielberg and Mathison's 10
passionate child partisanship. In *Peter Pan*, the children's special world was held together, in part, by the adults' inability to see Peter and Tinker Bell—a metaphor of Barrie's for adult insensitivity. In *E.T.*, the filmmakers work out the same idea in slapstick terms. The children's lovely mother (Dee Wallace), preoccupied with her own concerns, doesn't see the grotesque E.T. lying among the large teddy bears and other stuffed animals in the closet. She's merely busy and oblivious, but the other adults, all faceless, are presented as children's nightmare figures. The scientists who have been lurking in vans outside Elliott's house, spying and eavesdropping, finally crash in wearing frightening space suits. They wear the heavy gear, it turns out, to prevent themselves from contaminating E.T., yet Spielberg sustains, almost to the end, the children's view of them as sinister (doomy drumbeats accompany their entrance). The point of shooting them that way is that all their science and technology can't match what the children's love has done for E.T.

The poetic logic of animal stories requires that the horse, dog, or lion 11
finally "return to the wild," and that the child, who has created a private world with it, learn to accept the separation—in other words, he begins to acknowledge that he must grow up. The filmmakers make this resolution even more wrenching than usual by having the three children fight so hard to get the sickly E.T. home; out of love, they fight against their own desires to hold on to him forever. In the last 40 minutes or so,

Spielberg exhibits such a powerful grip on the audience's emotions (I have never seen so many grown men weeping at a screening) that some will accuse him of manipulation or even sadism. On the contrary, I welcome this return to the honorable emotional fullness that was taken for granted in movies of the thirties and forties (in, say, *Captains Courageous* and *How Green Was My Valley*).

Even when Spielberg is squeezing us for tears, there's eccentric detail   12
to marvel at. The impromptu hospital the scientists set up in Elliott's house is a terrifying white hell of milky plastic walls; the long translucent tunnel they stretch from the house to a waiting van is like a gigantic snake. Spielberg incorporates the tunnel in a terrific chase at the end that features a pack of boys on bikes splitting apart and shooting over hills like separate streams of water. His visual imagination never falters. At one point, as John Williams's music rises in triumph, Spielberg sends Elliott and E.T. riding a bicycle across the face of the moon, an image that recalls, in its mixture of homeliness and exuberance, the very origins of cinematic fantasy in Georges Méliès's *A Trip to the Moon*, from 1902. Just like those early audiences, the millions who see *E.T.* will stay rooted to their seats, astonished at what the movies can do.

Topical Considerations

1. How does Denby say *E.T.* will affect adults?

2. How does Denby interpret the appearance of E.T.? If you have seen the film, did the creature strike you this way or some other way?

3. According to Denby, how have past movie directors generally characterized alien life? How does Steven Spielberg differ in his film?

4. Denby makes the claim that *E.T.* and *Peter Pan* share some things. What do they have in common?

5. How has Spielberg characterized the adult world in *E.T.*, according to Denby? How has he characterized science and technology? What are some of Denby's supporting examples?

6. Why does Denby say in paragraph 11 that he would not accuse Spielberg of "manipulation or even sadism"?

7. How well do you think Denby reviewed this movie? Do you think he went overboard? Do you think his assessment was accurate and his reaction reasonable?

Rhetorical Considerations

1. Explain what Denby means by the last sentence in paragraph 1: "It's a Wordsworthian science-fiction movie." What does "Wordsworthian" mean?

2. In paragraph 6, Denby says that the opening of the movie was

"both majestic and witty." What evidence does he give for "majestic"? for "witty"?

3. In general, how well does Denby back up his observations with specific references to scenes in the movie? Could he have used more examples to support his statements? If so, where exactly?

Writing Assignments

1. Write a review of this review; that is, evaluate its style, its claims, its tone, the way it made specific reference to the movie. Did it have a clear focus and development? Did its interpretations and evaluations seem reasonable to you?

2. If you have seen the movie *E.T.*, write your own reaction to it—your own review. In the review, be sure to make specific references to the movie to support your general claims and analyses.

3. Denby makes the point that *E.T.* differs significantly from most other science fiction films in the way it depicts extraterrestrial life. Expand on this in a paper in which you explain how Spielberg's treatment of alien life differs from that in other science fiction movies you have seen. Specify the movies and the differences.

Is *E.T.* a Religious Parable?

William Deerfield

After seeing *E.T.*, William Deerfield, who identifies himself as "a writer on religious subjects," was struck by the number of parallels between that science fiction-fantasy film and the story of Jesus Christ. The following is a letter Deerfield wrote to the editor of the *New York Times,* in which he enumerates some of those similarities—intentional or unintentional on the part of Steven Spielberg. The letter is a good example of symbolic interpretation.

To the Editor:

After two tries to see the current Steven Spielberg blockbuster, "E.T. The Extra-Terrestrial," a friend and I succeeded one wet, muggy afternoon recently in getting into the packed movie house at Broadway and 47th Street.   1

Of course, it was well worth the wait—"E.T." is a delightful film on all counts. As a writer on religious subjects, though, I was struck by the number of parallels between this modern science-fantasy film and the story of Christ. I don't *think* I'm a religious fanatic. Has anyone else noticed the similarities—intentional or unintentional?   2

It would not be the first time. Mr. Spielberg's previous film, "Close   3
Encounters of the Third Kind," came off as a space-age version of the
Second Advent of Christ. But instead of the angel Gabriel descending
from the clouds with a shout and a blast on a golden trumpet, wonderful
all-wise aliens came down to whisk the enraptured hero off to a presumably better world, in a marvelous celestial ship that one critic described as
looking like Los Angeles piled on Manhattan or vice versa.

As for the Christian parallels in "E.T.": First, there is a benign being   4
who comes from "out there." He (or it) is a stranger and alien to this
world. He makes his first home in a shed. Christ also came into an alien
world and made his first home in a stable.

Am I straining at comparisons? Consider the following: 5

• E.T. can heal a bleeding cut with the touch of a bony, glowing finger.   6
Christ, with his work-roughened carpenter's hand, healed the severed ear
of the High Priest's servant. He performed many, many other miracles of
healing.

• E.T. causes objects and even people to levitate and fly. (Will we ever   7
forget the marvelous scenes with the boys flying high and free over
houses and mountains and trees? What magical, wonderful scenes!) But
according to the Gospels, Christ walked on the sea, turned water into
vintage wine; and, on two separate occasions, fed thousands of people
with a few rolls and dried fish—and had 12 basketsful of food left over.
(Top that, if you can, E.T.!)

• E.T., in the film's most uproarious scene, discovers a six-pack of beer   8
and proceeds to get "sloshed" while his young friend Elliott, sitting some
distance away in school, takes on all the symptoms of drunkenness and
ends up falling off his chair. In some way, not explained in the film, E.T.'s
mind or spirit influences the boy. In the same way, Christ's spirit (the
Holy Spirit in Christian doctrine) enters the "temple" of the believer's
body and influences him for the good.

• E.T. has a brilliantly lit heart that can be seen beating within his   9
breast. A striking parallel is to be found in the Roman Catholic cult of
the Sacred Heart—in which the Savior's wounded heart, topped with a
glowing flame, can be seen.

• In the most striking parallel to the story of Christ, E.T. dies and is   10
then miraculously restored to life. The linchpin of the Christian faith is
that Christ died and was miraculously raised to life—the doctrine of the
Resurrection.

• In the film, E.T. must leave the boy and return to his home "out   11
there." The obvious parallel is the Ascension of Christ. The Savior must
leave his grieving followers to return to his heavenly home, "up there."

• Finally, E.T., in parting, promises his young friend that he will always   12
be "in here"—indicating the boy's head and/or heart. Christ also promised His followers that He would abide with them forever—"lo, I am

with you always. . . ." Then in an act of almost religious devotion, the mother kneels down before the now nearly godlike E.T. One all but expects him to move a bony hand in the traditional Christian sign of blessing to the strains of the "Hallelujah Chorus." But the moment passes.

Of course, the same mythic elements predate the story of Christ—   13 sacrificial love, death and resurrection. One of the most striking of these ancient legends is that of the Phoenix—the wonderful bird that periodically returns to an altar in Egypt where it is consumed in the flames only to be miraculously resurrected. The Church has adapted the Phoenix as a symbol of the Resurrection of Christ. In the prescientific era, the traditional teaching was that all pagan myths of death and resurrection were prefigurings of Christ.

Even the fairy tales of our childhood are rich in this mythic symbolism.   14 The kiss of the prince (Christ) restores life to the princess (the sinner). Sociologists and scholars might say then that E.T. and Christ belong to the same tradition and that neither is more literally true than the other.

We have largely rejected the idea of a real Savior who comes to heal,   15 perform wonders, and to give up His life for mankind—and then, miraculously take it up again (as proof that good is stronger than evil, that life will triumph over death in the end).

Evidently there is still a need to believe (or at least long for) this   16 "myth" of a savior, for we are continually inventing fantasy versions that are entertaining and less demanding than the real thing.

WILLIAM DEERFIELD
West Orange, N.J.

Topical Considerations

1. Which of the various parallels cited by Deerfield strikes you as the most convincing? Which seems the least convincing or the most strained? If you have seen the movie, can you add any other parallels?

2. Does the author ever address the question of whether Steven Spielberg made such Christian parallels purposefully? Is that question important? Why or why not?

3. What mythic elements in *E.T.* predate the Christian era? What is Deerfield's point in this observation?

4. According to Deerfield, how does *E.T.* appeal to a modern need to believe in a savior? What does he mean when he claims that such science-fantasy versions of a savior are "less demanding than the real thing" (paragraph 16)? Does he mean that fantasies such as *E.T.* have replaced religious beliefs in people?

Rhetorical Considerations

1. What does Deerfield gain by opening his piece the way he does?

2. If Deerfield did not tell us that he was a writer on religious subjects, could you have guessed from the essay? Does he sound like a biblical scholar?

3. The author says he found *E.T.* a "delightful film." What word choices or comments in his analysis of the parallels reveal his affection for the film?

4. Does Deerfield ever show a sense of humor? If so, where?

Writing Assignments

1. Deerfield draws several Christian parallels in *E.T.* If you can recall the movie, select one specific parallel and discuss it in detail in an essay.

2. Deerfield says that E.T. and Christ can be seen to be in the same tradition. Can you think of any other science fiction movie that makes use of the Christian tradition and draws parallels? If so, write a paper describing how that movie made use of such traditions and parallels.

3. Bruno Bettelheim claimed in his essay that movies have the potential for being great art. Using his criteria for great art, write a paper evaluating the movie *E.T.* Does it qualify as great art in Bettelheim's terms?

Well, *I* Don't Love You, E.T.

George F. Will

As his title suggests, well-known *Newsweek* columnist George F. Will did not take kindly to *E.T.* He might be one of the few reviewers in the world who didn't. The childlike charm and innocent visions that moved both David Denby and William Deerfield represent to George Will the failure of Steven Spielberg's movie. What particularly bothers Will, however, is what he sees as the movie's prejudice against adulthood and science.

The hot breath of summer is on America, but few children feel   1
it. They are indoors, in the dark, watching the movie "E.T." and being basted with three subversive ideas:

Children are people.
Adults are not.
Science is sinister.

The first idea amounts to counting chickens before they are hatched. 2
The second is an exaggeration. The third subverts what the movie purports to encourage: a healthy capacity for astonishment.

The yuckiness of adults is an axiom of children's cinema. And truth be 3
told, adults are, more often than not, yucky. That is because they are
human, a defect they share with their pint-size detractors. (A wit once said
that children are natural mimics who act like their parents in spite of all
efforts to teach them good manners.) Surely children are unmanageable
enough without gratuitously inoculating them with anti-adultism. Steven
Spielberg, the perpetrator of "E.T.," should be reminded of the charge
that got Socrates condemned to drink hemlock: corrupting the youth of
Athens.

It is not easy to corrupt American youth additionally. Geoffrey Will, 4
8, like all younger brothers in the theater, swooned with pleasure while
sitting next to his censorious father watching the little boy in "E.T."
shout across the dinner table at the big brother: "Shut up, penis breath!"
"E.T." has perfect pitch for child talk at its gamiest. Convincing depictions of a child's-eye view of the world are rare. George Eliot's "The Mill
on the Floss" and Henry James's "What Maisie Knew" are two. But those
delicate sensibilities could not have captured the scatological sounds of
young American male siblings discussing their differences.

Ethnocentric

I feel about children expressing themselves the way Wellington felt 5
about soldiers. He even disapproved of soldiers cheering, because cheering is too nearly an expression of opinion. The little boy in "E.T." did
say something neat: "How do you explain school to a higher intelligence?" The children who popped through C. S. Lewis's wardrobe into
Narnia never said anything that penetrating. Still, the proper way to
converse with a young person is:

Young person: What's that bird?
Older person: It's a guillemot.
Young person: That's not my idea of a guillemot.
Older person: It's God's idea of a guillemot.

I assume every American has spent the last month either in line to see, 6
or seeing, "E.T." In the first month it earned $100 million—$17.5 million
during the Fourth of July weekend. But in case you have been spelunking
beneath Kentucky since May, "E.T." is about an extraterrestrial creature
left behind in a California suburb when his buddies blast off for home.

He is befriended by a boy in the American manner: the boy tosses a ball to E.T. and E.T. chucks it back.

It is, I suppose, illiberal and—even more unforgivable—ethnocentric (or, in this case, speciescentric) to note that E.T. is not just another pretty face. E.T. looks like a stump with a secret sorrow. (Except to another E.T. As Voltaire said, to a toad, beauty is popeyes, a yellow belly and spotted back.) E.T. is a brilliant, doe-eyed, soulful space elf who waddles into the hearts of the boy, his big brother and little sister. But a wasting illness brings E.T. to death's door just as a horde of scary scientists crashes through the door of the boy's house.   7

Throughout the movie they have been hunting the little critter, electronically eavesdropping on the house and generally acting like Watergate understudies. They pounce upon E.T. with all the whirring, pulsing, blinking paraphernalia of modern medicine. He dies anyway, then is inexplicably resurrected. He is rescued from the fell clutches of the scientists by a posse of kid bicyclists and boards a spaceship for home. This variant of the boy-sundered-from-dog theme leaves few eyes dry. But what is bothersome is the animus against science, which is seen as a morbid calling for callous vivisectionists and other unfeeling technocrats.   8

A childish (and Rousseau-ist) view of children as noble savages often is part of a belief that nature is a sweet garden and science and technology are spoilsome intrusions. But nature is, among other things, plagues and pestilences, cholera and locusts, floods and droughts. Earlier ages thought of nature in terms of such afflictions. As Robert Nisbet says, this age can take a sentimental view of nature because science has done so much to ameliorate it.   9

Wonder

Disdain for science usually ends when the disdainer gets a toothache, or his child needs an operation. But hostility to science is the anti-intellectualism of the semi-intellectual. That is in part because science undercuts intellectual vanity: measured against what is unknown, the difference between what the most and least learned persons know is trivial. "E.T." is, ostensibly, an invitation to feel what we too rarely feel: wonder. One reason we rarely feel wonder is that science has made many things routine that once were exciting, even terrifying (travel, surgery). But science does more than its despisers do to nurture the wonderful human capacity for wonder.   10

U.S. missions have revealed that Saturn has braided rings and a ring composed of giant snowballs. The space program is the greatest conceivable adventure; yet the government scants it and Philistine utilitarians justify it because it has yielded such marvels as nonstick frying pans. We live in (let us say the worst) an age of journalism: an age of skimmed surfaces, of facile confidence that reality is whatever be seen and taped and reported. But modern science teaches that things are not what   11 they seem: matter is energy; light is subject to gravity; the evidence of gravity waves suggests that gravitic energy is a form of radiation; to increase the speed of an object is to decrease the passage of its time. This is science; compared with it, space elves are dull as ditchwater.

The epigram that credulity is an adult's weakness but a child's strength   12
is true. Victoria Will (21 months) croons ecstatically at the sight of a squirrel; she sees, without thinking about it, that a squirrel is a marvelous piece of work—which, come to think about it, it is. For big people, science teaches the truth that a scientist put this way: the universe is not only queerer than we suppose, it is queerer than we can suppose.

Topical Considerations

1. What is Will's argument against the portrayal of adults in *E.T.*? How did David Denby feel about this?

2. Why does Will think it a "subversive" idea that "Children are people" (paragraph 1)?

3. In what ways did the movie *E.T.* show "disdain for science," according to Will? If you saw the movie, do you agree? What did David Denby say about how *E.T.* regarded science?

4. Explain Will's claim that "hostility to science" is a form of "anti-intellectualism of the semi-intellectual" (paragraph 10). Did you think that hostility was expressed in *E.T.*? Do you agree with Will's statement? Can't even scientists be hostile toward some aspects of science?

5. Do you think George Will would have liked *E.T.* better had he been his son's age? Do you think Will's own intellectualism stands in the way of his appreciation of the movie, or do you think he has leveled some valid criticisms at the movie?

Rhetorical Considerations

1. Will has three separate complaints about the movie *E.T.* Does he give equal weight to them, or does he discuss one more than the others?

2. Looking over the essay again, try to characterize Will's attitude toward children. Particularly examine his word choice.

3. What is the point of comparing *E.T.*'s child's-eye view of the world with those of George Eliot and Henry James in their novels (paragraph 4)? Is Will being sarcastic here? Is it unfair to compare the view of a 1982 movie with those of nineteenth-century novels?

4. What attitude of Will's is illustrated by the brief dialogue between the "young person" and the "older person"?

5. What is the topic sentence of paragraph 11?

6. From this brief essay, what general impressions do you get of George F. Will? What kind of temperament would you say he has? Is he a reasonable man? elitist? snobbish? liberal? intellectual? too serious? Be explicit, and cite specific words and statements of Will's to support your conclusions.

Writing Assignments

1. Imagine that you are George Will's 8-year-old son, Geoffrey. Write your father a letter telling him what you think of his reaction to *E.T.*

2. Write your own assessment of the movie *E.T.* if you have seen it.

3. One of Will's lines of criticism is that *E.T.* has a strong anti-scientific theme. If you have recently seen the movie, write a paper analyzing its attitude toward science.

4. The words that close Will's piece are from the late British astronomer J.B.S. Haldane: "The universe is not only queerer than we suppose, it is queerer than we can suppose." Have you ever seen a science fiction movie that illustrates both aspects of Haldane's statement—the "queerness" of the universe and the limitations of human imagination to comprehend that queerness? If so, write a paper about that movie in which you discuss how Haldane's observations were dramatized.

5. Imagine that you are reviewer David Denby, and write a response to Mr. Will regarding his statements about how *E.T.* disdained science and technology.

ADVERTISING

Advertising

Andy Rooney

Advertising is the prime mover in our consumer society. Advertising is also the creator and reflector—sometimes a distorted one—of the images and myths of ourselves. In this section, we will examine various aspects of advertising and some current ads. We begin with a wry and reasonable complaint about a basic fact of advertising: it is everywhere—and not just where it's supposed to be, such as in magazines and on billboards, but also on license plates, luggage, and underpants! The essay is written with the dry, rueful humor and down-home common sense that is characteristic of Andy Rooney. Since 1978, he has delighted millions of people with his observations of everyday life on CBS-TV's "60 Minutes." In addition to his television work, Rooney writes a syndicated column three days a week. The following piece is from a collection of his essays, *A Few Minutes with Andy Rooney* (1982).

1   My grandfather told me when I was a small boy that if a product was any good, they shouldn't have to advertise it.

2   I believed my grandfather at the time, but then years later my mother said that when *she* was a little girl he had told her that they'd never be able to build an automobile that would go up a hill. So I never knew whether to believe my grandfather or not.

3   Like so many things, I've really never made up my mind about advertising. I know all the arguments for it and against it, but the one thing I'm sure of is that there ought to be some sanctuaries, some places we're safe from being advertised at. There ought to be some open space left in the world without any advertising on it, some pieces of paper, some painted surfaces that aren't covered with entreaties for us to buy something.

4   Advertising doesn't belong on license plates, for instance. Of the fifty states, twenty-seven of them have slogans trying to sell themselves to the rest of us. It's offensive and wrong. The license plate has an important function and it's a cheap trick to tack something else on it. Most of the legends the states put on aren't true anyway.

5   Rhode Island, for instance, says it's the "Ocean State." There are fifteen states with more ocean than Rhode Island has. If they want to say something on their plate, why don't they explain why they call Rhode an island when it isn't one?

6   Florida says it's the "Sunshine State." I like Florida, but why don't they also say that Miami has more rain than any city in the whole United States except for Mobile, Alabama?

7   North Carolina says it's "First in Freedom." It doesn't say anywhere on the license plate who they think is *second* in freedom. South Carolina? Michigan?

8   Connecticut says it's the "Constitution State." I called the license

bureau in Connecticut and no one there could tell me why they call it the Constitution State. Connecticut is not the Constitution state, of course. *Pennsylvania* is the Constitution state. And Pennsylvania calls itself the "Keystone State." Does anyone really care?

Maine says it's "Vacationland." How would you like to drive a garbage truck for eight hours in Augusta with a sign hanging on the back that says "Vacationland"?   9

New Hampshire plates carry the pretentious legend "Live Free or Die." Some religious organization that apparently wasn't willing to die if they couldn't be free objected and taped over those words on all their license plates. The state said this was illegal and the case went to the Supreme Court. The Court ruled that the religious order did have the right to block out those words. New Hampshire would have saved us all a lot of time and money if they'd never put them on in the first place.   10

New Mexico calls itself "Land of Enchantment." This is not the kind of slogan that gets the work of the world done.   11

Hawaii says it's the "Aloha State." Hawaii ought to get over its palm-tree mentality and removing "Aloha" from its plates would be a good start. What sensible state would want to conjure up a picture of dancing girls draping flower ropes over the necks of visitors every time anyone thought about it?   12

Wisconsin "America's Dairyland"? Never mind that, Wisconsin, if you're dairyland why don't you tell us on your license plates what ever happened to heavy cream? That's the kind of stuff we'd like to read about when we're driving along behind a car from your state.   13

And then Idaho. How would you like to work hard, save your money and decide, when the kids were educated and the house paid for, to buy yourself a Mercedes-Benz. You plunk down your $28,000, the dealer screws on the license plate and there you are with your dream car, you drive away, and affixed to the bumper is the sign that says "Famous Potatoes."   14

"If a state is any good," I imagine my grandfather would have said, "it shouldn't have to advertise."   15

License-plate advertising is a small part of what we're faced with when we're driving. On the highways, trucks are turned into rolling billboards. The companies that own them look on it as easy advertising, too cheap to pass up. On major highways the commercials come along more often than on a late-night television movie.   16

On city streets, the billboards on Coca-Cola and Pepsi trucks are often double-parked while the driver makes deliveries. In most cities now, taxis and buses carry advertising. When you're paying a buck and a half a mile, you shouldn't have to carry a sign pushing cigarettes.   17

In California there's a company called Beetleboards. What Beetleboards will do for you is paint your Volkswagen, apply a commercial motif   18

from a sponsor who is paying them and pay you twenty dollars a month
to drive around in it.

And if you can understand businesses advertising their products on   19
our roads, how do you account for the private citizens who use the back
end of their cars to tell us about themselves or about some private campaign of theirs? A typical car or van in a parking lot outside a tourist
attraction in Washington, D.C., will announce, through the decals attached to it somewhere, that the owner is insured by Allstate, boosts the
Northern Virginia Ramparts—a team of some sort, I guess—is against
forest fires because he has a little Smokey the Bear stuck to his car, gives
to the International Convention of Police Chiefs and believes in God
because his bumper sticker tells us so.

If someone has to take pride in having people know what insurance   20
company gets his money, he's in trouble for things to be proud of.

A third of the cars on the road have reading matter stuck to them   21
somewhere trying to sell the rest of us a place, an opinion or a way of life.
Sometimes it looks as though half the cars in the United States have been
to a roadside stand in South Carolina called South of the Border, and for
some reason the entrepreneurs who have made tourist attractions out of
caves love to slap "Visit Secret Caverns" on visitors' bumpers.

One of the most incredible commercial coups of the century has been   22
pulled off by the designers who have conned women into thinking it's chic
to wear a piece of apparel on which the maker's name is imprinted as part
of the design.

The French luggage maker Louis Vuitton may have started the trend   23
when he made the brown LV the only design on his product, but the
women's fashion designers have taken it over. Bill Bass makes towels with
his name all over them. Why would anyone want to take a shower and buff
themselves dry on a piece of cloth bearing Bill Blass's name? Why would
a woman go around with the name "Bloomies" on the seat of her underpants? Is there something I don't understand here?

Why would I or anyone else want to lay me down to sleep with my head   24
on a pillowcase embossed with the signature of Yves Saint Laurent?

The first time I remember seeing a designer's name on something, the   25
name was Pucci. It seemed amusing enough but now they're all doing it.
Halston, Calvin Klein and Diane Von Furstenberg must all be wonderfully famous and talented, but if I buy anything of theirs I'd prefer to have
it anonymous. If I got a scarf with Diane Von Furstenberg's name on it,
which is unlikely, my first inclination would be to send it out to the
cleaners to have them try to get it out.

The advertisers are coming at us from all directions all the time. If we   26
were deer, a closed season would be declared on us to protect an endangered species. It just seems wrong to me that we're spending more time
and money trying to sell some things than we are making them in the first

place. I'm an all-American consumer but there are just certain times and places I don't want to be sold anything.

Topical Considerations

1. According to Andy Rooney, in what ways do license plates falsely advertise their states? In what ways are they silly advertisements? Do you think Rooney is making a lot out of nothing? Is he just being humorous? or is he making some valid points?

2. What are your own feelings about advertising on license plates?

3. What does Rooney feel about people who put bumper stickers and decals on their cars?

4. Why is Rooney most offended by designer towels and clothes that display the designers' names? Would you buy an Yves Saint Laurent pillowcase? Why or why not?

5. Summarize Rooney's stand in this essay.

Rhetorical Considerations

1. How does Rooney use his grandfather's wisdom at the beginning of this piece? How does it work throughout?

2. What is the thesis statement of this essay? Where is it? Does the author stick to this thesis throughout?

3. Which of Rooney's complaints are more tongue-in-cheek than serious? Which are serious criticisms against advertising?

4. How effective is Rooney's metaphor of the "endangered species" in his last paragraph?

Writing Assignments

1. Rooney mentions that a third of the cars on the roads have some form of reading matter on them—decals, bumperstickers, ads. The next time you're on the road, make note of the kinds of reading material on particular cars. Try to classify the kinds of material and slogans; then attempt to draw up a portrait of the person or persons in the cars, based on what they advertise about themselves. What kinds of images of themselves do they want to portray?

2. Do you agree with Andy Rooney that there is just too much advertising in our lives? If so, write your own response to advertising. Do you find it nearly impossible to avoid ads and commercials?

The Language of Advertising

Charles A. O'Neill

The language of advertising is very special. It is a language calculated to charm, to seduce—to separate the consumer from his or her money. Charles O'Neill has been a professional advertising writer for many years. In this essay, he explains just what advertising language does and how it does it. He examines some familiar television commercials and magazine ads and explains their continued prominence in those media. While admitting to some of the craftiness of his craft, O'Neill defends advertising language against critics who see it as a distorter of language and reality.

One night in 1964, a copywriter named Shirley Polykoff was   1
pacing around her office, thinking about Clairol's new hair coloring, Nice 'n Easy. The interesting, "saleable" thing about Nice 'n Easy—important to Clairol, to the advertising agency, and (at least potentially) to the hair-color–consuming public—was its basic difference from other hair colorings. Until the day Clairol put Nice 'n Easy on the market, a woman who wanted to dye her hair had to put the dye onto every strand. Coloring the older, longer hairs sometimes meant missing the roots. The result was an interesting, but somewhat less than fashionable, horizontal-striped look. New Nice 'n Easy, however, could be shampooed right through the hair, producing what Miss Polykoff calls that "beautiful, even, natural-looking color."

But that night, Shirley Polykoff's problem was to translate the product   2
feature into a benefit consumers could feel; she had to translate the idea of even coloring into a memorable, potent and attractive advertisement. So there she paced, searching for a way to motivate people to run out and buy Nice 'n Easy. She looked down at the rug, and as she remembers it, this is what happened:

> My mind wandered back to those early days when George and I used to meet each other after work and I'd spend the afternoon anticipating the rush of joy when I'd first glimpse him coming down the block. We'd be flying toward each other, but, compared to our eagerness to bridge the distance, it was like wading through molasses.
>
> Through the street was crowded, we were alone, the people in our path merely obstacles to cut around. On about the fourth time we met this way, he lifted me off my feet with a hug of sheer happiness. We were both a little breathless and as we stood there grinning at each other he said, "You know, you look pretty good from afar."

"And from near?"
"Even better."[1]

To anyone but Shirley Polykoff, that brief romantic reverie would   3
probably have been nothing more than a pleasant distraction, but way
back in her mind, she was still thinking about Nice 'n Easy.

> As I sat there recalling those delicious days, the cam-
> paign for Nice 'n Easy shampoo-in hair color unfolded
> like a dream. And, as if in a dream, the man and woman
> in the commercial would float toward each other in slow
> motion across fields or through crowds with arms out-
> stretched in anticipation. Though the message would
> have to express to the consumer that the color results
> would be even enough to pass closest inspection, it
> would have to capture the romance of the visual. And
> that is how I hit on the line, *The closer he gets . . . the better
> you look! With Nice 'n Easy, it's hair color so natural, the closer
> he gets the better you look!*[2]

Clairol found the concept appealing, and Nice 'n Easy sales proved   4
that Polykoff had indeed touched something deep in the psyche of the
public. The campaign had immediate, lasting impact: across America,
women who had feared that telltale, horizontal-striped, less than convincing look changed their minds and bought Nice 'n Easy. In the media-
advertising business, as elsewhere, imitation is the sincerest form of flattery. Suddenly, everybody who made television commercials wanted to
show slim, long-haired women running in slow motion across sunlit
fields.

Through a carefully chosen combination of visual images and spoken   5
words, one small group of human beings had caused a larger group to
take a specific, desired course of action. When Polykoff conceived "The
closer he gets . . . the better you look! With Nice 'n Easy, it's hair color
so natural, the closer he gets the better you look!" she set in motion a
sequence of events that changed the buying habits of hundreds of thousands (perhaps even millions) of people. Those who had previously
bought other brands of hair-color products now switched to Nice 'n Easy;
others who had never thought much about coloring their hair now felt
an impulse to do so. Creating that impulse—the impulse to *buy*—is the
reason for advertising. The final test of any advertising program (whether
for hair color, automobiles, detergents, cereals, life insurance, or
pantyhose) is simply the degree to which it creates the impulse.

What creates the impulse? The strategy may call for printed ads in   6

1. Shirley Polykoff, *Does She . . . or Doesn't She?* (Garden City, New York: Doubleday,
1975), pp. 98–99.
2. Ibid., p. 99.

magazines, 30-second spots on national television, handbills distributed on Main Street, T-shirts, or town criers. Whatever the strategy, advertisements derive their power from a purposeful, directed combination of two elements: visual images and words. The precise balance of words (either spoken or printed) and pictures is determined by the creative concept and the medium used; but that combination of images and words makes up the language of advertising.

Every member of our society soon learns that advertising language is   7
different from other languages. Most children would be unable to explain how "With Nice 'n Easy, it's color so natural, the closer he gets the better you look!" differed from ordinary language; but they *would* be able to tell you, "It sounds like an ad." Advertising language is different from most of the other languages we use in our everyday lives. Its differences exist because when Polykoff sits down to write an ad, she is attempting to change our behavior, to motivate us, to sell us something.

Over the years, the texture of advertising language has frequently   8
changed. Styles and creative concepts come and go. But there are at least four distinct general characteristics of the language of advertising that make it different from other languages.

1. The language of advertising is edited and purposeful.
2. The language of advertising is rich and arresting; it is specifically intended to attract and hold our attention.
3. The language of advertising involves us; in effect, *we* complete the advertising message.
4. The language of advertising holds no secrets from us; it is a simple language.

Edited and Purposeful

One easy way to develop a feeling for basic differences between adver-   9
tising language and other languages is to transcribe a television talk show.[3] An examination of such a transcript will show the conversation skipping from one topic to another, even though the guest and the host may attempt to stick to a specific subject. The conversation also is rife with repetition. After all, informal, conversational language transactions are not ordinarily intended to meet specific objectives. Advertising language cannot afford to be so desultory. It *does* have a specific purpose— to sell us something.

In *Future Shock*, Alvin Toffler draws a distinction between normal   10
"coded" messages and "engineered" messages. As an example of an uncoded message, Toffler writes about a random, unstructured experience:

3. The dialogue on a television talk show provides a good example of free-form, unstructured speech. An even better example is a casual conversation about an innocuous topic like the weather.

A man walks along a street and notices a leaf whipped along a sidewalk by the wind. He perceives this event through his sensory apparatus. He hears a rustling sound. He sees movement and greenness. He feels the wind. From these sensory perceptions he somehow forms a mental image. We can refer to these sensory signals as a message. But the message is not, in any ordinary sense of [the] term, man-made. It is not designed by anyone to communicate anything, and the man's understanding of it does not depend directly on a social code—a set of agreed-upon signs and definitions.[4]

The talk show conversation, however, is coded; the guests' ability to   11
exchange information with their host, and our ability to understand it, depend, as Toffler puts it, upon social conventions.

Beyond coded and uncoded messages there is another kind—the engi-   12
neered message—a variation of the coded message. The language of advertising is a language of finely engineered, ruthlessly purposeful messages. By Toffler's calculation,[5] the average adult American is assaulted by at least 560 advertising messages a day. Not one of these messages would reach us, to attract and hold our attention, if it were uncoded or completely unstructured. Similarly, even if they happened to attract us for a fleeting moment, coded but unengineered messages (for example, the conversation of talk show guests chatting about Nice 'n Easy) would quickly lose our attention. But when a woman runs through the field in slow motion and a voice says, "The closer he gets, . . . the better you look!" viewers who are looking for a hair color product pay attention, because the message has been carefully engineered, carefully compressed. Advertising messages have a clear purpose; they are intended to trigger a specific response.

Rich and Arresting

Advertisements—no matter how carefully "engineered" and packed   13
with information—cannot succeed unless they capture our attention in the first place. Of the hundreds of advertising messages in store for us each day, very few (Toffler estimates seventy-six) will actually obtain our conscious attention.[6] The rest are screened out. The people who design and write ads know about this screening process; they anticipate and accept it as a basic premise of their business. They expend a great deal of energy to guarantee that their ads will make it past the defenses and distractions that surround us. The classic, all-time favorite device used to penetrate the barrier is sex. The archetypal sex ad is simply headlined

4. Alvin Toffler, *Future Shock* (New York: Random House, 1970), p. 146.
5. Ibid., p. 149.
6. Ibid.

"SEX" with the text running something like this: "Now that we've got your attention. . . ." Whether it takes this approach or another, every successful advertisement contains a "hitch." The hitch can take the form of strong visuals (photos or illustrations with emotional value) or a disarming, unexpected—even incongruous—set of words:

"My chickens eat better than you do."	(Perdue Chickens)
"Introducing the ultimate concept in air freight. Men that fly."	(Emery Air Freight)
"Look deep into our ryes."	(Wigler's bakery products)
"Me. 4 U."	(The State of Maine)
"If gas pains persist, try Volkswagen."	(Volkswagen)

14   Even if the text contains no incongruity and does not rely on a pun for its impact, every effective ad needs a creative strategy based on some striking concept or idea. In fact, the concept and execution are often so good that many successful ads entertain while they sell.

15   For examples of ads where salesmanship and good ideas combine to achieve memorable results, consider the campaigns created by Ally and Gargano for Federal Express. By 1982, the "When it absolutely, positively has to get there overnight" campaign was five years old. Other competitors had entered the market, and a new twist was developed to position Federal Express as the company that would deliver packages, not just "overnight," but "by 10:30 A.M." the next day. The plight of the junior executive in "Presentation," one ad in the new campaign, is stretched for dramatic purposes, but it is, nonetheless, all too real: the young executive, who is presumably trying to climb his way up the corporate ladder, is shown calling another parcel delivery service and all but begging for assurance that he will have his slides in hand by 10:30 the next morning. "No slides, no presentation," he pleads. Only a viewer with a heart of stone can watch without feeling sympathetic, as the next morning our junior executive struggles to make his presentation *sans* slides. He is so lost without them that he is reduced to using his hands to perform imitations of birds and animals in shadows on the movie screen. What does the junior executive *viewer* think when he or she sees this ad?

1. Federal Express guarantees to deliver packages "absolutely, positively overnight."
2. Federal Express packages arrive early in the day, providing more time to use the information being sent.
3. What happened to that fellow in the commercial will absolutely not happen to me, now that I know what package delivery service to call.

A sound creative strategy, well executed, sells the service offered by Federal Express. The campaign was rated by TV viewers as one of the "outstanding" advertising efforts of 1982.

The *U.S. News and World Report* campaign by Ted Chin and Company   16
also has a readily apparent theme. The ads feature well-known people
making various straightforward remarks about why they read the magazine:

John Newcomb: "No sports."
Andy Warhol: "No gossip."
Jimmy Walker: "No jokes."
Truman Capote: "Not stylish."

The central idea: "*U.S. News and World Report* is a no-nonsense publication for people who want to read important news. It's such an important
publication, in fact, that Newcomb, the sportsman; Warhol, the trivialist;
Walker, the comedian; and Capote, the socialite, read it, even though it
doesn't cover the things they find most interesting personally."

The prominence of ads containing puns or cleverly constructed head-   17
lines would seem to imply that ads emerge, like Botticelli's Venus from
the sea, flawless and full grown. Usually they do not. The idea that
becomes the platform for an effective creative strategy is most often
developed only after exhaustive research. The product is examined for
its potential, and the prospective buyers are examined for their habits,
characteristics and preferences.

"Who will be interested in our product? How old are they? Where do   18
they live? How much money do they earn? What will they like about our
product?" Once an advertising writer has a sense of the answers to these
questions, information from other sources can be drawn on to develop
the creative strategy.

Research is one aspect of the science of advertising, the side of adver-   19
tising that made it possible for Shirley Polykoff to know that women were
afraid of the "zebra look."

The science of advertising plays an important role in the development   20
of the creative strategy. It provides the foundation on which a Polykoff
can practice her art.

The creative people in the advertising business are well aware that   21
consumers do not watch television or read magazines in order to see ads.
Ads have to earn the right to be seen, read and heard. Jerry Della Femina,
a man who earns a good living in the advertising business, sums up the
problem:

> There are a lot of copywriters who get mixed up and
> think they're Faulkner or Hemingway. They sit there and
> they mold and they play and when it's over they've writ-
> ten something that's absolutely beautiful but they forgot
> one thing. It's within the confines of a page. . . . What kills
> most copywriters is that people don't buy *Life* magazine
> to read their ads. People don't buy *Gourmet* to read their

ad for Bombay Gin. People are buying *Gourmet* to read the recipes, and the ads are just an intrusion on people's time. That is why our job is to get more attention than anything else.[7]

Involving

We have seen that the language of advertising is carefully engineered; 22
we have seen that it uses various devices to get our attention. Clairol has us watching the young woman running across a field in slow motion. Frank Perdue has us looking at a photo of his chickens at a dinner table. Volkswagen has us thinking about our "gas pains." Marlboro has us looking at the lean outdoorsman on horseback. Now that they have our attention, what will they do next? They present information intended to show us that the product they are offering for sale fills a need and, in filling this need, differs from the competition. The process is "product placement." On the night she developed the Nice 'n Easy campaign, Polykoff's problem was to express the differences between the Clairol product and its competitors. Nice 'n Easy *was* different. Its feature was that it could be shampooed through the hair. To the consumer, the benefit was that it did not cause telltale streaks. Once our attention has been captured, it is the copywriter's responsibility to express such product differences (when they exist), and to exploit and intensify them.

What happens when product differences do not exist? Then the writer 23
must glamorize the superficial differences (for example, differences of color, packaging, or other qualities without direct bearing on the product's basic function) or else *create* differences in the consumer's mind. At this point the language of advertising becomes more abstract, more difficult to define and analyze. It is also at this stage—the stage at which an image is fixed in the consumer's mind—that advertising becomes powerful, because now we, the consumers, are brought most directly into the process. As long as the ad is trying to get our attention, the "action" is mostly in the ad itself, in the words and visual images. But as we read an ad or watch it on television, we become more deeply involved. The action starts to take place in *us*. Our imagination is set in motion, and our individual fears and aspirations, our little quirks and insecurities, superimpose themselves on that tightly engineered, attractively packaged message. Polykoff did not create the consumers' need to feel attractive "up close." The drive to feel attractive was already there; she merely exploited and intensified it.

So the language of advertising is different from other languages be- 24
cause it holds up a brightly lit mirror. Once we have been brought into an ad we become participants.

7. Jerry Della Femina, *From Those Wonderful Folks Who Brought You Pearl Harbor* (New York: Simon and Schuster, 1970), p. 118.

This process is especially significant in ads for products that do not   25
differ significantly from their competitors. The running battle among
the low calorie soft drinks, for example, has spawned many "look alike"
advertisements, because the product features and consumer benefits
are generic, applying to all products in the category. Substitute one
product name for another, and the messages are often identical, right
down to the way the cans are photographed in the closing sequence.
Such commercials may happen to actually sell a particular product, but
they don't lead to lasting results. As with all advertising, the challenge
to marketers of low calorie soft drinks is to find or create differences
which set their product apart from the competitors. Specifically what
should you do, then, to stimulate better sales of your low calorie soft
drink, without falling into the "me too" advertising trap? Do what your
competitors do, but do it better. BBDO's solution for Diet Pepsi relied
on crisp, striking visuals and well paced music with lyrics that do not
disguise what the product is for—it's for people who want to have lean,
perfect bodies.

> Singers: Now you see it
> Now you don't
> Here you have it
> Here you won't
> Oh Diet Pepsi
> One small calorie
> Now you see it
> Now you don't.
> That great Pepsi taste
> Diet Pepsi
> Won't go to your waist
> So now you see it
> Now you don't.
> Oh Diet Pepsi one small calorie
> Now you see it
> Now you don't.

Quick cuts show a man and woman in poses intended to display their
bodies (what else?) to best advantage. The commercial is consciously
designed to build in our minds an association between the people and the
product. Even if we make a conscious effort to reject that association, we
will remember the Diet Pepsi woman and the Diet Pepsi man, and the Diet
Pepsi messages we see in the future will trigger the memory.

Symbols have become important elements in the language of advertis-   26
ing, not so much because they carry meanings of their own but because
we bring a meaning to them: we charge them with significance. Symbols
are efficient, compact vehicles for the communication of an advertising
message. As Toffler says:

Today, advertising men, in a deliberate attempt to cram more messages into the individual's mind within a given moment of time, make increasing use of the symbolic techniques of the arts. Consider the "tiger" that is allegedly put into one's tank. Here a single word transmits to the audience a distinct visual image that has been associated since childhood with power, speed, and force.[8]

Federal Trade Commission regulations are making it increasingly difficult for oil companies to say they put anything into the tank but fuel. But symbolism is, nonetheless, pervasive and powerful.   27

One example of a particularly effective use of symbolism is the campaign begun in 1978 by Somerset Importers for Johnnie Walker Red Scotch. Sales of Johnnie Walker Red had been trailing sales of Johnnie Walker Black, and Somerset Importers needed to position Red as a fine product in its own right. The Smith/Greenland Agency produced ads which made heavy use of the color red. One ad, often printed as a two page spread, is dominated by a close-up photo of red autumn leaves. At lower right, the copy reads, "When their work is done, even the leaves turn to red." Another ad—also suitably dominated by a photograph in the appropriate color—reads: "When it's time to quiet down at the end of the day, even a fire turns to Red." *Red.* Warm. Experienced. Bright. A perfect symbol to use in a liquor advertisement; all the more for the fact that it offers great possibilities for graphic design and copywriting: more fuel for the advertiser's creative art.   28

The reference to the tiger in the tank and the use of the color red are variations on the same theme. The tiger and the color are tangible; the advertiser makes no effort to disguise them as symbols. They appear on the surface of the ads.   29

From time to time a more abstract form of symbolism is also used— the "hidden message" symbol. Take a close, hard look at liquor ads and occasionally you will see, reflected in the photograph of a glass of spirits, peculiar, demon-like shapes. Are these shapes merely the product of one consumer's imagination? Or were they deliberately superimposed onto the product photograph by the careful application of ink and airbrush?   30

The art of advertising contains many such ambiguities. Some are charged, like this one, with multiple shades of meaning. The demons may be taken to represent the problems and cares which one can presumably chase away through consumption of the advertised product. Or they can, just as easily, be taken as representations of the playful spirits which will be unleashed once the product has been consumed. What did the advertising director have in mind? Take your pick. Not all the symbols of advertising are innocent; many are insidious.   31

8. Toffler, *Future Shock,* p. 149.

Another human desire advertising writers did not invent (although   32
they liberally exploit it), is to associate with successful people. Though
we may not like to advertise the fact, all of us tend to admire people who
are widely known for their achievements. We are therefore already
primed for the common advertising device of the testimonial or personality ad. Once we have seen a famous person in an advertisement, we
associate the product with the person. "I like Mr. X. Mr. X likes (en-
dorses) this product. I like this product, too." The logic is faulty, but we
fall for it just the same. That is how Joe DiMaggio sells Mr. Coffee,
Pac-Man sells vitamins, and Bugs Bunny sells Post Raisin Bran. The
people who write testimonial ads did not create our trust in famous
personalities. They merely recognize our inclinations and exploit them.

The language of advertising is different from other languages because   33
we participate in it; in fact, we—not the words we read on the magazine
page or the pictures unreeling before us on the television screen—charge
the ads with most of their power.

Simple

Clip a typical story from the publication you read most frequently.   34
Calculate the number of words in an average sentence. Count the number
of words of three or more syllables in a typical 100-word passage, omit-
ting words that are capitalized, combinations of two simple words, or verb
forms made into three-syllable words by the addition of -ed or -es. Add
the two figures (the average number of words per sentence and the
number of three-syllable words per 100 words), then multiply the result
by .4. According to Robert Gunning, if the resulting number is seven,
there is a good chance that you are reading *True Confessions.* [9] He developed this equation, the "Fog Index," to determine the comparative ease
with which any given piece of written communication can be read. With
this equation, the first passages of this essay measure somewhere between
Reader's Digest and *Time.*

Now consider the complete text of a typical cigarette advertisement: 35

> I demand two things from my cigarette. I want a cigarette
> with low tar and nicotine. But, I also want taste. That's
> why I smoke Winston Lights. I get a lighter cigarette, but
> I still get a real taste. And real pleasure. Only one ciga-
> rette gives me that: Winston Lights.

The average sentence in this ad runs seven words. *Cigarette* and *nicotine*   36
are three-syllable words, with *cigarette* appearing four times; *nicotine*, once.
Considering *that's* as two words, the ad is exactly fifty words long, so the
average number of three-syllable words per 100 is ten.

9. Curtis D. MacDougall, *Interpretive Reporting* (New York: Macmillan, 1968), p. 94.

    7 words per sentence
+ 10 three-syllable words/100
   17
× .4
  6.8 Fog Index

According to Gunning's scale, this particular ad is written at about the   37
seventh grade level, about the level of *True Confessions*. [10] This means the
ad is a little harder to read than a comic book but easier than *Ladies Home
Journal*. The level of the Winston Lights ad is representative of the ads
regularly found in most mass-circulation consumer magazines. Of
course, the Fog Index does not evaluate the visual aspect of an ad. The
headline, "I demand two things from my cigarette," works with the picture (that of an attractive woman) to arouse consumer interest. The text
reinforces the image. It is unlikely that many consumers actually take the
trouble to read the entire text, but it is not necessary for them to do so
in order for the ad to work.

Since three-syllable words are harder to read than one- or two-syllable   38
words, and since simple ideas are more easily transferred from one
human being to another than complex ideas, advertising copy tends to
use simpler language all the time. Toffler speculates:

> If the [English] language had the same number of words
> in Shakespeare's time as it does today, at least 200,000
> words—perhaps several times that many—have dropped
> out and been replaced in the intervening four centuries.
> . . . The high turnover rate reflects changes in things,
> processes, and qualities in the environment from the
> world of consumer products and technology.[11]

It is no accident that the first terms Toffler uses to illustrate his point
("fast-back," "wash-and-wear," and "flashcube") were invented not by
engineers, journalists, or marketing managers, but by advertising copy-
writers.

Advertising language is simple language; in the engineering process,   39
difficult words (which could be used in other forms of communication to
lend color or fine shades of meaning) are edited out and replaced by
simple words not open to misinterpretation.

Some critics view the entire advertising business as a cranky, un-   40
planned child of the capitalist free enterprise system, a noisy, whining,
brash kid who must somehow be kept in line, but can't just yet be thrown
out of the house. Because advertising mirrors the fears, quirks, and aspi-

10. Ibid., p. 95.
11. Toffler, *Future Shock*, p. 151.

rations of the society that creates it (and is, in turn, sold by it), it is wide open to parody and ridicule.

Perhaps the strongest, most authoritative critic of advertising language 41 in recent years is journalist Edwin Newman. In his book *Strictly Speaking*, he poses the question, "Will America be the death of English?" Newman's "mature, well thought out judgment" is that it will. As evidence, he cites a number of examples of fuzzy thinking and careless use of the King's English, not just by advertisers, but by many people in public life, including politicians and journalists:

> The federal government has adopted the comic strip character Snoopy as a symbol and showed us Snoopy on top of his doghouse, flat on his back, with a balloon coming out of his mouth, containing the words, "I believe in conserving energy," while below there was this exhortation: savEnergy.
>
> savEnergy. An entire letter e at the end was savd. In addition, an entire space was savd. Perhaps the government should say onlYou can prevent forest fires. . . . Spelling has been assaulted by Duz, E-Z Off, Fantastik, Kool, Kleen . . . and by products that make you briter, so that you will not be left hi and dri at a parti, but made welkom. . . . Under this pressure, adjectives become adverbs; nouns become adjectives; prepositions disappear; compounds abound.[12]

In this passage, Newman presents three of the charges most often levied against the language of advertising:

1. Advertising debases English.
2. Advertising downgrades the intelligence of the public.
3. Advertising warps our vision of reality, implanting in us groundless fears and insecurities. (He cites, as examples of these groundless fears, "tattletale grey," "denture breath," "morning mouth," "unsightly bulge," and "ring around the collar.")

Other charges have been made from time to time. They include: 42

1. Advertising sells daydreams; distracting, purposeless visions of lifestyles beyond the reach of most of the people who are most exposed to advertising.
2. Advertising feeds on human weaknesses and exaggerates the importance of material things, encouraging "impure" emotions and vanities.
3. Advertising encourages bad, even unhealthy habits like smoking.
4. Advertising perpetuates racial and sexual stereotypes.

12. Edwin Newman, *Strictly Speaking* (Indianapolis: Bobbs-Merrill, 1974), p. 13.

What can be said in advertising's defense? Advertising is only a reflec-   43
tion of society; slaying the messenger (and just one of the messengers,
at that) would not alter the fact—if it is a fact—that America will be the
death of English. A case can be made for the concept that advertising
language is an acceptable stimulus for the natural evolution of the language. At the very least, advertising may stimulate debate about what
current trends in language are "good" and "bad." Another point: *is*
"proper English" the language we actually speak and write, or is it the
language we are told we should speak and write, the language of *The
Elements of Style* and *The Oxford English Dictionary?* There are more questions than ready answers.

What about the charge that advertising debases the intelligence of the   44
public? Those who support this particular criticism would do well to ask
themselves another question: Exactly how intelligent is the public? How
many people know the difference between adverbs and adjectives? How
many people *want* to know?

This is not to suggest that people who care about the state of the   45
English language in America should abandon their cause. But they would
do better to look at more fundamental aspects of our society (our educational institutions, for instance) than to focus their attention on advertising, which is at best a reflection of the world as it is. An intelligent public
would:

1. Compare a product against its competitors, to determine rationally
   which product provides best value for their money.
2. Press advertisers to produce more accurate, fully descriptive ads.
3. Write letters to companies whose advertisements are racist, sexist,
   deceptive or otherwise offensive.
4. Recognize that ads are created by people, some more talented than
   others.

The fact is that advertisements are effective, not because agencies say   46
they are effective, but because they sell products.

Advertising attempts to convince us to buy products; we are not forced   47
to buy something because it is heavily advertised. Who, for example, is
to be blamed for the success, in the mid-70s, of a nonsensical, nonfunc-
tional product—Pet Rocks? The people who designed the packaging, the
people who created the idea of selling ordinary rocks as pets, or the
people who bought the product? Many tend to blame the advertiser, the
messenger.

Perhaps much of the fault lies not with the advertiser, but with the   48
public, for accepting advertising so readily. S. I. Hayakawa, for example,
finds "the uncritical response to the incantations of advertising . . . a
serious symptom of widespread evaluational disorder." He does not find
it "beyond the bounds of possibility" that "today's suckers for national
advertising will be tomorrow's suckers for the master political propagan-

dist who will, by playing up the 'Jewish menace,' in the same way as national advertisers play up the 'pink toothbrush menace,' and by promising us national glory and prosperity, sell fascism in America."[13]

Fascism in America is fortunately a far cry from Pet Rocks, but the   49
point is well taken. The intelligent consumer is the good advertiser's best friend. Emerson said it well: "Nothing astonishes men so much as common sense and plain dealing." Consumers should apply common sense, and they should expect advertisers to practice the art of plain dealing.

The advertising industry itself provides several formal mechanisms   50
through which ads are evaluated, not just for sales effectiveness, but for accuracy, clarity of expression, and excellence of design. Competition in the industry is fierce, and legislation is stringent and unforgiving. Today, awareness is no longer the responsibility of the buyer (*"caveat emptor"*), but of the seller as well.

Do advertisements sell distracting, purposeless visions? Occasionally.   51
But perhaps such visions are necessary components of the process through which our civilization changes and improves.

Other arguments may be made in support of advertising as it is prac-   52
ticed today. It has been said that advertising stimulates product development, thus helping people lead more comfortable lives. It has been said that the information presented in ads helps people make more intelligent purchasing decisions. As individuals living in a free society, we have the right to evaluate both sides of the various linguistic and social questions advertising—and the language of advertising—present to us. But we should recognize that advertising is likely to continue to influence our behavior, regardless of what we think of the process.

American companies are spending vast sums of money to drive their   53
messages home to us, and they are spending more every year: advertising expenditures have grown from about three billion dollars in 1944 to nearly 74 billion in 1983.

Advertisers are also aided in their efforts by a continuing stream of   54
technological developments. Beyond the development of the printing press and the advent of widespread literacy, radio and television have perhaps been most responsible for unleashing the advertiser's power. Print advertising appeals to only one of our senses—the visual—and in so doing, presents a static image. Radio added the auditory dimension, enabling advertisers to drive us crazy with jingles. Television combines the visual stimulation of print advertising with the auditory stimulation of radio and to these adds motion. And for the advertiser television is becoming increasingly potent. Consider these developments:

- Thanks to devices called speech compressors, producers can increase the speed of an audiotaped message without introducing distortion.

13. S. I. Hayakawa, *Language in Action* (New York: Harcourt, Brace, 1941), p. 235.

Listeners notice the difference; they pay more attention to the message, but they don't know why.

- The frequent use of computers and computer systems to drive and control systems of cameras enables producers to take best advantage of both film and television production techniques. The result: Television commercials which are more visually appealing, in many cases, than the programs they interrupt. Costs in the television industry are such that most producers cannot afford to rival the techniques available to the producers of commercials. For the most part, they do not even try.

Some of the best of the computer-assisted television commercials are those created for Levi Strauss by the Foote, Cone & Belding/Honig Agency. Creativity and excellence in production have been characteristic of Levi's commercials for many years, but one worth viewing for pleasure is the "Working Man" spot run in 1982:

> (Sound of hissing steam)
> Anncr. (Voice Over) He's the working man
> (Sound of sledge hammer striking metal)
> Anncr. (VO): Forging dreams with fire
> (Sound of hammer)
> Anncr. (VO): Building, moving mountains
> (Sound of hammer)
> Anncr. (VO): Always reaching higher
> (Sound of hammer)
> Anncr. (VO): He's the wheels that move a nation.
> (Sound of hammer)
> Anncr. (VO): The stitching in the seams
> (Sound of hammer)
> Anncr. (VO): He holds it all together
> (Sound of hammer)
> Anncr. (VO): He wears Levi's jeans
> (Sound of hammer)
> Anncr. (VO): 'Cause he knows
> (Sound of boards going up)
> Anncr. (VO): We still build the Levi's jeans
>   that helped build America.

As in the agency's earlier efforts for Levi's, this commercial makes use of state of the art production techniques, juxtaposing animation and computer-generated graphics with "real" scenes.

- The now commonplace presence of videotape recording equipment in the homes of consumers. While specialized nonbroadcast programming is now being actively marketed, studies show that most people who own home video equipment use it mostly to record programs they wish to see again. While the equipment can be put in stop or pause positions to prevent the recording of commercials while the viewer is present, the equipment is not "smart" enough to discriminate between commercials and ordinary programs on its own. As a result, by recording programs off the air, people who own this equipment are giving the commercials an extended shelf life, and are, in effect, almost guaranteeing that they will be viewed again by prospective consumers after the initial broadcast. Properly maintained, there is virtually no limit to the life of a video cassette.

Whatever we think of these developments—whether we view them with alarm for their power to shape our perception of the world around us, or greet them as new tools for communication and understanding— whatever we think of advertising itself, it is clear that advertising will continue to exert a profound influence on our lives.   55

Speaking one day on a New York City radio station, philosopher Rollo   56
May told his listeners that a line from a Nice 'n Easy ad ("If I've only one life, let me live it as a blonde!") was the "ultimate existential statement."[14] When Shirley Polykoff wrote that line, was she attempting to create an "existential statement"? No, she was simply trying to sell us something.

Advertising is a mirror. It is not perfect; sometimes it distorts. When   57
we view ourselves in it, we're not always pleased with the image. But perhaps, all things considered, that's the way it should be.

Topical Considerations

1. The author uses the phrases "advertising language" and "other languages." What assumptions about language is he making? Are they valid? Why or why not?

2. O'Neill describes several ways in which the language of advertising differs from other kinds of language. Briefly list the different ways he mentions. Can you think of any other characteristics of advertising language that set it apart?

3. In his last section, O'Neill presents several of the most frequent charges levied against advertising language. What are they? What does he say in defense of advertising? Which set of arguments seems the stronger?

4. "Symbols are efficient, compact vehicles for the communication of an advertising message" (paragraph 26). What symbols from the advertising world do you associate with your own life? Are they effective symbols for selling?

14. Rollo May's comments were broadcast by radio station WBAI in March, 1966.

Rhetorical Considerations

1. O'Neill's essay is constructed around a story about copy-writer Shirley Polykoff. How does this construction contribute to the essay?

2. O'Neill is an advertising professional. Does his style reflect the advertising techniques he describes? Cite examples to support your answer.

3. Describe the author's point of view about advertising. Does he ever tell us how he feels? Does his style indicate his attitude?

4. Why does O'Neill quote Rollo May in the second-to-last paragraph of the essay? Does the quotation tie into the discussion of advertising language and Shirley Polykoff?

Writing Assignments

1. The author believes that advertising language mirrors the fears, quirks, and aspirations of the society that creates it. Do you agree or disagree with this statement? Explain in a brief essay.

2. Choose a brand-name product you use regularly and one of its competitors—one whose differences are negligible, if they exist at all. Examine some advertisements for each brand. Write a short paper explaining what really makes you prefer your brand.

3. Write a description of a common object in "formal standard English." Now write an advertisement for the same object. Analyze what has happened to the language in your writing.

4. Write a paper on sexism or racism in advertising. Use specific examples from current ads and commercials.

Printed Noise

George F. Will

Most of us are so accustomed to the incessant roar of commerce that we hear it without listening. But if we stopped and thought about some of the names advertisers have given their products, we might recognize a peculiarly American form of language pollution. In this amusing essay, *Newsweek* columnist George F. Will takes a look at some of the fanciful and familiar names given to menu items—such as "Egg McMuffin," "Fishamigig," and "Hot Fudge Nutty Buddy." He concludes that all the asphyxiating cuteness amounts to a lot of verbal litter.

The flavor list at the local Baskin-Robbins ice cream shop is an   1
anarchy of names like "Peanut Butter 'N Chocolate" and "Strawberry
Rhubarb Sherbert." These are not the names of things that reasonable
people consider consuming, but the names are admirably businesslike,
briskly descriptive.

Unfortunately, my favorite delight (chocolate-coated vanilla flecked   2
with nuts) bears the unutterable name "Hot Fudge Nutty Buddy," an
example of the plague of cuteness in commerce. There are some things
a gentleman simply will not do, and one is announce in public a desire
for a "Nutty Buddy." So I usually settle for a plain vanilla cone.

I am not the only person suffering for immutable standards of propri-   3
ety. The May issue of *Atlantic* contains an absorbing tale of lonely heroism
at a Burger King. A gentleman requested a ham and cheese sandwich that
the Burger King calls a Yumbo. The girl taking orders was bewildered.

"Oh," she eventually exclaimed, "you mean a Yumbo."   4

Gentleman: "The ham and cheese. Yes."   5

Girl, nettled: "It's called a Yumbo. Now, do you want a Yumbo or   6
not?"

Gentleman, teeth clenched: "Yes, thank you, the ham and cheese."   7

Girl: "Look, I've got to have an order here. You're holding up the line.   8
You want a Yumbo, don't you? You want a Yumbo!"

Whereupon the gentleman chose the straight and narrow path of vir-   9
tue. He walked out rather than call a ham and cheese a Yumbo. His
principles are anachronisms but his prejudices are impeccable, and he is
on my short list of civilization's friends.

That list includes the Cambridge don who would not appear outdoors   10
without a top hat, not even when routed by fire at 3 A.M., and who refused
to read another line of Tennyson after he saw the poet put water in fine
port. The list includes another don who, although devoutly Tory, voted
Liberal during Gladstone's day because the duties of prime minister kept
Gladstone too busy to declaim on Holy Scripture. And high on the list
is the grammarian whose last words were: "I am about to—or I am going
to—die: either expression is correct."

Gentle reader, can you imagine any of these magnificent persons ask-   11
ing a teenage girl for a "Yumbo"? Or uttering "Fishamagig" or "Egg
McMuffin" or "Fribble" (that's a milk shake, sort of)?

At one point in the evolution of American taste, restaurants that were   12
relentlessly fun, fun, fun were built to look like lemons or bananas. I am
told that in Los Angeles there was the Toed Inn, a strange spelling for
a strange place shaped like a giant toad. Customers entered through the
mouth, like flies being swallowed.

But the mature nation has put away such childish things in favor of   13
menus that are fun, fun, fun. Seafood is "From Neptune's Pantry" or
"Denizens of the Briny Deep." And "Surf 'N Turf," which you might
think is fish and horsemeat, actually is lobster and beef.

To be fair, there are practical considerations behind the asphyxiatingly   14
cute names given hamburgers. Many hamburgers are made from portions
of the cow that the cow had no reason to boast about. So sellers invent
distracting names to give hamburgers cachet. Hence "Whoppers" and
"Heroburgers."

But there is no excuse for Howard Johnson's menu. In a just society   15
it would be a flogging offense to speak of "steerburgers," clams "fried
to order" (which probably means they don't fry clams for you unless
you order fried clams), a "natural cut" (what is an "unnatural" cut?) of
sirloin, "oven-baked" meat loaf, chicken pot pie with "flaky crust,"
"golden croquettes," "grilled-in-butter Frankforts [sic]," "liver with
smothered onions" (smothered by onions?), and a "hearty" Reuben
sandwich.

America is marred by scores of Dew Drop Inns serving "crispy green"   16
salads, "garden fresh" vegetables, "succulent" lamb, "savory" pork, "sizzling" steaks, and "creamy" or "tangy" coleslaw. I've nothing against
Homeric adjectives ("wine-dark sea," "wing-footed Achilles") but isn't
coleslaw just coleslaw? Americans hear the incessant roar of commerce
without listening to it, and read the written roar without really noticing
it. Who would notice if a menu proclaimed "creamy" steaks and "sizzling" coleslaw? Such verbal litter is to language as Muzak is to music.
As advertising blather becomes the nation's normal idiom, language
becomes printed noise.

Topical Considerations

1. What is George F. Will's major assertion here regarding the
language of American menus? Is he concerned that some items have been
given fanciful names to disguise inferior food? Or is he more concerned
with the way advertising hype reduces language?

2. Are you so used to fast food menu names such as "Fishamagig," "Egg McMuffin," or "Yumbo" that you never questioned them?
Or have they ever seemed silly and offensive to you? Can you think of
some other similar names?

3. In paragraph 15, Will attacks the language of Howard Johnson
menus. What is wrong with "steerburgers"? "oven-baked" meat loaf?
clams "fried to order"? "liver with smothered onions"? And what's
wrong with a "hearty" Reuben sandwich?

4. Will makes the point in the last paragraph that menus make
us adjective-blind (or deaf). But just how effective would a menu be if it
were stripped of all the empty adjectives? Is a "crispy green" salad more
attractive than "salad"? Is "sizzling" steak more tantalizing than just
plain "steak," or "tangy" coleslaw more appetizing than "coleslaw"? Are
we so accustomed to the adjectives that we need their assurance?

Rhetorical Considerations

1. How does Will use examples here? In other words, does he use examples to convince us of his position, or just to inform us?

2. How effective is the example of the *Atlantic* anecdote about the gentleman ordering a Yumbo? Did you find that example funny? Did it sufficiently dramatize Will's point?

3. How would you characterize Will's sense of humor? In what ways does he establish it? What humorous word choices can you find?

4. In the last paragraph, Will makes an analogy: "Such verbal litter is to language as Muzak is to music." What is Muzak, and how effective is the comparison?

Writing Assignments

1. Write your own essay on printed noise. Go through newspapers and magazines and find examples of advertisers' names for products to draw from.

2. Construct a menu of your own, using some of the advertising principles Will attacks here. Use silly, childish names, overblown adjectives, and euphemisms to make ordinary fast food sound tantalizing.

Resisting Those Awful Commercials

Diane White

Have you ever seen a television commercial that you found so offensive it made you refuse to buy the product? According to a poll of consumers, a majority of people refuse to purchase products whose commercials they didn't like. But there are some people, such as journalist Diane White, who out of some unexplained perverse impulse will buy a product whose ads they actually hated. The following is White's humorous confession—a confession, perhaps, of many a consumer who is torn between dark urgings to buy and to resist.

A story in *New York* magazine reports that companies called "monitoring services" are trying to pin down our tastes in TV advertising.   1

They've been sending pollsters out to shopping malls to stop people   2 at random and ask them which television commercials they hate most. One of the things they've found is that people have trouble remembering the commercials they don't like.

I was kind of surprised by this because, if somebody were to walk up   3 and ask me which commercials I really despise, I could bore them for hours singing awful jingles and describing hateful ads in detail.

After reading the *New York* magazine story, I realized something curi-   4 ous: Sometimes, when I find an ad particularly offensive, I deliberately run right out and buy the product.

For example, one of my least favorite television commercials pushes   5 a product called Murphy's Oil Soap.

You may have seen the ad. It features a man, a woman and a little girl   6 hopping around and singing, to the tune of "Turkey in the Straw," a jingle that goes, in part, like this:

> I've been using Murphy's Oil Soap
> On this wood floor of mine
> Now the dirt is finished
> But the finish is fine!

I can't even begin to tell you how much I hate this ad. I hate the jingle.   7 I hate the three people who sing it. I hate the grinning mom and dad. I especially hate the obnoxious little girl. I hate this ad so much I went out and bought a bottle of Murphy's Oil Soap.

I don't know why I bought it. Maybe because I couldn't get that stupid   8 jingle out of my head. Maybe because some part of my subconscious needs to be dominated by lousy advertising. Maybe because I felt guilty for hating that family so much. After all, what have they ever done to me? Maybe because I was curious to find out if the product could be as bad as the commercial.

Anyway, I went out and bought it. And, as much as I don't like to admit   9 it, the stuff really works. I don't know anything about the sales figures, but I bet they'd triple overnight if the company had a decent advertising campaign.

Unless, of course, there are lots of other people out there who respond   10 to offensive advertising the way I do.

However, according to the polling companies featured in the *New York*   11 magazine story, they don't. There's no evidence, they say, that annoying commercials increase sales or brand-name recall. In fact, one company found that 55 percent of the people they interviewed had vowed not to buy certain products whose commercials they didn't like.

Not me. Just the other day I bought some Close-Up Toothpaste be-   12 cause I hate the ads for it.

I don't know when I've ever seen a commercial quite as nauseating as   13 the Close-Up commercial featuring a young couple called Desiree and

Rob. These two are so in love that their eyes glaze over when they moon about each other, which they do in public, on television.

What, you may ask, does their passion have to do with toothpaste?   14
Well, it seems that the reason Desiree loves Rob is that his teeth are so white. And the reason Rob loves Desiree is that her breath smells like new-mown hay. Or maybe it's the other way around. Anyway, they owe it all to Close-Up toothpaste, and I say they deserve just what they get.

I could go on listing other awful commercials that have moved me to   15
buy the products. The Papa Gino's Pizza ad with the horrible adolescent who sings "Gimme that thick pan pizza, Papa . . ." and then sinks her teeth into a big slice of the stuff. Donny and Marie's Hawaiian Punch ads. The No Nonsense Pantyhose commercials featuring that woman who talks like Betty Boop.

There are some items I have actually had to restrain myself from   16
buying because, even though I may hate the ads, I have no use for the products. Arthritis Pain Formula is one. That woman who picks up the frying pan drives me crazy. Preparation H is another. I practically froth at the mouth when that man hops on his bicycle and starts pedaling like mad to show how well the stuff works.

Obnoxious advertising must work on some level, on some people. It's   17
possible, on the other hand, that there are some who don't find these ads as awful as I do. But I don't like to think about that.

What kind of perversity is at work here? I'm not sure. I only know I'll   18
never buy Carvel Ice Cream or Uncle Ben's Rice. And I'll never consult a Bache broker. Even I have my limits.

Topical Considerations

1. Why was Diane White surprised at the findings of the advertising pollsters?

2. What theories does White offer to explain why she went out and bought Murphy's Oil Soap even though she hated the commercial? Do any of her hypotheses seem more valid than others? Have you ever had similar reactions—that is, have you bought a product because you hated the commercial for it? What might have been your reasons?

3. What is there about the Close-Up commercial that makes White hate it so?

4. White reports that 55 percent of those interviewed by pollsters said they would never buy products whose commercials they didn't like. Are you such a person? Have you gone out of your way to avoid a product because a television commercial for it offended you? If so, which product? What was there about the commercial that you disliked?

Rhetorical Considerations

1. Is there something significant in White's claim that she can't understand why she buys products whose commercials she hates? Do you think her not knowing is part of her rhetorical strategy—part of her message about the way commercials work on us? If she did know, would her point be blunted?

2. Does White ever tell us exactly why she hates any of the commercials she cites? Where is she the most analytical? the least?

3. Comment on White's writing style. Is she formal? informal? conversational? friendly? Do you find her humorous in places? If so, try to evaluate her humorous effects.

Writing Assignments

1. Are there TV commercials that you just can't stand? If so, which ones in particular? Why do you hate them? Write a paper in which you try to analyze why these particular commercials are obnoxious to you. Would you still buy the products advertised? Or would you go out of your way to buy a competitive product?

2. Do you think the commercials that draw the most attention are the most successful, or the other way around? Analyze some television commercials that do and do not draw attention to themselves. Which seem the most successful?

"Ring Around the Collar!"

Michael J. Arlen

Speaking of obnoxious commercials, here is a close-up look at one of the most familiar commercials television has ever aired. Michael Arlen is a well-known author who writes regularly about television. Since 1956, he has been a staff writer for the *New Yorker.* He also contributes to *Atlantic Monthly, Cosmopolitan, Holiday,* and other periodicals. His best-known books include *Passage to Ararat* (1975), *The Camera Age* (1977), and *Thirty Seconds* (1980). His essay here is a fine example of analysis and interpretation.

This half-minute commercial for a laundry detergent called Wisk   1
appears fairly frequently on daytime and evening television. In a recent version, a young woman and a young man are shown being led down the

corridor of a hotel by a bellman who is carrying suitcases. The hotel seems to be an attractive one—not very elegant but definitely not an ordinary motel. Similarly, the young man and woman are attractive, but with nothing either glamorous or working-class about their appearance. Perhaps he is a junior executive. And she is probably his wife, though there is nothing so far that says that the two people are married. Since the framework of the drama is a commercial, the assumption is that they *are* married. On the other hand, against the familiar framework of similar modern movie scenes, there is no such assumption; possibly it is the beginning of an adventure. Then, suddenly, the bellman drops one of the suitcases in the corridor; some of the contents of the suitcase spill out; the bellman crouches down on the corridor carpet to put the items back in. He notices one of the man's shirts and holds it up. "Ring around the collar!" he says accusingly; these words are then taken up in the kind of singsong chant that has become a feature of these ads. The man looks puzzled and let down. The woman examines the offending shirt and looks mortified and aghast. By now, whatever slight elegance or intimations of adventure may have existed at the beginning of the scene have totally disintegrated, and, indeed, have quickly re-formed themselves into the classic hubby-and-housewife focus of most television commercials. The wife admits her mistake—to the bellman and her husband—of having used an inadequate detergent, and the scene changes to what is apparently the laundry area of her house, where the wife (now back in her regular "wifely" clothes) discusses the merits of using Wisk when doing the family wash.

In a number of ways, this is the most noticeably irritating of the housewife commercials. There is a nagging, whiny quality to the "Ring around the collar!" chant which is almost a caricature of the nagging, whiny voices of earlier Hollywood and TV-commercial housewives but which deliberately stops before the point of caricature is reached. In the manner of certain other ads—especially those for aspirin and "cold remedies"—it is a commercial that expressly announces its own irritatingness. We are going to repeat and repeat and repeat, these commercials say, and we are going to grate on your nerves—and you are going to remember us. At times, this sales approach has been given various fine-sounding methodological names by advertisers, but essentially it is the voice of the small boy who wants something: I want, I want, I want, I want—and finally you give it to him. In this case, the small boy wants you to buy his detergent, and who is to tell him no? 2

On the level of anti-female condescension, the "Ring around the collar!" ad seems to go even beyond irritation. In most housewife commercials, the housewife is portrayed as little more than a simpering, brainless jelly, almost pathologically obsessed with the world of kitchen floors or laundry, or of the celebrated "bathroom bowl." But in the Wisk commercials the standard trivializing portrait is accompanied by quite unusual 3 brutality. As if in a reverse Cinderella process, the young prince and his companion not only are stopped in their tracks by the hazard of the Dirty Shirt (and the curse cry of "Ring around the collar!") but, instantly, as if under a magic spell, are snatched from the hotel-palace and returned to their previous existence—she to profess folk-happiness among the laundry tubs, and he, presumably, to his northern New England sales route. Sex is back to what it used to be: the identityless woman in the traveling suit is replaced by the beaming housewife in housewifely attire. And it is all the result of *her* failure in not having properly attended to her husband's needs—in having exposed him to the scorn of the bellman who guarded the erotic corridor. The fable does not end in tragedy—for though Cinderella is back among the laundry tubs, she now has good magic on her side. But it has been a sobering experience.

Topical Considerations

1. What particular features of the Wisk commercial does Michael Arlen find irritating?

2. According to the author, how does this particular commercial show "anti-female condescension"? How is this one commercial even more brutal in its "trivializing portrait" than others?

3. How is the man portrayed in the commercial? What attitude toward marriage does Arlen object to in the commercial?

4. Do you agree with Arlen's interpretation of the commercial? Or do you think he has gone overboard in his analysis?

Rhetorical Considerations

1. What is the transition between paragraphs 1 and 2?

2. Toward the end of the last paragraph, Arlen calls the woman Cinderella. How appropriate is this name? What about the commercial drama suggests this fairy tale? What changes in the Cinderella tale does the commercial make?

3. Why does the author refer to the "erotic corridor" in the last paragraph? How does that choice of expression relate to a point raised in paragraph 1?

Writing Assignments

1. Arlen says that housewife commercials portray women as little more than "simpering, brainless jelly, almost pathologically obsessed with the world of kitchen floors or laundry, or of the celebrated 'bath-

room bowl' " (paragraph 3). Select a different housewife commercial and analyze the portrait of women in it. Is Arlen's assessment accurate? Try to describe the commercial in detail, as he does; then analyze its female images.

2. Select some other non-housewife commercials in which women are portrayed. Discuss the different images the advertisers are projecting, the different attitudes toward women they have created.

3. Are there any commercials on television that seem to avoid simple trivializing stereotypes of women? Are there any images of "liberated," independent women? Discuss these commercials, detailing how the images are portrayed.

4. Select different commercials in which men are portrayed. What different images or stereotypes are conveyed?

5. Select different commercials in which children are portrayed. What different images of children are conveyed?

Some Fancy Footwork from the World of Advertising: Sample Ads

On the following pages, we have reproduced nine recently published magazine ads. Although each of the ads represents a different manufacturer, they have one common theme: footwear. You will see ads for moccasins, duck shoes, cowboy boots, high-tech running shoes, and high-style Italian heels. And the ads are just as diversified in their approaches, their visuals, and their copy. Some are simply photographs, with no hard-sell copy, while others are informative, even chatty. Because the psychology of approaches and styles varies greatly in advertising, we have included three different ads for running shoes and three for boots in order to compare and contrast the different slants. The collection of ads is followed by a set of questions in which you are asked to analyze the individual ads and the comparative strategies. These questions were included to help stimulate class discussion, to provide ideas for papers, and to test what you have learned so far in this section on advertising.

THIS IS FOR ALL THE PEOPLE WHOSE FAVORITE CLOTHES ARE A 10-YEAR OLD PAIR OF JEANS, A FADED FLANNEL SHIRT, AND THE CREW NECK THEY WORE IN COLLEGE.

You finally have the shoes to go with those clothes: a pair of Timberland® handsewns.

Timberland's aren't made to just look good fresh out of the box. They're made to look even better a few years down the road.

Our handsewns are made with only premium full-grain leathers. They're soft and supple when new and, like any fine leathers, they get that beautiful aged look as they get old.

We use only solid brass eyelets, so they won't rust. Nylon thread on all stitching and chrome-tanned rawhide laces because they last longer. And long-wearing leather or rugged Vibram® soles because they're unbeatable for resistance to abrasion.

The final ingredient: Timberland's genuine handsewn moccasin construction. (We're one of the few companies still practicing this art.) This results in shoes so comfortable, and so well made, that you'll hold on to and enjoy them year after year.

Few things in life improve with age. A pair of Timberland handsewns are two of them.

Timberland®

The Timberland Company, P.O. Box 370, Newmarket, New Hampshire 03857

Courtesy of The Timberland Company

HOW TO IMPROVE A DUCK.

Sporto does it from the bottom up. Introducing our new Deluxe Duck. A duck shoe with a fashionable wedge sole and a little extra comfort in the comfort collar. Of course, it's got a waterproof bottom just like our classic duck shoe.

Because who can improve upon that? Available at May D & F, Macy's, Hudson's, Belk (Charlotte), Sanger-Harris and other fine stores.

 SPORTO®

Courtesy of Gold Seal Rubber Co.

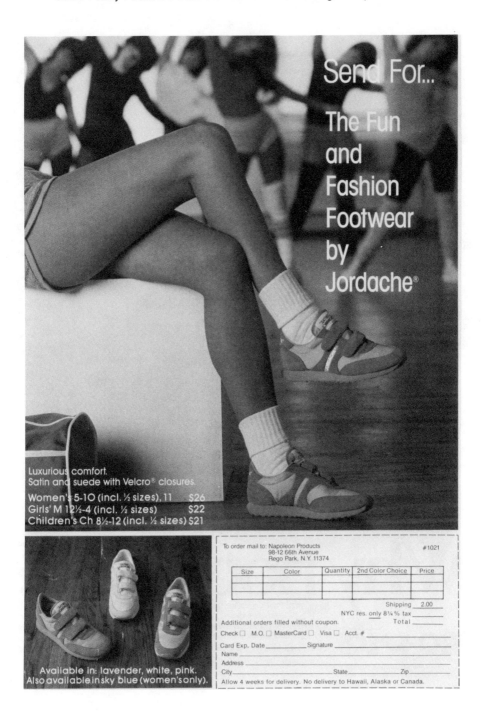

Courtesy of Jordache® Athletic and Leisure Footwear

Why not shoes?

PRO-SPECS®

Consumer Relations Department
Wales Avenue, Avon, Massachusetts 02322
Wats: 800-225-0475, Telex: SPECS AVNO 924313

GUARANTEE Pro-Specs is the first sport shoe brand to offer a written guarantee on its performance shoes . . . right in the box. You wouldn't consider buying other high technology products without a written guarantee. Now you don't have to buy high-tech sport shoes without a written guarantee . . . direct from the manufacturer.

Guaranteed durability, guaranteed quality, guaranteed value, guaranteed performance. In the competitive world of athletic footwear, we back our performance in writing . . .
. . . why not Pro-Specs shoes?

Courtesy of New Specs, Inc.

One of the most difficult things any runner has to endure is being sidelined by a running injury. And the most common forms of running injury are knee injuries

caused by pronation and supination, the side-to-side motion your foot makes when you run.

So at Converse, we've engineered a line of 4 hi-tech running shoes with built-in stabilizers designed specifically to help reduce pronation and supination.

All of them have their own unique injury prevention features to fit different running styles. Like the Force-5's™ dual medial support and extra dense midsole. The Phaeton's™ and Selena's™ heel stabilizer. The Laser's™ midfoot and rearfoot support. And the Tribune's™ lateral stability.

Converse. When it comes to helping prevent running injuries we're with you every step of the way. Because we know how important it is for you to stay off the road to recovery if you're going to stay on the road to success.

©1983 Converse Inc.

CONVERSE

The Official Athletic Shoe of the 1984 Olympic Games

O.S. DINGO

The man knows all there
is about fancy footwork. Listen:
"When you dress up, your
boots have got to dress up with
you. That's when you step up
to the Baron Collection.
"Just one look at those rich,
smooth leathers and you'll know
that Nobody Puts Leather
Together Like Dingo."

dingo®

Acme Boot Co., Inc., P.O. Box 749, Clarksville, Tenn. 37040. A subsidiary of Northwest Industries, Inc. Or call toll-free 800-251-1382. (except in Tenn.).

Courtesy of Acme Boot Co., Inc., and O.J. Simpson Enterprises

The power of Dan Post.

Uncompromising boots handcrafted from fine leathers and exotic skins. For the store nearest you, write Dan Post Boots, P.O. Box 749, Clarksville, Tenn. 37040. Or call toll-free: 800-251-1382.
(Except in Tenn.)

Courtesy of Dan Post Boots

Courtesy of John A. Frye Shoe Company, Inc.

Courtesy of Mario Bologna

Discussion Questions

1. The first ad, for Timberland shoes, is a two-part–two-page statement—one part visual, one verbal. Looking at both pages, try to summarize in your own words what the theme of this ad is.

2. For many advertised products, image is everything. As Charles O'Neill pointed out in his essay, much of the advertising image is created out of the associations the consumer makes with his or her own experience. Consider the image projected by the male model in the Timberland ad. How well does he fit the image of the shoe? Consider his expression, his body language, his clothes, his age, and his style. From all this, what profession do you think he might be in? What kind of car would he drive? Describe what he might wear (besides his shoes) when going out to dinner. What sport (or sports) might he be interested in? What kind of music would he listen to? What might be his favorite drink? How would he vote in the 1984 presidential election?

3. Like any other visual ad, the Timberland photograph is loaded with messages that help create the manufacturer's desired image. Discuss the different effects on this image if the following changes were made:

   a. The lawn is a neatly manicured turf; the path and steps are poured concrete.
   b. The house has new aluminum siding and a fancy storm door.
   c. The man has a cat instead of a dog.
   d. The man's dog is a toy poodle, a Doberman pinscher, or a Great Dane.
   e. The man is wearing an earring.

4. Advertising copy is subtly designed to suit the image of the product being sold. Consider the copy for the Timberland ad—that is, the sentence structure, the vocabulary, the descriptive details, the tone. How well does the copy fit the shoe? Why does the fourth paragraph in the copy contain sentence fragments? What effect do they produce? Vibram soles are synthetic; so is Nylon thread. Do these facts affect Timberland's all-natural, handsewn image for you? Explain your answer.

5. Compare the visual strategy of Sporto duck shoes with that of Timberland. What do you think the advertisers had in mind when they put a duck in a pair of shoes? Does the picture call more attention to the duck or to the shoes (they are bright green with tan trim and yellow soles in the original ad)? What would the effect be if the duck weren't wearing a rain hat?

6. Consider the advertiser's fanciful statement that Sporto improves a duck "from the bottom up." What does this claim say about Sporto shoes versus duck feet? What about the rest of the duck? Do you think Sporto makes rain hats, too?

7. Which do you think is the more effective ad, the one for Timberland or that for Sporto? Explain your answer.

8. The next three ads—for Jordache, Pro-Specs and Converse —are selling athletic shoes. As you can see, each takes a distinctly different approach. Look at the Jordache ad and try to determine what specific "fun" activities these shoes are for. Are they shoes you would wear for running? jogging? tennis? boating? softball? dancing? aerobic exercises? dating? shopping? class?

9. Jordache claims that their shoes are for fun *and* fashion. How does their ad suggest this double claim? How do they mean "fashion" here? Just what kind of fashion are they talking about—that is, what kinds of clothes would these shoes be worn with?

10. Why do you suppose the model in the photo is bare-legged and shown only from the waist down? How would the ad be affected if the model were shown full body, or if she were wearing pants, or leggings, or warm-up socks, or a skirt?

11. Consider the effect of the background in the Jordache ad. Why do you suppose the background figures are out of focus? How do they function in the ad—that is, how do they help create the Jordache image? Since the shoes can be ordered for girls and women only, the ad is obviously aimed at females. But what age group, social class, economic level, and life style does the ad target?

12. The Jordache ad is the only ad in our collection that includes an order form. In fact, the ad begins with the imperative, "Send for . . ." What does the inclusion of the order form say about the Jordache shoe? Why would you not expect to find an order form with an ad for Pro-Specs or Converse shoes?

13. Jordache makes a variety of apparel. Find ads for other Jordache products and compare the styles and techniques to those in this ad. What common images are created? What kinds of people and life styles are targeted in Jordache ads?

14. Explain how each of the four background products in the Pro-Specs ad functions. Do any of these products not quite fit the message of the copy? If so, explain why.

15. According to Charles O'Neill, advertising has been criticized for selling us daydreams and fantasies. What daydreams and fantasies are being sold in the Jordache ad? What ones are being sold in the Pro-Specs ad? Consider the effect on the Pro-Specs ad if the gold Seiko watch were replaced by a plastic-strapped Timex, or the Porsche 928 by a Ford Escort, or the ReVox sound system by a GE clock radio, or the diamond replaced by an onyx.

16. Pro-Specs claims that its shoes are high-tech products with a written guarantee. Does this claim make you want to buy the shoes? Why or why not? Do you think the ad should have spelled out the exact conditions of the guarantee?

17. The appearance of an ad is of crucial importance, since it might determine whether a reader will read the rest of the copy and consider the product. Evaluate the appearance of the Converse ad. Does it grab your attention? Is the picture provocative? Does the headline make you want to read the rest of the copy? How does this ad compare in appearance with that for Pro-Specs? Be specific.

18. Both the Pro-Specs and the Converse ads stress the high-technology aspects of their shoes. Examine the copy in each ad. Which ad uses the most technical terms? What particular appeals are being made with each ad? What do the following terms mean: *pronation, supination, stabilizer, dual medial support*? Does the Converse ad assume that we know the meaning of these terms? Does it make any difference if we don't?

19. Explain as fully as you can the message in the photograph below the headline in the Converse ad. Consider the subtle emotional appeal of the elements in the photo—the crutches, the closed window, the blue sky, the sun-lit, empty road, the endless perspective, the lighting, the shadow in the foreground, and so on.

20. If you were a judge in an athletic-shoe ad competition, which of the three ads would you award first prize. Why exactly?

21. The next three ads in our collection use three different slants to sell boots. The first, the Dingo ad, uses a familiar strategy—celebrity endorsement. Why is O. J. Simpson an appropriate person to push Dingo boots? Does his endorsement make you want to buy Dingo boots for yourself or for a male friend?

22. What is the point of photographically giving O. J. Simpson a third leg? How does this gimmick relate to the model? to the ad copy? to the image Dingo is trying to sell?

23. Some advertisers believe that the headline is the most important ingredient of an ad—that it is a kind of telegram that determines whether or not the reader will read the rest of the ad. What is the immediate impact and implication of "O. J. Dingo"? Consider the headlines of all the ads in our collection. Attempt to rate them on a scale from 1 to 10, with 10 being the most inviting and effective and 1 the least.

24. Although the Dan Post Boots ad does not use the celebrity endorsement strategy, it was carefully designed to create a particular appeal. What would you say that appeal is? Consider the face and expression of the male model and try to characterize it and the kind of man behind it. Does this man resemble any celebrities? What kind of man wears Dan Post Boots?

25. What is the function of the image of cowboys and cattle in the Dan Post ad? How does this add to the overall advertisement? Would the ad have the same effect without this image? Explain.

26. The headline of the Dan Post ad says simply, "The Power of Dan Post." What exactly is that "power"?

27. Write a profile of the man to whom the Dingo ad and the Dan Post ad are addressed. Describe the target customer, based on the different styles and images of these two ads. Consider the language and the visuals. Which of the two ads has the greater appeal to you? Why?

28. Unlike the two preceding ads, the ad for Frye boots features more than one model. What is the message of a group of Frye boot wearers? Try to describe the spirit and energy level of the Frye ad. How does it contrast in this regard with the last two boot ads? What are the Frye people trying to suggest about people who wear their boots?

29. Each of the three boot ads appeals to different kinds of people. What kind of person is the Frye ad targeting? Consider the age group, gender, social set, economic level, life style, and so on. In your answer, also consider the appearance of the models, their attitudes, and their clothes.

30. How well does the copy in the Frye ad fit the visual images? What does "real staying power" mean? How is it dramatized in the photograph?

31. The final ad in our collection, for Mario Bologna shoes, is perhaps the most bizarre. Except for the name and address of the manufacturer, there is no copy—just the photograph, which is black and white in the original. If you didn't know that Mario Bologna made women's shoes, would you be able to determine that from the ad? Explain.

32. Looking at the photograph in this ad, try to come up with a story of what happened. In other words, why is the man lying on the floor with his drink spilled? What might have happened to him? What state might he be in? What role did the woman in the picture play? Why is she dressed the way she is and sitting as she is? Why is there a closed-circuit television camera and monitor operating? After you have come up with a reasonable story behind the scene, try to explain what all this has to do with women's shoes.

33. Try to explain just what the advertiser had in mind in deciding on this particular visual for the Mario Bologna ad. Why was the apparently violent scene chosen? What image associations are we supposed to make with the shoes and the wearers? Is this picture geared simply to catch our attention, or is there more here than immediately meets the eye?

34. Examine the ad again and try to characterize the kind of woman who wears Mario Bologna shoes. Consider temperament, social set, economic level, age group, and life style.

35. Look over all nine ads in our collection. Try to determine which ad you thought was the best and which the worst. Explain your choices as fully as you can.

36. Select one of the ads and revise its language and visuals in any way to appeal to a completely different audience. For instance, try to

redo the Timberland ad so that it appeals to a young, swinging set. Or revise the Dan Post ad so that it appeals to executives.

37. Using a library, try to determine the ways in which advertising strategies for a particular product have changed over the years. (You might select one of our manufacturers here, such as Frye boots.) Find magazines from 15 or 20 years back and trace the evolution of a manufacturer's ads for the same product. Write a paper in which you analyze some of the changes in styles and approaches. Do any of these changes reflect changes in social attitudes over the years?

38. Imagine that you are a professional ad writer and that you have been assigned to write advertising copy for a brand-new product. Select a product. (You may stick with footwear, such as motorcycle boots, sandals, or bedroom slippers, or choose some other product, such as a new beer, screwdriver, or perfume.) Make up an appealing brand name; then design three or more ads for the product, using some of the different selling approaches we have seen in our ad collection.

Sport and the American Dream

Jeffrey Schrank

For nearly a century, Americans have had a love affair with sports. It has had something to do with the belief that competitive games are healthy—not only for the body, but for the national psyche. In this section, we will examine different sports and the ways they influence our lives inside and outside the fields of play. We begin with an explanation of how three American sports— football, baseball, and golf—are ritualistic enactments of national values and myths. Jeffrey Schrank has written widely on communications and popular culture. He is the author of several books, including *Snap, Crackle, and Popular Taste: The Illusion of Free Choice in America* (1977).

Sport is a ritual, an acting out of a myth or series of myths. A sport   1
that can be considered a national pastime can be expected to reflect
national values and wishes. Sports that capture the national fancy are
ritualistic enactments of the American Dream. Baseball is still called our
national pastime but is rapidly being replaced by American football. That
football should become our "national pastime" is understandable to
those who can see sports as reflections of national character.

American football is passionately concerned with the gain and loss of   2
land, of territory. The football field is measured and marked with all the
care of a surveyor and the ball's progress noted to the nearest inch.
Football is a precise game and its players are often trained like a military
unit on a mission to gain territory for the mother country. The players
are the popular heroes but the coaches and owners run the game, using
the players to carry out their plans—there is comparatively little room for
individual initiative. A score comes as the result of a strategic series of
well-executed maneuvers and is bought on the installment plan, yard by
yard.

The regulation and almost military precision of American football is   3
a reflection of national psychology. Even the words we use to describe the
game include throwing the bomb, marching downfield, game plan (which
has become nearly a national phrase for any field, from selling toothpaste
to covering up political scandals), guards, executions, blitz, zone, platoon, squad, drills, attack, drives, marching bands for entertainment,
stars on helmets, lines that can be blasted through and even war paint.
Much of the verbal similarity comes from the fact that war was originally
the ultimate game played within the confines of certain rules agreed upon
by both "teams."

Football, more than any other sport, is a game for spectators to watch   4
superhuman, mythical heroes. Football is a sport that more people watch
than play. The game requires too many people, too much space and is
simply too dangerous for the weekend athlete. The size and speed of
professional players and their uniforms make them into heroic figures

capable of feats that invite admiration but not imitation. The football spectator is in awe of the armored monsters. The viewer of a golf match or even baseball or tennis dreams of going out the next day and doing likewise, but football is played only by the gods who can run the 100 yard dash in ten seconds, stand six feet three and weigh 260 pounds.

The demise of baseball as our national pastime reflects a change in national character. The change does not mean the disappearance of baseball, merely its relocation to a position as just another game rather than *the* game. Professor John Finlay of the University of Manitoba, writing in *Queen's Quarterlay,* compares baseball to an acting out of the robber baron stage of capitalism, whereas football more clearly reflects a more mature capitalism into which we are now moving. Hence, the rise in popularity of football and apparent decline in baseball. He notes that Japan, still in the early stages of capitalism, has taken avidly to baseball but not to football. It is not a question of Japanese physique serving as a determinant since rugby has a large Asian following. He predicts that when their capitalism moves into a higher stage, the Japanese will move on to football as have Americans. 5

Baseball is a game of a quieter age when less action was needed to hold interest, when going to the park was enjoyable (baseball is still played in ball parks while football is played in stadiums), when aggression was subservient to finesse. Baseball players did not need exposure as college players to succeed as football players do; they play a relatively calm game almost daily instead of a bruising gladiatorial contest weekly. Baseball has room for unique and colorful characters, while football stresses the more anonymous but effective team member. Baseball is a game in which any team can win at any given contest and there are no favorites; only football has real "upsets." Football's careful concern with time adds a tension to the game that is lacking in the more leisurely world of baseball. 6

Football has replaced baseball as the favorite American spectator sport largely because of television. A comparison between a telecast of a football game on one channel and a baseball game on another could reveal baseball as a game with people standing around seemingly with little to do but watch two men play catch. Football would appear as twenty-two men engaged in almost constant, frenzied action. To watch baseball requires identification with the home team; to watch football requires only a need for action or a week of few thrills and the need for a touch of vicarious excitement. 7

Baseball is a pastoral game, timeless and highly ritualized; its appeal is to nostalgia and so might enjoy periods of revitalization in comparison to football. But for now, the myth of football suits the nation better. 8

According to a 1974 Harris survey, baseball has already been statistically dethroned. In a sports survey a cross section of nearly fourteen hundred fans was asked, "Which of these sports do you follow?" 9

The decision to play or "follow" a certain sport is also the decision to live a certain myth. The team violence of football, the craftiness of basket- 10 ball, the mechanistic precision of bowling, the auto racer's devotion to machinery are all subworlds within the universe of sport.

Golf, for example, is a unique subworld, one of the few left as a sport (unlike hunting which does not involve scoring or teams) in which the game is played between man and nature. The winner of a match is one who has beaten the opponent, but the game itself is a person versus the environment. To understand the appeal of golf it is again necessary to consider the game as a ritual reenactment of an appealing myth.   11

Golf, perhaps more than any other sport, has to be played to be appreciated. Millions who never played football can enjoy the game on TV, but only a dedicated participant can sit through two hours of televised golf. Golf is growing in participation but still has the stigma of an upper-class game. Eighty percent of the nation's golfers must play on 20 percent of the nation's courses that are open to the public. The ratio of public to private facilities hurts public participation in the game but mirrors the inequities of society and provides a convenient status symbol for those who can afford club membership. Its TV audience is not the largest of any sport but it is the most well heeled.   12

Golf is a reenactment of the pioneer spirit. It is man versus a hostile environment in search of an oasis. The goal is a series of lush "greens," each protected by natural hazards such as water, sand and unmanageably long grass. The hazards are no threat to physical life but they are to the achievement of success. Golf is a journey game with a constantly changing field. Golfers start the eighteen-hole journey, can rest at a halfway point and then resume until they return to near the point of origination.   13

The winner of the match is one who has fallen victim to the fewest hazards and overcome the terrain. Many golf courses have Indian names as if to remind the golfer of the frontier ethos. A local course called Indian Lakes invites golfers to use either one of two courses—the Iroquois trail or the Sioux trail.   14

Golf, like baseball, is a pastoral sport—with a high degree of tensions and drama but relatively little action. It is a game in which players are constantly in awe of the magic flight of the golf ball. To hit any kind of ball 100 or 200 or more yards with accuracy or to hit a small target from 150 yards is an amazing feat to be appreciated only by those who have at least tried the game. Golf is very likely the most difficult game to master, yet one in which the average player occasionally hits a shot as good as the best of any professional. It is this dream of magic results that keeps the golfer on course.   15

Topical Considerations

1. Why is watching a football, baseball, or golf game a ritualistic act? What myths are Americans acting out when they participate in this way?

2. How is football a reflection of the American character? In other words, what does the game of football reveal about ourselves, our life styles, and our values as Americans?

3. What does "pastoral" mean? How are baseball and golf pastoral sports? Can you think of other sports that would fit this category? How is golf's television audience "well-heeled"?

4. Do you have a favorite sport? How does this preference reflect your personality?

5. According to Schrank, a 1974 Harris survey revealed that baseball has been "dethroned." How have we as Americans changed to cause the national pastime to shift from baseball to football?

6. What is a "robber baron"? How was the "robber baron stage of capitalism" a less mature capitalism than we have now? Why does Schrank feel that the Japanese, too, will eventually prefer football to baseball?

Rhetorical Considerations

1. What underlying idea links the descriptions of football, baseball, and golf together? Where in the essay is it introduced? Is this the thesis? Where else in the essay does Schrank rephrase, restate, or touch on this idea?

2. Outline the essay. Identify its major sections. Show how Schrank orders his ideas within each section. Cite the transitional words and phrases Schrank uses to move from one section to another.

3. Does Schrank use topic sentences effectively? Cite specific paragraphs to prove your answer.

4. Schrank begins four of his last five paragraphs with the word *golf*. Why does he do this? What effect does it have on the development of the essay?

Writing Assignments

1. What is your favorite sport? Write an essay showing how this sport is a reflection of your own personality.

2. Identify another leisure time activity that a majority of Americans like to either watch or participate in. In an essay, explain how it is a reflection of the American character.

3. Television programs and motion pictures also often portray ritualistic enactments of the American dream. Choose a television program or motion picture that does this and write about it. Show how it is "an acting out of a myth or series of myths."

Attitude

Garrison Keillor

Garrison Keillor has done a remarkable thing. He has managed, in this
television age, to pull two million Americans to their radio sets each Saturday
night. He has been doing that since 1974, when he created and began hosting
the live variety show, "A Prairie Home Companion," from Minneapolis. What
has made Keillor's National Public Radio production so popular is just the kind
of warm wit and wisdom that characterizes the following article. Here he gives
some thoughts about playing softball—particularly about attitude and about
how it might be the most important part of the game. This essay is taken from
a collection of Keillor's essays, mostly from the *New Yorker—Happy to Be
Here* (1983).

Long ago I passed the point in life when major-league ballplayers   1
begin to be younger than yourself. Now all of them are, except for a few
aging trigenarians and a couple of quadros who don't get around on the
fastball as well as they used to and who sit out the second games of
double-headers. However, despite my age (thirty-nine), I am still active
and have a lot of interests. One of them is slow-pitch softball, a game that
lets me go through the motions of baseball without getting beaned or
having to run too hard. I play on a pretty casual team, one that drinks beer
on the bench and substitutes freely. If a player's wife or girlfriend wants
to play, we give her a glove and send her out to right field, no questions
asked, and if she lets a pop fly drop six feet in front of her, nobody
agonizes over it.

Except me. This year. For the first time in my life, just as I am entering   2
the dark twilight of my slow-pitch career, I find myself taking the game
seriously. It isn't the bonehead play that bothers me especially—the pop
fly that drops untouched, the slow roller juggled and the ball then heaved
ten feet over the first baseman's head and into the next diamond, the
routine singles that go through outfielders' legs for doubles and triples
with gloves flung after them. No, it isn't our stone-glove fielding or
pussyfoot base-running or limp-wristed hitting that gives me fits, though
these have put us on the short end of some mighty ridiculous scores this
summer. It's our attitude.

Bottom of the ninth, down 18–3, two outs, a man on first and a woman   3
on third, and our third baseman strikes out. *Strikes out!* In slow-pitch, not
even your grandmother strikes out, but this guy does, and after his third
strike—a wild swing at a ball that bounces on the plate—he topples over
in the dirt and lies flat on his back, laughing. *Laughing!*

Same game, earlier. They have the bases loaded. A weak grounder is   4
hit toward our second baseperson. The runners are running. She picks
up the ball, and she looks at them. She looks at first, at second, at home.
We yell, "Throw it! Throw it!" and she throws it, underhand, at the

465

pitcher, who has turned and run to back up the catcher. The ball rolls across the third-base line and under the bench. Three runs score. The batter, a fatso, chugs into second. The other team hoots and hollers, and what does she do? She shrugs and smiles ("Oh, silly me"); after all, it's only a game. Like the aforementioned strikeout artist, she treats her error as a joke. They have forgiven themselves instantly, which is unforgivable. It is *we* who should forgive them, who can say, "It's all right, it's only a game." They are supposed to throw up their hands and kick the dirt and hang their heads, as if this boner, even if it is their sixteenth of the afternoon—*this* is the one that really and truly breaks their hearts.

That attitude sweetens the game for everyone. The sinner feels sweet   5
remorse. The fatso feels some sense of accomplishment; this is no bunch of rumdums he forced into an error but a team with some class. We, the sinner's teammates, feel momentary anger at her—dumb! dumb play!—but then, seeing her grief, we sympathize with her in our hearts (any one of us might have made that mistake or one worse), and we yell encouragement, including the shortstop, who, moments before, dropped an easy throw for a force at second. "That's all right! Come on! We got 'em!" we yell. "Shake it off! These turkeys can't hit!" This makes us all feel good, even though the turkeys now lead us by ten runs. We're getting clobbered, but we have a winning attitude.

Let me say this about attitude: Each player is responsible for his or her   6
own attitude, and to a considerable degree you can *create* a good attitude by doing certain little things on the field. These are certain little things that ballplayers do in the Bigs, and we ought to be doing them in the Slows.

1. When going up to bat, don't step right into the batter's box as if it   7
were an elevator. The box is your turf, your stage. Take possession of it slowly and deliberately, starting with a lot of back-bending, knee-stretching, and torso-revolving in the on-deck circle. Then, approaching the box, stop outside it and tap the dirt off your spikes with your bat. You don't have spikes, you have sneakers, of course, but the significance of the tapping is the same. Then, upon entering the box, spit on the ground. It's a way of saying, "This here is mine. This is where I get my hits."

2. Spit frequently. Spit at all crucial moments. Spit correctly. Spit   8
should be *blown*, not ptuied weakly with the lips, which often results in dribble. Spitting should convey forcefulness of purpose, concentration, pride. Spit down, not in the direction of others. Spit in the glove and on the fingers, especially after making a real knucklehead play; it's a way of saying, "I dropped the ball because my glove was dry."

3. At the bat and in the field, pick up dirt. Rub dirt in the fingers   9
(especially after spitting on them). Toss dirt, as if testing the wind for velocity and direction. Smooth the dirt. Be involved with dirt. If no dirt is available (e.g., in the outfield), pluck tufts of grass. Fielders should be

grooming their areas constantly between plays, flicking away tiny sticks and bits of gravel.

4. Take your time. Tie your laces. Confer with your teammates about possible situations that may arise and conceivable options in dealing with them. Extend the game. Three errors on three consecutive plays can be humiliating if the plays occur within the space of a couple of minutes, but if each error is separated from the next by extensive conferences on the mound, lace-tying, glove adjustments, and arguing close calls (if any), the effect on morale is minimized.

10

5. Talk. Not just an occasional "Let's get a hit now" but continuous rhythmic chatter, a flow of syllables: "Hey babe hey babe c'mon babe good stick now hey babe long tater take him downtown babe . . . hey good eye good eye."

11

Infield chatter is harder to maintain. Since the slow-pitch is required to be a soft underhand lob, infielders hesitate to say, "Smoke him babe hey low heat hey throw it on the black babe chuck it in there back him up babe no hit no hit." Say it anyway.

12

6. One final rule, perhaps the most important of all: When your team is up and has made the third out, the batter and the players who were left on base do not come back to the bench for their gloves. *They remain on the field, and their teammates bring their gloves out to them.* This requires some organization and discipline, but it pays off big in morale. It says, "Although we're getting our pants knocked off, still we must conserve our energy."

13

Imagine that you have bobbled two fly balls in this rout and now you have just tried to stretch a single into a double and have been easily thrown out sliding into second base, where the base runner ahead of you had stopped. It was the third out and a dumb play, and your opponents smirk at you as they run off the field. You are the goat, a lonely and tragic figure sitting in the dirt. You curse yourself, jerking your head sharply forward. You stand up and kick the base. How miserable! How degrading! Your utter shame, though brief, bears silent testimony to the worthiness of your teammates, whom you have let down, and they appreciate it. They call out to you now as they take the field, and as the second baseman runs to his position he says, "Let's get 'em now," and tosses you your glove. Lowering your head, you trot slowly out to right. There you do some deep knee bends. You pick grass. You find a pebble and fling it into foul territory. As the first batter comes to the plate, you check the sun. You get set in your stance, poised to fly. Feet spread, hands on hips, you bend slightly at the waist and spit the expert spit of a verteran ballplayer—a player who has known the agony of defeat but who always bounces back, a player who has lost a stride on the base paths but can still make the big play.

14

This is *ball*, ladies and gentlemen. This is what it's all about.

15

Topical Considerations

1. What does Keillor believe is the wrong attitude to have toward playing softball? the right attitude? If it's just a game, why is attitude so important?

2. Why does Keillor encourage his teammates to tap the dirt off their spikes when they are only wearing tennis shoes without spiked soles? What other apparently unnecessary acts does he insist they perform? Why does he feel these acts are so essential to the way the game is played?

3. How could Keillor's thesis and his comments about how to approach a game of softball be related to other activities? How could it help a student pass a course? earn a promotion on a job? get along better with a girlfriend or boyfriend?

4. How familiar is Keillor with professional baseball practices? Is he writing from first-hand or little, if any, experience? Cite specific passages to prove your point.

5. In comparing football to baseball, Schrank remarks that baseball has more "finesse." If Schrank were to happen by one afternoon while Keillor and his team were playing a casual game of slow-pitch softball, do you think Keillor would be likely to invite him to play? Why or why not? While sitting on the bench with Schrank, what comments might Keillor make about baseball as a reflection of American character?

Rhetorical Considerations

1. Keillor introduces his thesis in installments. Where does he actually state it? Identify each of the stages that leads up to it.

2. Writers strive to use specifics to show their readers what they mean and to avoid speaking in vague generalities. Is Keillor successful in this? Cite specific passages that prove your point.

3. Keillor refers to the "Bigs" and the "Slows." He describes a member of the opposite team as "a fatso" and his team as "no bunch of rumdums." Given these examples, how would you characterize the diction of this essay? Can you cite other examples?

4. Keillor often uses verbs that create a vivid word picture. In paragraph 4 he states: "The batter, a fatso, chugs into second." What image does "chugs" convey? What other interesting verbs does Keillor use?

5. Reread Keillor's list of things to do to create a proper attitude toward playing softball. What kind of sentence does he use here? What effect does it have on a reading of the essay?

6. What does Keillor's last sentence remind you of? Why is this a good concluding line?

Writing Assignments

1. Write an essay in which you explain your own views on the proper attitude to take toward some other sport. Draw on ideas from Keillor's essay that you agree with. Select incidents and examples that illustrate the points you want to make.

2. Attitude is important for professional athletes, musicians, singers, actors, and other performers. Write an essay about the effect the right attitude has on a nonathletic activity such as playing a musical instrument, singing, or writing.

On the Ball

Roger Angell

The name Roger Angell is synonymous with baseball. No, he doesn't play professional ball. He just writes about it better than most people. He is the author of *The Summer Game* (1972), *Five Seasons: A Baseball Companion* (1977), and *Late Innings* (1982). He is also an editor and sportswriter for the *New Yorker*. In the following brief piece, Angell describes the essential ingredient in the game—the baseball. Notice how he moves from near-scientific objectivity to some strong feelings about the ball and the game.

It weighs just over five ounces and measures between 2.86 and 2.94 inches in diameter. It is made of a composition-cork nucleus encased in two thin layers of rubber, one black and one red, surrounded by 121 yards of tightly wrapped blue-gray wool yarn, 45 yards of white wool yarn, 53 more yards of blue-gray wool yarn, 150 yards of fine cotton yarn, a coat of rubber cement, and a cowhide (formerly horsehide) exterior, which is held together with 216 slightly raised red cotton stitches. Printed certifications, endorsements, and outdoor advertising spherically attest to its authenticity. Like most institutions, it is considered inferior in its present form to its ancient archetypes, and in this case the complaint is probably justified; on occasion in recent years it has actually been known to come apart under the demands of its brief but rigorous active career. Baseballs are assembled and hand-stitched in Taiwan (before this year the work was done in Haiti, and before 1973 in Chicopee, Massachusetts), and contemporary pitchers claim that there is a tangible variation in the size and feel of the balls that now come into play in a single game; a true peewee is treasured by hurlers, and its departure from the premises, by fair means or foul, is secretly mourned. But never mind: any baseball is beautiful. No other small package comes as close to the ideal in design and utility.

It is a perfect object for a man's hand. Pick it up and it instantly suggests its purpose; it is meant to be thrown a considerable distance—thrown hard and with precision. Its feel and heft are the beginning of the sport's critical dimensions; if it were a fraction of an inch larger or smaller, a few centigrams heavier or lighter, the game of baseball would be utterly different. Hold a baseball in your hand. As it happens, this one is not brand-new. Here, just to one side of the curved surgical welt of stitches, there is a pale-green grass smudge, darkening on one edge almost to black—the mark of an old infield play, a tough grounder now lost in memory. Feel the ball, turn it over in your hand; hold it across the seam or the other way, with the seam just to the side of your middle finger. Speculation stirs. You want to get outdoors and throw this spare and sensual object to somebody or, at the very least, watch somebody else throw it. The game has begun.

Topical Considerations

1. Why do you think Angell wrote this essay?
2. Do Angell's feelings about the baseball reflect your own?
3. Angell points to a "pale-green grass smudge" on his baseball, which he explains is "the mark of an old infield play, a tough grounder now lost in memory." What does this remark suggest about Angell's past association with the game of baseball? What associations does it have for you?
4. Is there any other sports equipment that might evoke the same response in an avid sports fan like Angell?
5. Why does Angell say that the baseball is a *sensual* object? What connotations does the word have within the context of his essay?

Rhetorical Considerations

1. What is Angell's attitude toward his subject? Cite specific phrases to illustrate your point.
2. Identify the primary rhetorical pattern used to develop this essay.
3. Why are there no paragraphs in this essay? Does it need these divisions? Explain.
4. Angell moves from an objective to a subjective description of a baseball. How does one relate to the other? Where and how does he make the transition? What can you point out about the way he orders his ideas in each section?

Writing Assignment

1. Write an essay about an object that has fond associations for you. Adopt Angell's method of organization, moving from an objective to a subjective description. Include numerous details.

On the Bench

Robert B. Parker

There was a time when men who pumped iron were regarded as densely wadded muscle freaks whose manhood was questionable. Over the last decade, however, weightlifting—and body building—not only has become popular, it is positively *au courant*. In nearly every city and suburb across the nation, you can find big, flossy health clubs full of physical fitness-minded men and women on the benches of fancy weight machines, pumping chrome. What follows is a rather humorous and insightful narrative of a man who has been on the bench since before it was fashionable. In his characteristic style, Robert B. Parker tells how he got interested in weightlifting, why he continued for 25 years, and what it has done for his body and psyche. Since 1974, Parker has written ten novels about a tough and wisecracking private eye named Spenser —the most notable of which include *Looking for Rachel Wallace* (1980), *Early Autumn* (1981), *Ceremony* (1982), and *The Widening Gyre* (1983). (Like Parker, Spenser is occasionally on the bench.) Parker is also author of several non-Spenser books, including the thriller *Wilderness* (1979)—which has been contracted for a movie—*Love and Glory* (1983) and his *Sports Illustrated Training With Weights* (with John R. Marsh, 1974).

When I came home from Korea in the early '50s I weighed 148 pounds. While I was cat-quick and a trained killer, I did have to hold onto my wife Joan's arm in a strong wind, and the only reason people couldn't kick sand on me was that I stood sideways and they missed. Judicious management of food and drink helped me get up to 160 by the time my first son was born. But neither Pabst Blue Ribbon nor meatloaf sandwiches has much positive effect on biceps or pectoral muscle, and I remember thinking in the first rush of parenthood, a boy needs a strong father. So, at age 26 I got my first set of weights.   1

It was a big step, because when I was a boy, weightlifting was not fashionable. Only muscle-bound freaks lifted weights, and, while one would hesitate to actually tell a weightlifter that he was a muscle-bound freak, one knew it to be true. His manhood was open to speculation as well.   2

When I got my first set of weights I had Joan buy them for me. I hid   3 in the bedroom when they were delivered and she signed for them. After the delivery man left, I scurried out and assembled the weights and began to do the exercises described in the accompanying pamphlet. That was 25 years ago and I am still shoving away at the irons. The results have been mixed, but now when it's windy Joan holds onto *my* arm.

My first set of weights allowed me to lift a maximum of 110 pounds,   4
if I put all the weights on the bar. I especially wanted to do bench presses. So I made a bench out of two-by-fours and plywood and added a rack for the barbell. I put the bar on the rack, put all the weights on the bar, lay on the bench on my back, feet on the ground, hands comfortably apart, grasped the bar firmly near each end, tested the balance, hoisted it off the bar and lowered it to my chest: step one of the bench press. Step two is to press the barbell back up to arm's length. Ah, there's the rub. The bar, resting with nice balance on my chest, would not move. After a manful struggle I faced the hopelessness of my situation and called for Joan. She arrived, helped me tip the barbell off my chest, smiled her Mona Lisa smile, and went away without comment.

I tried again with less weight until I could do one bench press, then   5
several, then ten, and then three sets of ten. The muscles in my chest and arms got stronger. I added a little more weight and started the same routine again.

When I got too powerful for my 110-pound barbells, I graduated to   6
the big York barbells at the local Y. York barbells are the kind they use in the Olympics. The poundage plates slide onto a 45-pound bar easily and needn't be locked in place. The 100-pound weight plates for a York set look like spare wheels for a McCormick reaper.

The trick to weight training is simple: you isolate one muscle, or   7
muscle group, and exercise it repeatedly; then you exercise another, and another, *voila*—Franco Columbo. A good deal of ingenuity is required to find positions that will isolate, say, the upper abdominals, or the trapezius muscles.

After some regular congress with the Yorks (though I tended to es-   8
chew the 100-pound plates), I was presentable enough to go public at the Universal Trainer in the weight room at Northeastern University. During my Babylonian captivity, when I had access to the Universal, I more than doubled my earliest bench pressing efforts and was able to mingle with the weight room crowd undetected. No one suspected me of being an English teacher (this was, unfortunately, also true in the English Department).

One of the charms of the Universal is that it is a weight lifting machine   9
with several lifting stations. The weights are fixed on pulleys or runners, and poundage can be adjusted by simply moving a pin. Now that I am no longer at Northeastern, the Universal is denied me. But, ever venturesome, I have signed up to try the new Nautilus system at the Colonial in

Lynnfield. Remember Yaz in '67? Next summer I will tear up the Lynn-field Men's Softball League.

I didn't devote myself exclusively to the irons all this time. Joan and   10
I had another son. Further motivated, I built up to 190 pounds of bone and sinew. At this writing there are still 190 pounds of bone and sinew. It is, however, almost entirely disguised by about 30 pounds of what could generously be called tissue. If you think weightlifting is sure to trim you down you haven't been watching Vasily Alexyev.

Why have I spent several hours each week for 25 years, straining to   11
exercise, with weights, at the outer limits of my strength, and trying to do it again and again at the outer limits of my endurance? In 25 years I've had to thrash no bullies on behalf of my sons. I have occasionally glared at someone who got uppity with Joan. But she needs my protection about as much as Marvin Hagler does. I am good at picking up one end of something. Over the last twenty years my friend, John Marsh, and I have picked up and carried about an impressive assortment of refrigerators, pianos, sofas, washing machines, boulders, bags of Portland cement, stoves, timbers and beer kegs. But that seems small recompense for 25 years of Ben-Gay.

There *are* drawbacks to all that lifting. I'm probably heavier (though   12
not fatter) than I would have been if I hadn't started lifting. I have distorted my upper body so that I am nearly impossible to fit off the rack. Clothing salesmen blanch when I enter. At 5'10" I take a size 46 suit. The pants have to be shortened so much that the cuffs catch in the zipper.

You are also brought face-to-face with the validity of an old truth: 13
never a horse that couldn't be rode; never a rider that couldn't be throw'd. If you can bench press 250 pounds you're certain to have a friend who can do 350, and he knows someone who can do 450. I'm fairly strong for a 51-year-old fat man. But in any weight room in the country there are twenty people (mostly men) who are stronger than I am and maybe one that's better looking. Weightlifting is very useful in under-standing the inequality of nature's dispensation.

Of course it is embarrassing at first when you go into the weight room   14
with your little potbelly and your skinny white arms wearing the brand new gym suit your spouse bought you at K-Mart; and there are a lot of people who look like the Great Blue Hill pumping iron with their sleeves cut off. But progress is rapid, and you can learn from watching others. Most of them will be preoccupied with the wall mirrors and won't notice you anyway.

For a man who makes his living sitting down, alone, all day, weightlift-   15
ing has much to offer. It pays off promptly, it fits conveniently into my schedule, it provides exercise that my profession does not (helping to offset typists' hump), and, perhaps more to the point, it makes me sweat. I *like* to sweat. Inelegant, but true. I like the feeling of effort, of tension

followed by release (Arnold Schwarzenegger has already pointed out the sexual parallels; I try to write only of what I know). I like the sense of work carried through to resolution, and I like the sense of near endless possibility in goals accomplished and new goals set.

But most simply I lift weights for the reason with which I began. I want   16
to be strong. I want to be strong the way I want to be smart. So I study to be smart and lift to be strong. (Joan says I'm oh-for-two, but she's never admitted my resemblance to the young Olivier either.) In the case of strong, as in the case of smart, there are limits to what can be made of the raw material. Like study, exercise can only improve on the basics. It can't supply them.

But within the limits of how you start, it seems to me that the renais-   17
sance ideal of the warrior poet (Sir Philip Sidney, say) isn't a bad one. It needn't, of course, be weights. My son is a dancer and he can do things with his body that no one else I know can do. It could be running. It could be gymnastics. Physical accomplishment doesn't have to include the ability to pick up the front end of a Buick. To be physically accomplished would seem as much a fulfillment of one's humanity as to be intellectually accomplished. To be both would seem most fully human.

Topical Considerations

1. What were Parker's original reasons for buying a set of weights? Back then, what was the general attitude toward men who were weightlifters, according to Parker?

2. What has 25 years of pumping iron done for Parker? How has it physically changed him? What has it done for his self-image? What drawbacks has he had to face as a result? How has it helped him?

3. What reasons does the author give for continuing to lift weights after 25 years? Is it for phsyical accomplishments alone?

Rhetorical Considerations

1. What is the organizing principle of this essay?

2. What is there about the first paragraph that makes you want to read on?

3. What kind of humor does Parker use in this piece? What is the source of his humor? How does his wife Joan serve his humorous effects?

4. Could you tell from this essay that Parker was once a professor of English? What literary allusions does he make directly and indirectly?

5. Could you tell from this essay that Parker is a successful novelist? If so, how?

6. Explain the following allusions and how they sustain the humorous tone of this essay: Mona Lisa, Franco Columbo, Marvin Hagler, Ben-Gay, Vasily Alexyev, Arnold Schwarzenegger, Sir Philip Sidney.

Writing Assignments

1. Parker says that 25 years ago the attitude toward men who were weightlifters was not complimentary. What is the current attitude toward people who lift weights? Write a paper about how the general attitude toward weightlifters has changed.

2. If you lift weights regularly, write a report on how you got started. Try to capture the experience and explain how it has affected your physical development as well as your attitude.

3. If you are not a weightlifter but play a sport regularly, write a paper in which you tell how you first got interested in that sport, why you enjoy it, and what it has done for you physically and mentally.

Female Athletes: They've Come a Long Way, Baby

P. S. Wood

There was a time when sports were all-male experiences. As reported here, however, there has been a rush of women into athletic competition on every level—schools, colleges, Olympic games, and professional sports. But just how good are female athletes? How do they compare with males? Are they built to take the punishment of some competition? In the following essay, P. S. Wood reviews new research on the comparative prowess of men and women and comes up with some surprising answers to these questions.

There has been an explosion in women's competitive sports. If   1
women have not yet achieved equal time on the playing fields of America, or equal space in the halls of fame, they have come a long way, and are moving up fast. For example:

• Thirty-three percent of all high-school athletes are female, a sixfold   2
increase since the early 1970s, according to figures supplied by the Women's Sports Foundation. In colleges, the figure is 30 percent, an increase in ten years of 250 percent.

• Since 1970, the number of women tennis players in the country has   3
jumped from about 3 million to 11 million, the number of golfers from

less than a half million to more than 5 million. According to one survey, of the nation's 17.1 million joggers, well over one-third are women—in 1970, there were too few to count.

• In 1980, according to six sports federations (tennis, golf, bowling, skiing, racquetball, basketball), financial rewards for female athletes topped more than $16 million, up from less than $1 million a decade ago.   4

As women rush into athletic competition, certain questions are being raised: How good are women as athletes? How do they compare with men? Are women's bodies strong enough, tough enough, to take the battles?   5

New research on the physical and athletic differences between men and women shows that in some respects women may be at least as tough as men. Some evidence suggests that women's endurance may be equal or perhaps even superior to men's. Women's bodies are constructed so that certain crucial organs are better guarded from injury; ovaries, for instance, lie inside the pelvic cavity, far better placed for protection than the testicles.   6

Furthermore, the folk wisdom that other elements of the female anatomy make women athletes more vulnerable seems incorrect. The suspicion that severe bruises cause breast cancer is not borne out; breasts are less susceptible to injury than knees or elbows, whether male or female. And the old idea that, at certain times of the month, women do not operate at peak performance is generally not true for athletes. World and Olympic records have been set by women in all stages of their menstrual cycles. Moreover, at certain intense levels of training, menstruation conveniently turns off for many women, a phenomenon that has been linked in some studies to a reduction in body fat, in other studies to physical and emotional stress.   7

The point is that, if concern for safety is a determining factor, women should have the same opportunities to participate in competitive athletics as men. And, by and large, they have the same reasons for wanting to do so. Says tennis star Billie Jean King: "Athletics are an essential part of education for both sexes. Girls and boys are going to grow up easier in each other's company."   8

No one suggests now that equal experience is going to lead to equal performance in all things athletic. Men are bigger and stronger, can run faster, throw and jump farther. But the fact that women are genetically ordained through most of life to compete with less powerful bodies, far from tarnishing their performance, makes it more worthy.   9

Actually, boys and girls start out with nearly identical equipment so far as fitness for sports goes. If anything, girls, because they mature faster, may have an edge, as youth soccer-league coaches, for example, are finding out.   10

At puberty, the situation abruptly changes. Estrogen levels begin to build in the female body. There is a growth spurt which peaks at about   11

12 years, then tapers off by 14 or 15. Most boys begin to mature sexually a year and a half to two years later than girls, and then keep on developing much longer, in some cases up to six years longer.

On the average, men end up ten percent bigger. They have longer   12
bones, providing better leverage; wider shoulders—the foundation for a significant advantage in upper-body strength—and bigger hearts and lungs. In addition, while the body of the female adolescent is preparing for childbirth by storing up fat reserves, the male body is growing muscle. And this occurs quite apart from exercise. Exercise adds strength and endurance, and increases the size of the muscles. But on average, men have more muscle fibers than women; and they have an added advantage in the hormone testosterone, which adds bulk to those fibers.

When the Army first accepted women at West Point in 1976, it found   13
it necessary to quantify the strength differences of the incoming plebes. The upshot of numerous tests indicated that women had approximately one-third the strength of men in the upper body and two-thirds the strength of men in the legs, and about the same amount of strength as men in the abdomen. The implications are obvious for those American games that have dominated the sports pages for years: women are no match for men in football, baseball and basketball, all of which place a high premium on upper-body strength. Tennis, too, illustrates the female disadvantage. Tracy Austin has mastered the basic strokes of the game every bit as well as most of the top male players. But she simply cannot match them in the serve, which demands upper-arm strength and happens to be the key stroke of the game.

Sometimes the special combination of female traits works to women's   14
advantage. Ever since Gertrude Ederle swam the English Channel in 1926, two hours faster than any man had ever done it, women have dominated the sport of long-distance swimming. Women generally have ten percent more fat than men. This appears not only in the characteristic deposits on the thighs, buttocks and breasts, but in an overall layer of subcutaneous fat. The result is that women are more buoyant than men and better insulated against cold. An added edge is their narrower shoulders, which offer less resistance through the water.

Another advantage long-distance swimmers may share with other well-   15
trained female athletes is the ability to call on reserves of energy perhaps unavailable to men. Running the marathon, women get tired, but few report "hitting the wall," an expression for the sudden pain and debilitating weakness that strike many male runners after about two hours, when most of the glycogen that fuels their muscles is gone. The training necessary to run the marathon conditions the body to call directly on fats after the glycogen is used up. One controversial theory is that women, because of hormonal differences, utilize their fat more efficiently than men. Another is that, since women have more stored fat than men, their staying power is greater.

Beyond physical characteristics, past social attitudes have had a sub- 16
stantial influence on the sex factor in athletics. The old attitude was
epitomized in the expression "throwing like a girl." At first glance there
does appear to be a certain innate awkwardness in the way girls throw a
ball. But Prof. Jack Wilmore of the University of Arizona, in researching
female and male relative athletic ability, had a number of right-handed
men throw lefty: the men proved equally awkward. Wilmore said it
seemed apparent from his studies that throwing is an acquired trait. The
broader shoulders and bigger muscles of men give them an advantage in
speed or distance, but not, innately, in grace.

The effect of such subtle forces on women's competitive athletics 17
seems clear. A coach at an Ivy League university says, "Women have
taken up athletics so recently that they don't understand what it takes to
be good. They are greener and they lack competitive experience. Beyond
that, and the greater strength and speed of men, there is no fundamental
difference. Girls make the same mistakes boys do—and have the same
youthful enthusiasm. It will just take time."

It already has taken time, but the first step may have been the hardest: 18
shucking the encumbering skirts and petticoats in which Western women
had been trapped. Another early milestone was the introduction around
1900 of the "safety bicycle," the basic two-wheeler used today. It is
credited with getting women actively out on their own in large numbers
for the first time. Then came World War II and the opportunity for Rosie
the Riveter and her sisters to prove themselves.

Shortly thereafter, the communist world began to score propaganda 19
points in the Olympics with the formidable showing of its female athletes.
Eastern-bloc sports factories turned out such superior goods that when
at Rome, in 1960, a hitherto unknown American sprinter named Wilma
Rudolph ran off with three gold medals, she became an instant national
hero. The vehicle that carried Rudolph to her fame was television—and
from that year on, the upstart medium, with its voracious appetite for
sporting events, would find ample fare in women's sports.

In the past decade, more milestones went by. In 1972, Congress 20
passed Title IX of the Education Amendments of 1972, providing that
"no person in the United States shall, on the basis of sex, be excluded
from particpation in any education program or activity receiving federal
financial assistance." It took most of the remainder of the '70s for the
Department of Health, Education and Welfare to define the law, and for
schools across the country to begin to comply.

In 1973, New Jersey ruled that qualified girls must be allowed to play 21
Little League baseball. Male coaches across the country screamed that the
sky was falling. The following year, Little League changed its bylaws to
include girls.

Even so, as the '80s begin, Donna Lopiano, director of women's athlet- 22
ics at the University of Texas at Austin, assesses women athletes as still

ten years from realizing their potential. "The kids we think are super now," she says, "are going to be the rule, not the exception. We are just starting to get kids who are good already, who have received coaching from the age of 15."

Some believe the day is coming when women will compete head to   23
head with men in more and more sports events, particularly in track and swimming events of longer distance. Australian scientist K. F. Dyer sees the difference between some men's and women's track and swimming records closing so fast he expects it to disappear altogether in the not too distant future.

There are predictions, too, that women will eventually surpass men in   24
the super-marathons—those of 50 miles or more. Lyn Lemaire, a 29-year-old Harvard law student, proved that last year when she joined a field of 15 for the Iron Man Triathlon, a 140.6-mile non-stop race around the Hawaiian island of Oahu, combining swimming, cycling and a final, conventional 26-mile marathon. Of the 12 finishers, Lyn Lemaire placed fifth. The event may have to be renamed.

Topical Considerations

1. How *have* female athletes come? What are some of the myths about female athletes that have been disproved? What disadvantages remain?

2. Wood mentions a number of surprising predictions about female athletes. What did you find most surprising? Why?

3. In which two sports do women have a physiological advantage? What do analysts predict women's future performance will be in these sports?

4. Athletic training programs for girls have changed gradually since the Education Amendments of 1972. What signs of these changes have you see in your own elementary and high school athletic training experiences?

5. Wood notes a number of historical events that have contributed to women's freedom to pursue athletic excellence. What are some of these events? Can you think of others?

Rhetorical Considerations

1. Succinct, clear beginnings are important if an essay is going to be understood, appreciated, and *read* by an audience. How well does Wood achieve this in his essay? How does he achieve it?

2. Wood doesn't confine his remarks about female athletes to generalities but uses concrete specifics to illustrate his points. Cite pas-

sages where he uses specifics effectively. You might discuss, for example, how he supports his claim: "There has been an explosion in women's competitive sports" (paragraph 1).

3. What rhetorical pattern does Wood use when he explains how there has been an explosion in female athletic contests?

4. Wood's second, third, and fourth paragraphs are developed by means of comparison. The remainder of the article is also one extended comparison. Point out what these comparisons are and how they are ordered.

5. Does this essay have a beginning, a middle, and an end? What is discussed in each section? How does Wood achieve transition between sections? Note, particularly, how he moves from his introduction to the body of the essay.

Writing Assignments

1. Do you see any difference in the athletic training you and your classmates received and that of your parents? Talk to your parents about this, or find a magazine article that discusses this point. Write an essay in which you compare your athletic training with that of one or both of your parents. Show how the results have been different. Include personal experiences to illustrate these differences.

2. Identify an outstanding male and female athlete in a national sport that you follow. Write a comparison essay that illustrates how each has demonstrated excellence in the field. Point out some of the physiological factors that have contributed to this success.

Take the Plunge . . .

Gloria Emerson

If you had any doubt that women have come a long way in the world of sports, the following piece should dispel it. Here is a gripping personal account of Gloria Emerson's first jump out of an airplane. Skydiving has been called the "world's most stimulating and soul-satisfying sport." That may be true, but, as Emerson suggests, skydiving requires some of the most mind-grueling preparation. In mounting detail, Emerson describes the full experience of parachuting—from instruction class to the open door of the Cessna through the 2,300-foot plunge to the target pit below. Gloria Emerson was an award-winning foreign correspondent for the *New York Times,* covering, among other crises, the last years of the Vietnam War. In 1978, she received the National Book Award for her *Winners and Losers,* a book about that war.

It was usually men who asked me why I did it. Some were amused, others puzzled. I didn't mind the jokes in the newspaper office where I worked about whether I left the building by window, roof or in the elevator. The truth is that I was an unlikely person to jump out of an airplane, being neither graceful, daring nor self-possessed. I had a bad back, uncertain ankles and could not drive with competence because of deficient depth perception and a fear of all buses coming toward me. A friend joked that if I broke my bones I would have to be shot because I would never mend. 1

I never knew why I did it. It was in May, a bright and dull May, the last May that made me want to feel reckless. But there was nothing to do then at the beginning of a decade that changed almost everything. I could not wait that May for the Sixties to unroll. I worked in women's news; my stories came out like little cookies. I wanted to be brave about something, not just about love, or a root canal, or writing that the shoes at Arnold Constable looked strangely sad. 2

Once I read of men who had to run so far it burned their chests to breathe. But I could not run very far. Jumping from a plane, which required no talent or endurance, seemed perfect. I wanted to feel the big, puzzling lump on my back that they promised was a parachute, to take serious strides in the absurd black boots that I believed all generals wore. 3

I wanted all of it: the rising of a tiny plane with the door off, the earth rushing away, the plunge, the slap of the wind, my hands on the back straps, the huge curve of white silk above me, the drift through the space we call sky. 4

It looked pale green that morning I fell into it, not the baby blue I expected. I must have been crying; my cheeks were wet. Only the thumps of a wild heart made noise; I did not know how to keep it quiet. 5

That May, that May my mind was as clear as clay. I did not have the imagination to perceive the risks, to understand that if the wind grew nasty I might be electrocuted on high-tension wires, smashed on a roof, drowned in water, hanged in a tree. I was sure nothing would happen, because my intentions were so good, just as young soldiers start out certain of their safety because they know nothing. 6

Friends drove me to Orange, Massachusetts, seventy miles west of Boston, for the opening of the first U.S. sports parachuting center, where I was to perform. It was the creation, the passion, of a Princetonian and ex-Marine named Jacques Istel, who organized the first U.S. jumping team in 1956. Parachuting was "as safe as swimming," he kept saying, calling it the "world's most stimulating and soul-satisfying sport." His center was for competitions and the teaching of skydiving. Instead of hurtling toward the earth, sky divers maintain a swan-dive position, using the air as a cushion to support them while they maneuver with leg and arm movements until the rip cord must be pulled. 7

None of that stuff was expected from any of us in the little beginners 8 class. We were only to jump, after brief but intense instruction, with Istel's newly designed parachute, to show that any dope could do it. It was a parachute with a thirty-two-foot canopy; a large cutout hole funneled escaping air. You steered with two wooden knobs instead of having to pull hard on the back straps, or risers. The new parachute increased lateral speed, slowed down the rate of descent, reduced oscillation. We were told we could even land standing up but that we should bend our knees and lean to one side. The beginners jumped at eight A.M., the expert sky divers performed their dazzling tricks later when a crowd came.

Two of us boarded a Cessna 180 that lovely morning, the wind no   9
more than a tickle. I was not myself, no longer thin and no longer fast. The jump suit, the equipment, the helmet, the boots, had made me into someone thick and clumsy, moving as strangely as if they had put me underwater and said I must walk. It was hard to bend, to sit, to stand up. I did not like the man with me; he was eager and composed. I wanted to smoke, to go to the bathroom, but there were many straps around me that I did not understand. At twenty-three hundred feet, the hateful, happy man went out, making a dumb thumbs-up sign.

When my turn came, I suddenly felt a stab of pain for all the forgotten   10
soldiers who balked and were kicked out, perhaps shot, for their panic and for delaying the troops. I was hooked to a static line, an automatic opening device, which made it impossible to lie down or tie myself to something. The drillmaster could not hear all that I shouted at him. But he knew the signs of mutiny and removed my arms from his neck. He took me to the doorway, sat me down, and yelled "Go!" or "Now!" or "Out!" There was nothing to do but be punched by the wind, which knocked the spit from my mouth, reach for the wing strut, hold on hard, kick back the feet so weighted and helpless in those boots, and let go. The parachute opened with a plop, as Istel had sworn to me that it would. When my eyelids opened as well, I saw the white gloves on my hands were old ones from Saks Fifth Avenue, gloves I wore with summer dresses. There was dribble on my chin; my eyes and nose were leaking. I wiped everything with the gloves.

There was no noise; the racket of the plane and wind had gone away.   11
The cold and sweet stillness seemed an astonishing, undreamed-of gift. Then I saw what I had never seen before, will never see again; endless sky and earth in colors and textures no one had ever described. Only then did the parachute become a most lovable and docile toy: this wooden knob to go left, this wooden knob to go right. The pleasure of being there, the drifting and the calm, rose to a fever; I wanted to stay pinned in the air and stop the ground from coming closer. The target was a huge arrow in a sandpit. I was cross to see it, afraid of nothing now, for even the wind was kind and the trees looked soft. I landed on my feet in the

pit with a bump, then sat down for a bit. Later that day I was taken over to meet General James Gavin, who had led the 82nd Airborne in the D-day landing at Normandy. Perhaps it was to prove to him that the least promising pupil, the gawkiest, could jump. It did not matter that I stumbled and fell before him in those boots, which walked with a will of their own. Later, Mr. Istel's mother wrote me a charming note of congratulations. Everyone at the center was pleased; in fact, I am sure they were surprised. Perhaps this is what I had in mind all the time.

Topical Considerations

1. In his essay, Schrank states: "Sport is a ritual, an acting out of a myth or series of myths." How is skydiving a way for Emerson to act out a myth? What does she mean, for example, when she remarks that she wanted "to take serious strides in the absurd black boots that I believed all generals wore" (paragraph 3)?

2. Schrank comments that the day she decided to try skydiving, her mind was "as clear as clay." Why "clay"? What connotations does this word have?

3. When Emerson finally takes the plunge, what are some of the first things she things about? Is this typical? (Think back to a moment of crisis in your life. What did you think about while it was happening?)

4. If you were to ask yourself what Emerson's purpose was in writing this essay, you might conclude that she was actually asking herself a question. What is the question? How do the last few lines suggest an answer?

5. How would you act if you had the opportunity to go skydiving? Describe any comparable experience you have had.

Rhetorical Considerations

1. The specifics in Emerson's first paragraph create a vivid picture of her aptitude for skydiving. How do these specifics reinforce the main idea of the paragraph? Find other paragraphs in which Emerson's specifics help show what she means.

2. In paragraph 9, Emerson describes how she felt before she jumped out of the plane. In paragraph 11, she describes what it was like as she descended to the ground. Cite specific word choices in these paragraphs that help the reader vicariously experience what it was like.

3. How does Emerson order the events of her narrative?

4. In what way does the last sentence serve to tie the essay together? Explain how it is relevant to the beginning.

Writing Assignments

1. Describe an experience you have had that is like Emerson's skydiving adventure. Include an explanation of why you did it, what others thought about it, and how you felt before, during, and after it was over. Imitate Emerson's use of concrete details to show what you mean.

2. Skydiving is becoming a popular leisure-time activity. Write an essay in which you analyze why you believe people might want to spend their free time parachuting out of airplanes.

Jogging

Russell Baker

This essay seems an appropriate one with which to end this book. No, it is not about the joys of jogging—although Russell Baker once jogged. Nor is it about the joys of any other sport Baker used to play. Just the opposite—this is a middle-aged man's justification for inactivity—for never having to prove himself again on field or track. It has something to say about attitude, youth, and competition—as have several of the essays in this section. And there is some characteristic Russell Baker humor here. That is another reason we close the book on this piece—we want to leave you smiling. Russell Baker has been writing entertaining columns for the *New York Times* since 1962. He is also the author of several books, his latest being *Growing Up* (1982).

I don't jog. If this makes people who do jog feel smug about their   1
muscle tone, so be it. One old geezer, a friend who chuffs and wheezes through Manhattan each dawn, assures me that refusal to pound arches on concrete signifies a yearning for the grave.

It pleasures him to visualize the interment of persons who are happily   2
snoozing in their beds while he is chugging through the dawn. Health faddists of all eras have sustained themselves on the belief that people pass to the great beyond only because of perverse refusal to humor their muscles and innards, and it would be petty to disabuse them.

To my observation, the decision about who passes over and who lin-   3
gers on in the earthly domain is based entirely on whim, but if contemplating imminent demise among the sedentary helps the athletic to endure their suffering, I shall not dispute them. Having been a jogger at one stage, I know too well the dreariness and boredom with which they cope. It is more humane to leave intact any compensating delusions which make their lot easier.

My refusal to join them in shin splints stems from an oath sworn years   4 ago after two seasons on the high-school track team. Mere jogging, of course, doesn't qualify a runner for track, but it is an indispensable part of the program. He jogs before the race, he jogs after the race, he jogs most of the time between races. It is exceedingly dull, although not at all tiring for people of high-school age.

The racing, on the other hand, is worse than tiring, at least for persons   5
to whom torture is more painful than fatigue. The aim is to achieve a complete physical collapse just short of death simultaneously with hitting the finish tape. Not being permitted to die, at least when I was in high school, one was permitted to vomit, after which you jogged a little to "cool off."

I should add that I never actually hit the finish tape. Four or five other   6
runners had usually hit it well ahead of me and were already there writhing and jogging and evacuating their lunches by the time I arrived on the scene. ˙

Why, you will ask, should anyone submit to such torment, particularly   7
after learning that he is never going to be the first to collapse? What a question. This was high school. Why do people contend with algebra in high school? Why do they go on wrestling endlessly with a French that always wins?

Youth is a time of enduring agonies without asking why. I knew that   8
even then. I would endure, I told myself, but when I grew up, I would never run again. Or jog. To me, being grown up meant, besides being able to buy beer without having to prove my age, never having to engage in athletics for which I was inadequately constructed.

Very quickly it became apparent that this included almost all athletics.   9
Pressed into the military, I was placed at the mercy of a cabal of professional coaches who were fighting Fascism by subjecting the short-winded and the spindly-shanked to the zest of All-American sports competition.

Their theory held that everybody could become superior on the bat-   10
tlefield by experiencing the thrill of actual sport. For two weeks we played football. I was placed near the center of the line. Periodically, a dense wad of muscle that had played football for Ohio State would run over me with the determination of a runaway locomotive. I swore never to play football again, and haven't.

During the second two weeks we boxed. I was placed in a ring with a   11
light-heavyweight who had been a finalist in some Marine Corps boxing festivity. My left jaw still aches occasionally. I swore never to lift another fist, and haven't.

Some years later, the papers reported that this Marine had been shot   12
down over China, captured and brainwashed. I was depressed to hear this, for the Chinese had obviously stayed well clear of his right hook, which showed they were smarter than I was.

No need to dwell on the two weeks we spent in gymnastics. Who in his   13
right mind would send a giraffe up against Nadia Comaneci in the cart-

wheel and back somersault? I swore I would never leap, flip, swing, shinny or dive again, and haven't.

As for wrestling, it was not only humiliating—one was accustomed to   14
that by then—but also terrifying, despite the coach's assurances that gorillas did this sort of thing constantly without ever having their necks broken.

One of the few rewards of being grown up is not having to carry on   15
in this fashion. Now and then I feel an urge to do something vigorous in order to refresh the pleasure of being able to stop doing it, but I am always quick to lie down again.

One owes it to friends who jog. Contemplating the imminence of my   16
demise helps them to endure.

Topical Considerations

1. What did you find humorous about Baker's essay? Why? Did you identify with it, or not? Explain your answer.

2. How accurate are Baker's observations about why his "old geezer" friend runs? What are some reasons why bank presidents, corporate lawyers, salesclerks, homemakers, and teenagers are running more than they ever have?

3. Baker graphically describes why he dislikes jogging. Have you experienced what he describes? How accurate is he?

4. How do Baker's complaints about jogging and other athletics compare with those of Mike Royko (see "Farewell to Fitness")?

5. Baker makes a curious comment about growing up. In paragraph 8, he says: "Youth is a time of enduring agonies without asking why." Do you agree with this? Give reasons for your answer.

Rhetorical Considerations

1. Where does Baker first establish the thesis for his essay? Where does he expand it? How does he make the transition to this broader thesis?

2. Baker claims that his refusal to jog provides his friends with an incentive to continue jogging. How does he work this idea in with his thesis? How does this give him a way to tie the essay together in the end?

3. Baker's friend "chuffs and wheezes through Manhattan each dawn" and "pound[s] arches on concrete" (paragraph 1). Why are these verb choices more effective than if he were simply to say that his friend went running? What connotations do these words have? Find other examples of unusual verbs.

4. Baker also has a flair for vivid noun phrases. His friend is an

"old geezer" and a football opponent is a "wad of muscle" who runs over him like "a runaway locomotive." Find other examples of vivid noun phrases in Baker's essay.

5. Baker often achieves his humor through absurdity and exaggeration. Cite examples of this.

Writing Assignments

1. In paragraph 8, Baker remarks: "Youth is a time of enduring agonies without asking why." What agonies did you find typical of your teenage years? Did you endure them without asking questions, Or did you rebel? Write an essay in which you discuss these questions.

2. Adopt the point of view of Baker's "old geezer" friend. Write a humorous essay ridiculing deadweights who refuse to get out of their easy chairs.